Jolene Mayo
1442 N Hampshire Pl
Mason City, Iowa 50401

do Chart

Page 107-1.

By the Authors of

NEW WORLD OF SCIENCE

R. Will Burnett

To Live in Health
Biology for Better Living (with E. E. Bayles)
Life Through the Ages
Aviation Education Source Book
Education in Wartime and After (with others)

Bernard Jaffe

New World of Chemistry
Men of Science in America
Outposts of Science
Crucibles—The Lives and Achievements of the Great Chemists
Chemical Calculations

Herbert S. Zim

Rockets and Jets
Man in the Air
Submarines
Minerals (with F. K. Cooper)
Mice, Men, and Elephants
Air Navigation
Parachutes
Plants
Elephants
Goldfish
Rabbits
This Is Science
Science Interests and Activities of Adolescents

NEW WORLD

Drawings by

ROBERT DOREMUS

MATTHEW KALMENOFF

F. R. GRUGER

OF SCIENCE

R. WILL BURNETT

Professor of Science Education, University of Illinois

BERNARD JAFFE

Chairman, Department of Physical Science, James Madison High School, New York City

HERBERT S. ZIM

Science Consultant, Ethical Culture and Manhasset Bay Schools, New York

New York   *Chicago*   *San Francisco*

PREFACE

To be effective, a general science program should help young people become more scientific in their ways of thinking and acting. In addition, it should provide the scientific basis for intelligent thought or action concerning personal and social problems important to young people. It should enable young people to develop the ability to think critically and to solve problems of many kinds by using the methods of science. It should develop the kinds of initiative and self-reliance so necessary to the responsibilities of democratic citizenship. By no means of least importance, it should enable young people to acquire a store of *useful* scientific facts and principles.

Forward-looking science teachers and school administrators agree that most general science programs do not reach these goals in spite of the earnest efforts of good teachers. Why not? Is it not possible to build a program that will achieve these results and yet will not call for radically different methods of teaching?

We believe that such a program is possible. NEW WORLD OF SCIENCE was built with these goals in mind. We do not claim that it is the only program that will reach these goals, but it is one way to reach them.

At least three approaches have been used in building science programs. The first, the "field-covering" approach, attempts to acquaint students with the many branches of science through a sampling of materials from these many branches. The second, the "generalizations" approach, consists of materials and experiences built around generalizations of science that have greatly influenced man's thinking or that may lead to improvements in important aspects of living. The third, the "interests" or "needs" approach, consists of science experiences related to problems of a personal or social nature in which young people express interest.

None of these ways of building science programs provides the science experiences young people need to help them solve the many problems that confront them. The branches of science have become so many and varied that a "field-covering" general science textbook cannot be more than a highly selective sampling of the branches of science. In addition, in such programs scientific data current some 40 to 50 years ago outweigh and often exclude developments of the past few years.

In practice, a "generalizations" general science textbook is seldom as effective as it might be. Students rapidly learn to repeat the generalizations, sometimes with considerable understanding. But all too often they fail to develop enough understanding of how the generalizations may be used to make them effective in improving their ways of living. Thus students may repeat the generalization "Communicable diseases are caused by microorganisms," without realizing what they can do to help prevent or secure treatment for communicable diseases.

The "interests" or "needs" approach too often serves as a springboard from which to launch an unorganized science program based solely on what students are interested in at the moment. This may exclude the scientific aspects of personal problems that valid research has shown them to be concerned about or that mature minds consider to be significant social problems.

Obviously, a sound general science program will combine the good points of each of these approaches. It will provide an organized program of learning experiences designed to provide new insights into the ways science functions in our world. This is the "functional" approach on which NEW WORLD OF SCIENCE was built.

The personal concerns and interests of young people, important social problems, and values and attitudes necessary to intelligent living in a democracy—these were the screens through which the science materials and experiences were selected, organized, and built into NEW WORLD OF SCIENCE. For example, one of the important social problems facing us today concerns the ways in which atomic energy will be used. Basic to this problem is an understanding of what atomic energy is, how it may be produced, what its potentialities are, and what social, economic, and political problems are bound to arise from its use. These aspects of atomic energy are discussed in NEW WORLD OF SCIENCE, for young people today must become familiar with both social *and* scientific implications of major scientific developments.

Another important social problem is that of securing better health for all. The scientific, social, and economic aspects of this problem are discussed—a discussion led into and built around problems that concern young people. Still another social problem is that of our "shrinking" world. The developments of modern science have made world-wide cooperation no longer merely a desirable humanitarian goal but a very real necessity.

Some of the differences between what science has promised us and what has actually been achieved are discussed on an appropriate level. The use of science in health, production and distribution of goods, conservation of natural resources—soil, forests, water, minerals, fuels, and wildlife—and similar important areas has been explored. No dividing line between the natural sciences and the social sciences is drawn in society, nor is one drawn in NEW WORLD OF SCIENCE. Thus students obtain a factual basis for sound consideration of various social problems on which democratic action must sooner or later be taken. In this way the gap between what is scientifically possible and what has been achieved may be somewhat lessened.

Science is interesting, challenging, and dramatic—it does not need to be made so. While science textbooks are often dull, usually this is the result of the way in which the subject matter is presented. NEW WORLD OF SCIENCE was written to be exciting and challenging—a pleasurable experience for both students and teachers. Great care was exercised to make the presentation of materials appealing to young people, psychologically sound, and scientifically accurate. The language is simple, clear, and direct. Sentences and paragraphs are short, and the pages are open and attractive. Photographs and illustrations are physically attractive as well as educationally useful.

Throughout the book, interesting episodes from the history of science show how science has changed our ways of living. In this connection, Chapter One and the full page of illustrations with which each chapter opens are particularly valuable. But more than this, these episodes and illustrations show that the scientists who have made important contributions to scientific progress were not the cold, unemotional persons that popular myth has made them. Scientists are, after all, just people, and the great scientists of both past and present got excited about things that count. We want young people to get excited about things that count also but, like good scientists, we want them to get excited on a firm foundation of facts. We want them to learn to deal with problems that have strong emotional aspects on a rational, critical, and scientific basis rather than on pure emotion, blind prejudice, or unsound superstition.

Some of the problem areas that concern young people include problems of adolescence (psychological and physical), personal and social adjustment, economic security, and youth's stake in the future. The potentialities as well as the achievements of science are emphasized because young people must become so thoroughly aware of what is possible through science that they will work both now and as adults toward achieving at least some of the possible goals.

Thus NEW WORLD OF SCIENCE comes honestly by its name. Most of the subject matter that general science teachers expect to find in a general science textbook is included. But the emphasis and the focus are different. No science subject matter is included only because it is expected. If the subject matter could not be shown to contribute to an understanding of the problems and concerns of today, it was not included.

A sound science textbook is one very effective tool for good science teaching—but it is only one of several tools. To help provide a series of rich and significant science experiences, NEW WORLD OF SCIENCE includes numerous suggestions for science activities of many kinds. These include suggestions for experiments, demonstrations, field trips, class discussions, exhibits, individual library or laboratory "research," committee reports, and class projects. These suggestions, called "Working With Science," appear at the close of each section of each chapter throughout the book. Detailed, step-by-step instructions are given if the activity is complex or requires caution. Detailed instructions are not given for the simpler activities, for if students are to develop self-reliance and initiative, they must have opportunity to plan and carry out activities with only a small amount of guidance.

References for both students and teachers are included at the close of the chapters under "Reading You Will Enjoy." Brief annotations describe them. Some of the books are appropriate for any student, while others are for the students whose interest in a particular topic is such that they would like to go beyond an elementary treatment of the subject. Some deal with human problems that can be treated or perhaps solved through science. Others show the impact of scientific developments on society. Fiction as well as nonfiction is included.

Teaching aids designed solely for the teacher are included in the pamphlet entitled *The Resourceful Teaching of New World of Science* which is available to teachers who use this book. In addition to many concrete suggestions for teachers, this pamphlet includes a list of 150 carefully selected, up-to-date teaching films that the authors have found useful in presenting the course. The pamphlet also contains an objective test for each of the book's units.

We are indebted to many persons and to many organizations for valuable help in building this book. We wish to thank them all and, in particular, those students and teachers who read and used parts of the manuscript in its earlier stages of development, who tried out the many activities, and who made many helpful suggestions for their improvement; those representatives of industrial, educational, and government agencies who checked many sections of the manuscript and who were more than generous in supplying data and illustrations; and Encyclopaedia Britannica Films, Inc. for furnishing many teaching sequences from their sound films.

We wish to express our thanks to the publishers for their gratifying desire to produce textbooks built on sound psychological and educational principles and in keeping with the demands of today's schools. In conclusion, we wish to acknowledge our indebtedness to Earl E. Welch, Editor-in-Chief, and Homer E. Shaw, High-School Editor, of Silver Burdett Company who, in addition to their functions as editors were members of the author-publisher team that made this book possible.

R. Will Burnett
Bernard Jaffe
Herbert S. Zim

CONTENTS

Unit One: The World That Science Has Built

1. How Science Has Changed the World 1
2. How Science Changes the World 21

Unit Two: Your Body-Machine and How It Works

3. The Body-Machine and Its Use of Food 31
4. Fuel and Air for the Body-Machine 45
5. How We Keep in Touch With the World 61

Unit Three: Health to You

6. Check Up on Your Health 75
7. Communicable, or "Catching," Diseases 79
8. Eat Healthfully to Live Healthfully 91
9. Be Yourself 101
10. Modern Medicine and America's Health Plans 109

Unit Four: Using Biological Resources for Better Living

11. The Kinds of Living Things 121
12. The Life of Living Things 135
13. The Wise Use of Living Things 145
14. The Control of Living Things 159
15. The Improvement of Living Things 169

Unit Five: Using Mineral Resources for Better Living

16. These Are Our Resources 179
17. Mining the Land 199

18. Mining the Seas. 215
19. Mining the Air 229
20. Mining the Laboratory 243

Unit Six: Energy and Machines for the World of Tomorrow

21. The Machines We Use 253
22. Simple Machines and Complicated Machinery 267
23. Energy Turns the Wheels 287
24. Heat Engines 301
25. Electricity, the Modern Power 321

Unit Seven: Time, Measurement, and Mass Production

26. Precision Measurement for Modern Science 347
27. Production for All 361

Unit Eight: The Weather and What We Can Do About It

28. The Atmosphere 373
29. The Air Masses 393
30. Can We Control the Weather? 407

Unit Nine: Astronomy

31. The Solar System in Which We Live 417
32. Billions of Stars and Other Universes 435

Unit Ten: Science for Our Homes

33. Heating Our Homes 441
34. Lighting Our Homes 451
35. Electronics in the Home 463
36. Sound in the Home 477
37. Science and People 489

Index 493

We live today among many of the results of science. You may not know it, but science has made possible many, perhaps most, of what we call the good things of life. Science has made great changes in our ways of living. Most of these changes have been to the good, but not all have been. And even in those results that have improved our ways of living lie possibilities of undesirable effects.

The big point, and one that is often overlooked, is that science and society interact and react. For example, a chemist discovers how to make a dye that has long been obtained from a plant. The new dye is better and far cheaper than the old. Cloth dyed with it does not fade and the color does not run. People as a whole benefit (1)—all except those who made their living raising the plant (2) from which the dye was made. In turn, the needs of society spur on the scientists. When light metals were needed for making aircraft parts, scientists developed methods of getting magnesium from sea water.

Science makes possible a world of peace and plenty. But we must always be on guard to see that science is used for the good of man rather than for his destruction. We must choose between ruin, as at Hiroshima (3) and Nagasaki, and the use of atomic energy for the good of all (4).

The World That Science Has Built

1

HOW SCIENCE HAS CHANGED THE WORLD

Overhead roars a mighty airliner. In the city below, engines and power plants throb and hum to provide the energy needed for modern living. Great buildings tower high into the sky. Vast roadways, filled with cars and trucks, thread from city to countryside. Modern machinery and farming methods produce an abundance unknown even 50 years ago.

That airplane and most of the things we use in our everyday living were made possible by science. We can understand today's world best by learning what men and women of science, that is, *scientists*, have accomplished. Scientists have worked, observed, thought, and experimented to get information from nature. This information has produced the electric motor and generator, the airplane, the rocket, modern medicine, and the vast array of materials, machines, and methods that make today's world possible.

We can see the dim outlines of tomorrow's world by learning what scientists are doing today. The promise of the future lies in the research now being carried on by scientists all over the world. However, only the promise of the future can be seen in the newer scientific developments. Many of them can be used either to advance man's interests or to destroy him. Man must decide whether the future will bring progress or destruction.

A NEW WORLD OF SCIENCE IS BORN

Science makes possible a world of peace and plenty. At the same time, it makes possible a world of destruction and want. Man must choose how he will use his rapidly advancing knowledge. In fact, it is up to you. You and millions of young people like you will help control the world not many years from now. Your understanding of the part that science plays in the affairs of men and your determination that science be used for better living will help to decide the future of the world.

THE FUTURE COMES

It is the morning of July 16, 1945. A drizzling rain drips from the leaden skies. The first grayness of dawn has not yet disclosed the vast stretches of the New Mexico desert or outlined the flat-topped hills.

Far from any dwelling place, a steel tower rises some 100 feet into the cold morning air. At the top of the tower rests a ball of metal. Many cables and wires spread out from the tower.

U. S. Army-Navy Task Force One photo

Atomic explosion among ships at Bikini. What does the terrific "power" of an atomic bomb come from?

Ten miles away from the giant tower, men hug the ground and adjust goggles of double-thick, dark glass. Somewhat nearer the tower, other men sit nervously behind heavy earth banks and massive timbers, watching instrument boards covered with dials.

The Blast. It is a few seconds before 5:30. An announcer speaks into the microphone of a loudspeaker system. He ticks off the swiftly fleeting seconds until zero hour, 5:30. Fifteen seconds! Ten seconds! Five seconds! If he an-

Control and observation posts for the test.

U. S. Army Signal Corps photo

nounces the exact time when the switch is closed, no one hears. For the earth rocks and sways in a mighty explosion that lights the skies as if a dozen noonday suns suddenly beamed down upon the desert.

A great fiery cloud of brilliant colors mushrooms skyward. Smoke and particles swirl 8 miles into the sky. The blast knocks down two men who stood behind the earth and timbers more than 5 miles away from the tower. Mountains as much as 150 miles away from the blast are lighted up very brightly for about 3 seconds.

What had taken place? What was this terribly violent explosion? Why were these men —many of them foremost scientists of the world—gathered in this remote desert land? Why did they want to observe the thundering, blinding crash of a small bomb so powerful that the tower on which it rested disappeared completely, and the ground over which it had hung yawned open in a hole ½ mile wide and ¼ mile long?

2

The Research behind the Bomb. America was at war—a war fought chiefly by methods and with materials that modern science had produced. For example, scientists had developed "eyes" that enabled airmen to "see" through heavy clouds or through the blackness of night. These "eyes" also made it possible to detect the approach of enemy ships and planes hundreds of miles away. With instruments produced by scientists, guns were aimed and fired far more accurately than ever before.

But here, in the remote desert of the southwestern United States, was a terrifying test of the most dramatic wartime science research of all. Two billion dollars, the time and work of more than 100,000 people, and mountains of materials had been spent in a great cooperative search. This vast research project ended in a bomb, easily carried by a single airplane but more powerful than 20,000 tons of TNT.

In this bomb man first used successfully the tremendous *energy* locked up in the small particles, or *atoms*, of which all things are composed. Energy is extremely important in our lives. Very simply, energy is the ability to act or to do something. Even atoms, the tiny particles that make up matter, have energy.

What happened on July 16, 1945 may make a greater difference in your life than any single discovery or invention in history. When scientists released the energy of the atom, they unlocked a source of energy so vast that even today its greatness is hardly realized.

POWER FOR GOOD OR ILL

The fact that we live in a world in which the atomic bomb exists is very important to all of us. Everyone must live with this terrific energy that scientists have loosed on the earth. We cannot go back to the time before scientists developed this bomb. We do not want to go back. For the same energy that has been released for destruction may someday do most of the work of the world.

The next 10 or 20 years may see atomic energy harnessed to heat and light our homes, and to move heavy machinery in factories and on farms all over the world, perhaps for a fraction of the cost of present forms of energy. Note well the word *may!* It is certain that this terrific energy will someday be controlled and harnessed. But how quickly that day will come

Removing material from an atomic pile. The Geiger counter tells whether dangerous rays are present.

U. S. Army Signal Corps photo

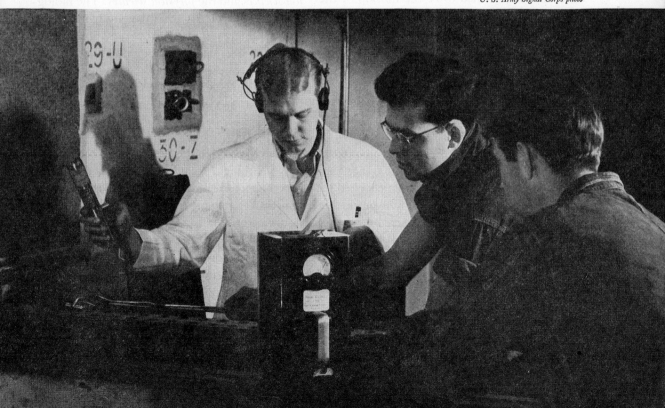

cannot be safely predicted at this time.

The release of atomic energy, an achievement of science that actually began many years ago, can be used to make man happier and to free him from drudgery, or it can be used to destroy him. As such, this discovery does not differ, except in its great power, from any other scientific discovery. Every important scientific discovery has brought the possibility of both good and ill. It is up to us to decide how the great discoveries and inventions of science are used. The future is being shaped today. Your study of science is part of that process.

WORKING WITH SCIENCE

1. You may want to read and report to the class the story of the release of energy from atoms. Now is a good time for you to learn how to find articles in magazines and newspapers, that is, *periodicals*. Your teacher or librarian will show you how to find articles by referring to *Readers' Guide to Periodical Literature*. *Readers' Guide* indexes all articles in certain periodicals. Look under *atomic energy*, *atomic bombs*, or *atoms* for magazine articles on the study of atoms. The August 20, 1945 issues of *Life* and *Time* have excellent articles and illustrations on the subject.

2. Start a scrapbook of scientific news and notes. Collect photos of great scientists and reports of scientific phenomena, such as flashes of lightning hurricanes, eclipses, new synthetic chemicals, and so forth. Consult newspapers and magazines like *Science News Letter*, *Science Illustrated*, *Popular Mechanics*, *Scientific American*, *Science Digest*, *Life*, *Newsweek*, *Reader's Digest*, *Coronet*, and so forth.

WHAT IS SCIENCE?

Science is not wholly "modern." It is not something new. The first man who experimentally wrapped himself in a skin to keep warm was something of a scientist. So was the first man who wondered about and carefully watched what seemed to be the motion of the stars or who made what to him was the mysterious thing we call *fire*. Man's early observations of wild plants finally led to the practice of agriculture. His need for food, clothing, and shelter and his plain, ordinary curiosity about things led to the inventions and discoveries that we consider important today.

In the thousands of years since the dawn of history, men have built up a vast amount of knowledge about the earth and the things that are on it. This knowledge has been checked by experience. It has been proved by experiments and organized and made clearer by mathematics. We call this organized knowledge *science*. Even more important than the knowledge itself, are the constantly improved methods scientists use in getting knowledge. These methods, too, are science.

BRANCHES OF SCIENCE

As you may imagine, the field of science is very large. One person cannot completely grasp all of it. Science has many branches, but all these fall into two large groups: the *biological sciences* and the *physical sciences*. The biological sciences deal with living things: plants, animals, human beings—how they are formed, how they live, and what they do. The physical sciences deal with nonliving things: rocks, chemicals, machines, stars—their composition, formation, measurement, and uses.

WHAT SCIENCE DOES

The *study of science* enables us to find out how the things around us really work and how they happen to be as they are. Most of us use household appliances, drive automobiles, and buy various foods and medicines with little real knowledge of these things. Just think how often you flip on an electric switch, but do you really know how an electric light works?

The study of science enables us to check what we already know from common observa-

How our energy sources and the value of goods produced by a man or woman in working 1 hour have changed. The symbols stand for three sources of energy: human beings, animals, and nonliving things. The numbers above the symbols are percentages of the total energy supply obtained from each source. Study these graphs carefully. How has the percentage of energy obtained from each source changed? Do you know why these changes have occurred?

tion about an everyday thing and to gain a real understanding of it. It also provides the chance to learn about new things that are rapidly becoming very useful, such as delicate instruments, new drugs, and modern airplanes that travel swiftly and safely.

What happens when you plug an electric iron into a wall socket? How is it possible to travel in an airplane 20,000 feet aboveground without ill effects? By what means do scientists predict the weather days and weeks in advance? What has made it possible to treat and cure, and even prevent, many diseases?

We constantly find new and different kinds of food products on the market, and some of us—wisely or unwisely—take various preparations to give us additional pep and to help keep us well. But how many people know why and how these products are made available to us? Many of our buildings and some of our homes are made comfortable by air-conditioning. We make the best use of such things as air-conditioning and new food products when we really understand them.

All these things, and many more, were made possible by science. They make our way of living and our civilization different from those of other times and places. The study of science is a way of finding out how changes have come about.

AMERICA YESTERDAY AND TODAY

Science is used all over the world and has developed throughout all time. However, we can best understand the changes it has brought about by looking at our own small part of the world—the United States of America.

Many scientific discoveries had already been made before the American Colonies were settled. Many basic scientific ideas that we have today were already known and some were in practical use. There were tools and some manufactured goods in Europe, but it was difficult and expensive to transport these things across the Atlantic Ocean. So the early American Colonists lived a rather simple life. They used the tools they brought with them in carving out their lives on a new continent.

Since those early days, Americans have contributed much to the world's store of scientific knowledge. One of our earliest scientists was Benjamin Franklin, born in 1706. The contrast between the life of a city-dweller or a typical frontiersman in Ohio or Pennsylvania in Franklin's day and their modern descendants in the same area is very great.

Better Living through Science. Because of improvements made possible by science, people live better today than they did in Franklin's time. Better living means good health, plenty of food in variety, proper medical care, good housing, rapid transportation, freedom from drudgery, and pleasant surroundings. It means also an opportunity for education, employment, and recreation. All sorts of important little things—a plentiful supply of pins, a stove that heats up at the press of a button, a refrigerator that works automatically, and soap, bread, and butter that can be bought instead of being prepared at home—have helped to make our living not only better but a great deal easier.

5

A home in Colonial times. Compare this home with the one on the next page. How do they differ?

HOMES PAST AND PRESENT

Modern conveniences in our homes are among the chief items in our picture of better living through science. Houses are carefully planned and built to protect us from cold winters and hot summers. We know how to provide them with adequate heat and light. Plumbing and other sanitary conveniences make our houses considerably different from those in the last half of the eighteenth century. Even the homes of the richest of Franklin's friends lacked such essentials as plumbing for bathtubs, hot water, and drains.

The style and even materials of the furniture used in Colonial America were very different from what we see today. Most frontier families made their own furniture, and only such essential pieces as tables, chairs, beds, and cupboards were found in ordinary homes. Of course, there were some great mansions in the 1700's, and these were elegantly furnished, often with materials brought from abroad. But even the very wealthy people did not have electric lights, or even gaslight. There were no vacuum cleaners, no linoleum, no refrigerators, no central heating, no phonographs or radios, because science had not yet made such things possible.

A modern home. List its improvements over the Colonial home. Which were made possible by science?

LIFE-EXPECTANCY THEN AND NOW

Life-expectancy means the average number of years a person is likely to live. A baby born in Franklin's time had a life-expectancy of about 30 years. In the early eighteenth century, thousands of babies died in their first year of life. On the other hand, thousands of people lived to be 60, 70, 80, and more. If 100 babies died at birth and another 100 lived to be 60 years of age, the life-expectancy of a new-born baby would be the average of those two groups, or 30 years. It can be shown, of course, that although a baby had a life-expectancy of only about 30 years in Franklin's time, a man or woman of 20 could expect to live to an age much greater than 30. In fact, many did.

Science and Life-Expectancy. Chiefly because of scientific progress, a baby born today has a life-expectancy of about 63 years. This means that the average life-expectancy at birth has more than doubled during the last 200 years. This great change was brought about largely by our increased knowledge of the cause, prevention, and treatment of diseases such as smallpox, diphtheria, malaria, typhoid fever, and tuberculosis. Increased life-expectancy has also been made possible by our knowledge of the kinds of food to eat, by improved water and milk supplies, by general sanitary conditions, and by public health services.

Making a carriage by hand. How do handcrafts differ from mass production, as shown on the next page?

MAKING THE THINGS WE USE

Many changes have taken place in agriculture and industry during the past 200 years. Most of these changes have been made possible by science and have brought about entirely new ways of living. The Colonists who settled in the "wilderness" cut down trees to clear the land and to get logs to build their houses. They sawed lumber by hand and with it built furniture, spinning wheels, and weaving looms. They plowed and planted by hand or with the aid of animals hitched to crude tools.

Only about 200 years ago, iron plows replaced wooden ones. Today a steel gang plow pulled by a tractor can plow an acre of wheat land in less than 1 hour. The same job with a two-horse team required 7 hours before the steel plow was invented. With a tractor, combine, and motor truck, a present-day farmer can, in less than 1 hour, reap, thresh, and haul away more than 20 bushels of wheat, a task that required more than 50 hours before the development of modern farm machinery.

After harvesting the grain, early American families ground the flour and made their own bread. They preserved foods for winter by smoking, drying, and curing meat and by preserving, pickling, and storing fruits and vege-

Automobiles on an assembly line—mass production. What are some advantages of mass production?

tables. Each family made its own soap and dipped its own candles to light its cabin.

Almost every family raised sheep and sheared them. The women spun the wool, wove it into cloth, dyed the cloth, and made the family clothing. Geese were plucked to obtain feathers for pillows. Other family tasks were the dressing and tanning of leather and the making of shoes.

Handcrafts versus Mass Production. Some people especially skilled in certain kinds of work went from house to house or traveled from village to village and offered their services. These were the *craftsmen*. They included weavers, blacksmiths, carpenters, cobblers, and artists, teachers, and so on. Even though many of them turned out fine products, their work took many hours. For example, it took a nail-maker a full 12 hours to turn out 100 flat-headed nails. Compare this with modern factories, where 100 such nails are manufactured by a single machine in 1 minute. Nails at the rate of 100 per minute are only one of the smaller gifts of *mass production.*

Mass production means turning out goods in huge quantities by specialized machinery. It is possible because of scientific developments— new sources of energy, such as electricity— and the invention of machinery, such as the lathe, plane, drill press, and hydraulic press.

Some of the means of transportation of earlier times. How did such transportation affect the people?

HOW WE TRAVEL

Changes in transportation show one of the greatest contrasts in our way of living with that of people who lived 150 to 200 years ago. Most of these changes were brought about through science. In 1790 about 90 percent of the American people lived on the narrow plain that lies between the Atlantic Ocean and the Appalachian Mountains. Within the next quarter of a century, thousands of people moved farther inland and westward.

Rivers were the first routes of travel on the American continent, and in the eighteenth century the Colonists traveled by canoe, rowboat, and barge. They also sailed small vessels be-

tween coastal towns. Some traveling was done on foot or horseback over trails that had been cut by Indians and exploring pioneers. By 1769 more trails had been marked out by Daniel Boone and other frontiersmen.

As homes and stores were built, trails were widened and improved to accommodate packhorses. Companies were organized to run stagecoaches on weekly or biweekly schedules. One such company operated between New York and Philadelphia, another between Boston and New York. In 1750 the trip from Boston to New York required a week of hard traveling. About 40 years later, it took George Washington 2 whole days to travel by coach

Some modern means of transportation, all made possible through science. How do they affect us?

from New York to Philadelphia, at that time the capital of the United States. Today this same distance—about 100 miles—can be traveled by airplane in less than 20 minutes' flying time.

Not only do we travel faster and more comfortably today, but we have many different kinds of vehicles. Magnificent liners sail the oceans, and smaller ships travel on rivers, lakes, and along the coasts. Fast, streamlined trains roar over a network of railways that completely covers the continent. Millions of automobiles, trucks, and buses travel our paved highways. Only a few crude motor cars had been built before 1900. By 1940 there were almost 35 million automobiles in the United States.

Now, we are in an age of aviation. Great airliners make the 2683-mile trip between New York and San Francisco in a few hours' flying time. The trip has been made in less than 6 hours by a giant airliner. Widespread travel by air will mean more changes in our way of living. People will be able to move from one place to another in much less time, and food and other merchandise will be transported long distances very quickly. Fruits and vegetables from faraway places may become as common to us as oranges, lemons, bananas, and string beans.

Mail just off the boat in Colonial times. Persons expecting mail gathered in a coffee-house to receive it.

CARRYING MESSAGES

In the early days of our nation, communication was almost entirely dependent on transportation. Messages were almost always carried by word of mouth or by letters. This meant that someone had to travel by ship, stagecoach, horseback, or on foot to take a message from one place to another.

Paul Revere's breath-taking ride to spread the news of the coming of the British is typical of the limited means of communication even in cases of great urgency. According to Longfellow's famous poem, Paul Revere received information of the approach of the British soldiers by means of light signals, which he had planned with a friend who watched from North Church. The light signals worked very well in this instance because both persons involved knew what they meant. However, light signals were not used for general communication.

When a Letter Was News. To receive a letter in eighteenth-century America was a rare experience for an average person. Neighbors quickly gathered to hear the news. To send one line from Virginia to Boston cost as much as a telegram does today and required more time than it now does to send a letter from

Some modern means of communication. What are some changes resulting from improved communications?

New York to Shanghai. There was mail service of a sort, and Benjamin Franklin helped greatly to improve the service during the period from 1753 to 1774, when he served as Postmaster General of the Colonies.

Originally mail was carried entirely by post rider. About 1770, stagecoaches took over the job. Since then steamboats, railroads, motor vehicles, and airplanes have carried the mail.

Science "Carries the Mail." In addition to our use of mail service, we now transmit messages by telephone, telegraph, radio, and television. The invention of the telegraph has been largely responsible for the development of the railroad

system, the modern newspaper, and, above all, the final welding of the people of America into a nation. The telephone made conversation possible between persons separated by great distances.

Transmission of messages without wires was the next step. Now, by radiotelephone, our voices can be carried to any part of the world in a fraction of a second.

Thus, through science in a relatively few years, the speed of carrying messages increased from about 10 miles per hour, to the almost unbelievable speed of more than *600 million miles per hour,* by radio!

A blacksmith's shop in Colonial times. What hand tools and handcrafts are important today? Why?

CHANGES IN THE TOOLS WE USE

The development of tools in America has played a large part in the growth of our nation. American Colonists of the eighteenth century had crude tools, in keeping with the conditions under which they lived. Of course, the first Colonists arrived from England with shovels, spades, sickles, hoes, axes, adzes, saws, and iron points and plates for plows. But even these tools were simple. In addition to tools for farming and building, they brought tools for fishing, whaling, shoemaking, tinkering, hat-making, leather-working, harness-making, saddle-making, distilling, dyeing, barrel-mak-ing, rope-making, milling, and so forth.

The tools were the simplest that could be made to serve well in frontier surroundings. All tools were so crude that parts from one tool could not be used in another of the same kind. Men had not yet learned to make tools by making a large number of the different parts required and fitting the parts together. Each gun, plow, or simple lathe was made complete, and was somewhat different from any other like it.

In the houses were tables, benches, chairs, and stools put together with wooden pegs. Tubs, buckets, and churns were made of

Cutting many steel plates at once. How do such tools affect our standard of living?

wood. There were some iron and copper utensils, but most of these were brought over from England and Europe. Tableware was made of pewter and did not include forks. Housewives swept their floors with split-birch brooms.

One look in your mother's kitchen or in your father's tool chest or even in any "10-cent store" will impress you with the difference in the tools we use today. As a result of scientific progress, our hammers, saws, and tableware are very much easier to use and are more attractive. And we have such things as fountain pens, electric drills, and power saws,

which were not heard of in the last half of the eighteenth century. More important are the modern machine tools that make possible the modern production of cars, airplanes, and refrigerators. Both the design and materials used in modern tools show our progress from a simple way of living to a highly refined and complex existence.

Today, most of the things we use are made by mass-production methods. We use automobiles, clothing, cooking utensils, books, and thousands of other things constantly, with little or no thought of their low cost or of the amount of time and labor saved by machinery.

1. Science and the ways of living that science has brought are not the same in all parts of the world. For example, the automobiles that most Americans take for granted are quite rare, or even unknown, in some parts of the world. As another example of the effects of science on ways of living, find the answer to the following question. Do people in other countries live, on the average, as long as they do in the United States? If there is a decided difference, can you account for it?

2. Read about soap-making at home. List some other commonly used things that once were made by each family but are now manufactured in large quantities.

3. Name five things that are relatively unchanged after 200 years of progress. Can you account for this lack of change after such a long time?

GROWTH OF SCIENCE

As you have seen, scientific knowledge has been very important in the development of the United States. We are especially interested in the United States because it is our home. But many of the changes brought about by science have occurred throughout the world. How did science bring about such changes? The answer to this question is one of the most important and thrilling stories in the history of mankind. It is the story of the development of modern science, which has transformed the ways of living of millions of people.

Some inventions and some scientific progress were made even before the dawn of recorded history. For example, hammers, levers, knives, drills, and wheels were invented so long ago that no one knows for sure who invented them. The ancient Egyptians and Greeks had some knowledge of heavenly bodies, and early alchemists discovered many truths about nature in their efforts to turn common substances into gold. But science as we know it today came much later.

OPPOSITES OF SCIENCE

Before careful thinking based upon observation and experiment gave people tested information, they often believed that many things happened magically. For example, when sickness struck down thousands of people in a short time, early physicians attempted to find its natural causes. They tried desperately to cure the victims and stop the spread of disease with all the means they had. In this they were just as scientific as any modern doctor. *Science is essentially the search for natural causes.*

Because of lack of knowledge and their poorly developed methods and instruments, the attempts of early physicians often failed. Thousands of people fell ill and died. Overcome by fear, many people—sometimes even the physicians themselves—turned to strange beliefs and mysterious remedies. Many thought that evil spirits were in a sick person's body and attempted to get rid of such spirits by elaborate hand-waving and meaningless words. Such beliefs we call *magic*. Magic is born of lack of knowledge and fear. It is an opposite of science, for science holds that anything that occurs has natural causes.

Early Medicine. Many early people depended upon strange remedies in their efforts to cure diseases. One remedy of earlier days read something like this, "For all sorts of aches, cut the patient's fingernails when the fever is coming on, and put the parings in a little linen bag, and tie the bag about a live eel's neck in a tub of water. The eel will die, and the patient will recover."

Such a remedy is not based upon belief in evil spirits or other supernatural beings. But it is an example of an idea that has no basis in tested information. Such a belief—accepted without thinking and in spite of the lack of tested information to support it—is commonly called a *superstition*. A superstition is an opposite of science, for science demands tested information for belief.

The day of magic and superstition is not

over. Many people still believe that 13 is an unlucky number. Few hotels have a floor numbered 13 because many people would not accept rooms there. For the same reason, airplanes rarely have seats numbered 13. Many people still believe that spilling salt, breaking a mirror, seeing the moon over the left shoulder, or allowing a black cat to run across their paths means that they will have bad luck. The study of science should cause people to be less superstitious, to see why it is necessary to look for natural causes, and to demand tested information in support of ideas and beliefs.

MEN FIGHT AGAINST FEAR

Fortunately, there were always men who tried to find the natural causes of disease, lightning, earthquakes, and other occurrences that threatened them. They believed that if they could find the causes, they might find ways to protect themselves and their fellow-citizens from sickness and destruction.

In their fight against superstition, ancient tradition, and ignorance, these brave men often met stubborn opposition. For example, an epidemic of smallpox struck Boston in 1721. Dr. Zabdiel Boylston, a self-educated physician, tried to stop the spread of the disease by injecting, or *inoculating*, people with cowpox— a procedure that had been used successfully in England.

The people of Boston were against Dr. Boylston, although the success of the procedure in England was in his favor. They refused to accept his treatment. They were afraid of it and called it evil work. Someone wrote a pamphlet attacking Dr. Boylston. A howling mob threatened to take his life and even attempted to bomb the house of Cotton Mather, who had persuaded him to inoculate.

But Boylston would not be browbeaten by superstition and ignorance. He went ahead with his plans and inoculated his own son, another boy, and two servants against smallpox. Boylston's courage was repaid, for inoculation saved the lives not only of these four persons, but of millions of others since his day.

THE SEARCH FOR CAUSES

Sometimes the inquisitive, truth-seeking men met in groups to discuss various questions that puzzled them. In America one of the earliest of such groups was a club organized in Philadelphia by Benjamin Franklin in 1727. It was the Junto Club, which met every Friday evening in a tavern or a home or in the open air. The members discussed such questions as "Why does smoke rise?" "Why does water appear on the outside of a glass of water?" "What causes storms?" "What is lightning?"

Franklin and his friends refused to accept the belief that lightning was a bolt shot from heaven and aimed at some evil-doer on earth. They considered it a perfectly natural occurrence that might be similar to sparks. So they searched for a *natural* explanation.

In 1747 one of Franklin's friends who lived in England sent him a large glass tube. When rubbed with silk, the tube became charged with electricity, or *electrified*, and gave off electric sparks.

During his experiments, Franklin found that he could electrify a metal ball by means of the glass tube. When a tiny ball of very light wood suspended on a thin string touched the electrified metal ball and then was held near the metal ball, the wooden ball swung away from the metal ball. In other words, the tiny wooden ball was *repelled*. Later, Franklin touched the metal ball with the sharp point of a needle and reported that when he did this in the dark, " . . . you will see, sometimes at a foot distant or more, a light gather upon it like a firefly."

Franklin reasoned that perhaps a lightning flash in the heavens might be like the light produced by the needle and the electrified metal ball. He wanted information to support his belief or to show that it was wrong, and he devised an experiment to find out the truth.

FLYING A KITE TO FIND ELECTRICITY

Franklin hoped, by flying a kite during a storm, to bring a lightning flash down to earth for examination. The kite was made of a piece of silk cloth stretched over two sticks placed crosswise. A pointed metal wire was attached to one of the sticks and also was connected to the cord of the kite. A metal key was tied to the lower end of the cord.

Franklin and his son waited under a shed in an open field. As clouds gathered and the sky became dark, the kite was sent aloft. Suddenly, Franklin noticed that the unraveled strands at the end of the cord began to spread out. They were repelling one another. He quickly brought his bare knuckle to the metal key. A strong spark jumped to his knuckle. He felt the slight shock and saw the miniature flash. The proof was actually in his hand. There could be little doubt that the lightning flash was a long electric spark.

Through the kite and its cord, electricity had passed, or been *conducted*, from the clouds to Franklin's hand. Franklin did not realize at the time the great danger of this experiment. He knew that electricity passed through wet objects more readily than through dry objects, but he did not know that if the cord had been thoroughly wet, he might have been killed.

HUMAN NEEDS SHAPE SCIENTIFIC PROGRESS

Scientific discoveries and inventions are stimulated by man's curiosity about his surroundings and his desire to live longer, more safely, more comfortably, and more attractively. The old adage, "Necessity is the mother of invention," is often quite true.

Not *all* experiments and *all* inventions result because they are needed at a particular time. Many discoveries occur because some person becomes inquisitive about an apparently useless question or problem. He starts thinking about it and then experiments to find the answer, regardless of any practical value it may have.

Often, however, discoveries provide new information that leads to other research which may produce very practical results in men's lives. The atomic bomb is a good example of how research on an apparently useless problem may result in world-changing ideas and de-

vices. For centuries scientists have worked and studied to learn more about the basic nature of all the material in the world.

Sir Isaac Newton, an English scientist who died in 1727, revived and developed an ancient Greek theory that all things are composed of tiny particles called atoms. Newton also developed certain ideas concerning motion. These ideas hold generally true for large objects and even the unbelievably tiny atoms.

Among the modern scientists who have studied the nature of matter and provided knowledge, without which the atomic bomb and the promise of controlled atomic energy for man's use could not have been made possible, are an Englishman, Sir James Chadwick; a Dane, Niels Bohr [bōr]; an Italian, Enrico Fermi [fär′mē]; a French woman and man, Irene and Frédéric Joliot [zhô-lyô′]; a German, Albert Einstein; an Austrian, Wolfgang Pauli [pou′lē]; a Russian, Peter Kapitza [kȧ′pyĭ-tsŭ]; and an American, Ernest O. Lawrence.

These, and many other scientists of various nationalities, colors, and religions worked without much regard for the practical applications of their research on the nature of the atom. It took urgent war needs and the organized attempt of thousands of scientists to make practical use of the knowledge disclosed by their research. But the wartime research could not have been carried on successfully without the information and ideas that the earlier scientists had provided through their study of "useless" problems.

KNOWLEDGE IS POWER

Science is the tested knowledge that has given man power to change his world. To a large extent, this tested knowledge has made the modern world possible. It is up to all of us to use science for better living. We can do so only as we come to know some of the important ideas of science and as we come to understand the methods used in scientific work to discover answers to problems and questions. Your study of general science should provide you with a beginning of such knowledge.

WORKING WITH SCIENCE

1. You may find it interesting and worthwhile to form small committees from your class to report on various scientific advances. Subjects and articles of possible interest are indicated under *Reading You Will Enjoy*.

2. Consult a number of people among your own family and friends about any superstitions which they may follow. Make a list of the superstitions. Report on how your friends first began to practice them and whether they really believe that they are true.

3. You have a friend who believes it is unlucky to walk under an open ladder, break a mirror, or who has some other superstition. How would you proceed to convince your friend that there is no scientific basis for these beliefs?

4. To get the same effect as Franklin did when he rubbed glass with silk, shuffle your feet across a rug and then bring your knuckle to a metal object, such as a radiator. Explain the result of your experiment. What other method could you use to get a similar effect?

5. In 1831 when Michael Faraday demonstrated his first simple dynamo, Gladstone, the great British statesman, asked him what it was good for. Faraday replied, "Some day, Mr. Gladstone, you will be able to tax it." Try to find some other examples of the skepticism of political leaders concerning the inventions and discoveries of scientists.

READING YOU WILL ENJOY

Ilin, M. *Turning Night into Day*. J. B. Lippincott Co., Philadelphia, 1936. A fascinating account of the history of lighting.

Jaffe, Bernard. *Men of Science in America*. Simon and Schuster, Inc., New York, 1944. Extremely interesting account of the advance of science in America.

Kummer, Frederick A. *The First Days of Knowledge*. Doubleday & Co., Inc., New York, 1923. Fanciful descriptions of the invention and development of many things before the time of recorded history, based on probable situations that brought about the inventions.

Readers' Guide to Periodical Literature will be your guide to many exciting stories and articles concerning new developments through science. Check in this guide on a few topics, such as electronics, plastics, synthetics, atoms, genetics, soilless agriculture, rockets, jet propulsion, radar, television, radio, DDT, penicillin, cancer. Some of these terms may not mean very much to you now. However, they will take on meaning and interest as you see what your world of tomorrow may be through the development of such new things and ideas in science.

Towers, Walter K. *From Beacon Fire to Radio* (rev. ed. of *Masters of Space*). Harper & Bros., New York, 1924. Excellent accounts of the invention and development of the telegraph, radio, and other communication devices.

Science is an endless search. As problems are solved, new ones arise. Progress is made, but there is always more to learn.

Little progress was made toward conquering malaria until after America was discovered. Jesuit priests, who came to South America with the explorers, found the Indians (1) using the bark of an evergreen tree to treat the disease. This bark, known as Cinchona, or Peruvian bark, became famous. It was studied by many scientists, but more than a century passed before pure quinine was extracted from it.

Meanwhile other scientists were tackling the problem of how malaria is transmitted. In 1880, Laveran discovered the malaria germ, and Ross, in 1897, gathered the facts that tied malaria to mosquitoes. Grassi (2) and others helped find the kind of mosquito. Knowing how malaria was transmitted, scientists developed public health measures to help control it: swamps were drained, houses screened, and insect repellents invented.

When the supply of quinine from the East Indies was threatened by World War II, work on substitutes went ahead at full speed. Atabrine was a reasonable substitute, and thousands of soldiers (3) used it during World War II. Finally, in 1944, two American chemists, Woodward and Doering (4), made synthetic quinine. This did not mark the end of malaria. The disease is still serious in many parts of the world. The malaria problem, like many in science, still needs much more work.

2

HOW SCIENCE CHANGES THE WORLD

Science is far more than just a body of knowledge. It also consists of the ways in which knowledge was discovered and organized. It is the open-minded, critical attitude toward what we know, or think we know, that enables us to find new knowledge and to modify old knowledge if we find it partly or wholly incorrect. It is the belief that all things have explainable causes, and that man can discover answers to problems through careful observation, experimentation, and critical thinking.

The ways by which we find and use knowledge through such methods of acting and thinking are called *scientific methods*. The story of how one scientist attacked and solved a baffling problem will make clearer how scientific and unscientific methods differ. One such story concerns the disease now called by a name that means *bad air*.

A FAMOUS SCIENTIFIC SEARCH

Before the days of modern medicine, natives of a swampy, coastal region of Italy noticed that persons who went out into the night air often became ill and developed a fever that lasted for some time. They were correct in observing that going out at night had something to do with the disease. However, these Italians knew nothing about the very small beings that cause disease, that is, *germs*, and how they are carried. They thought that night air was responsible for the disease. Hence, they called it *malaria*, meaning *bad air*.

You can easily see how this idea spread. Foreign sailors stopping at Venice brought the idea to France and England. Immigrants carried the idea to America. Parents passed the word on to their children, "Night air is bad for you. It causes disease."

SCIENCE DEMANDS CAREFUL OBSERVATION

There were good reasons for the original observation that night air was responsible for malaria. The Italians who named the disease simply observed that night air and the disease seemed most of the time to go together.

On the other hand, there was nothing particularly scientific about their observation. Science demands *careful* observation. We all observe things with varying degrees of care. However, a person trained to do scientific work makes very careful and detailed observations.

Careless observations often do more harm than good. This was the case with the observation that night air and malaria went hand-in-hand. The observation saved lives, it is true. Many people refused to go out into the night air and thus did not get malaria. But, on the other hand, the belief was passed along from parents to children and became accepted as entirely true. As truth, it stood in the way of more complete knowledge of the disease.

Fortunately, *careful* observations were finally made. Not by one man, but by several. Two men deserve credit for special detective work in locating the "criminal" responsible for transmitting malaria: Ronald Ross, an

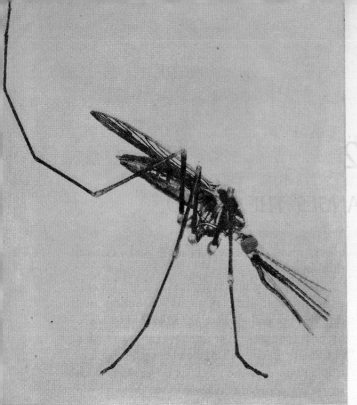

An enlarged *Anopheles* mosquito. See if you can find out how to tell *Anopheles* from the common *Culex*.

Englishman; and Battista Grassi [grä'sě], an Italian. Grassi's story is particularly interesting.

FINDING THE "CRIMINAL"

Many people realized that malaria struck only in or near swampy areas or lowlands. A few, including Grassi, guessed that this might be because there were many mosquitoes in such places. It had already been proved that certain kinds of six-legged animals called *insects* carry diseases from person to person. This gave support to the idea that swamp mosquitoes might be the carriers of malaria.

With the care of a trained scientist, Grassi thought the matter over. And he observed. He went here, there, and everywhere in his native Italy, searching out the places where malaria struck. He compared conditions in such places with conditions where no malaria existed. His careful observations showed that:

1. There were places in Italy without

malaria. In some of these places, there were no mosquitoes. But in other places also without malaria, the air buzzed with countless mosquitoes!

2. In every place where malaria was common, there were mosquitoes.

This was as far as Grassi's most careful observations could take him. Was his guess wrong, as his first observation might appear to make it? If mosquitoes carried malaria, why did not people in certain mosquito-ridden areas he investigated get the disease?

But note his second observation. Wherever he discovered malaria to be common, he also discovered mosquitoes. What would you make of such a situation?

This is what Grassi decided. "There is only one answer. I am almost certain that mosquitoes carry malaria, for I never find it without also finding mosquitoes. *But it must be one particular kind of mosquito.* How else can I explain why human beings do not get malaria in many places where mosquitoes are common?" This was Grassi's guess—scientists call such carefully made guesses *working theories*—and he set out to find out whether his guess was right or wrong. *Science requires experiments.*

First, Grassi hunted for all the different kinds of mosquitoes he could find. He was still very carefully observing, you see. With a sack of glass bottles and tubes, he went to many marshes, swamps, stagnant pools, and lowlands and scooped up mosquitoes. He studied them carefully. When he found a new kind, he checked to find out whether or not human beings in the region had malaria.

Grassi went into hospitals, churches, and stores, swooping down on mosquitoes, identifying them, and always finding out whether anyone in the localities had malaria or knew about malaria cases nearby. In this way he identified 15 or 20 different kinds of mosquitoes that he ruled out as probably not being carriers of malaria.

He asked questions. He would approach a sick man, "Are there mosquitoes around here?" "Did mosquitoes bite you shortly before you became ill?" "Did they look like this one? or this one? or this one?" This was careful observation for you.

Finally, Grassi began to realize that he had almost certainly tracked down the carrier. Time after time, he found that a mosquito of a particular kind was in the room, or had recently bitten a chill-chattering malaria patient or his next-door neighbor tossing with a violent fever.

But this was not complete proof. It just narrowed the problem so that it could be studied more closely. Grassi was nearly sure he had located the guilty mosquito, for in Rome in 1898 he made a speech in which he said, "It is the *Anopheles* mosquito [a light brown, spotted-winged mosquito that stands on its head when it sucks blood] that carries malaria if any mosquito carries malaria . . . ." But he knew that he had to put his theory to the test of an experiment under conditions that he could control. Scientists call such an experiment a *control*, or *control experiment*.

MR. SOLA GETS BITTEN

Grassi went to a hospital high on one of the highest hills of Rome. There, no one had ever contracted malaria. Furthermore, the *Anopheles* mosquito that Grassi suspected did not fly that far from its swampland home. It was an ideal spot for the experiment Grassi had in mind.

In this hospital was a man named Sola. We do not know what Sola was doing in the hospital, but he did not have malaria. He had never had malaria. Grassi interested Sola in his experiment, and Sola agreed to help. Sola was placed in a small room that mosquitoes could not get into or out of. Then Grassi let loose in the room mosquitoes that had bitten people with malaria. But these were mosquitoes of a particular kind.

Grassi first tried the common *Culex* mosquito—the one that often bites us on summer evenings. Night after night Sola let those irritating, buzzing mosquitoes bite him. But he stayed healthy and as happy as such a well-bitten man could expect to be. As a result of

U. S. D. A. photo

Cutting cinchona bark in Ecuador. Quinine for treating malaria is made from this bark.

this experiment, it seemed clear that the *Culex* mosquito does not carry malaria.

But what about the *Anopheles* mosquito? Now came the big test. You can imagine Grassi's nervousness as he shut Sola in the room and then turned loose a horde of *Anopheles* mosquitoes—mosquitoes that earlier had feasted on the blood of malaria victims. Next day Sola was covered with his usual itchy bumps. Then Grassi waited. One day passed and nothing happened. Another day, and still no malaria. Three days—a week! Was he wrong? Could all his careful, painstaking observation have been of no value? Nine days went by. You can well imagine that Grassi was about to give up in disgust.

On the morning of the tenth day, Grassi went into the hospital and opened the door to Sola's room. He rushed to the bedside. His eyes danced. Perhaps he had to stifle his joy. For Sola was a sick man. His body was shaking with the violent chill typical of malaria. When Grassi examined a drop of Sola's blood

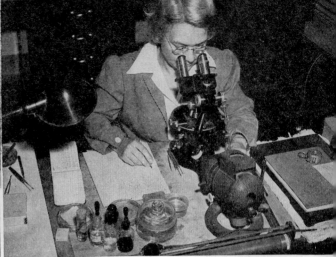

These Department of Agriculture scientists use scientific methods. Left: Getting ready to make tests to determine the quality of canned foods. Right: Working on problems of inheritance in plants.

under a microscope, he found it swarming with the tiny germs of malaria.* Sola was given immediate relief through the use of medicine. And he had the glory of being in on an experiment that has saved hundreds of thousands of lives since.

THE FINAL TESTS

Grassi had not finished. How do *Anopheles* mosquitoes get malaria germs into *their* bodies? Grassi believed that they get the germs by sucking them up with the blood of malaria victims. But he was not sure. He decided to make sure. He raised some *Anopheles* mosquitoes. He kept them carefully so that they did not have a chance to bite anyone. Then he let them loose in a room and every evening for 4 months he and several close friends sat in this room. Some of his friends were bitten as many as 50 times a night. Yet not one of them got malaria. Apparently *Anopheles* mosquitoes can carry malaria germs only after sucking them up with the blood of malaria patients.

The next summer, Grassi went to the worst malaria spot in all Italy. There he chose 10 tiny homes of railroad workers and put up wire screens on all the windows and doors. He used screens of such fine mesh that no mosquito could get through. He chinked up the

* Malaria is caused by a very small being called a *malarial parasite.*

cracks and holes in the 10 houses so that they were absolutely mosquito-proof. One hundred twelve persons lived in those 10 tiny houses. Grassi had them stay indoors with windows wide open from early evening until morning. He kept them there every evening for months.

While these 112 persons stayed there, breathing the "bad air" that had always been considered the cause of malaria, 415 other persons lived in the same little community in houses unprotected from *Anopheles* mosquitoes. Almost without exception, these 415 persons got malaria and suffered the chills and fever of the disease.

What of the 112 protected individuals? Only five got the disease during the entire summer. As you can see, Grassi could never be certain that a few of them could not be bitten by mosquitoes during the day.

Through careful observation and controlled experiments, Grassi demonstrated to the world that the *Anopheles* mosquito is the carrier of malaria. Bad air? Bad only in the sense that the *Anopheles* mosquito could fly in it from a sick person to a well one. Get rid of the *Anopheles*, and you get rid of malaria.

WHAT ARE SCIENTIFIC METHODS?

Let us take stock of what Grassi did. It is typical of the way scientific methods are used

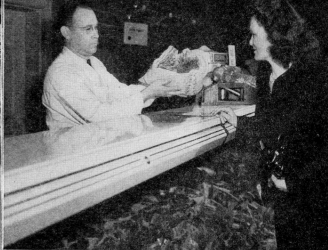

You do not need to be a scientist to use scientific methods. For example, in what ways are this boy and this housewife using scientific methods in buying things? How scientific can they be?

by all scientists in solving a problem. Grassi *carefully collected and sorted out all the information that seemed to be related to the problem.* And he made many very *careful observations* of his own.

After examining all this information and his own observations, Grassi *made a guess*, or a *working theory*, as to the cause of malaria. He improved on the general belief that night air often "carried" malaria. He "guessed" that night air was dangerous only when a certain kind of mosquito (*Anopheles*) was present.

Grassi did *careful and critical thinking* throughout his work. He thought through the problem carefully. He did not jump to any conclusions but was content to develop a working theory that he could modify later if necessary.

After developing a working theory, he *put it to the test of controlled experiments.* Controlled experiments really put theories, which grow out of careful thinking, to the test of observation under controlled conditions.

After the working theory was tested by means of controlled experiments, Grassi and others were willing to *accept it as an established theory.* An established theory is called a *law*, or *principle.* Scientific laws, or principles, are statements that describe what man has found always to hold true about natural occurrences.

The fact that Grassi went at the problem as he did, shows that he did not accept even widespread beliefs without investigation. That is to say, *he did not accept a belief just because almost everyone else did.* He had a *vast curiosity* about things and wanted to answer the why, how, and what of the troublesome malaria problem.

These are all parts of what we call scientific methods of work. Other parts might be listed, but these are among the most important.

WORKING WITH SCIENCE

1. A discussion has arisen regarding the relative mileage obtainable from two advertised brands of gasoline. How would you proceed to find a scientific answer to the question?

2. Examine the advertising page or pages of your favorite magazine. Select five advertisements and explain why you would or would not accept the claims made for various products on the basis of scientific facts. If possible, clip the "ads" and exhibit them to the class.

3. A Frenchman accompanied by his 13-year-old son arrives in the United States for a short visit. They spend practically all of their time in one home in Cambridge, Massachusetts. Upon their return to Paris, the young boy tells his friends that America is a land of very educated, fairly well-

25

You can easily study common living things scientifically by direct observation, reading, and experiment. In reading about them, be sure to pick books written by experts. Check your observations in such books.

to-do people. Everybody is happy, polite, and un-troubled. What would you say about the boy's report of America? Give reasons for your criticism.

4. If you have recently read a Sherlock Holmes or any other detective story, briefly describe how the mystery was solved by "scientific methods."

YOU AND SCIENTIFIC METHODS

Do not think that only trained scientists can work scientifically. Training in science does provide a rich store of scientifically tested information. And it helps to develop the ability to work scientifically. But everyone can, and should, use scientific methods to help reach sound conclusions on all kinds of problems met in everyday living.

One of the finest things about scientific methods is their common-sense quality. As a matter of fact, science has been called *organized common sense*. Consider Grassi's work for a moment. Isn't that just about what his methods amounted to?

BELIEFS AND FACTS

Most of us do not take any stock in the once-common belief about the bad effects of night air. But what about the old saying, "Stuff a cold and starve a fever." Is that true? How about the belief that sunlight is good for you or that you should always sleep with your windows wide open? Does smoking stunt your growth? Test your answers to these questions against the latest scientific information. You may be surprised at what you find out.

We cannot afford to run our lives and make important decisions in ignorance of facts that have been shown to be true. If we are to bene-fit by the knowledge that science has pro-duced, we must take the trouble to determine the *facts* and use them.

You must understand clearly what a scien-tist means by a fact. He means simply that study and experimentation have shown a cer-tain thing to be apparently true. Nothing known now makes it appear false. But a scien-tist knows that methods of study are always being improved, and he fully expects that someday new knowledge will make him change his mind about *some* things he now thinks of as facts.

Grassi's work, with that of Ronald Ross and others which merely gave further support to Grassi's conclusions, resulted in the "fact" that only the *Anopheles* mosquito carries ma-laria fever. But research carried on during World War II seems to indicate that a few kinds of mosquitoes in addition to *Anopheles* may also carry malaria.

One of the most important of the attitudes

of a scientist is that there may be no such thing as unchanging truth. A scientist has an open mind, always ready to re-open a problem and to change his views if new facts are found.

ABUSE OF SCIENCE

Scientific knowledge, and the methods that produce it, are powerful instruments for good. Unfortunately they may be used for destructive purposes also. We have seen this to be true of atomic energy. For another example, consider the explosive *dynamite* which was invented by a Swedish scientist, Alfred Nobel [nȯ-běl'], in 1867. He made this explosive to break apart huge rocks in order to build roads, and to blast deep channels in rivers and harbors so that ships might pass through safely. Dynamite was a great advance, for it saved the labor of many men. But dynamite and other explosives have also been used in wars to destroy life and property.

A steam shovel, a case of dynamite, a rocket, or a tank of gasoline is *neither* good nor bad. But they can be put to constructive or destructive use. The uses to which inventions and discoveries are put are either good or bad, depending on the people who use them.

When the Wright brothers of Dayton, Ohio produced their first airplane in 1903, they did not dream that their invention would lead to the horrible destruction caused by aircraft in World War II. They were interested in a new and more rapid way of getting people and supplies from one place to another.

Can scientists be blamed for producing such death-dealing weapons as atomic bombs, high explosives, airplanes, and poison gas? No, they cannot, for it is the *way* in which the products of science are used that is the important thing. Scientists—as scientists—are not to blame for the horrors they have made possible. But scientists—as men—along with everyone else, should take responsibility for watching how their inventions or discoveries are used by others.

SCIENCE AND DEMOCRACY

As men reasoned, observed, and experimented, scientific methods evolved. These made possible *organized* study and resulted in an unending stream of discoveries and inventions. Thus, scientists have helped to improve and increase the material things of living, such as more nourishing food, better clothing, electric lights, refrigerators, and automobiles. They have made it possible for men to control famines, floods, and pestilences.

Some scientists have also helped to make possible the democratic way of life that we enjoy in the United States. Democracy and science arose and developed together in our country. Because they needed freedom to experiment and invent, scientists helped to build a country where men would be free to work and think—a country where democracy is the form of government.

Many of the heroes of the Revolutionary War and some of the greatest American statesmen were also good scientists or men who believed firmly in science. Benjamin Franklin, George Washington, and Thomas Jefferson are good examples.

Scientists joined with other men in insisting that all men belong to the same human family and that they are all entitled to life, liberty,

To buy scientifically, what facts should a shopper know? Are such facts always available? Why?

Philip Gendreau

27

and the pursuit of happiness. They helped destroy false beliefs, such as the divine right of kings to govern and enslave other people. They refused to accept the old Greek idea that "slavery is the natural position of certain men."

Scientists built machinery that took away much long and back-breaking work. Thus, scientists gave men more leisure in which to think, to experiment, and to enjoy themselves. They destroyed the age-old beliefs that illness is punishment and that work is degrading. More recently, they fought against the unscientific belief that one particular people is superior to all other peoples.

SCIENCE IS WORLD-WIDE

Scientists' search for truth and for ways of making better living more widespread is carried on in all parts of the world. The discoveries of a scientist working in Paris may be reported in a scientific journal. Scientists in New York, Leningrad, London, Mexico City, Peking, or elsewhere may read and use it. Except in wartime, the laboratories of scientists are generally open to scientists from other parts of the world.

Very often in the history of science a final achievement has been reached by slow steps made by many men. A good example is the final mastery of radio communication. Michael Faraday, an Englishman, had an idea that electric sparks travel in all directions, even through empty space. James Clerk Maxwell, a Scotsman, proved the idea according to mathematics. Using this information, Heinrich Hertz, a German, discovered radio waves.

Guglielmo Marconi, an Italian, then devised a practical way of sending radio messages across the Atlantic Ocean. Thomas A. Edison, an American, discovered a strange occurrence in a glass bulb from which air had been removed. John A. Fleming, an Englishman, devised a way to control the passage of electricity through this glass bulb. Finally, an American, Lee De Forest, introduced a wire net, or *grid*, in the bulb and produced the first radio tube, which provides the foundation for modern radio communication all over the world.

The development of the electric motor, the automobile, penicillin, the sulfa drugs, and even the atomic bomb are other examples of cooperation of scientists from all parts of the world. Science advances through the sharing of information and the efforts of many people of different nations, classes, colors, and creeds.

True science and true democracy are one.

WORKING WITH SCIENCE

1. Have you ever heard the belief that crops must be planted only at a certain time of the month when the moon is "right"? From local farmers, find out if that belief exists in your locality. Develop a method of attacking the problem through careful observation, experimentation, and critical thinking to determine whether the belief is based on facts.

2. Is there a scientific basis for the common belief in the absolute authority of the printed page? Take several newspapers and compare the *differences* in their reports of some news item with the complete *agreement* of the stock-market quotations of these same newspapers.

3. *Astrology* is the belief that the stars influence human affairs. Bring to class clippings on astrology from newspapers and magazines, and discuss them. Form theories about the correctness of such articles. In Unit 9 you will study the nature of the stars and can, at that time, check the theories you now form with the facts that have been discovered by science.

4. It is sometimes easier to see that scientific developments make war possible than that they make peace more likely. Consider how the invention of the telegraph, radio, and airplane and the release of atomic energy have made peace more likely.

5. From your science department or school library select one of the books listed at the end of this or any other chapter and write a book report after you have read the book chosen.

READING YOU WILL ENJOY

Coe, Douglas. *Marconi, Pioneer of Radio.* Julian Messner, Inc., New York, 1943. An interesting biography of this famous man.

Darrow, Floyd L. and Hylander, Clarence J. *The Boys' Own Book of Great Inventions* (rev. ed.). The Macmillan Co., New York, 1941. An unusual and excellent book that describes all kinds of inventions. Includes experiments you can perform to demonstrate the principles involved in these inventions.

de Kruif, Paul. *Microbe Hunters.* Harcourt, Brace & Co., New York, 1926. An exciting book about men of science in their fight against the tiny plants and animals that cause many of man's diseases. Chapter X is an absorbing account of the work of Grassi and Ross in hunting down the mosquito that carries malaria.

Slosson, Edwin E. *Creative Chemistry* (rev. ed.). D. Appleton-Century Co., New York, 1930. A delightful book that tells the part science has played in industry and in our lives. Somewhat old, but still worthwhile.

Slosson, Edwin E. *Short Talks on Science.* D. Appleton-Century Co., New York, 1930. About 100 articles on science collected from Dr. Slosson's writings in magazines.

1

2

Before man learned how the human body uses food, he could do very little to help keep the digestive system working smoothly. As he learned more about how the digestive system actually works, he became able to eat more wisely and to treat more effectively a digestive system that does not work as it should.

Early peoples had many explanations of digestion. Among these were that food is cooked or rots or ferments in the digestive system and thus becomes part of the living body. Some persons believed that the "vital touch" is necessary and that whatever digestion is, it cannot be carried on outside the body. However, careful experimentation proved otherwise. In 1782, Spallanzani (1)

showed that gastric juice is secreted in the stomach and that its action is different from fermentation. In 1883, William Beaumont (2), an American army surgeon, demonstrated that digestion can take place outside the body. In 1835, Schwann (3) isolated and named the enzyme pepsin, which is responsible for protein digestion in the stomach.

Since the days of these early experimenters, our knowledge of digestion and nutrition has grown rapidly. Much of this was made possible through direct study of human beings and the use of animals (4) in research. Today we know much about how the digestive system works. As a result, we can all live more healthfully.

3

4

UNIT TWO

Your Body-Machine and How It Works

3

THE BODY-MACHINE AND ITS USE OF FOOD

Joe Jones swung into the front seat of his new car and pressed the starter. The engine turned over rapidly a few times, backfired, wheezed, and quit. Joe frowned and pressed the starter again. The motor turned over slowly and then stalled. Again Joe pressed the starter. This time he got a tired "Arhhhuuu," and that was all.

Joe sat for a few moments thinking. He was proud of that new car. He had had it for only about 6 months and it had given him no trouble before. "Must have a short somewhere," he said to himself. Then he got out and went into his house.

JOE CALLS AN EXPERT ·

Joe picked up the telephone and called the neighborhood garage. In a few minutes a service car pulled up in front of his house. "What's the trouble, Joe?" said the mechanic.

"If I knew, and could fix it, I wouldn't have called you out here," grinned Joe. "A short somewhere must have run down my battery."

"Well, I'll take it to the garage and have a look at it," said the mechanic. "You can't pick it up before tomorrow, though. Give you a lift to town?"

Next day, Joe took a taxi to the garage. His car was waiting, just three cars from the grease rack where another car was getting a regular lubrication and checkup. Under the windshield wiper on Joe's car was a bill. Joe read, "Bearing replacement, starter motor. Labor $6.50. Parts, $0.60."

As Joe looked at the bill, the mechanic came up and said, "She's as good as new again."

"Well she ought to be," said Joe. "That car isn't more than 6 months old. Say, how in the world do you know what's wrong and how to fix these cars so easily. I thought it must have a short, but it looks like the trouble was something entirely different."

The mechanic smiled. "Joe," he said, "every man to his own business. I've worked at this trade for more than 10 years. A car has lots of parts. And it isn't easy for someone like you to know what has happened when something goes wrong. Certainly it wouldn't pay you to try to fix it. You don't have the know-how, and you don't have the right tools. But it's my business to know what goes wrong with cars, and to fix them right."

JOE'S CAR AND JOE'S BODY

Two years later, almost to a day, Joe Jones got into his car and drove away from his home. It was not the car just discussed, for Joe bought a new car every year. Joe always said, "Trade them in before they start to wear out. Treat them right while you drive them. Have them checked regularly and keep them lubricated. Then you don't have the expense of

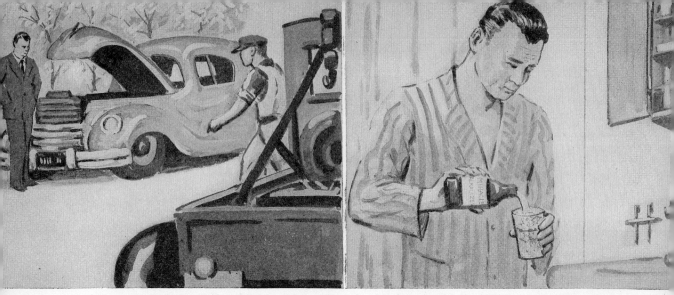

People who would not think of trying to fix their own cars try to treat their own illnesses. Why?

major repairs. A few hundred dollars and you have a new car."

Joe drove to his office. He went into the building, nodded hello to his secretary, shut the door to his office, and sank heavily into his chair. He had not been feeling very well lately. That pain in his chest again. Besides, he had trouble getting his breath when he climbed the stairs. His wife had insisted that he see a doctor. But not Joe. "It's nothing," he would say. "Just a little indigestion. A little of that 'Miracle Alkalizer' and I'll be all right in a jiffy."

Joe sat up and tried to put his mind on his work. That pain—it was pretty bad today. "Maybe I had better see a doctor," said Joe to himself. He started to get up, but he did not make it. He slumped forward over his desk. His secretary found him there a few minutes later. Joe had had a heart attack. He was soon on the way to a hospital.

THE BODY-MACHINE

Few persons would think of tinkering with a modern car when something goes wrong. Unfortunately, far too many of these same persons attempt to figure out, or *diagnose*, their own ills and to treat themselves.

The man who takes good care of his car and neglects his body does not understand that his body-machine is far more complex and delicately adjusted than his car. If he realized how the working, or *functioning*, of one part of his body affects other parts of his body, he would never decide on medicines for himself, unless he was sure he knew what his trouble was and how to treat it.

Actually there are far better reasons for persons to have periodic checkups on themselves than on their cars. Spare parts for cars can be secured and installed. Not so with the body-machine. You get one new model when you are born. Spare parts are not available, and repairs, when they are possible, are likely to be more than a little expensive.

You are the most remarkable, complex, and smoothly running machine in the world. You are more than a physical machine, of course. You are also a chemical factory and a powerhouse. And finally, the real marvel of you is that you think, love, hate, enjoy. You dream and plan and create. You are life!

When asked for the source of true wisdom and a happy life, an ancient philosopher always answered, "Know thyself!" That is a large order. You will spend your life learning more about yourself and how to understand and control your actions. One part of that growing knowledge is an understanding of your physical make-up—your body-machine.

What is life, anyway? This is a question that man has asked always and is still asking. Although much more is known about life than ever before, scientists find that for every question they answer, new questions arise.

LIVING AND NONLIVING THINGS

The question "What is life?" is too broad and too general for a complete answer. Scientists have found it more useful to narrow the problem to questions such as, "How do living things differ from nonliving things?" "What do all living things have in common?" "How do living things grow and act, or behave?"

As scientists studied such questions, many facts—important to human health and well-being—have been learned. What are some of these facts? In the first place, living things—whether they are plants, bugs, or elephants—have certain ways of acting, called *functions*, in common. What are these *life-functions?*

Life-Functions. All living things take in certain materials from outside their bodies, make new products out of them, secure energy from them, and throw off waste products from their bodies. Scientists use the general term *metabolism* in referring to this life-function.

All living things grow. Tiny animals that can be seen only under a microscope grow at different rates of speed and to different sizes than do men or elephants, but they all grow. The important point about the *growth* of living things is that they grow by manufacturing more of the same stuff of which they are made. So growth is a second life-function.

All living things are suited to their surroundings. This is called *adaptation*, a third life-function. Adaptation includes the many ways in which living things adjust themselves to the world about them. All living things are sensitive to certain conditions, such as pain, pressure, sound, light, warmth, cold, and moisture. And all living things are able to adjust, or *adapt*, themselves to these conditions.

All living things are able to produce other living things like themselves. This is called *reproduction*. Life comes from life. Reproduction is a fourth life-function.

THE WHOLENESS OF LIVING THINGS

There are several differences in the behavior of living and nonliving things. In the first place, there is a sort of *wholeness* to living things that does not exist in nonliving things.

Nonliving things may grow. For example, a snowball may grow by rolling downhill or being patted with more snow. However, it grows from the outside without changing the form of the inside. How different this growth is from that of a living thing! You cannot make a puppy grow by rolling it down a snow-covered hillside. Snow may get in its ears, but it has not actually grown. When a puppy grows, something happens to cause the entire animal to grow *from within* and as a whole. Every small part of its body changes to produce growth.

Reproduction is another example of the difference between living and nonliving things. Think of breaking a toy doll or wooden train in two. You do not get two smaller dolls or trains. You have two parts of one broken train or doll. On the other hand, when a plant or animal reproduces, an entirely new living being, or *organism*, develops. Like its parent

What life functions are shown here?

Lambert from Frederic Lewis

or parents it has complete parts and the proper relationship of those parts to carry on its life.

PURPOSE AND MOVEMENT

There is another important difference in the way living and nonliving things behave. It is frequently called *purposiveness*. Nonliving things may move. But they move because of some outside force, and they are not able to control their movement.

If you kick a small rock, it is moved in the direction of your kick. If you kick a dog, it moves also. But you cannot be sure in which direction it will move. It may go ki-yiing down the street, heading for home. Or it may leap up and grab you by the leg. You cannot be sure, for it is a living thing and its movement is purposive. It determines things for itself.

Furthermore, a living thing generally starts, or *initiates*, its own movements. A stone or stick cannot decide all of a sudden to go somewhere or do something. A dog or a human being can and does. Mercury in a thermometer expands and is forced up the tube when the temperature rises; it cannot do anything else

But it is impossible to predict what a man will do when the temperature rises. Put a thermometer by a fire, and the mercury will rise. Put a man by the fire, and he may go to sleep, move toward it to warm his hands or to roast a wiener or run to get some water to put it out. In short, living behavior is purposive and usually self-initiated.

WORKING WITH SCIENCE

1. Compare an automobile with a living animal, such as a dog, for evidences of each of the life-functions. Do any life-functions appear to be performed by the automobile? How are such functions different from those performed by a living animal?

2. Consider the life-functions carried on by a living plant, such as a bean plant. Are all life-functions represented?

3. A living seed, stored in a box, shows little evidence of any of the life-functions. It does not move or grow. Can you explain its life in terms of life-functions?

4. You have probably seen a chicken whose head has just been cut off, thrashing and jumping around. Is the chicken dead or alive? Explain.

5. Plant bean or pea seeds in a flower pot. Water the soil daily. Observe the growth of the plant. Can you detect purposiveness and wholeness in the life of this plant? Explain.

BUILDING BLOCKS OF LIFE

Are the building materials of living and nonliving things as different as their functions and behaviors? Nonliving things are constructed from many different substances. Great bridges are made of steel beams, huge spans of wire rope, and concrete towers and supports. Buildings may be constructed of steel, concrete, wood, brick, marble, limestone, and so forth. Thus, both the arrangement of parts, or *structure*, and the substances used as building blocks, or *units*, of nonliving things vary enormously.

On the other hand, all living things, plant and animal, are composed of similar substances. And living things are remarkably the same in structure as well as in requirements and functions.

DISCOVERY OF THE CELL

In 1665 an Englishman named Robert Hooke looked at a piece of cork (the inner bark of the cork tree) through a microscope. The cork was really dead, and all the living material, or *protoplasm*, had decayed away. Hooke noted that the cork seemed to be a network of small structures which reminded him of a honeycomb. He called these structures *cells*, although what he saw were really the woody walls of cells.

A little more than 100 years ago, two German scientists, Matthias Schleiden [shlī′ dĕn] and Theodor Schwann [shvän], described the structure of cells and presented the theory that all plants and animals are made up of one or

All living things are composed of one or more cells.

more cells. In other words, they believed cells to be the building blocks of *all living things*.

The cell theory has been verified many times since Schleiden and Schwann announced it. However, there is one possible exception to the cell theory. The tiny substances called *viruses* seem to be alive, but no one has been able to prove that they are living things.

Viruses are so small that they cannot be seen under the strongest ordinary microscope, which enlarges up to 2000 times. Only recently they have been observed under the great new electron microscopes, which can enlarge more than 100,000 times. But no cells have been found. If viruses are ever proved to be living things, they will be an exception to the cell theory.

CELL STRUCTURE

Although cells differ widely in size and shape, most of them have about the same parts. The illustration shows the structure of cells. The animal cell is enclosed in a jelly-like envelope called the *cell membrane*. The cell itself is also jelly-like, but it is more liquid than the membrane. Within the cell, near its center, is the *nucleus*, the dark, round area. The nucleus is the most complex and important part of the cell. It contains strands of material that are easily stained with certain dyes so that the cell can be studied.

If the cell and the nucleus are cut in two, each part cell usually rebuilds, or reproduces,

Which is the plant cell? Animal cell? Why?

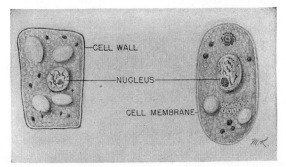

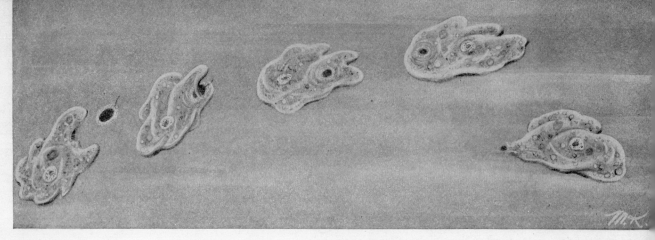

An ameba engulfing a food particle. Explain these drawings.

the part of the cell that is missing. But if one part cell contains the entire nucleus, this grows into a complete cell again, while the part without the nucleus dies. The nucleus is necessary to reproduction.

ONE-CELLED AND MANY-CELLED ORGANISMS

All living things, from tiny animals and plants that can be seen only under a microscope to the largest plants and animals, are composed of cells. Some living things consist of only one cell. Others are made up of billions.

Ameba. One-celled animals must perform the same life-functions as human beings. An *ameba* is one such animal.

An ameba feeds itself simply by flowing around food in the water in which it lives, and staying there until the food is absorbed. It removes wastes from its body largely by "walking off" and leaving them behind. No fuss or bother with complicated intestines, kidneys, and so forth. An ameba takes in *oxygen* directly through its cell membrane. Oxygen is a gas from air, which you must get by breathing through an elaborate lung apparatus.

An ameba does not have blood, heart, or blood vessels, for it does not need them. After all, a heart is a pump that pushes blood through blood vessels to all parts of the body. Since an ameba is only one cell, it obviously does not need a heart or blood vessels because there is no place for blood to go.

Man. Your body is composed of billions of cells, instead of just one. Unlike an ameba,

most of these cells cannot possibly soak themselves in water and absorb food directly through their cell membranes. Therefore, cells that perform special functions, or *specialized cells,* handle your food needs.

If you poke an ameba with a needle, it simply flows away from the needle. But if you poke the cells of the tip of your toe with a needle, they cannot possibly flow away. Cells are all around and above them, so that those in your toe cannot move of their own accord away from the danger. Of course, *you* get away fast enough. But you do so because other cells in your body cooperate, especially two groups of specialized cells: *nerve* cells and *muscle* cells.

SPECIALIZED CELLS

The human body has many types of cells, but they all have the same general structure. Most of them have become massed together in groups and changed, or *modified,* to do specialized tasks. Groups of similar cells that perform specialized tasks are called *tissues.* Nerve tissue, for example, is a group of nerve cells.

The other main types of cells and tissues are *epithelial; muscle; connective,* such as *cartilage* and *bone; blood; fat;* and *gland.* Epithelial cells are generally flat or like cylinders. They form the skin and membranes that line the mouth, intestines, chest, and other cavities.

There are three types of muscle cells. The muscles that move the arms and legs are called *skeletal muscles.* They are striped in appearance

36

and draw up, or *contract*, at our will. We call them *voluntary muscles*. Smooth muscle cells cannot be controlled at will. They make up the *involuntary muscles*, the muscles that move food along the digestive tube, control the size of eye pupils, and perform similar tasks. *Heart muscle* is the third type of muscle cell. It is striped, like skeletal muscle, but is not under voluntary control.

Connective tissue cells manufacture long strands that contain nonliving material. These strands are interlaced to form the strong, tough tissues that hold together, or support, other cells and tissues. Cartilage is tough, semitransparent tissue more elastic than bone.

Blood may be hard to think of as a tissue, for it is not sheetlike in appearance. However, it is a tissue, since groups of blood cells perform special functions.

The cells that make up fat tissue can take up particles of oil or fat and store them. Since fat is transparent, a fat cell has the appearance of a finger ring with the cell nucleus forming the thickened part of the ring.

Gland cells produce and throw out, or *secrete*, certain chemicals. Some of these chemicals are important in regulating metabolism, that is, energy changes in the body.

ORGANS AND SYSTEMS

When several kinds of tissue, such as muscle, nerve, blood, and fat tissue, work together to perform a particular function or functions, they form an *organ*. For example, the heart is an organ. It is made of muscle, nerve, blood, fat, connective, and epithelial cells and tissues.

A group of organs and tissues that work together form a *system*. For example, the heart,

The human body is composed of many different kinds of cells and tissues.

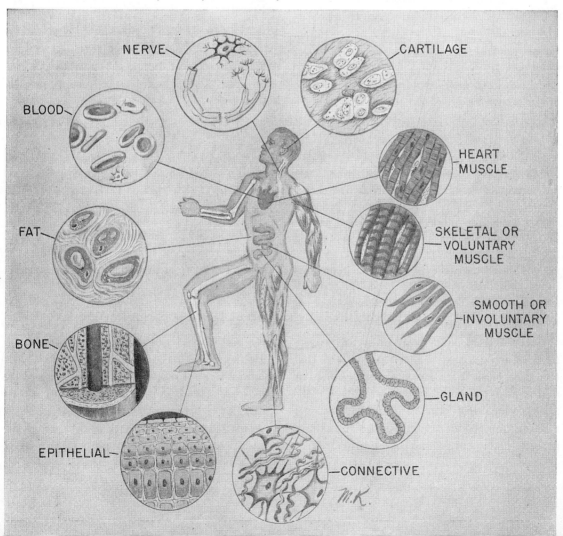

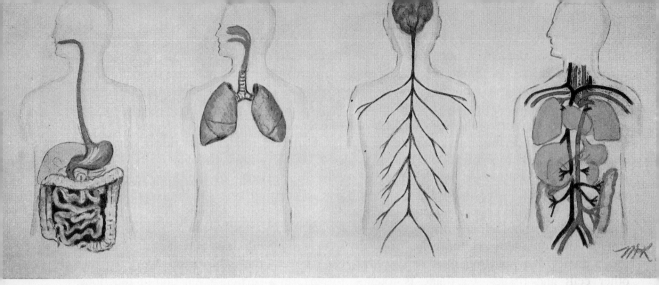

Four body systems: digestive system, respiration system, nervous system, and circulation system.

blood, and blood vessels make up the *circulation system*. The brain, spinal cord, and nerves form the *nervous system*.

INTERDEPENDENT PARTS

Like a great city, the human body is made up of parts. If something should slow down or stop the activities of one part—for example, transportation of foods—in the city, every other activity would quickly be affected. Such parts are called *interdependent* parts. Similarly, in the human body, if something should harm the circulation system, every other system and cell in the body would be affected.

A feeling of pain in one part of the body may actually be the result of an illness in an entirely different part of the body. For example, headaches may mean that the eyes, the stomach, or other parts of the body are ill. Hence, it is dangerous to diagnose your own ills and to take medicines for them. Only a trained physician knows enough about the human body to do an intelligent job of treating it.

WORKING WITH SCIENCE

1. Carefully scrape the inside of your cheek with the edge of a spoon or very dull knife. Place the scrapings on a microscope slide and smear them flat with the edge of another microscope slide. Place a drop of ink on the smear and leave it for about 1 minute. Wash off the ink by immersing the slide for a few seconds in a jar of water. The ink will stain some of the *epidermal* (outer epithelial layer) cells that you scraped from the lining of your cheek. This makes them more easily seen. Place your slide under the microscope lens and observe the cells. Can you detect a darkened nucleus in some of the cells?

2. If your teacher has prepared slides of animal and plant cells, look at some of them under the microscope. Some of these may show the nucleus and its contents well.

GETTING FOOD INTO THE BODY-MACHINE

Every cell in your body is actually surrounded by a watery substance, or *fluid*, that contains foodstuffs, oxygen, and salts, or *mineral* materials. In this way, your body cells are not very different from an ameba. But your millions of cells are organized into specialized groups. The job of getting food into your body belongs to the cells of the *digestive system*.

Perhaps you have thought that, once you swallow food, it is inside your body. In a way it is, of course. It is in your stomach or intestines. But is it really inside your body?

Your body is covered with a sort of sack of skin. If you look at your mouth in a mirror, you see that the skin becomes thin at your lips and nostrils, *but it does not stop.* The lips, insides of the nostrils and mouth and throat are reddish because the blood shows through the thin membrane. The skinlike membrane that lines your mouth is called *mucous membrane.* It is a continuation of the skin and forms a continuous sheet that lines every part of your digestive tube.

If you put a lump of sugar inside the hole in a doughnut, would you say that the sugar had gone into the doughnut? In the same sense, a piece of sugar swallowed into the stomach is still not *inside* your body. Before it gets inside, it must pass through the mucous membrane.

The digestive tube is a long, twisted passageway into which food passes when we eat. In the digestive tube the food changes so that it can go through the membranes and to the cells that need it.

DIGESTION IN THE MOUTH

What happens to food when you eat it? Even before eating, your body prepares to get busy when you smell good food cooking. If you are hungry, your mouth begins to water. Even the thoughts of tasty food will start the flow of *saliva*, a digestive juice that is secreted by the *salivary glands* of your mouth.

As you chew food, it is broken up and ground into tiny pieces. It is mixed with a large amount of saliva that pours from the three sets of salivary glands of your mouth, located as in the illustration on page 40.

What is the function of saliva? If you have ever attempted to eat dry crackers fast, you know one of the answers. Saliva moistens food so that it can be swallowed easily. But there is a second and even more important function of saliva. Saliva contains a chemical called *ptyalin*, which changes, or *digests*, starch. Starch cannot pass through cell membranes so it is changed into substances that can pass through the mucous membrane and be used.

Starches are foods; so are *sugars.* Starch cannot go through mucous membrane, but a *simple sugar*, such as the *glucose* in corn syrup or mo-

lasses, can. So ptyalin digests starch by changing it to simple sugar.

Enzymes. Only a few of the foods we eat—minerals, vitamins, and simple sugars—can go directly through the walls of the digestive tube and into our bodies. The rest must be broken down mechanically and changed chemically to simpler substances before they can reach the cells where they will be used. This mechanical and chemical process is *digestion.*

The mechanical part of digestion begins when we chew food. Chemical changes in food are brought about by substances called *enzymes.* The ptyalin in saliva, which digests starch, is an enzyme. Enzymes really digest food for us.

It is not necessary to know the names of all

The chief internal organs.

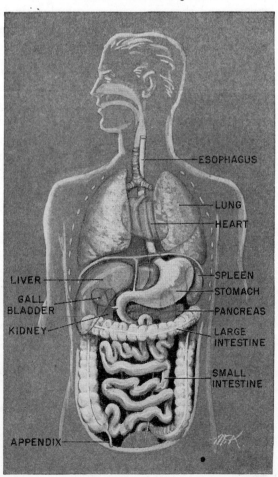

ESOPHAGUS

LUNG

HEART

LIVER

GALL BLADDER

KIDNEY

SPLEEN

STOMACH

PANCREAS

LARGE INTESTINE

SMALL INTESTINE

APPENDIX

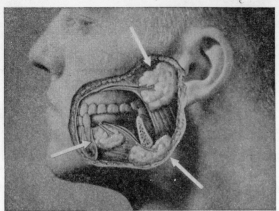

One of each of the three pairs of salivary glands.

the enzymes or to know the names of all the substances that are formed when beefsteak, butter, bread, and so on are digested. The important point is that digestive enzymes are produced in various parts of the digestive system and that they change complex foods into simple substances that can pass through the mucous membranes.

Could You Swallow While Standing on Your Head? After you swallow a mouthful of food, it goes through a tube called the *esophagus* to your stomach. Foods may "fall" down the esophagus, but they are also pushed along by a series of ringlike muscles that contract one after another. You can swallow even water, you know, while standing on your head.

The contraction of muscles in the esophagus is very much like the effect you would see if you slipped a rubber tube through a tight ring and pushed the ring along the tube. Such contraction and movement in the human body is called *peristalsis* and occurs in all parts of the digestive tube.

Food is prevented from going into your windpipe, or *trachea*, by action of the throat muscles, which lift the end of the windpipe against a sort of lid, called the *epiglottis*. You can feel this action by holding your *Adam's apple* and swallowing.

Foods do not go up into your *nasal cavity* because the soft part of the roof of your mouth —the *soft palate*—lifts up like a trap door to seal off the opening to the nasal cavity. If you examine the inside of your mouth in a mirror, you can see the soft palate and its tip, called the *uvula*, which hangs down at the back.

DIGESTION IN STOMACH AND SMALL INTESTINE

Perhaps you think of the stomach as the chief organ of digestion. But this is not true. Most digestion takes place in the *small intestine*. The stomach serves as a storage bin. It takes in a fairly large amount of food at one time and slowly releases it in semiliquid form to the small intestine.

The stomach secretes a liquid called *gastric juice*. This acts upon *proteins*, a type of food of which meats are largely composed. Periodically, the strong circular muscle at the end of

Both uvula and epiglottis change their positions when we swallow. Why?

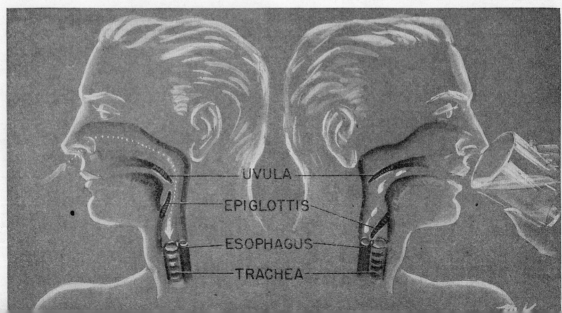

UVULA

EPIGLOTTIS

ESOPHAGUS

TRACHEA

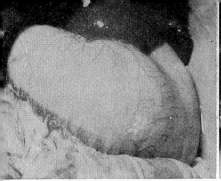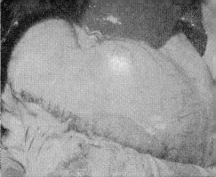

From Encyclopaedia Britannica film Digestion of Foods

In peristalsis a wave of contraction moves along part of the digestive tube. These are stomach waves.

the stomach relaxes, and some of the stomach contents pass through into the small intestine. Starch digestion, which was started in the mouth, and protein digestion, which was started in the stomach, are both completed in the small intestine. *Fats*, which are not digested at all before reaching the small intestine, are broken up and completely digested there.

The digestive juices in the small intestine all flow into the first 10 inches or so of the small intestine. Small glands line this region of the intestine and pour out large amounts of *intestinal juice*, which contains several enzymes and digests sugars and proteins.

Bile, another digestive juice, enters the small intestine through a tube from the *liver*. Bile does not contain a digestive enzyme, but it does break up fat into extremely fine droplets so that it can be digested. The *pancreas* is a digestive gland that lies just under the stomach. It is shaped something like a dog's tongue. The pancreas pours *pancreatic juice* into the small intestine. This juice contains three enzymes and digests starches, proteins, and fats.

ABSORPTION FROM THE SMALL INTESTINE

The mucous membrane that lines the small intestine has many folds, which give it a very large absorbing surface—much larger than if the membrane were smooth. The intestinal lining is also covered with millions of tiny finger-like projections called *villi*. The villi increase greatly the actual surface of the intestine in contact with digested food materials.

Osmosis. Foods are absorbed from the inside of the small intestine. That is, they go through the mucous membrane into the blood stream. Whenever a membrane, such as the lining of the small intestine, separates two liquids, some of the liquid on each side goes through the membrane to the other side. When the liquid on one side contains more dissolved material than that on the other side, the transfer, or *diffusion*, of liquid is greater in the direction of the liquid containing the most dissolved material. This process is called *osmosis*.

The mucous membrane that lines the digestive tube separates liquid foodstuff in the intestine from the blood that is contained in millions of tiny blood vessels on the other side of the membrane. When the liquid foodstuff is composed of simple sugars and the end-products of protein and fat digestion, it passes through the membrane and into the blood stream.

ABSORPTION IN THE LARGE INTESTINE

After absorption in the small intestine, only the indigestible materials remain. These indigestible materials contain much water at this

Into one container of starch in water, saliva is poured. Explain photo at right. Why two containers?

From Encyclopaedia Britannica film Digestion of Foods

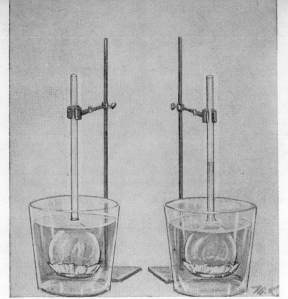

Apparatus for demonstrating osmosis. Explain.

large intestine, more water than usual may be absorbed. The indigestible materials become hard and dry and are hard to push out. Such a condition is called *constipation*.

LAXATIVES CAN BE DANGEROUS

The preparations used to relieve constipation are called *laxatives*. There are three types of laxatives. One type stimulates peristalsis by increasing the bulk of the indigestible materials. Another lubricates and softens the materials. A third type softens the materials by causing water from the intestinal walls to be forced into the large intestine.

You have probably heard that poisons, or *toxins*, are absorbed from the large intestine. These toxins are supposedly produced by the tiny plantlike organisms called *bacteria* which live in millions in the large intestine. Now, *if* the waste products of these bacteria were absorbed into the body, they undoubtedly would cause trouble. But it is extremely doubtful that they ever are, except perhaps in unusually severe and prolonged constipation.

One of the most common forms of constipation occurs when the large intestine becomes irritated as a result of the too-frequent use of laxatives. Do not take laxatives unless they are prescribed. If you tend to have constipation, eat more fruits and vegetables.

stage—water that was secreted as a part of the various digestive juices. The unabsorbed, indigestible materials are pushed from the small intestine past a little finger-like organ called the *appendix* and into the *large intestine* (see illustration on page 39). In the large intestine, much of the water in the indigestible materials is absorbed.

From time to time, the indigestible materials are pushed out of the large intestine. Usually this occurs once a day, although longer intervals are normal for some persons. If indigestible materials pass very slowly through the

WORKING WITH SCIENCE

1. Mix a little cornstarch with water and pour it into a test tube. Fasten an animal membrane or vegetable parchment over the end of the tube with rubber bands so that it is watertight. Make a

A section through the small intestine looks like this.

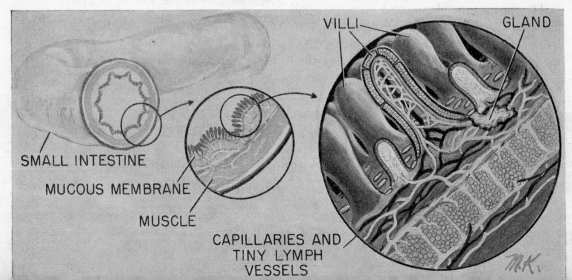

SMALL INTESTINE

MUCOUS MEMBRANE

MUSCLE

VILLI

GLAND

CAPILLARIES AND TINY LYMPH VESSELS

sugar *solution* by mixing some corn syrup or molasses with a little water and pour it into another test tube. Fasten another piece of animal membrane tightly over the end of the second test tube. Pour some water into each of two glasses or beakers and turn one tube upside down in each glass of water. Let the tubes stay in the water until the end of the class period. In the meantime, do Exercises 2 and 3.

At the close of the period take a small amount of the water surrounding the tube that contains starch and test it for starch (see Exercise 2). Did any starch go through the membrane?

Take a small amount of the water surrounding the tube that contains simple sugar and test it for sugar (see Exercise 3). Did any sugar go through the membrane?

Let the tubes remain in the glasses of water until the next day and test the water again for starch and sugar to see whether the results are the same after a longer period of time.

2. To test for starch: Prepare an iodine solution by placing a drop of iodine in a tablespoonful of water. Place some of the material to be tested in a container and pour in a little of this iodine solution. If starch is present, a blue-black color will result. If starch is not present, this color change will not take place.

3. To test for glucose, a simple sugar: Pour a small amount of the substance to be tested into a test tube and pour into the same tube one-half this amount of Fehling's solution A and the same amount of Fehling's solution B. (Or use equal amounts of the material to be tested and Benedict's solution.) Heat the contents of the test tube over a flame until it comes to a boil. If a simple sugar is present an orange-red or brick-red color will result, and a solid substance of this color will settle out.

4. The change from starch to sugar can be easily demonstrated outside the human body. Place a small amount of bread or cracker which has been broken into tiny pieces in a test tube. Pour in just enough water to soak the bread or cracker. Place another small amount of bread or cracker into another test tube and add enough saliva of your own to soak it. (Or chew the bread or cracker for a few minutes until it is well mixed with saliva and then put it into the test tube.) Let both tubes stand until near the end of the class period. Then test some of the contents of each tube for starch and for sugar. What do you discover?

5. Osmosis occurs constantly in living things, and understanding the process will help you to understand many things about the functions of human bodies and other living things.

Set up apparatus as shown on page 42. Use corn syrup, glucose, or other simple sugar to make a sugar solution and place it in a thistle tube, or glass funnel. Fasten a piece of animal membrane over the end of the tube with a rubber band so that it is watertight. Place the thistle tube in a glass or jar of water and use a support to hold it erect (see page 42). With a gummed label, mark the height of the sugar solution in the thistle tube at the start of the experiment.

Look at the tube at the end of the class period and again at the beginning of the period next day. What do you observe?

Test the water surrounding the thistle tube for simple sugar. You will note that some of the simple sugar has apparently passed through the membrane into the water.

READING YOU WILL ENJOY

de Schweinitz, Karl. *Growing Up* (2nd rev.). The Macmillan Co., New York, 1935. A valuable book that presents the story of how we develop before birth, are born, and grow up.

Disraeli, Robert. *Seeing the Unseen* (rev. ed.). The John Day Co., New York, 1939. A remarkable book about the world that may be seen only through a microscope. It has many marvelous photographs taken through microscopes.

Hawley, Gessner G. *Seeing the Invisible*. Alfred A. Knopf, Inc., New York, 1945. The subtitle of this book is "The Story of the Electron Microscope." It contains remarkable pictures taken by this most up-to-date of all microscopes.

Strain, Frances B. *Being Born*. D. Appleton-Century Co., New York, 1936. Another excellent book describing in simple terms how we develop before being born.

"Authorities" often stand in the way of progress even in science. For example, Aristotle (1), a great Greek teacher who lived in the fourth century B.C., carefully studied the bodies of fishes and other lower animals, but probably not those of human beings. However, he concluded that the blood of human beings obtains "food" from the liver from which it flows to various parts of the body where it is "consumed," with no return flow to the liver. He also believed that the blood is "cooled" by air taken into the lungs.

Galen (2), a Greek physician who practiced in Rome in the second century A.D., believed that blood is formed from food in the liver and passes back and forth through the veins like the tides.

Aristotle and Galen had such great reputations that what they had believed was considered correct for hundreds of years. Because of their influence, many later students refused to carry on their own experiments. Other students would not believe their own observations when their observations did not agree with what Galen or Aristotle had said.

But William Harvey (3), an English physician, was not such a man. His studies convinced him, in 1628, that the heart pumps blood out through arteries and back to the heart through veins. People called him a fool for contradicting Aristotle and Galen. But Harvey's conclusions were finally accepted. As a result of our present understanding of the blood and the circulation system, examination of the blood (4) tells modern doctors many things about the state of a person's health.

4

FUEL AND AIR FOR THE BODY-MACHINE

A siren wails in the night. An ambulance screeches to a stop. Men in white jump out, examine an injured man with expert fingers and eyes. He is bleeding badly and his face is drawn, white, and covered with tiny beads of perspiration. He seems to feel no pain.

The flow of blood is stopped. A bottle of clear fluid hangs from a small stand that has been erected. A rubber tube connected to the bottle ends in a long hollow needle. Carefully this needle is thrust into a large blood vessel in the mid-arm of the injured man and the clear fluid flows slowly into the man's blood stream.

A few minutes later he is enroute to a hospital for further treatment. But already he is on the way to recovery. His face has a healthy glow. He breathes deeply and regularly. The look of distress has left him. If his injuries have not been too serious, he will live because of the clear fluid now coursing through his blood vessels.

WHAT IS BLOOD?

What is the clear fluid? How will it enable the injured man to recover? How did it save the lives of hundreds of thousands of fighting men at battlefronts in World War II? How does it save other thousands of lives in America as well? The clear fluid is *plasma*, the fluid part of human blood.

PLASMA

If you measure out, say, a pint of blood, one-half or a little more of it is plasma. That is to say, plasma makes up about 50 percent *by volume* of your blood. This percentage changes a little from time to time. For example, if you perspire heavily, the fluid part of your blood is decreased somewhat, for perspiration actually comes from blood. If you drink a large amount of water, the fluid part of your blood is slightly increased for a short time. But such changes are really slight and temporary.

Incidentally, you cannot "thin" your blood with sassafras tea or "blood tonics." If you could, it would probably kill you. Such tonics are generally a waste of money, to say the least.

The Blood's Job. About 90 percent of plasma is water. The rest is composed of many substances that are dissolved or mixed in the water. Only through the blood can the cells of your body get the things they need and get rid of their waste products. Therefore, your blood must carry all these things at one time or another.

Water and foods enter the blood stream from the small intestine. Oxygen enters from the lung tissues and is carried by the blood. Glands in your body throw other materials into the blood stream. *Carbon dioxide*, a waste gas produced by the cells of the body, is carried to the lungs, and other wastes are carried to the liver, kidneys, sweat glands, and so forth.

SOLID PARTS OF BLOOD

Besides the plasma, blood is composed of a number of solid objects. If you examine blood

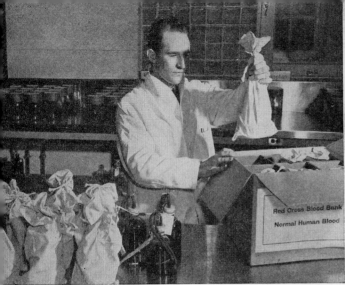
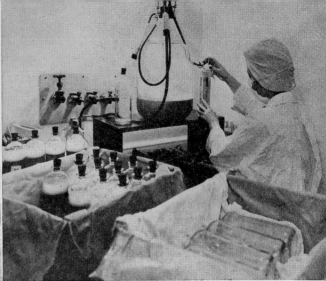

American Red Cross photos

Red Cross blood banks are maintained in many hospitals. Left: Bottles of whole blood arriving. Right: Filling bottles with plasma after the blood cells have been removed. The plasma will be frozen.

under a microscope, you will see objects that look like tiny, straw-colored, balloon-tired disk wheels (see illustration below). These are the *red blood cells*, also called *red corpuscles*, and your blood contains many millions of them. In fact, a drop of blood equal in volume to a cube each side of which is the size of this block ▪ contains from 4½ to 5 million red blood cells!

These red blood cells contain a reddish substance made up of iron and protein and called

Looking into the end of a small blood vessel. Point out red and white corpuscles and platelets.

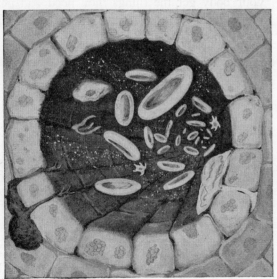

hemoglobin. Hemoglobin is a remarkable substance that combines, or unites chemically, with oxygen in the lungs. (The union of any substance with oxygen is called *oxidation*.) As the red blood cells circulate through the blood stream, they release oxygen to the cells of the body.

The Body's Warriors. There are other solid objects in the blood. Under a microscope, some of these look very much like amebas. These are *white corpuscles*. They are the warriors of your body and battle with disease germs that get into your body (see Chapter 7). A drop of blood small enough to rest on the head of a pin normally contains about 7000 of them.

Very small, disk-shaped bodies, called *blood platelets*, are the third kind of solid substance in the blood. These are well named, for they look like tiny plates. They are much smaller than red corpuscles, which they resemble somewhat, and they are not red since they contain no hemoglobin. The drop of blood mentioned earlier contains about 250,000 platelets. Their chief function is to make blood clot. This is a very important function, for if the blood did not clot when a blood vessel was cut, a person would bleed to death in a short time.

How Blood Clots. The process of clotting is

not completely understood, but it is known that the platelets always break up just before clotting begins. Just as soon as the platelets start breaking up, clotting begins. Apparently, both the platelets and plasma release substances which produce a stringy, or *fibrous*, substance that collects the red blood cells into clots.

WORKING WITH SCIENCE

1. Would you like to examine some of your own blood under a microscope? With your teacher's supervision, secure a drop of blood from your finger in the following manner. Wash your index finger carefully. Soak a bit of absorbent cotton in rubbing alcohol. Dab the cotton on the ball of your finger. Let the finger tip dry without touching it. Heat a needle to redness in a flame. Place your index finger, nail down, on a table. Hold the needle about an inch or 2 from the finger and jab lightly down but with sufficient force to penetrate the finger. (This procedure is painless or, at most, causes just a pinprick sensation.) A drop of blood should well out at the puncture. Increase the amount of blood by squeezing the finger.

Touch the drop of blood to the center of a clean microscope slide. Place the edge of another microscope slide on the first slide and wipe firmly from one end to the other so that the drop of blood smears thinly over the slide. Examine the blood smear under a microscope. For best results, find a place on the slide where the blood smear is very thin and use the high-power lens of the microscope. The red corpuscles should be readily seen.

2. Have you ever watched blood clot? You will be able to see the fibrous material that enmeshes the red cells to make the clot. Secure a drop of blood from your finger in the manner described in Exercise 1. Place it on a clean microscope slide. Move the point of a needle through the drop of blood with a circular motion. Soon fibrous strands of blood fasten to, and are dragged by, the needle as you move it. Determine the amount of time required for this to occur and compare with the time required for clotting by blood from other members of the class.

CIRCULATION SYSTEMS

A circulation system is a transportation device. Some animals do not need one. For example, an ameba with a circulation system would be something like a hermit in a desert who built a streetcar system but had no place to go.

On the other hand, many-celled animals need a transportation, or circulation, system. For example, a starfish is composed of many thousands of cells. Even though a starfish lives in water, not all of its cells are in direct contact with the water, and they would die without some way to bring food to each cell and carry away wastes. Therefore, materials are distributed to the body cells by small whiplike organs called *cilia*, which cause a slow movement of a fluid contained in the body cavity of the starfish.

Higher forms of sea life depend on the fluid blood to circulate materials in their bodies. Their circulation systems include some sort of major internal pumping device, or heart. Hearts range from very simple to very complex structures.

Animals with Several Hearts. The heart of an earthworm or insect is very simple compared with that of man. Actually, an insect or earthworm has several hearts. These are thickened places in some of the blood vessels. In the walls of these thickened places are muscles, which contract and push the blood along.

Not All Hearts Are Alike. A fish has a definite heart. But it also is simple compared with the hearts of the generally furry or hairy, milk-producing animals called *mammals*. A fish heart has two parts, or *chambers*. A frog heart has three chambers. Birds and mammals have four-chambered hearts. Man is a mammal and, therefore, his heart is typical of other mammals, such as dogs, cats, bats, pigs, cows, and whales.

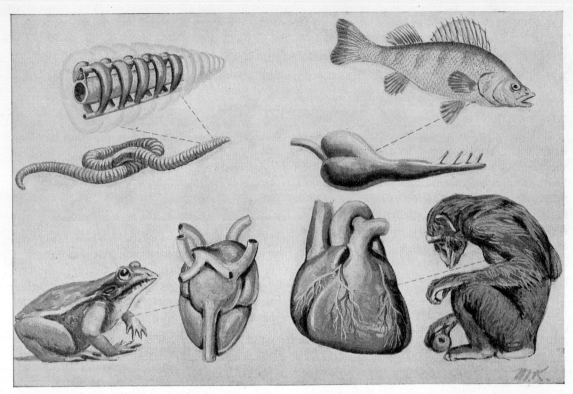

How many chambers has the heart of an earthworm, fish, frog, monkey? Which is most like ours?

THE HUMAN BLOOD STREAM

One way to understand the nature of the human blood stream, or circulation system, is to follow the blood from some point until it returns to the same, or similar, part of the body. Since food materials enter the blood stream from the small intestine, that point is one of the very best places to start.

The Capillaries. Digested foods leave the small intestine and enter the blood stream by moving into one of the millions of very short, very thin-walled, and very fine blood vessels called *capillaries.* Capillaries are so small that red corpuscles often must pass single file through them.

Blood flows slowly in the capillaries. It takes a red blood cell almost a second to go through a capillary about 0.04 inch in length. This slow rate of flow allows time for blood to pick up food materials that pass through the intestinal walls, and oxygen from the lungs, and to give off these materials to the cells of the body and pick up waste products there.

Capillaries join other capillaries, like tiny branches of a creek, and form larger blood vessels. These vessels are the *veins*, which carry blood from all parts of the body back to the heart. Veins have thicker walls than the capillaries. They meet other branches of veins, just

Red blood cells moving in capillaries.
From Encyclopaedia Britannica film The Heart and Circulation

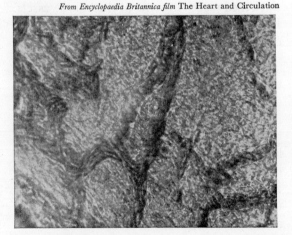

48

as creeks flow into large rivers. As small veins unite with, or merge into, larger and larger veins, the speed of blood flow increases greatly. As blood moves into middle-sized veins, it travels along at a speed of about 8 or 9 inches a second.

THE LIVER—ONE OF MAN'S "FUEL TANKS"

Where is the blood going? Remember that your study began at a capillary in the small intestine. All the millions of intestinal capillaries that carry food from the small intestine finally merge into one vein that goes to the liver. The liver (see illustration on page 39) is a huge organ. In fact, it is the largest organ in the body.

Why does the blood go from the small intestine to the liver? This question was answered in large part by a Frenchman, Claude Bernard [bĕr-nàr'], in the nineteenth century. He made careful measurements of the amount of sugar in the vein going into the liver and compared these with measurements of the amount of sugar in the vein leaving the liver. He found that when food is being absorbed from the small intestine, there is considerably more sugar in the large vein leading to the liver than in the large vein leaving the liver.

What Happens in the Liver. Further investigations showed that the liver changes some of the sugar into a form of starch called *animal starch*, or *glycogen*. Now this is an interesting fact. For some reason, the liver takes sugar from the blood stream and changes it into starch. It is interesting because much of the

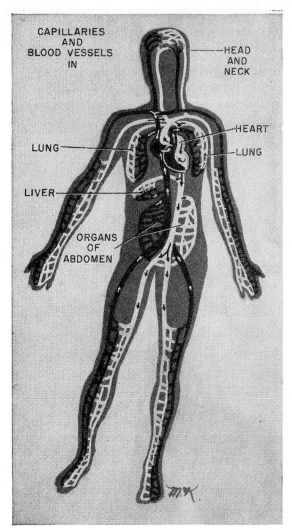

Simplified human circulation system.

sugar is the end-product of digestion of starches.

The starch in a potato or piece of bread, for example, is changed to sugar so that it can pass through the membrane lining the small intestine and into the capillaries of the villi. It is then carried by the blood to the liver, and some of it is changed back into starch. Why is it so changed?

Just as an automobile needs gasoline stored in a tank to make it run, so the body-machine needs a reserve of food to draw on. In each case, when gasoline is used in an automobile or food is used by a human body, energy is produced. Sugar in the human body produces

Construction of small arteries, veins, and capillaries.

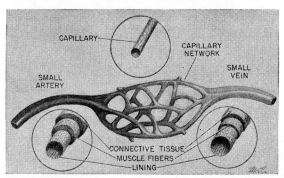

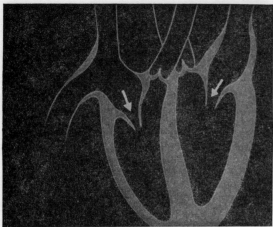

From Encyclopaedia Britannica film The Heart and Circulation

Top: Ventricles filling with blood from the auricles. Bottom: Ventricles contracting and forcing blood into arteries. Note the valves that are open and the valves that are closed in each drawing. Explain action of the valves.

energy when it is combined with oxygen. This combination of sugar—or any other substance —with oxygen is known as oxidation. *Burning* is rapid oxidation.

But the energy requirements of our bodies vary from time to time. When we are asleep, we use very little energy. But at other times we work, play, or exercise violently. Obviously, there must be some means of storing sugar so that it will be available when needed. Part of it is stored in the muscle cells where it is used to produce motion. A large amount is taken from the blood and stored in the cells of the liver.

Of course, the liver cells could not possibly store sugar as such. As you know, a simple sugar can go through an animal membrane but a starch cannot. Osmosis cannot be turned on and off at will. Simple sugar dissolved in a fluid will continually diffuse through a membrane that separates it from another fluid. So, if sugar is to be stored in liver cells for future use, it must be changed into starch, which will not go through the cell membranes.

Not all the sugar is changed to glycogen in the liver. Some of it passes through this organ and continues the trip with the blood, which goes next to the heart.

THE MOST AMAZING PUMP ON EARTH

Your heart is really two pumps fastened together. Each pump consists of a thin-walled chamber, into which blood flows from the veins, and a thick, muscular chamber, which is the real pump part of the heart. The thin-walled collecting chambers are called *auricles*, and the thick-walled pumping chambers are called *ventricles*.

Flaps called *valves* are between the auricles and the ventricles. Other valves are between the ventricles and the vessels that carry blood away from the heart. The blood vessels that carry blood away from the heart are called *arteries*. The illustration at the left shows the way in which these valves work as the heart beats.

Heart Valves. When an auricle contracts, the valve between it and its corresponding ventricle opens, and blood is pushed into the ventricle. When the ventricle contracts, the valve between the auricle and the ventricle flies shut, and the blood is pushed into an artery. When the ventricle relaxes, the valve between the ventricle and artery flies shut so that blood in the artery cannot flow back into the heart again.

When a doctor places a *stethoscope* over your heart and listens to its beat, he is actually listening to the sound made when the valves fly shut. Certain diseases can injure these valves so that they do not close properly. When this happens, blood leaks back into the chamber it has just left and in so doing produces a murmuring or gurgling sound, which the doctor can hear.

Circulation in the Heart and Lungs. Blood enters the heart on the right side. That is, the vein that collects blood from all over the body (except the lungs) empties into the right auricle. From there the blood is pushed down into the right ventricle, and then—wham— the ventricle gives a powerful contraction, the valve above flies shut with a thump, and the blood is pushed out into a large artery with two branches. These two branches are called *pulmonary* (from a Latin word meaning *lung*) *arteries*. Through the pulmonary arteries the blood is rushed to the lungs. There it is pushed into tinier and tinier arteries that carry it directly into the millions of capillaries in the lung tissue.

Carbon dioxide, produced when food is burned in the body cells, is removed from the blood in the lungs. Oxygen is picked up by the red corpuscles in the lungs. The blood then goes to the left side of the heart. It travels through the left auricle and into the thick-walled left ventricle.

The heart is actually in the center of the body. We think of it as on the left side only because the left ventricle is so large and thick-walled that it pushes out on that side.

AMONG THE CELLS OF THE BODY

When the left ventricle contracts, the valve between the left auricle and ventricle flies shut. The blood is then plummeted from the ventricle through the open valve between the ventricle and artery into the largest artery of the body—the *aorta*. This great artery divides and redivides (see illustration on page 49) so that some of the blood is eventually pushed into every part of the body.

As the blood is pushed into smaller and smaller arteries, its speed decreases. Finally, it reaches capillaries again and moves along very slowly. There the oxygen and food materials diffuse through the capillary walls into the

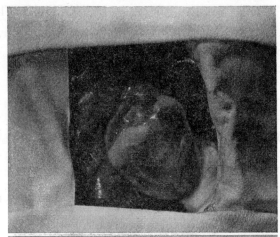
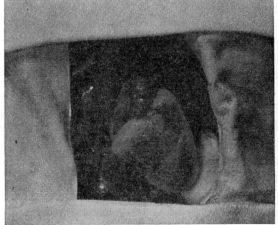

From Encyclopaedia Britannica film The Heart and Circulation

These photographs of a beating heart correspond to the drawings on page 50. Note the difference in size before and after the ventricles contract. How do you account for this difference in size? What has happened to the blood in the ventricles?

cell liquid called *lymph*, outside the capillaries.

Lymph. Lymph is the clear, watery substance that fills a blister. It is very similar to sea water in chemical make-up. Actually, lymph is the fluid part of the blood that is able to diffuse through the capillary walls. You recall that this fluid part of the blood is called plasma when it is in the blood vessels. It is called lymph when it is outside the blood vessels. Every cell in the body is surrounded by lymph, from which it gets oxygen and food, and into which it throws off carbon dioxide and other waste products.

1. Did you ever listen to a heartbeat? A local physician will probably loan you a stethoscope for class use. If you cannot borrow a real stethoscope, you can make one that will do fairly well.

Fasten a small glass or metal funnel to a rubber tube about 1½ feet long. At the other end fasten a Y-tube, which you can get from the science or chemistry laboratory of your school. Fasten a piece of rubber tubing about 1 foot long to each arm of the Y-tube. Fasten a piece of rubber from a toy balloon over the funnel. Place the funnel over the heart of a class member and hold the two ends of tubing in your ears. You should be able to hear the thump as the auricle-ventricle valves fly shut when the heart contracts, and a less distinct and hard noise as the valves between the ventricles and the arteries fly shut when the ventricles relax.

EXERCISE AIDS CIRCULATION

Here is a little experiment that is fun. Whirl your arm around your head a few times so that the blood is forced down into your lower arm and hand. Now press your upper arm closely against your body or against a book placed between your arm and your body.

You will note that the veins in your arm and hand stand out because they contain more blood than before the whirling. You have pressed the walls of the veins together, so that the blood is prevented from flowing back toward the heart.

Veins, for the most part, are near the surface of the body. Arteries are generally deeper in your flesh, where they are better protected from injury. At some places your arteries come nearer the surface, and at those spots you can feel the *pulse* as blood is pushed through them at every beat of the heart. The rate of heartbeat is commonly determined by counting the pulse in the *radial artery* of the wrist, just at the base of the thumb.

While the veins still stand out, pick out a prominent vein on the back of the hand. Place the middle finger of the other hand on this vein at a place near the finger, and press down firmly. Place the index finger near the finger holding the vein down, and slowly wipe up the vein toward the heart. Release this finger, but keep the middle-finger in place. Probably you cannot see the vein now. Try the same experiment on other veins or at other places in the same vein.

ACTION OF VALVES IN THE VEINS

Valves are spaced along the veins. They allow blood to flow toward the heart but not away from the heart. When you press on a vein, you prevent more blood from flowing into that vein. When you wipe another finger along that vein toward the heart, you push the blood along in the vein. When you raise that finger you might expect the blood to flow back again to fill the vein.

But if you wipe the blood up to or past one of the valves, it snaps shut when you release your finger, and the blood is prevented from flowing away from the heart. The illustration on page 53 indicates the action of these valves.

How Valves Aid Circulation. The heart is helped by the many valves in the veins. Many of the veins lie between or against muscles,

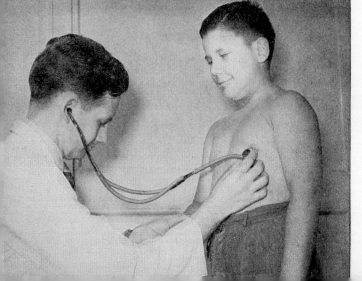

Listening to the heartbeat with a stethoscope.
U. S. Public Health Service photo

and this position aids the heart. Look at your hand and arm again. Flex your muscles and bend your hand forward. Note how the blood is squeezed along by the action of the muscles. The blood cannot move back toward the capillaries, because the tiny valves fly shut. Therefore, it is squeezed along toward the heart, just as it was when you squeezed it along with your finger.

VALUE OF EXERCISE

Exercise is a valuable aid to circulation because the action of the muscles helps to keep the blood moving. Patients in hospitals who are unable to move about are given massages whose chief effect is to push the blood along, just as in exercise.

You undoubtedly know how tiring it is to stand perfectly still. You tire more quickly than when you are walking, because the blood tends to stagnate in many tiny veins, and waste products which produce fatigue are not carried away rapidly. You undoubtedly know also how tired you can become when you lie in bed too long on a Saturday morning. Too much inactivity can cause fatigue.

NOT ENOUGH BLOOD TO GO AROUND

Have you ever tried to control blushing? The more you try, the redder your face becomes. What happens in blushing? When you go out into cold air, why does your skin get red, particularly at your ears and nose where the tissues are quite thin? The answer is that the blood supply in those parts of your body has increased.

There are only 4 to 5 quarts of blood in your entire body. This amount is by no means enough to fill all your blood vessels at one time if all of them were always as large as they sometimes are. In fact, it is not enough to fill all the vessels in the lower part of your body, let alone those in your head and chest.

The walls of the arteries and veins contain many muscles. These muscles are connected to two different sets of nerves. One set of nerves controls the contraction of the blood vessels. The other set so controls the vessels

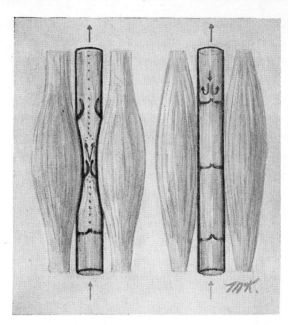

How valves in the veins are affected by exercise.

that they can enlarge and hold much more blood.

VASOMOTOR ACTION

The nerves and smooth muscles in blood vessels work automatically and are beyond our control. At any one time some of the blood vessels are contracted and others are enlarged. You can see this easily by thrusting one arm into a pail of hot water and the other into a pail of cold water. The hot water relaxes and expands the blood vessels just under the surface of the skin, and the hand becomes red.

At times when a person becomes embarrassed, the blood vessels in the face expand and blood rushes to the face. It turns red and feels fiery hot. It is hotter, of course, because warm blood from vessels deep in the body has rushed to the surface as a result of the expansion of the surface capillaries.

This general action of the blood vessels in expanding and contracting is called *vasomotor action*. Understanding this action will help you to understand a number of interesting things about your body. For example, it enables you to explain why you often feel sleepy after a large meal. Remember that there is not

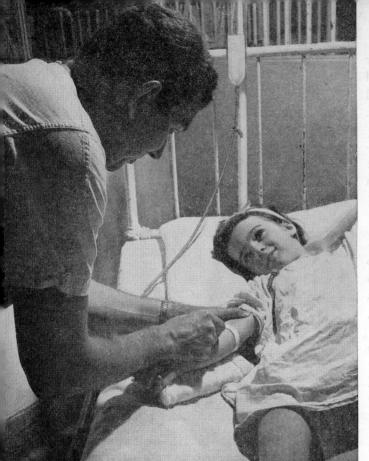

American Red Cross photo by Riordan

A transfusion of blood plasma.

Blood tends to flow out into the open space and cause swelling, pain, and a bluish discoloration resulting from stagnant blood that has lost its oxygen.

SHOCK AND THE BLOOD STREAM

Under certain conditions, such as following a bad accident, most of the veins in the body expand. Hence, there is not enough blood to enable the organs most necessary to life to carry on their functions. Also, more plasma than usual seems to diffuse through the capillary walls into the spaces between cells, that is, *intercellular spaces*. The veins in the *abdominal* organs and certain other parts of the body seem to dilate greatly, and large amounts of blood tend to stagnate or move slowly in these regions. Such a condition is known as *physical shock*.

Shock is often the result of severe wounds, surgical operations, or even strong emotional experiences. In other words, an emotional shock can bring about a physical shock.

Many persons have died of physical shock. It was once a principal cause of death on battlefields and in traffic accidents. The present treatment, however, saves many lives, because it is in keeping with what we know about shock. A person suffering from shock is kept quiet and in a horizontal position, with the head slightly lower than the rest of the body. Do you see why?

The most important shock treatment, however, is the injection of blood into the blood stream. If plasma is not available, even salt water will help, for it supplies additional fluid when there is not enough blood to provide all parts of the body with the blood needed.

enough blood to fill all the vessels when they are expanded, and it takes a lot of blood to digest and absorb food.

Perhaps you can now see why persons who swim soon after eating a large meal may be seized with cramps. Remember that it takes much blood to enable the large muscles to function properly during exercise such as swimming. For the same reason, a cold compress or bandage, rather than a hot one, should be applied to a sprained ankle. When an ankle is sprained, a number of blood vessels are broken.

WORKING WITH SCIENCE

1. It would be interesting to observe the action of the circulation system of a transparent man if that were possible. As a substitute, however, you might construct a model of the circulation system and observe its action. To do so, you will need an *aspirator bulb*, which you can obtain at a local drugstore, about 4 feet of rubber tubing, about 5 feet of glass tubing, and some rubber bands.

The aspirator bulb becomes the model heart. Really, its action is very much like that of the ventricle of the human heart. There are valves at both ends of the bulb, just as there are between the auricle and ventricle of your heart and between the ventricle and the artery which carries the blood away from the heart. The rubber tubing is flexible and will expand and contract, just as arteries do when blood is pushed through them. The glass tubing represents the human capillaries.

Hold the middle of a piece of glass tubing in the flame of a bunsen burner or alcohol lamp until it produces a red flame and turns red. Pull on both ends of the glass tubing until you pull the tube apart. You will then have two tubes, and one end of each will have pulled out into a glass thread. Allow the tubes to cool and then break off the tip of one of them so that a very fine hole results. Your teacher will show you how to file and cut the other end of this tube so that you will have a glass tip the total length of which is about 4 inches.

Slip this glass tip into one end of the rubber tubing and fasten it tightly with rubber bands. Now fasten the other end of the rubber tubing to the aspirator bulb by means of a short piece of glass tubing (see illustration below).

How to use the model circulation system: Place the end of the aspirator bulb in a large beaker of water as shown below. Squeeze the bulb. This removes the air in the bulb. Remove your hand and allow the bulb to fill with water. Alternately squeeze and release the bulb. When you squeeze the bulb, a valve at the beaker end of the bulb flies shut, and the water cannot return to the beaker. The valve at the other end of the bulb opens, and the water squirts into the rubber tubing. When you release the bulb, the valve at the tubing end flies shut and the other valve opens, and the bulb again fills with water. Thus, this action is very much like that of the heart.

If you squeeze rapidly, a continuous stream of water will squirt out of the "capillary" tip of the glass tube. If the stream is not continuous, you may need to replace this tip with another one of smaller diameter. As you squeeze the bulb, feel the rubber tubing. You will notice that it expands and feels just like the pulse of the large artery at your wrist.

One function of the elastic arteries and the tiny capillaries of your body is the maintenance of a constant flow of blood through the capillaries. When the heart contracts and pushes blood into the arteries, it cannot immediately be taken up entirely by the capillaries, because they are too tiny. But the arteries are elastic and expand under pressure.

As the heart relaxes, the arteries contract, thus pushing blood continuously through the capillaries.

To see what would happen if human blood did not flow through tiny capillaries or if the arteries were hard and nonelastic, do the following. First, remove the "capillary" glass tip from your model circulation system. Now squeeze rapidly on the bulb. The water is pushed out of the rubber tubing in squirts and does not flow steadily. If this were the situation in the human body, the cells would suffer from a lack of constant blood supply.

Now replace the entire rubber tubing and "capillary" tip with a piece of glass tubing of the same length whose end has been heated and drawn out into a "capillary" tip. Now squeeze rapidly on the bulb again. The glass tube cannot expand. Therefore, despite the pressure when the bulb is released, water immediately stops flowing.

2. Determine the rate of your heartbeat by taking your pulse where the wrist, or radial, artery is near the surface, just at the base of your thumb. Now stand in front of the class and make a speech. If you are even a little frightened or nervous when you do this, your heartbeat will be affected. Have someone take your pulse as you are speaking. What has happened to the rate of beat?

Now try running and again have someone take your heartbeat. What do you find?

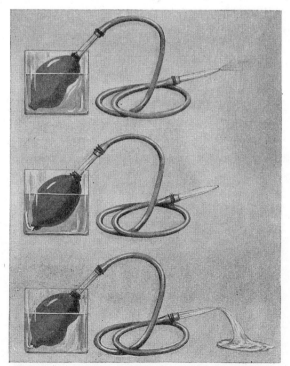

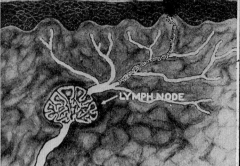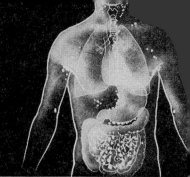

From Encyclopaedia Britannica film Body Defenses Against Disease

When germs get into the body, some of them get into the lymph ducts and reach the lymph nodes, where they are attacked by white blood cells. Major lymph nodes are shown at the right.

THE LYMPH—AND NO HEART TO PUMP IT

Another set of vessels in the body makes up the *lymph system.* You remember that the fluid part of the blood is called lymph when it is in the intercellular spaces. Some of this lymph is picked up by veins, but some of it diffuses into tiny tubes called *ducts* that join other tiny tubes leading finally to large tubes that empty into one of the large veins in the left shoulder. The fluid in these tubes is lymph, not blood. It does not have red blood cells or platelets in it.

The lymph ducts, or *lymphatics,* do not make a complete circuit to the heart. They are closed off at one end, much like the branches of a tree.

Lymph system (white) and circulation system.

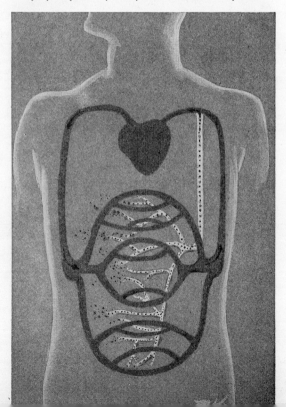

Why is some of the lymph picked up by the lymphatics and some of it by the veins? The answer is not clear. However, the heart is not directly connected to the lymphatics and, therefore, does not pump lymph. The lymphatics contain thousands of valves spaced closely together. Only the squeezing action of contracting muscles moves the lymph along, for the heart does not pump lymph at all.

LYMPH NODES

Hundreds of tiny groups of gland cells, called *lymph nodes,* are distributed throughout the body. The lymphatics pass through them. Lymph nodes are packed with white blood cells which destroy disease organisms.

Not only are disease organisms destroyed in the lymph nodes, but all kinds of other solid particles are filtered out of the stream at the nodes and kept there. A surprising number of solid particles get into the body. Old cell fragments are filtered out at the nodes; so are smoke and dust particles.

Tonsils. Two of the largest lymph nodes are the *tonsils,* about which you may know from personal experience. These serve an important function in the body, for they are near the throat membranes where disease organisms and solid particles frequently enter. But these nodes may be overworked and become infected themselves. When this happens repeatedly, tonsils become a source of infection and fail to serve their normal function. Then the doctor removes them.

56

WORKING WITH SCIENCE

1. Examine your tonsils in front of a mirror. Even if they have been removed, you may see the "roots" of the tonsils at the sides of the throat. What is the purpose of tonsils?

2. Rub carefully the sides of your neck and the sides of your chest directly under your armpits. Do you feel the bumpy glandular tissue? Try this again when you have a cold or other infection. You will note that this tissue probably has become swollen and prominent. Can you explain why in terms of the function of the lymph glands?

THE RESPIRATION SYSTEM

Below is a drawing of the *respiration system*. Study it for a moment. It looks something like the roots of a plant or the branches of a tree. At the top leading to the neck and

The respiration system with a highly magnified bronchus and air sacs. Trace the path of the air breathed in.

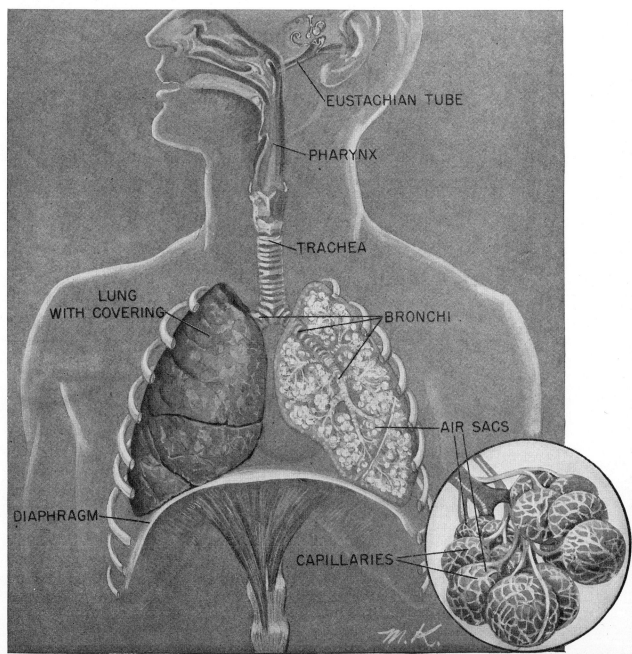

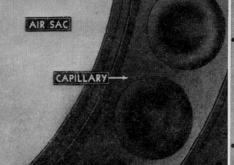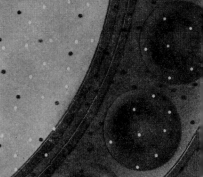

From Encyclopaedia Britannica film Mechanisms of Breathing

An air sac compared with a fine thread. In the air sacs, oxygen passes through the walls of the capillaries to the red cells. Carbon dioxide leaves the red cells and passes into the air sacs.

mouth is the trachea. The trachea divides into two main branches, like the fork of a tree. These branches, or *bronchi* (singular, *bronchus*), then branch into tinier and tinier tubes.

The inset at the lower right of the drawing is an enlargement of one of the small bronchi. Notice that each tiny branch finally ends in an enlargement called an *air sac*.

LUNGS

The air passageways themselves branch into smaller and smaller tubes that enable air to pass from outside the body, through the trachea, bronchi, and finer tubes to the air sacs. The capillaries of the lung surround hundreds of thousands of air sacs.

In texture the lungs are something like sponges. They are pinkish in color, because of the many capillaries that carry blood in close contact with the air sacs. The outside of each lung is covered with a thin membrane. The lungs are very elastic. They expand when filled with air and contract somewhat when the air is expelled.

The illustration on page 57 gives a fair idea of the position of the lungs in the body and the relationship of the various parts of the respiration system. Note that there are open passageways from the nostrils and mouth into the trachea. The roof of the mouth separates the nasal cavity from the mouth cavity. At the soft palate, the two passageways join to form the organ called the *pharynx*. Also opening into the pharynx are two tiny tubes, each of which goes to the middle part of one of the ears. These are called the *Eustachian tubes*. At the lower end of the pharynx, the esophagus leads to the stomach, and the trachea leads to bronchi and lungs.

WHAT HAPPENS WHEN YOU BREATHE?

Breathe in and notice the expansion of your chest cavity. Every time you breathe in, or *inhale*, your ribs lift up and the volume of the chest is increased. Another action, which you cannot observe, also increases the volume of the chest. Look again at the illustration on page 57 and notice the thin, sheetlike muscle, which forms the floor of the chest cavity and separates this cavity from the abdominal cavity. This muscle is called the *diaphragm*. When you inhale, the diaphragm flattens out and is drawn downward. When you breathe out, or *exhale*, the abdominal organs push the diaphragm up, thus making the chest cavity smaller.

Breathing seems merely to be a process whereby the chest cavity is changed in volume. How does this action cause air to enter the lungs? Between the walls of the chest cavity and the lungs, there is no air. That is, there is a good *vacuum*. Outside our bodies there is air, of course. Now air has weight, and on the surface of the earth we are at the bottom of a deep ocean of air. Consequently, this air exerts much pressure on our bodies (see Unit 5).

Usually, there is more than a ton of air pressing on every square foot of your body. Naturally then, when the volume of the chest cavity is increased, air is forced into the lungs and keeps the lungs expanded and pressed against the chest walls. When the chest cavity

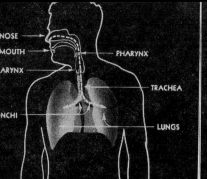
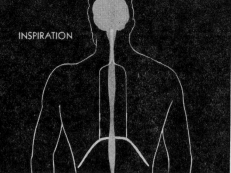
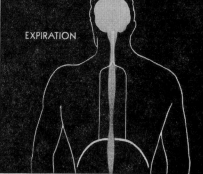

NOSE
MOUTH
LARYNX
PHARYNX
TRACHEA
BRONCHI
LUNGS

INSPIRATION

EXPIRATION

From Encyclopaedia Britannica film Mechanisms of Breathing

Air gets into and out of the lungs chiefly as a result of the action of the diaphragm. Using these drawings, explain the action of the diaphragm in inhaling (inspiration) and exhaling (expiration).

is decreased in breathing out, the air is forced out because the air pressure inside the lungs becomes greater than that outside the body.

THE SELF-REPAIRING MACHINE

If man could invent a machine half as complicated as the human body, he would have produced a miracle. For the body-machine, as represented by the circulation system and the respiration **system**, is self-operating and self-adjusting.

Most amazing, however, is the fact that the body-machine is largely self-repairing. For example, the heart does a tremendous amount of work and beats steadily from before birth until the instant of death. Cells of your heart are dying at this moment. Yet you need not be alarmed. For the heart repairs itself, removing the dead cells and replacing them with new, young, healthy cells. This constant repair job is going on in every part of your body every second of your entire life.

WORKING WITH SCIENCE

1. To get a firsthand idea of the spongelike texture of the lungs, remove the lungs and trachea from a small animal, such as a rabbit, chicken, or white rat. Why are the lungs pinkish in color? Insert a glass tube into the open end of the trachea. Blow into the glass tube and observe the lungs' elasticity.

2. Would you like to see how the movements of your diaphragm push air out of your lungs and admit air to them? Fasten two old rubber balloons to the arms of a Y-tube. (If new balloons are used, blow them up several times to stretch the rubber.) Insert the stem of the Y-tube through a one-hole rubber stopper that has been placed through the top of a bell jar. Fasten a large rubber diaphragm (from a large toy balloon) on the bottom of the bell jar with rubber bands.

Pull down on the rubber diaphragm and you will increase the volume inside the bell jar. Since no air can get into this space, the air pressure inside the jar is lessened. As this occurs, the air pressure outside the jar pushes air through the tube and into the tiny balloons. When you push up and in on the diaphragm, the space in the jar is decreased and the air is compressed. This pushes against the tiny balloons and forces some of the air in them out of the glass tube at the top.

This action is almost exactly like the action of the human diaphragm in changing the volume of the chest cavity and pushing air in and out of the lungs. Remember that, in your chest, there is a vacuum between the lungs and the chest walls, whereas in the model there is air. Yet, in each case, when the "chest" cavity volume is increased, the outside air pressure forces more air into the "lungs."

READING YOU WILL ENJOY

Andress, J. Mace, Goldberger, I. I., Dolch, Marguerite P., and Hallock, Grace T. *Safe and Healthy Living*, Bk. VII (rev. ed.). Ginn & Co., Boston, 1945. A good health and physiology book.

Burnett, R. Will. *To Live in Health*. Silver Burdett Co., New York, 1946. An interesting and clear account of the body-machine and how to keep it healthy.

1

2

Not until man understood how the sense organs and the nervous system work could he do much to help correct those that did not work well. For example, many early peoples, including some as recent as the Greeks, believed that vision is produced by "rays" or "beams" of light that shoot out from the eyes (1) and hit the object being seen in much the same way that a flashlight sends out light. This idea was widely held even several hundred years after it was disproved by the Arabian scientist, Ibn-al-Haitham, or Alhazen (2), who lived in Egypt during the early eleventh century. Alhazen's work with light and lenses led to the introduction of glasses to improve poor vision some two centuries later.

Although nerves had been recognized by others before him, Andreas Vesalius (3) in the sixteenth century showed how they help control various parts of the body. Vesalius was a very careful observer and experimenter and dissected many human bodies. Because Vesalius studied the bodies of human beings and was such a careful student, his observations corrected many of the errors of Aristotle and Galen. As a result of the work of these and thousands of other research workers, specialists, such as an oculist (4), are now able to find out what is wrong with various sensory organs. In this way they help us to keep in better touch with the world around us.

3

4

5

HOW WE KEEP IN TOUCH WITH THE WORLD

Suppose that you are sitting in the yard, reading a magazine. Suddenly someone yells, you look up and see a baseball about 15 feet from your head and coming fast. Without thinking, you duck your head. Perhaps you scramble away from the spot on which you are sitting.

Without a nervous system, you would not even realize that the ball is coming toward you. You would not hear the yell, you would not see the ball, and if it hit you, you would not even feel it. No messages would be sent from one cell of your body to another.

Your body has special apparatus for keeping you in touch with the world around you, just as it has for digestion and respiration. Not all cells are equally affected by all the different things to react to, or *stimuli*, that exist. Stick your finger around a corner and it does not see a thing even though light falls on it. However, if you look around a corner, you not only detect light but see what is around the corner. Some cells of your eye are highly specialized for seeing.

THE NERVOUS SYSTEM

If your eyes see something dangerous approaching, nothing is gained unless that message is sent to other parts of the body. However, you have a remarkable system of specialized nerve cells, which carry messages from one part of the body to other parts as needed. When you see a ball flying toward your head, that message travels through nerves from the eyes to the brain. From the brain, messages then go through nerve cells to the various parts of the body that must move, or react in some way, to avoid the danger.

FUNCTIONS OF NERVOUS SYSTEM

Without proper timing and control of all messages throughout the body, you would not be able to move away from danger. For example, if the messages from the brain to your neck and body muscles are not exactly timed, you probably would just flop aimlessly around when you see a ball flying toward your head. But the nerve cells work together in harmony and the messages to and from them are, therefore, *coordinated*. Proper timing and control, or *coordination*, is an important function of the nervous system.

Essentially then, the nervous system detects, or is *sensitive* to, such stimuli as light, sound, heat, and pain. It carries, or *communicates*, messages from one part of the body to another. And it *coordinates* the parts of the body so that they act in cooperation to produce motion or other reactions.

Sensations without Sense Organs. If you experiment with the one-celled animals called *paramecia* (singular, *paramecium*), you will find that they are sensitive to light, though they have no eyes. They are sensitive to heat, though they have no heat-sensitive nerves. They are sensitive to touch, though they have no touch-sensitive nerves.

Since a paramecium is only a single cell, it cannot have these separate cell structures.

A paramecium. Its entire cell is sensitive.

More to the point, a one-celled animal has no need for special organs, called *sense organs*, or nerves to detect things. The entire cell is sensitive to the things around it. Now, you must understand that this does not mean that a paramecium or an ameba sees things as we do, or that it is aware of heat, light, touch, and pain as we are. But the cell is sensitive and does react to the outside world to protect itself and adjust to its surroundings.

IS A NERVE MESSAGE ELECTRIC?

The nerves in the human body look surprisingly like a telephone system with its switchboards and many branches to separate buildings. This resemblance gave rise to the idea that a nerve message, or *impulse*, might be electric.

A reflex arc begins in a sensory nerve ending, travels through a sensory nerve to the spinal cord, through ganglia, and through a motor nerve to a muscle.

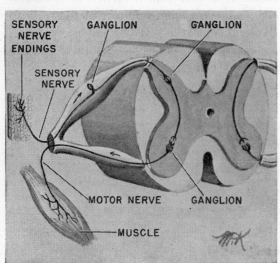

SENSORY NERVE ENDINGS

GANGLION

GANGLION

SENSORY NERVE

MOTOR NERVE

GANGLION

MUSCLE

Microscopic examination shows that the nerve cells make contact with one another, not directly, but through apparent gaps (see left below). These gaps look somewhat like the jacks and plugs in a telephone switchboard. Furthermore, millions of these tiny gaps exist in the brain and the spinal cord. In many cases, several nerve endings come together to form tiny centers, or *ganglia* (singular, *ganglion*). In such centers, incoming messages are received and outgoing messages are sent to the various parts of the body as needed.

Wires and Nerves. Despite the resemblances, there are great differences between an electric current and a nerve impulse. For one thing, a wire can carry electricity in two directions. However, in the body certain nerves, called *sensory* nerves, carry messages from sense organs to the brain and spinal cord (the *central nervous system*). Other nerves, called *motor* nerves, carry messages from the central nervous system to the muscles and glands of the body. And direction of messages cannot be reversed in either set of nerves.

The real nature of a nerve impulse is not fully understood. It seems to be a combination of electric and chemical actions. We do know that electric effects are produced. Dr. Ralph Lillie [lǐl'ĭ] has made a model of a nerve, using soft iron wire immersed in a chemical (nitric acid). The iron wire changes chemically and conducts electric impulses in a manner very similar to the way in which nerves conduct impulses.

REFLEX ARC

The simplest nerve path is a *reflex arc*. In a reflex arc, a sensory message—pain, for example—is carried by a sensory nerve to the spinal cord. From the spinal cord, a motor impulse is sent out through a motor nerve and back to muscle fibers, causing the muscle to contract.

The interesting thing about a simple reflex arc is that it does not depend upon awareness or knowing what is going on, that is, *consciousness*, for its action. If you hit your thumb,

This boy has hit his thumb with a hammer, a not unusual occurrence. Explain the drawings in terms of sensory and motor nerve endings and nerves, and reflex arcs.

you do not wait to move your hand until the message reaches your brain. You do not have to think and say, "Ah, a message from my thumb tells me that I have just hit it with a hammer. I believe I will lift that hand and move it away from the hammer." Not at all. The message goes from your thumb to your spinal cord and another message goes back to the muscles of your arm and hand, causing you to lift the hand.

In the meantime, of course, the sensory message is still traveling, over other nerves, up your spinal cord to your brain. When it reaches the brain, you feel pain and decide on other things to do, such as putting iodine on the wound, or whatever else occurs to you. But you lifted the hand *before* you actually were aware of the pain. Your reaction was not under conscious control. Such an action is called an *involuntary action* (see the three illustrations across the top of this page).

INVOLUNTARY NERVOUS SYSTEM

Many nerves are entirely beyond conscious, or voluntary, control. These include the nerves that cause the heart to beat, the digestive glands to secrete, the stomach and intestines to mix food and move it along, and many other vital reactions. Such nerves make up the *involuntary nervous system*.

In general, this involuntary nervous system controls the more important organs essential for life, that is, the *vital* organs, and functions of the body. It is better for us that we cannot voluntarily control the heartbeat, the secretion of digestive juices, and so forth. If we could, there would be danger that we would interfere with these functions to such an extent that our health would be affected and our lives endangered.

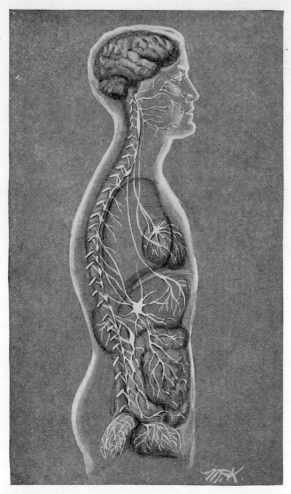

The involuntary nervous system. Why is it so called?

VOLUNTARY NERVOUS SYSTEM

The arrangement of sense organs, nerves, brain, and spinal cord that keeps us informed about the outside world and enables us to move about, think, and act as human beings is called the *voluntary nervous system.*

The voluntary nervous system is organized somewhat like the general staff of an army in the field. There are outposts in both cases. In the army, officers and men at the front lines and in planes above the lines are in contact with all that is going on and relay that information back to the field headquarters. In the human body, the contact jobs are done by the eyes, ears, nose, sense of touch, pain, cold, and heat, and the senses of balance and position.

Messages from army outposts are sent back to headquarters over radio, field telephones, and similar devices. Messages from the sense organs of the body are sent to the brain over sensory nerves.

In the army, decisions and explanations of field reports are made by officers at field headquarters. These men put information together, make their decisions, and send messages to front lines so that proper action can be taken.

In a somewhat similar sense, the brain of the human body takes incoming messages, sorts them, and considers this information in connection with the "files" of the human memory. Then messages for action are sent out over motor nerves so that the body may take whatever action is appropriate.

The Brain. The main, or "thinking," part of the brain of man is the *cerebrum.* This is the part of the brain that makes man more intelligent than other animals. Your cerebrum enables you to look at these peculiar little marks on this page and to understand what they mean. In the cerebrum is your consciousness, thinking, imagination, and memory. Here, indeed, is your humanness. Here—and in certain glands—is the physical basis of your love, pity, sorrow, joy, and understanding.

Lower animals such as snakes, birds, and monkeys have cerebrums, but they are not so well developed as in man. The cerebrum of a monkey is far better developed than that of a snake, and a monkey is far more intelligent.

What Happens When Parts of the Brain Are Removed? The function of the cerebrum and its importance to various animals can be determined by experiments in which the cerebrum is removed. When the cerebrum of a frog is removed, the animal behaves almost as it always did, because the cerebrum in a frog is poorly developed and its function is not great.

On the other hand, when the cerebrum is removed from a bird or dog, the behavior of the animal is markedly different. The bird or dog will generally sit or lie for hours or even days without much movement. There seems to be little or no voluntary action. If the animal is prodded with a stick or startled by a loud noise, it will move. Such an animal will starve to death with food placed directly before it. If food is placed in its mouth, it will swallow. It can walk (or fly, as the case may be) but all movement is at random and shows no intelligence behind it.

What controls the voluntary muscles and coordinates them so that an animal can move about when its cerebrum has been removed? Control and coordination are supplied by the *cerebellum*. A pigeon whose cerebellum has been removed cannot fly or walk. It is not paralyzed, for the legs and wings will thrash about. But it has lost all coordination. The muscles are able to move, but all of them seem to move at once without rhyme or reason.

When the cerebellum of a human being is partially destroyed through disease or injury, the same trouble usually results. Small or fine movements, such as picking up pins or threading a needle, are not possible. The hands move jerkily, as may the entire body.

Apparently, the cerebrum sends out the messages for voluntary action of the body, and these messages pass through the cerebellum where they are coordinated before going to the muscles. It is the same as if a central office sent out an order to men in a factory to do a certain job and this order went first to a sub-office where assistants worked out the plans, indicating just how much and at what time each man in the factory would do his bit.

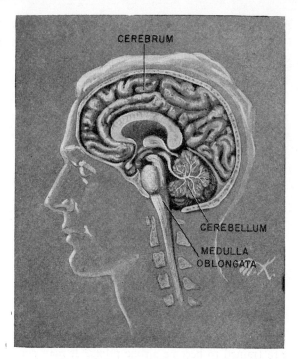

The chief parts of the human brain.

The third part of the brain is the enlarged top of the spinal cord, called the *medulla oblongata*. The medulla controls respiratory action and controls or modifies the rate of the heartbeat, vasomotor muscles of the blood vessels, swallowing reflexes, and some eye actions (see page 68). All these actions are beyond our conscious control. The spinal cord is essentially a main pathway for nerve impulses from sensory nerves to the brain and for motor impulses from the brain to the muscles and glands of the body.

WORKING WITH SCIENCE

1. Have one of your classmates stand in front of you and tell him that you are going to strike at his face. Assure him that you will not actually hit him (and be sure that you do not). Tell him to try his best not to "bat" his eyes. Watch what he does when you strike at him. Why?

2. You can demonstrate involuntary reactions in another way. If you will kill a frog by using chloroform or ether, you will cause no pain to the animal. Immediately cut off the frog's head. Run a bent pin or hook through the neck and connect it to a string, which can be fastened to an overhead support or held in your hand.

Obviously, the frog does not feel pain, since its entire head is gone and it cannot have the slightest bit of consciousness. Furthermore, no actions can possibly be conscious and voluntary. Pinch one of the feet rather hard and suddenly. What happens? How do you account for the reaction? A simple reflex arc is involved, as you can see.

Now place a tiny bit of acid on the back of the frog and watch closely. You will see a definite attempt on the part of the frog to rub the irritating substance off. The feet will even be rather successful in their attempts to reach the place where the acid is. The animal feels no pain, but the sensory nerves of the back carry the message to the spinal cord, where many other motor nerves carry rather well-coordinated messages to various muscles, causing the legs and feet to move in an effort to scrape the acid off the back.

3. One of the easiest evidences of the involuntary nervous system to see is the change in the size of the *pupil* that takes place when the eye sees lights of various degrees of brightness. Look at a classmate's eye in a dimly lighted room. You will note that the pupil is quite large. Then light a match or turn on an electric light, and look closely at his eye. The pupil immediately gets smaller. This is an involuntary adjustment for better seeing and is entirely beyond his control.

4. Did you ever wonder why only *young* men are trained to become airline pilots? It may surprise you to know that a certain amount of time elapses between the moment a person decides to do something and the moment he actually begins to do it. This time is called *reaction time*. It is the time required by the nerve impulse to travel from the brain to the muscles that must move the body to perform the act decided upon. Only young men are trained to become airline pilots largely because their reaction time is generally much less than that of older men and because their total coordination of bodily movement is quicker and better.

Here is a way to check your own reaction time approximately. Have members of the class join hands in a large circle. Each person closes his eyes and keeps them closed. One member of the class, previously selected, starts a signal by squeezing the hand of the person next to him. That person in turn squeezes the hand of the next person, and so on around the circle. When you feel your hand squeezed, squeeze the hand of the next person as quickly as possible. Your teacher will watch the progression of these hand squeezes and, at the instant the person who started the signal has his other hand squeezed, will note the total time in seconds.

Divide the time required for the signal to move around the circle and back to the person who started it by the number of people in the circle. The result will be the average reaction time for each member of the class. What is it? What actually happened in each person's body, in terms of the nervous system, during this time?

SENSATION AND SENSORY APPARATUS

For most of us the world is full of light, color, form, movement, noise, words, music, and things that taste and smell both pleasant and unpleasant. Through our sense organs, we learn about the world and contact the people in it. Sight, hearing, touch, smell, taste, pain, and other sensations are recorded in different groups of sensory cells located in the cerebrum. In these cells we become conscious of things and events in the world outside our bodies.

The sensory cells are totally dependent upon the stimuli they receive from the outside world. For example, seeing is dependent upon light. Have you ever stopped to think just what light is? Do you know how we see? Why is it that we cannot see things in a dark closet or at night when all lights are out? The answer to this last question is simply that there is not enough light to see by. Now, keep this point in mind, because some of the following statements may astonish you.

WHAT DOES MAN SEE?

Look at some person you know. Do you think you see him? Do not be too sure. What if you were told that you do not see him, that you never have seen him, and that you never will see him? These suggestions bring out a very interesting point.

Suppose you look at your friend in complete darkness. Can you see him then? Why not? He is still there, as you can discover by touching him. Why can you see him in a lighted room but not in the dark?

What you see in a lighted room is simply the light that has gone from the light bulb to your friend's body and has bounced off, or *reflected*, back to your eyes. Therefore, it is not far wrong to say that you have never seen the person next to you. All you have seen is light that was reflected from his body into your eyes. You recognize the person because light reflects differently from noses of different sizes, from eyes of different colors, and so forth. In other words, reflected light follows the shapes and colors of whatever it hits, so that you recognize objects and people.

WHAT IS LIGHT?

In order to understand how your eyes work, you must understand a few things about light. (You will study light in more detail in Unit 10.) Our standard of light is the direct sunlight at noonday and is called *white light*. White light is made up of all the colors that you see in a rainbow. When the sun comes out during or after a rain, the tiny droplets of water in the air break white light into its parts, and a rainbow appears. White light is a combination of all the colors you see in a rainbow—red, orange, yellow, green, blue, indigo, and violet. However, white light can be produced by a proper combination of only red, green, and blue light. When these are blended together in different proportions, the other colors— orange, yellow, indigo, violet—are produced.

DIFFERENT COLORS

When white light hits a piece of white paper, all colors are reflected at the same time and go into the eyes. Then we say that the paper is white. If white light hits a piece of very black paper, none of the light is reflected.

In other words, the light is *absorbed*. The paper looks black simply because black is what we "see" when there is no light.

Now suppose that you look at a piece of red paper. Why does it look red? White light has hit the paper. But knowing that white light is composed of all colors, you can guess what has happened. All the green and blue in the white light are absorbed by the red paper. Hence, only the red light is reflected into your eyes, and the paper looks red. In the same way, a blue object appears blue because it does not absorb blue light.

AFTERIMAGE

Very often when you look at a colored object for a long time and then transfer your gaze to a light-colored wall or white paper, you see another color. This color is called an *afterimage*. It is produced because the nerves sensitive to any one color become "tired" and do not register that color when you look at a white surface. The afterimage you see is the color left when the original color is removed from white light.

For example, if you look at a red object until your eyes become tired, you will probably see a blue-green afterimage when you transfer your gaze to a white piece of paper. The red-sensitive nerves do not work well, and you see only the blue and green in white light. If you look at a green object first, you will probably see a reddish afterimage on the white paper.

WORKING WITH SCIENCE

1. You can easily produce a rainbow by adjusting a garden hose so that it makes a fine misty spray. Stand with your back to the sun and slowly turn around until you see a distinct rainbow. The tiny droplets of water break up the sunlight into the colors that actually make up white light.

2. To produce a rainbow of really brilliant colors, place a small mirror in a metal pan so that it rests at an angle with the surface of the water. Allow a beam of sunlight to fall on the water and slowly move the pan around until a bright display of colors is thrown on the wall or on a sheet of

white paper. If it is impossible to get sunlight into the room, the beam of light from a glass-slide projector or arc projector will produce a rainbow of fair brilliance.

3. To produce an afterimage, lean or hang a piece of red cardboard on the wall. Look directly at the card for a minute, or more, and *do not blink your eyes* any more than you can help. After looking at the red card until your eyes are tired, look at a sheet of white paper on the wall. What do you see? Repeat, using green cardboard, instead of red.

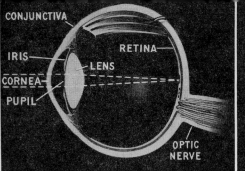
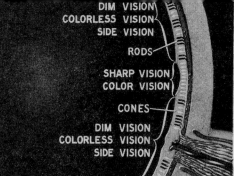
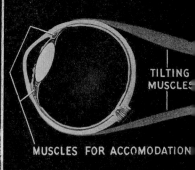

CONJUNCTIVA
IRIS
CORNEA
PUPIL
RETINA
LENS
OPTIC NERVE

DIM VISION
COLORLESS VISION
SIDE VISION
RODS
SHARP VISION
COLOR VISION
CONES
DIM VISION
COLORLESS VISION
SIDE VISION

TILTING MUSCLES
MUSCLES FOR ACCOMODATION

From Encyclopaedia Britannica film Eyes and Their Care

Left: The chief parts of the eye. Middle: A section through the retina. Right: Some eye muscles.

YOUR EYES

The nerve endings that are sensitive to light are located in the inner surface of the back part of the eyeball. The middle illustration above shows this region. It is called the *retina*. Not all light-sensitive nerves can detect color. In fact, your retina contains two different types of nerve endings. Some of these are long and rodlike and are called *rods*. Some look something like inverted cones and are called *cones*.

The cones are sensitive to color. Some apparently are sensitive to one color and some to another color. Most cones are directly in the field of vision. In other words, when you look directly at something, the light falls on the place in the retina where there are many cones.

The rods are sensitive to light but cannot detect colors. In the edges of the retina there are only rods. Therefore, things that you see out of the "corner of your eye" are colorless. You can demonstrate this by having a friend bring two objects of different colors slowly into the field of your vision from one side while you look steadily straight ahead. You can distinguish the two objects long before you name the color of the objects.

STRUCTURE OF THE EYE

Your eyes are amazing and accurate organs. The illustrations above show the parts of the eye. Six muscles move it in its *socket*. Two move it up and down, two move it from right to left, and two cause it to turn slightly in the socket.

You can see your eyeball turn if you look in a mirror and tilt your head slowly so that your head rests on your shoulder. If you look at the tiny blood vessels near the surface of the eye, you will note that the eyeball is actually turning in its socket. As your head tilts, the eyeball maintains its original position in relation to the horizon for a little while.

As you probably know, a screen called the *iris* changes the size of the pupil which is just an opening in the iris. Its action is controlled by the medulla. The iris is blue or brown, or whatever color your eyes are. But the pupil, since it is really a hole in the iris, is black.

The outside of the eye is covered and protected by a continuation of your skin, which folds down under the lids and becomes transparent as it goes over the eyeball. The skin covering the eyeball is called the *conjunctiva*. The conjunctiva may become infected through unwise rubbing of the eye. It often becomes inflamed if the eyes are used with improper lighting, such as glare or not enough light. *Pink eye* is a disease of the conjunctiva.

The eye is constantly bathed in tears, which seep out of the *tear glands*, one above each eye. Tears ordinarily drain out of the eye through

How the eye focuses on an object.

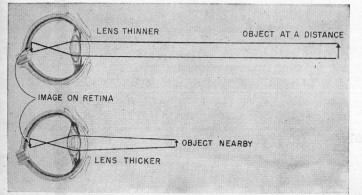

LENS THINNER
OBJECT AT A DISTANCE
IMAGE ON RETINA
OBJECT NEARBY
LENS THICKER

a tiny duct at the inner, lower, edge of the eye. This duct ends in the nose. When you cry and tears come very fast, you may get the sniffles because so much liquid goes into the nostrils.

FOCUSING—WITH AND WITHOUT GLASSES

Just behind the pupil is a transparent tissue called the *lens*. Without it a person could see light and things at a distance, but everything—particularly things near—would be blurred. The human lens is like the lens in a camera. It adjusts, or *focuses*, light so that a picture, or *image*, of what you are looking at falls sharply on the retina.

Why is light reflected from objects near at hand different from, or require a different focus than, light reflected from objects at a distance? The illustration at bottom of page 68 will help answer this question. Light goes out from an object in all directions. For example, suppose that you light a match. Wherever you stand in the room, the match can be seen. Light from the match or any other object spreads out. The shafts of light, or *rays*, are at an angle. That is, they *diverge*.

Therefore, if you are near an object, the rays that go through the pupil and into your eye diverge widely, as shown on page 68. But if you are some distance from an object, only those rays that are nearly parallel are close enough together to enter the pupil.

The lens bends light so as to make an image, as shown on page 68. The more curved a lens is, the more sharply it bends light. Therefore, if rays entering the eye are nearly parallel, as from objects at a distance, and a lens is so rounded that it bends them enough, the image forms on the retina, as shown on page 68. If the lens does not change its shape after the eye observes an object at a distance, and light from a nearby object enters, the image of the nearby object is formed behind the retina (see middle illustration at the right). This produces blurring.

If you look at something out of a window or at a distance and hold a hand in your line of vision, the hand is blurred. Now, if you look

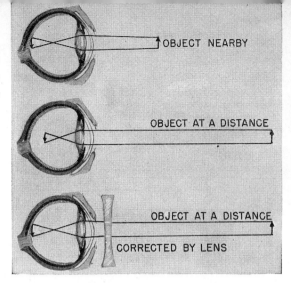

Correction of nearsightedness.

directly at the hand it becomes clear, but the distant object becomes blurred. The lens has thickened and become more curved so that it can bend the diverging rays more, and they now fall on the retina.

Sometimes a person's ability to change the curvature of the lens—changing the curvature of the lens is called *accommodation*—is weakened. In some cases, the eyeballs are too long or too short; that is, the lens is too far away from or too near the retina for proper focusing. If a person can focus nearby objects on the retina but cannot focus far-away objects, he is *nearsighted*. If a person can see things clearly at a distance but not near at hand, he is *farsighted*.

The illustrations above are of a nearsighted eye. This eye focuses well things close at hand. But when light enters it from a distant

Correction of farsightedness.

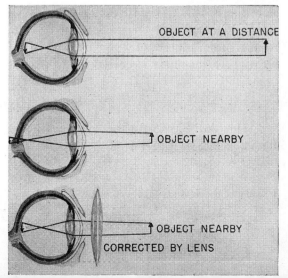

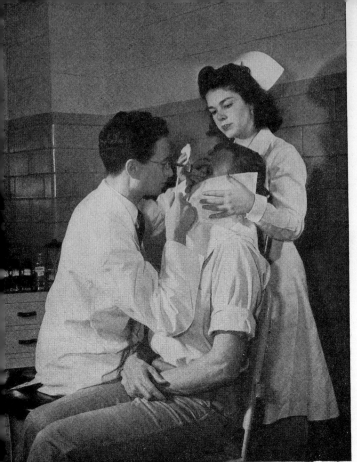

"Something in the eye" often requires a doctor.

that bend the light rays from nearby objects together so that they still enter the eye nearly parallel, just as they do from an object that is far away.

Sometimes the lens or the clear part of the eyeball's outer coat known as the *cornea* is curved unevenly. When this occurs, a person is said to have *astigmatism*. Part of the light from an object forms a sharp image on the retina, and part of it does not.

EYE HEALTH

The eyes, like other organs, are fed by the blood stream. By means of the nervous system, they are in contact with all other parts of the body. For these reasons, diseases in other parts of the body can and do affect the eyes. Nervousness, fatigue, or other general body conditions may produce definite reactions in the eyes, such as soreness or cloudiness of vision. On the other hand, the eyes themselves affect other parts of the body. Eyestrain may produce violent headaches, sleeplessness, digestive upsets, and so forth.

Because the eyes are so closely related to other parts of the body, a person should always have his eyes examined by a competent medical doctor who has specialized in eye treatment. Such a doctor is called an *oculist* or *ophthalmologist*. Quite often he is an "eye, ear, nose, and throat specialist."

For your good health, perhaps the big point you should remember is that the eyes, although rugged, are delicate and are a part of your total body. Mistreatment of them will affect other parts of your body, and poor health of other body parts will often affect the eyes. Remember these facts and you will understand the advisability of securing competent medical advice on troubles that appear to be in the eyes.

object, the parallel rays come to a focus before reaching the retina, ordinarily because the eyeball is too long. Nearsightedness is corrected by glasses that bend the light rays out so that they are diverging when they enter the eye, just as they are when coming from a nearby object.

The illustrations at bottom of page 69 are of a farsighted eye. This eye focuses well things at a distance. But when light enters it from a nearby object, the image falls behind the retina, ordinarily because the eyeball is too short. Farsightedness is corrected by glasses

WORKING WITH SCIENCE

1. How do the lens and cornea of the human eye form a picture on the retina of the eye? How do glasses correct nearsightedness and farsightedness? Here is an interesting experiment that will help you to answer these questions.

Secure an inexpensive lens, such as a reading glass, or take the focusing lens from the school's motion-picture projector or glass-slide projector. Place a sheet of white paper on the wall opposite the windows. Bring the lens in front of the paper and move it slowly toward or away from the paper until a bright, sharp image of the window is produced. Examine this image closely. Is it right side up or upside down? The picture your eye forms is in the same position. However, you have learned to think of it as right side up.

Now move the lens slowly toward the paper. Note how the image becomes blurred and indistinct. The lens is too near the paper. This is similar to the condition in the human eye that causes nearsightedness.

How is nearsightedness corrected? Leave the lens in front of the paper and so near it that the image is blurred. Now place another lens in front of the first one and move it back and forth slowly until a distinct image is again formed. Glasses can be fitted to the human eye so that nearsightedness is overcome. Other shapes of lenses correct farsightedness and astigmatism. See the illustrations on page 69 for an explanation of types of lenses.

2. You can get a good idea of the nature of the eye by examining a fresh beef, pig, or sheep eye, which you can probably obtain from your butcher. If you cut it open, you will find that it is filled with a light liquid. This liquid helps the eye to retain its rounded shape.

Toward the front of the eye you will find the roundish lens. Take out the lens and, while it is still fresh, hold it up toward the daylight and place a white paper at the other side. The lens will produce an image of the window on the paper. In the living eye, the lens forms distinct images on the retina of the eye by becoming thicker when the eye is looking at something nearby and thinner when the eye is looking at something at a distance.

YOUR EARS

We learn much through our eyes, but our ears are also a chief source of contact with the outside world. Just as we need to know something about light to understand how we see, so we need to know something about sound to understand our ears and how they enable us to hear. When anything moves rapidly back and forth, or *vibrates*, it starts waves in the air around it, just as something moving in water starts waves in the water. Some of the waves in air are *sound waves*. These waves cause *hearing*.

The illustrations below show the structure of the ear. The *outer ear* is a sort of funnel that collects sound waves. From the outer ear, a little canal leads to the *middle ear*. At the inside end of the canal is a thin, stretched membrane, which vibrates when sound waves hit it. This membrane is the *eardrum*.

The vibrations of the eardrum are carried over three bones in the middle ear—*hammer*, *anvil*, and *stirrup*—to the *inner ear*, which consists of three *semicircular canals* and the *cochlea*. The cochlea looks like a snail, for it is a long hollow tube that is coiled, as shown in the middle illustration. In the cochlea, sound vibrations are converted into nervous impulses that enable us to hear sound.

This series of drawings explains how we hear. Beginning with sound waves in the drawing at the right, trace the various steps in hearing.

From Encyclopaedia Britannica film
Fundamentals of Acoustics

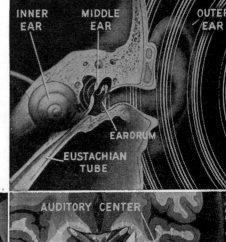

INNER EAR — MIDDLE EAR — OUTER EAR — EARDRUM — EUSTACHIAN TUBE

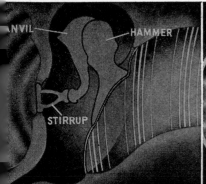

ANVIL — HAMMER — STIRRUP

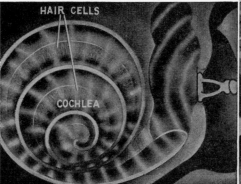

HAIR CELLS — COCHLEA

AUDITORY CENTER — AUDITORY NERVE

Chewing gum or swallowing is not necessary to relieve ear pressure in the pressurized cabins of some planes. But the gum is distributed anyway.

HOW DO WE HEAR?

Look inside a piano case, and you will find that the strings which make the low, or *bass*, notes are longer and heavier than the strings which make the high, or *treble*, notes. The situation in the human ear is similar. Inside the cochlea are *hair cells*, which are connected to tiny stringlike membranes of various lengths. The longest ones are at the tip of the cochlea and—just like piano strings—the membranes gradually become shorter until very short ones are at the base of the coiled cochlea.

How do we tell the difference between sounds? The theory commonly accepted is that low notes cause the long membranes in the cochlea to vibrate, and high notes, which are vibrating very fast, cause the short membranes to vibrate. The vibrations cause nerve impulses to go to the brain. When the long membranes vibrate, we hear the sound as low. When the short membranes vibrate, we hear the sound as high.

FLYING AND EARS

The middle ear is connected with the nostril-throat area by the Eustachian tube (see illustration on page 57). This is an extremely important little tube. It is even more important now, in an age of flight, than before.

The pressure of the air is not always the same. It changes with the weather to a small extent, and decreases considerably with a gain in altitude—for example, at the top of a high mountain, flying high in an airplane, or even at the top of a tall building.

Air enters the middle ear through the Eustachian tube. Ordinarily, the pressure on both sides of the eardrum is the same. If there were no way of changing the pressure in the middle ear, a person could not go up, say, 20,000 feet, in an airplane without serious consequences. At 20,000 feet, the outside pressure on his eardrum would be roughly half of the pressure on the inside of the eardrum, and this difference in pressure would be more than enough to burst the eardrum.

Usually the Eustachian tube is closed. During swallowing, talking, or yawning, the tube opens, and air gets into or out of the middle ears thus keeping the pressure of the air the same on both sides of the eardrum.

Colds and other infections may cause the Eustachian tubes to become clogged. When this occurs, pain and distress result if a person changes altitudes rapidly. Something similar occurs if a person does not swallow, talk, or yawn while changing altitudes rapidly.

You may have noticed how your ears sometimes "pop" when you go up in an elevator or airplane or up a mountain road. Ears "pop" when the Eustachian tubes open up and the pressure is suddenly equalized. Pilots on going into extreme dives yell loudly. Yelling forces open the Eustachian tubes.

The fact that the Eustachian tubes connect your nose and throat with the delicate middle ears may result in trouble. Deafness may result if infections in the respiratory passages spread to the middle ear through the Eustachian tubes. Some diseases, such as measles, scarlet fever, and even the common cold, often involve the middle ear. Hence, such diseases should be controlled and treated properly, particularly if earache develops. If treatment is delayed or is improper, an infection of the middle ear may be extremely serious.

OTHER SENSORY MEANS

There are many other sensations—far more than the "five senses" we ordinarily talk about. There is the sense of balance. There is the sense of smell, which accounts, by the way, for most flavors. There is the sense of taste: salt, sour, bitter, and sweet. (You smell a chocolate milk-shake. You taste only its sweetness.) There are the sensations of touch, pain, cold, and heat. You can study more of these and other interesting things about your remarkable human body in other books and in later science courses, such as biology.

THE NERVOUS SYSTEM AND MODERN LIVING

It is amazing how the body-machine is able to maintain itself and avoid trouble. Man's nervous system allows him to detect danger and to avoid it. Before the time of the automobile, the airplane, and other inventions growing out of the Industrial Revolution, this nervous system was generally capable of keeping an individual out of trouble.

But the reflexes that protected a man driving a team of horses will not protect a man driving an automobile 60 miles an hour, or an airplane 200 miles an hour, nearly so well. The deaths from automobile accidents in this country are tremendously high. Over 35,000 people are killed and 90,000 permanently crippled annually from automobile accidents. These deaths represent the fact that even man's highly developed nervous system has limitations. When a man slows down his reaction time by drinking—and then drives a car—he not only risks his own life but that of others on the highways. The body-machine must be kept fit for the demands of modern living.

WORKING WITH SCIENCE

1. If you do not believe that you smell rather than taste most foods, try the following experiment. Blindfold a member of the class. Have on hand several types of food which the blindfolded person has not seen. These should all be liquid, such as maple syrup, meat broth, and castor oil, so that the blindfolded person cannot recognize them by their texture. Hold his nose securely so that he cannot smell anything, and place a small bit of each substance in turn in his mouth.

Ask him to name each substance after he spits it out. What things could he taste? How does castor oil taste? What is its odor?

READING YOU WILL ENJOY

American National Red Cross. *American Red Cross First Aid Textbook*. The Blakiston Co., Philadelphia, 1945. A standard and sound reference for first-aid work.

Carlson, Anton J. and Johnson, Victor. *The Machinery of the Body*. University of Chicago Press, Chicago, 1941. Contains excellent photographs and drawings of all parts of the body-machine.

Stack, Herbert J., Seaton, Don C., Hyde, Florence S. *Safety in the World of Today*. Beckley-Cardy Co., Chicago, 1941. A safety textbook for young people. You will find particularly valuable the section on safety in driving.

Zim, Herbert S. *Man in the Air*. Harcourt, Brace & Co., New York, 1943. An interesting book that relates the adjustments man's body must make in taking to the air. Particularly interesting are the sections on sensory illusions and adjustments of the senses of balance and vision in flying.

As man has learned more about how a healthy human body works, he has become better able to detect differences between good health and poor health by means of scientific instruments. For example, people long ago realized that disease is usually accompanied by fever. The first person to use a thermometer to measure fever was Sanctorious (1), an Italian physician, early in the seventeenth century. Sanctorious also devised an instrument for measuring the pulse rate. The practice of tapping the chest to discover the presence of fluid in the lungs is thought to have originated early in the nineteenth century with a young Austrian doctor named Auenbrugger (2). His father had been an innkeeper and he remembered slapping the wine casks to see how much wine was in them. The stethoscope for listening to the heart-beat was invented in 1814 by Laennec (3), a French physician, who got the idea by watching some children listening to messages being scratched out on a seesaw.

Modern doctors are aided by instruments undreamed of even a few centuries ago. Roentgen discovered x-rays in 1895. Because x-rays pass through

flesh and bone, they can be used in studying conditions inside the body (4) as well as in treating certain diseases. The electrocardiograph (5) "listens" to a heart-beat and makes a complete "picture" of every phase of its movements. By studying the record made by an electrocardiograph, a doctor can tell exactly how a particular heart is working. In many cases this gives the doctor the clues he needs to tell what is wrong. Thus, scientific instruments help man to live longer through helping him to learn what is wrong when he is in ill health.

Health to You

6

CHECK UP ON YOUR HEALTH

If you have good health, it is hard to imagine what poor health is like. No one can expect you to be very much disturbed about heart disease while your own heart pumps right along without causing trouble. On the other hand, it is hard to understand what really good health is like if you do not have it or have never had it.

WHAT IS "GOOD" HEALTH?

First and obviously, good health is the condition of a person who is free from disease. Diseases are of two general types. One type is caused by plants or animals so tiny they can be seen only under a microscope. These tiny plants and animals are called *microorganisms*. Microorganisms that cause disease are often called germs.

Diseases caused by microorganisms may be transferred from one person to another. Such diseases are called *communicable diseases*. Among the communicable diseases are *measles, mumps, smallpox, colds, influenza*, and so forth.

In addition, there are the diseases that are the result of some serious body lack or improper functioning. Such diseases are called *noncommunicable diseases. Cancer, heart disease*, and *diabetes* are among these diseases.

Good health, however, is far more than just freedom from disease. It means also that the various parts of the body are functioning properly and together as a whole. The eyes are keen and working well. The teeth are in good condition. Digestion takes place easily and without distress. The head does not have periodic aches, and so on. Good health also means freedom from body injuries and freedom from constant nervousness or worry.

A person in good health finds that the world looks pretty rosy. A person who is constantly worried, gloomy, nervous, or fretful is not in good health. All the factors of good health taken together mean that a person who possesses them is living fully. He is energetic and enjoys a full day's work and play. He has endurance and poise. And, over long periods of time, his body is in such good condition that he "doesn't know he has one."

HEALTH CHECK

How is good health acquired? How is it maintained? No one knows the whole answer. But we know many ways to healthful living. And you can improve and maintain your health by following a plan of healthful living. But it is a long-term undertaking. It is a way of life.

A brief health-check list appears on page 76. Fill it out carefully and honestly. But before you do, read the entire list and study the explanation that follows the list. (Do not write in your book. Use another sheet of paper and copy off each heading.) You may not understand the importance of some of the questions and statements. If not, your teacher will help you now, and later study in this unit will enable you to understand them very much more thoroughly.

CHECK UP ON YOUR OWN HEALTH

Some of the following questions deal with your past and present health. Some deal with your knowledge of how to maintain health. Your health in the future depends a good deal on how well informed you are about ways to keep healthy.

1. Which of the following diseases have you had: measles, mumps, scarlet fever, chicken pox? List any others.

2. How often do you have a cold or sore throat?

3. Do you have pains in joints, arms, or legs?

4. About how often are your tonsils swollen and painful? Or have your tonsils been removed?

5. Have you been *vaccinated* (inoculated) against smallpox? When?

6. Have you ever had a *tuberculin* test? a chest x-ray? When?

7. Has anyone in your family or with whom you have lived had *tuberculosis?*

8. How often do you have headaches? What do you do for headaches?

9. How many hours do you sleep each night?

10. About how much time do you spend each day in outdoor exercise?

11. Keep a record of what you eat for breakfast, lunch, and dinner for 3 days and attach it to the sheet on which you are answering these questions.

12. Have you ever had your eyes examined by a medical doctor? When was the last time?

13. How often do you see a dentist? When was the last time?

14. How much do you weigh? Are you gaining weight or losing weight?

15. Do you ever take laxatives? How often?

16. Do you very often feel tired and exhausted?

17. Do you like gym activities or such sports as baseball, basketball, and football?

18. Would you ordinarily prefer to read an interesting book or to go to a party or to meet with a group for an evening?

19. Make a brief list of your hobbies.

20. How many good friends do you have? How many of them are boys? How many are girls?

21. What are the causes of common diseases, and how can you help prevent such diseases as colds, measles, malaria, and typhoid fever?

22. What health services are provided by your community, county, state, and the nation? List those you know about.

EXPLANATION OF ITEMS IN CHECK LIST

Items 1 and 2. These items refer to communicable diseases that you may have had. Some persons have had many diseases; others, few. The diseases you have had are not as important as how often you have been sick.

If you very often have colds or if you have had many childhood diseases, you should consider carefully the possible reasons for this. It may be that you are not in good general condition because of improper diet, not enough rest and exercise, overwork, or something of the kind. It may be that you are not careful to avoid people with colds or that you pay no attention to rules for healthful living.

Item 3. This item refers to an all-too-common condition of youth known as *rheumatic fever*. Aches and pains may mean many things, but if you do have pains in your joints, arms, and legs, and if you find that you are unusually nervous, see your doctor. Rheumatic fever often injures heart valves, and if by chance you have it, you need medical attention.

Item 4. This merely calls your attention to the danger of repeatedly infected tonsils. If you have had *tonsillitis* often and your tonsils have not been removed, you may be harboring germs that can harm you. This does not necessarily mean that your tonsils should be removed. It does mean that a physician should advise you what to do.

Item 5. Item 5 refers to the disease smallpox. Smallpox is very easily prevented. You should be vaccinated about every 7 years at most.

Item 6. This item refers to the importance of periodic physical examinations to detect tuberculosis. The tuberculin test is made by injecting tuberculin between layers of the skin. If the reaction is negative, you are all right. If the reaction is positive (that is, if a reddening and swelling occurs), it indicates the presence of living tuberculosis germs in your body. They may or may not be active.

If the reaction to the tuberculin test is positive, a chest x-ray should be made. An x-ray will show evidences of active tuberculosis if it is present. Safeguard yourself by periodic chest x-rays all through your life.

Item 7. This item suggests the importance of chest x-rays if you have been long exposed to anyone who has had tuberculosis. Tuberculosis is being stamped out. But it still exists, and people ordinarily get it through long contact with persons who have it.

Item 8. Item 8 is intended as a warning that something is wrong if you have headaches frequently. Remember that the body is complex, and headaches may mean a number of things. Certainly you should avoid the temptation to take aspirin or other headache remedies for headaches that occur frequently without consulting a doctor in order to determine the underlying cause of the pain.

Items 9 and 10. Those items refer to the general health practices of getting enough sleep and exercise. It is hard to set a general rule for the amount needed by all people. Eight or 9 hours of sleep a night seem to be required by most persons, but some need more. Young people should not try to get along with less. You know the effect of exercise on the circulation. Even more important is the effect of healthful, active recreation on morale and general outlook. Get an hour or more each day.

Item 11. Save this record for use when you study Chapter 8.

Items 12 and 13. All of us should have our eyes and teeth checked from time to time. Too often we do not realize that we are having eye trouble and lay the blame for headaches, irritability, and just plain distaste for study on something else. Have your eyes checked by a competent physician and treated if necessary. Have your teeth cleaned and examined twice a year and have minor cavities filled to keep them from becoming major ones.

Item 14. The number of pounds you weigh is not as important as whether you are gaining weight, as you should be at your age. If you are not gaining weight, or if you are losing weight, by all means see your doctor.

Item 15. Laxatives are generally needless and often downright dangerous. Sometimes a pain in the abdomen and constipation mean an acutely inflamed appendix. If so, a laxative might make it burst. Proper diet and healthful living should make laxatives unnecessary.

Item 16. If you answered this item *Yes,* clearly something is wrong. Just what the trouble is can be determined only by your physician. You should certainly secure his services to help you begin living with zest again.

Items 17, 18, 19, and 20. These items are to help you think about your tendencies and tastes in getting along with other people. Some of us prefer to "hole up" with a book and to develop hobbies that enable us to be by ourselves. This is often good, of course. But we should all learn to live and play with others. If you do not like sports or parties, the chances are that you are a little too self-critical and afraid of the criticism of others. Try to get over this feeling. You *can* learn to enjoy group games and the company of other people.

Items 21 and 22. These items refer to two aspects of disease control about which everyone should be informed. You should know something of the general nature and control of communicable diseases and be aware of the services available to you through your local, county, state, and Federal health resources.

1

2

Until man learned what causes various diseases, he could not treat them very successfully. Many early peoples thought that illness is caused by "evil spirits" or "demons" that somehow get into their bodies. Early "healers" (1) used magical ceremonies in trying to drive out the demons. Such ceremonies cured no one who was really sick. A few early doctors got the idea that diseases spread because of something passed from person to person. Fracastoro, an Italian physician of the early sixteenth century, talked of the "seeds of disease," but it is not likely that he meant germs. Von Plenciz, an eighteenth century Austrian physician, stated that diseases that spread are caused by living things. But no one had actually seen germs.

The microscope enabled man to see and study germs. Louis Pasteur (2) the great nineteenth century French chemist, proved that certain diseases of animals are caused by "microbes," and developed vaccines to treat and even prevent various diseases. In this, he had been preceded by Jenner, an English physician, who developed a vaccine against smallpox near the end of the eighteenth century. In 1882, Robert Koch (3), a celebrated German doctor, proved that specific germs cause specific diseases of human beings. Modern methods of combatting communicable diseases (4) are based on the work of these and other research workers. Today, it is possible to prevent or to treat successfully many of the diseases that killed thousands only a few centuries ago.

3

4

7

COMMUNICABLE, OR "CATCHING," DISEASES

It took a long time to find out that communicable diseases are caused by living organisms. However, long ago the ancient Egyptians believed that organisms that live on or in another organism at its expense caused certain illnesses. Such organisms are called *parasites*. But the Egyptians had little definite evidence to support their belief. It was really just a good guess, that is, a good working theory.

Actually, less than 100 years have elapsed since the fact that germs cause communicable diseases was firmly established. And today thousands of scientists are still working hard to discover the exact nature and cause of certain diseases that are still beyond man's control.

GERMS AND DISEASE

Many of the great discoveries in medicine awaited the invention of the microscope, which enlarged the tiny world of microorganisms to visible size. Although the microscope was invented near the close of the sixteenth century, it served no very useful purpose until it was improved by a Dutch lens-grinder named Anton van Leeuwenhoek [vän lā′ věn-hŏŏk] in the middle of the following century.

But long before that time, some understanding of communicable diseases had developed by trial-and-error methods. As a result, persons suffering from certain diseases were kept by themselves in an effort to keep others from getting the diseases. For example, *quarantines* (meaning, originally, a *40-day isolation*) were established in Venice in the fourteenth century to protect well people from the deadly black death, or *bubonic plague*.

The First Man to See Germs. In 1675 Leeuwenhoek actually saw many microorganisms through the microscopes that he made. He saw and sketched the tiny one-celled animals we call *protozoa* (singular, *protozoan*) and the various shapes of bacteria—rod-shaped, cork-screw-shaped, and spherical-shaped. Probably he did not have any idea that some of these tiny plants and animals could cause diseases.

PASTEUR PROVES THAT GERMS CAUSE DISEASE

About 1857 Louis Pasteur [päs-tûr′], a French chemist, began to study the change that takes place when grape juice turns into wine. This process is called *fermentation*. With the aid of a microscope, he discovered that this fermentation results from activities of certain tiny plants called *yeasts*.

How Pasteur Saved the French Wine Industry. Carrying on his studies, Pasteur found that wine was soured and changed to vinegar by certain bacteria. He also found that the harmful bacteria could be killed by applying heat several times—just enough heat to kill the bacteria but not enough to harm the wine.

Pasteur's discovery was very important, for the wine industry of France was being ruined by the bacteria that soured the wines. Later discoveries showed that germs of several common communicable diseases are easily killed by heat. The process of heating foods,

Did Leeuwenhoek realize that some one-celled plants and animals could cause disease?

such as milk, thus making them free from dangerous bacteria is called *pasteurization*, in honor of Pasteur.

Pasteur, the Germ Detective. In 1865 Pasteur made his greatest discovery. Before that time there had been no direct proof that some of the strange little plants and animals visible only under a microscope were the cause of disease. The French government asked Pasteur to study the disease *pébrine*, which was killing the silkworms and thus crippling the silk industry of France. Pasteur performed many experiments and finally proved that bacteria were causing the trouble. He even showed the silkworm-growers how to study the silkworm's eggs under a microscope to select for raising only those free of germs.

Most important of all was Pasteur's proof that the disease of a living organism was definitely caused by a microorganism. Knowledge of this fact has saved countless millions of lives since Pasteur's day. The discovery about the silkworm disease opened the door for other investigations on the cause of diseases of other animals, including man. Pasteur himself continued his studies on the diseases anthrax and chicken cholera.

KOCH AND HUMAN DISEASES

The final proof that some diseases of man are caused by certain microorganisms was developed by another scientist who lived during the same period as Pasteur. Robert Koch [kŏk], a German physician, was a brilliant and methodical experimenter. He set out to conquer *anthrax*, which killed whole flocks of sheep and cost his country millions of dollars each year. It also attacked human beings. What was the cause of this destroyer?

How Koch Studied Germs. Koch went at his investigation carefully, critically, and patiently. He found ways to grow bacteria on food suspended in gelatin. In biological terms, by transferring bacteria from the blood of a diseased animal to gelatin, he prepared a *culture* of bacteria. Then he separated out a single bacterium by dipping a needle into a culture of the bacteria and stroking it lightly across the top of clean gelatin.

As the needle first touched the gelatin, millions of bacteria were wiped off into the gelatin. But as the needle continued across the gelatin, a single bacterium would finally be wiped off by itself. Koch found that he could keep a single bacterium alive and that it would reproduce itself by dividing and redividing until a colony large enough to be seen by the naked eye was formed.

This method enabled Koch to separate one kind of germ from other kinds of germs. That is, he obtained a *pure culture*. You will realize the importance of this method if you stop to think that a diseased person or animal may be harboring several kinds of germs. If the kinds of germs could not be separated, it would be impossible to tell which kind was responsible for a disease.

Koch took the fluids from various organs of animals that had anthrax and examined them under a microscope. He found that the fluids were filled with swarming masses of tiny, rod-shaped bacteria. He examined the fluids from organs of animals that did not have the disease. Never did he find these rod-shaped plants. All rod-shaped bacteria have the general name *bacilli* (singular, *bacillus*).

Using his method of separating germs on gelatin, Koch obtained a group of germs that were definitely of one type, the bacilli. He dipped the end of a clean splinter of wood into the culture of bacilli and then plunged the splinter under the skin of a healthy mouse. The next day the mouse was dead. And it had all the usual symptoms of anthrax.

Koch did not jump to conclusions. The evidence seemed convincing as far as it went. But possibly something had slipped. Maybe it was not really those bacilli but something else that had killed his mouse. So he continued his experiment.

Koch Proves His Theory. He took fluids from healthy animals, which did not contain the bacilli, and injected them into healthy mice. None of these animals contracted the disease. Then he transferred the bacilli from a sick mouse to a healthy one, and the animals always contracted anthrax.

Koch repeated these procedures many times. The animals that were not injected with bacilli never got the disease. The animals that contracted anthrax always had the bacilli in their body fluids. The healthy animals did not have the bacilli in their fluids. Koch was finally convinced. For a time many people did not accept his findings, but Koch had proved beyond a doubt that living germs of a particular type cause anthrax.

KOCH'S POSTULATES

Koch made many other important discoveries. In 1882 he made known his discovery of the *tubercle* bacillus—the germ that causes tuberculosis. At the same time, he announced the now famous principles called *Koch's postulates*.

These postulates outline the four steps that are necessary to prove that a particular organism is the cause of a particular disease. They

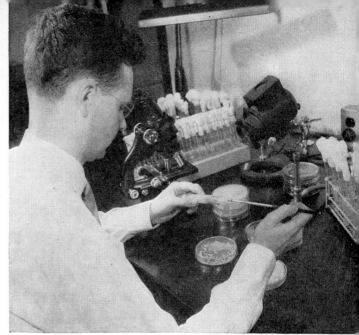

U. S. D. A. photo by Forsythe

Culturing a specific microorganism from a Petri dish with colonies of several microorganisms.

summarize Koch's experiments and the conclusions based upon those experiments. They grew out of experimental work to which was added good hard thinking. They are an excellent example of the use of the experimental method in the study of diseases.

1. Large numbers of the microorganism must be found in the fluids, tissues, or discharges of an animal suffering from a disease.

2. These germs must be taken from the animal's body and separated, so that individual germs and their descendants may be studied with the certainty that no other types of germs are in the same materials.

3. These germs—known definitely to be of a single type—must be capable of producing the original disease.

4. The same type of germs must then be found in large numbers in the fluids, tissues, or discharges of an experimentally infected animal.

Modern Germ Detectives Carry On. Many scientists have continued the magnificient work that was started by Pasteur and Koch. Many of their own students carried on bril-

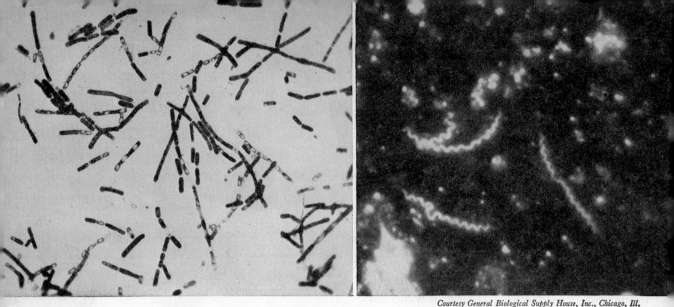

Courtesy General Biological Supply House, Inc., Chicago, Ill.

Highly enlarged photographs of germs. Left: Anthrax. Right: Syphilis.

liant research. Throughout the world today many men and women are working in laboratories and in the field to increase our knowledge of the cause and nature of diseases. Some of you may someday join in searching for the knowledge that will lead us to better living through better health.

To profit most from the studies scientists have made, all of us should know the basic facts about the diseases that are caused by germs. For, in spite of all our progress, germs are still with us. Hundreds of thousands of persons die each year following the invasion of their bodies by germs.

WORKING WITH SCIENCE

1. The biographies of some of the early investigators of the causes of disease are as interesting as adventure or detective stories. To help you see how the work of many different people living at different times and in different places contributed to our knowledge of the cause and cure of diseases, read and prepare reports on the lives and works of some of the early investigators. The references given at the end of this chapter will help you locate suitable reading material.

2. You may perform a number of experiments in the laboratory that will make Koch's experiments clearer to you. In order to prepare a culture of gelatin-like food, you will need the following materials: agar-agar, 10 grams or ½ ounce; beef extract, 10 grams or ½ ounce; peptone, 10 grams or ½ ounce; salt, 10 grams or ½ ounce; water, 1000 milliliters or 1 quart and 13 fluid ounces; baking soda, pinch.

It is a good idea to prepare a number of agar cultures at one time. Place the agar-agar in a large pan

or beaker. Add the water and heat slowly, stirring occasionally, until the agar-agar is dissolved. Then add the beef extract, peptone, and salt. Continue stirring until all the materials are dissolved in the broth. Test the broth with red litmus paper. If the red litmus paper does not turn blue, add very small pinches of baking soda until it does.

Pour the agar culture into test tubes until each is about one-third full. Plug the mouths of the tubes with cotton. Sterilize the tubes and their contents by heating in a pressure cooker or other steam sterilizer. Tubes of culture, so prepared, will become jelly-like, and remain fresh and sterile for a long time if kept in a cool dark place. Sterilize also twice as many Petri dishes as you have tubes of culture.

When you are ready to do an experiment, heat the number of tubes of culture that you need in boiling water until the cultures melt. Remove the plug of sterile cotton and pour about half the contents of one tube into a sterilized Petri dish. Pour the remainder into another Petri dish. Immediately re-place the lids on the Petri dishes to prevent the entry of any nonsterile substance. Allow the cultures to cool. They are then ready for inoculation with bacteria.

If you have been careful in preparing your cultures, no bacteria will be present. Try inoculating the cultures (1) by exposing them to the air at various places, (2) by running a dirty finger over the surface, (3) by washing the finger carefully and then passing it over the surface, (4) by sneezing into a culture, and (5) by allowing a fly to walk over the surface.

After inoculating your cultures, keep them in a warm, dark place. A shaded 40-watt electric-light bulb burning in a small box makes a good incubator. Bacteria grow best at about body temperature (about 95° to 100°F).

3. If equipment and materials are not available to make the agar cultures, as suggested in Exercise 2, you may find it interesting to try the following experiment. Boil a large potato until it is tender. After it has cooled, cut it into slices ½ inch thick. Place each slice in a separate Petri dish (or turn a small glass upside down in a saucer on which the potato slice is resting). Sterilize the Petri dishes and contents by heating for 20 minutes in a pressure cooker. Remove the dishes from the pressure cooker. Keep one potato slice sterile. Perform each of the experiments suggested in Exercise 2 with the remaining slices.

(Note: The potato culture will not allow the growth of bacteria as well as the agar cultures, but you should find colonies of some microscopic plants after inoculating the slices and incubating for a few days.)

FACTS ABOUT COMMUNICABLE DISEASES

To profit most from what is known about communicable diseases, you must first of all remember the fact that communicable diseases *are* caused by germs. Second, there are several types of germs. Some are microscopic plants, some are animals, some are the extremely tiny viruses. Third, germs cause disease in different ways. Waste products called toxins are thrown off by some germs. These are sometimes poisonous to human beings and cause the symptoms of illness. Other germs cause illness by actually destroying human cells or by blocking off blood vessels or important passageways.

WHAT GERMS REQUIRE TO LIVE

With the possible exception of viruses, disease germs are living organisms. In general, they have the same basic requirements as you or any other living thing. They must have food, a reasonable degree of warmth, and moisture in order to grow and be active. They will eventually die if they do not have suitable food. They can be killed by very high temperatures. Extreme cold does not kill many types of germs, but it does make them inactive. Some germs can be killed by drying.

Like human beings, germs can be poisoned or killed by certain chemicals. Fortunately, some chemicals affect certain germs more quickly and easily than they do the cells of your body. For this reason, it is possible to use such chemicals to destroy germs in your body without seriously affecting the cells of your body.

Because of their requirements for life, germs do not exist just anywhere. They come from other human beings or animals suffering from a disease. They may pass directly from one person to another, or they may be carried from one person to another by foods, insects and other animals, or in such things as water, dirt, and even books.

But in every case, disease germs come originally from persons or animals who have or have had germs of the same kind in their bodies. We can escape disease germs best by avoiding contact with persons suffering from communicable diseases.

Finally, you must remember that the human body is complex and the parts are interdependent. Consequently, it is impossible for a person who is not a trained physician to do an intelligent job of diagnosing illnesses and prescribing treatment.

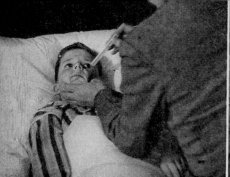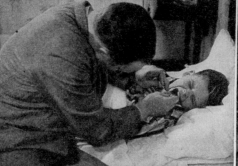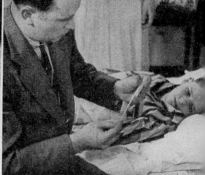

From *Encyclopaedia Britannica* film Defending the City's Health

The germs obtained will be identified so that the doctor can tell what causes this boy's sore throat.

MANY MICROORGANISMS ARE HELPFUL

Despite our loathing of disease germs, we must understand, of course, that there are hundreds of thousands of microorganisms, and only a very few cause diseases. Many are exceedingly beneficial to man. Some of them cause rotting, which releases chemicals that would otherwise be locked up in dead plants and animals and would, therefore, not be available to future generations for the materials they need for life.

Others make cheeses, cause bread to rise, and make the alcohol that is the basic chemical for many modern products and processes. Microorganisms do a thousand and one important things. But the few types that cause diseases cause much suffering and death.

AVOID CONTACT WITH SICK PERSONS

We contract most diseases from diseased people. Experiences during World War II provided additional proof of this fact. One navy doctor who worked for two years on a small group of islands in the South Pacific reported that his men did not suffer from colds, although they were often exposed to heavy rains, cold weather, winds, and so forth. They had colds only when new groups of men with colds arrived on the islands. Cold germs were transferred from the sick to the well.

We cannot avoid people completely. But we can protect ourselves from other people's diseases better than most of us do. Direct contact, such as kissing or shaking hands, is the most common source of infection for communicable diseases.

Most disease germs die quickly when away

from the warmth and moisture and food that they find in the human body. However, some germs can live without the protection of the human body. That is, they are *resistant*. Resistant types of germs can be carried on such dry objects as books and tables, but these are not usual sources of infection.

Many diseases are transferred by the tiny droplets of moisture that are ejected from the mouth in sneezing, coughing, or even speaking. Since these generally do not travel far, a person is fairly safe if he is more than 3 feet away from another person. However, it is extremely important that all of us cover our faces with handkerchiefs when we sneeze or cough.

AVOID CONTAMINATED FOOD AND WATER

Some disease germs thrive especially in foods and water. These are the germs of intestinal diseases, such as *dysentery*, *typhoid fever*, and some of the most deadly diseases of historical importance—for example, *cholera*.

Therefore, it is important that we drink water only from sources approved by health authorities or boil water for 5 minutes or longer if its purity is in doubt. We should eat at places where eating utensils are properly washed and sterilized. If we drink only pasteurized or certified milk, we can avoid the danger of typhoid fever, undulant fever, other intestinal diseases, and some types of tuberculosis that are easily carried in raw milk.

SOME ANIMALS CARRY DISEASE GERMS

Insects and other animals carry the germs of some diseases. Wood ticks carry *Rocky Mountain spotted fever*. Lice carry *typhus fever*. Fleas carry bubonic plague. Flies can carry almost

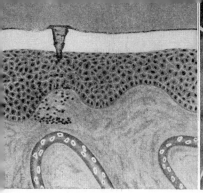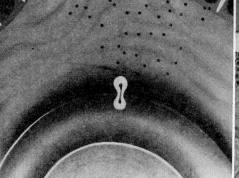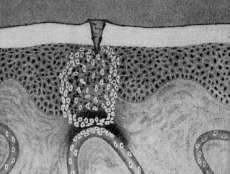

Left: Germs entering. Middle: White blood cell leaving capillary. Right: Invaders walled off.

any kind of intestinal disease, for they live and breed in filth where germs are likely to be.

Mosquitoes carry diseases, too. One kind carries malaria; another kind, *yellow fever*.

WORKING WITH SCIENCE

1. What would happen if every person would immediately go home and stay away from others when he first started having a cold? It is possible that the spread of colds would be much less, although medical scientists believe that the most infective stage of a cold occurs before a person realizes that a cold is beginning.

Your general science class can carry out a project of great interest and possible value to the school by making a careful check on what the boys and girls of the school and their parents do for colds. Form working committees to collect this information and determine how many people stay at home when they begin to sneeze and cough. Arrange the information in a chart and display at the school or sub-

mit to the local newspaper with suggestions from medical doctors on the correct procedures to combat a cold and to prevent the spread of colds.

2. Individuals or a committee of your class might visit or telephone the eating places in your community and inquire what procedures are used in washing and sterilizing dishes. Find what local and state laws help to protect people from disease spread by unclean dishes and silverware.

3. Find out from your local health office, a local doctor, or the state department of health what diseases are considered particularly prevalent in your area. Find out what, if anything, young people and adults of your community can do to reduce the number of cases of these diseases.

THE BODY'S FIGHT AGAINST DISEASE

Every person should realize that the state of his general health is a large factor in preventing illness. Some persons have one cold after another, while others living and working in the same places seem never to have colds. This is because the *general resistance* of some persons is high and that of others is low—or at least much lower.

The whole story about resistance to disease is not known. However, we do know that a person whose diet is well rounded, who gets plenty of sleep and rest, who secures enough exercise, and who, in general, is "in the pink" is less likely to develop diseases than a person who is run down.

WHITE BLOOD CELLS

Medical research has given us much information on how the body resists disease, and the story is interesting and important. To make the story simple, suppose that you have stepped on a nail. It does not matter much whether the nail is rusty, except that a rusty nail is often dirtier. Hence, more germs are likely to be rubbed into the wound.

Look at the illustrations on this page. They represent a wound in the skin. The wound extends through the outer, dead cells of the outer layer of the skin, or *epidermis*, through the living epidermis cells, which are bathed in lymph, and on into the inner layer of the skin,

85

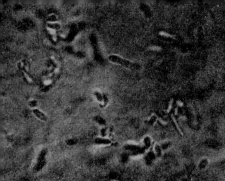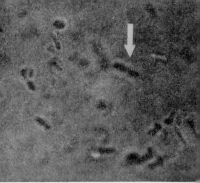

From Encyclopaedia Britannica film Body Defenses Against Disease

Substances called **antibodies** are produced by the body and result in specific immunity. One kind of antibody has a dissolving action on germs, as can be seen here. This helps the white cells.

or *dermis*. It penetrates capillaries and tiny veins. The germs released might cause the death of body cells and even of the entire human organism if they were allowed to reproduce and develop. But see what happens.

How the White Warriors Kill Germs. The amazing little white blood cells begin to move to the wound area. Millions upon millions settle there. They move around in a sort of slow, flowing motion. They look and act as if they were independent one-celled animals, instead of being a part of your body. They ac-

Inoculation is good insurance.

Courtesy National Tuberculosis Association

tually devour the germs. Of course, the germs kill many of the white blood cells by the toxins they throw off. But—if everything goes well —the white blood cells eventually devour all the germs, and the wound heals.

The accumulation of dead germs, white blood cells, body cells, and lymph is known as *pus*. Pus commonly collects in an infected area. The action of the white blood cells is a part of the general resistance that we all have against disease germs.

TOXINS AND ANTITOXINS

Another type of resistance is to particular, or specific, disease germs. This type of resistance is known as *specific immunity*. Your body is a remarkable chemical factory. If you get a disease—*diphtheria*, for example—the disease germs produce a dangerous poison, or toxin. But your body begins immediately to produce a chemical to counteract the effect of the toxin.

This chemical—called *antitoxin*—neutralizes to a certain extent the effect of the poison produced by the germs. Your fight for life is chiefly a race between the antitoxin produced by the body and toxins produced by the germs. The white blood cells take part in this battle, too. If the germs win, you die. If your body wins, the germs are destroyed.

But the most remarkable part is that the antitoxin your body produced will *ordinarily* protect you against diphtheria for many years. This particular antitoxin will not protect you against other diseases. It is specific in acting only against diphtheria germs.

86

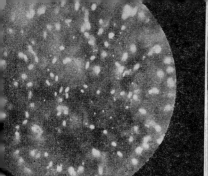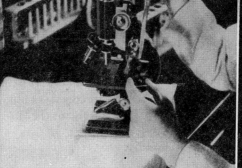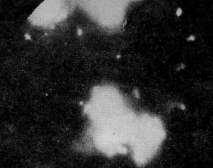

From Encyclopaedia Britannica film Body Defenses Against Disease

The action of this antibody differs from that shown on page 86. When this antibody is added (middle), the germs clump together and become easy prey to the white blood cells.

INOCULATIONS SAVE LIVES

We do not need to suffer and survive a dangerous disease to develop specific immunity. Fortunately, Pasteur, Edward Jenner, and other scientists developed a method of inoculating the human body with substances that give protection against a disease as well as if a person had contracted the disease and been cured.

Diphtheria. No one today need ever have diphtheria. Small amounts of the toxin produced by diphtheria germs or the dead or weakened germs themselves may be injected into a healthy body without danger. This toxin or the dead germs will cause the body's chemical factory to begin work much as if the active, dangerous germs had invaded the body. The antitoxin produced not only protects the body against the injected toxin but also provides specific immunity against diphtheria germs for a long time to come. A toxin so treated that it can no longer produce disease but still causes the body to develop specific immunity is called a *toxoid.*

The Miracle of Antitoxins. Even if a person has not been inoculated with toxoid and has contracted diptheria, his life can be saved. If a physician is called in when the first symptoms of sore throat and mild fever are observed, he will inject diphtheria antitoxin into the patient's body.

Small doses of toxin would not be injected at this time, for the dangerous, fully active disease germs are already producing toxin, and the body has all it can do to fight this toxin. Therefore, the doctor injects antitoxin pro-duced in the bodies of animals. Immediately this antitoxin protects the body against the toxin of the germs, and the white blood cells devour the germs.

There is no excuse for death from diphtheria. Yet, in the United States more than 1200 persons have died from this entirely preventable disease every year since 1940.

Lockjaw. Suppose that you step on a nail that penetrates deeply into the skin. The germ that produces lockjaw, or *tetanus*, is very widespread in soil, particularly where barnyard manure has been. When this germ is away from the warmth, moisture, and food of an animal's body, it forms a hard, capsule-like covering in which it can live for an amazing length of time—many years, in fact—and still cause death if carried into a human body. Such a germ in its covering is called a *spore.*

There is a chance that the nail that punctured your skin carried some tetanus spores into the wound. The toxin produced by the tetanus germ is one of the most powerful poisons known. Mice have been killed by injections of less than 0.000000002 ounce of this toxin—so small an amount that it cannot be seen with the naked eye!

If the white blood cells kill the germs before they start growing and producing toxin, a person would never know that he had the germs in his body. But if this does not happen and the germs start growing, a person is in deadly danger. Five days to 4 or 5 weeks may pass before the symptoms of tetanus appear. This is called the *incubation period* and is the time it takes the germs to get really underway

American Museum of Natural History, New York

The bite of infected body lice is responsible for transmitting typhus fever.

in living, eating, reproducing, and throwing off toxin in the body. All diseases have incubation periods. Their lengths vary.

After the symptoms of tetanus appear, the chances of recovery are gravely reduced. Consequently the services of a physician should be obtained for any deep or torn wound and especially for puncture wounds, such as caused

The housefly is a real villain. He helps spread many serious diseases.

American Museum of Natural History, New York

by a nail, or injuries caused by gunpowder or the explosion of fireworks. If a physician gives tetanus antitoxin before the symptoms appear, recovery is almost certain. In fact, the symptoms of the disease should not even appear.

Smallpox. You probably have never seen a case of smallpox. Would it surprise you to know that smallpox was once very common? Sixty million Europeans were killed by this dread disease in the eighteenth century. As late as 150 years ago, 10 out of every 100 deaths were caused by smallpox. Many persons who recovered were disfigured for life with deep scars, or *poxes.*

Smallpox has been all but wiped from the face of the earth by vaccination. It could be wiped out completely. But we have forgotten how dangerous this disease is. And in many parts of the United States today, smallpox breaks out and spreads locally simply because people neglect to be vaccinated. In 1941 more than 2000 persons died of this disease, and more than 1000 in 1942. The number of deaths continues at about these totals to the present time. Be vaccinated at least every 7 years to be certain that you do not get smallpox.

COMMON-SENSE RULES TO PREVENT DISEASES

Weeks and months could be spent on the study of diseases—their causes, nature, and means of prevention and cure. But this discussion is going to stop right now with just a review list of common-sense rules of living which—if followed—will give you excellent protection against diseases.

1. Stay away from people who are ill. Be especially careful to stay away from people who are sneezing and coughing.

2. Protect others from yourself. Cover your mouth and nose with a handkerchief when you sneeze and cough.

3. Protect yourself as well as others when you do not feel well. Do not keep on going. And do not try to treat yourself. Many diseases—some of them deadly—have similar symptoms. Call a

doctor right away and let him do the worrying for you. You will live longer.

4. Be sure that the food and water you take are clean. Be sure that milk is pasteurized or certified. Try to eat only at those places where the equipment is carefully washed.

5. Kill that fly! Keep your body clean to avoid lice and fleas. Remove ticks after walking in woods. Get rid of mosquitoes, and protect yourself from them.

6. Protect yourself against the diseases for which inoculations are available. (Partial or complete protection can be secured against many diseases. Everyone should be vaccinated for smallpox every 7 years, and children should be given injections protecting them from

Infected fleas spread typhus fever and bubonic plague.

whooping cough, diphtheria, and possibly tetanus and scarlet fever. Your doctor's judgment is likely to be best—follow his suggestions in regard to inoculations.)

WORKING WITH SCIENCE

1. The microscopic world teems with invisible life. A fascinating way to spend a few hours is to examine this world through the enlarging eye of a microscope. If you drop some dry grass into a jar of water, after a few days you will find that microscopic animals have multiplied until there are millions in a few drops of water.

Take a drop of water from this *hay infusion* and place it on a microscope slide. Place a cover glass on the slide and examine the slide under the microscope. The chances are good that you will find many tiny slipper-shaped animals, paramecia, swimming merrily around.

2. If you are fortunate, you may find an ameba in a drop of hay infusion. If not, you can purchase cultures of live amebas from a biological supply house. Watch the amebas closely. They flow around bits of material in the water in much the same way that the white corpuscles of your body flow around and devour germs that enter your body.

3. If possible, examine a prepared slide of white blood cells and note their general nature.

4. If the school doctor or school health service provides vaccinations during the school year, arrange to have vaccinations done at a time when the class can observe the technique and ask the doctor to discuss inoculations with you.

READING YOU WILL ENJOY

de Kruif, Paul. *Microbe Hunters*. Harcourt Brace & Co., New York, 1926. The stories of the discoveries of inoculations against disease are excellently told in this book.

Disraeli, Robert. *Seeing the Unseen* (rev. ed.). The John Day Co., New York, 1939. A remarkable book about the world that may be seen only through a microscope. It has many marvelous photographs taken through microscopes.

Thone, Frank E. A. *The Microscopic World*. Julian Messner, Inc., New York, 1940. The life-histories of some microscopic plants—bacteria, molds, algae—presented through interesting writing and excellent photographs and drawings.

Watson-Baker, W. *World beneath the Microscope*. Studio Publications, Inc., New York, 1935. Contains 80 excellent illustrations of the invisible world that becomes visible when seen through a microscope.

Early peoples were hungry much of the time, so they ate almost everything good to eat that they could lay their hands on. They ate the glands and internal organs as well as the flesh of animals. When roots and greenstuff were available, they ate them also. Of course, they knew nothing about vitamins and minerals, but by eating what they did (1) much of the time, they got enough of them.

When man began to eat "refined" foods and did not eat or could not get fresh fruits and vegetables, diseases caused by lack of enough vitamins and minerals showed up. British sailors on long voyages used up their supplies of fruits and vegetables and developed scurvy, a disease caused by lack of vitamin C. However, as early as the seventeenth century, ship captains learned to prevent and cure the disease by giving the men limes or lemons (2). In the 1890s, Dr. Christian Eijkman (3) showed that a disease of chickens resembling beriberi in man could be cured or prevented by feeding the chickens rice bran, later shown to contain vitamin B_1.

As a result of the work of Eijkman and thousands of other research workers, we now know the important part that good diet (4) plays in keeping us healthy. We know that we must eat healthfully to live healthfully.

8

EAT HEALTHFULLY TO LIVE HEALTHFULLY

Your health—to a large extent—is what you make it. Take the matter of diet and eating, for example. The man who wrote a book entitled *You Are What You Eat* was not too far wrong. A great deal of evidence from experiments in *nutrition* and from human experience shows that diet greatly influences human life. Nutrition is the sum total of body processes involved in absorbing and using food. It is part of metabolism, one of the life-functions.

You were born with a particular tendency to fatness, or slimness, or tallness, or shortness. If your natural tendency is to be small-boned, thin, and wiry, you could eat huge quantities of food regularly and you would never become very heavy. But within the limits set by your natural tendency, you can greatly influence your health—and in turn your personality and your life—by what you eat.

The important thing to understand is that people may die of starvation, even though they eat tremendous amounts of food. To live in good health, you need many substances in your diet. You might be able to live on only sugar or candy bars for a short time, but your health would very quickly suffer.

NUTRITIONAL REQUIREMENTS

Your body is a remarkable and complex organism. It needs many different chemical *elements*,* such as oxygen, carbon, iron, and phosphorus, and combinations of these elements, such as proteins and sugars, in order to live, grow, and be active. The serious lack of any essential foodstuff results in inadequate absorption, or *assimilation*, of food. Such a condition is called *malnutrition*, usually the result of an inadequate diet. When malnutrition becomes very serious, certain diseases may result. These are known as *deficiency diseases*.

ENERGY FROM CARBOHYDRATES

Sugars and starches are the chief sources of energy for the human body. They are called *carbohydrates*. Carbohydrates form a basic and important part of our diet.

* Anything that has weight and takes up space is made up of *matter*. Matter, in turn, is made up of substances that cannot be broken down into simpler substances by ordinary means. Such substances are called *elements*.

When produced in the human body, energy is in the form of heat. Heat is measured in units called *Calories*. A Calory is the amount of heat required to raise the temperature of 1 kilogram (about a quart) of water 1 degree centigrade. One degree centigrade is equal to 1.8 degrees Fahrenheit. A given amount of food taken into the body will release a certain number of Calories of heat when used by the body. For example, 1 ounce of carbohydrate (starch, sugar) will furnish 116 Calories of heat energy.

Your own activities are a pretty safe guide to the number of Calories that you need. When you exercise, you generally are hungrier than when you do not. Thus, your hunger is a rather safe guide to the *amount* of food you need. But not to the kinds of food needed for health. You should be careful not to fill up on starchy foods to the exclusion of milk, fresh fruits, and vegetables.

This girl has selected a well balanced meal at the school cafeteria.

FATS AND VITAMINS

Our bodies obtain fats from such foods as butter, salad oil, oleomargarine, peanuts, fat meats, and so forth. Fats provide a great amount of energy, but this is not their only function in the diet. Carbohydrates would supply all the energy needed at lower cost than fats.

Fats are also important because they carry a number of *vitamins*. And vitamins are necessary because they act as regulators and controllers in the body. Some vitamins dissolve, or are *soluble*, only in fats or oils. Therefore, we must have certain amounts of fats to maintain health and to get enough of certain vitamins. However, there is little danger that your diet will not include sufficient fats.

One of the fat-soluble vitamins, *vitamin D*, is manufactured, or *synthesized*, in the human body from substances in the skin when it is exposed to sunlight. Some animals, especially certain fishes, store vitamin D in their livers. Hence, fish-liver oils are rich sources of this essential vitamin.

Generally vitamin D must be added to the diets of babies to be sure that they do not suffer from malnutrition and develop *rickets*, a disease that results in weak and poorly formed bones. In some cases, adults should take cod-liver oil or other sources of vitamin

D, particularly if they are not able to be out in the sunshine very much.

Why British Sailors Are Called Limeys. Long ago many sailors suffered seriously from the disease *scurvy* when they were on long voyages. Scurvy is an ugly disease. The walls of small blood vessels become fragile and break easily. Thus, bleeding occurs under the skin. The teeth become loose and the gums swell and bleed. The joints get stiff and sore. And a person becomes easy prey to disease germs.

Through experience, it was found that something in *citrus* fruits (oranges, lemons, grapefruits, for example) and green vegetables prevented and cured this disease. British sailors are still sometimes called "limeys" because before the time of modern canning and refrigeration, they were given limes to suck as part of their food rations on voyages. Now, of course, it is possible to carry canned fruits and juices and fresh vegetables on ships. Scurvy is the result of a great lack of *vitamin C (ascorbic acid)* in the body.

In this country scurvy is rare today. But many people do not get enough vitamin C. The lack of this food chemical, in some cases, causes a general restlessness, irritability, and laziness. Many people do not eat enough foods containing vitamin C, especially in wintertime when such foods are more expensive and less easily obtainable.

Vitamin C is easily destroyed by heat in cooking. Hence, it is wise to eat a certain amount of *raw* leafy, green or yellow vegetables and fruits.

Why Bread Is Made of "Enriched" Flour. Vitamin B_1 *(thiamin)* is another chemical regulator, the lack of which causes serious difficulties in the body. In 1883 the disease *beriberi* was widespread in the Japanese navy. It had been common for centuries among oriental people, who were accustomed to diets of polished rice and dried fish. Later, the husks of rice were found to contain vitamin B_1. A Japanese scientist named Takaki placed a group of sailors on a diet of meat, vegetables, and milk, in addition to the usual polished rice. Very quickly the terrible nerve inflammations, paralysis, listlessness, and deaths were stopped.

Like scurvy, beriberi is almost unknown in the United States. However, thousands of people undoubtedly suffer from some lack of vitamin B_1. They are irritable, constantly tired and nervous, and do not know what is wrong. Many cases of such continual, or *chronic*, tiredness and nervousness have been relieved by changing the diet to include whole grains, "enriched" flours or bread made from flour to which vitamin B_1 has been added, and a variety of leafy and other vegetables.

Vitamin B_1 is a rather delicate chemical and is destroyed when vegetables are overcooked or is lost in the water in which vegetables are boiled. Hence, use only a little water in boiling vegetables and avoid overcooking.

Have You Ever Seen a Pellagra Victim? Pellagra, another deficiency disease, *is* widespread in the United States. It is chiefly a disease of poor people—people who, through ignorance or poverty, live on a very restricted diet. It is particularly common in regions of the southern part of the United States but is also found throughout the country.

The symptoms of pellagra vary. Generally a person becomes weak and may lose weight. His appetite is poor, and he finds that he has little strength, particularly in his legs. His skin breaks out in eruptions and then sores. The mucous membranes become red and swollen, and pus-filled sores, or *ulcers*, form on them. Finally, violent headaches and a feeling of doom occur. Many untreated pellagra victims become insane.

Joseph Goldberger, a scientist of the United States Public Health Service, began a study of pellagra in 1914. At that time it was thought to be a germ disease like measles or tuberculosis. His discovery that pellagra is simply the serious lack of *vitamin B_2 (riboflavin)* made it possible to wipe out the disease. But even today—and as often as depressions and poverty strike our people—pellagra and death stalk the land.

The way laboratory animals respond to various diets helps us learn many facts about nutrition.

According to the United States Department of Agriculture, as many as 400,000 cases of pellagra have been reported annually in the United States. There are claims that 10 percent of the inmates in mental hospitals of the South are victims of pellagra. Adequate diet would have prevented or cured the pellagra if established before nerve tissue injury had resulted.

Pellagra, as well as the more common and really widespread general poor health that results from a lack of vitamin B_2, can be prevented by including milk, whole grains, lean meats, green vegetables, and fruits in the diet. Yeast contains a large amount of riboflavin and is often used in treating persons with symptoms that indicate lack of this necessary vitamin.

Other Vitamins. There are several other vitamins, including *A, E, K*, and so forth. Definite lack of any of them causes disturbances, and sometimes serious ones, in the human body.

You may have wondered about the names of vitamins and why they are often called by letters and—as in the case of B_1—by numbers as well. The original researches on vitamins did not give much information about what they are. Hence, they were given letters rather than names. The vitamin named B was later found

In addition to the vitamins they contain, why should we eat foods such as these?

to be really a whole group of vitamins. So one of them—thiamin—was renamed B₁, and another in the group—riboflavin—was called B₂. Vitamin B₂ was also called *vitamin G*.

PROTEINS AND ALPHABETS

Our bodies are composed largely of protein. This food is necessary for growth, maintenance, and repair of the body. It also provides some energy.

Proteins are found chiefly in lean meats, eggs, peas, beans, and similar foods. Gelatins, such as "Jello," are proteins to which sugar

Poor teeth and bad diet are related. Trace the path of the invaders in this bad tooth.

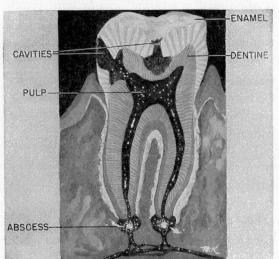

and flavoring have been added. They are excellent as far as they go. But just a single kind of protein is not sufficient. The proteins that make brain cells, for example, are different from those that make skin, liver, bone, heart, or lung cells.

Proteins are made of simpler substances, in somewhat the same way that words are made up of simpler things—the letters of the alphabet. There are only 26 letters in our alphabet. Yet, by putting these letters in various positions, we can form hundreds of words.

The simpler substances that make up proteins are called *amino acids*. Just as letters of the alphabet are put together to form words, so the various parts of the body put the amino acids they need together to make brain cells, or liver cells, and so forth. It is not known just how many amino acids there are in all the proteins, but at least 22 are now known.

Apparently, the body actually manufactures some amino acids. But at least 10 must be secured from foods; otherwise, illness and death may result. Since many proteins do not contain all 10 of the essential amino acids, it is a good idea to eat a variety of foods containing proteins. Vegetable proteins are likely to contain only a few amino acids. Animal proteins—lean meat, milk, cheese, eggs, and such internal organs as sweetbreads and liver—are particularly good sources of the necessary amino acids.

MINERALS FOR BODY BUILDING

Some of the elements that your body needs are minerals, such as iron and calcium. These must be obtained in foods. Calcium and phosphorus are necessary for the building of bones and teeth. Phosphorus is found in many protein foods. But it is difficult to secure enough calcium in the diet, for few foods contain adequate quantities. The blood and nerves also require calcium and suffer seriously if there is not enough. Milk, an excellent source of calcium, should be a part of everyone's diet. Poor teeth probably are more often the result of poor diet than anything else. If you want

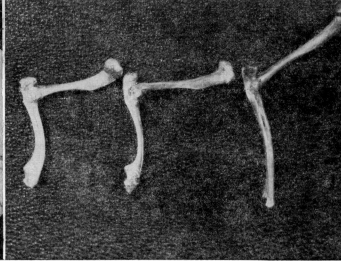

Not all needed amino acids are found in all proteins. The rat at the left lived on a diet having the same amount of protein as the other rat, but all body-building amino acids were not present. Right: Manganese is related to bone formation. The bones at the left and center are from a rabbit whose diet lacked manganese. The bone at the right is from a rabbit whose diet included manganese.

good teeth, cut down on the sweets and eat plenty of vegetables and milk.

Other Needed Minerals. We need iron, iodine, and fluorine, too. In some regions of the United States, the soil and water are lacking in iodine. Therefore, vegetables grown there—and meat from animals that eat those vegetables or grains—do not have sufficient iodine to form an adequate diet for human beings.

Many cases of *goiter*, a disease of the *thyroid gland* (one of the "ductless" glands; see page 103), are found in these regions, which are called by doctors the *goiter belt.* For this reason, iodine is supplied in the diet by adding small amounts of it to salt. The goiter belt covers the Appalachian Mountains, extends north to Vermont, and goes through the Great Lakes region and west to the state of Washington.

Fluorine helps to prevent tooth decay. In some cities, small amounts of compounds of fluorine are added to the water supply.

Even copper is needed by the human body. Small amounts are required in the formation of hemoglobin. We need many other elements in very small amounts. Boron, nickel, cesium, barium, silver, silicon, cobalt, and even the deadly arsenic, are thought to be necessary in very small amounts for an adequate diet.

WORKING WITH SCIENCE

1. Examine the food chart on pages 96–97. Make a list of the foods you ate yesterday. Compare this list with the food chart. Are any essential food stuffs lacking in this diet? What is the most complete food you ate, in terms of the proteins, vitamins, and minerals that it contained?

2. Make a list of the vitamin preparations advertised in the daily paper. Add to this list the vitamin preparations on sale at a local drugstore.

Besides concentrated vitamins in capsules, fluids, and pills, vitamins are sold in candy form, in gum form, and even mixed with cold cream to apply to the skin. What is your present judgment about the wisdom of buying such vitamin preparations rather than securing them in a well-balanced diet? Delegate one member of your class to ask a doctor about the need for such vitamin preparations and to report to the class.

ADEQUATE DIETS AT

	MILK					POTATOES AND SWEET POTATOES	MATURE, DRY LEGUMES, AND NUTS	TOMATOES AND CITRUS FRUITS
GOOD *Expensive*	3 CUPS DAILY FOR CHILD UNDER 2	4 CUPS DAILY FOR OTHER CHILDREN	3 CUPS DAILY FOR SEDENTARY PEOPLE	1 QT. DAILY FOR EXPECTANT OR NURSING MOTHER	1 PT. DAILY FOR EACH ADULT	1 SERVING A DAY	ABOUT 1 SERVING A WEEK	1 SERVING A DAY
GOOD *Moderate cost*	3 CUPS DAILY FOR CHILD UNDER 2	4 CUPS DAILY FOR OTHER CHILDREN	3 CUPS DAILY FOR SEDENTARY PEOPLE	1 QT. DAILY FOR EXPECTANT OR NURSING MOTHER	1 PT. DAILY FOR EACH ADULT	10 OR 11 SERVINGS A WEEK	1 OR 2 SERVINGS A WEEK	5 OR 6 SERVINGS A WEEK*
GOOD *Low cost*	3 TO 4 CUPS DAILY FOR EACH CHILD		3 CUPS DAILY FOR SEDENTARY PEOPLE	1 QT. DAILY FOR EXPECTANT OR NURSING MOTHER	1 PT. DAILY FOR EACH ADULT	10 OR 11 SERVINGS A WEEK	2 OR 3 SERVINGS A WEEK	4 OR 5 SERVINGS A WEEK*
FAIR *Economical*	2-3 CUPS DAILY FOR CHILDREN UNDER SEVEN	2 CUPS DAILY FOR CHILDREN 7 YRS. & OLDER	2 CUPS DAILY FOR SEDENTARY PEOPLE	1 QT. DAILY FOR EXPECTANT OR NURSING MOTHER	1 CUP DAILY FOR EACH ADULT	10 OR 11 SERVINGS A WEEK	4 OR 5 SERVINGS A WEEK	3 OR 4 SERVINGS A WEEK*

*(4 to 6 tablespoons of tomato juice or 2 tablespoons of orange juice daily for each child under 4 years.)

HOW TO BE SURE OF AN ADEQUATE DIET

Careful studies made by the Bureau of Human Nutrition and Home Economics of the United States Department of Agriculture have shown that malnutrition is really common in this country. According to these studies, American diets seldom lack enough starches and proteins. But there is a lack of fresh leafy vegetables, fruits, milk, and eggs, which contain vitamins and minerals. Such foods are called *protective foods*.

What Is a Good Diet? Unfortunately, the foods that contain the most vitamins and minerals tend to be more expensive than such foods as bread, rice, and cornmeal. And malnutrition is most common and serious among the people who do not have too much money to spend on foods. Farm families are better nourished, on the average, than city families because they generally produce many of the protective foods on their farms. But it is possible for almost all of us—even if we do not have much money—to have complete and adequate diets.

Actually, our *eating habits*, more than poverty, prevent many of us from eating the foods we need. The Army and Navy found this to be true. Boys who grew up on a diet of salt pork and corn bread wanted this type of food, even though the meals served them provided a well-balanced and complete diet.

96

VARIOUS COST LEVELS

LEAFY, GREEN AND YELLOW VEGETABLES	OTHER VEGETABLES AND FRUITS	EGGS	LEAN MEAT, POULTRY OR FISH	BUTTER	OTHER FATS	CEREALS	BREAD	DESSERTS
11-12 SERVINGS A WEEK	ABOUT 3 SERVINGS A DAY	1 A DAY PER PERSON	9 OR 10 SERVINGS A WEEK	4/5 LB. A WEEK	SMALL AM'TS.	AS DESIRED	AS DESIRED	AS DESIRED
10 OR 11 SERVINGS A WEEK	2 OR 3 SERVINGS A DAY	5 OR 6 EGGS A WEEK PER PERSON	7 OR 8 SERVINGS A WEEK	ABOUT ½ TO ⅔ LB. A WEEK	ABOUT ½ LB. A WEEK	DAILY	AT EVERY MEAL	ONCE A DAY, SOMETIMES TWICE
9 OR 10 SERVINGS A WEEK	9 OR 10 SERVINGS A WEEK	ABOUT 4 A WEEK PER PERSON	6 OR 7 SMALL SERVINGS A WEEK	ABOUT ½ LB. A WEEK	ABOUT ½ TO ⅔ LB. A WEEK	USUALLY ONCE A DAY. SOMETIMES TWICE	AT EVERY MEAL	ABOUT ONCE A DAY IF DESIRED
8 OR 9 SERVINGS WEEK	1 SERVING A DAY	2 OR 3 EGGS A WEEK PER PERSON	3 OR 4 SERVINGS A WEEK	½ LB. A WEEK	ABOUT ½ LB. A WEEK	ONCE OR TWICE A DAY	AT EVERY MEAL	OCCASIONALLY**

Pictograph Corporation, from To Live in Health   ** (Occasionally, such as cereal pudding, dried fruit, one-egg cake, and other inexpensive kinds.)

These boys—and many like them from all parts of the country—simply would not eat green vegetables. A study made by the Army showed that more than 50 percent of the "greens" were left on soldiers' plates. There lay the rich sources of vitamins, which would help produce really vital, buoyant health.

We have to learn to eat correctly. If you find that you do not like many of the foods listed in the table, just remember that you can *learn* to like them and that your health will be much better if you do learn to eat a wide variety of foods containing milk, eggs, leafy vegetables, and fruits.

The table above will help you to choose a good diet. It lists foods according to major *food groups* and is easy to understand, remember,

and follow. The basic information was prepared by the Bureau of Human Nutrition and Home Economics of the United States Department of Agriculture.

In using this table you must remember that you can safely substitute foods within a food group, but that it is unwise to substitute foods from one group for those in another. In other words, it is all right to use cheeses instead of milk, but it is not healthful to cut out milk and milk products in favor of more potatoes or bread.

It is not suggested that you follow this table strictly day in and day out for breakfast, lunch, and dinner. If you have a good appetite and eat all kinds of foods including the protective ones, you can forget diets and not

U. S. D. A. photos by Forsythe

Nutritious meals may be planned for various income levels as the table on pages 96 and 97 shows. The family at the left is eating baked beans and bread. The family at the right is eating meat, mashed potatoes and gravy, beets, lima beans, bread, and milk. Compare the two meals with respect to nutrition and current cost. What do you conclude? For the same cost, could the meal at the left be improved nutritionally? What about the meal at the right?

worry about them. However, over a period of time, you should eat plenty of foods in each of these broad groups.

VITAMIN FOOLISHNESS

Recently we have been bombarded through the press and radio with advertisements of vitamin preparations and "health foods" of all kinds. This is the latest of the health fads. Of course, vitamins are necessary in your diet. But if your diet is well balanced and you get plenty of the protective foods, you need not waste money on vitamin pills and capsules.

Of course, if your doctor finds that you need more of certain vitamins and prescribes them, then you should take them. It is often hard to get enough vitamin B_1, for example, because we tend to eat foods that contain too little of this vitamin. The best way to correct this lack is to eat foods containing vitamin B_1 rather than to take pills.

In a recent year, vitamin preparations amounted to one-third of all drug sales. That is big business. In cold cash, Americans spent around 200 million hard-earned dollars for vitamins and vitamin preparations. The tremendous sale of vitamins, backed by extravagant advertising, is proof that we must be always on guard against unscientific claims.

There are no "health foods" really. Any food that is wholesome and provides for some body need is healthful. No special "health food" can do more than this.

WORKING WITH SCIENCE

1. Experiments on nutrition in white rats or mice will give you dramatic proof of the serious results of dietary deficiencies. Write to the General Biological Supply House, Chicago, Illinois for the pamphlet on nutrition experiments. This pamphlet gives instructions for diet experiments that show the effects of dietary deficiencies in a few weeks if you use young rats or mice from the same litter. (a) Feed them materials that are deficient in carbohydrates or proteins. Food materials for these experimental diets may be obtained from local merchants. (b) If you want to perform experiments with vitamin-lacking foods, it is easier to order the diet materials from a biological supply house.

2. In Chapter 6 you made a list of the foods you ate in several days. Check this list against the table on pages 96 and 97. How adequate is your diet? Are you eating enough protective foods? Does your diet include some items from each of the food groups? Discuss your diet with other members of your class. List the foods or food groups that you should add to your diet or eat more of to have a well-balanced diet.

READING YOU WILL ENJOY

Crampton, Charles W. *The Boy's Book of Strength*. McGraw-Hill Book Co., New York, 1936. This book tells how you can build your body through proper diet, exercise, and sound living.

Verrill, Alpheus H. *Foods America Gave the World*. L. C. Page & Co., Boston, 1937. The interesting story of how many native American food plants were developed and adapted to varying situations.

Webster, Hanson H. and Polkinghorne, Ada R. *What the World Eats*. Houghton Mifflin Co., Boston, 1938. This book tells, in an informal and interesting style, what the people of the world eat. You will be amazed at the different kinds of diets even in the United States.

"Growing up"—the road to maturity— is a time of many problems. You may even think that the problems you face have never been faced before. But they have. Each person who becomes an adult passes through the growing-up period, and most persons successfully cope with the same problems you face.

Perhaps you feel awkward, that you have grown too fast, and that you cannot control your movements as well as you would like (1). Don't worry. You will get over your awkwardness. It is just a stage through which most young people pass. Perhaps you believe that you are not as "good" as you would like to be in doing something you want to do (2). Don't worry. Not everyone can excel at the same thing. Incidentally, you might be surprised to learn that the boy or girl you most admire wishes to be as good at something as you are. Perhaps you think you are too "plump" or too tall (3). Don't worry. Most likely you will be entirely normal for your framework within a few years. Perhaps you feel ill at ease or out of place in a group (4). Don't worry. Most likely you will quickly get over that feeling.

The most important thing to remember about this period of "growing up" is that it is a time when most persons are most critical of themselves. This is normal and to be expected. But don't worry. Learn to be just yourself.

9

BE YOURSELF

Have you ever seen a cow or a horse pressing against a fence and stretching its neck so that it could eat grass on the other side of the fence? Almost any time you drive through the country you can see such a sight. If you think the situation over, you will notice a curious fact. As often as not, the grass outside the fence is actually no better or perhaps is even worse than the grass right under the animal's feet.

In this respect, human beings are somewhat like the cow or horse. We so often think that the grass on the other side of the fence is greener. For example, every one of us has qualities that others respect and sometimes even envy. Too few of us take advantage of this good fortune by attempting to develop fully our own abilities, or *talents*, and our own good qualities. Too often we think that Joe Ross and Mary Todd are getting all the "breaks" and too seldom really understand how well off we are in our own lives.

Of course we must face our own faults and shortcomings, and attempt to correct them. But most of us are far too critical of ourselves and spend too much time wishing we were like someone else or daydreaming that we actually are.

You may wonder why such things as envy and daydreaming are discussed in a unit on health. The answer is easy. The health of the body cannot be separated from the health of the mind. You know already that diet strongly influences the health of a person. You know that the lack of certain vitamins can cause laziness, irritability, and nervousness. Characteristics that involve the mind and the total characteristics of a person, we call *personality*.

The mind also greatly influences the health of the physical body. You already know this, too. Perhaps you have experienced stage fright when speaking before a group, or have been frightened or worried for some other reason. Remember how you were weak in your knees and your stomach seemed to turn flip-flops? Worry can decrease the secretion of digestive juices and seriously hinder digestion. Thousands of people in this country have chronic stomach distress and even stomach ulcers as a result of constant worry or unhappiness. The mind certainly does influence the health of the body.

ARE YOU NORMAL?

Some persons with the notion that they are less able or less attractive than others go to great lengths in trying to change themselves. Often they injure themselves, both through mental distress and by their practices.

For example, many young people feel that they are not quite "normal" in body build.

101

Is the grass greener outside the fence?

U. S. D. A. photos by Osborne and Mead

These two girls and the boy are healthy and normal, yet in physical size and body build they may differ somewhat from other boys and girls the same age. This is to be expected.

Usually, they fail to understand that they were born with a certain tendency in body build: fatness, slimness, tallness, or shortness. There is little that anyone can do about his natural tendency in body build. Of course, some people are too fat or too thin because of illness or some body deficiency. These cases should be diagnosed and treated by a physician.

Thousands of boys of small build grow up wishing that they were big and strong with muscles and shoulders like some football hero or "muscle man" pictured in a magazine. So they buy gadgets made of springs or weights and work frantically trying to develop big muscles. If they have a natural tendency to small build, they will do little but wear themselves out and be terribly disappointed. For they will never look like the football hero.

HOW TO LOSE WEIGHT AND YOUR HEALTH TOO!

Girls who think that they are too thin or too fat often go to extremes in trying to adjust their weights to what they think is more "normal." Some even are so unwise as to take patent medicines to help them reduce.

Reducing medicines fall into three types. The most common are simple laxatives, which force digested material through the intestines so rapidly that the body does not have time to absorb much from it. Some of these are salt-type, or *saline*, laxatives, which force water from the body into the intestines, thus causing the body to lose water. Naturally, these laxatives cause a person to lose weight for a little while—just until more water is drunk or more food is eaten.

Another type of reducing medicine is offered for sale along with a diet that is to be followed. The diet is low in carbohydrates so that a person who follows it is bound to lose weight. The reducing remedy is often of no worth whatever, or it is a laxative.

A Dangerous Way to Reduce. A third type of reducing medicine is more dangerous than the other two, because it contains products of the thyroid gland. In human beings the thyroid gland is located like saddle-bags, one part on each side of the Adam's apple, or *voice box.*

If there is too little secretion from the thyroid gland, a person becomes sluggish. If young children suffer from serious lack of thyroid secretion, a form of feeble-mindedness results in which the mind seldom develops beyond that of a child 5 years of age. Body growth is retarded and permanent *dwarfism* may result.

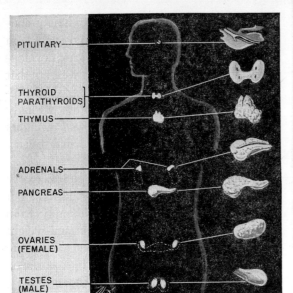

PITUITARY

THYROID
PARATHYROIDS

THYMUS

ADRENALS

PANCREAS

OVARIES
(FEMALE)

TESTES
(MALE)

The ductless glands produce hormones. Why are they called "ductless glands"?

On the other hand, too much thyroid secretion produces a general speeding up of body functions. A person with an overactive thyroid may eat heartily yet actually lose weight. Such a person is likely to be extremely nervous and high-strung. If the secretion is greatly in excess, the person may be highly emotional and unstable.

You can see, then, what the effects of taking thyroid extract without medical supervision might be. Will a person lose weight? Very likely, for the thyroid secretion increases the rate at which the body burns its fuel. Of course, a person's appetite might be increased, and if more food is eaten, loss of weight might not result. But other—and serious—changes might be taking place. The person might become irritable and high-strung. If the reducing remedy is continued, the person might actually have a nervous breakdown. The heart might be damaged and the loss of weight might be difficult to check; it might continue until his weight is dangerously low.

If you feel that you are seriously overweight, see a doctor. He will probably work out a simple diet by which you can reduce without danger to yourself.

HORMONAL CONTROL

The thyroid gland is one of a number of glands whose actions greatly influence the health of both the body and the mind. These glands produce, or secrete, amazing substances that seem to regulate or control the development and action of the body. Such chemical substances are known as *hormones*. Hormones pass directly into the blood stream as blood passes through the glands without flowing through ducts. Hence the glands that produce them are called *ductless glands*.

Hormones from the *sex glands* (*testes* in boys and *ovaries* in girls) start and control body changes that produce the deepened chest, low voice, and whiskers of a man, and the higher voice and general feminine characteristics of a woman.

The "Master Gland" of the Body. Secretions from the *pituitary gland*, a pea-sized gland at the base of the brain, have many effects on the human body. Too much secretion from one part of the gland produces *giantism* and is the cause of the giants you may have seen in circuses. Too little secretion prevents the body from growing as it should and results in a dwarfing of the body. The pituitary gland seems to be the "master gland" of the entire ductless gland system. If it does not secrete normally, the thyroid gland, the sex glands, the *adrenal glands*, *parathyroids*, *pancreas islets* and others do not function normally.

The chick at the right received injections of male sex hormones. The control chick did not.
U. S. D. A. photo by Stenhouse

Capitalize on your own talents rather than envying someone else.

AVERAGES AND NORMALCY

All of us cannot be exactly alike in anything. What does it matter if you are smaller or larger than someone else? Does it matter if someone else is better in sports than you? or in schoolwork? or in anything else? Be yourself. You have your own talents and strengths. Capitalize on them. Find out what you can do and what you like, and develop ability in these things. Do not try to be someone else.

You probably have seen the height-and-weight tables that are commonly used in checking an individual's physical development. These tables show certain weights that are *average* for certain heights. Unfortunately, these tables are very often wrongly used. They do not give *normal* weights for each height. It is perfectly normal to vary considerably.

Look at the illustrations on page 102. Every one of these persons is perfectly normal. But their weights would vary considerably from those indicated on the height-and-weight tables of averages. These tables simply are *averages*, which are determined by measuring thousands of individuals from the 6-foot-5's to the 4-foot-8's.

In other words, if you weighed each of the three 14-year-3-month-old boys in your schoolroom, you might find that one of them weighs 118 pounds, another 123 pounds, and the third 134 pounds. Now, to find the *average* weight of these boys, you add their weights and divide by the number of boys. The average weight of these boys is 125 pounds. But not one of the boys actually weighs that.

Do not worry if you are not average in anything, from school marks to body build. The average is just the general picture given by thousands of *normal* persons like yourself. If you are greatly under the average weight for a person of your height or are losing weight, see your school nurse, teacher, or doctor.

WORKING WITH SCIENCE

1. Place two headings on a sheet of paper. One of these headings should read, "My Strengths"; the other, "My Weaknesses." *Do not* place your name on the paper. Under each heading make as honest and complete a list as you can. Place the unsigned papers in a box so that no one will know who wrote any particular paper.

The teacher, or a member of the class, can now place these same two headings on the blackboard. Under them list all the different statements of strengths and weaknesses that appear on the papers. Every time that the same strength or weakness is suggested, place a check mark on the board alongside that statement. When the list is complete, examine it carefully. How many of your fellow-students listed the same weaknesses you listed? This list may provide the basis for an interesting and worthwhile discussion by the class.

2. Take the height and weight of each member of the class. Determine the average height and weight of the class members. Does anyone in the class exactly fit this average height and weight?

3. Note how much your classmates differ in size of bone structure. Place your fingers around the wrist bones of different classmates. Do you notice that some have much thicker and heavier bones than others? Those with thin bones generally are slimly built compared with those with heavy bones. Much exercise would not produce, on a thin-boned individual, the heavy muscles that are possible on a heavy-boned individual. The difference is inborn. In other words, the normal variation is large, and a person should not attempt to do what his basic structure does not allow.

MILESTONES TOWARD ADULTHOOD

Early one Saturday morning, three Boy Scouts stepped out of a car at the edge of a large city and strode briskly down a country lane. They were Second-Class Scouts starting on the 14-mile hike that is a necessary part of the work toward a First-Class badge.

Fourteen miles is quite a long distance. Their scoutmaster had marked off this particular route with markers 1 mile apart. As the scouts passed the first marker, they grinned merrily. "Only 13 more to go," said one.

"Doesn't sound hard now," said the second. "But wait 'til we've passed ten more of those markers and still have 3 miles to go. We'll be plenty glad to see those last three markers go by."

"Sure we will," said the third. "But you know—it's a big help to have those markers there. They help a lot. You can always see that you are making progress. Every time you pass one you feel good because you know you have that much less distance to go."

Growing up is much like that 14-mile hike. It is filled with delightful surprises and some that we would just as soon skip. It has its tough miles and its pleasant ones.

Growing up is not particularly easy. We all do it, but in doing so we meet many problems we must overcome. It helps to realize that the problems of growing up are really milestones toward adulthood. Every young man and woman who ever lived has had similar problems and difficulties. Remember that *such problems are actually evidences that you are growing up.*

YOU'LL GET OVER THOSE PIMPLES

Sometimes young persons worry about having pimples that keep coming and seem almost impossible to clear up. Such a condition is called *acne.* Just why some people have acne and some do not is not known. Acne generally commences about the time that the sex glands begin to function—that is, at the time called *adolescence.* Everyone goes through adolescence. The possibility that you may develop acne should not cause you mental distress, for you will get over it eventually, although it may last for several years.

Acne is really an infection of the *oil glands,* which are numerous in the face. When the ducts that lead from these glands to the surface of the skin become clogged and infected, pimples result. Acne is not communicable, and you will not "catch" it from others.

Both exercise and relaxation are provided by a good hobby.

U. S. D. A. photo by Forsythe

Courtesy American Airlines; Lil and Al Bloom

Although there are many things we like to do and do well, we must learn to do well certain things that will equip us to live more intelligently and with greater satisfaction. This is especially true of some of the things you may be called upon to do at home or at school.

Diet may have something to do with acne, but this relationship is not certain. However, eat well-balanced meals that are not too heavy in sugars and starches. Acne can generally be helped by very careful and frequent washing of the face with soap and water. Washing removes some of the oil and helps to prevent clogging of the oil glands and resulting irritation of the cells of the skin. Some people develop acne after taking drugs, such as *bromides*, which are found in certain headache medicines.

If you have acne, it might be a good idea to consult a doctor. He may treat the condition in several ways, depending on what he finds. But do not worry about it. Acne is a common condition and will clear up. No one else minds it as much as you do, anyway.

EVERYONE FACES THE SAME TYPES OF PROBLEMS

As you grow up, you will meet many problems and you may do things about which you may worry or be ashamed. You must realize that millions of boys and girls have grown up before you, and many will be growing up after you have become a happy and successful man or woman. Remember that everyone faced the same kinds of problems that you do

and had similar disappointments and heartbreaks.

Above all, do not be ashamed about some of the things you do that you do not seem to be able to help. Eventually you will cease to do many of the things that distress you now, and no harm will be done if you do not worry about yourself.

According to some interesting studies, thousands of young people have feared that they were "losing their minds." Although this worry is common, it is needless because there is no real basis for this particular fear. If you ever should become insane, the chances are good that everyone else will know it and you will not. Besides, insanity is only another disease. Between 25 and 40 percent of the patients in hospitals for the mentally ill are released to live normal, happy lives again.

Every boy and girl in the world has had feelings and problems similar to yours. Life is a lot of fun if you will only take yourself for what you are and the world for what it is. Develop and improve yourself according to your own talents, but do not try to do the impossible. Enjoy life as you go along. And remember: Be yourself!

WORKING WITH SCIENCE

1. Class reports on hobbies and recreational interests will help you to see that many people in the world have interests and abilities similar to yours and many more have interests and abilities different from yours. Each of you might talk briefly about your hobbies and demonstrate your interests to the group. A display table might be arranged to show some of the work done by class members.

2. If you are unacquainted with the recreational areas near your community, it might be worthwhile to form a committee to secure information and speakers to talk with you about nearby recreational facilities.

3. A science club can be an exciting group in which you conduct experiments, take trips, and meet socially with others who find science fun. If your school does not have a science club, your class might take the leadership in organizing one. It is not necessary to have a president, treasurer, and other officers, but it is a good idea to appoint a committee to plan a program of meetings and projects for the group to work on. You might start with a study of problems of adolescence.

READING YOU WILL ENJOY

Becker, May L. *Under Twenty*. Harcourt, Brace & Co., New York, 1932. A collection of short stories and articles showing girls how common their experiences are. If you want to see some of the problems, experiences, and attitudes of other women as they grew up, you will find this book valuable.

Crew, Helen C. *Saturday's Children*. Little, Brown & Co., Boston, 1927. Here are interesting stories about working children in many foreign countries. It will help you better understand people of other lands and learn in what ways they are the same as and in what ways different from you.

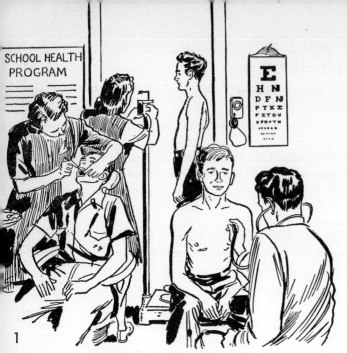

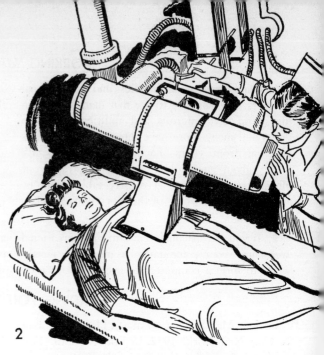

Modern medical science can promise for nearly everyone health such as few had even a century ago. Nearly all communicable diseases *can* be controlled. Medical research, government health agencies, and organizations such as the Red Cross and the National Tuberculosis Association have helped make such control possible (1). The battle against heart disease, cancer, and some others is still to be won, but organizations like the American Heart Association and the American Cancer Society are making a good fight (2).

However, lack of knowledge keeps people from getting competent medical attention until it is too late. Lack of knowledge leads people to try to treat their own illnesses without knowing whether they are serious or trivial. Lack of knowledge sends people to quacks who promise "miraculous" cures for troubles that only good doctors can treat (3).

Lack of money keeps people from getting the expert medical care that is available. Lack of money sends people to quacks for cheap "cures" and halfway measures. Lack of money keeps needed clinics and hospitals from being built and staffed. Lack of money forces some people to live in conditions that make getting diseases easy and curing them almost impossible (4). Until these two barriers—lack of knowledge and money—are removed, no nation can be as healthy as it should be. And in our own nation, the richest and greatest, these barriers still stand.

10

MODERN MEDICINE AND AMERICA'S HEALTH PLANS

Modern medical scientists have the information to provide a much higher level of health than we, as a nation, now enjoy. *Penicillin* is not the only "wonder drug." There are many. There are the toxoids and antitoxins, which can prevent or cure many diseases that formerly ravaged the populations of the earth. There are the sulfa drugs, or *sulfonamides*, which are extremely effective against certain diseases. There are *synthetics*, such as *atabrine*, which is very similar to *quinine* in its nature and general effectiveness against malaria. Quinine itself, ordinarily secured from plants, has also been synthesized.

In addition to the many new drugs, there are modern ways of using the specialized knowledge of medical scientists. There are well-equipped hospitals, clinics, and surgeries. There are trained and specialized medical doctors.

THE NATION'S HEALTH

Despite all these medical advantages, our health as a nation is not good—not as good as it could be by a whole lot. Our national health is poor, partly because of ignorance on the part of the great mass of people and partly because we fail to take measures to protect ourselves against disease even when we know what should be done.

Many of us do not take such proved safety measures as drinking pasteurized or certified milk. We do not eat the proper foods. We fail to get the sleep, exercise, and rest that we need to keep our general resistance high.

We do not protect others from our colds and other diseases. We allow diseased tonsils and decayed and abscessed teeth to injure our hearts. We abuse our eyes. Many of us, without knowing it, go to "quacks" instead of to competent doctors.

Instead of going to a doctor when a disease is in an early stage or seeking his advice periodically, we wait until we are really ill. We treat ourselves with worthless or even harmful patent medicines and thus delay effective treatment until serious illness strikes us down. Sometimes it is too late then. We would consider it disgraceful to neglect and mistreat our automobiles, furnaces, or lawnmowers half as much as we neglect our bodies.

The health of the nation is the sum total of the health of the individuals that make up the nation. Individual ignorance and carelessness add up to a tremendous amount of needless illness and death in our nation.

HEALTH COSTS MONEY

Another problem must be solved before our national health will be what it could be, medically speaking. That is the problem of paying for medical services.

Paying for medical care is a big problem. But there is disagreement on how it should be

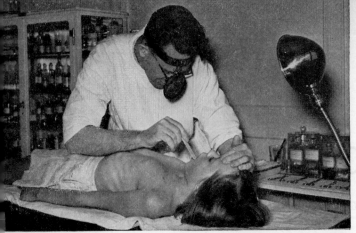

Everyone should have complete physical examinations at regular intervals throughout life.

solved. In a sense, health can be bought. This has been proved by studies, such as the National Health Survey, conducted by the United States Public Health Service a few years ago. This study showed that families on relief had about 85 percent more chronic illnesses than families of the highest income groups. Other studies have supported these facts.

Such facts are obvious if you think about the situation. It costs money for treatment by a doctor when you are ill and for regular check-ups and visits to a doctor when you are not feeling "up to par." It costs money to live in pleasant homes and to have good food and opportunities for exercise, rest, and recreation.

Of course, almost every physician devotes much time to people whom he treats without charge. But few of us want something for nothing. We would rather consider health as our right, just as we consider education our right. We all are entitled to good health, and the health of each one of us is endangered as long as others are in poor health.

ENGLAND'S HEALTH PLAN

Plans to meet the problem of medical costs have been proposed, and some are in practice in the United States and in other countries. Some countries have gone very far in providing for medical care. England, for example, has had a National Health Insurance Plan in operation for many years. The most recent plans of the British government for extension

of the health services state that complete medical facilities will be free and easily available to all. The plan protects the freedom of the patient to select his own doctor.

Such a program will cost about $600 million each year. This money will come partly from national and local taxes and partly from insurance to which each person contributes a set fee in much the same way as we pay premiums for fire insurance or life insurance. In any country the cost of allowing preventable illness and physical disability to go without correction is greater than the cost of an adequate health program.

AMERICA'S HEALTH PLANS

The United States as a nation does not have a plan like the British one, but several have been proposed, and some local ones are in operation. There are three broad possibilities in the establishment of a health plan:

Medical care can be financed for some by voluntary insurance in which they [individuals] pay the full cost; for others by compulsory insurance in which the insured pays part of the cost and the government or the government and industry pay the balance. Or it can be paid entirely by the government on the theory that health, like education, is a proper concern of the government.

In order to extend the use of any of these methods, we do not have to renounce the others. We now have all three. At the same time, we can maintain the individual fee-for-service practice of medicine for those who want and are able to pay for such service.*

Among the plans already established in the United States is the Hospital Service of California, sponsored by the California Physicians' Service. Through insurance payments a person is entitled to a number of excellent hospital services. The California Physicians' Service provides the services of licensed physicians and surgeons, also on an insurance basis.

* William T. Foster, *Doctors, Dollars and Disease*, Public Affairs Pamphlet No. 10 (Public Affairs Committee, Inc., New York, 1944), p. 13.

In Washington, D.C. there is the Group Health Association. This is another nonprofit organization which provides medical service and hospital care on an insurance basis. Voluntary hospitalization insurance plans have grown rapidly in the United States. For example, the Blue Cross Hospitalization Plan had 6000 members in 1933; in 1945 it had almost 19 million.

INDIVIDUAL RESPONSIBILITY FOR WELL-BEING

Many persons cannot afford even the small monthly payments required for health and medical insurance. Perhaps some plan other than insurance is necessary for such persons.

But whether everyone can afford good health is not the whole question. The other part of the question is whether we as a nation can afford to continue to pay the costs of poor health now that the skill necessary to improve health is available. The whole problem is tough. And in our attempt to secure freedom from poor health, we want to be sure that we do not lose some of our other freedoms. Undoubtedly, many plans for an adequate national health program will be proposed in the years to come. Keep yourself alert and well informed about the suggested plans.

In the long run, good health depends largely on us as individuals. Dietitians cannot help you if you will not eat wholesome foods. The best doctors cannot help you much if you "doctor" yourself. Tuberculin tests and chest x-rays cannot detect tuberculosis unless you take them. In spite of the good work of all health agencies, there will be unnecessary diseases and poor health if we fail, as individuals, to maintain our health and control or remove sources of infection. In addition, we must be aware of the unhealthful aspects of using such substances as tea and coffee, tobacco, and alcohol.

WORKING WITH SCIENCE

1. Bulletins are available on almost any health problem that you can think of. They can be obtained from the Superintendent of Documents, United States Government Printing Office, Washington, D.C. If you want to see the range of subjects, write for the list of publications on health.

2. You will probably read or hear many discussions of the British health plan. Details of the plan can be obtained by writing to the British Information Services, 30 Rockefeller Plaza, New York 20, N.Y. In your letter ask for ID 250. If you study this plan, point out its good and bad features.

X-ray photographs reveal conditions inside the body. The doctor at the left is interpreting such photographs. The doctor at the right is checking his interpretations of the boy's x-ray photograph.

American Cancer Society photo

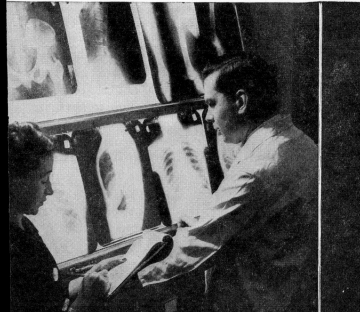
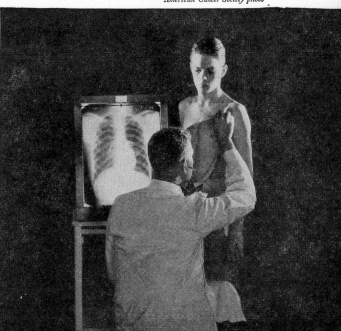

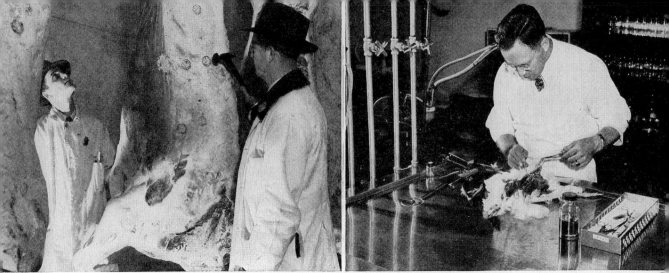

U. S. D. A. photos by Knell and Osborne

Many government agencies help protect our health. The inspector stamping the meat approves it for human consumption. The biologist at the right will find out what disease killed the chicken.

PERSONAL HYGIENE

It is possible to get along with little sleep, improper food, and no active exercise, and still remain in fair health—for a while! Some persons appear to get by for long periods of time and still remain apparently healthy.

But do not be fooled. Such unhealthful living is taking its toll of the body. The body-machine is remarkably able to stand punishment. But it records every experience it has just as certainly as a phonograph record records the blare of a trumpet or the soft singing of a violin. The record of unhealthful living builds up and builds up. Then, one day, the effects of such living become noticeable. Finally, in later life, all sorts of symptoms, and in some cases actual impairment of body functions, play back some of the record of bad living practices.

EXERCISE

The effects of exercise on the body have already been discussed. Circulation is aided by exercise, and muscles that are flabby become firm and able to do the work for which they were designed. Appetite is increased, and body wastes are generally eliminated without difficulties. Perhaps the greatest value of exercise is that it releases the mind from worries and concerns and allows a joyous period of wholehearted physical and mental activity that refreshes the body for more effective work. To the old adage, "All work and no play makes Jack a dull boy," should be added "and a sick boy."

Organic diseases cannot be cured by exercise. In many cases, in fact, doctors will not allow exercise while a person is recovering from an illness. But such troubles as headaches, nervousness, constipation resulting from nervousness, and other similar conditions are often greatly relieved through regular exercise. Exercise for fun, preferably out-of-doors, should be a part of the daily program of every young man and woman!

FATIGUE AND REST

We all become very tired, or *fatigued*, at times. The sensation is produced by the action of toxins, resulting from the burning of fuels in the body. Such fatigue is normal. There are individuals, however, who refuse to recognize and accept the warning signals of fatigue and attempt to keep going. Reducing the amount of time reserved for rest and sleep, they fool themselves into thinking that they are getting more work done.

It is true that the body-machine can work for an extended period of time without rest and sleep—if forced! But again, the body records the forcing. If attempts are maintained to cut down on sleep and rest, the body-machine simply refuses to operate as it should. It is sluggish and slow-witted. It is irritable, high-strung, and loses its judgment.

If you find that your enthusiasm for living is low, you are nervous and irritable, and the whole world looks pretty gloomy, consider carefully the amount of time you allow yourself for rest and sleep. Rest and sleep are required for maintaining the body-machine. You fool no one—above all, not your own body—in trying to cut corners on rest.

INFECTIONS AND CONSTANT FATIGUE

You will recall how tired and listless you have been following a cold or other illness. The toxins produced by germs that invade your body produce strong symptoms of fatigue. Obviously, during and following such illnesses, one of the most important things you can do is to allow yourself a large amount of time for rest and sleep.

Certain infections of the body produce a constant fatigue and wear down the body-machine to the point of exhaustion. Abscessed and diseased teeth, tonsillitis, and similar continuing infections are among the most common and serious diseases. The first warning of tuberculosis and various other serious diseases is a tiredness that has no relationship to hard work or exercise. If you find that you are almost always tired and nervous, see a doctor for a complete check-up. It is no fun living if you feel too tired for a full day's activities.

TOBACCO

Why do people smoke? Very often the first attempt to smoke results in violent sickness. Why do they repeat that experience until they become so habit-bound to it that they are uncomfortable without it?

Several factors are involved. Without much question, they begin smoking despite severe discomfort because they see others doing it and want to "be one of the gang." Why do they keep it up? That is a little easier to answer. It becomes a habit. Moreover, the body has become accustomed to the nicotine, and a strong will is required to break the habit.

Does Smoking Have Benefits? Smoking produces no physical benefits whatever. It is difficult to get a confirmed smoker to say what values he gets from smoking. He really does not know.

Does a smoker really enjoy smoking? Probably, because he has the habit and his body literally aches for tobacco. When he smokes, that ache is relieved. In that sense, he enjoys smoking.

What Is the Harm in Smoking? Tobacco contains *nicotine*, and nicotine is a powerful poison. It is the chief ingredient of many insecticides.

The amount of nicotine absorbed in smoking varies with the form of smoking. Of course, the amount absorbed is very small compared with concentrated forms of the drug. However, that it does have a poisonous effect on the body is shown by its nauseating effect to the inexperienced. Even a confirmed smoker will sometimes smoke so much that

Plenty of fresh air and sunlight, freedom from overcrowding, and a sense of well-being all help to improve physical and mental health.

Penicillium notatum highly enlarged. This is the mold from which penicillin, a wonder-working drug, is obtained. During World War II, it was produced in quantity through the cooperation of scientists, government agencies, and business organizations.

he becomes somewhat faint, dizzy, and nauseated.

Nicotine is not the only substance that affects a smoker's body. The smoke contains other substances that are irritating to the mucous membranes. Excessive smoking frequently results in inflamed mucous membranes and a constant, hacking, "cigarette" cough. Smokers often complain of a "hot spot" at the back of the throat, and that the mouth is hot, dry, and irritated.

TEA AND COFFEE

Both tea and coffee contain a drug known as *caffeine*. An ordinary cup of tea and one of coffee contain about the same amount of this drug. Caffeine increases the rate of blood flow, the rate of breathing, and the speed with which the body burns fuel. These are measurable, immediate effects. There is no clearcut evidence that moderate use of tea or coffee makes people nervous and irritable. However, many persons find that they cannot sleep for several hours after drinking a cup of coffee or tea. Because caffeine is a stimulant, it is clearly unwise for anyone who is already nervous and high-strung to use much coffee or tea.

Even cocoa contains a drug. This drug is *theobromine*, and its effects are much like those of caffeine except that it does not seem to stimulate the nervous system as much.

ALCOHOL

The chief point to keep in mind about alcohol is that it is not a stimulant as so many people believe. On the contrary, it depresses and slows down the body-machine.

Why is alcohol so commonly believed to be a stimulant? The answer is based on the fact that the chief effects of alcohol are on the nervous system. If alcohol is given in large amounts, its effects are much like ether or similar anesthetics. It produces complete unconsciousness by paralyzing nerve centers.

What happens when a smaller amount of alcohol is drunk—say the amount contained in an ordinary "drink"? The alcohol is absorbed into the body very quickly. The blood carries it to the brain. Immediately it begins to paralyze or anesthetize nerve centers. The feeling of exhilaration that persons appear to feel when drinking is merely a result of the fact that the highest centers of the brain—in the cerebrum—are becoming more and more paralyzed. The cerebrum cannot carry on its normal functioning.

You will recall that man's cerebrum is the seat of his judgment, restraint, memory, thinking, and decision. With this center of higher activities lulled to sleep, he is unable to use the good judgment and caution he ordinarily has. He believes that he is being very witty when he is but stupidly boring. He thinks that he is more clever, accurate, quick, and generally able when, as a matter of fact, he tends to be far less so than normally.

The chief harm in alcohol rests in this matter, for man's "brakes" are released by it. Behind the wheel of an automobile, he has the feeling that he can drive better than he can when sober. The ghastly number of automobile accidents that result from drunken driving shows how wrong he really is. His judgment is impaired and his sense of moral values affected. Thus he will do, while under the influence of alcohol, things he would never do when sober.

Physiological Effects of Alcohol. There are other measurable effects of alcohol on the body-machine. It causes a dilation of the surface blood vessels, resulting in a flushing of the skin and a sensation of warmth. Usually there is a drop in blood pressure, and the heart beats slightly more rapidly. Increased amounts of alcohol reverse this condition; the blood pressure increases and the heart action is slowed down.

YOUR PERSONAL HEALTH PLAN

To be healthy, a person must live healthfully. To live healthfully, you must know something of the rules of the game. It is possible to live like any of the lower animals without planning, without self-control. It is also possible to plan ahead to a life of effective, happy living through playing the rules of the game of healthful living. No one can make your plan for you. Science can show you the rules of the game. It is up to you to accept those rules and plan your own life for better living.

Penicillin does not kill germs directly but prevents them from multiplying. As a result, the germs fall easy prey to the body's normal defense mechanisms. Such drugs are called antibiotics. The mold from which penicillin is obtained is being grown in the bottles at the left. The clear areas in photo at the right surround colonies of *Penicillum notatum* that are growing in a culture of bacteria. What do these clear areas mean?

U. S. D. A. photo by Knell; photo from Merck & Co., Inc.

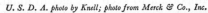

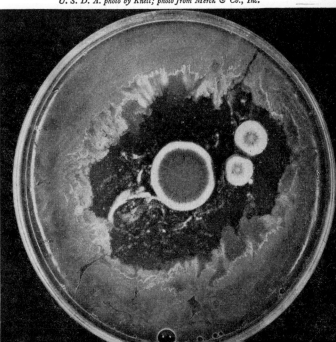

1. In Chapter 6 you were asked to check yourself against a list of health items. Refer to that list now and determine what steps you need to take to improve your health. Perhaps the meaning and importance of some of the items are clearer now than when you checked the list.

FIRST AID—BE PREPARED TO SAVE LIVES

If you have ever seen a serious accident, you were probably struck by the fact that so many people are unable to give aid to the injured. When such an accident occurs, crowds gather but do nothing. You can almost hear the crowd sigh with relief when someone who knows first aid orders the crowd to stand back, and assists the injured in such a way that the crowd knows, almost instinctively, that real help is being provided. Often such a person is a Boy Scout or other young person who has learned the "do's" and "don't's" of first aid.

WHAT IS FIRST AID?

Each year about 100,000 persons in the United States die from accidental injury. Each year about 300,000 more persons are permanently disabled. In 1941 accidents killed or disabled one out of every 14 persons in the United States. First aid could have saved many of those lives and prevented much of the permanent disablement.

First aid is just what its name suggests, the first aid that is given before the skilled services of a trained physician are available. It is important to keep this fact in mind. Many injured persons have been killed by the attempts of well-meaning people to provide more aid than their understanding and skill made possible with safety.

If you want to be prepared to save lives in case of serious accidents, learn well these three points: Your job is simply to (1) call a physician immediately, (2) make the injured person as comfortable and free from pain as possible, and (3) prevent further injury to the body. It is the doctor's job to take over after such emergency aid has been provided.

DO NOT MOVE THE PATIENT

An injured person should never be moved until the extent of his injuries has been determined by a physician. Many deaths have resulted from ignoring this basic rule. Broken ribs jab into the lungs or the heart. Broken bones with razor-sharp edges cut through arteries, causing death from bleeding. A broken back presses with fatal force against the spinal cord. Shock drains the blood from vital organs. These are common and often fatal results of moving an injured person.

Even though an injured person is lying on the street in the middle of traffic, do not move him. Direct traffic around him but keep him lying quiet. If care is taken, a coat may be slipped under him and another over him to keep him warm. But that is all.

CONDITIONS REQUIRING FIRST AID

There are many injuries, small and large, requiring first aid. But there are four conditions that cost so many lives that all of us should know about them and what to do if they arise. These are shock, suffocation such as drowning, arterial bleeding, and poisoning.

First Aid for Shock. Shock was discussed on page 54. It results quite commonly from serious injury. Occasionally, even a slight injury, accompanied by great fear or other emotional reaction, may bring about the condition of shock. You will recall that in shock there is insufficient blood to enable the vital organs to carry on their work.

The symptoms of shock may be any or all of the following: The injured person may feel weak, faint, sick, and his body will quite often be cold and clammy. His face will appear pinched and pale and he may have an anxious expression. He may be unconscious or in a stupor. His breathing may be irregular and generally his pulse will be weak and rapid. What should be done? The purpose of the following rules will be clear if you will recall the nature of vasomotor action of the blood stream and that shock is draining blood away from vital organs.

1. Place the patient in a horizontal position with the head low.

2. Control bleeding to prevent loss of blood.

3. Allow no movement of the patient. Often a patient is not aware of his condition, insists he is all right, and wants to move about. Do not allow him to do so until you are certain he is not suffering from shock or until a doctor comes.

4. Keep the patient warm. Apply blankets, coats, or artificial heat if possible.

5. Give the patient hot drinks *if he is conscious*. Do not attempt to force liquids into an unconscious or partially conscious person.

6. Call a doctor! Shock is serious. It is one of the biggest killers. The above treatments are just first aid. They do not replace the services of a physician.

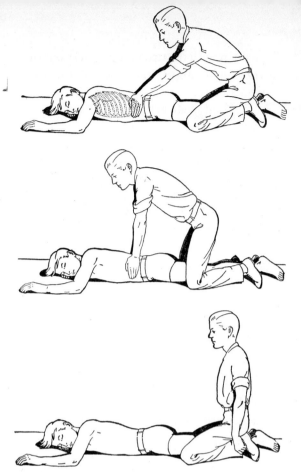

Steps in artificial respiration.

First Aid When Breathing Stops. Suffocation, or *asphyxia*, generally results from drowning, electric shock, or gas poisoning. If for any reason a person has stopped breathing, artifical respiration should be applied. It should be continued for at least 2 hours even though no signs of life are apparent. Many times breathing has been started over an hour after it had stopped.

The purpose of artificial respiration is to press on the body in such a way as to force air in and out of the lungs in the way that the diaphragm and ribs normally do. The following rules and diagrams should enable you to practice artificial respiration successfully. Keep in mind, however, that giving artifical respiration is much like riding a bicycle. You could read many books on how to ride a bicycle but you will not be able to ride without considerable actual practice. With the supervision of your teacher, Scout Leader, or other trained person, practice artificial respiration

until you *know* you can provide it if the need arises.

1. Lay the patient face down, remove any objects that might be in the mouth, and be sure that the tongue has not turned backwards, stopping up the throat.

2. Place one of the patient's arms under his head and extend the other arm over his head (see the diagrams).

3. Kneel astride the patient in the position shown in the first diagram. Place your coat or some padding under your knees. If you cannot be relieved by someone else, you may be on your knees for 2 hours and they will get extremely sore.

4. Place the palms of your hands on the small of the patient's back so that your little fingers are just touching the lowest ribs. Your thumbs and fingers should be in a natural and comfortable

position with the tips of the fingers out of your sight around the sides of the patient's body.

5. Hold your arms straight and push forward slowly so that your weight is pushed down on the patient's body. Do not bend your elbows. Say slowly, as you push down, "Out goes the bad air." This will help you to time your pushing which must be done rhythmically (see the second and third diagrams).

6. Snap your hands off smartly and swing back and sit on your heels, so as to remove the pressure suddenly and completely. As you do so say, "In comes the good." This will enable you to time your work (see the first diagram again).

7. Now begin the entire procedure again. You should work steadily and rhythmically. If you are timing it correctly, it will allow you about 12 to 15 such pressing and releasing operations per minute.

8. Remember to keep up the work for at least 2 hours if necessary. If you tire and another person takes your place, be sure that the rhythm is maintained. Have your assistant kneel alongside you and swing back and forward with you until he has caught your rhythm.

First Aid to Stop Bleeding. Bleeding may be one of three types. Slight wounds allow blood to ooze from capillaries and small veins. Such bleeding stops of its own accord. It is important, however, to guard against infection by applying iodine or some other germicide. If larger veins are cut, the blood will continue to flow. Such blood will be rather dark in color and will flow steadily. Unless a great amount of blood is being lost, do nothing except keep the patient quiet until the doctor comes. If a great quantity of blood is being lost, apply a germ free, or *sterile*, dressing directly over the wound and then apply pressure by binding a cloth around it and pulling it tight.

If an artery has been cut, the blood will be bright red and will spurt with every contrac-

tion of the heart. Such bleeding is dangerous. The heart may pump the blood out of the body and death result in a few minutes. Such bleeding must be stopped as quickly as possible. Since the arteries carry blood away from the heart, arterial bleeding may be stopped by applying pressure *between* the wound and the heart. The chief places where such pressure

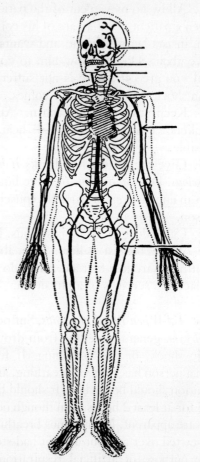

Chief pressure points for stopping arterial bleeding.

may be applied are shown in the diagram immediately above.

Pressure must be maintained until a doctor comes. To do so it is often necessary to apply a *tourniquet*. This can be a strap, handkerchief, piece of torn shirt, or anything else that can be tightened around an arm or leg between the heart and the wound. It should be wide enough to prevent cutting the skin when tightened and should be used with a pad.

The pad—a tight roll of cloth or handkerchief—should be placed directly over the artery. The tourniquet should be wrapped around this and twisted to tighten it. Tighten until the blood stops spurting. *The tourniquet should be loosened every 15 minutes* to allow the circulation to start again for a few minutes. Otherwise food would not be brought to the injured part and cells would die.

First Aid in Poisoning. There are so many different types of poisons, each having a different effect in the body, that it is difficult to remember precisely what to do for each type of poisoning. Two general rules, however, may be followed in all poisoning. If you follow these rules in case of need, you will save a life. First, the stomach must be emptied as soon as possible. This will remove all the poison not already absorbed. Second, dilute the poison as much as possible or provide some substance that will soak up the poison so that as little of it as possible gets into the blood stream.

Both of these rules can be observed by getting a person who has swallowed poison to vomit. Vomiting can be started by giving at least 5 glassfulls of lukewarm soapsuds, *strong* salt or soda water, or warm water to which a tablespoon of mustard has been added. Call a doctor immediately if a person has taken poison or is even suspected of having taken poison.

WORKING WITH SCIENCE

1. Locate on your own body or that of a classmate each of the pressure points shown in the diagram on page 118. Feel the pulse at the wrist of a classmate. Now press at the pressure point in the upper arm until you have stopped the blood so that the pulse cannot be felt. Why does it stop?

2. Practice artificial respiration with a classmate or friend. Work at this until you have established an easy rhythm and the "patient" is forced to "breathe" as a result of your procedure.

READING YOU WILL ENJOY

Brown, Esther L. *Physicians and Medical Care.* Russell Sage Foundation, New York, 1937. A discussion of the education and training of doctors and the demand for their services.

de Kruif, Paul. *"Toward a Healthy America,"* Public Affairs Pamphlet No. 31. Public Affairs Committee, Inc., New York, 1939. The progress of medical science is revealed in our health gains, yet this booklet shows there is a great lag between the discoveries of our life-saving sciences and our uses of them.

"Fitness for Freedom," Special Number VI (March, 1942) in *Calling America* series. Survey Associates, Inc., New York. This special number of *Survey Graphic* contains illuminating articles by "life-conservation experts" giving practical advice and information on various aspects of health to Americans.

Foster, William T. *Doctors, Dollars and Disease,* Public Affairs Pamphlet No. 10 (rev.). Public Affairs Committee, Inc., New York, 1944. This pamphlet is based on the studies of the Committee on the Cost of Medical Care, the Twentieth Century Fund, the Julius Rosenwald Fund, the National Health Survey, the American Medical Association, and the United States Public Health Service, as well as reports of many medical and hospitalization plans. An excellent summary of known facts of the relationship between economics and health in America, and proposals and plans for achieving a healthier America through cooperative means.

Living things live almost everywhere—from the deepest depths of the seas to the highest reaches of of the air around us, from the coldest arctic waters to the heated waters of natural hot springs. And of course, they vary greatly in size and complexity—from simple one-celled plants and animals to organisms such as man with his billions of cells and complex organ systems. Even the most conservative estimates indicate that there are more than 1 million different kinds of animals and about one-fourth as many different kinds of plants.

No one person could hope to know very much about all of these different kinds of living things without some systematic method of learning about them. So the biologists have grouped them to make their study and control easier.

They have made groups of plants and groups of animals that have similar characteristics of structure. For example, man belongs to a large group of animals with backbones. This large group in turn is divided into five groups. Man belongs to one of these groups which includes all animals with backbones that have hair and feed their young with milk.

The animals without backbones are far more numerous and are divided into nine large groups. The plants are divided into four groups.

Fascinating and varied, and seemingly everywhere, living things carry on their eternal battle to eat and avoid being eaten. All, that is, except the green plants. Green plants manufacture their own food and do not eat.

Using Biological Resources for Better Living

11

THE KINDS OF LIVING THINGS

Has it ever occurred to you that a vacant lot is not really vacant and empty? You will immediately agree when you stop to think that a vacant lot is usually covered with weeds and may have a tree or two. But you may be surprised to learn that there are many, many kinds of living things in the vacant lot.

How many kinds of living things could be found in a vacant lot? With great care and the use of proper instruments, you could probably find several thousand kinds of living things.

About how many individual living things could you expect to find? The answer would run high into the billions. Just a pinch of garden soil taken between your thumb and fore-finger contains from 600,000 to 800 million bacteria. That same pinch of soil contains many thousands of tiny animals, called protozoa.

Suppose the vacant lot were expanded to include all the vacant lots in the world. Then add all the forests, rivers, creeks, valleys, mountains, oceans, cities, grasslands, croplands, and the air above. Do not forget the deserts, teeming jungles, and arctic wastes. The living things throughout the world are numbered in such billions upon billions that it is almost beyond understanding. Regardless of size or shape, however, they are all made up of one or more cells and must perform the essential life-functions.

ANIMALS WITH BACKBONES

There are well over 1 million different kinds of animals, and they vary considerably in the way they look, the way they act, and the way they live. Among the animals, however, is an important group whose members have one characteristic in common. All the animals in this group have an internal backbone of bone or cartilage. Inside or very near this backbone is a nerve cord running down the back. Such animals are called *vertebrates*.

Man, bat, frog, and fish—all are vertebrates. Although the vertebrates are very important, in number of kinds they make up only about 5 percent of the animal kingdom. Except for spinal cord and backbone, animals in this group vary greatly in structure and function.

MICE, MEN, AND ELEPHANTS

You yourself are an example of the most complex and highly organized living thing in

Except for the birds, these animals are all mammals. They are shown in surroundings typical of where they live. Such surroundings are called habitats.

the world. Man is one of a large group of animals that have some hair or fur on their bodies and feed their young from milk glands, called *mammary glands*. These are the mammals.

Some mammals live in the sea, some in the air, and some on the land. A bat is a mammal, although it looks much like a bird. It is a

A chicken is a bird. Note how its internal organs differ from those of a human being.

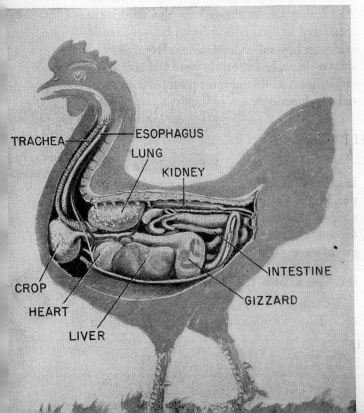

TRACHEA — ESOPHAGUS
LUNG
KIDNEY

CROP
HEART
LIVER
INTESTINE
GIZZARD

mammal because it is furry and because it feeds its young from mammary glands, just as does a cow, a dog, an elephant, or a mouse. Seals and whales look somewhat like fishes. But they breathe with lungs, have hair on their bodies, and feed their young with their own milk. They, too, are mammals. Altogether there are about 15,000 kinds of mammals.

PENGUINS, HUMMINGBIRDS, AND EAGLES

Another large group of animals is the *birds*. Birds breathe by means of lungs, all have feathers, and nearly all have wings. The wings of some birds enable them to fly in the air for long periods of time. Some birds, for example, the penguin, have lost the ability to fly. The penguin spends much time in the water where it catches fish and swims swiftly.

The tiny hummingbird can hover over a flower from which it sucks a sweet substance called *nectar*. The giant vulture, condor, and eagle all are meat-eaters and soar for hours without beating their wings. They keep aloft without beating their wings, just like a glider, by riding the rising currents of air. Other birds, such as the sparrow, robin, and thrush, live almost entirely on seeds or on tiny insects. There are more than 20,000 kinds of birds.

Warm Blood and Cold Blood. Regardless of outside temperature, the body temperature of

American Museum of Natural History, New York

A bullfrog is an amphibian (see page 124). The developing bullfrog tadpole at the left developed into the young bullfrog at the right. Frogs and toads are found in all parts of this country.

mammals and birds varies only slightly. Consequently, mammals and birds are called *warm-blooded animals*. For example, man's body temperature is about 98.6°F, whether the outside temperature is 10° below zero or 110° above zero. When the temperature drops, the body burns fuel faster to produce more heat to maintain this constant temperature. When the temperature goes above 98.6°F, the body adjusts and more blood is sent to the surface for cooling, and perspiration increases. As the perspiration evaporates, it cools the body. All other groups of animals are *cold-blooded*.

SNAKES, LIZARDS, AND CROCODILES

The *reptiles* include snakes, lizards, turtles,

alligators, and crocodiles. They are good examples of cold-blooded animals. "Cold-blooded" is not a very accurate description of these animals, for their temperature is always just about the same as that of their surroundings. If the weather is cold, their blood is cold. The temperature of a garter snake lying on the ground when the temperature is 102°F, is also about 102°F.

There are about 6000 kinds of reptiles. All of them have dry, scaly skins. Some of them lay eggs from which the young hatch, and others, such as the garter snake, hatch their eggs internally and bear their young alive.

By and large, reptiles are quite valuable because they eat large numbers of insects,

The spotted turtles at the left are just emerging from the eggs from which they developed. The common hog-nosed snake at the right surrounds her eggs.

Lynwood M. Chace; American Museum of Natural History, New York

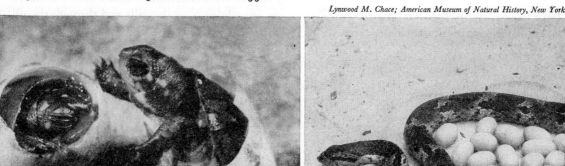 

A fish with gill covers removed. What is the function of the gills?

lie just under the skin of a frog. Air dissolves in the moisture on the skin and is absorbed into the blood stream.

You are undoubtedly familiar with frogs and toads but perhaps not with salamanders. They have four legs and a tail and look much like lizards. Their skins are moist rather than dry and scaly. Like frogs and toads, they begin life as eggs laid in water.

All tadpoles breathe by means of *gills.* These gills project out from the sides of the neck of certain tadpoles and are inside the neck and connected to the outside by *gill slits* in other forms. As the tadpole grows older, the tail becomes shorter and shorter and finally disappears. Legs begin to form, first the front ones and then the hind ones. Finally, the gills are absorbed and lungs develop. The adult frog or toad and many salamanders breathe through both lungs and skin. They would drown if held under water.

Frogs, toads, and salamanders live in the water when young. In general they become lung-breathers and live most of the time on land as adults. Such animals are called *amphibians.* About 3000 kinds are known.

mice, and other gnawing animals. The only poisonous snakes in the United States are the rattlesnake, the copperhead, the cottonmouth water moccasin, and the coral snake. The Gila monster is the only poisonous lizard in the United States. It lives only near the Gila River in Arizona.

TOADS, FROGS, AND SALAMANDERS

Many persons think that snakes are "slimy." They are not, but most toads, frogs, and salamanders are. There is good reason for the moistness of their skins. Although these animals have lungs at maturity, they also breathe through their skins. Many heavy blood vessels

EELS, SHARKS, AND CATFISH

Fish, as you know, live in water. They vary tremendously in details, but most of them are covered with scales and have fins with which they swim through the water. They breathe through gills.

The next time you catch or buy a fish, examine the gills. These are behind slits at the sides of the head. Water taken in at the mouth is forced out over the gills and through the gill slits. As the water passes over the gills, oxygen is taken up and carbon dioxide is given off. The redness of the gills shows that the blood is close to the surface of these breathing organs. Eels, sharks, catfish, bass, salmon, and tuna are common fishes.

WORKING WITH SCIENCE

1. Select a vacant lot convenient to the school. Arrange a field trip to the lot for the entire class.

Each member of the class should carry pencil and paper to jot down the different kinds of living things discovered. Carry a spade with which to dig into the ground, and a small ax with which to split open rotted logs. If your class has the use of a microscope, be sure to carry back to the class samples of dead grass. Place the grass in a jar of water and wait for about 2 weeks. Now examine a drop of water from this jar under a microscope.

How many different kinds of living things did you discover at the vacant lot? How many different kinds of living things were discovered when the lists of each class member were put together? Do you think it likely that you discovered all the living things that existed in the lot?

2. Arrange field trips to creeks, wooded regions, or seashores to discover the variety of living things that may be found in each place. Such trips should be planned in advance. A small spade should be taken in order to dig into the ground. A small hatchet is useful to break up rotted logs. Paper should be taken on which to record the types of living things discovered.

If certain plants or animals cannot be identified, you may wish to take them back to the classroom for further study. Cigar boxes or other small containers are useful for carrying such materials. A small amount of carbon tetrachloride poured into a small wad of absorbent cotton and placed in a bottle with a tight stopper is useful to kill insects for later study and mounting. Your teacher will help you make such a killing bottle or one using *potassium cyanide*. **Caution**: *Potassium cyanide is a deadly poison.*

3. There is great fun in observing the life and antics of various forms of life. Here is a list of some things you may enjoy doing:

(a) Dissect snakes to see modifications in usual vertebrate structure because of the shape of the snakes.

(b) Secure tadpoles from ponds and watch them develop into frogs (or toads, as the case may be). Keep them in an aquarium or large glass bottle.

(c) Observe aquarium fish moving about in the water. Note that they can rise and sink in the water without moving a single fin. How do they do it?

(d) Examine the gills of a fish and note the redness showing the nearness of the blood to the surface of the skin.

(e) Collect and study insects of various kinds.

THE SPINELESS ANIMALS

Animals without backbones far outnumber those with backbones. For every ground squirrel, there are *millions* of tiny crawling creatures without spinal columns. For every fish, there are *millions* of tiny swimming creatures without the fish's spinal cord. For every bird, there are *millions* of flying insects without skulls and backbones. The spineless animals, or *invertebrates*, make up about 95 percent of the animal kingdom.

SPIDERS, "BUGS," AND CRAYFISH

You are quite familiar with one large group of spineless animals. These are the *jointed-legged* animals, which include all the insects, the thousand-legged worms, the crabs, lobsters, and crayfish, and the spiders. More than 650,000 different kinds of jointed-legged animals are known.

Perhaps the most interesting characteristic of the jointed-legged animals is that they wear their skeletons outside their bodies. The muscles on the inside are attached to the outside covering. In the crayfish and crabs, the skeletons are quite heavy and hard. In the spiders and flies, the skeletons are rather soft. The soft parts of the body are protected by the more or less hard outside covering.

Insects. All insects have six legs. Most insects have certain other features in common. If you catch a grasshopper and examine it closely, you can see some of these common features yourself. Note the hard outside skeleton. Look carefully and you will see that the grasshopper has, not two eyes, but five. Two of the five are easily seen. These are the large eyes at the sides of the head. Each of these is made up of many, more or less separate, parts arranged so that they look somewhat like a bundle of tall tin cans. Such

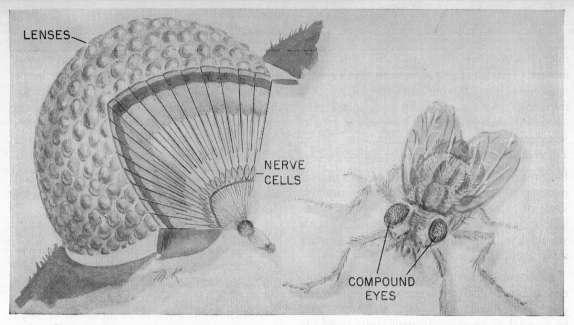

LENSES

NERVE CELLS

COMPOUND EYES

Flies and many other insects have compound eyes. Their vision differs greatly from ours.

eyes are called *compound eyes*.

Many insects, as well as crabs and crayfish, have compound eyes. Such animals see moving things easily, for light goes from one unit of a compound eye to another, thus indicating motion. A grasshopper also has three *simple eyes*. Probably these simple eyes do not form good images. Many insects have only simple eyes.

Most insects have two pairs of wings. The first pair of a beetle's wings are just hard cases that cover the soft second pair. The second pair fold up under the cases when not in use. Some insects, such as the housefly, have only one pair of wings. The second pair, however, exist as tiny "balancing" organs. When these are clipped off, the fly gets into all kinds of trouble when it attempts to fly.

A few kinds of insects have no wings at all. Can you find any of them? Others, such as the ants, grow wings during the mating season.

A grasshopper's ears are not at the sides of its head. They are at the sides of its body, just above its large jumping legs. The ears are only large eardrums and do not have outside flaps like the ears of a human being. Katydids and crickets have ears inside their first pair of legs, just below the "knee" joint.

Most insects have a pair of "feelers." These "feelers" are the chief organs of touch and are called *antennae*. As an ant crawls along, it waves its antennae, touching everything in its path with them.

An insect does not have lungs. If you look carefully along the sides of a grasshopper's belly, or *abdomen*, you will notice a dot on each side of each part, or *segment*. These dots are tiny holes that open into the breathing tubes of the insect. If you watch a live grasshopper closely, you will see that its abdomen seems to expand and contract. This muscular action helps push air in and out of the breathing tubes.

Spiders. A spider has eight legs. Clearly, then, it is not an insect. Spiders, ticks, mites, scorpions, and the common daddy longlegs belong to a different group of jointed-legged animals called *arachnids*.

Arachnids do not have compound eyes or antennae, and they differ from insects in many other ways. Spiders usually have eight simple eyes. They have large hollow fangs that are used in killing or paralyzing prey by injecting poison from glands in the head.

In most spiders the tip of the abdomen has three pairs of *spinnerets*. Each of these is made up of 100 or more tiny openings through which liquid silk is forced by the spider. As the silk hits the air, it hardens into tiny strands.

Different kinds of silk glands in a spider's body produce different kinds of silk. You can easily discover that the silk of a spider web

126

is of at least two types by touching different parts with your finger. The heavy framework is not very sticky, but the rest is. The sticky strands entangle insects or other tiny animals so that the spider can rush out from its hiding place and paralyze the victim.

Crabs and Lobsters. Crabs and lobsters live in ocean water. Like their fresh-water relative, the crayfish, they breathe by means of gills attached to the top of the leg joints and extending up into the chest region under the hard limey covering. They feed chiefly on decaying animal and plant matter but may catch small fish. Their chief means of protection from their enemies is their hard covering. Lobsters and crayfish can move backward suddenly by flipping their tails under them.

Crayfish, shrimps, lobsters, and crabs have an interesting balancing organ, a water-filled sac at the base of the antennae. The bottom of this sac is covered with tiny sensory hairs. Grains of fine sand are always found among these hairs. The grains of sand are always pulled toward the center of the earth. The weight of these grains on the hairs tells the animal it is right side up. When it is flipped over, the grains of sand do not press against the hairs, and the animal knows it is upside down.

OYSTERS, SNAILS, AND DEVILFISH

If you have eaten clams or oysters on the half-shell, you have seen the animals in one-half of their limey homes. Clams and oysters are commonly called *bivalves*, which means *two-shelled*. The shells protect the little soft-bodied animals, for two very powerful muscles hold the shells together. Oysters, clams, octopuses, snails, and so forth are *mollusks*, which means *soft-bodied*.

A clam lives buried in the mud or sand under shallow water of the ocean or fresh-water streams. It lies with the hinged part of its shell up and the two parts of the shell usually slightly open. A clam secures both food and oxygen by pulling water into its body through a tiny tube called a *siphon*.

Squids, snails, and octopuses are much like

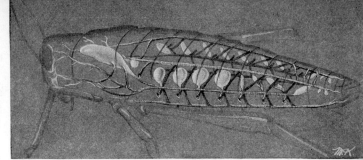

The breathing tubes and air sacs of a grasshopper.

clams and oysters, in spite of their different appearance. Squids and devilfish have large eyes that are much like our eyes. The arms, or *tentacles*, of a squid press together when the animal shoots through the water and help to steer the animal. Two of the tentacles of a squid, like the many arms of an octopus, have sucking disks by which food is seized and drawn toward the mouth. The mouth has two large, horny jaws something like the beak of a bird. These kill the prey and tear it to pieces so that it can be swallowed.

Slugs and snails may be found both in the sea and on land and, therefore, vary in their method of breathing. All common seashells are the former homes of mollusks. About 80,000 kinds of mollusks are known.

EARTHWORMS, ROUNDWORMS, AND MORE WORMS

Worms are found everywhere. Not earthworms, of course, but other kinds of worms.

Where are a katydid's ears?

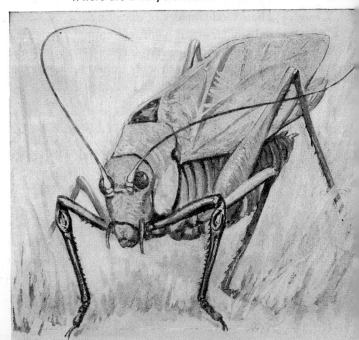

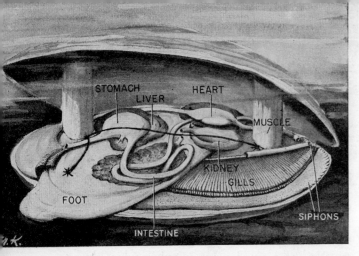

STOMACH
LIVER
HEART
MUSCLE
KIDNEY
GILLS
FOOT
INTESTINE
SIPHONS

A clam has many body parts even though it is a simple animal. How does it obtain food?

Earthworms belong to a fairly small group of rather large worms. Roundworms and flatworms are far more numerous. Most roundworms are very small. Flatworms are of various sizes. Of all worms, the roundworms exist in greatest numbers.

Earthworms. Earthworms live in moist, rich earth. They burrow through the soil in search of particles of food. An earthworm breathes through its skin. It has no lungs or gills. Oxygen dissolves in the moisture of its skin and is absorbed into the animal's body.

Earthworms come out of their burrows at night, usually sticking just their head ends out. If you join the early birds, you may find some worms that stay out a little late, busily thrusting their heads around searching for food. Their food consists of decaying leaves, seeds, and similar small plant and animal particles.

Earthworms spend most of their time swallowing soil as they extend their burrows. The soil goes through a storage chamber, or *crop*, into a gizzard where tiny pebbles grind up digestible particles, and then into a long intestine. Food material is absorbed from the intestine. The undigested material is deposited as a ring of *castings* at the top of the burrow.

The excreted earth at the top of the burrow is of great value to man. In one year as many as 18 tons of earth have been brought up from burrows and deposited on the surface of an acre of ground by earthworms. This helps to mix and in many ways to improve the soil.

Earthworms and leeches are common examples of segmented worms, of which about 8000 kinds are known.

Roundworms. Roundworms are very different from segmented worms. About 100,000 kinds of roundworms are known.

One of the commonest roundworms is the "horsehair snake," or hairworm. You may have heard that horsehairs in watering troughs turn into these horsehair snakes. The belief is natural enough, for the hairworms appear suddenly, and they look much like horsehairs. They appear so suddenly in watering troughs because the young worm lives inside the body of an insect and may drop from the insect when it settles on the edge of the trough.

Very tiny roundworms are common in garden soil. In addition, they live in water, trees and other plants, and in the bodies of our pets. More than 50 different kinds of roundworms may live as parasites in man.

Ascaris is a common parasitic roundworm that may live in, or *infest*, dogs, pigs, and even man. An adult female *Ascaris* may lay hundreds of thousands of eggs each day in the intestines of an infested animal. These eggs pass out of the body with the undigested materials. If deposited on open ground, they may be taken into another person's body.

A more serious parasitic roundworm is the tiny *hookworm.* The hookworm fastens onto the lining of the intestines and sucks blood and fluids from the body. Its eggs pass out of the body with undigested materials. The eggs hatch into tiny worms which can live for a short time in the soil. Human beings who walk barefoot on such soil are almost sure to become infested sooner or later.

Trichinosis is a disease caused by living worms often found in undercooked pork. The meat of pork may be infested by millions of tiny trichina worms. These are about $\frac{1}{25}$ of an inch long and are curled up in tiny capsules called *cysts.*

Flatworms. Most of the 5000 kinds of flatworms are parasites. The common beef tapeworm is a good example. The tapeworm attaches itself to the inside wall of the intestine by suckers on the head. Sections of the body develop, and the worm grows longer and longer. The worm does not have a digestive system, for it simply soaks up the food that its host has eaten and already digested.

URCHINS, SAND DOLLARS, AND STARFISH

Almost everyone has seen starfish. These spiny-skinned creatures live only in sea water, but they have been dried and carried to all parts of the country. Other members of this group of animals are the sea urchin and the sand dollar. All these animals live in sea water and all have a wheel-like shape and spiny skin.

The eating habits of a starfish are interesting. Its stomach is directly above its mouth, which is at the center of the underside of the body. Most starfish live on clams or oysters. The starfish humps itself over the two shells of the clam, attaches its hundreds of tube feet, and starts pulling on the two shells.

For a long time nothing happens, for the clam's muscles are far more powerful than those of the starfish. But the starfish pulls for a while with some of its tube feet and then it lets them rest while it attaches others and pulls. It can keep this up for a long time. The clam, on the other hand, has only two large muscles with which it keeps its shells closed. It cannot give them a rest. So finally it is completely worn out, its muscles begin to relax, and the shells open.

When this happens, the starfish turns its stomach wrong-side out through its mouth so that the inside surface of the stomach is in contact with the clam's soft body. The starfish keeps it there until the clam's body is digested and then draws the stomach back in.

Starfish eat so many oysters that they are dredged up and killed where large oyster "beds" are grown. When men first tried to kill off the starfish, they cut them in two, and dumped them back again into the ocean. To their surprise, they found that soon there were

almost twice as many starfish as before. The reason for this is that the starfish can grow anew parts that have been lost. This is called *regeneration.*

The sea cucumber, another member of this group, throws out its internal organs when it is in danger. This gives it time to get away while the animal that is after it eats the "insides." The sea cucumber then regenerates a set of internal organs.

CORAL REEFS AND JELLYFISH

Look carefully at the illustration below. It shows the floor of the ocean about 15 feet below the surface. You are looking at what seems to be a variety of flowers and plants. Some of these flower-like structures are brilliant orange, others are red, others purple, blue, white, pink, and other colors.

These flower-like structures are not plants. They are animals that belong to the large group which includes jellyfish and the corals that build the great barrier reefs and atolls of the Pacific Ocean.

A jellyfish swims by contracting and relaxing the bell- or parachute-shaped part of its body. Water is forced out of the bell when it contracts, thus forcing the jellyfish forward.

The Portuguese man-of-war is a common sight in warm seas throughout the world. This creature is really a colony of specialized animals that live together. One of these animals, or "parts," has become specialized into a sail-like float. This blue, gas-filled part catches

The floor of a shallow part of the ocean contains many living things. How many can you name?
American Museum of Natural History, New York

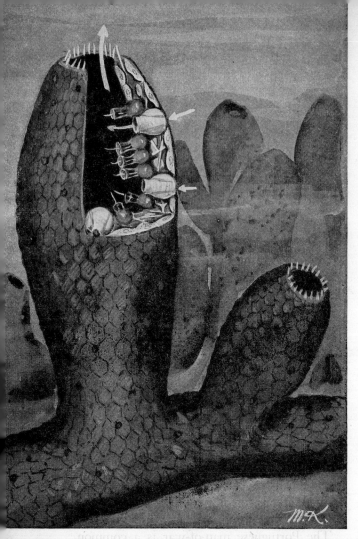

Sponges look like plants, but they are animals. How does a sponge get its food?

the wind, and the Portuguese man-of-war sails merrily along.

SPONGES AND COLONIES

These animals are known as *pore-bearers*, because their bodies have many tiny pores, or holes. They are probably far better known by their skeletons, for such skeletons are the common sponges we use to wash cars and windows. Most sponges live in the sea, but a few live in fresh water. Large sponges are made up of great numbers, or colonies, of simple sponges formed together.

Protozoa. One animal group includes simpler creatures than the sponges. That group is composed of the one-celled animals, known collectively as protozoa. There are more than •15,000 different kinds of these one-celled, microscopic creatures. The ameba and paramecium are common examples of protozoa.

Most protozoa live in a free state, but some are parasites and cause some of man's most serious diseases. *African sleeping sickness* is one of these diseases. Man cannot live in large parts of Africa because of the danger of sleeping sickness.

Another protozoan that causes much suffering and death is the malarial parasite. This protozoan is carried from man to man chiefly by the *Anopheles* mosquito.

WORKING WITH SCIENCE

1. Study the variety of spider webs in your locality. Note particularly the large, perfect webs of the orb weaver, or garden, spider. Touch the various parts with your finger. Which are sticky? See if you can find the funnel opening of the small wolf spider. Generally, these are found on the ground in open fields.

2. Catch some crayfish and place them in a glass jar with a little water. Dangle a small piece of raw meat in front of the crayfish and watch how he "captures" the meat and eats it.

3. Obtain some common land snails. Place them in a glass jar and watch the action of the muscular "foot" as the snails crawl up the sides of the jar.

Place some tender, young leaves in the jar and watch the snails eat. Sprinkle a small amount of water in the jar occasionally.

4. Observe the castings left on the top of the ground by earthworms. Go out early some morning, before the sun has come up, and observe earthworms in rich soil by using a flashlight. You may be fortunate enough to see them sticking their heads out of their burrows and eating bits of vegetable matter.

5. Dig into the ground or search the twigs or trees to discover insect larvas. Place such larvas in small cages together with some of the plant material or earthy material on which you found them, and observe them from time to time. If you can secure the pupal case, or *chrysalis*, of a butterfly, you may be able to see the adult butterfly emerge. Be sure that you check the chrysalis daily or you may miss this dramatic event.

6. Place several earthworms in a small jar that contains enough water to cover the worms completely. Place a few small pieces of dead leaves or decaying vegetable material in the jar for food. Determine how long the worms live. Compare this life-span with that of other worms placed in soil that is kept moist by regular sprinkling. Is it easy to drown a worm?

THE KINDS OF PLANTS

In numbers of separate living things the plants are more than a match for the animals. For example, every blade of some kinds of grass is part of a single plant. A square foot of your yard contains several hundred separate living plants. Multiply that by the number of square feet of grass in your yard and you will see that there may be a million or more grass plants in your yard.

TREES, GRASSES, AND FLOWERING PLANTS

Grass plants belong to a large group of plants that have leaves, stems, roots, and flowers. All the 130,000 or more different kinds of plants in this group bear seeds from which new plants develop. In fact, these plants are called *spermatophytes*, meaning *seed plants*. Trees, bushes, grasses, our common grain crops, vegetables—all are members of this large group.

Flowers and Seed Formation. The ways in which the spermatophytes produce seeds is interesting. Take an apple tree as an example. In spring, the branches of the tree become loaded with many tiny blossoms, or flowers. These flowers, of which there are many, are the *reproductive*, or *sexual*, *organs* of the apple tree.

At the base of a flower are tiny, green, petal-like structures that covered the tender blossom as the flower was developing from a bud. Just inside this are the petals of the flower. At the base of the petals are small glands that produce the perfume that makes the flower such a delight to man—and to bees!

Inside the petals are a number of tiny stalks. These are the male parts of the flower and are called *stamens*. At the tips of the stamens is a large amount of tiny, dustlike particles called *pollen*. Each pollen grain contains a living male cell. At the center of the flower is a large stalk which is the female part of the flower. It is called the *pistil*. The end of the pistil is sticky so that pollen will stick to it. At the base of the pistil is an enlarged part in which are living female cells.

If a young apple blossom is covered with a sack before it opens and the sack is left there until the flower has wilted and died, no apple will form. Observe carefully what happens to an apple blossom that is uncovered. Bees buzz from flower to flower. They are attracted by the odor of the flowers and secure the sweet nectar from the base of the flower. They make

The chief reproductive organs of a flowering plant. What part do insects play in this process?

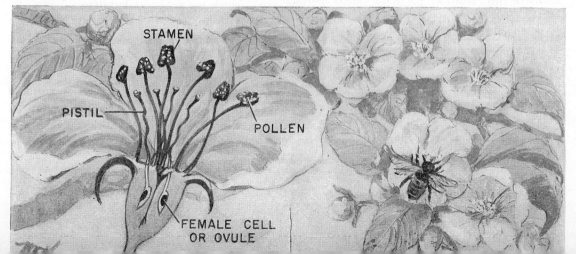

honey from nectar they get from the flowers.

As the bees get this nectar, they rub against the stamens and their bodies become covered with pollen. Then, as they push farther into a flower, the pollen from their bodies rubs off on the sticky pistil. This process of transferring pollen to the pistil of a flower is called *pollination*. Without pollination, fruit would never form.

After pollination, the pollen grains grow long tubes that thrust down into the pistil. The tube grows until its end comes in contact with the female cell at the base of the pistil. When this occurs, the male cell unites, or joins, with the female cell. We say that the female cell is *fertilized*. The fertilized cell then grows into a seed. If properly planted, this seed will develop into another apple tree. Large numbers of our common plants, including most vegetables and garden flowers, are pollinated by insects.

Many plants are pollinated by the wind. This is true of most of the grasses, grains, corn plants, and such trees as willows, maples, cottonwoods, poplars, and oaks. Plants that are pollinated by the wind usually have tiny flowers that are not easily seen. Plants that are pollinated by insects generally have showy flowers and perfume to attract insects.

FERNS, MOSSES, AND POT-CLEANING PLANTS

Not all plants produce seeds. About 5000 kinds of plants that belong to the fern group do not produce seeds. Neither do any of the 17,000 kinds of plants that belong to the group composed of the mosses and the flat, small plants known as *liverworts*.

Ferns reproduce by the production of thousands of tiny, dustlike particles called *spores*.

The underside of a fern leaf with the spore sacs.
American Museum of Natural History, New York

These are produced in tiny sacs, or pockets, on the under surface of the leaves, or *fronds*. Each spore is capable of becoming a new plant. Because sexes are not required, such reproduction is called *asexual*, meaning *without sex*.

The plant that develops from the spore is different in appearance from the fern plant that produced the spore. This tiny spore-produced plant produces female cells, or *eggs*, and male cells, or *sperms*. The sperms swim to the eggs through a film of moisture and fertilize them. The fertilized eggs develop into fern plants like the ones that produced the original spores.

Most ferns have stems that run underground with only the fronds aboveground. This is true of the ferns in our woodlands and of those used as house plants. But some kinds of tropical tree ferns have long stems that grow in an erect manner above the ground.

The fern group of plants also includes the horsetails, or "scouring rushes." Can you see how these plants got the name *horsetails?* Pioneers used scouring rushes in cleaning pots and pans. The plant stems contain minerals that are useful in scouring, valuable since our ancestors could not go to the corner store for a can of scouring powder.

MOLDS, POND SCUMS, AND GOOD AND BAD BACTERIA

Most of us think of plants as being green and having stems, roots, and leaves. However, one large group of plants contains about 80,000 kinds, and only a few of these—the *algae*—are green. And none of them have stems and leaves that are like the green plants with which we are most familiar.

This group of plants includes the bacteria, a few of which cause diseases. But most bacteria are beneficial because they bring about the rotting of dead organisms. Without their action, the earth would soon become cluttered up with dead plants and animals. But its greatest importance is that it releases materials that are needed by plants and animals yet to be produced.

132

Perhaps you have never thought of it this way, but your body is made up of substances that once were parts of the bodies of plants and other animals. If there had been no bacteria to help release these materials, most of them would be locked up in a form that you could not use.

Besides the bacteria, this group includes the molds, the rusts, the yeasts, toadstools, and similar *fungi*. The group includes plants so small—the bacteria—that many millions could easily rest on the point of a pin; and others—the algae—some of which are several hundred feet in length. Another kind of alga is the green scum that floats on the surface of stagnant water in the warm summer months.

WORKING WITH SCIENCE

1. Observe insects pollinating flowers as they attempt to obtain nectar from the flowers. Observe pollen being blown by wind from wind-pollinated types of flowers. Shade trees are typical of this extremely large group of wind-pollinated plants.

2. Obtain some bread mold, and examine it under a microscope or hand lens. See if you can identify the spores.

READING YOU WILL ENJOY

Beebe, William. *Exploring with Beebe*. G. P. Putnam's Sons, New York, 1932. A fascinating book of Beebe's adventures and explorations.

Buchsbaum, Ralph M. *Animals without Backbones*. University of Chicago Press, Chicago, 1938. A book, extremely well illustrated by photographs and good drawings, to help you study all kinds of animals without backbones.

Ditmars, Raymond L. *A Field Book of North American Snakes*. Doubleday & Co., Inc., New York, 1939. A useful handbook or reference to snakes in this country, written by a great snake specialist.

Edey, Maitland A. *American Songbirds*. Random House, New York, 1940. A small but excellent book to help you identify common songbirds.

Fabre, Jean H. *Insect Adventures*. Dodd, Mead & Co., New York, 1917. A great French scientist's interesting accounts of the lives of common insects.

Hegner, Robert W. *Parade of the Animal Kingdom*. The Macmillan Co., New York, 1944. A standard book about animals, their habits and nature. Parts of the book are slightly difficult, but you will find some interesting material in it.

Morgan, Ann H. *Field Book of Ponds and Streams*. G. P. Putnam's Sons, New York, 1930. A book to help you study and enjoy the plants and animals in ponds and streams near you.

The Book of Birds, Vols. I–II. National Geographic Soc., Washington, 1939. Excellent reference books that show, in full color, all of the types of birds that are found in the United States.

The Book of Wild Flowers. National Geographic Soc., Washington, 1933. Excellent accounts of wild flowers and 250 color pictures of them.

Zim, Herbert S. *Plants*. Harcourt, Brace & Co., New York, 1947. Interesting things to do with plants.

1

2

3

One of the aims of every living thing is to keep on living. Another is to produce offspring so that in spite of the fact that individuals die, other similar individuals live on. The fight for survival is hard and tough. It is always won by those living things that are best fitted for the lives they lead. Biologists call this *adaptation*, and adaptations are of many kinds.

Most adaptations improve a living thing's chances of keeping on living and producing offspring. For example, a rabbit (1) is so constructed that it can run very fast and dodge this way and that in escaping from dogs and other natural enemies. A cat (2) has teeth that are well suited for tearing meat from bones. It also has sharp claws for protection. Some animals, such as an insect called "walking stick" (3), look so much like their surroundings that their enemies have a hard time finding them.

Of all living things, man possesses the most remarkable and probably the most useful adaptations. One of these is man's brain, the organ that enables man to solve complex problems (4), to create new things, and to learn by the experience of others. Another is man's hand in which the thumb is so placed that an endless variety of manipulating, fingering, and grasping movements is possible (5). Another is the group of adaptations that enables man to speak (6) and thus to communicate his thoughts to others. Because of these and other adaptations, man, and not some other group of living things, is master of the earth.

12

THE LIFE OF LIVING THINGS

Probably well over 1 million different kinds of plants and animals exist in the world. Regardless of size and shape and where they live, they all have certain functions in common. These are the life-functions that were discussed in Unit 2. Food-getting is part of metabolism, one of these life-functions.

An automobile or an airplane must have fuel to operate. Without fuel the pistons cannot move up and down. The gears and wheels will not revolve. Energy is required to produce this motion. In the case of the automobile or airplane, the source of this energy is the fuel that is burned.

FOOD-GETTING AND THE GREEN PLANT

In a sense, living things are somewhat like automobiles or airplanes. All need a source of energy—fuel of some kind. In the case of living things, energy comes from food. Every living thing must have food to live.

The basic law of life seems to be: Eat, and do not be eaten! Where do the millions of animals get food to eat? What do they eat? Many of them eat one another. But you probably realize that something is missing from this picture. After all, animals cannot continue to get the energy they need for life by eating one another. Of course, man can get food by eating, let us say, beef. And it is true that tapeworms and roundworms may live as parasites in a cow's body. But where does the cow get its food?

PLANT FACTORIES

Without exception, every animal's source of food may be traced to green plants. Now the question becomes: Where do green plants get their food? If they ate other forms of life, then it would be necessary to trace the source still farther. For somewhere food must be made. Somewhere we must find food factories

in operation. We find them in the green plants.

Green Plants Trap Sunlight. With the exception of toadstools, bacteria, yeasts, and similar plants, almost all plants have a green coloring matter, a substance called *chlorophyll*. Why is this green chlorophyll so widespread in plants? What does it do? These are questions that many men over long periods of time have asked and tried to answer. The answer has to do with the food-getting of green plants.

The ancient Greeks observed that the roots of plants thread their way into the earth like so many fingers. Also, it was clear to them that green plants did not eat food as did animals. They saw the tiny seeds grow into great trees or bushes or plants. So they thought that green plants in some way got food from the earth. They considered the earth a sort of great stomach.

Not until early in the seventeenth century were experiments made to find out what plants took from the soil. At that time, a Belgian scientist named Jan Baptista van Helmont [vän hĕl' mŏnt] weighed a twig from a willow tree and also a tubful of dry earth. Then he planted the twig in the tubful of earth and watched it

Van Helmont's willow-tree experiment. Why did the soil lose so little weight?

grow. Finally he removed the tree that had grown and weighed it and the earth in which it had grown. Amazingly enough, he found that the willow twig had gained 169 pounds in weight, but the soil had lost only a very few ounces.

Where did this additional weight come from? The ancient Greeks must have been wrong in believing that plants get food for life and growth from the ground. Of course, van Helmont had watered the soil frequently. But the tree was obviously more than just water. Furthermore, no plant or animal could live for long on water alone, for it is not a fuel or source of energy.

Green plants have been broken down, chemically, to find out what they are made of. They are made of certain carbohydrates, proteins, fats, minerals, and water. But chiefly they are made of a woody material called *cellulose* and contain large amounts of starch and sugar. In 1864 a German named Julius von Sachs [fŏn zäks'] showed that under certain conditions green plants can *manufacture* starch. Sugar is made first. Green plants make starch, cellulose, and even fats and proteins from this sugar.

What are the conditions necessary for starch manufacture? If you take a green leaf from a plant that has been in sunlight for an hour or more and remove the chlorophyll from it (instructions are given at the end of this

section), you can test it to see if it contains starch.

This experiment can be modified to help find out what conditions are necessary for starch to be made by a green plant. Test the leaves of a green plant that has been kept in a dark closet for several days. In the closet the plant does not get light.

Is chlorophyll necessary for starch manufacture? Place a plant with leaves that have white or colorless areas in the light for an hour or more and then test the white or colorless areas for starch.

There are ways of removing carbon dioxide from the air around a plant. Water can also be removed from around the plant's roots. After all these experiments are performed, a list similar to the following could be prepared.

The root systems of some plants are very large. How do roots serve a plant?

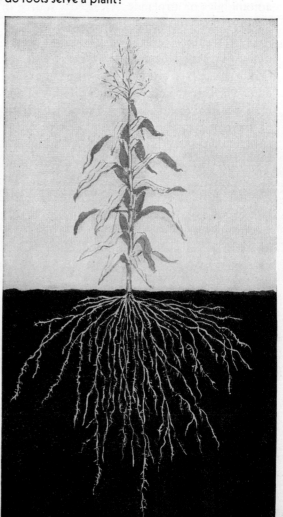

Conditions Necessary for Starch Production by Plants

	Starch Is Found	Starch Is Not Found
When green plants in air are placed in light	X	
When light is not present on the green plant		X
When nongreen parts of leaves are tested		X
When carbon dioxide is removed from the air		X
When water is removed from around plant roots		X

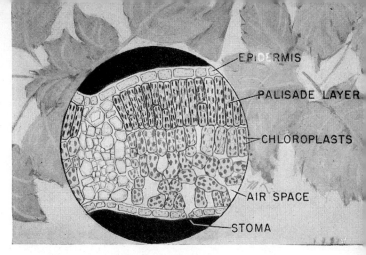

Section through a leaf. Air enters through a **stoma.** The **chloroplasts** contain chlorophyll.

Photosynthesis. Here, then, is what happens in green plants when they are in light and are getting enough moisture and enough carbon dioxide from the air. Chlorophyll enables water and carbon dioxide—with energy from light—to combine, forming sugar. This sugar is quickly changed to starch in the leaf.

The green plant actually manufactures food by *trapping* sunlight. The plant uses this energy to change two simple substances—water and carbon dioxide—to another substance—sugar. Sugar and starch can be burned in the bodies of living things. In burning, they release the sun's energy for growth, work, motion, heat, and so forth. When we eat plants or animals, we indirectly take into our bodies some of the sun's energy.

The process of manufacturing food with the energy of light is called *photosynthesis. Photo* means *light,* and *synthesis* means *manufacture,* so the word means *manufacture with light.* Here, in the green plant, is the source of food for all living things, plant and animal alike. Animals, even the meat-eaters, depend on green plants for food and energy.

WORKING WITH SCIENCE

1. Remove a *variegated leaf,* a leaf that has uncolored or white parts, from a living plant. Various ivy plants and geraniums have such leaves. Boil the leaf for a few minutes in water to soften it. Place the leaf in 95 percent alcohol and leave it until all the green chlorophyll has been dissolved and the leaf left colorless or nearly so. Then place the decolorized leaf in a dish and test it for starch as in Exercise 2, page 43. Do the parts of the leaf that were originally white or uncolored show evidences of starch manufacture? Explain.

2. Secure a potted green plant, such as a geranium. Place it in a dark room and leave it for a day. Fasten a square of heavy black paper to the top side of one of the leaves, using pins. Fasten the same sized piece of black paper to the under side of the green leaf, directly under the other piece of paper. Now take the plant to the window and leave it in the light (direct sunlight is best) for an hour or two. Remove the leaf, take off the pieces of paper, and test the leaf for starch as in the preceding exercise. Explain the results.

HOW LIVING THINGS ARE ADAPTED

All living things have certain characteristics—color, physical structure, ability to run or fly, and so forth—that enable them to live successfully and reproduce their kind. Some of these characteristics, or *adaptations,* protect them from other living things. Some adaptations enable them to obtain food. Other adaptations protect them from rain, cold, heat, and dryness. All plants and animals are adjusted, or *adapted,* to their surroundings.

Living things are adapted to the lives they lead. These jawbones are highly adapted. Study them and see what you can conclude about the food habits of a human being, deer, leopard, and beaver.

ADAPTATIONS FOR FOOD-GETTING

The wolf and the wildcat have sharp-pointed teeth. With these teeth they tear the throats and eat the flesh of animals on which they live. The dog and cat families, to which the wolf and wildcat belong, are meat-eaters. Such animals are called *carnivorous animals.* Their claws, teeth, jaws, muscles, digestive systems, and even their ways of living make them successful in stalking, killing, eating, and digesting other animals.

A deer, on the other hand, belongs to a large group of animals that are plant-eaters. Such animals are called *herbivorous* animals. If a deer had sharp-pointed teeth it would starve, for it eats certain grasses and the leaves and bark of certain bushes and trees. A deer is adapted for such food. It has flat front teeth, or *incisors*, that meet so as to provide a good edge for cutting such food. It has large flat back teeth, or *molars*, that are well adapted for mashing and grinding plant food. Its jaw

muscles, digestive system, and, to an extent, even its digestive juices are different from those of a carnivorous animal.

If you look at the molars of a dog, you will see that they are not flat like those of a cow or horse. A dog's molars have points, or *cusps*, on them. They are used to crush bones.

Did you ever see a dog trying to eat a piece of "chewy" candy? It has a terrible time. Its jaws move straight up and down, for it does not have muscles to swing its lower jaw back and forth, as we can. A dog has trouble chewing candy because it cannot move its lower jaw sideways. The candy sticks to its pointed teeth, which can only move straight up and down and are unable to move sideways to roll the candy over and mash it. The lower jaw of a cow moves sideways so that the grinding molars can slide over each other and mash plant food.

Mouth parts are not the only food-getting adaptations. Even the digestive enzymes of

138

carnivorous animals differ from those of herbivorous animals. For example, the saliva of a dog does not contain an enzyme that can digest starch. Starchy foods, such as potatoes, may make a dog sick. A dog should not be fed sweets or starches because it has trouble digesting them. A dog is a meat-eater and is not adapted for such foods.

Food-getting adaptations are many and varied. Reconsider the structure and living habits of the plants and animals discussed in Chapter 11. An ameba's ability to flow around particles of food in the water in which it lives is a food-getting adaptation. So are the cilia of sponges that whip water through pores in its body walls. The wings of a bat are a food-getting adaptation that enable it to fly through the night air in search of flying insects.

ADAPTATIONS FOR PROTECTION

Many of the most interesting structures of plants and animals protect them against enemies. Adaptations useful in food-getting may also be useful for protection against an enemy. Carnivorous animals protect themselves with the teeth and claws they use to get their food. Many wasps have stingers that are used to paralyze other insects or spiders which are then used as food for the wasp's young.

The same stinger can wound any animal that dares to try to harm the wasp.

Herbivorous animals often have structures used entirely for protection against enemies. Quite often such animals can run very fast and are very nimble. Rabbits often outrun coyotes and wolves that attempt to catch them. This is possible not only because of their speed in running straight but also because of their zigzagging and running under brush and other cover.

The great antlers and sharp front hoofs of many deer are a protective adaptation common among herbivorous animals. Among the many protective adaptations of plants and animals are the quills of a porcupine, the overpowering odor released by a skunk, the shape and color of many insects that keep them from being seen among leaves and twigs that they closely resemble, and the thorns and prickles of such plants as roses, thistles, cactuses, and blackberries.

OTHER ADAPTATIONS

Living things are highly adapted to the lives they lead. Adaptations help in reproduction. For example, the seeds of plants are tremendously varied in form and structure. Many, like dandelion and milkweed, have

What kinds of adaptations do you see in this illustration? If wolves ate mostly plant life, how might their appearance differ from that of this wolf?

American Museum of Natural History, New York

A mother skunk traveling with her brood. What kind of adaptation is a skunk's powerful scent? Why does a skunk need such an adaptation?

light structures that enable the wind to carry them far and thus distribute the plant widely.

Others, like appleseeds, are embedded in fruits that are good to eat. Animals eat the fruits and drop the indigestible seeds some distance from the parent plant. The coconut palm produces a seed, or coconut, with a light, fibrous husk. A coconut can float for hundreds of miles on the sea. Finally, it may be washed ashore, become buried, and develop into a young palm tree.

The cells lining your nose have adaptations that help move dust and germs out of the body.

From Encyclopaedia Britannica film Body Defenses Against Disease

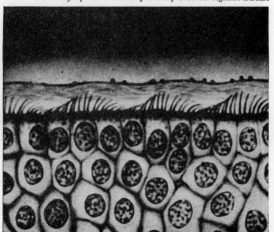

Many seeds, like the cocklebur, wild oat, and "sticktight," have hooks or stickers that catch in the fur of passing animals. They may be carried far before they become dislodged and fall to the ground with the chance of developing into a plant.

Other adaptations fit plants and animals to the climate of their surroundings. Some plants are well fitted for desert life, but would die in the moist soil and air of temperate regions. For example, a cactus is adapted to save what little moisture it can get in its surroundings. It has surface tissues that are thick and waxy so that water will not evaporate from the surface. The leaves of a cactus have been reduced in size and shape until they are not recognizable as leaves—but as the prickly spines and needles with which you are familiar.

The large reservoir stomach of a camel enables it to go for several days without water. Other animals would die under such conditions. The feet of a camel have great pads that spread out and keep the camel from sinking into the sand. Animals not adapted to life on the desert would find it hard to travel over the shifting sands.

Animals like the whale live in the deep cold waters of the ocean. Such animals often have thick layers of fat, called *blubber*, that protect the body against the cold.

MAN, THE ADAPTABLE

Man, of course, is no exception to adaptation. His habits vary greatly under different conditions. For example, an Eskimo eats much fat, for fat provides about twice as much heat per pound as sugars, starches, or proteins.

Men and women whose ancestors have lived for a long time in tropical or desert conditions usually have much dark coloring matter in their skin. This helps to protect the body from the intense heat of the sun. Not only Negroes, but also Caucasians ("white men") who have lived for many generations in such conditions have dark skins. The Arab and East Indian are good examples.

Man's most useful adaptations are these: He stands on his hind legs and, instead of two front legs, he has two marvelously adapted arms and hands. With them he can touch things, grasp objects, and move them about very gently or with great force.

Second, man has a chin, a mouth, and muscles of jaw and face that enabled him to develop speech. Thus, man can exchange his experience with others and learn from others. All other animals learn only what they experience directly. Speech enables man to cooperate with man so that together they may plan and work for their happiness, safety, and comfort. Third, man's brain is highly developed. Man is far more intelligent than the great apes, the next animals lower down the scale.

Man's intelligence, coupled with his ability to speak and to make tools, has made him undisputed master of the living world. Man can live in the cold parts of the earth, for he can make clothes and shelter and control fire to keep warm. He can live in the hot parts of the earth, for he can make shelter and cooling devices that no other animal can approach.

Man does not need sharp fangs and great claws or horns, for he can make weapons far more deadly than those of any animal. He does

141

A milkweed seed is attached to a silky windcatcher. How does this windcatcher serve the milkweed?

not starve if wild herds move away from where he lives, for his intelligence has enabled him to tame, or *domesticate*, animals and to plant grains, trees, and vegetables for food.

Animals that are highly adapted to particular conditions may become extinct when conditions change. Changed conditions make it hard for them to live. But man is not only highly adapted. His adaptations—intelligence, speech, and a grasping pair of hands—have made him able to adjust to changing needs and conditions. That is, man is not only highly adapted, but is also highly *adaptable*.

A flying squirrel glides through the air on an adaptation consisting of loose skin.

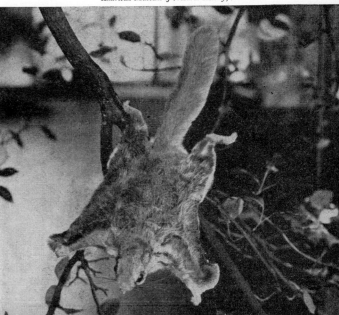

American Museum of Natural History, New York

What adaptation enables a beaver to cut down small trees to use in building dams and homes?

Man lives more widely over the earth and under greater differences in conditions than any other animal. Even so, except for a few unimportant differences, such as skin color and shape and color of hair, man is much the same wherever he lives. Man is adaptable. In addition, man changes or molds his surroundings to meet his needs and interests.

WORKING WITH SCIENCE

1. Trace several kinds of foods you eat to determine their original source. Do so for fish, beef, lamb, and other commonly eaten animals. What do you find is the original source of all our food?

2. It should be interesting to repeat van Helmont's famous experiment. Use a young sapling willow tree. Allow sufficient time for noticeable growth before final weighing. Be sure that you dry the earth carefully before you begin your experiment. Keep a record of the total weight of the water you use. How does the plant use this water? Does it use all of it? What happens to some of it?

3. See if you can figure out how plants get rid of waste materials. All living things, including plants, form waste materials that must be removed from their bodies in some way. Here is a hint: What happens to most trees as winter approaches? How do evergreen trees get rid of their waste materials? To answer this last question, look carefully at the ground under an evergreen tree.

4. Test some saliva secured from a dog's mouth

Man's hands are highly adapted. What highly specialized adaptation do man's hands possess?

Courtesy National Broadcasting Company

for its ability to digest starch. What do you find? (See the test for starch on page 43.)

5. Stock a school aquarium with water plants and with small fishes, water snails, and similar water life. The plants release oxygen that the animals need and serve as food for such small animals. The animals, on the other hand, release carbon dioxide that plants need and nitrogenous wastes that are useful in plant development. By properly balancing the number of plants and animals, you can maintain the aquarium so that it will need no attention other than the occasional addition of water that is lost through the process of evaporation.

6. Take a field trip to a fresh-water pool or ocean tidal pool and observe carefully the types of living things you find. Consider how they live together.

READING YOU WILL ENJOY

Bianco, Margery W. *All About Pets*. The Macmillan Co., New York, 1929. The care and training of pets, including material about turtles, toads, and other less common pets as well as cats and dogs.

Comstock, Anna B. *The Handbook of Nature-Study* (24th ed.). Comstock Publishing Co., Inc., Ithaca, New York, 1939. An interesting reference book in natural sciences.

Conant, Roger and Bridges, William. *What Snake Is That?* D. Appleton-Century Co., New York, 1939. A field guide to the snakes that are found east of the Rocky Mountains. Contains over 100 drawings to help you identify snakes.

Daglish, Eric F. *The Life Story of Birds*. William Morrow & Co., New York, 1930. Interesting and complete information about the lives of birds.

Ditmars, Raymond L. and Bridges, William. *Snake-Hunters' Holiday*. D. Appleton-Century Co., New York, 1935. An absorbing book describing the vampire bat and many other types of animals captured by the authors on one of their expeditions.

Emans, Elaine V. *About Spiders*. E. P. Dutton & Co., Inc., New York, 1940. A well-illustrated book about the interesting habits and lives of about 40 common American spiders.

Hoogstraal, Harry and Martinson, Melvin. *Insects and Their Stories*. Thomas Y. Crowell Co., New York, 1941. Delightful accounts of almost 50 insects, how they live, and where they are found. Well-illustrated with excellent photographs.

Hornady, William T. *Tales from Nature's Wonderlands*. Charles Scribner's Sons, New York, 1924. Absorbing stories about past and present animals, written by a former director of the New York Zoological Park.

Nelson, Edward W. *Wild Animals of North America* (rev. ed.). National Geographic Soc., Washington, 1930. Interesting and valuable photographs and writing about the most important big and small animals in this country, taken from articles in *National Geographic Magazine*.

Sanderson, Ivan T. *Animals Nobody Knows*. The Viking Press, New York, 1940. A book about 21 unusual animals with excellent illustrations as well as interesting writing.

The Book of Fishes (rev. ed.). National Geographic Soc., Washington, 1939. Contains almost 500 color pictures and over 150 photographs of fishes in addition to interesting accounts of their lives.

Our country has great natural resources. We still have vast forests, some wildlife, and rich croplands. Almost one-third of the United States is covered with forests or brush. In many parts of the country it is still possible to catch fish and to find enough wildlife for a successful hunt. Our croplands still produce abundant crops.

However, our resources can be exhausted. The United States Forest Service estimates that bad lumbering practices, fire, insects, and disease have reduced our valuable forests by some 40 percent in the last 30 years (1). With wise use—careful lumbering, replanting, cropping, and adequate protection from fire, insects, and disease—our forests can last forever and still produce all of the lumber and game we normally need (2).

Our wildlife has been greatly reduced in many areas. Over-hunting, destruction of normal living conditions and food supply, and general lack of regard for living things did the trick (3). But better wildlife management is possible and under the leadership of such agencies as the Fish and Wildlife Service, great progress is being made (4).

In many parts of our nation bad farming practices have resulted in serious erosion. Much valuable topsoil has been washed or blown away (5). As much as 60 percent of our farm land has been affected in some degree. But better farming practices are possible and are in effect in many parts of the nation. Under the leadership of agencies such as the Soil Conservation Service, much destruction has been stopped and farming practices that will prevent erosion have been started (6).

Bad practices are generally the result of lack of knowledge. With your knowledge of these problems, you can help greatly in the fight to conserve our resources.

13

THE WISE USE OF LIVING THINGS

One Saturday morning in July, 1945, a two-engined Army airplane crashed into the side of the Empire State building in New York City. Fog had made the building invisible. The airplane, flying dangerously low, struck at the 78th floor. Flaming gasoline was scattered throughout several floors of the great building.

For many hours fire raged on these floors. Fire, in a building of reinforced concrete and steel? What fed the flames? What did the fire burn? Many persons were surprised that such a modern building could burn. They did not realize how much wood is used in building and furnishing our most modern buildings. This fire was fed by the wood paneling in modern offices. It burned wood furniture, wood flooring materials, and wood used for decoration in various offices and rooms.

MAN'S USE OF THE FORESTS

Wood is more than holding its own with plastics, concrete, and steel. America is now using more wood and wood products than ever before.

Less than half the wood cut from our forests is used as lumber. Science has made possible many new ways to use wood. More than 10,000 different wood products have been listed. What are a few of these uses?

PAPER

The softwood forests, such as pine, fir, and spruce, are the main sources of paper. All our newsprint, many of our magazines, catalogs, paper bags, wrapping paper, cardboard cartons, and other similar products are made from *pulpwood* cut from softwood forests. These uses alone require tremendous amounts of timber. For example, about 80 acres of forest must be cut to produce paper for just one edition of a New York City Sunday newspaper.

SYNTHETICS

A product that man has made, usually by chemical means, is called a synthetic. Cellulose from wood is used in making many modern synthetics. Many plastics are made from a gluelike substance obtained from wood pulp. This substance is called *lignin*. Perhaps the comb in your pocket or purse is a plastic made from wood.

Rayon and cellophane are other familiar synthetics. They are made chiefly of cellulose from wood. This cellulose is treated chemically and then forced through tiny holes to form long fibers, or *filaments*. These filaments are twisted into threads, and the threads are woven into fabrics. In making cellophane the treated cellulose is forced through slits to form sheets.

Many dresses and other clothing are thus made from trees. Almost 80 percent of the rayon used in this country is made from wood. Rayon dresses, hose, robes, and fabrics are common today.

AIRPLANES FROM TREES

In making any modern airplane many wood products are necessary. Plastics are used in instrument cases, in electric equipment as

In hilly or mountainous areas bad floods may follow forest fires. Why?

panels, and so forth. One of the largest airplanes ever built is almost entirely a wooden plane. It is an eight-engined, 212-ton giant with a wingspread of 320 feet. It can carry 65 tons of cargo, or more than 750 passengers besides the crew. And it is made chiefly of thin sheets of wood glued together. Such wood is called *plywood*.

Plywood is made by a machine that holds a long knife against a rotating log so that it cuts off a thin sheet of wood. The sheet of wood unrolls much like a large sheet of paper. Several of these thin sheets are glued together with the fibers of the wood of the separate sheets placed alternately lengthwise and sidewise. The glue used is very strong. It is made synthetically from substances obtained from trees. Plywood has tremendous strength and is very light in weight. As a result, it is used widely in airplane construction.

OTHER USES OF WOOD

Other uses of wood range from lumber used in building to sugar and candy made from wood sawdust. Wood is still the chief or only fuel of many farm and country homes. Turpentine and rosin are obtained from certain pine trees, generally grown in the southern part of the United States. Charcoal is made by heating wood in the absence of air. Much leather is tanned by chemicals obtained from forest products. Many dyes and some wood alcohol are made from trees.

The annual value of forest products is more than $1 billion. Nearly one million workers are required to produce and process forest products into goods that we use. Forests are clearly one of our most important resources.

FORESTS HOLD THE SOIL

Forests have important values besides the products we make from them. For one thing, forests and brush keep soil from washing away. Not long ago in California a fire swept through a canyon whose sides and bottom were covered with brush and shrubs. In almost no time, some 5000 acres were laid bare. Just one month later, a 12-inch rainfall hit the canyon, causing a flood. The flood destroyed 200 homes and 34 lives in the valley below.

Just a few miles away was another canyon. The 12-inch rainfall hit this canyon too, but its natural plant life was still there. There was no flood down this canyon. The runoff of surface water was less than one-twentieth of that in the burned-over canyon. And the loss of fertile soil through wearing and washing away, called *erosion*, was only *one-thousandth* of that in the burned-over canyon.

FORESTS AND EROSION

When steep slopes are swept clear of timber, brush, or other natural cover by fire or other means, there is nothing to hold the soil and nothing to prevent water from rushing away in angry floods. To see why this is true, you have only to go to a timbered or forested area and dig down into the soil. In addition to brush, shrubs, and grass, a thick pad of dead leaves, twigs, and other material lies under the trees. This thick pad acts as a blanket that prevents the raindrops from hammering into the naked soil.

Furthermore, it acts as a blotter that soaks up much of the water and lets it pass slowly into the soil below. The leaves of the trees and shrubs break the fall of the raindrops.

146

Haven't we all ducked under the shelter of a tree during a rain?

Capillary Action. A forest prevents soil erosion and flooding in another way. Did you ever try to mop up water with a dry rag? If not, try it. Then try it again with a slightly damp rag. The dry rag does not work very well. The water does not seem to be soaked up, or absorbed. This is because water is absorbed by *capillary action*. In capillary action, a fluid rises in thin tubes or tiny spaces.

Dry soil, like a dry rag, absorbs water very slowly because the particles are too far apart for capillary action to take place. The thick pad on forest soil generally keeps the ground somewhat moist, so that rainfall is absorbed more quickly. Thus there is far less danger of water running off so rapidly that it floods the lowlands and carries away much

soil. The moist pad protects the soil.

Snows melt slowly when protected by trees because the sun's rays are broken by the branches. Thus, in the spring, snow on tree-covered land does not melt quickly enough to produce floods.

Forests as Reservoirs. Forests prevent flooding and soil erosion in even other ways. For example, they serve as reservoirs for water. Great quantities of water evaporate from the leaves of trees in the process of bringing water up from roots into the leaves for photosynthesis. Careful experiments indicate that one medium-sized tree will lose about 5 or 6 tons of water in a single hot day. This evaporated water becomes liquid again, or *condenses*, in very tiny droplets as clouds and finally as rain or snow. Remove forests and the rainfall and level of water in the ground are reduced.

WORKING WITH SCIENCE

1. Write to the American Forest Products Industries, 1319 Eighteenth Street, N.W., Washington, D.C. for the pamphlet *New Magic in Wood* or for other pamphlets that explain the many new uses of wood products. Write a report on the subject or give an oral report to the class.

2. If you live near a forested area, arrange a field trip to the forest. Note the nature of the soil and the litter of tiny twigs, leaves, and rotted material that covers the surface of the soil. Take a

sample of this material back to the classroom for the exercise that follows. While in the forested area, examine the trees. Do you find evidences of insect pests? Do you find trees that are rotting as a result of torn branches that have been cut off, leaving stubs? Note how a tree attempts to heal a cut by the growth of new tissue over the wound. You will note that a tree can heal a tiny cut, but that large cuts begin to rot.

3. Place the sample of forest soil with its top

Left and middle: Forest areas are covered with a thick pad of living and decaying plant materials. Right: Roots help keep topsoil from washing or blowing away. The subsoil lies below the topsoil.

Soil Conservation Service and other U. S. D. A. photos

litter in an open pan. Place a similar sized sample of soil without top litter in another open pan. Tilt the pans so that the surfaces of both soil samples slope the same amount. Now slowly pour water on the tops of the soil samples. Notice the absorption power of both samples. Examine the water that runs down to the bottom of the tilted pans. Pour this water out of each pan into separate glasses. Let the water settle. From which soil sample was there greater runoff of water? From which soil sample was a greater amount of soil washed away? Explain your results in terms of what occurs in a forested, hilly area before and after lumbering or fires have removed the trees.

WHAT IS HAPPENING TO OUR FORESTS?

At present almost one-third the area of the United States is still forest. The Pilgrims landed in 1620. More than 325 years later, we still have many forests in this country. But let us examine this situation more closely.

We still have about 630 million acres of forests. But not much of this is virgin forest. About 170 million acres are covered with trees and brush of no commercial value. Such forests and brush are valuable in preventing erosion and in providing watersheds. But they cannot be used for wood products.

That leaves 460 million acres of commercial forests. But according to the Forest Service, United States Department of Agriculture, about 77 million of these acres produce almost nothing because fires and harmful lumbering have ruined much of the timber. Of the remaining acreage, all but about 100 million acres have been cut over for lumber. And the cut-over forest is now able to produce only a small part of what it once produced.

Trees grow and develop like any other plants. It takes time for small trees to grow to maturity. In 1943 timber cut or destroyed was 50 percent greater than the amount of timber that grew to maturity in our forests.

Another way to look at the problem is to compare the standing trees that can be used for timber with those available some years ago. The Forest Service estimates that in the United States such trees have been reduced almost 40 percent in the past 30 years. It is clear that our forests are being destroyed faster than they are being replaced with new growth. What are the important destructive agents?

FIRE, INSECTS, AND DISEASE

A tree is a living thing. Like other living things, it has diseases and is damaged by insect pests. Fire, however, is the deadly enemy of the forests. The Forest Service estimates that the loss of timber from forest fires is $50 million every year and has been as high as $450 million in a single year.

Fires, insects, and diseases together destroy a tremendous amount of our forests every year. Much of this is preventable. But this loss is only about one-ninth of the total loss. Even more serious than fire is the carelessness of man.

BAD LUMBERING PRACTICES

Timber can be cut so that young trees are protected and continue to grow. By such lumbering practices, trees can be cut for lumber and be steadily replaced by young trees reaching maturity. Such lumbering practices require care and planning. Often they are more costly than to cut down all the trees and clear the ground.

About 90 to 95 percent of wood products are produced from trees owned by private citizens and corporations. A 1938 survey reported by the Forest Service states that about 80 percent of the lumbering on private lands was without regard to future crops of trees from the lands. On the other hand, increasing numbers of private owners of forests now follow sound lumbering practices.

WHERE DO WE STAND TODAY?

The facts appear to be these. We waste our forests through bad lumbering practices, neglect and carelessness, and fires. Most of this waste can be prevented. We still have enough forests to provide all the wood we are likely to need if better practices are used. But if we continue to waste our forests, before long we must reduce our use of wood and have a great tree-planting program to get back to the place where we can again use the wood we need. How can we conserve our forests so that such restricted use will not be necessary?

FORESTS ARE CROPS

A basic principle of the wise use of forests, that is, forest *conservation*, is that our forests can, and must, be thought of as crops much like crops of corn, wheat, or cotton. We must manage the forests and cut the lumber so that the forests continue to grow and maintain themselves. Many of our forests have been cleared to produce croplands. To an extent, this was necessary and desirable. Yet in vast regions totally unsuited to agriculture the forests have been so ruthlessly cut over, slashed, and burned that the land erodes badly and becomes worthless for generations to come.

Such waste is needless. Forests can be made to reproduce themselves so rapidly that for every tree that falls another tree reaches maturity. For example, in one southern state, a large grove of timber was bought by a lumber company. This company employed scientific foresters who worked out a program of lumbering with an eye to the future. They considered the timber as a crop to be cut and yet maintained so that it would produce lumber indefinitely.

They built mills and other plants so that the sawdust, slash, and wood wastes could all be put to use. This company has now operated at a good profit for more than 25 years, and *has as much timber in its grove now as when the company began operations.*

FIRE CONTROL

Next to careless lumbering, the forest's chief enemy is fire. Because more than 90 percent of forest fires are caused by man, we might say that 90 percent of forest fires can be prevented. Prevention of forest fires is largely a matter of using common sense in a forest. Here are common-sense rules to follow if we are to camp, play, or work in the forests. These rules are suggested by the United States Forest Service.

1. *Matches:* Be sure your match is out. Break it in two before you throw it away.

2. *Making camp:* Before building a fire, scrape away all inflammable [burnable] material from a spot 5 feet in diameter. Dig a shallow hole in the center, and in it build your campfire. Keep your fire small. Never build it against trees or logs or near brush.

3. *Breaking camp:* Never break camp until your fire is out—dead out.

Forest rangers of the Forest Service, U. S. Department of Agriculture, are constantly on the lookout for forest fires. After one is spotted, men and equipment for controlling it are rushed to the scene.

U. S. D. A. photos

4. *How to put out a campfire:* Stir the coals while soaking them with water. Turn small sticks and drench both sides. Wet the ground around the fire. If you cannot get water, stir in dirt and tread it down until packed tight over and around the fire. Be dead certain it is clean dirt containing no humus [decaying plant or animal matter]. Humus will hold fire. Better use lots of water and no soil when you can get the water. Be sure the last spark is dead.

5. *Brush burning:* Never burn slash or brush in windy weather or while there is the slightest danger that the fire will get away. Have water and tools at hand for instant use if the fire should unexpectedly start to spread. In some localities it is necessary to obtain a permit from a forest officer before brush-burning is allowed.

6. *Put out any small fires you can:* Report all fires to the nearest warden, ranger, or telephone operator.

UNITED STATES FOREST SERVICE

Forest conservation practices have developed as a result of the help of informed citizens throughout the country. The picture is still not as good as it could and should be. It will not be until our annual cut of timber is no greater than our annual growth and until our losses through fire, improper lumbering, insects, and disease are far smaller than they now are.

The situation demands that you keep informed about our forests—even if you do not live in the regions where forests are. Ask your state forester for information regarding forest problems. If you live in an area that was once forested but is now cut-over, you should be greatly interested in the scientific problems of rebuilding the forests.

Your state forester and his associates work under regional foresters of the Forest Service of the United States Department of Agriculture. The Forest Service maintains 12 forest experiment stations in various parts of the country. In these experiment stations research in forest growth and management, insect-and-disease-control, firefighting procedures, and so forth is carried on.

The Forest Service also maintains the Forest Products Laboratory at Madison, Wisconsin. There scientists study the uses of wood and develop new wood products.

WORKING WITH SCIENCE

1. If you live in a forested area, talk with your local forester about local forest problems. Write a report of the talk.

2. Arrange a field trip to a lookout station, if one is nearby. Describe its activities in a report to the class.

CONSERVING OUR WILDLIFE

Have you ever gone on a bear hunt or a deer hunt? Chances are that you have not unless you live in a forested or open brush-covered area.

Actually bear and deer are not hard to find in many parts of this country. In Yosemite and Yellowstone National Parks, black bears are so common that they often frighten campers by stealing food. And, of course, deer are plentiful and very tame.

In the national forests of the Sierra Nevada Mountains, it is not uncommon to see a hunter dragging out of the woods a large brown bear he has just killed. Such hunters seem to be having the time of their lives. And so are the dogs that prance around as if to say, "Look what we did!"

In certain parts of the country, geese and ducks are so plentiful that their cries sound much like the roar of a baseball or football crowd. Ducks, snow geese, "cracklers," "honkers," and other types of geese wing across the skies by the hundreds of thousands during the fall as they start their long flight southward.

OVERPOPULATION IS POSSIBLE

Believe it or not, in a few parts of the United States deer and other wild game are still so numerous that they occasionally become a menace both to people and to themselves. Proof that deer may become so numerous that they are a menace to themselves is shown in the experience of the Kaibab Plateau area of Arizona.

Some animal lovers believe that it would be kind to prohibit all hunting and killing of deer. Furthermore, some of these people believe that it is good policy to destroy all mountain lions and other *predatory animals* that kill and eat deer and other herbivorous animals. These groups were able to have their ideas supported by law in the Kaibab Plateau area of Arizona.

What happened? Most of the animals that kill and eat deer, that is, the deer's *natural enemies*, were killed and men were prohibited from hunting deer. The deer were so well protected that in a few short years their numbers increased tremendously. And then, one stormy, cold winter, thousands upon thousands of these deer died of starvation. There were so many of them that they literally ate one another out of all available food.

Most experts on wildlife management believe that not all bears, mountain lions, and other predatory animals should be killed. Enough of them should be left to maintain some sort of balance with the deer and other herbivorous animals. This is necessary to limit deer and other animals to numbers that can be maintained safely on the available food supply. For this reason, limited deer hunting is desirable in the interests of the deer themselves.

Unfortunately, two extreme points of view exist among people who are interested in hunting and fishing. Some people believe that no hunting should be allowed. Others believe that governments should not impose *any*

American Museum of Natural History, New York

The Kaibab Plateau lies across the Grand Canyon from these mountain lions.

restrictions on hunting. If we want to maintain our stock of wildlife, the second viewpoint is completely unwise. Without control, ruthless men would exterminate many kinds of wildlife just as they exterminated the passenger pigeon. The Kaibab Plateau experience shows that the other extreme is also unwise.

WILDLIFE MANAGEMENT

Our wildlife, like our forests, is a "crop" to be "harvested" but still maintained. Limitations on killing, trapping, and fishing are an important part of such management. In the natural balance of the forest, field, or stream—without man—each animal really lives off the excess wildlife.

If wolves or mountain lions kill too many deer in one year, next year there are so few deer that because of starvation the wolves and mountain lions themselves decrease in number or are forced to move on to other areas where deer or other food are in excess. In nature the weak and poorly equipped are the first to be killed by other animals or disease. The strong are likely to survive and reproduce.

When man enters their picture, he changes the balance seriously. For example, he kills most or all of the wolves and mountain lions. Then the deer become so numerous that they may starve. The most active and strong die just as quickly as the small and weak, for they

Soil and water conservation practices are closely related to good wildlife management. This farm pond, made from the eroded gully, was stocked with young fish and provides both recreation and food.

require more food than the small and relatively inactive ones.

Man may cut down the forests, drain the swamps, plant the grasslands in crops, and fence off areas that once provided food for grazing animals. Then the animals may starve. Certainly, if men hunted, fished, and trapped without restrictions, our wildlife would disappear or would be cut down to the few animals available in protected national parks or forest areas.

Good wildlife management does not mean no hunting, no fishing, no trapping. It means that experts, who study the food and shelter requirements of animals and make careful check on their numbers and changes in numbers from year to year, should limit the "take" of wildlife so that the population is stabilized on a sound level. In other words, man—who destroys the balance—must maintain the natural environment in which wildlife can reproduce and grow.

Hunting and Fishing Restrictions. How can you help in the conservation of wildlife? First of all, you must realize that hunting, fishing, and trapping regulations are not just to stop your fun. On the contrary, they exist so that you may continue to enjoy the outdoors and the pleasure of learning about the creatures of the wild. They are *for* you, as a hunter, fisher, trapper, or individual who likes wildlife.

If you play the game fairly, buy your licenses, and follow the rules, we need not fear that wildlife will be destroyed. If you refuse to play the game, wildlife will be harder and harder to find and hunting will disappear as a sport.

Money paid for licenses helps in many ways to maintain wildlife. It helps to pay the experts who study wildlife. It helps to pay for raising various kinds of wildlife for restocking. It helps to pay the game wardens who protect our wildlife from those few persons who insist on being game hogs in spite of the regulations. It is money well spent.

Individuals Can Help. All of us can help in the general program of wildlife management in several ways. One way is to try to make farms, fields, and yards good places for wildlife to live. Quail will not live on a farm if all ground is cleared, all brush burned, and all grass and fence rows cleaned up. Quail, rabbits, and other small game must have cover to live.

Those who live in towns or cities can do some things of value. Put out water and scraps of bread, suet, grain, and other food for birds in both summer and winter. Every year when the snow is deep thousands of birds die of starvation. In summer if water is not available, birds will go to outlying areas where they can get water. You can plant shrubbery and trees that will attract birds and at the same time beautify your home.

152

Above all, do not kill wildlife needlessly. Many persons have killed snakes, hawks or other wildlife because they had a mistaken idea that they were dangerous or harmed man's crops or domesticated animals. More commonly such animals are killed just for the fun of killing. This is particularly true of snakes and hawks. Snakes eat quantities of small gnawing mammals, or *rodents*, which are our real mammal pests. Kill the snakes, and the rats, mice, and gophers will increase.

The same situation is true of hawks. For years, experts of the United States Fish and Wildlife Service have kept careful records of the contents of the stomachs of all kinds of birds. From this work reliable information on the kinds of food that birds eat and the value or harm of birds has been obtained.

Certain of the sharp-shinned hawks, such as the Cooper, Goshawk, and Sharp-shin, which have no feathering on the lower leg, may occasionally eat a young chicken. But an occasional chicken is small price to pay for the mice and other rodents that are killed by these birds and the consequent saving in grains and other crops. Other kinds of hawks do not eat chickens at all.

It is entirely all right to kill game animals within the law, for such animals are an important contribution to the food of America. But it is another matter to kill needlessly, wastefully, and uselessly.

Organizations That Help. Among the organizations working to conserve wildlife are many private associations and governmental agencies. The governmental agencies include the United States Fish and Wildlife Service, the United States Department of Agriculture, the United States Forest Service, and the National Park Service. These agencies are all interested in wildlife conservation and have prepared interesting bulletins on the subject.

WORKING WITH SCIENCE

1. Study the hunting and fishing restrictions in your state. Why are the closed seasons when they are? Talk with an expert about the wildlife in your area. A Forest Service or a Fish and Wildlife Service man is an expert. Write a report of your findings.

2. Put out feeding stands, and feed and water birds around the school. This is a year-round project.

3. Make cages and learn to care for a variety of wild pets: snakes, white rats, turtles, frogs, lizards, salamanders, insects. Remember to release pets (except white rats) after you have studied them.

TOPSOIL, OUR MOST IMPORTANT RESOURCE

The soil is now, and may always be, the primary source of our food supply. Thus it is our most important natural resource. What have we done to our soil, and what can we do to conserve it?

First, just what is soil? Can't we dig deep into the earth and still find soil? Why worry about a wastage of that little bit of surface soil in which our crops grow?

Consider the size of this globe of ours, for a moment. Eight thousand miles in diameter. In a thin film on the outer surface of this globe are water areas and the land that we know. Covering some of this land is an extremely thin layer of material called *topsoil*. Topsoil varies in depth from one part of the world to another, but seldom is it deeper than the spade or plow that is plunged into the earth.

Beneath this extremely thin layer of topsoil is a heavier material called *subsoil*. You can generally see the difference between topsoil and subsoil. Where roads have cut through tiny hills or where land ends in small cliffs, you can generally see a thin surface layer of dark topsoil and beneath it a lighter-colored layer of subsoil.

But the differences between topsoil and subsoil are much more important than differences in color. Gather up samples of the two. Feel them and work them between your fingers. You who have gardened or farmed know what the difference is. Topsoil is "rich" and loose and crumbly, or *friable*. In it crops or luxuriant grass will grow. Subsoil is harder, less crumbly, and is generally clayey or sandy. Crops grow very poorly or not at all in subsoil.

FROM ROCK TO SOIL

Soil is made from rock. Soil lies like a skin over the rocky skeleton of this globe. Just under the subsoil is a layer of loose rock and broken rocky and sandy materials. These finally merge into the solid rock known as *bedrock*. In many places the bedrock has thrust through the soil, like bones through broken skin. And you know how useless it would be to plant a garden on such rock.

But the soil came from rock. The rock was broken up as rains and winds hit it and washed it, and as millions of years of heating and freezing of water forced particles of the rock apart. Such action is called *weathering*. Sand is the result of the wearing and weathering of some kinds of rocks. Sand does not look like soil, and it does not act like soil. It is not soil, but it is the first stage in the weathering of one kind of rock out of which soil is made.

LIFE IN THE SOIL

Through millions of years, tiny plants and animals have lived in this rocky, sandy material. Through their living and their dying, they have slowly changed it. As the animals and plants died, the minerals of which these living things were made settled into the rocky material, enriching it, and adding to the stuff that would become soil. Leaves, twigs, roots, and decayed body parts of millions upon millions of animals and plants mixed with the rocky materials. Thus soil was born.

Soil was born? That sounds as if it has a life of its own. Of course, it does not have. But the soil under your feet is teeming with life. It contains microscopic living things—worms, grubs, plant roots, fungi, algae, and a host of others. Without these, dirt would not be soil.

The living things in soil constantly change living and nonliving substances into different forms. Bacteria tear down dead plants and animals and release the elements so that new life may be born. Carbon is changed to carbon dioxide. Nitrogen from the air is trapped by certain bacteria which change this element into useful nitrogen compounds, such as nitrates, which plants use for food.

You noticed that topsoil is darker in color than subsoil. This color is caused by the decaying bodies of plants and animals or the waste products from living things. Such materials are called *humus*. Humus is extremely important to soil, for this material is partly protein and contains nitrogen, phosphorus, calcium, and other materials that are essential to life. Besides this, humus keeps the soil loose and acts like a blotter that absorbs and holds the life-giving water without which plants cannot live or manufacture food. Humus is the chief characteristic of rich soil; poor soil usually does not contain much humus.

ESSENTIALS FOR PLANT GROWTH

Plants manufacture sugar, but a plant cannot live on sugar alone. Plants, like man, need minerals. They can get them only from the soil and soil water. Twenty elements necessary for the fullest development of plants are listed in the table below.

Elements Necessary for Complete Development of Plants

Carbon	Manganese
Hydrogen	Copper
Oxygen	Zinc
Phosphorus	Boron
Potassium	Aluminum
Nitrogen	Iodine
Sulfur	Chlorine
Calcium	Fluorine
Iron	Molybdenum
Magnesium	Silicon

Of these elements only carbon and oxygen are secured directly from the air. Only hydrogen and oxygen are obtained from pure water. Each of the other elements must be secured from soil water and soil, or must be added to

U. S. D. A. photos by Forsythe

Left: Portable soil testing kits enable anyone to find out what minerals may be lacking in soil. Right: Applying lime with a homemade spreader to soil that tests showed to need it.

the water or soil for the fullest development of plants. Some of these elements are needed in such small amounts and are so commonly present in soil that we seldom need to be concerned about them.

But nitrogen, potassium, and phosphorus are used in large quantities by plants. These elements are easily lost through the runoff of water from land. They are also removed from soil, as rain water dissolves them and then flows to lower levels of the soil or to bedrock, forming a thin, sheetlike, underground lake. The underground lake may feed slowly out to streams, rivers, or the ocean.

WORKING WITH SCIENCE

1. Plant some pea seeds or other seeds in a sample of topsoil and subsoil. Water the soils equally, and give them the same treatment. Watch the results over a period of several weeks. What do you find?

2. Pick up some sand from the seashore if possible and examine it. Or get some sand from your local dealer in building materials. Try planting some seeds in this material, and let them grow for several months. At the same time that you plant these seeds, plant some of the same kind in rich topsoil. Be sure to provide the same moisture, light, and warmth to both. Compare their growth after a few months.

3. Study a cut in a hill where a road goes through, or examine a cliff. Notice the darker topsoil and the lighter subsoil. Examine several such cuts and notice variation in the depth of the topsoil. Look at various farm lands. Do you find some places where the lighter subsoil is showing through? If crops are growing there, is there a difference in their size and appearance from that of the plants growing around it? What do you conclude about the value of topsoil?

SOIL CONSERVATION

Probably 400 years or more are required to produce an inch of topsoil. When this country was settled the soil, like the forests and wildlife, seemed inexhaustible. A man could always move on when his land quit producing. He could farm it hard and savagely—sapping its strength and killing the soil. Although many good farmers farmed their land wisely, thousands crippled the soil and moved on.

In part they crippled the soil by removing forest and brush cover from slopes and land that should never have been cleared. They did it by farming too heavily with crops that sapped the minerals from the soil. They did

Left: Some soils have everything needed to grow good crops except water. Needed water may be supplied by irrigation. Right: Strip cropping on the contour helps prevent water erosion in sloping lands. Why?

it in dozens of ways—not willfully, but because of lack of knowledge.

OUR LAND TODAY

And how do we stand today? The Soil Conservation Service of the United States government makes careful studies of the condition of our land. They estimate that about 250 million acres—about 60 percent—of our agricultural land is eroding badly or is already so wasted that it does not provide a decent income.

Four hundred years to produce 1 inch of productive topsoil! And we have jerked the "skin" off the American earth in a few years. As stated by the Soil Conservation Service, "What it has taken nature thousands of years to give us, we have despoiled in two or three centuries at the most, and often in as little as 20 or 40 years, a mere clock-tick, in the span of eternity."

TO CONSERVE OUR SOIL

What can be done to save the soil? A basic principle is that the land should be studied very carefully and used only in keeping with the results of the study. Such conditions as rainfall, soil minerals, and slope must be considered.

Some land can safely be planted in corn, wheat, cotton, or tobacco. Other land should never be planted in such crops because they are planted in rows, and the soil between the rows is worked to keep weeds down. Such crops are called *intertilled crops*. Under certain conditions, intertilling increases erosion.

Conversion. Some land that is now farmed should be turned, or *converted*, to other uses. Land in regions of hot winds and little rainfall often cannot produce a crop that even pays for itself. Such land should be returned to forest, brush, or cover. Many steep hillsides that have been cleared and farmed should be returned to brush and forest. Only study of the land will indicate what should be done in any particular case. But beyond doubt some of our present farm land should be turned to other uses, including grazing.

Crop Rotation. One of our biggest soil conservation problems is created by the farmer who plants his land, year after year, in the same crop.

Plants vary in their requirements and in the minerals they take from the soil. By changing, or *rotating*, the crops planted in any particular plot of ground we can prevent the taking of too much of certain minerals from the soil. Such plants as alfalfa, beans, and peas, called *legumes*, should be included in the rotation, for they return nitrogen to the soil.

Fertilizers. Much land, including most backyard gardens, because of its nature or because of the crops planted, should be enriched by the addition of enriching materials, or *fertilizers*. Commercial fertilizers usually contain potassium, nitrogen, and phosphorus.

Irrigation. Very dry or desert regions may be successfully farmed by supplying water not naturally present. This is called *irrigation*.

Some of the richest and most productive land in this country lies in the great Imperial Valley of southern California. This land is rich with humus and minerals that were deposited long ago when this land was the bottom of a sea. The sea dried up long ago. Only water was lacking to make this land productive. Through irrigation, water was made available. The land is now farmed very successfully.

Strip Cropping. In certain regions very heavy rains fall in spring just when the land is ready for crops. In such regions, the crop rows, or *furrows*, should follow lines of equal height on the land. When furrows are plowed up and down the slopes, water rushes down the furrows in trickles or torrents, tears loose tons of soil, and bares the worthless subsoil in a few years.

There are many ways to prevent erosion of such land. These include *strip cropping, terracing,* and *basining.* You may be interested in studying more about them in the references at the end of this chapter. The Soil Conservation Service pamphlets are especially valuable.

Soil Conservation Service. The Soil Conservation Service of the United States Department of Agriculture is the chief organization that studies and works with our people on soil conservation problems.

The Soil Conservation Service carries on research into all kinds of problems connected with soil conservation. It sets up experimental plots of ground and demonstrates scientifically how various practices affect the soil, and which practices will conserve the soil and make possible the greatest production by the farmer. The Soil Conservation Service works closely with farmers and with experts of other governmental departments and agencies.

WORKING WITH SCIENCE

1. Attempt to find a farm in your community or near it which illustrates plowing around hills rather than up and down them. Ask the farmer what have been the actual benefits of this procedure.

2. See if you can find a farm on which rotation of crops is practiced. Talk with the farmer and report to the class on the advantages of crop rotation.

3. Talk with your agriculture teacher or county agricultural agent about the fertilizers recommended for use on land in your community. Report your findings about fertilizers to the class.

4. If you live in or near a forest or brush area, check on the litter on the forest floor. Dig into this litter and note the condition of the soil by examining it and crumbling it between your fingers.

5. Write to the Soil Conservation Service, United States Department of Agriculture, Washington, D.C. to secure information on soil erosion in the United States and what can be done to control it. Write a report based upon the pamphlets you receive.

READING YOU WILL ENJOY

DuPuy, William A. *The Nation's Forests.* The Macmillan Co., New York, 1938. A well-written and well-illustrated presentation of the history, present problems, and best practices in saving our nation's forests.

Gaer, Joseph. *Men and Trees.* Harcourt, Brace & Co., New York, 1939. The story of our trees and of the United States Forest Service. The problem of forest conservation that America is faced with is well presented, together with sound programs for maintaining this vital resource.

Lord, Russell, ed. *Behold Our Land.* Houghton Mifflin Co., Boston, 1938. The story of soil erosion, interestingly told.

The United States Forest Service and the Soil Conservation Service have many interesting and valuable pamphlets on conservation. To secure these materials write to the United States Department of Agriculture, Forest Service, Division of Information and Education, Washington, D.C.; and to the United States Department of Agriculture, Soil Conservation Service, Washington, D.C.

Not all living things are man's friends. Tiny plants and animals cause many diseases. Pests of many kinds attack and destroy many of the things he needs.

Science is continually working on new ways and new materials to fight pests of all kinds. Methods of control differ, but, if possible, they include killing the pest outright, increasing or protecting its natural enemies, destroying its breeding and living places, destroying its young, and at least attempting to keep it from getting at its normal food supply. In most cases, taking only one of these measures provides only temporary and local relief.

The fight against mosquitoes is an excellent example of the scientific use of all these methods of control. Mosquitoes (1) lay eggs and grow in either fresh or salt water. The egg hatches into a larva, or "wriggler," that requires air. This it gets through an air tube thrust above the surface of the water. The larva changes to a pupa and from the pupal case the adult mosquito emerges. Adult mosquitoes are

killed by many kinds of sprays, such as DDT and pyrethrum (2). Since fish eat mosquito larvas, increasing the number of fish in places where mosquitoes breed is an effective control measure (3). Digging ditches in swamps (4) may drain them, removing the breeding ground. Or it may allow water to flow in and out with the tide. Since mosquitoes do not lay eggs in running water, this measure is effective.

Mosquito larvas are killed by spraying water containing them (5) with light oils or pyrethrum larvicides. The oil kills the larvas by closing up their breathing systems. Screens with mesh not larger than 16 to the inch and new insect repellents keep us from getting bitten (6). Unfortunately, depriving the mosquitoes of human blood does not result in their starvation and death, but merely drives them to look for other animals. Only female mosquitoes bite. Male mosquitoes feed on nectar from flowers.

14

THE CONTROL OF LIVING THINGS

One way to conserve the plant and animal resources that man uses is to destroy the many pests that eat and destroy them. There are many kinds of pests. They include animals and plants from almost every one of the large groups mentioned in Chapter 11. But weeds, rodents, and insects are among the most important pests.

A *weed* is any plant that is out of place or unwanted where it grows. For example, Bermuda grass is a weed to many people who try to grow fine bluegrass lawns. Yet this so-called weed makes a very common and successful lawn in certain places where other grasses will not grow.

The definition of weed could be broadened to include all types of pests—weeds or otherwise. It would be hard to say that any living thing is always a pest, wherever it is found. Nevertheless, certain animals and plants are so constantly "out of place" or are so unwanted that they are considered as pests throughout the country.

Many of us put off controlling pests until serious damage is done. We plant fine gardens, and we study good books on how to control insects and other pests. Then we forget all about pests until they have become so numerous that our crops are pretty well ruined and the cost of killing the pests has increased greatly.

Keeping in mind our tendency to lock the barn door after the horse has been stolen, let us survey the pests that are common all over the United States and about which we should be informed.

RODENT PESTS

No group of animals can be more safely condemned as outright pests than the rodents, the gnawing mammals. The rodents include some of our most destructive pests and carriers of some diseases. Their small size, very high rate of reproduction, and their gnawing and burrowing enable them to thrive in the midst of the greatest cities as well as in our homes and on farms.

The United States Department of Agriculture estimates that our nation's loss of crops resulting from rodents is about $500 million a year. Think of the food and other crops that such a sum of money represents!

Sometimes huge fields of sunflowers are grown for poultry feeds. But in other places sunflowers grow where they are not wanted. Are they ever a weed?

U. S. D. A. photo by Forsythe

159

House rats spread diseases and destroy foodstuffs.

POCKET GOPHERS

This rodent burrows under the ground and eats the roots of valuable crops and young trees. Experts estimate that pocket gophers cost California alone about $8 million every year.

Pocket gophers may be controlled by traps, poisoned grain, and by *fumigation* with poisonous gases. Unfortunately, gardeners generally ignore gophers until they have cut off the stems of many of the best plants just under the ground. Then the gardeners set traps or place bait. But much damage has already been done.

MICE AND RATS

Mice and rats probably are the greatest rodent pests. Certainly they are the most widespread. They eat almost any kind of food and produce several litters of young a year. Control is difficult, largely because it is seldom carried out on a community-wide basis. Mice and rats move from one building to an-

Gophers do not eat money. Why are they pests?

other. For this reason it does little long-range good for a single home-owner to get rid of mice or rats, for they will spread out from the buildings of his neighbors. Then how can these pests be controlled?

Control of Rats and Mice. In the first place, every person should do what he can with traps, poisoned baits, or by fumigation. **Caution:** *Poisoned baits and fumigation should be handled by experts or by responsible persons only after they have studied carefully the suggestions made by experts.* Detailed instructions on control of rats and mice can be obtained from your county agricultural agent or the United States Department of Agriculture.

In the second place, everyone should encourage and cooperate with a community attack on rats and mice. City dumps and garbage piles where rats may breed should be controlled. Home garbage and refuse should be placed in covered metal or rat-proof cans. Storage bins for foodstuffs should be rat-proofed. All new buildings should be made rat- and mouse-proof. With such a program, poisons, traps, and fumigation will have lasting effectiveness.

Natural Enemies of Rodents. A third—and very important—part of rat and mouse control in rural areas is the protection of snakes, hawks, and owls that eat rats and mice. Weasels and skunks also eat large numbers of rats and mice. One expert of the United States Department of Agriculture has stated that all hawks, owls, and weasels in the country combined do not destroy one-sixth as much poultry and game as the common brown rat, and many of them are efficient enemies of both rats and mice.

Studies of the stomach contents of hawks and owls have proved their usefulness as natural controls of rodent pests. For example, owls eat small animals whole and then disgorge the bones and skin after digesting the meat. One study of 675 lumps of disgorged materials from the stomachs of barn owls showed 134 house rats, 452 house mice, and

160

1119 meadow mice! In a study of the stomach contents of 99 rough-legged hawks, 5 house mice were found in one stomach, 4 meadow mice in another, and 15 mice in a third.

There are other rodent pests and many, such as the cottontail rabbit, may be serious pests in some regions. Your county agricultural agent can give you reliable information on those that are pests in your area and on what you can do to control them.

WORKING WITH SCIENCE

1. Talk with your county agricultural agent or with farmers to determine what rodent pests are common in your locality. What methods of rodent control does he recommend? Are his services available to people living in your county for pest control?

2. Talk with your town or city health officer regarding the health problems resulting from rats in your community. Is there much of a problem? What is being done to lessen the problem? What suggestions has your health officer that you might follow in your home or neighborhood?

INSECT PESTS

Insects are undoubtedly man's chief competitors. An expert of the United States Department of Agriculture has estimated that our annual loss from insects averages more than $1½ billion. After all, more than 600,000 kinds of insects are known and probably many more have not been identified.

Most insects are tiny and evade detection. They are generally well adapted to the lives they lead and seem capable of considerable adaptation to differing conditions. They reproduce in tremendous numbers. Usually, the young of the insects cause damage to our crops and materials.

HOW INSECTS GROW UP

You would never fail to recognize the young of human beings, horses, cats, or dogs. But the young of many insects are totally unlike their parents. Insect young are called *larvas* (singular, *larva*). Examine the pictures on this page.

161

Most insects go through these four stages of change from egg to adult. These four stages of change are called *complete metamorphosis*.

Steps in complete metamorphosis, eggs enlarged.

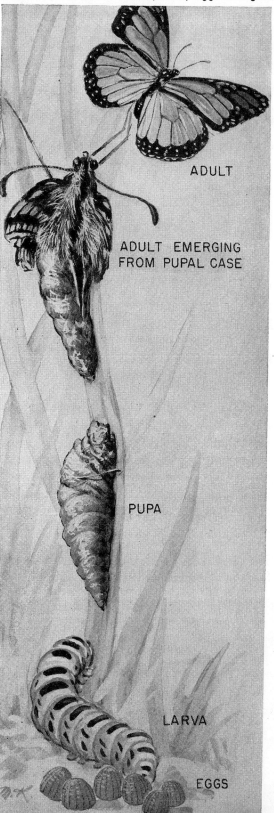

ADULT

ADULT EMERGING FROM PUPAL CASE

PUPA

LARVA

EGGS

Clothes moth eggs, larvas, and adults.

It is very interesting to place pupal cases of insects in wire cages and watch the adult insect break out sometime later on. It is even more interesting to take a caterpillar, together with the branch or plant on which it is feeding, and place it in a fine wire cage. Place the end of the plant in water or in moist earth and watch the larva form its pupal case. Then some months later, watch the adult moth or butterfly emerge with wet, folded wings. Watch it stretch its wings and finally, fully formed and beautiful, take to the air.

CONTROL OF INSECTS

Since much of the eating—hence, the damage—of insects is done in the larval stage, control measures often are based upon these eating habits.

Clothes Moths. Much damage is done by the larva of the clothes moth. The illustration at the left shows what the egg, larva, and adult look like. These are not actual size. The adult clothes moth does not eat and lives for only about a month. The adults lay tiny eggs on woolens, silks, or furs. Each egg hatches in a few days into a tiny larva with a tremendous appetite. Clothes and goods not used often are particularly subject to destruction.

Control of clothes moths is best carried on by dry-cleaning materials before storage to kill all eggs or larvas and then storing in bags or containers that moths cannot get into. Storing clothes in moth-proof containers does no good if the clothes already have moth eggs or larvas on them. Moth balls keep adult

Other insects, for example the grasshopper, go through *incomplete metamorphosis*, and the larva resembles the adult but is much smaller.

All insects that undergo complete metamorphosis hatch out of tiny eggs as small wormlike larvas. Caterpillars are the larvas of butterflies and moths. With the exception of earthworms, most of the "worms" and grubs that you find in the earth or on the ground and in trees and bushes are the larvas of insects.

After eating great amounts of food, the larva *pupates*. That is, the larva forms a hard covering, or spins a *cocoon*, in which remarkable changes occur. Out of the pupal case comes the adult insect.

Japanese beetles have two enemies—a tiny wasp and the milky-white disease. Middle: a larva of the wasp feeds on a Japanese beetle grub. The grub at the far right has the milky-white disease.

Bureau of Entomology and Plant Quarantine and other U. S. D. A. photos

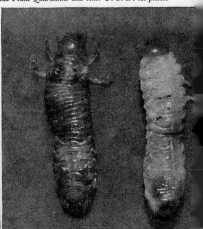

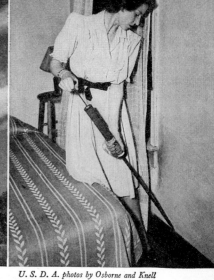

U. S. D. A. photos by Osborne and Knell

Left: Spraying an apple orchard to control insect pests. Middle: Many insecticides may be spread by airplane or helicopter over large areas. Right: Dusting or blowing insecticides behind baseboards is often necessary in controlling household insect pests.

moths away but do not destroy moth eggs and larvas already present. Paradichlorobenzene, in sufficient quantity, will destroy both eggs and larvas.

Houseflies. Houseflies hatch from eggs laid in garbage and refuse. Their eating preferences range from the best that baby's bottle and our table afford to the garbage can, toilet, and manure pile. Flies are filthy creatures and carry many food- and water-borne diseases.

One female fly in the spring may be the ancestor of millions of flies before the end of summer. Kill a fly in the spring and you will prevent millions from being hatched. "Swat that fly," is a slogan that we all should heed. However, the best method of fly control is to destroy the garbage, animal wastes, and filth in which flies lay eggs.

Fleas and Lice. Adult fleas and lice feed on the blood of animals which they suck through tubelike mouth parts. Their "bite" is irritating and can carry such diseases as typhus (carried by lice) and bubonic plague (carried by fleas).

A female flea lays eggs usually on the body of a dog, rat, or other animal. These eggs often drop off and lie in cracks, on rugs, or on the open ground. In places where the weather is never very cold, the eggs on the ground and the larvas and adults into which they grow may be a constant source of infection for household pets.

The eggs hatch into very tiny larvas. These eat animal or vegetable matter for a few days and then pupate. Finally they emerge as high-jumping adults, ready to attack your pets. Certain kinds of fleas attack human beings. Fleas and lice may be controlled by keeping clean and by regular dusting of pets with flea powders.

Common Garden Pests. Any insect has one of two kinds of mouth parts. Some, like the flea, have sucking mouth parts. Some, like the larva of the flea, butterfly, or clothes moth, have biting or chewing mouth parts.

These two kinds of mouth parts are adaptations for different eating habits. Control of garden pests rests largely on two ways of poisoning, one of which is useful for the sucking insects, and the other for biting insects.

INSECTICIDES

One group of insect-killers, or *insecticides*, consists of poisons that are sprayed or dusted on plants that are eaten by biting insects. Such poisons are known as *stomach poisons*. Biting insects actually bite off particles of plants and swallow them. A stomach poison attacks an insect on reaching its digestive tract. Arsenic

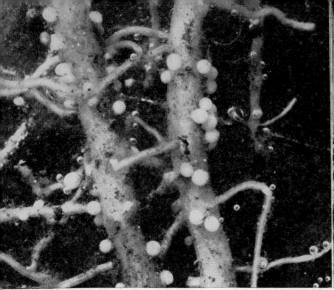

U. S. D. A. photos by Mead

The roots of the potato plant at the right were attacked by a tiny garden pest called the *golden nematode*. Each of the enlarged golden balls at the left contains from 200 to 500 nematode eggs. See if you can find out how this pest is controlled.

and its compounds are among the most common stomach poisons used. In using arsenic poisons caution must be observed, for arsenic is a poison to man and must be washed off fruit or vegetables that have been sprayed.

Stomach poisons have no effect on insects that stick a needle-like sucking tube into a plant and suck juices from the inside. Such sucking insects must be killed by spraying or dusting materials directly on the insect itself. Such poisons are known as *contact poisons*. Among the most common contact poisons are nicotine preparations, lime-sulfur sprays, and certain oils. The oils work by stopping up the openings of the breathing tubes of the insects.

Biting-Insect Pests. Among the common biting-insect garden pests are the grasshoppers, the "June beetles," and similar beetles whose larvas are white grubs with biting mouth parts. The Japanese beetle is in this group also. It was introduced from abroad in 1916 and has created havoc since then in the eastern United States. Cutworms, which are the larvas of moths, do great damage. They stay underground during the day and emerge at night to eat the leaves and stems of garden plants. Quite often they cut off the plants completely just at the base of the stem.

The chief control of biting insects is spraying or dusting with stomach poisons. Other methods are useful, too. Cutworms may be picked off plants at night or dug out of the top inch or so of soil during the day. Potato bugs or any large insect, for that matter, can be picked off plants by hand.

Aphids. By far the most numerous and widespread of the sucking insects is the plant aphid. This insect has a very efficient sucking tube and a very large appetite. There are many kinds of aphids, and they attack a wide variety of plants, including roses, corn, trees, and vegetable plants. They jab their beaks into the tissues of the plants and suck so much of the plant juice that the plant may wilt and die. Often their attack so weakens a plant that it becomes easy prey to fungi and bacterial diseases.

An interesting point concerning aphids is that they secrete a sweet fluid known as *honeydew*. Cars parked under trees are sometimes covered by this sticky fluid. Some kinds of ants are fond of this liquid. They actually care for the aphids and "herd" them about to good, juicy plants.

Plant aphids are controlled by contact sprays. These must reach the undersides of leaves as well as the tops, for the spray must actually hit the aphid to kill it. Control of ants by means of poisonous syrups and by destroying their nests aids in controlling aphids.

Scale Insects. Another common and destructive group of insects consists of the *scale insects.* Probably you would not recognize most of them as insects at all. Many of their body parts have become so changed that they do not look like insects. In addition, they secrete a scaly or mealy covering. The mealybug is a scale insect that causes great damage to citrus trees, such as orange, grapefruit, and lemon. In controlling scale insects, oil contact sprays and lime and sulfur sprays are useful.

CLEAN-UP CONTROL

Two other methods of controlling insects are important. The first is to clean up weeds, refuse, and trash from gardens. These should be burned or treated to make fertilizer so that eggs, larvas, or adult insect pests cannot pass the winter in them.

NATURAL ENEMIES

The second method is to encourage natural enemies of the insect pests. Sparrow hawks, woodpeckers, and above all the *perching* birds, such as the robin, song sparrow, junco, bluebird, and similar small birds, eat great quantities of insects and weed seeds.

Every such bird aids effectively in the war against insects. Other animals help, too. Even certain insects are of great value. For example, the ladybird beetle was imported to California from Australia to combat the cottony-cushion scale, which was ruining gardens and orchards. It was most effective in controlling the scale. Ladybird beetles are of great value in controlling other insect pests.

The chief insects that live parasitically on insect pests are the wasps. Ichneumon flies and other members of the wasp family have done invaluable service to man in combatting insects. The illustration on page 162 shows how the larvas of tiny wasps and flies destroy harmful insects.

DDT IN INSECT CONTROL

One of the newest and most powerful weapons for fighting insect pests is a chemical called *DDT.* DDT was introduced and used widely during World War II. It is a contact poison, and it paralyzes many kinds of insects and brings about their death. DDT's chief advantages are that only a small amount is needed to kill insects, and the substance is effective for several months.

DDT need not be sprayed directly on insects to kill them. In experiments walls have been sprayed with DDT. For several months, flies

Left: A Mormon cricket shedding its skin at one stage in its growth. Middle: Sweet clover plants stripped of leaves by grasshoppers. Should stomach or contact poisons be used in controlling crickets and grasshoppers? Why? Right: Identifying an insect is the first step in controlling it. Why?

U. S. D. A. photos by Forsythe, Hufnagle, Rothstein

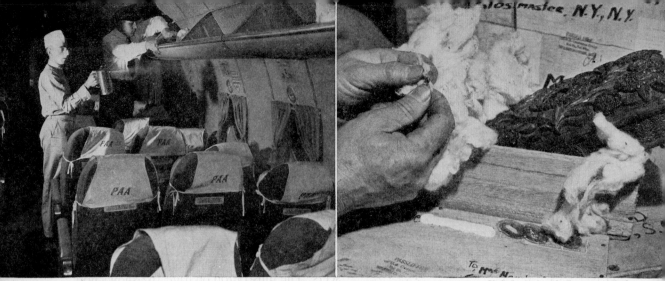

U. S. D. A. photos by Forsythe and Knell

Officers from the U. S. Department of Agriculture and U. S. Public Health Service inspect a plane just in from a foreign country for diseased plants and disease-carrying insects. Right: A Foreign Plant Quarantine inspector removing pink bollworms from cotton packing from a foreign land.

and other insects that walked on the walls became paralyzed and died.

The biggest disadvantage of DDT is that it kills many useful insects as well as insect pests. For example, if DDT is sprayed on crops before or while they are blooming, the bees and other insects that pollinate the flowers are killed along with the insects that eat and destroy the crop. Thus, such crops do not produce fruit. Great care should, therefore, be taken in using DDT particularly when it is to be used over large areas.

WORKING WITH SCIENCE

1. Make a collection of insects found in your area. Which are pests? Get information from textbooks and from your county agent. What control should be used? Study mouth parts with hand lens.

2. Look up recent articles on DDT in papers and magazines. Compare the information obtained from these articles with the information on DDT obtained from the United States Department of Agriculture.

3. Spray DDT on the screens or window sills of the schoolroom. Observe what happens to flies that come in contact with either the screens or the window sills.

WEED CONTROL

The task of removing weeds from a garden or lawn is reason enough—so many have decided—to live in a city apartment where only a potted plant can be grown. Weeding is hard, back-breaking work. Yet it must be done, for weeds compete with garden plants and grass for light and moisture. If weeds are not removed from gardens, crops are seriously stunted. If they are not removed from lawns, they eventually crowd out the grass.

2,4-D WEED CONTROL

The announcement of the development of the chemical called *2,4-D* was good news for those who love attractive lawns and yet hate weeding. This chemical, when sprayed in proper dilution, kills broad-leaved weeds, such as plantain and dandelion, but does no serious harm to the narrow-leaved grass plants. 2,4-D poisons the entire plant and kills it, roots and all.

166

Unfortunately, 2,4-D cannot be used to destroy weeds in vegetable or flower gardens unless it is sprayed very carefully directly on each separate weed, for this chemical kills all broad-leaved plants—crops, flowers, and weeds alike. So there is still work for man to do in weed control. Besides, the ground would still need cultivating even if no weeds were present. Cultivating breaks up the soil, providing the roots with needed air and conserving the moisture in the soil. If the surface soil were not broken up, the water would rise to the surface as ink travels in a blotter, only to evaporate uselessly into the air.

THE ETERNAL FIGHT AGAINST PESTS

Man has learned to control many natural enemies. But his fight is never won, for living things adapt themselves to changing conditions. Almost as fast as man discovers how to control a pest, new forms develop or more resistant types of the old ones appear, requiring further research and new techniques of control. The fight appears to be endless.

WORKING WITH SCIENCE

1. Look up recent articles on 2,4-D in papers and magazines. Compare information obtained from these articles with the information obtained from the United States Department of Agriculture.

2. Experiment with 2,4-D by spraying weeds in the schoolyard and observing the results.

READING YOU WILL ENJOY

Duncan, Carl D. and Pickwell, Gayle. *The World of Insects*. McGraw-Hill Book Co., New York, 1939. A well-illustrated book that gives information on the habits and values of insects as well as on how to control the harmful ones.

Our Insect Friends and Foes and Spiders. National Geographic Soc., Washington, 1935. Pictures and accounts of over 500 insects and spiders, taken from articles on these subjects that have appeared in the *National Geographic Magazine*.

1

2

3

One way for man to conserve biological resources is to increase production. This often means that types of plants and animals that will give a greater return for the time and money spent on them are required. For example, a typical hen produces about 80 eggs a year. But man has developed hens that produce as many as 300 eggs a year at little additional cost for feed. If you were raising chickens to market their eggs, which kind would you prefer?

Modern plants and animals differ from their early ancestors in many respects. Some of these changes occurred naturally over millions of years as conditions on the earth changed. The plants and animals that adapted themselves successfully to the changed conditions survived; those that did not perished. But man himself is able to promote changes in living things. This he does by using principles of genetics, the science of how living things inherit various characteristics.

Changes that occur naturally usually occur more

slowly than those produced by man. For example, Eohippus, the ancestor of the modern horse lived about 55 million years ago and was a tiny animal about the size of a domestic cat (1). By the time man domesticated the horse, it had become an animal about 4 feet tall. From this "wild horse" (2), all modern horses have been developed—from the giant draft horse to the agile race horse (3). The changes promoted by man have all occurred in just a few thousand years; most of them within the last few hundred.

Modern corn probably developed from a wild type of corn that grew long ago in the lowlands of South America. By the time of the discovery of America, corn was being grown in many parts of North and South America. The Incas of Peru (4) and North American Indians (5) grew corn, but it was different from modern varieties. Modern hybrid corns (6) produce much greater yields of far better quality than native varieties.

4

5

6

15

THE IMPROVEMENT OF LIVING THINGS

World War II required many new kinds of machines and devices. It also required the improvement of many already in use. New vehicles called ducks, capable of moving swiftly on land or water, were invented. Jet-propelled planes with speeds almost as fast as sound were made. Radar equipment for locating enemy planes and ships came into being. Atomic bombs were developed and used.

When necessary, man has amazing ability to invent devices to meet his needs.

However, man cannot invent a new living thing. Man is not able to produce living substance in any form. He cannot decide that he wants a very speedy horse or a corn plant 10 feet tall or a fox with blue fur or a grapefruit with pink flesh and then sit down in his laboratory and invent them.

MAN TAKES OVER FROM NATURE

While man cannot invent new living things, he has developed horses of great speed and corn plants far more than 10 feet tall. He did so by taking a tip from nature. Long before man appeared on earth, plants and animals had lived for millions of years. During these millions of years, they had changed tremendously. The record of these changes is told by the remains of plants and animals that lived millions of years ago. Such remains are called *fossils*. They consist of rocky likenesses of animals and plants or their parts.

LIVING THINGS HAVE CHANGED

From fossil remains, we know that the earliest horses were only about as big as rabbits. Through millions of years, such changes occurred that the descendants of the early horses finally became modern horses. Plants and animals of all kinds have changed and become varied naturally. Then, long ago, man began to domesticate plants and animals. And man learned how to speed up the changes that produce new kinds of living things.

Just when man began to domesticate plants and animals, no one knows. It seems likely that early man was first a hunter. Later on he became a wanderer, or nomad, following his tiny herds of domesticated animals from one pasture land to another. Finally he settled down and became a farmer, or agriculturist.

We can guess how these changes took place, but only guess. Probably at some stage in human history man realized that it was too much trouble to follow herds of animals. He captured some of them and kept them tied up until they became accustomed to him and to the food and shelter that he could give them. In this way man learned to domesticate animals. He killed enough of the offspring for food and clothing but always kept enough for reproduction. He learned to make animals serve as beasts of burden.

Later on, man must have realized that there were great differences, or *variations*, among the animals he kept. Some were big-boned and lean, and others were relatively small-boned and fat. Some were short-legged, and some

U. S. Coast Guard photo: U. S. D. A. photo

Man invents new devices, but he develops new plants and animals by speeding up natural processes.

were long-legged. Some were strong, and some weak. In other words, man realized that *living things vary.*

SELECTIVE BREEDING

Early man probably most often killed for food the animals that were weak or in other ways not adapted to the use for which he kept them. Probably he kept the best animals and allowed them to bear young more commonly than the animals of poor quality. Consciously or unconsciously, he was improving his animals by *selective breeding.*

Changes in Wheat. Probably the same development is true of grains and other plant crops. Wheat has been found in the Egyptian tombs—wheat that is at least 6000 years old. Wheat is a grass. We do not know from what wild grass or grasses the modern wheats have come. Some experts believe that a wild grass called *emmer,* which has been found in Pales-

tine, may be the forerunner of modern wheat.

But whatever its origin, wheat is now grown in almost all parts of the world. The United States, Russia, China, Canada, India, Australia, France, Argentina, Spain, and Italy all raise large amounts of wheat. But the kinds of wheat often grown in one country differ from the kinds of wheat grown in another. In most cases, wheats are adapted to the land on which they are grown. None are like the Egyptian wheat. All of them bear far more heavily than the emmer plant.

Many modern wheats have been developed by man through careful scientific work. Some of them produce fat, heavy heads of grain of much better quality than wheats commonly planted just a few decades ago. Hardy wheat varieties that are resistant to cold and frosts have been developed. Wheats have been developed that are resistant to the *rusts,* fungus diseases that cause great losses to wheat crops.

WORKING WITH SCIENCE

1. Use an encyclopedia to determine what is known concerning the history of the development of various forms of crop plants such as corn, wheat, rye, and oats. Write a brief report on the probable origin and development of one of these crops.

2. Use an encyclopedia to determine what is known concerning the origin and development of various forms of animals such as dogs, cats, horses, sheep, pigs, and cattle. Write a brief report concerning the changes in one of these animals.

HOW ARE NEW VARIETIES PRODUCED?

Several years ago the celebrated and widely grown *Marquis* wheat was developed.

Its parents were kinds of wheat that are called *Red Calcutta* and *Red Fife.* Wheat

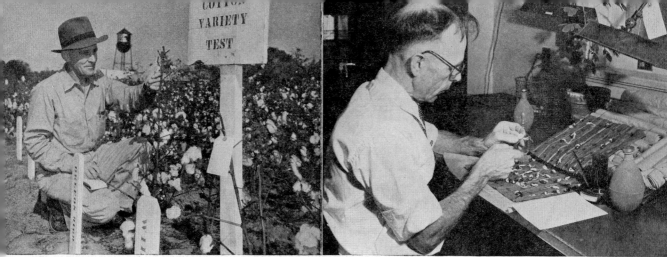

U. S. D. A. photos by Forsythe and Knell

Comparing new varieties with older or parent varieties of plants. Left: Testing new varieties of long-staple cotton. Right: Testing seeds of a variety of garden bean to see how well they sprout.

plants, like many other plants, produce pollen grains, which contain male sex cells, in male flowers. They produce eggs, or *ova*, which contain female sex cells, in the female flowers.

HYBRIDIZATION

Ordinarily, the pollen of one kind, or *variety*, of plant fertilizes the ova of a flower of the same variety. For example, Red Calcutta is a variety of wheat. Ordinarily it is fertilized by pollen from Red Calcutta. The same is true of Red Fife wheat. But often man can take pollen from one variety of plant and *artificially fertilize* a different variety of the same group, or *species*. This process is known as *hybridization*.

When Red Fife was crossed, or *hybridized*, with Red Calcutta, a hybrid wheat superior to both was produced. Marquis wheat matures early and generally escapes rust. It produces high yields of grain that are excellent for flour. Since about 1915, it has been the chief spring wheat grown in this country.

Sometimes one variety of plant or animal can be crossed with a plant or animal of another closely related species. For example, wheat has been crossed with rye, barley, and other grasses. At present, experts are trying to cross certain grain grasses with grasses that are particularly able to grow in dry country and to hold eroding soil. The hybrids produced may conserve the soil in addition to producing crops. Scientists hope to produce a wheat that does not have to be planted each year. New plants would grow from the previous year's roots.

Left: Collecting pollen from a parent corn plant in developing a new hybrid. Right: Using the collected pollen in pollinating the other parent. The silk is then bagged to keep out other pollen.

U. S. D. A. photos by Purdy

Left: A new breed of cattle that resists high humidity, heat, and insects, obtained by crossing Brahman and Africander cattle with Aberdeen-Angus. Right: A champion milk-producer, a Holstein-Friesian.

Cross-Breeding Animals. Our chief breeds of horses, cattle, sheep, poultry, dogs, and cats have been developed by selective breeding combined with *cross-breeding*. For example, outstanding *Brahman* cattle were crossed with the best selection of *Aberdeen-Angus* cattle in efforts to produce a *cross-breed* superior to either parent type. Cross-breeding is followed by careful breeding of closely related stock, such as brother-sister or father-daughter. Breeding closely related stock is known as *inbreeding*.

MUTATION

Occasionally among animals and plants an offspring that is quite different from any of its parents develops without hybridization. When such a change occurs and the offspring is able to reproduce more of its kind, that is, it *breeds true*, we say that a *mutation* has occurred.

One valuable mutation occurred in 1791 when a lamb with very short legs was born. The Massachusetts farmer who owned the lamb saw that such sheep could not jump high and hence could easily be fenced in. The animal was bred with ordinary sheep, and some of the offspring were also short-legged. These were inbred and bred true, thus establishing the line of sheep that became known as the *Ancon*.

WORKING WITH SCIENCE

1. Ask your county agricultural agent or a farmer to talk to your class about new forms of hybrid crop plants that are being used. Ask him to explain how seeds of hybrid corn are produced.

2. Mutations are produced in scientific laboratories by the use of x-rays. The animals used for such experimentation are the tiny gnats known as fruit flies. Use *Readers' Guide to Periodical Literature* to locate articles about this work. Check under *genetics, fruit fly, mutations,* or *drosophila* (the scientific name of the fruit fly). Report to the class on your findings.

HOW DO HYBRIDIZATION AND SELECTIVE BREEDING WORK?

Hybridization and selective breeding produce offspring that are different, and often better, than their parents. The modern science of *genetics,* the science of how living things pass on certain characteristics to their offspring, has discovered many important facts.

These facts are of great importance in modern plant and animal improvement. The fundamental study of inheritance upon which much of more recent scientific study has been based was made by a monk whose hobby was gardening.

172

MENDEL STUDIED THE INHERITANCE OF PEAS

In 1866 an Austrian monk named Gregor Mendel [měn′ děl] published the results of his many experiments in producing different types of plants. His work consisted mainly of studying varieties of the common garden pea plant. He crossed, or hybridized, certain pea plants, such as tall with dwarf varieties and those that had wrinkled peas with those that had smooth peas in the developed pod.

Mendel's Experiments. He found out an interesting fact. When he crossed tall peas with dwarf peas, the offspring—the first generation—were not middle-sized, as you might think, nor were they of all sizes from tall to dwarf. *They were all tall.* When the plants producing wrinkled peas were crossed with those producing smooth peas, the offspring all produced smooth peas.

But here is the truly remarkable fact that Mendel discovered. When the first generation of offspring of tall and dwarf parent peas were crossed among themselves, their offspring—the second generation—varied in the ratio of three tall to one dwarf. The second generation of the original wrinkled and smooth pea plants were in the ratio of three smooth to one wrinkled, although the first generation had all been smooth.

Dominance. Mendel realized that something in the tall pea plant made tallness overcome, or *dominate*, the dwarfness of the other pea plant. Tallness and dwarfness, smoothness and wrinkledness are *physical characteristics* of the pea plants. His many experiments led him to conclude that when different *purebred varieties* of pea plants are crossed, certain characteristics of one (such as tallness) will dominate the contrasting characteristic (in this case dwarfness) in the offspring. A purebred variety is a variety whose ancestors are all alike, that is, belong to the same variety.

HOW ARE PHYSICAL CHARACTERISTICS INHERITED?

Mendel did not know why one characteristic dominated another, for he did not know

Gregor Mendel in his garden.

how physical characteristics are inherited. Even today, our knowledge is far from complete. But geneticists have learned much since the time of Mendel.

We know that the young of all higher plants and animals are the result of the union, or joining, of sex cells. In animals these sex cells are the egg, or female, and the sperm, or male. If you examine an egg and a sperm under a microscope, you find that the nucleus of each contain strands of material called *chromosomes.*

Chromosomes and Genes. The number of chromosomes in the cells of any plant or animal is always the same. For example, each cell of a rat always has 16 chromosomes in its nucleus; each cell of a man always has 48. These chromosomes are believed to carry material that determines what the offspring will be like. In other words, the chromosomes

White are dominant characters; black, recessive.

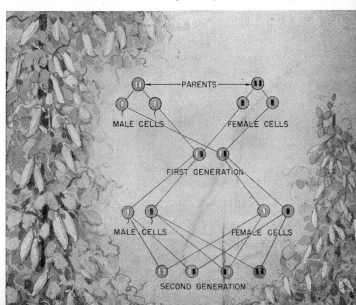

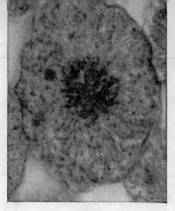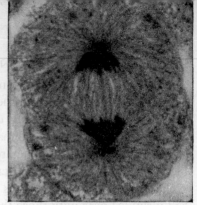

Courtesy Bausch & Lomb Optical Company

In cell division the chromosomes split lengthwise and the two cells end up with the same kinds of chromosomes. In the last photomicrograph, the cell is about to divide.

carry determiners, or *genes*, that enable the offspring to inherit physical characteristics, such as eye color, shape of nose, and so forth.

The photomicrograph below is an enlargement of the giant chromosomes in cells of the salivary glands of the little fruit fly which so often hovers over ripe or rotten fruit. Notice the dark bands on these chromosomes. These dark bands are thought to be the genes, or determiners. When some of these bands in the sex cells of a fruit fly are destroyed or changed, the offspring of that fly lack some characteristic or are different in some respect from a normal fly. Thousands of experiments with fruit flies have enabled scientists to learn, in some cases, just what part of a chromosome carries a gene for a particular characteristic, such as eye color.

Any plant or animal receives half its chromosomes from its father and half from its mother. Thus, each parent contributes one gene for any characteristic. For example, your father and mother have each given you one

Chromosomes, highly enlarged.

Courtesy Bausch & Lomb Optical Company

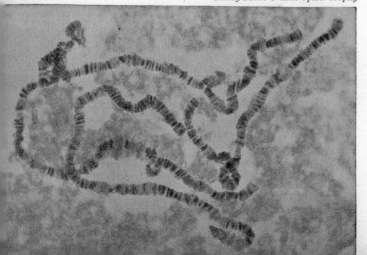

basic gene for eye color. Perhaps the gene from your father was for blue eyes and from your mother for brown eyes, but regardless of the color, each gives you one—and only one—gene for eye color and one for every other characteristic you possess.

Pairing Off. Just before an egg or a sperm is produced, the pairs of chromosomes come to lie side by side. Thus, the genes for any particular characteristic, such as eye color, pair up as well. As you can see, this means that the 48 chromosomes of man are really 24 pairs of chromosomes. In the production of an egg or sperm the pairs of chromosomes separate so that each sperm or egg receives only one of the pair.

To understand what happens when sperms and eggs are produced and fertilization occurs, examine the illustration on page 173. This diagram shows what happened when Mendel crossed purebred varieties of peas.

ACCOUNTING FOR MENDEL'S RESULTS

In terms of genes, why did Mendel get only tall plants in the first generation when he crossed tall plants with dwarf plants? Why did these tall plants produce offspring in the ratio of three tall to one dwarf in the second generation? We now have a basis for answering these questions.

The illustration on page 173 shows that Mendel crossed purebred varieties of peas. Cells of the pea plant that produced the sperms had two chromosomes carrying genes for tallness. They did not have any genes for dwarfness and were, therefore, purebred tall. When the sperms were produced, the pairs of chromosomes separated so that each sperm received only one gene for tallness. Cells of the pea plant that produced the eggs had two chromosomes carrying genes for dwarfness. They did not have any genes for tallness and were, therefore, purebred dwarf. When the eggs were produced, the pairs of chromosomes separated so that each egg received only one gene for dwarfness.

Lines show the union of sperms and eggs (fertilization) for production of plants of the first generation. All of the plants of this generation contained both the gene for tallness and the gene for dwarfness. They were *hybrid*. Yet they were not middle-sized, because tallness is dominant over dwarfness, which is *recessive*.

When the sperms and eggs from this first generation were produced, the chromosomes and genes again separated. Some sperms and eggs carried the gene for tallness and some carried the gene for dwarfness, but none for both. Any sperm might have united with any egg. Possible unions are shown by lines.

If a sperm with a gene for tallness united with an egg with a gene for tallness, the offspring would be tall and purebred, that is, would carry no genes for dwarfness. If the sperm carrying a gene for tallness should unite with the egg carrying a gene for dwarfness, the offspring would be hybrid, for it would carry genes for both tallness and dwarfness. Again, as in the first generation, the plant would be tall, because tallness is dominant over dwarfness.

All possible combinations of sperms and eggs are shown. If a large number of offspring

A mule is a well-known hybrid.

were produced, this proportion of one tall purebred to two tall hybrids to one dwarf purebred would hold true.

HYBRIDIZATION MAY PRODUCE NEW CHARACTERISTICS

First-generation hybrids are not always like one parent. Characteristics may mix, or *blend*, rather than one dominating another. When this happens, hybridization may produce new varieties of plants or animals. For example, when Red Fife wheat was hybridized with Red Calcutta, the offspring, Marquis wheat, had characteristics that were superior to those of either of its parents. When a female horse, or *mare*, is mated with a male ass, known as a *jack*, the offspring is a hybrid, the well-known *mule*. Many of our best breeds of crop plants have been produced by hybridization.

SELECTIVE BREEDING AND GENES

Selective breeding includes selecting the offspring that most nearly have the characteris-

The guinea pigs at the right are the offspring of the two at the left. Using the diagram in the middle, explain why one of the offspring is white.

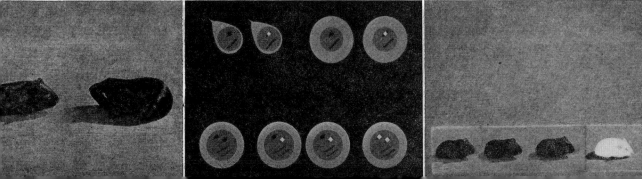

U. S. D. A. photos

Left: American "wild" hog, actually a descendant of liberated razorback hogs, such as those at the right. Middle: highly selected and well-bred hogs developed especially for pork production.

tics desired. These offspring are then mated and again the offspring are carefully selected for further mating. After a time, offspring with the characteristics desired and which breed true are secured. In terms of genes and chromosomes, the goal of selective breeding is to get rid of unwanted genes and continually remate desired genes until the plants or animals have only desired genes. These plants or animals are purebred and will produce offspring like themselves.

Mutations often produce desirable characteristics. Mutations result from changes in genes. What causes mutations is not clear, but certain mutations have been experimentally produced by placing animals under x-rays. Whatever the cause, mutations are likely to breed true if offspring with the desired mutation characteristic are mated with similar offspring until purebred characteristics are obtained. When the mutations breed true, a new variety has been established.

WORKING WITH SCIENCE

1. In human beings, black hair is dominant over recessive blonde hair. Using the letter *B* for black hair and *b* for blonde hair, work out the following crosses. Describe the hair color of the offspring and indicate which are hybrid and which are purebred in hair color: one parent is purebred with respect to black hair and the other is purebred with respect to blonde hair; one parent is hybrid with respect to black hair and the other is purebred with respect to blonde hair.

2. Repeat Exercise 1 using *B* for dominant black eyes and *b* for recessive blue eyes.

MODERN BIOLOGICAL PRODUCTION

Our wildlife is a source of pleasure to all of us. We conserve deer, bears, geese, and ducks because so many of us find them interesting or enjoy hunting as recreation. Wildlife is one of our sources of clothing and food. The annual value of the meat and fur of wild birds and mammals is estimated at about $190 million. Another $100 million worth of fish are caught each year in the United States and Alaska and off their coasts.

But this is a "drop in the bucket" compared to domesticated crops and livestock in the United States. Our total crop production has provided the farmer well over $6 billion annually during the past few years. Our cattle, sheep, hogs, and poultry have given the livestock producer more than $8 billion per year.

One way to conserve biological resources is to develop better plants and animals so that we can get more for our investment of time

176

and money. The illustrations on page 168 show some of the changes that man has made in horses and corn. Our production today would be far less than it is if man had merely domesticated wild animals and plants and raised them without improvement.

But man has found that he could improve plants and animals to suit his purposes. He has produced certain breeds of cattle that give large amounts of rich milk. He has produced other cattle that are heavy with meat. He has developed horses of tremendous strength and endurance and other horses that are very swift.

GREATER PRODUCTION THROUGH GENETICS

There are many examples of the great value of the science of genetics in increasing biological production. For example, the average hen produces about 80 eggs in a year. But certain flocks of carefully bred hens produce as many as 300 eggs per hen per year. And these hens do not cost much, if any, more to feed and care for than the average hen.

A cow produces milk to feed her calf. She does not produce milk just so you and I can drink it. A few centuries ago the cattle kept by man produced little more than enough milk for their calves, and the milk "dried up" about the time the calves were weaned. Even today an underdeveloped, or scrub, cow usually produces less than 4000 pounds of milk in a year; this amount normally includes about 190 pounds of butterfat.

The table below shows highest yearly production records of certain dairy breeds that man has developed. Naturally the average yield of cows of these breeds is less than this. But the figures show how we can conserve by improving plant and animal life.

*Maximum Annual Records of Dairy Breeds**

Breed	Pounds of Milk	Pounds of Butterfat
Holstein Friesian	38,606	1,402
Milking Shorthorn	32,522	1,614
Ayrshire	31,156	1,356
Brown Swiss	27,512	1,106
Guernsey	24,008	1,098
Jersey	23,677	1,197

* Adapted from E. E. Stanford, *Man and the Living World* (The Macmillan Co., New York, 1940), p. 792.

WORKING WITH SCIENCE

1. Examine a dairy herd in your area. Talk with the farmer or production expert. How much milk is produced by the average cow? How does this compare with that of ordinary cows?

READING YOU WILL ENJOY

Burnett, R. Will. *Life through the Ages*. Stanford University Press, California, 1947. An interesting and well-illustrated little book on the changes in living things since the beginning of life on the earth.

Carter, William H. *The Horses of the World*. National Geographic Soc., Washington, 1923. A beautifully illustrated book that shows the development of various breeds of modern horses from earlier stocks.

Fenton, Carroll L. *Life Long Ago: The Story of Fossils*. The John Day Co., New York, 1937. An excellent and authoritative account of fossils—the animals and plants that lived on the earth many millions of years ago in various geologic times.

Knight, Charles R. *Before the Dawn of History*. McGraw-Hill Book Co., New York, 1933. Contains excellent reproductions and accounts of the many extraordinary murals painted by the author for the American Museum of Natural History.

Reed, W. Maxwell and Lucas, Jannette M. *Animals on the March*. Harcourt, Brace & Co., New York, 1937. Ancient forms of life and the history of living things down to the present time.

Verrill, Alpheus H. *Foods America Gave the World*. L. C. Page & Co., Boston, 1937. The interesting story of how many native American food plants were developed and adapted to varying situations.

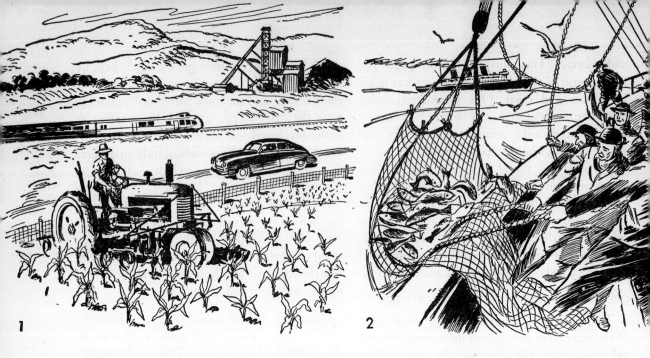

1

2

All that man has depends on earth's natural resources and how man uses them. From the land (1) comes most of man's food—crops and meat—and his mineral and agricultural raw materials—metals, rocky building materials, lumber, and fuels. From the seas (2) come some of man's food—fish of many kinds, and either directly or indirectly, many of his minerals—salt, magnesium, and bromine for antiknock gasoline. From the air (3) come gases that make life possible—oxygen for breathing and burning, carbon dioxide for food-making by green plants, and nitrogen for building into fertilizers.

As man's knowledge has increased, a fourth resource has become more and more important—the laboratory (4). In the laboratory, raw materials of the land, seas, and air are built into an endless stream of products for better living. Some of the products of the laboratory are the same as those produced naturally, either by living things or by other natural forces. Other products of the laboratory are some that nature never got around to making. Still others make it possible to use the resources of the land, seas, and air more effectively.

Without the laboratory, many of the good things of life we all enjoy would not be possible. And, as some of our present natural resources become less plentiful, we must depend on the laboratory to develop substitutes for them.

3

4

Using Mineral Resources for Better Living

16

THESE ARE OUR RESOURCES

What is the earth—the continents, islands, seas, and air—made of? "Simple," says the chemist. "About 92 substances make up the entire earth, and as far as we can tell, the planets, moons, and stars also." These substances are called elements.

Some elements have been known since the earliest days. A few were discovered by the alchemists in the sixteenth to eighteenth centuries. Many were discovered by the early chemists, and some were brought to light as recently as within your own lifetime. Four new elements were produced in connection with the research that led to the atomic bomb.

EARTH'S BUILDING BLOCKS

The ancients thought that all things were made up of only four elements—earth, air, fire, and water. "It is very clear," they said. "When a branch of a tree is burned, fire is produced. Water is forced out of the wood and can be seen boiling at the cut end of the branch. A smoky gas (air) drifts upward, and a grayish material (earth) is left behind."

The ancients could give many examples to support their theory of the four elements. Even today, we sometimes talk of "the elements" when we mean the air or the seas. Only in the past 2 centuries have scientists given us a picture of a world made up of 92 natural elements.

THE ELEMENTS

The word *element* may be new to you, but you can name several without much thinking. Iron, copper, lead, mercury, tin, gold, and silver are all elements. So are carbon, nitrogen, sulfur, magnesium, and chlorine. Caesium, germanium, gallium, and xenon may be strange names to you. These, too, are elements.

At ordinary temperatures, some elements are gases, like oxygen; some are liquids, like mercury; and some are solids, like sulfur. The elements include silvery metals, gray earthy materials, and substances that are red, yellow, green, and colorless. Regardless of form, color, or weight, all elements have one characteristic in common: *they cannot be broken down by ordinary means into other simpler substances.*

Burn a piece of wood and it changes to smoke, certain invisible gases, black charcoal, and gray ash. You have broken down the wood into simpler substances. But almost no matter what you do to the element gold or the element

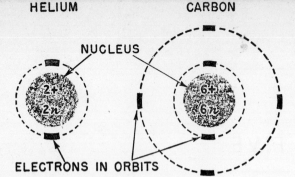

HELIUM   CARBON

NUCLEUS

ELECTRONS IN ORBITS

Helium and carbon atoms may be drawn like this.

oxygen, you cannot break them down into simpler substances.

Our definition of element contains the phrase *by ordinary means*. Some 50 years ago that phrase would not have been necessary. However, in 1898 Pierre and Marie Curie [kü-rē'] discovered radium, an element that breaks down naturally into other simpler elements, such as lead.

From this beginning, scientists have found ways to break down some of the heavier elements into simpler elements. In this process, tremendous amounts of energy are set free. This energy gives the atomic bomb its terrific power. However, the methods of breaking down, or smashing, atoms are still too complex to be called ordinary.

COMBINATIONS OF ELEMENTS

Elements combine with one another. Millions of combinations are possible. These combinations of elements make up the materials we usually find in the earth and which we use.

A few elements are found *pure*, or uncombined with other elements. Gold, copper, nitrogen, and oxygen are examples. Iron, aluminum, tin, and magnesium are never found pure. These, and most other elements, are combined with one or more other elements. Such combinations of elements cannot be separated except by chemical or electrical means. They are called *chemical compounds*.

There are millions of chemical compounds. Sugar, salt, cotton, baking soda, sand, and water are common chemical compounds. Each is always made of the *same* elements combined in the *same* proportions. For example,

water, wherever it comes from, is always composed of two parts of hydrogen and one part of oxygen by volume. Salt, whether you eat it in South Africa or San Francisco, is always composed of about 39.3 percent of sodium to about 60.7 percent of chlorine.

ATOMS AND MOLECULES

The smallest particle of a substance that can exist as that substance is called a *molecule*. For example, the smallest particle of water that can exist as water is a molecule. If it is broken up still further, it breaks down into two particles of hydrogen and one particle of oxygen. Thus, a molecule is usually made up of still smaller particles of two or more elements. However, a molecule may be made up of one or more particles of a single element. Thus, a molecule of carbon is made up of one particle of carbon; a molecule of oxygen, of two particles of oxygen.

These smallest possible particles of an element are called atoms. You can have an atom of oxygen, tin, or sulfur. You can also have a molecule of each of these substances. By combining different elements, you can have a molecule of sugar, salt, or baking soda.

As shown by the example of oxygen, certain gases exist as molecules composed of two atoms. Although it is possible to have oxygen as a single atom, it does not normally exist in that form. Thus, every molecule of oxygen contains two atoms of oxygen.

Atoms are composed of still smaller particles called *electrons*, *protons*, and *neutrons*. These particles are the basic particles of which all substances are composed.

The electron is the smallest particle of all. It is a particle, or unit, of negative electricity and weighs about 2000 times less than the lightest and smallest atom, that of hydrogen gas. The proton is a unit of positive electricity and weighs about the same as an atom of hydrogen. The neutron, discovered in 1932, is a very compact particle that has almost the same weight as a proton but is electrically neutral.

How are these units arranged in the atom? A great deal of experimentation has led sci-

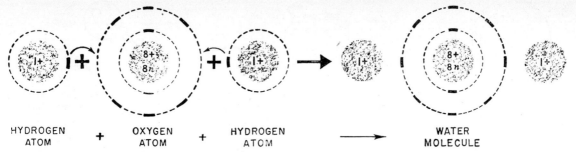

HYDROGEN ATOM + OXYGEN ATOM + HYDROGEN ATOM ⟶ WATER MOLECULE

In this chemical change, hydrogen and oxygen atoms combine, producing a molecule of water.

entists to picture the center of the atom as made up of a tiny nucleus. This nucleus consists of different numbers of protons and neutrons. The electrons move at terrific speeds around the nucleus in orbits similar to the orbits of the planets around the sun. For this reason the picture of the atom is often referred to as the *solar-system arrangement of the atom.*

During a *chemical change,* for example when hydrogen combines with oxygen to form a molecule of water, electrons shift from one atom to another so that electrons are shared in the molecule formed. During a chemical change, the nucleus is not affected. When the nucleus of an atom breaks up of its own accord, as in the case of an atom of radium, the nucleus throws out one or more protons and becomes a new element, such as lead. This process is called *radioactivity.* The nucleus of an atom can also be artificially smashed. For example, when an atom of the element uranium-235 or of the element plutonium is bombarded with neutrons, the nucleus is broken up and other neutrons are thrown out. Such an event is accompanied by the release of tremendous amounts of energy, that is, atomic energy. Such a change is called *atomic fission* and the result is *nuclear change.*

ELEMENTS, MIXTURES, AND COMPOUNDS

Everything in the air or sea or on the land is either an element, a compound, or a *mixture* of either or both. If molecules and atoms are mechanically mixed and a new chemical compound is not formed, the result is a mixture. You breathe oxygen (an element) which you take from the air (a mixture). You eat bread and meat (both mixtures) which you may flavor with salt (a compound). If the food does

not agree with you, you may take bicarbonate of soda (a compound).

PHYSICAL AND CHEMICAL CHANGES IN MATTER

The world we live in is a place of constant change. All around us things change before our eyes. Water changes to water vapor, or *steam,* and ice. Coal burns in our stoves and furnaces and changes into hot gases, soot, and ashes. Gasoline from the fuel tanks of automobiles, airplanes, and tractors changes to a vapor, enters the engine, and is burned. Huge chunks of marble are pulverized between the steel jaws of giant rock crushers, green plants grow, silverware tarnishes, iron rusts, and bronze statues become discolored.

These changes are of two kinds. In some only the *form* of the original substance is altered. For example, when water changes to steam or ice, only its form changes. It is still water. When a piece of marble is ground into a powder, it is still the same marble that was dug from the quarry. Such changes are *physical* changes. In a chemical change, the *composition* is changed, and new substances with new

This glacier consists of ice formed by pressure from snow. What kind of change is this?

Ewing Galloway

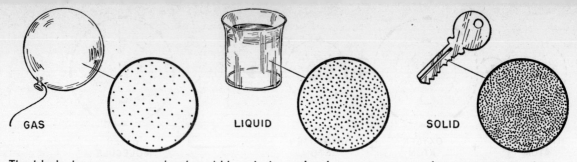

GAS   LIQUID   SOLID

The black dots represent molecules. Although the molecules are in motion, this motion is not shown.

properties are formed. For example, when a piece of paper burns, it is completely changed into hot gases and ashes, neither of which resembles the original paper.

GASES, LIQUIDS, AND SOLIDS

The atoms or molecules of which a substance is composed are in continual motion. Furthermore, even though the substance appears to be composed entirely of matter, there is much space between the atoms or molecules. There is more space between the atoms or molecules of a gas than between the atoms or molecules of a liquid. And there is more space between the atoms or molecules of a liquid than between those of a solid.

The atoms or molecules of a gas are in more rapid motion than the atoms or molecules of a liquid. And the atoms or molecules of a liquid are in more rapid motion than the atoms or molecules of a solid.

When a substance is heated, its atoms or molecules move more rapidly and over greater distances. For example, when iron (a solid) is heated enough, it becomes a liquid. Heat the liquid iron to a high enough temperature and

As pressure on a liquid increases, its boiling point increases. A pressure pan uses this principle.

Courtesy Revere Copper and Brass Incorporated

the liquid changes to a gas, or *vapor*. Vapor is the name of the gaseous state of a substance that normally exists as a liquid or a solid.

When a substance is cooled, its atoms or molecules move less rapidly and over shorter distances. For example, when water vapor, or steam, is cooled enough, it becomes a liquid (water). Cool the liquid water enough and the liquid changes to a solid (ice).

Evaporation. The molecules of a substance are held together by certain forces. Whenever a molecule of the substance moves fast enough to overcome these forces, it can escape. Thus, when water is exposed to air, some of the molecules at its surface escape into the air. This is known as *evaporation*. Evaporation takes place most rapidly in warm places.

Boiling and Melting. When water is heated, its molecules begin to move more rapidly. Many of the water molecules below the surface escape from the liquid and bound away. This is known as *boiling* and is true of liquids other than water. The temperature at which a liquid changes from a liquid to a vapor is a definite temperature known as its *boiling point*. Pure water boils at 100°C or 212°F. A liquid may evaporate at temperatures well below its boiling point.

Like liquids, the molecules of a solid move more rapidly when heated. The temperature at which a solid changes from a solid to a liquid is a definite temperature known as its *melting point*.

Condensing and Freezing. When a gas or vapor is cooled, its molecules move less rapidly. As a result, the molecules are closer together. When a gas or vapor is cooled enough, it changes from a gas to a liquid. Thus, steam changes, or condenses, from a vapor to a liquid—water. This change takes place at the boiling point. When a liquid is cooled enough, it changes from a liquid to a solid. This change takes place at the *freezing point*. The freezing point and the melting point are at the same temperature. The freezing point of pure water is at 0°C or 32°F.

SOLUTIONS

If you place a spoonful of sugar in a cup of water and stir the two, the sugar disappears. We say that the sugar *dissolves* in the water. The resulting liquid is called a solution. If you take several samples of the solution from different parts of the cup, you will find that one sample tastes just as sweet as the others. The molecules of the sugar have become uniformly mixed with the molecules of the water.

A spoonful of salt in a gallon of water makes a solution that contains little salt compared with the amount of water. Such a solution is called a *dilute solution*. Half a pound of salt in a gallon of water makes a solution that contains much salt compared with the amount of water. Such a solution is a *concentrated solution*.

Solutions are very important substances. Almost all life-processes and most processes not connected with living things are carried on by means of solutions.

SHORTHAND OF CHEMISTRY

All elements and compounds have names. But scientists use a shorthand that helps them to see a whole problem at a glance and to think and write precisely. Instead of writing out the names of elements and compounds, chemists use *symbols* that stand for the names.

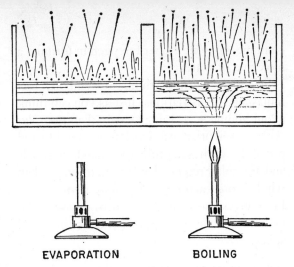

EVAPORATION   BOILING

In both evaporation and boiling, molecules escape through the surface of a liquid and get away.

The capitalized first letter of either the common or Latin name of an element stands for the element. It represents one atom of the element. If the names of two or more elements begin with the same letter, a second letter is written as a small letter after the first. Thus, C is the symbol for one atom of carbon. Ca is the symbol for one atom of calcium. Cl is the symbol for one atom of chlorine.

The shorthand for the name of a compound is called a *formula*. A formula stands for one molecule of a compound. It is written by joining the symbols of all the elements that compose the compound. The formula for copper sulfide is CuS. The formula for hydrogen chloride is HCl. If the number of atoms of an element in a compound is greater than one, a small number is written below and to the right of the symbol of the element to indicate the number of atoms. Thus H_2O, the formula for water, means that two atoms of hydrogen

In solutions, molecules of a dissolved substance mix uniformly with those of the dissolving substance.

combine with one atom of oxygen in forming a molecule of water.

Scientists learn to think in symbols, formulas, and abbreviations. Just as you can think about adding 4 + 3 more easily than *four plus three*, so scientists can work more quickly and precisely with scientific shorthand. Symbols and formulas require less space to write than whole words and they give more information. H_2O gives more information to anyone who understands the symbols than does the word *water*.

ELEMENTS OF THE EARTH'S CRUST

Not all elements are equally common. Some are downright rare. However, we know about how much of each element is available in the earth's crust. This estimate is based on years of scientific study of rocky substances, the seas, and air.

The facts are somewhat astonishing. Oxygen, a colorless gas essential to life, makes up close to 47 percent of the materials of the earth's outer crust. Silicon, a grayish solid, is the second most abundant. Practically 28 percent of the earth's outer crust is silicon.

If silicon is so common, why is it not often seen? The answer is that silicon does not occur naturally as an uncombined, or *free*, element. Most commonly it is combined with oxygen in the ratio of one atom of silicon to two atoms of oxygen. This is a compound you all know—sand. A chemist calls this compound silicon dioxide, SiO_2, a name that explains its composition.

Sand, white or colorless and glassy, consists of broken up fragments of *quartz*. Silicon dioxide (quartz) occurs in most of the rocks of the earth, so that the two elements in it make up practically 75 percent of the earth's crust.

The most common 10 elements in the earth's crust are shown in the table below.

Composition of Earth's Crust in Approximate Percentages

Oxygen	47	Potassium	2.5
Silicon	28	Magnesium	2.1
Aluminum	8	Titanium	0.6
Iron	5	Hydrogen	0.1
Calcium	3.5	All other elements	
Sodium	2.5	less than	1.0

METALS AND NONMETALS

Iron, copper, and gold are shiny elements that conduct heat and electricity well. They can be rolled and hammered into sheets or pulled into wire. They dissolve in some acids and act in special ways with other chemicals. Iron, copper, and gold are *metals*. Lead, aluminum, tin, uranium, and magnesium are metals also. So are a dozen or more less well-known elements, some of which are of great value to us, such as, cadmium, vanadium, tungsten, molybdenum, thorium, and plutonium.

Elements that are not metals are called *nonmetals*. Nonmetals are quite different from metals. Nonmetals conduct heat and electricity poorly. Elements such as carbon, sulfur, phosphorus, and oxygen are nonmetals.

Both metals and nonmetals are very important to us. Our modern world, with all its machinery, could not exist without metals. Life itself would be impossible without oxygen, phosphorus, and other nonmetals. Enough of most metals and nonmetals exist to supply all of our needs if we could locate and obtain them cheaply.

This is certainly a big IF. It sent Cortez to Mexico, and other explorers throughout the world, in search of gold. It guides the work of thousands of scientists today—men who are

Granite, a rock, is composed of several minerals.
U. S. Geological Survey photo

seeking better ways to locate the needed materials and to extract them from the earth.

MINERALS

Earth scientists rarely speak of compounds, but they frequently speak of *minerals*. A mineral is an element or compound found naturally in the earth. A chemist can make sodium chloride from the elements, sodium and chlorine. The same compound is found by the ton in the underground rock of New York and Michigan. It is known as the mineral *halite*. Sodium chloride, halite, and table salt are the same thing.

Every mineral is a compound except those few elements found free, or native, in the earth. Thus, a lump of gold found in rock is both a mineral and an element.

Diamonds, rubies, flint, quartz, iron ore, mica, gypsum, sulfur, and borax are all minerals. Literally thousands of minerals exist, but only a few hundred are of great importance to us.

A look around your classroom shows many objects that come directly from minerals— glass in the window, iron in the radiator, copper wires that carry electricity to the electric light, and the tungsten filament of the bulb

U. S. Geological Survey photo

This quartz contains tourmaline, another mineral.

itself. The plaster on the wall and probably the coloring material in the paint are mineral products. The point of your pen and probably the ink are also.

Almost all industries and trades use minerals. Check in your own town to see what ones do. How does a farmer use minerals? A radio repairman? A bricklayer?

WORKING WITH SCIENCE

1. Make a collection of elements. Mount them on a chart with properties and uses of each. About 20 elements are common enough so that you can get them without much difficulty.

2. Look up the story of radium and its discovery. Make a chart to show how radium changes to other elements and explain to class.

3. Add some vinegar to a teaspoonful of baking powder. What happens? Is this a physical or a chemical change? Explain.

4. Demonstrate the properties of sulfur powder and iron filings and the separation of a mixture of iron and sulfur by the use of a magnet. Heat the mixture of sulfur and iron filings over a *hot* flame for some time and demonstrate a chemical change and the formation of a new compound.

5. Check through the classroom and list all the elements and compounds you can find. Skip the mixtures—there are too many of them. With some help, you should get 25 or more compounds and perhaps 10 elements.

6. Use a battery, flashlight socket, bulb, and connecting wire to show the conductivity of metals and nonmetals. Conductivity can be judged by brightness of the light.

7. Demonstrate the effect of an acid on metals and nonmetals by gently placing a bit of zinc in dilute hydrochloric acid in a test tube. Repeat using a bit of sulfur in hydrochloric acid.

8. Add table salt, bit by bit, to a glass of water. Stir after each addition of salt. Report what happens, step by step.

U. S. Geological Survey photos

Sedimentary rocks. Left: Alternate layers of limestone and shale make up this formation. Right: The sandstones of the Grand Canyon have been cut by water and wind.

EARTH'S ROCKS

A *rock* is a large mass of mineral or mineral-like material that forms part of the earth's crust. Rock may be one mineral as, for example, a mountain of quartz. But more often rock is a mixture of several minerals. These are mixed together in a definite way so that it is possible to tell one kind of rock from another.

Minerals and compounds are identified by the elements they are made up of. Rocks can be identified that way also, but such a system is too complicated. Usually we name and identify rocks according to the way they were formed and according to the minerals that make them up.

SEDIMENTARY ROCKS

As nearly as we can tell, the earth came into being some 3 billion years ago. How the earth looked at that time, we can only guess. Possibly the first rocks were formed by the cooling of hot, melted lava just as new rock is being formed at the famous volcano of Paricutín in Mexico.

Whatever the form of this original rock, it no longer exists. No rock that gives evidence of being part of the original crust of the earth has ever been located. The oldest known rocks were formed from sand, gravel, and mud washed into the oceans by streams that ran over the land. So other rocks must have existed before them.

Rocks like the oldest known rocks are still being formed as the land is worn down and materials from it are washed into the sea. Rocks formed from parts, or fragments, of other rocks are called *sedimentary rocks*. Some sedimentary rocks were formed from parts of the bodies of animals. Others were formed as water evaporated, leaving mineral substances.

The kind of sedimentary rock that is formed from other rocks depends on the size and material of the fragments. The action of running water separates the fragments according to size. Running water carries the finer, lighter particles longer and farther then the heavier ones. You can see this yourself by placing some gravel, sand, and mud in a milk bottle, filling it with water, and shaking it vigorously. When the mixture is completely shaken, set it on a table and watch the particles as they settle to the bottom. Let the bottle stand overnight and then notice the layers of material that have formed.

As a swift stream flows into the ocean, it deposits pebbles and gravel just as soon as the stream loses its speed and thus its carrying power. Particles of sand are smaller and lighter and are carried farther to sea. Fine muds and

Some 400 to 500 million years ago, these plants and animals lived in the seas that covered various parts of the earth. Their remains are found in sedimentary rocks.

clays may be carried miles out to sea before they finally settle to the ocean bottom.

Rocks formed from gravel held together by such natural cements as iron rust, lime, or silica are called *conglomerate*, or *puddingstone*. The individual pebbles stand out like plums in a pudding. Grains of sand held together by the same cements form a rock called *sandstone*. The hardness of sandstone depends on the strength of the cement that binds the grains together. An iron rust cement produces a weak and crumbly sandstone. A silica cement produces a hard and durable rock.

Particles of mud and clay are so fine grained that under pressure they form a compact rock. Such a rock is called *mudstone*, or *shale*. Pure shales are soft, almost greasy rocks. The process by which coarse particles are separated from fine particles is not perfect. Therefore, shales that contain traces of sand are common. So are sandstones that contain shale or even bits of conglomerate.

The commonest kind of sedimentary rock varies greatly in appearance. This rock is called *limestone*. Vast amounts have been formed and are being slowly built up today from tiny sea animals that die and whose limey skeletons settle to form deep-water lime muds. These animals secured this lime by chemically separating it from sea water. Vast areas of limestone consist largely of sea shells loosely or tightly cemented together. *Coral* reefs and islands are the limestone skeletons of coral, a marine animal. Many midwestern states, such as Kansas, are underlaid with this type of limestone.

Carbon dioxide is given off when a drop of acid is placed on limestone. This is a simple test for limestone. The shorthand expression, called a *chemical equation*, for this chemical test is

$$CaCO_3 \;+\; 2HCl \;\rightarrow\; CaCl_2 \;+\; H_2O \;+\; CO_2$$

calcium + hydrochloric → calcium + water + carbon
carbonate   acid   chloride   dioxide

When CO_2 gas is bubbled through limewater, the limewater turns milky.

Do these fossils resemble any of the plants or animals at the top of this page?

187

From Encyclopaedia Britannica film Volcanoes in Action

When magma flows into or between layers of other rocks, intrusive rock is formed.

There are many more kinds of sedimentary rocks. Those discussed are the most common and the most important. All our cement, lime, and most of our clay comes from these rocks. Limestone and sandstone are commonly used in building. Limestone is used widely in agriculture, too.

Since most sedimentary rocks are formed under water, those composed of fine-grained material often bury and preserve impressions or living parts of plants or animals. Such buried materials or imprints are called fossils. Since fossils are as old as the rocks in which they are found, they give us many clues about early living things.

IGNEOUS ROCKS

Sedimentary rocks are one of three large groups of rocks. The other groups of rocks are much different in form and appearance. One of these groups of rocks was formed from melted or *plastic* (matter that will flow although solid) materials. This means, of course, that they were very hot, since the melting point of most rock is more than 1000°F. Under great pressure, however, even solid rock becomes plastic and flows.

Rocks that have flowed into the outer crust of the earth from deeper regions are called *igneous rocks*. Their name comes from the same Latin word as *ignite* and *ignition* and refers to fire or heat. However, do not conclude that igneous rocks all came from volcanos or from bubbling material inside the earth. Neither of these ideas is entirely right, yet neither is entirely wrong.

Place both of your palms together, push as hard as you can and rub your hands together. You are soon aware that heat can be produced by rubbing and pressure. On a very small scale, this is like what is happening inside the earth at many places. The pressure is so great that enough heat is produced to melt the rocks when other conditions are favorable. This melted rock material is called *magma*. When it cools and crystalizes, it forms igneous rock.

There are many kinds of igneous rocks and they can be classified in many different ways. One of the simplest is to classify them according to where they were formed. If the pressure was gradually relieved so that magma cooled inside the earth or flowed into and filled cracks in other rocks, the rock formed is known as an *intrusive rock*.

Intrusive rocks sometimes form several miles beneath the surface. Because they cool very slowly, the elements and compounds in the magma separate out, forming mineral

A *cinder cone* is formed by the piling up of ashes and cinders from several eruptions.

From Encyclopaedia Britannica film Volcanoes in Action

crystals. Compounds of metals sufficiently abundant or concentrated to be mined profitably may settle out, forming an *ore*. Most of the deposits of gold, silver, lead, zinc, and copper are found in or near intrusive rocks. An example of an intrusive rock is *granite*.

When igneous material flows out on the surface of the earth, *extrusive rock* is formed. Because the rock cools very rapidly, extrusive rocks have not had the time required to form large, well-developed crystals as are found in intrusive rocks. Neither are they as rich in concentrated minerals.

Volcanos. The melted rocky materials resulting from great pressure inside the earth break through to the surface under proper conditions. This break-through may be violent and noisy or relatively quiet. A *volcano* is a mound-shaped or cone-shaped hill or mountain formed as a result of one or many such break-throughs.

All the gases, ash, and molten rock, or *lava*, that come from a volcano are extrusive. In many places lava has simply flowed out of the ground through cracks, or *fissures*, without forming a true volcano. The lava has spread far and wide like molasses poured on the center of a rather rough table. Much of the Columbia Plateau in the northwestern part of this country was formed by such lava flows.

In Mexico there have been lava flows so recently that Indian villages have been buried beneath them. You may have heard of the volcano Paricutín which a few years ago began pouring out lava and ashes from what used to be a cornfield of a poor Mexican farmer. More recently—1946—a new volcano manufactured an island off the coast of Japan.

American Museum of Natural History, New York
Paricutín in eruption.

Volcanos get more attention than they deserve. They are not nearly as important as mineral-bearing intrusive rocks. But some of them are spectacular, so they steal the show. There is only one semiactive volcano in the United States—Mount Lassen in California.

Most of the world's volcanos lie in a ring that borders the Pacific Ocean. This "ring of fire," as it is commonly called by scientists, runs along the west side of South America, up our Pacific coast into Alaska, through the Aleutians, down through Japan and the Philippines, and through the East Indies. This Pacific ring is an area of strain in the crust of the earth. Along this ring there is constant readjustment, movement, and pressure.

METAMORPHIC ROCKS

Sedimentary and igneous rocks can and have been altered by natural forces. Intrusions heat

A composite cone is a flatter cone made up of ashes, cinders, and lava.

From Encyclopaedia Britannica film Volcanoes in Action

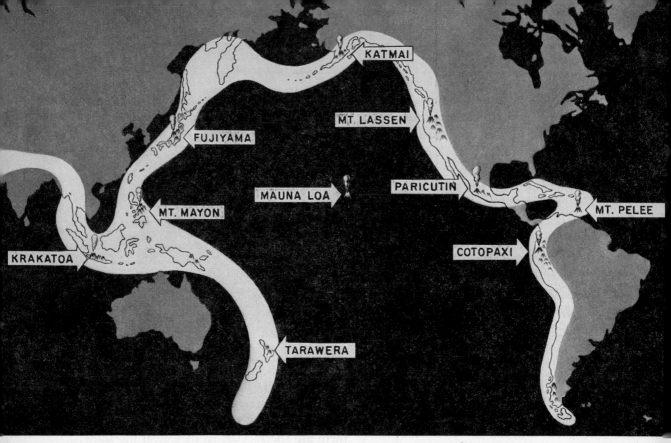

The "ring of fire." Not all of these volcanos are now active but have been so relatively recently.

and bake the rocks with which they come in contact. The pressure of overlying sediments squeezes and binds lower layers together. Large-scale earth movements bend and fold layers of solid rock as if they were paper, and the resulting physical and chemical changes produce new kinds of rock. All rocks produced by directly altering some earlier rock—commonly through pressure and heat—are called *metamorphic rocks*.

Mud hardens into shale, a sedimentary rock. Shale, when heated and pressed, becomes *slate*, a partly metamorphosed rock. Sandstone becomes *quartzite*, and limestone may become *marble*. Often the heat and pressure are so intense that it is practically impossible to identify the original rock that has been altered. *Gneiss*, a streaky granular rock with small flakes of mica, is often formed from altered granite, though it may be formed from a sedimentary rock also.

Metamorphic rocks are important because new materials are formed as they change. *Soft*, or *bituminous*, *coal* is altered into *hard coal*, or *anthracite*. Dull limestone becomes brilliant marble. At the same time, the process of change may recombine the elements and compounds into new kinds of minerals. Mica and garnet are minerals often formed in metamorphic rock.

ROCKS AND ROCK PATTERNS

The crust of the earth is made up of different varieties of sedimentary, igneous, and metamorphic rocks. Some varieties are so common that you can travel for hundreds of miles seeing chiefly the same kind of rock. Other varieties are found only in one small place in the world.

As a result of years of careful study, earth scientists, or *geologists*, of the United States Geological Survey know rather accurately the kinds of rock in every part of this country. They know the rocks even though layers of soil cover much of the crust of the earth. They tell us that the coastal plain that runs along the

Atlantic coast and around the Gulf of Mexico consists of sedimentary rocks in most places not cemented into something hard and rock-like. The Catskill Mountains of New York are sedimentary rocks also. So is most of the Mississippi Valley and the Great Plains region.

The northwestern states have large deposits of igneous rocks. So have the Sierra Nevada and Rocky Mountains and the Black Hills. Other igneous deposits are widely scattered through most of the country, especially in the southwest.

Metamorphic rocks are characteristic of New England, the Adirondack Mountains, parts of the Rockies, and huge areas in Canada.

WORKING WITH SCIENCE

1. Make a collection of any kinds of sedimentary rock found in your neighborhood. If possible, show the original kind of rock fragments from which it was formed. Are the rocks found in layers? Are the individual particles of rock smooth or rough?

2. There may be a place in your region where fossils are found. Arrange a trip there and dig some. If not, examine a fossil. Try to figure out how the print was formed. Make artificial fossils with clay and a shell or leaf.

3. Obtain a piece of granite. Break it apart with a hammer. Pick out crystals of quartz, marble, and mica.

4. Collect igneous rocks if they occur in your locality, or examine samples of granite, lava, or other kinds. Prepare an exhibit of igneous rocks.

5. Make a model volcano of clay or papier-maché. An artificial eruption can be made by filling the crater with 2 tablespoons of lump ammonium dichromate and heating from below. In a half-darkened room this gives a good imitation of an eruption.

6. Find out about Pompeii (buried by volcanic ash) or about Mt. Vesuvius, Mt. Etna, Mt. Lassen, Katmai, Crater Lake, or any other famous present or extinct volcano. Report to class on a famous eruption.

7. If information is available, make a model or chart showing the crust of the earth in your region. Show the kinds of rocks and relative amounts of each.

EARTH'S RESOURCES

All living things are directly dependent on rocks or on materials formed from them. Chemicals from the rocks form a basic part of the soil and are dissolved in the waters of the sea. They are just as essential to tiny ocean plants as they are to the giant redwoods of California. When we speak of the "good earth" or the "bountiful earth," we have in mind the soil that nurtures all life.

THE ATMOSPHERE

The earth contains some 6 sextillion tons of rocks and minerals. Around the solid earth, or *lithosphere*, is an all-important blanket of air, the *atmosphere*. The atmosphere weighs less than one-millionth as much as the rocky earth —a mere 5 quadrillion tons. The atmosphere is just as much a natural resource as a gold mine or a forest. In fact, it is far more important to our living.

The colorless gas nitrogen makes up about 78 percent of the atmosphere. The colorless gas oxygen makes up 21 percent. The remaining 1 percent includes about a dozen elements and compounds, all colorless gases. There is always some water vapor in the air, varying from almost nothing to about 5 percent.

About 90 percent of the air lies within 12 miles of the earth's surface. The remaining 10 percent thins out so gradually that traces of air may be found 600 to 750 miles up. To get an idea how thin a blanket the atmosphere is, consider drawing a circle to represent the earth and another to represent the atmosphere. If the atmosphere is 1 inch thick, the earth must be 800 inches in diameter (67 feet) to make the

These two pictures and those at the top of page 193 show how the solar system may have been formed.

ratio correct. If the atmosphere is $\frac{1}{10}$ of an inch thick, the earth must be 6.7 feet in diameter. If the atmosphere is $\frac{1}{100}$ of an inch thick—about the thickness of a fine pencil line—the earth is about 8 inches in diameter.

THE SEAS

About five-sevenths of the surface of the earth is covered with water—140 million square miles of oceans and lakes compared with 58 million square miles of land. This third great part of the earth, the *hydrosphere*, is a natural resource of great importance. We think of fishing and swimming when we think of the seas, but the seas are also the source of much of our rain. Most of the molecules of water that you drink have one or more times been part of the seas.

But the seas contain more than water. In them are dissolved many elements and compounds. These are present in small amounts, but the totals are tremendous because the seas are so large. No one mines gold from the seas because the percentage of gold in sea water is very small—about one part in 200 million. Small as this is, the gold in the seas totals thousands of millions of tons—far more than has been obtained in centuries of mining. We have just begun to learn how to obtain some of the valuable minerals from the seas.

Everything that man has today has come from hydrosphere, atmosphere, and lithosphere. The only exceptions are stray bits of iron and rock that have fallen from the skies. These are called *meteorites*, and they are of scientific interest only. They contain iron, nickel, and other metals but not enough to meet any modern need.

ORIGIN OF THE EARTH

Have you ever looked out your window day after day at the same street or the same trees or the same hills? Perhaps you have felt that nothing ever happens, that things are always the same. Nothing could be farther from the truth. The hills that to you seem unchanging are very changing things. "As everlasting as the mountains" is not an accurate phrase.

Most of us judge the world on our own time-scale. We consider everything on a scale of days or weeks or 70-year lifetimes. But the time-scale of the earth is very different. A lifetime is not even a second on the time-scale of the earth. The earth's changes, which have been very great, must be considered on a time-scale of millions of years. A geologist uses such a time-scale and to him the earth is a continually changing planet.

A geologist would like to start his story of the earth's changes at the beginning. However, there is no evidence that enables him to do so. Changes have hidden all the evidence. The best he can do is to explain most reasonably the facts that he observes today.

What do geologists and astronomers observe today? Through telescopes they see a rather small, middle-aged, hot *sun* with a diameter of 866,000 miles. Its surface temperature is about 6000°C (11,000°F). Inside, it is much hotter. Around this sun travel nine rounded fragments of material, the *planets*. The planets are much smaller than the sun. What we know of them causes us to conclude that they must have come from this larger body.

The earth would fit into the sun a million times over. Jupiter, the largest of the planets, has a diameter only $\frac{1}{10}$ that of the sun. Many

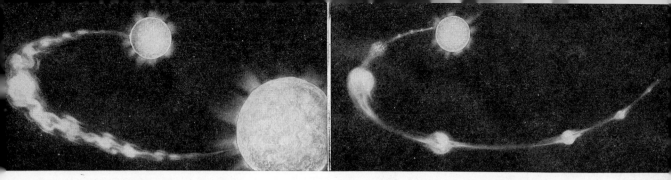

All four illustrations are based on the modified theory of Chamberlin and Moulton.

facts tie the sun, planets, and their moons into one *solar system* that undoubtedly began and continues as a single unit.

The best theory to account for the solar system is a modification of a theory of two American scientists, Thomas C. Chamberlin [chăm′bẽr-lĭn] and Forest R. Moulton [mōl′tŭn]. According to this theory, about 3 billion years ago a very large star passed close to our parent sun. The attraction of the passing star was so great that a long streamer of hot material was pulled from the sun. This material was moving so fast that most of it was not pulled back into the sun as the other star moved away. It broke up in sections that traveled around the sun in paths that are almost perfect circles. These sections of hot materials formed the planets which all move in the same plane and in the same direction around their parent sun.

EARTH IS STILL CHANGING

We do not know for sure how long ago the earth cooled into a solid body. Scientists believe it was perhaps 3 billion years ago. The oldest rocks yet discovered are about 1.85 billion years old.

However, we can be certain of one thing. Ever since the earth was formed, it has been changing. The greater changes probably have taken place on the surface. The interior of the earth is very hot, so hot that the rocks would melt if it were not for the terrific pressure of the solid rock layers that make up the crust of the earth.

All the changes that have taken place on the earth's surface can be put into two main classes: those that are wearing down and levelling off the surface of the earth, and those that are building up or raising the surface of the earth. Every hill, mountain, valley, and canyon on the earth today is a direct result of the work of these opposing forces.

The Destructive Processes. The earth's crust is worn down in many ways. The chemicals of the atmosphere, notably oxygen, carbon dioxide, and water, help decompose rocks and dissolve the substances of which they are made. Water is especially active. Rain fills cracks in rocks, freezes, and expands. The resulting pressure pushes the rock apart and breaks masses of rock into smaller fragments.

Water not only breaks up the rock but very slowly dissolves such rocks as limestone, actually carrying millions of tons of lime into the seas every year. Running water in streams, rivers, or ocean waves, cuts away the hardest rocks. Plants force rock fragments apart with

Water freezing in cracks in rocks helps wear down the earth's surface.

Soil Conservation Service photos

Dry winds and chemical weathering have worn away the softer parts of these rocks.

their roots, and chemicals produced by mosses and lichens wear away the rocks also.

The three chief agents that wear down the surface of the earth are water in rain or rivers, glacial ice, and chemical weathering. Each acts in its own way, but the net results are always the same—the land surface is lowered. The action of wind is also most important, particularly in desert regions. Ice wears down Arctic lands, and in ancient days, greatly changed the appearance of much of the now-temperate regions. Running water does most of the job in temperate regions.

Chemical weathering or decay of rocks is also extremely important, particularly in regions where a great amount of moisture exists in the air—the *humid* regions.

As rocks are broken into smaller and smaller fragments or are chemically changed, some mix with decaying plant material, forming soil. The particular kind of soil depends on the kind of rock and the amount of *organic* material (formed from material once a part of living organisms) mixed with it. Limestone forms one type of soil, granite a very different type. Sandy soils contain much quartz; lime soils contain very little.

The final action in the wearing down process is the carrying of rock fragments from high places to low. Valleys become filled, and rivers carry fine rock material from valleys to the still-lower oceans. There the fragments settle on the lowest land, the ocean bottom.

This continual process lowers the surface of the earth very slowly—by inches or parts of inches. Yet it is estimated that each year about 800 million tons of rocky materials are carried into the oceans from the United States alone. Add to this the millions of tons of minerals dissolved in the river water, and you begin to get an idea of how tremendous this process is.

The process of wearing down and removing rocks and soil material is called erosion. Erosion is not a new process or one that exists only to plague farmers. It has been going on ever since there was wind and water. How-

The cutting action of moving water continually lowers the earth's surface.

From Encyclopaedia Britannica film Work of Running Water

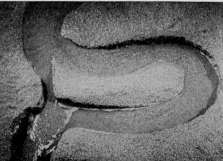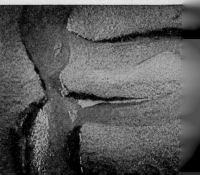

U. S. Geological Survey photos

This juniper widened a split in granite. Temperature changes may cause splitting, as at the right.

ever, in places where man has removed the natural plant covering to grow his own crops, erosion, formerly held in check by the plant covering, has become a very serious problem. The thin layer of soil so invaluable to man can be washed away in a few years unless erosion is prevented.

The Constructive Processes. The processes that build up, or raise, the earth's surface are more exciting than those that tear down. Volcanos make exciting reading. They build up the surface of the earth and raise the level of the land. Mountains and plateaus of lava are evidences of this kind of land building.

The land surface is also raised by movements within the earth. For example, large blocks of rock are pushed upward to relieve pressure along a crack, or *joint*. When such movement along a joint takes place, a slippage, or *fault*, occurs and an *earthquake* results. The Sierra Nevada Mountains are blocks of rock that are still being pushed upward. The result-

ing earthquakes are part of the long process of building up the earth.

Other slower earth movements of even greater extent raise the level of large areas of land. For example, the entire Atlantic coast is rising slowly from the sea. The section we call the *coastal plain* was all under water not so very long ago.

Pressures developing in the crust of the earth squeeze and push the rock layers as if they were paper. Layers of rock hundreds or even thousands of feet thick are folded into huge up-and-down *folds*. The Appalachian Mountains are long ridges of folded sedimentary rocks. The pressure is often so great that the rock layers break and are pushed over one another.

In the Blue Ridge Mountains, rock layers have been pushed 50 miles or more as part of the action that has lifted and folded rock layers all through eastern United States. From the evidence left behind, geologists can compute the extent of this folding. For example, they

A glacier carries rocks and boulders that scrape and scar and end up as piles called **morraines.**

From Encyclopaedia Britannica film Geological Work of Ice

From Encyclopaedia Britannica film Mountain Building

How a fault occurs and how a real fault looks in cross section.

can tell that mountains higher than the Alps once stood over what is now New York City.

Intrusions of magma beneath the surface raise the level of the earth also. Sometimes they swell up surface rocks like a huge blister. The Black Hills of South Dakota look like such a blister, partly worn open by the erosion of deep-cutting streams.

Living things also build up the earth's surface. Some of these build up miles and miles of land. Coral animals are best known for this activity. Thousands of south Pacific islands are the result of the slow piling up of their limey skeletons. Beavers dam up streams and provide a place where mud and silt can settle. In time, a beaver pond becomes filled in and becomes a rich swamp meadow.

EARTH CHANGES AND NATURAL RESOURCES

The building up and wearing down of the crust of the earth have had great effect on our natural resources. More coal has been carried away from Pennsylvania by erosion than we will ever mine. From careful studies of mineral deposits, geologists can estimate their original size. In many cases most of the minerals have been eroded away long before man discovered the deposit.

While some processes rob us of raw mate-rials, others provide new ones. The folding of the Pennsylvania rock layers produced high-grade anthracite from what would otherwise be bituminous coal. Without folding, tilting, and other earth movements, oil and natural gas probably would not collect in amounts large enough to be used. The flows of igneous rock, which often accompany the larger earth movements, bring to the surface minerals that otherwise could not be reached.

Man can do very little about the changing earth beyond controlling erosion that carries away soil. He can take advantage of those places where minerals have been concentrated and use those minerals as carefully as possible. Once they are gone, it may be millions of years before new deposits are formed. Man can do little more than use wisely and cautiously the raw materials he has found.

This is the earth on which man must live and from which he must get all that he needs to maintain his life. Air, water, and food come directly from the earth. So do all the minerals and plant and animal materials that we use in so many ways. Man's progress is the story of how he has utilized the plant, animal, mineral, and human resources he finds around him. The mineral resources may be the most important. They will be impossible to replace once they

When the earth's rock layers are pushed up and down, or from the ends, folds occur.

From Encyclopaedia Britannica film Mountain Building

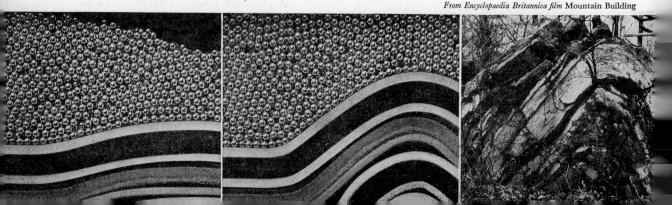

From Encyclopaedia Britannica film Mountain Building

Can you explain what has happened in the illustrations at the top and bottom of this page?

are gone. We can grow new forests and re-stock our rivers with fish, but we know of no way to replace the minerals in a mine that has been exhausted.

WORKING WITH SCIENCE

1. Make a list of all the obvious relationships between the atmosphere and the lithosphere. Oxygen in the air causes rocks to decay; rain dissolves minerals from the soil; and so forth. If rock is exposed near school, study fresh and weathered rock. How have the atmosphere and water changed the rock?

2. If there is a museum nearby that has a meteorite, get a good look at the only material we get from outside the earth.

3. List the natural resources that are now used in your own community, in agriculture, industry, recreation or in other ways. Make a list of resources of your region that are not used because we have no need for them or have not developed ways of using them.

4. Get more facts on the modified Chamberlin-Moulton planetesimal theory. Find out how this theory accounts for the size of planets, for the fate of the passing star, and so forth. Does it fit the facts?

5. By digging sample holes in a number of places, measure the thickness of the topsoil in your region. Measure along the clean edge of the hole to the place where a distinct change in color of the soil can be noticed. This may vary from 1 inch to well over a foot.

6. Both constructive and destructive processes have played an important part in the history of your own region. If this history is known (and it is for most of the United States), find out what processes built up your locality and which are most important in wearing it down.

READING YOU WILL ENJOY

Hawksworth, Hallam. *Strange Adventures of a Pebble.* Charles Scribner's Sons, New York, 1921. A simple geology textbook for young people. Written in an interesting style.

Lucas, Jannette M. *The Earth Changes.* J. B. Lippincott Co., Philadelphia, 1937. How the earth has changed its form to become as it is today. Interestingly told with excellent color maps and illustrations.

Reed, W. Maxwell. *The Earth for Sam.* Harcourt, Brace & Co., New York, 1930. One of the best books about the earth and how it came to be as it is.

From Encyclopaedia Britannica film Mountain Building

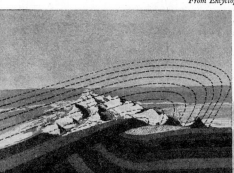

1

2

3

As man's knowledge has increased, he has become able to use natural resources in better ways. Thus he has brought up his standard of living from barely enough to live on to the relatively high standard we have today. Knowledge has made this improvement possible. Earth's resources have been here always, but man has not always had the "know-how" to find and use them to the greatest advantage.

One of the early ways in which man used the land was as a place on which to hunt, fish, and collect wild foods (1). He also collected useful rocks and minerals. Later on man learned to raise cattle and sheep (2). This new knowledge enabled man to become a herdsman and made him a little more certain of enough to eat and enough to wear. When

man learned to till the soil and to raise food crops, he became a farmer and settled down to live on the land rather than wandering over it from place to place in search of good pastures for his cattle or good wild crops to harvest (3).

All the while man was learning more about finding, getting, and using more of the earth's mineral resources and fuels and natural building materials such as wood and rock. Today giant mechanical shovels mine most of our coal and ores (4). Powerful machines help us obtain lumber (5). By means of small explosions (6), scientific fingers probe deep into the earth for raw materials. And man's standard of living has continually improved.

4

5   6

17

MINING THE LAND

One misfortune after another left the Ancient Mariner becalmed and dying of thirst in the middle of the ocean. No wonder he said, "Water, water everywhere, Nor any drop to drink."

Human beings are in a somewhat similar situation. We need raw materials. They exist in abundance, but we cannot get hold of them easily. In the crust of the earth, there is more iron, copper, gold, and many other metals than we will ever need. The trick is to extract them at a cost that makes their use possible.

Every resource has its price. Like the water in the seas surrounding the Ancient Mariner, abundance in itself means nothing. The resources must be both abundant and usable.

HOW MINERAL DEPOSITS ARE FORMED

We are lucky that the earth is continually changing. Many of these changes have helped to bring together, or *concentrate*, minerals so we can extract them easily at low cost. Man continually searches for such mineral concentrations. Once found, they have changed the course of history time after time. The search for gold and petroleum are good examples.

How are minerals concentrated? Why are there deposits of gold in California and none in Kansas? Answers to such questions take us right back to the rocks of the earth and how they were formed.

FORMATION OF VEINS

Many minerals, especially metals, originate in intrusive igneous rocks. A large mass of magma may be forced by pressure into a pocket between layers of rock. This mass of molten rock may be miles wide and very thick. Such a mass of rocky material cools very slowly, because it is protected by layers of rock. While it gradually cools, several things happen. Elements that have great "attraction" for each other come into contact. Heavier minerals settle toward the bottom.

Melting Point and Concentration. Minerals with the highest melting points change to solids first. Many minerals that contain metals have lower melting points. These usually remain liquid. With hot gases and steam, they flow from the main mass of hot rock into cracks in the surrounding rock. Thus they become concentrated.

A mass of minerals that fills a crack in rock is called a *vein*. Veins do not all contain valuable minerals. Veins of quartz are common, but they have no value. In some other place, however, the quartz may carry gold with it.

Veins of valuable minerals are usually beneath the surface. However, erosion often wears away the surface until part of the vein is exposed. A prospector or geologist learns the clues that lead him to such veins. Rust stains on the rock are one of them. He takes a sample of rock from the vein and has it analyzed.

What Is an Ore? An ore is rock that contains enough of a metal or nonmetal to be profitably extracted. This is true of all ores—for example, gold ore, tin ore, iron ore, and lead ore. Only a few of the rocks or minerals that con-

From Encyclopaedia Britannica film Volcanoes in Action

Intrusions help concentrate minerals in rocks. Intrusions vary greatly in length, width, and thickness.

tain iron, gold, tin, or lead are rich enough to be considered ores.

Mineral veins are the richest source of metal ores. Most mines are dug to follow a vein so that minerals can be removed.

EFFECTS OF RUNNING WATER

Erosion often removes the local rocks and the mineral veins. When this occurs, running water may concentrate the ores if they are heavy enough. For example, ores of gold and tin are much heavier than the rock in which they occur. Pebbles or nuggets of these ores settle to the bottom and are not washed away rapidly by eroding streams.

California Gold Rush. These facts led to the discovery of gold in the American River near the present site of Sacramento, California. In 1848 on land belonging to John A. Sutter, a

Panning for gold.

Soil Conservation Service photo

millrace for a new sawmill was being dug. In the gravel of the streambed, gold was found—gold deposited there as the stream carried gravel from rich gold veins toward the sea.

Soon thousands were *panning* the streams—shaking gravel in flat pans with a motion that allowed the lighter gravel to wash out and left the heavier flakes of gold on the bottom of the pan. Huge dredges now do the work that the early miners did by hand. Much of our gold and tin is obtained from deposits along what either are or once were river beds, or bottoms.

EFFECTS OF EVAPORATION

Certain lakes and seas do not have outlets to the oceans. Evaporation of water from such *landlocked* lakes and seas is another means of concentrating minerals. The rivers that empty into Great Salt Lake are no more salty than other American rivers. But the lake has no outlet. Water continually evaporates, but the salt and other minerals do not.

The salt content of Great Salt Lake has risen slowly. Now it averages about 18 percent. The oceans have become salty by the same process. Since they are so much larger than Great Salt Lake, their salt content is still only about 3 percent.

EFFECTS OF LIVING THINGS

Certain plants and animals are able to concentrate minerals. Coral animals extract lime from sea water and build it into coral rock. Thousands of islands have been built up of the mineral produced by these small sea animals. Certain bacteria extract iron and concentrate

200

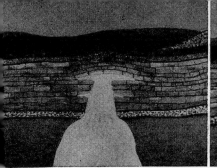

From Encyclopaedia Britannica film Volcanoes in Action

A shaft mine extends down to the ore body, and passages lead out into the ore.

it. These bacteria are believed responsible for many of the large iron deposits in this country —for example, around Birmingham, Alabama and Duluth, Minnesota—and in Europe.

EFFECTS OF SOLUTION

Oxygen and rain water from the atmosphere also aid in concentrating minerals. When a vein is exposed, oxygen and rain water may break down and dissolve the minerals in it. If the rock is porous, these dissolved minerals are carried into the rock and enrich the deeper deposits.

Circumstances determine which concentration agencies are at work. Coral animals work only in tropical oceans. Evaporation is most effective on bodies of water without outlets and that are in warm regions.

It is far more profitable to find a concentrated ore than to try to concentrate ores that contain only a small amount of worthwhile minerals. You can readily see how costs enter this picture. An iron mine with ore that contains 30 percent iron is not as profitable as a mine in which the ore contains 60 percent iron.

In this country it scarcely pays to mine iron-bearing rocks that contain less than 30 percent iron. But a gold ore that contains $\frac{1}{1000}$ of 1 percent gold is ordinarily enough to make mining it worthwhile. The reason is simple. Iron is worth about 5 cents a pound; gold is worth about 35 dollars an ounce.

Mine operators take advantage of changing prices. When prices of metal are high, they mine the *lowest-grade* ores that will give them a profit. When metal prices drop, they stop mining the low-grade deposits, on which they would lose money, and mine *higher-grade* ores. Thus they keep their mines operating in bad times as well as good.

WORKING WITH SCIENCE

1. Veins are found in nearly every kind of rock. In a quarry or roadcut where rock is exposed, look for veins. Most likely you will find veins of calcite ($CaCO_3$) or quartz (SiO_2), the most common vein-forming minerals.

2. Evaporate a weighed amount of sea water—preferably 2 to 5 pounds. It can be boiled over a burner or evaporated slowly over a radiator. Care should be taken to evaporate the last bit of water slowly. Weigh the salt and compute the concentration of salt in sea water.

3. Obtain some crystals of copper sulfate (bluestone) and dissolve them in water. Hang an iron nail in the solution for a few minutes. Report your observation and explain what has happened. Consult some book on chemistry used in your high school classes for the chemical explanation. Can this method be used to obtain pure copper? Explain.

LOCATING ORE DEPOSITS

Concentrated ores are a precious natural resource. Men have searched all their lives for them. Wars have been waged over them. The finding of a rich mineral deposit today is more than pure chance. In the old days prospectors went alone through the mountains looking for iron stains on the rock, flecks of gold in the gravel, or for any other clue to minerals.

Standard Oil Co. (N.J.) photos by Bubley and Lofman

Exploring for oil, using seismic methods. The small explosion at the left resulted in the record at the right. From this record, scientists can map fairly accurately rock formations beneath the surface.

Prospectors no longer work alone. A team of geologists goes into the field with elaborate equipment. They use the latest scientific methods and locate bodies of ore that cannot even be seen on the surface.

These men use airplanes to take photo-graphs of the land. The photographs indicate the structures of the rock and the kind of rock that is present. They often enable the geologists to tell if closer search is needed.

SEISMIC METHODS

In locating new ore deposits, geologists make use of the different properties of different kinds of rock in the crust of the earth. Let us watch a team of scientific oil geologists at work on the swampy plains of southern Texas. They have come in several trucks and set up stations with sensitive receiving apparatus several miles apart. When everything is ready, one man pushes a button. There is the roar of an explosion. Soil and sand are scattered in all directions.

Interpreting the Results of the Explosion. After the soil and sand have fallen and the smoke has blown away, do the men rush in to see what their dynamite explosion has uncovered? Oddly enough, they pay no attention to the hole. They study some wavy lines on a roll of moving paper in the instruments placed thousands of feet away from the source of the explosion. These lines tell the story.

The explosion started vibrations, or waves, travelling through the earth. These waves travel faster and farther through some

How seismic prospecting methods work.

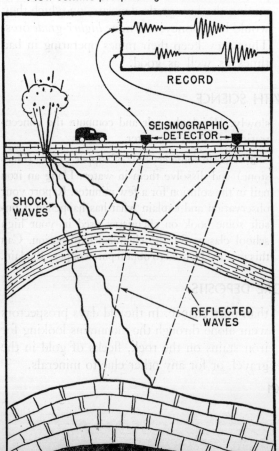

202

substances than through others. The elaborate apparatus set up by the scientists measures the speed and *intensity* (size or bigness) of the waves from the explosion.

If the rock under the entire area is the same, the vibrations travel equally well in all directions. If the rock varies, so does the speed of the vibrations. The vibrations, or waves, travel faster through the heavier rocks. By studying the record of the waves as they travel through the earth, geologists learn of differences in rock structure that cannot be seen at the surface. Large salt "domes" and oil deposits are found by this method.

Perhaps this idea of explosions and vibrations, or waves, strikes a familiar note. Probably you have heard of something like it before. It is like the method used in locating earthquakes. An earthquake, caused by slipping of tremendous blocks of rock, produces three kinds of waves that travel very far. The recording instrument is similar in each case. It is a vibration recorder, or *seismograph*.

GRAVITATIONAL METHODS

Could you take a sealed box containing an unknown number of blocks of different substances, such as iron, wood, cork, and lead, and find out the weight of *one* of them without opening the box? Geologists do almost that when they locate a mineral deposit by the use of an instrument called a *gravimeter*.

Minerals that contain metals weigh more, volume for volume, than most rock. That is, they are more *dense* than the rocks. A gravimeter is so sensitive to gravitational pull that it turns more when it is near a dense mineral deposit than when it is near the surrounding lighter rock. Thus, without digging, geologists can locate and get an idea of the size of a mineral deposit that is completely covered by layers of rock.

OTHER METHODS

Some metallic ores can be detected by measuring the electricity set up in the earth as water seeps through the ores and the surrounding

rock. In another electric method, electricity is sent through the earth. The ease with which it flows depends on the nature of the rock. Ores of metals offer less resistance to the electricity than do other rocks.

Locating Uranium. Two special methods are used in locating ores of uranium. Even before the release of atomic energy, there were many reasons for finding ores of this rare element. Since uranium ores are the source of uranium-235, one of the sources of atomic energy, uranium has become a key element.

Uranium's peculiar properties make it easy to detect its ores with proper equipment. Uranium ores and a number of other ores glow in the dark when they are exposed to ultraviolet light. This is called *fluorescence*. A geologist can expose ore specimens to ultraviolet light and if a specimen glows brightly with a characteristic color, he will recognize it as an ore of uranium.

Uranium ores contain small amounts of radium, an element that gives off telltale electrons, electrified helium atoms, and gamma rays similar to x-rays. These rays and particles are invisible but easy to detect. For example, if a piece of unexposed camera film is carefully

Examination of cores obtained with diamond drills gives information on underlying rocks.

wrapped and sealed in dark paper and then placed in a dark cabinet beneath a piece of uranium ore, nothing that you can see happens. But about a week later if you develop the unexposed film, you will find an image of the uranium ore. This image was produced by gamma rays that passed through the dark paper and affected the film.

In searching for uranium and radium deposits, geologists use a device known as a *geiger counter*. This instrument detects one kind of particle given off by uranium and radium ores. It is so sensitive that it has located very tiny pieces of radium that have been lost in hospitals. As the operator comes nearer and nearer to the uranium deposit, the clicks in the counter come faster and faster. Thus, deposits can be located and mapped.

These ways of locating ore deposits are all useful and very important. But geologists cannot get far unless they understand the science of geology. This requires long and detailed study of rocks, the way they are formed, the way they are altered, and how they now appear. A geologist must be as alert for clues as a detective.

EXPLORING FOR MINERALS

Why don't our geologists find more mineral deposits, if they know how to do it so well? The answer to this question is not a very happy one. Most large mineral deposits in this country have been found. Even the wildest parts of our country have been explored and prospected. Some parts do need more study, but the chances of finding any large mineral deposits are very slim.

Farther afield, in northern Canada, in the Antarctic continent, in Siberia and Alaska, are large areas still to be explored. But unfavorable climate makes mining difficult and costs are necessarily higher. It does not pay to tap any but the richest deposits in such regions.

Drilling with Diamonds. After an ore deposit is located, it is difficult to judge the wealth inside the earth's crust. The size, depth, and richness of the ore are still not certain. Some mines get richer with depth, some get poorer. The deeper the mine, the greater the cost of extracting the ore.

Use of *diamond drills* helps get information on ore deposits. Diamonds are the hardest minerals, and many more are used in industry than are suited for gems. Drillers use the dull, irregular, black, or discolored stones.

A diamond drill cuts a circular hole, leaving a core of rock in its center. This core is hauled to the surface and gives an accurate sample of the rock through which the drill has cut. It shows exactly how thick and how rich the ore is at that spot. By drilling in many places, a costly procedure, information on the size of an ore deposit may be obtained.

WORKING WITH SCIENCE

1. Listen to the ticking of a watch about a yard away from your ear. Then listen to the watch at the same distance but with a yardstick between the watch and your ear. Hold the watch against the end of the yardstick and place the other end against your ear. Is sound transmitted better through air or wood?

2. In a swimming pool, determine transmission of sound under water by banging two stones together. Is sound transmitted through water better than through air?

3. Find out how a seismograph receives earthquake waves and how the earthquake can be located when waves are picked up by two or more stations.

4. Set up a circuit to test electrical conductivity, using a lamp as an indicator. Test several mineral samples, including *magnetite*. How well do these conduct electricity?

5. If an ultraviolet lamp is available, test the fluorescence of various substances—the "radium" dials of watches contain uranium salts. **Caution:** *Direct exposure to ultraviolet light is dangerous to the eyes.*

MINES AND MINING

Mining the earth is not a new occupation nor is it a romantic one. It is plain hard work that requires careful planning and some luck. Knowing how to recognize a valuable mineral from one that is not is only the first step.

The structure of the earth determines what miners must do to obtain ores. A mine is much more than just a hole in the ground. Before any mining is begun, the ore deposit is studied and mapped to find out its size and extent. Then mining is begun.

OPEN-PIT MINING

The oldest and simplest kind of mining consists of an open hole, or pit, from which ore is removed. This is called *open-pit mining*. Such methods can be used only when the ore lies at the surface. Open-pit mining is usually relatively cheap. Therefore, low-grade ores can be mined profitably by the open-pit method.

The largest copper mine in the United States at Bingham, Utah is an open-pit mine. Here, huge mechanical shovels actually dig away an entire mountain of low-grade copper ore. In the Great Lakes Region are iron mines that produce over half of our country's iron ore. Many of these are open-pit mines from which steam shovels take 10 to 15 tons of ore at a bite.

Sand Pits. Two kinds of open-pit mines are so common that probably you have seen both of them. The first is the *sand* or *gravel pit* from which deposits of sand or gravel are dug.

Quarries are another kind of open-pit mine from which rock is dug. Drilling and blasting are required to loosen the rock. The rock may be fine building stone for houses or monuments. Or the rock may be crushed for making concrete, railroad ballast, road building, or other local uses.

STRIP MINING

Strip mines are similar to open-pit mines. Layers of rock, sand, or soil that cover the ore must be stripped off before the ore can be mined. This is usually done by huge electric or steam shovels. Strip mining is profitable when the ore is in horizontal layers that are not too deeply covered. The strip coal mines of Illinois are examples of this type of mining. After the coal has been removed, the torn-up land is of little value.

HYDRAULIC MINING

Another kind of surface mining is used in panning for gold. By the use of water and simple apparatus, ore is mechanically separated from gravel. Huge gold dredges work on the same principle. They swallow gold-bearing gravel by the ton, separate the gold from it, and spew the gravel out. Such dredges work so efficiently that it is profitable to operate them in gravel with only 10 cents worth of gold per ton.

If gold-bearing gravels do not lie in stream beds, the gravels are washed loose by powerful streams of water. This method is known as *hydraulic mining* and is used in many of the Alaskan gold deposits.

SHAFT MINING

Most of us think of a mine as a *shaft* leading down into the earth to the ore deposit. There are many mines of this type. If the ore deposit is uniform in thickness and tilted, like some layers of coal, the shaft is dug at an angle to follow it. Inclined shafts are quicker to dig and

The pencil points to a diamond embedded in conglomerate from a shaft mine.

American Museum of Natural History, New York

205

U. S. Bureau of Mines, Department of the Interior photos

Left: This huge electric shovel is strip mining for coal. Each of its caterpillar feet is as tall as an automobile. Right: Mining for gold by hydraulic methods.

cheaper to operate than are the vertical shafts.

In many mines one or more vertical shafts are dug down to the ore deposit. At various levels, side passages are dug into the ore. Mining takes place in the side passages. Ore cars are hauled by electric engines to the elevator shaft. Then the ore is raised to the surface and dumped.

Hazards. Mining is hazardous. In spite of safety rules and safety programs, more accidents occur than in many other industries. Besides accidents, there are other health hazards: the effects of working in a humid atmosphere in cramped space and of breathing silica dust which may cause a disease of the lungs called *silicosis.* More safety devices and stricter rules are needed to make our mines safer.

WORKING WITH SCIENCE

1. Make a collection of minerals and rocks of your own locality. In some places you can find a hundred or more kinds of minerals. In others, at least a half-dozen. Look in roadcuts, quarries, and other places. For directions on mineral collecting, see Zim and Cooper, *Minerals*, Harcourt Brace & Co., 1943.

2. Demonstrate the preparation of carbon dioxide by the action of acid on limestone ($CaCO_3 + 2HCl \rightarrow CaCl_2 + H_2O + CO_2$). Test for carbon dioxide with limewater which turns milky in the presence of CO_2. Passages in shaft mines often contain carbon dioxide.

3. Demonstrate the physical properties of carbon dioxide. Pour a jar of carbon dioxide on a bank of burning candles. What happens?

4. If there is a mine or quarry in your region, try to arrange to visit it. The chances are you will NOT be allowed to go down in the mine, but you may be allowed to see the workings above ground and find out details from the superintendent or the mine union representative.

MINING AND SMELTING TYPICAL METALS

Iron makes up about 5 percent of the earth's crust. There is more iron deep in the earth, but we cannot get at it now and may never be able to. Iron is rarely found pure. Usually it is combined with either oxygen or sulfur. One ore in which it is combined with oxygen (iron oxide) is called *hematite.* Hematite is this country's most common and most important iron ore. It is very similar in composition to ordinary iron rust.

MINING IRON

Hematite contains two atoms of iron to three atoms of oxygen, Fe_2O_3. Its appearance varies from a soft, earthy red powder to black, shiny crystals. Sometimes it is in the form of tiny red pellets about the size of buckshot, cemented together.

The hematite of Minnesota is in a metamorphic rock in which it shines and sparkles because of the mica found with it. When hematite is scratched, a *red* powder results even if the sample of hematite is black in color. Because of its iron content, hematite is a heavy mineral, almost twice as heavy as any of the common rocks.

Nearly 90 percent of the iron and steel products manufactured in this country come from the hematite ores of the Great Lakes region and Alabama. Much of the hematite is dug from open-pit mines by shovels that scoop up rock that contains 50 to 60 percent hematite. This ore is shipped in huge ore boats through the Great Lakes to the ore ports of Illinois, Indiana, Ohio, and Pennsylvania. At the ports, it is unloaded mechanically and is ready to be changed into iron.

SMELTING IRON

Since hematite is a compound of iron and oxygen, the making, or *smelting*, of pure iron involves chiefly the removal of the oxygen. This is not easy, since the two elements are strongly bound together chemically. The element carbon performs this function of removing the oxygen from iron oxide very well. Such an element is called a *reducing agent* by chemists. A supply of carbon is necessary. The carbon comes from soft coal, which contains about 66 percent carbon plus some hydrogen, oxygen, and sulfur compounds.

When soft coal is heated in a closed container, it does not burn. It *decomposes*, or breaks apart. Compounds containing hydrogen, sulfur, and other substances are driven off as gases, together with a number of compounds important in the manufacture of drugs, dyes, explosives, solvents, and other products. Left behind is a mass of pure carbon, known as *coke*. Coke is used as a reducing agent in the smelting of iron.

If the iron ore were pure hematite, coke would be the only substance needed to release the iron. But the iron ore contains sand and other mineral impurities. To remove these, crushed limestone is used. The limestone unites with the silica of the sand, forming a dark, glassy substance known as *slag*.

The Blast Furnace. A huge tower, lined with firebrick, is used in smelting iron. This tower is known as a *blast furnace*, because a blast of hot air blown in through a circular pipe around the bottom of the furnace raises the temperature to about 3000°F. A small trolley hauls the iron ore, coke, and limestone to the top of the tower and automatically dumps them. The coke is soon ignited by the molten material below.

Some of the coke, C, unites with the oxygen of the hematite, Fe_2O_3, and leaves the iron, Fe, free. The chemical equation for this change is

$$Fe_2O_3 + 3C \rightarrow 2Fe + 3CO.$$

Some coke combines with the oxygen of the hot air, forming carbon monoxide gas. The carbon monoxide gas joins with oxygen from the iron ore, forming carbon dioxide gas and leaving more molten iron. The liquid iron runs to the bottom of the furnace. The melted limestone unites with the sand, forming a slag that floats on top of the iron.

Pig Iron. This process continues until the reservoir at the bottom of the furnace is filled with white-hot liquid iron. Then the furnace is tapped. The molten iron pours through a hole in the furnace wall into molds made of sand. Such iron is called *pig iron*.

The iron produced by one blast furnace may amount to 700 tons or more daily. The huge furnaces are kept going day and night. They are very hard to rekindle once they have gone out. To produce 500 tons of iron requires 1000 tons of ore, 250 tons of limestone, 500 tons of coke, and about 60,000,000 cubic feet of air.

Pig iron contains 4 or 5 percent impurities. The chief impurity is carbon. Compounds of silicon, sulfur, and phosphorus are present also. Pig iron is a grayish, brittle metal.

Courtesy of the Bituminous Coal Institute

White-hot coke being removed from a byproduct coke oven. Much coke is used in smelting iron.

Cast Iron. The impurities can be removed from pig iron, and this is usually done. Frequently, the iron is treated to remove the impurities even before it cools, thus saving the cost of remelting. The molten iron may be poured into shallow furnaces, where it is heated and rusty scrap iron or iron ore are added. The oxygen of the scrap iron or iron ore unites with and removes the excess carbon.

Partially purified pig iron is called *cast iron.* Cast iron has many uses, such as in making furnace parts, radiators, and drain pipes. It is easily cracked, however, and cannot be used when strain may occur.

Wrought Iron. If more completely purified pig iron is rolled and squeezed until the slag is pressed out, a definite structure forms within the iron. It is then rolled into sheets or formed into tubes, rods, or bars. Such iron is known as *wrought iron.* It is a very pure form of iron and is tough, pliable, and resistant to rusting.

MAKING STEEL

Most of the metal that we call iron is not iron. It is an *alloy,* formed by melting iron with other metals or other substances that change the properties of the iron. Iron alloys are called *steel.* There are many different kinds of steel.

The commonest steels contain carbon and iron. When about 0.5 percent carbon is present, the steel is fairly soft and is used in making rails, axles, nails, and building mate-

rials. When 0.8 to 1.5 percent carbon is present, the steel is harder and more brittle. Such steel is used for cutting tools, for springs, and for magnets.

Special Steels. Steel that contains manganese is tough and resists wear. Chromium and nickel increase the strength of steel and prevent rusting. Steel that contains tungsten or molybdenum is very hard and tough. Such steels are used in lathes, drills, and other cutting machines. Even when red hot, these "high-speed" steels retain their sharp edges. Most large-scale manufacturing would be impossible without these special steels.

Bessemer Steel. Steel is made in several ways, but the most spectacular is the *Bessemer process.* In this process the impurities are "burned out" of the molten iron by blowing a blast of air through it. When all impurities are removed, the right amounts of carbon and manganese are added, and the mixture is cooled.

Open-Hearth Steel. A slower but more accurate method of making steel is the *open-hearth process.* This process takes longer, but the chemical reaction can be controlled better and steels can be made to meet more exact specifications. The finest steels are made in huge electric furnaces in which even closer control is possible.

The scientific study of steel has resulted in ways of improving this important alloy. By controlling the speed with which the steel cools, it may be hardened or softened. Slow cooling produces a soft but tough steel. Fast cooling produces a hard but brittle steel. In *case hardening,* a heated steel axle or wheel can be made to absorb carbon on the surface, thus making the outside hard while the inside remains softer but tougher.

Modern Steel Production. It is scarcely a century since man first learned to manufacture steel in commercial quantities. An American, William Kelly, worked out a process in 1851. But steel production did not begin in quantity until the end of the Civil War when the improved furnace of the Englishman, Henry Bessemer, came into use. Now about 5 million tons of Bessemer steel are made yearly, with about 70 million tons from the open hearths.

MINING COPPER

Copper was used for centuries before iron was discovered. In fact, copper is the first metal that man learned to use as he emerged from the Stone Age. The reason for this is that copper commonly occurs as a pure element. Early man found deposits of pure copper and learned to use this soft metal.

The greatest uses of copper have developed during the past 50 years. Copper is essential in all electric and electronic industries because it is such a good conductor of electricity. Besides, copper can be drawn into wire, made into tubes, and shaped into many useful forms.

In addition to the deposits of pure copper, there are a number of copper ores. Two beautiful green and blue ores are carbonates of copper, $CuCO_3$. Other ores are compounds of copper and oxygen, and copper and sulfur.

SMELTING COPPER

The separation of copper from a compound of copper and sulfur is not as easy as separating iron from oxygen. Carbon cannot be used because it does not unite as easily with sulfur as it does with oxygen. But the solution to this problem is not difficult.

The copper ore is finely ground and heated in a furnace with a blast of air. The sulfur unites with oxygen from the air, forming a gas, sulfur dioxide, SO_2. The copper also unites with oxygen, forming copper oxide, Cu_2O. The copper oxide is heated in a furnace and reduced with coke. The carbon unites with the oxygen, forming carbon monoxide, and the copper is left behind. The copper is then refined by electricity and sheets of practically pure copper are obtained.

USES OF COPPER

There is enough copper wire in this country to reach from the earth to the sun, with some left over. It is used in the telephone, telegraph,

radio, and in television. But copper has other uses. Nearly 22 million homes in the United States are wired for electricity. Many major industries depend entirely on electricity.

Every automobile requires about 50 pounds of copper. Most of this is used in making the radiator, for copper is a good conductor of heat as well as electricity. Trolley cars, buses, airplanes, steamships, and locomotives could not run without copper. A steam locomotive requires about 4 tons of copper; an electric locomotive, about 30 tons.

The most common alloy of copper is an alloy with zinc. This alloy is known as *brass* and is widely used in home and industry. *Bronze* is an alloy of copper, zinc, and tin. Copper is also alloyed with gold. Only 24-karat gold is pure gold. Gold less than 24-karat is an alloy, usually of gold and copper.

Copper compounds are widely used. Copper sulfate, $CuSO_4$, is poisonous and is used in sprays for fruits and vegetables. This same compound is used to kill microscopic plants that give drinking water a bad flavor.

A Bessemer converter during a "blow" is a fiery and noisy spectacle.

Courtesy Bethlehem Steel Company

ALUMINUM, THE FIRST LIGHT METAL

Every year, more and more aluminum is used. Airplanes are about 90 percent aluminum and aluminum alloys. Even freight cars and houses are being made of this light metal.

The story of the discovery of the method of separating aluminum from its ore is the story of a young college boy, Charles Martin Hall. This boy was interested in science. He experimented at school and at home until he found a way to separate aluminum from its ore by means of electricity. This was not easy. Even today, making aluminum is more complicated than making most other metals. Luckily, America produces much electricity from water power at low cost. Many aluminum refineries have been set up near such sources of electricity.

Preparing Aluminum. Aluminum ore, called *bauxite*, is a compound of aluminum and oxygen. It must be dried and concentrated until pure aluminum oxide, or *alumina*, Al_2O_3, is obtained. This purified ore is placed in a carbon-lined tank with a compound called *cryolite* that enables electricity to flow through it. Carbon rods are lowered into the tank, and electricity heats and melts the ore. The electric current at the same time separates the oxygen from the alumina. This oxygen unites with the carbon of the rods. The metal aluminum is set free and settles to the bottom in molten form.

The molten aluminum is drained from the bottom of the tank and cast into bars. The bars are made into rods, tubes, sheets, foils, or powders. Aluminum is alloyed with copper, magnesium, and nickel. Aluminum alloys are both light and strong, so they are used widely. Besides such common things as kitchen utensils, aluminum is used to make most of the "tinfoil" we use. Aluminum is also used in making aluminum paints, toothpaste tubes, wires for electricity, radio parts, and so forth.

OTHER IMPORTANT MINERALS

Mining the earth includes more than mining the three major metals. There are a dozen other metals of importance. Some of the rarer metals are used in making alloys of iron, copper, or aluminum.

The nonmetals in the earth's crust are of great importance also. One of these is sulfur, necessary in making useful chemical compounds and in processing rubber. Chlorine purifies our water. Bromine is used in making antiknock gasolines. Carbon is another essential non-metal. Salt, gypsum, asbestos, and borax are other minerals used in large quantities.

Clays—commonly compounds of potassium, aluminum, silicon, and oxygen—are used in the manufacture of bricks and porcelain ware. Such materials are known as *ceramics* and are used in industry and in the home. Porcelain insulators are as necessary for electric lines as the wires that carry the electricity.

WORKING WITH SCIENCE

1. Demonstrate the coking, or destruction distillation, of coal by heating crushed soft coal in a test tube with a rubber stopper and a delivery tube. Burn the gas that comes from the end of the delivery tube. When the tube has cooled, remove the coke. Examine specimens of coal and coke.

2. Iron can be manufactured in the classroom by the *thermit process* in which aluminum powder is used to reduce the powdered hematite to iron. Scientific supply companies sell thermit mixture ready to use. This mixture is ignited by means of a strip of magnesium and precautions against fire must be taken as the hot slag and molten iron are dangerous. When demonstrated properly, this is a most striking classroom experience. About an ounce of iron can be safely produced at one time.

3. With the help of a mechanic or someone who knows metals, make an exhibit of different iron alloys and show how they are used. You will have no difficulty in finding cast iron, low- and high-carbon steel. You can borrow a vanadium steel tool and perhaps can get other alloys as well.

4. Make a collection of copper objects from coins to tubing, wires, and so forth. Include illustrations of objects too large to exhibit of which copper is an essential part.

THE MINERAL FUELS

Anything that will burn well enough to supply reasonable amounts of heat may be called a *fuel*. Most fuels contain carbon. Coal and petroleum are two of our most important fuels. They are derived largely from plant and animal material of past ages. Both are sources of energy and will continue to be necessary until atomic energy is so well developed that it can take their place.

COAL

Coal consists of the remains of buried plants that have been altered by chemical changes and the weight of overlying rock. Many feet of plant material have been compressed and altered in making 1 foot of soft coal.

Kinds of Coal. There are three chief kinds of coal. *Lignite* has been altered least from the original plant material. It is often called *brown coal*. It contains about 56 percent carbon and about 35 percent moisture. Soft, or bituminous, coal contains about 66 percent carbon and about 10 percent moisture. It is by far the most common coal used in the United States. We produce more than 500 million tons of soft coal in this country in a normal year.

Hard coal, or anthracite, contains about 80 percent or more carbon and less than 3 percent moisture. On burning, anthracite gives off a little less heat than soft coal. However, it produces much less smoke. Anthracite deposits in the United States are limited to two areas in Pennsylvania, where the coal deposits have been folded and compressed.

Soft coal contains many compounds of hydrogen and carbon as well as pure carbon. These compounds can be liberated by heating the coal in the absence of air. This is known as *destructive distillation*. Coal gas and many other chemical compounds are driven off. These compounds condense as a sticky material called *coal tar*. From the chemical compounds in coal tar, many of our medicines, dyes, and other important substances are made.

The material left behind after the gases have been driven off is pure carbon, or coke. In the early manufacture of coke, the coal gas and coal tar were wasted. Now they are carefully collected and are valuable *byproducts*. The value of these byproducts is an example of how science has transformed an industry—in this

Left: Mining copper far underground in Montana. The miner is using a compressed-air drill to make holes for explosives. Right: Pouring an aluminum casting from a ladle of molten aluminum.

Courtesy Copper & Brass Research Association; Courtesy Aluminum Company of America

case the manufacture of coke—into a more useful and profitable undertaking.

PETROLEUM

Petroleum is thought to be the product of the decomposition of billions upon billions of microscopic sea plants or possibly equally small animals. These plants or animals settled to the bottom of the seas and were buried under deposits of mud and sand. Most of our petroleum deposits were raised above water by the great earth movements that formed mountains and valleys.

Sometimes oil seeps out from the surface rock. Under such conditions, petroleum was first obtained in Pennsylvania. Later, in 1859, Col. Edwin Drake had a well dug at Titusville, Pennsylvania that struck oil at a depth of about 70 feet. Modern oil wells go down hundreds and thousands of feet. Borings of 2 or 3 miles in search of oil have been made and some of the best geologists devote all their time to locating new oil deposits. We have used our oil deposits rapidly. Perhaps the largest reserves that still exist are under the seas along the continental shelf. These are now being located.

Uses of Petroleum. Petroleum is the substance from which gasoline is produced. The amount of gasoline produced from a barrel of petroleum has been increased from 5 gallons to 18 gallons through chemical methods.

Besides being a source of fuel, petroleum furnishes the lubricating oil used in keeping machinery in operation. Asphalt, used in surfacing roads, is made from petroleum. From petroleum we obtain compounds used in making synthetic rubber. Vaseline, paraffin, and benzine are well known petroleum products. Farmers living far from town may now have gas for stoves—gas made from petroleum.

Deposits of *natural gas* often are found with or near deposits of petroleum. This gas consists mainly of a compound of carbon and hydrogen called *methane* that burns readily and gives off much heat. It is another excellent fuel. Natural gas is piped hundreds of miles from the gas fields and provides fuel for many kitchen stoves and for many industries as well.

MINING TOMORROW

Long before Columbus landed, Indians had mines in this country. These were crude pits from which they dug flint for weapons and tools, brown or red iron ore for paint. They were mines, but the quantity of minerals they took from the earth was very small indeed.

In the past 250 years—especially in the last 50—we have used the earth's minerals with reckless speed. Luckily, we have been able to locate new deposits of metals, nonmetals, and mineral fuels—but the supply is definitely limited. Luckily also, scientists have worked out methods for using low-grade ores, for extracting more of the mineral from the ore, and for using the final products to better advantage. However, our prospects for mineral supplies in the future are not too bright. Minerals cannot be obtained from empty mines.

Reserves of Mineral Resources. One of the difficulties in planning for the future is the almost impossible job of estimating how much ore still remains in the earth and how much we can get out at reasonable cost. We now have better methods of estimating our mineral resources than we once had. As a result, we know of reserves that we did not know about 25 years ago.

Another problem is that the earth's mineral resources are not evenly distributed among the nations. America is fortunate and the United States is even more so. We have most of the minerals that we need. However, ores of tin, chromium, aluminum, manganese, and nickel must be imported. Our own supplies of iron, coal, petroleum, copper, gold, potash, phosphates, zinc, lead, and perhaps aluminum are sufficient for most of our needs. Yet, at times, we import some of these minerals, too.

What of the Future? We need not be concerned over the supply of some of our minerals. Some of them will last for generations unless we use them much faster than we have in the past. For the minerals that are more nearly used up, we have two hopes. New

Left: In drilling an oil well, the drill rotates in the hole. Cuttings are removed by pumps. Middle: A petroleum refinery. Right: Crude petroleum, natural gas, and finished products may travel by pipeline.

methods of mining and better ways of smelting the ore and preparing alloys may make them last longer.

If necessary, scientists are likely to develop good substitutes. Gasoline can be made from coal if need be. Oil can be extracted from low-grade sources such as oil shales and oil sands. At present these are too costly to use. Nevertheless, they are important reserves of petroleum. Plastics can take the place of some metals and scientists are finding ways of making wood products very much stronger and better.

Our use of minerals depends on the fact that they have been concentrated in certain parts of the earth's crust. Naturally, we use the most concentrated deposits first. Now we can supplement our mining of the earth's concentrated deposits by mining less concentrated sources— the seas and the air.

WORKING WITH SCIENCE

1. Set up an experiment to see what happens to wood when it is heated without air. Place some wood shavings in a test tube with a one-hole rubber stopper in which a small glass jet tube has been inserted. Heat the test tube over a flame. Try to set fire to the gas issuing from the jet. Examine the solid left in the test tube and the brownish substance that collects on the sides of the test tube or the jet tube. What kind of change has occurred?

2. A sample of crude petroleum can be distilled with simple apparatus and the fractions representing gasoline and kerosene extracted over a bunsen burner. **Caution:** *The vapors are flammable.*

READING YOU WILL ENJOY

Hibben, Thomas. *The Sons of Vulcan.* J. B. Lippincott Co., Philadelphia, 1940. A history of metals, their production, and uses. This book clearly indicates how the metals available at any particular time in history have made possible the type of culture that existed.

Ilin, M. *Men and Mountains.* J. B. Lippincott Co., Philadelphia, 1935. Chapter 8 of this fascinating book tells how men search for ores.

Jaffe, Bernard. *New World of Chemistry.* Silver Burdett Co., New York, 1947. The making of iron, steel, copper, aluminum, and petroleum and coal are discussed.

Strack, Lilian H. *Aluminum, A Magic Mineral.* Harper & Bros., New York, 1942. A profusely illustrated book which tells how aluminum is obtained and used.

Zim, Herbert S. and Cooper, Elizabeth K. *Minerals.* Harcourt, Brace & Co., New York, 1943. An excellent book that tells how men search for ores and also deals with rock-collecting as a hobby.

1

2

3

Early man used the seas, the lakes, and the rivers for several purposes. They provided him with water for drinking, washing, and bathing (1). They furnished him a route for travel after he had learned to build rafts, dugout canoes, and later on better and larger boats (2). They provided him with a plentiful supply of fish after he had learned to catch them by means of spears, seines, traps, and lines. Directly or indirectly the seas provided early man with salt. Some early peoples obtained salt from natural salt licks used by animals. Such salt licks came indirectly from the seas. Other early peoples (3) obtained salt by gathering it from dried-up pools at the seashore or by trapping the sea water in shallow basins and letting the heat of the sun drive off the liquid.

Modern man uses the seas much more effectively but not very differently. The seas still provide man with water, salt, fish, and routes for travel and commerce. Although man has long known that the seas contain tremendous quantities of minerals, only recently has he learned how to obtain a few of them at a cost low enough to make the project worthwhile. Bromine for use in antiknock gasoline (5) and magnesium (6), a very light metal, are now obtained directly (4) from sea water. But man is only beginning to mine this vast resource.

4

ETHYL

5

6

18

MINING THE SEAS

Erosion is constantly wearing away the land, carrying rocky material into the seas. As a result, many minerals are dissolved in sea water. Other minerals occur in deposits that lie beneath the seas. The seas are thus a great natural resource.

The seas are greater in area than the land. The earth's surface is about 72 percent water. The *average* depth of this water is more than 12,500 feet. The *average* elevation of the land above the seas is only 2400 feet. If this land were levelled off and spread evenly over the entire earth, its thickness would be only 660 feet. It would be covered with water to a depth of about 2 miles.

THE SEA FLOOR

The sea floor provides an interesting study. Only recently, a device for automatically measuring the depth of the ocean by means of sound waves has made extensive mapping possible. The bottom of the Atlantic Ocean has now been mapped more accurately than parts of North America were 100 years ago.

About 75 percent of the sea bottom is a flat basin, averaging more than 2 miles in depth. This relatively level bottom is broken by lower areas, or depressions, known as *deeps*. About 75 of these deeps are known. In several, the water is more than 5 miles deep. Near the Philippine Islands is the greatest deep—6.5 miles. In some places tremendous mountains rise from the sea bottom. Some of these are so tall that they rise through 2 miles of water and another mile or more of air. The mountains that form the Hawaiian Islands are of this type.

The sea floor is more than just the bottom of the water. It is the resting place of about 3 billion tons of solids that are carried into the seas each year. Much of this material is topsoil, our key resource, which through erosion is continually removed.

THE WATER OF THE SEAS

Of greater interest is sea water—the salty water that is so irritating to anyone who gets a mouthful when swimming. The most remarkable thing about sea water is that there is so much of it. It is a tremendous reservoir—not only of water, but of many elements and other compounds. It is also a reservoir of heat—such an important reservoir of heat that its importance in this respect alone can hardly be estimated.

SEA WATER AND TEMPERATURE

Fortunately for us, water is not a good conductor of heat. It heats more slowly and cools more slowly than land. The seas absorb heat from the sun. They absorb a great amount of heat during the summer when both land and air are warmer than the water and release it during the winter when both land and air are cooler.

The Gulf Stream. The stored heat of the seas is always on the move. Warm waters from the tropics flow in streams through the seas. Such a stream is the famous *Gulf Stream* which brings enough additional warmth to the British

Isles and the Scandinavian countries to modify the climate, agriculture, and industries.

New York State, which lacks the influence of the Gulf Stream, has temperatures in January that average between 14° and 32°F. Great Britain, which lies from about 300 to 600 miles farther north than New York, has January temperatures of 32° to 50°F because of this natural hot-water heating system.

Effects of Sea Temperature. The sea temperature affects winds and produces the famed San Francisco fogs and the more dangerous ones off the Newfoundland fishing banks. Cold sea currents off the west coast of South America and northern Africa have much to do with the deserts that make both those regions barren.

But let us consider sea water itself. Have you ever looked at sea water? A sample of it is clear and nearly colorless. Just to look at it you would not suspect how valuable a resource it is. But great wealth is dissolved in sea water. Possibly you will say, "What is all this fuss about salt?" But salt is only one of the many valuable substances that sea water contains.

GASES IN THE SEAS

Sea water is in continuous contact with air, and there is a continuous interchange between the two. Water continuously evaporates from the sea into the air. Microscopic bits of salt find their way into the air. Gases from the air are continuously being dissolved in the water of the seas.

Most of the earth's surface is covered by water.

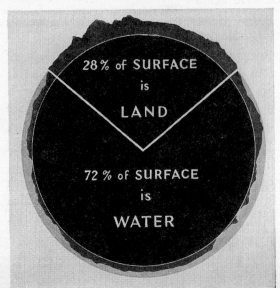

28% of SURFACE is LAND

72% of SURFACE is WATER

Oxygen makes up about 21 percent of the air. But when air dissolves in water, the percentage of oxygen in the total gases dissolved is *greater* than 21 percent, because oxygen is more soluble in water than are the other gases of the air. Thus, air dissolved in sea water contains as much as 34 percent oxygen. The total amount of air dissolved in sea water varies from about 1 to 2 cubic inches per quart, depending on the temperature. The colder the water, the more air will dissolve in it. This has a direct bearing on the quantity of living things the water can support.

The carbon dioxide of air does not all come directly from combustion or from the exhaled air of land animals. These do produce carbon dioxide, but the vast reservoir of carbon dioxide is the seas. Sea water contains from 18 to 27 times as much carbon dioxide as does the air. Most of this carbon dioxide is produced by living things in the water. Sea water is the reservoir that keeps the carbon dioxide content of air nearly constant.

SOLIDS IN THE SEAS

The solids dissolved in sea water vary from about 1 percent, where rivers enter the sea, to about 5 percent, where the circulation of water is partly restricted. But they average about 3.5 percent. One hundred pounds of sea water, if boiled away, will leave behind close to 3.5 pounds of solids. Most of this solid material is ordinary salt.

Considering the dissolved material as elements and simple groups of elements, the solids in sea water are shown on page 217.

These numbers mean much more when the size of the ocean is considered. For example, although calcium makes up only about 1 percent of the solids in sea water, the total amount of calcium in sea water is about 550 trillion tons. Calcium is found in all coral deposits, in shells, and in limestone.

The calcium of sea water is the source of all this—from a tiny shell to the thousand-mile Great Barrier Reef off Australia. The sodium in the ocean totals more than 14 quadrillion

216

Composition of Solids in Sea Water

Nonmetals	Percent
Chlorine	55.0
Bromine	0.2
Sulfates (SO_4)	8.0
Carbonates (CO_3)	0.2
Metals	
Sodium	30.0
Potassium	1.1
Calcium	1.2
Magnesium	4.0
Other	0.3*
Total	100.0

* Traces of gold, iron, copper, and many other elements and compounds.

tons, and the grand total of all dissolved solids in the ocean reaches the stupendous figure of 46 quadrillion tons.

In themselves, these figures on the dissolved solids in the ocean may not mean much to you. But perhaps another example will make them clearer. There is very, very little iron dissolved in sea water—less than one-thousandth of 1 percent. But the total amount of iron comes to about 11.5 trillion tons. If we could extract this iron from the seas, it would be sufficient to supply the world for more than 100,000 years at our present rate of use.

The fresh water that flows into the seas from rivers carries small amounts of dissolved minerals as well as undissolved solids. These dissolved minerals add about 3 billion tons of elements and compounds to the seas every year. This dissolved and suspended solid material is removed from the land as rain water runs over and through it. It amounts to about 87 tons from every square mile of land. For the 6 million square miles of North America, the minerals removed amount to nearly 500 million tons each year.

These figures indicate the riches that the seas contain. The substances listed in the table at the left are only the most common. A by-product of this figuring is an interesting estimate of the age of the seas. To make this estimate, scientists assume that all water was

The Gulf Stream's heat modifies the climate in many places.

Courtesy of the International Salt Co., Inc., Scranton, Pa.

Left: Brine pumped from salt wells is stored in tanks outside a modern salt plant. The water is removed by evaporation under reduced pressure. Right: Mining salt underground with special machinery.

fresh in the beginning and that the elements and compounds have all been added by rivers at rates similar to the present. With allow-ances for a number of other factors, the seas are estimated to be at least 100 million years old.

WORKING WITH SCIENCE

1. Using a convection tube or a glass beaker with sawdust and a color indicator, demonstrate convection currents in water. The convection currents result from unequal heating caused by the fact that water does not transmit heat very well.

2. Allow a glass of tap water to stand for several hours. Notice the bubbles that collect on the sides of the glass. Where do these bubbles of air come from? Why?

3. Fill a small aquarium with water that has been boiled and allowed to cool. Put a goldfish in this water and watch. Have another aquarium of fresh tap water ready to put the goldfish into if things go too badly with it.

SALT FROM THE SEAS

The most abundant dissolved substance in sea water, of course, is the salt that gives the sea its taste. This salt, common table salt, is one of the wonders of chemistry. The small white grains you eat every day are absolutely necessary to life. An animal placed on a diet without salt would soon die. Yet this life-giving salt is made of two elements, both of which are dangerous poisons.

WHAT IS SALT?

It is fortunate that the properties of a chemical compound are not related to the properties of the elements in it. If they were, salt would be a peculiar combination of a silvery metal and a greenish-yellow gas.

The metal is *sodium*, Na, which is a most common and yet most rare metal. Sodium in compounds is common. It is found in salt and in many rock-forming minerals. Sodium, the metal, is rare because it is so active that it is never found free. It can be obtained from its compounds only by means of electricity under special conditions. The greenish-yellow gas is *chlorine*, Cl_2. Chlorine is as active as sodium and is never found free.

The 15 million tons of salt used in the United States every year are obtained by mining the seas or by mining the land for salt from seas that long ago dried up. But whether the seas are mined directly or indirectly, almost all our salt comes from them. The only other source worth noting is the salt lakes which really are small seas. Great Salt Lake and the Dead Sea are examples of salt lakes.

MAKING SALT FROM SEA WATER

The oldest method of mining the seas for salt is still widely used in places with warm climates. It consists of building an earthwork, or *dike*, that cuts off a shallow piece of shore. At high tide, sea water enters. The dike is shut and the sea water is trapped. Heat from the sun evaporates the water, making a more and more concentrated salt solution.

Soon the salt solution becomes so concentrated that salt crystals begin to form. At this point, more sea water is allowed to enter. Evaporation continues. This process is repeated again and again, until a large amount of salt is deposited. The salt is scraped into piles, drained, and dried. Though crudely prepared, it is ready for many uses. It is further cleaned and purified for human consumption.

MINING SALT

Salt-bearing layers of rock lie along the south side of the Great Lakes. These alone produce two-thirds of the American salt supply. Michigan is the leading salt-producing state. New York, Ohio, Louisiana, Kansas, Texas, and Utah are producers also.

Salt is mined in two different ways. The simplest and most typical method of mining is to sink a shaft like that at Retsof, New York, the largest salt mine in the world. Here, a quarter of a mile underground, is a thick layer of salt. The workings of the mine extend over a thousand acres, with galleries running 1.5 miles along the salt layer. Electric trains and other mechanical equipment bring the lumps of salt to the surface where the salt is crushed and refined.

SALT FROM WELLS

Under other conditions, the producers make use of an important property of salt—the ease with which it dissolves in water. A well, containing several pipes within one another, is sunk into the salt layer. Fresh water is pumped down to the salt for several months. The salt dissolves.

By the end of several months, the water has dissolved all the salt it can hold. A chemist would say that a *saturated solution* of salt has been produced. This solution is pumped up into large tanks where it is fed into a series of evaporators. In the evaporators, the water is evaporated off under reduced pressure and the salt crystallized.

USES OF SALT

The uses of salt include all those common ones such as flavoring food, preserving fish and meat, making pickles, melting ice from the street or sidewalk, and freezing ice cream. Other uses are less well known. In farming, salt blocks for livestock are necessary. Most cattle do not get enough salt and need an extra supply. Deer and buffalo were known to travel miles to *salt licks* or natural salt springs.

In the home, salt is used in foods and in preserving meats. The medical uses of salt are varied. Salt is used in making solutions that

Left: In this rotating drier, the last traces of moisture are removed from crystallized salt. Right: Cattle gathered around a salt block. Why are such salt blocks necessary?

Courtesy of the International Salt Co., Inc., Scranton, Pa.; U. S. D. A. photo

must mix readily with blood, the plasma of which is similar to a dilute salt solution.

This solution of 0.6 to 0.8 percent salt in distilled water is called a *physiological saline solution* and is used in medicine and in biological experiments. Many kinds of injections are mixed with such a salt solution. Salt is used as a gargle and mouthwash and is taken as an aid in preventing heat exhaustion. Teeth may be cleaned effectively with a bit of salt on a toothbrush.

Industrial Uses of Salt. Important as these uses may be, the industrial uses of salt require the greatest quantities. The tanning of leather, the making of soap and chlorine, the smelting of copper, lead, and silver ores all require salt. The manufacture of ice requires a strong salt solution. In addition, it is used in the making of many chemical compounds, such as washing and baking soda and lye.

CHEMISTRY OF SALT

When electricity flows through a solution of salt (sodium chloride), electrified particles, or *ions*, of sodium and chlorine in the solution separate. Ions are electrically charged atoms or groups of atoms. Pure chlorine gas would be liberated and pure sodium would be released if water were not present. But a chemical reaction between the sodium and the water occurs. This liberates part of the hydrogen of the water and leaves a compound of sodium, oxygen, and hydrogen called *sodium hydroxide*, or lye. The final result may be written:

$$2NaCl + 2H_2O \rightarrow 2NaOH + Cl_2 + H_2$$
salt + water → sodium + chlorine + hydrogen
hydroxide

This process is carried on in factories where low-cost electricity, usually from water power, is available. It is carried on in special tanks called *Vorce cells*. These produce a steady supply of chlorine gas, hydrogen gas, and sodium hydroxide. All three of these substances are valuable. The chlorine is used in making bleaching powder and solutions, and in purifying drinking water.

Hydrogen gas is the lightest of all the elements. It is highly flammable. It is used industrially in large quantities. Most margarines and cooking fats are made by chemically treating such oils as cottonseed oil with hydrogen. Sodium hydroxide is used in making rayons, dyes, soaps, and many other products.

Salt is used in another important chemical process in making a series of important compounds. In this process, known as the *Solvay process*, ammonia gas, NH_3, and carbon dioxide, CO_2, are passed through a solution of salt. Sodium bicarbonate, $NaHCO_3$, and ammonium chloride, NH_4Cl, are formed:

$$NaCl + NH_3 + H_2O + CO_2 \rightarrow NaHCO_3 + NH_4Cl$$
salt + am- + water + carbon → sodium + ammo-
monia dioxide bicar- nium
bonate chloride

Ammonium chloride is used in making dry batteries, or "dry cells." Sodium bicarbonate is used as baking soda and in baking powders. When sodium bicarbonate is heated, water and carbon dioxide are given off and *washing soda*, or sodium carbonate, remains:

$$2NaHCO_3 \rightarrow Na_2CO_3 + H_2O + CO_2$$
sodium → sodium + water + carbon
bicarbonate carbonate dioxide

Washing soda is used in industry as well as in the home. It is most important in the manufacture of glass and in the manufacture of cleansers, soaps, and many other chemical compounds.

WORKING WITH SCIENCE

1. Experiment with formation of crystals by letting saucers of salt, sugar, alum, copper sulfate, and other solutions evaporate on a quiet shelf or over a radiator.

2. Prepare a hot saturated salt solution. What happens when this solution is allowed to cool? What happens when some of the water is evaporated?

3. Find out about evaporation under reduced pressure. What principle is involved? How is this method used in making evaporated milk, penicillin, and salt?

4. Boil some water and add sugar to it until no more will dissolve. Hang a piece of string down the middle of the glass of hot water. Leave over-night in a cool place. Report on what you find the next day. What kind of candy does it look like?

5. Make a collection and exhibit of different forms of salt—table, rock, tablets, and so forth; also products containing salt or made with or from salt. Salt pork, glass, baking soda, lye, and bleaching powder might be included.

OTHER SUBSTANCES FROM THE SEAS

Until relatively recently, salt was the only substance of importance to be obtained directly or indirectly from the seas. Yet chemists knew that many other substances were present in sea water. However, it has been difficult to develop profitable ways to extract the other substances found in sea water.

Living Things Mine the Seas. Oddly enough, some things that our scientists have not done, have been done by other living things. Oysters concentrate copper from sea water in their tissues, though not nearly enough to make into wire.

Seaweeds, especially the giant kelp plants that grow in the Pacific Ocean, concentrate iodine from the seas, even though in sea water it occurs in concentrations of only about two parts per million. The kelp plants are gathered and burned, and the iodine is separated from the ashes.

ANTIKNOCK GASOLINE DEPENDS ON THE SEAS

The story of bromine is the first of the new ventures in mining the seas. Bromine is related to iodine. It is a reddish-brown, heavy liquid that evaporates into a poisonous gas of the same color. Bromine has many uses. Bromine and silver are used in making the compound silver bromide. Silver bromide is used in great quantities in making photographic films and papers.

Bromine from the Seas. But the real need for bromine developed only recently. It came with the perfection of tetraethyl lead, a compound added in small amounts to gasoline to eliminate the "knock" in gasoline engines and increase the engine's power. Chemists found that ethylene dibromide, a compound containing bromine, made tetraethyl lead much more effective.

Sea water contains bromine, 2 ounces per ton or about 70 pounds in 1 million pounds of sea water. So huge plants were built to extract bromine from sea water. Because there is so little bromine in sea water, the amount of water that passes through the plants each day

Left: In this plant at Freeport, Texas, bromine is extracted from sea water. Sea water enters the plant through the huge channel on the left. Right: A cell in which magnesium is produced electrically.

Courtesy The Dow Chemical Company

is enough to meet the drinking-water requirements of a city as large as New York.

The chemical process of producing bromine from sea water is simple. The bromine in sea water is in the compound magnesium bromide, $MgBr_2$. To release the bromine, chlorine, a more active element, is added. The chlorine *replaces* the bromine in the compound as follows:

$$MgBr_2 \; + \; Cl_2 \; \rightarrow \; MgCl_2 \; + \; Br_2$$

magnesium + chlorine → magnesium + bromine
bromide   chloride

This method of mining the seas has increased the production of bromine tremendously. The capacity of these plants is measured in millions of pounds of bromine each year.

MAGNESIUM FROM THE SEAS

A metal now coming into wide use, and of which the seas contain vast amounts, is magnesium. Magnesium is a very light metal, only about two-thirds as heavy as aluminum.

Until recently, this very light metal was not widely used. Magnesium compounds, such as Epsom salts and asbestos, had many uses. But the metal magnesium itself was known mostly for the intense heat and white light produced when it burned. This made magnesium an important ingredient in flares, fireworks, photoflash bulbs, and flashlight powders.

But magnesium is very light and can be alloyed with aluminum, copper, and other metals to make very strong alloys. Furthermore, large pieces of magnesium do not burn easily. Consequently, magnesium alloys are used in making aircraft and in other places where lightness and strength are necessary.

Whenever there is a demand for a material, scientists redouble their search for a supply. Magnesium had been obtained from mines that tapped salt layers in sedimentary rocks. Such deposits are found in British Columbia, Michigan, Germany, and elsewhere, but they were not great enough to meet the demand.

So chemists turned to the seas for magnesium. Huge plants were set up along the Gulf of Mexico and on the Pacific coast. Here in the ocean an inexhaustible supply of magnesium compounds, chiefly magnesium chloride, is available. However, only one-tenth of 1 percent of sea water is magnesium and not all of this can be removed. At best, only 7 pounds of magnesium can be extracted from a ton of sea water.

Pure magnesium is obtained from magnesium chloride by means of electricity. The magnesium chloride is first separated from the sea water. It is then melted and broken up into its two elements, magnesium and chlorine, by electricity. The magnesium is collected as a light, silvery metal at the negative electrode, or *cathode*, and the chlorine is liberated at the positive electrode, or *anode*.

No other metal has had so many new uses in so short a time. No doubt we will be using

Left: Magnesium castings are lighter than aluminum, and certain of its alloys are very strong. Right: A photoflash bulb contains magnesium foil. When flashed, it produces an intense white light.

Courtesy The Dow Chemical Company; Courtesy General Electric Company

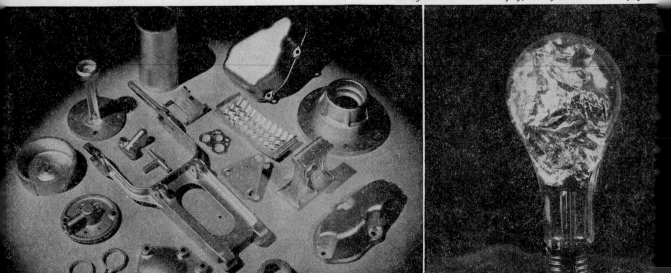

magnesium more and more and will depend more and more on the seas as a source of the metal.

What of the Future? The future of mining the seas is uncertain because mining the seas deals with the lowest-grade ores yet used. We naturally use more concentrated ores when these are available. Only when the more concentrated ores are exhausted do we use less concentrated deposits.

However, the substances in sea water are in excellent form to be used. They are all present as soluble salts that are fairly easily separated from other substances in sea water. Our ability to use the seas as a source of raw materials depends on the supply of low-cost energy available. Since the substances in sea water are present in such small amounts, more energy is used in obtaining them than in mining more concentrated deposits. It is possible that the development of atomic energy power plants may make mining of the seas much more common and extensive than at present.

WORKING WITH SCIENCE

1. Bromine can be prepared by passing chlorine gas into a beaker containing a weak solution of sodium bromide. A few drops of carbon tetrachloride added to the water and shaken will dissolve the bromine out of the water and concentrate the brown element in the carbon tetrachloride.

2. Prepare a chart of as many chemicals as you can that contain or are made with the use of bromine. Use actual samples of chemicals wherever possible.

WATER FROM THE SEAS

The seas have one other tremendous resource —water! Of course, the seas are not often mined for water. Only rarely must this be done, but such occasions are often matters of life and death.

Why You Cannot Drink Sea Water. Mining the seas for water is the reverse of mining for magnesium or bromine. The idea is to get rid of the substances dissolved in the water and retain the water.

Left: A lake or a reservoir is the product of a natural distillation and condensation process known as the water cycle. Right: A laboratory still is a very efficient producer of pure distilled water.

Philip Gendreau; Courtesy Barnstead Still & Sterilizer Co., Inc.

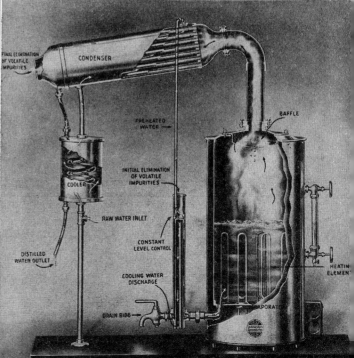

Sea water cannot be drunk because the salt concentration in the blood is less than 1 percent and that of sea water about 3.5 percent.

Because of osmosis, water would flow *from* the blood and body tissues toward the more concentrated solution in the stomach and intestines. Thus, drinking sea water only aggravates thirst.

CHEMICAL TREATMENT

One method of making drinking water from sea water consists of adding special silver compounds to a measured amount of sea water. These compounds react with the salts in the water and produce insoluble compounds. After standing awhile, the insoluble compounds settle out and fresh drinking water can be drained off.

DISTILLATION

The most important method of preparing fresh water from sea water involves heating the water until it turns into water vapor, or steam, and then cooling the water vapor until it condenses back into water again. Since only the water molecules of the salt water change into vapor, they condense into pure water, thus separating the water from the salt.

Ordinarily, distilling is carried on in an apparatus with a long spout and a cooling coil. The water is heated until it changes to steam. The steam is condensed by a stream of cold water running around the steam tube. The fresh distilled water drips out at the end. No better method of purifying water is known and no water is as pure as water that has been distilled several times. Distilling not only removes salts, minerals, and gases, but bacteria as well.

Distillation is ordinarily too expensive a method to use, except in laboratories where very pure water is needed for experimental work. However, ships use distillation on a large scale. It keeps them from having to carry large supplies of water for boilers and bathing, cooking, and drinking.

When we turn on a faucet to get a drink of water, we are, in a sense, mining the seas for water. The water we drink is prepared in a gigantic natural still that uses heat from the sun.

Heat from the sun is constantly evaporating water from the seas and from rivers, lakes, green plants, and the soil itself. With such a large surface area, the amount of evaporation is tremendous. This water vapor is present in air even though clouds are not to be seen. When a part of the air is cooled, it can no longer hold as much moisture as when it was warmer and the excess moisture falls as rain or some other form of falling water.

Annual Rainfall Varies. The annual rainfall on the earth varies from place to place. In the driest deserts it is less than 1 inch a year. In the world's wettest place, Cherrapunji, India, the rainfall averages 426 inches a year. This means that if the rain did not evaporate, sink into the ground, or run off, its depth would be 35½ feet at the end of the year. The average annual rainfall in the United States is about 29 inches.

Actually these figures do not give a clear idea of the amount of rain that falls on the earth. One scientist has estimated that the rainfall each year amounts to about 30,000 cubic miles of water. This figure becomes very impressive when you realize that 1 cubic mile of water weighs more than 4 billion tons.

What Happens to Rain Water? This tremendous amount of distilled rain water is not 100 percent pure by the time it reaches the ground. It contains dissolved gases and dust particles from the air. Over half the rain falls in the oceans from whence it came. Part evaporates into the air. The part that remains is the part that interests us most.

Two other things can happen to rain, and both usually do. It can run off over the ground or it can sink into the ground. In either case, the water dissolves traces of soil compounds and picks up soil bacteria and clay particles.

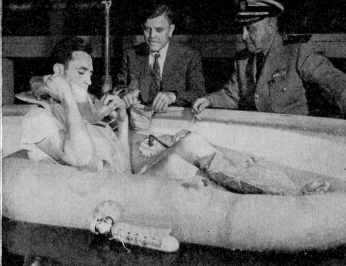

U. S. D. A. photo by Forsythe; Official U. S. Navy photo

Left: Even in areas of little rainfall, water may be obtained by tapping underground sources by means of wells. Right: Testing a device that produces drinking water from sea water by means of chemicals.

It rapidly becomes less pure. It may pick up disease germs or so much clay or mud that it becomes cloudy. Surface water is not often pure enough to drink without purification.

The water that sinks into the ground helps support plant life. Some of it flows underground along layers of rock through which it cannot pass. Occasionally such water reaches the surface on a hillside, forming a spring. At other places, wells must be drilled into the earth to tap the underground supply.

Sources of Water in Rural Areas. Springs and wells are adequate sources of farm water. Usually treatment or purification is not necessary. However, during periods of little or no rainfall, the source of such water may be cut off and springs and wells become dry. Water from springs and wells may become contaminated by disease germs unless proper safeguards are taken. Garbage and sewage disposal must be so planned that contamination from those sources is impossible.

City Water Supplies. Towns and cities usually do not use wells as sources of water unless the wells extend down into deep water-bearing layers that cannot be contaminated and that will provide a steady supply of water. Such supplies are often obtained. But many large cities use rivers and lakes for their supplies of water.

If lakes are not available, artificial lakes may be made. Rivers are dammed up to build large *reservoirs* where water is collected and stored. If possible, such reservoirs are built at an elevation higher than the city so that water flows by gravity to the places where it will be used. If this is not possible, pumps are used to force the water through the city's water mains.

PURIFYING WATER SUPPLIES

Storage in reservoirs helps purify water. Mud and fine particles in the water settle to the bottom, carrying bacteria with them. Chemical compounds, such as filter alum, may be added. These compounds help any particles in the water to settle out. This method is called *coagulation*. But this, in itself, is not a sufficient safeguard for large cities where polluted water might easily start an epidemic of typhoid fever or dysentery. Further purification is obtained in several ways. One or more of these ways may be used, depending on what the water supply needs.

Filtering traps and holds most bacteria or other very small living things in water. The water moves slowly through thick filter beds of sand and gravel. These act as a very fine strainer and catch and remove most harmful material. The filter beds gradually become

225

choked with material and from time to time must be flushed out and cleaned.

Filtering removes most substances from water except material that is dissolved in it. Dissolved materials can be removed only by distillation or chemical treatment.

Chlorination. A common method of protecting the water supply is by adding some substance that kills the living things it may contain. Chlorine, which comes indirectly from the seas, is commonly used for this purpose. The method is called *chlorination.*

A small flow of chlorine into a water supply is enough to kill any disease germs. Excess chlorine is soon removed by the sun and air, and the quality of the water is not harmed. In places where the chances of contamination are very great, as in swimming pools, larger amounts of chlorine may be used.

Aeration. Another method of purifying a water supply is by spraying it into the air in many fine sprays. This process is called *aeration.* In aeration, the water comes into contact with oxygen of the air and with sunlight. Both are effective in killing disease germs.

IMPORTANCE OF THE SEAS

Thus we see how important the seas are to us. Directly or indirectly, our water, much of our food, and many of our raw materials come from the seas. As the years go by, probably we will get more and more from the seas—not only foods but metals and other substances.

Man has a peculiar problem in dealing with his mineral resources. He must wage a constant struggle to keep his topsoil, minerals, and other precious resources from being washed into the seas by erosion. But once they get into the seas, man can use the seas as a resource and thus make up somewhat for the damage that has been done. However, the products we get from the seas, valuable as they are, do not balance and cannot replace the most important resource lost by erosion—topsoil. We must use the seas as a resource, but we must preserve the land also.

The seas are a resource that all nations and all men can use together. When our land reserves of metals get too low, chemists will turn to the seas for new supplies. Russia, England, France, Brazil, Australia, and America can all take magnesium, bromine, and whatever they need from the seas. There never need be wars or rivalries to obtain the minerals of the seas. The seas are the reservoir into which millions of tons of metals are washed from the land. They are abundant, and the seas bring them to the shores of almost all nations that need them.

WORKING WITH SCIENCE

1. Set up a demonstration based on osmosis to show why a person cannot drink sea water.

2. Prepare distilled water by the use of a still and condenser or if this apparatus is not available, use an ordinary teakettle and a sheet of glass cooled on its upper surface by a cold moist cloth.

3. To demonstrate the effect of surface area on evaporation, take two identical washcloths, wet both and wring out equally well. Hang one to dry and leave the other crumpled up. Estimate surface area in each case and note time of drying.

4. Study any wells and springs in your locality. What is their rate of flow? Where does the water in them come from? How well do they work in dry spells?

5. If you live on a farm or in a rural community, find out from your county agricultural agent or health officer how to check your own water supply. Many states will test the purity of your water free of charge. Samples of the water must be taken carefully.

6. Find out how people in your neighborhood choose the location for the sinking of a well. What information do they use in deciding which is the best location?

7. By the use of a funnel as a reservoir and rubber tubing and glass tubes, demonstrate the flow of water in a water system where the reservoir is higher than the place of use.

8. Demonstrate the difference between a solution and a suspension and the filtering of water, by building a filter of layers of sand and charcoal. Add a bit of salt and some clay to water until it becomes cloudy. See if the filter removes the clay and salt.

9. Visit a swimming pool where chlorine is used. Find out how it is bought, what care must be taken in using it, and how the user knows how much chlorine to put in the water.

READING YOU WILL ENJOY

Croneis, Carey G. and Krumbein, William C. *Down to Earth: An Introduction to Geology*. University of Chicago Press, Chicago, 1936. Chapters 7–12 tell the part played by water in making the earth what it now is.

Holmes, Harry N. *Out of the Test Tube* (4th ed.). Emerson Books, New York, 1945. Chapter 7 deals with "the water of life."

Reed, W. Maxwell and Bronson, Wilfred S. *The Sea for Sam*. Harcourt, Brace & Co., New York, 1935. One of the most popular books dealing with the rich resources of the seas.

Strack, Lilian H. *Magnesium, A Magic Mineral*. Harper & Bros., New York, 1943. The story of this increasingly important light metal, now obtained from sea water.

1

2

From the day man first drew breath, and for millions of years before that, plants and animals (1) have been using the air—mining it—for oxygen and carbon dioxide. But man did not know that this was going on for many thousands of years. When he discovered how to use fire and later learned to make fire himself (2), oxygen was being used. It came then, as it does today, from the air around us. Even earlier than this, millions of years earlier, green plants were using the carbon dioxide of air for making their woody stems and their sweetish fluids and their starchy flesh. All the while, soil bacteria were robbing air of its nitrogen to furnish plants with necessary raw material to build into proteins. But man did not know that these things were going on. Most of these secrets he has learned relatively recently, within the past two or three centuries.

3

4

As man's knowledge of the air grew, he used it for many purposes. He harnessed the fickle winds and made them drive his sailing ships and his windmills (3). He learned how to travel through the air in balloons, airships, and airplanes (4). He learned how to take nitrogen from the air and to build it into synthetic fertilizers (5) and explosives. He learned how to compress the air and imprison it in rubber tires to smooth his travel. He also learned how to put compressed air to doing such things as breaking up concrete pavement and spraying paint. He learned how to change air into a liquid so cold it freezes mercury and alcohol. He learned how to put the air's inert gases, such as neon and argon, to work in selling his products (6) and lengthening the life of his electric light bulbs. The air that surrounds you may not seem to be of much importance commercially, but it is, and many new uses are being found for it as the days pass by.

5

6

19

MINING THE AIR

The atmosphere is another of our three great resources. It is often called the *ocean of air* and rightly so. The atmosphere has no upper surface, however. But it has much in common with the hydrosphere, or seas. Both are composed of substances that flow and fill up space. Such substances are called *fluids*.

The atmosphere, even more than the seas, is a resource that any nation can use and that most living things *must* use. Only a few kinds of bacteria can get along without air. As you know, air dissolved in the seas is the source of oxygen for marine life. Without an atmosphere, life as we know it could not exist.

PROPERTIES OF AIR

There are important differences between the ocean of air and the ocean of water. The ocean of water is largely a single chemical compound—water, H_2O. This water contains many substances dissolved in it. Air contains a number of elements and compounds that are mixed together but are not united chemically. The currents of the air are more changing and affect the earth more than the currents of the oceans.

AIR IS COMPRESSIBLE

Air can be squeezed together, or *compressed*, whereas the seas, for all practical purposes, cannot. As you know, the molecules of a gas are in motion and are relatively far apart. The molecules can be squeezed together so that the gas occupies less space. Such squeezing is called *compression*.

You can put a quart of air in a heavy container and, by pressing sufficiently, you can squeeze the air until its volume is a pint or less. But if you try the same thing with a quart of water, you will find that even the most powerful machines can compress water only very slightly. The container will break

long before the water is compressed to any extent.

The physical properties that make air so different from water result in its many uses. If air could not be compressed, we could not breathe, for our method of breathing takes advantage of changes in pressure to force air into and out of our lungs. All compressed-air devices from air brakes to drills and pumps are based on this property, too.

The physical properties of air have made the atmosphere useful in transportation. The first practical balloon was made in 1793. While balloons are not closely related to airplanes, balloons did open up the atmosphere

In compression, molecules are squeezed together.

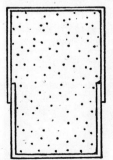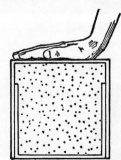

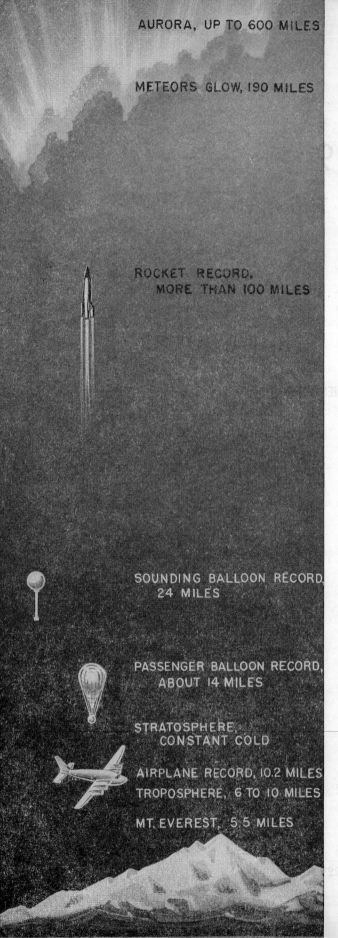

AURORA, UP TO 600 MILES

METEORS GLOW, 190 MILES

ROCKET RECORD,
MORE THAN 100 MILES

SOUNDING BALLOON RECORD,
24 MILES

PASSENGER BALLOON RECORD,
ABOUT 14 MILES

STRATOSPHERE,
CONSTANT COLD

AIRPLANE RECORD, 10.2 MILES
TROPOSPHERE, 6 TO 10 MILES

MT. EVEREST, 5.5 MILES

to exploration and made experiments possible. Rockets do not need air to support them in flight. They actually travel faster when they are high up where there is very little air.

Before man could make intelligent use of air, he had to discover that there was such a thing. This was not easy. Even today we speak of an empty bottle when we know it is filled with air. Early men thought space was empty. They thought that the wind was a spirit breath and rain was caused by a whim of the gods. Gradually men learned that air was a physical substance and since all air looked alike, they assumed that air was a single, simple substance. So it is not surprising that the ancients thought of air as one of the "four elements."

Priestley Discovers Oxygen. Scientific knowledge of the air is as about as new as the United States. In 1774 Joseph Priestley discovered the pure gas oxygen, and this element was soon shown to be necessary to burning and to life itself. Nitrogen, the other major gas in air, was studied about the same time. Since then, discoveries about the composition of the atmosphere were not so rapid, and our knowledge of the lesser gases in the atmosphere is scarcely 50 years old.

COMPOSITION OF THE ATMOSPHERE

Samples of air from most places in the atmosphere show that the same substances are present almost regardless of where the samples are taken.

The carbon dioxide that pours into the atmosphere from the respiration of organisms, from fires, furnaces, and exhaust pipes of cars does not increase the carbon dioxide present in the air to any great extent. It is roughly matched by the vast amounts of carbon dioxide used by plants in photosynthesis.

The table on page 231 shows the approximate composition of dry air.

But air is rarely dry. Water vapor is usually present to some extent. By volume, the amount varies from just a trace on cold dry days to as much as 5 percent on hot, humid days. The composition of the atmosphere may be somewhat different today than it was millions of years ago. While evidence is uncertain, there is some reason to believe that slight changes in the composition of the atmosphere have had marked effects on climate and on living things.

Approximate Composition of Dry Air

Gas	Percent by Volume
Oxygen	21
Nitrogen	78
Argon and other similar gases	0.96
Carbon dioxide	0.04
Total	100.00

WORKING WITH SCIENCE

1. Compressibility of air can be shown by corking a bottle with a one-hole stopper though which runs a *long* glass tube with funnel attached. Water poured into the funnel will partly fill the bottle even though no air can escape. This is because the air is compressed slightly.

2. To demonstrate the percentage of oxygen in air, place some iron filings in a large test tube whose inside walls have been moistened with water. The iron filings stick to the wet inside of the test tube. Invert the tube over colored water in a jar and leave overnight. Note rise of water in tube and change of color of the iron. Explain.

3. To show that air occupies space, place a two-hole stopper in a bottle. Insert a *short* glass tube connected to a funnel. Water will run into the bottle only when the second hole is opened to permit air to escape. Pouring the water from a narrow-mouthed bottle demonstrates that air bubbles enter to take the place of the water which leaves.

4. That air has weight can be demonstrated with any simple balance or even a balance improvised from a yardstick suspended on a string. Weigh an empty balloon. Weigh it again filled with air. If balance is adjusted correctly, this is enough air to be weighed.

5. Air weighs about 0.08 pounds per cubic foot. Measure your classroom and compute the volume and weight of air in the room. Make an estimate for the school. How much does a cubic mile of air weigh?

OXYGEN FROM THE AIR

The chief benefit you get from the air you breathe is its oxygen content. Oxygen can be obtained from several substances that contain the element. It can be obtained by passing electricity through water—the simplest and commonest compound that contains oxygen. The water breaks down into the two elements of which it is composed, and these two gases are easily collected. The equation is as follows:

$$2H_2O \rightarrow 2H_2 + O_2$$

Oxygen has many uses in industry, medicine (in oxygen tent), high-altitude flying, and deep-sea diving. It can be separated from the other gases of the air by first freezing the air to a liquid and then boiling off the other gases.

Oxygen has many uses. Left: Oxygen tent provides oxygen for persons whose respiratory systems do not function normally. Middle: Tanks of oxygen for industrial uses. Right: Oxyacetylene torch cutting through several metal plates.

Courtesy Air Reduction Co., Inc.

LIQUID AIR AND OXYGEN

In 1883 two Polish scientists prepared the first good-sized sample of *liquid air*. Methods have since improved and now air is liquified in large quantities. It is made by compressing air and cooling it many times in a continuous process.

Liquid air is a light-blue liquid almost as heavy as water. It boils at about $-310°F$. It does not have a definite boiling point, since each of the elements and compounds in it boils at a different temperature. The boiling point of liquid nitrogen is nearly $-321°F$, while liquid oxygen must be warmed to $-297°F$ before it boils. This difference of $24°F$ makes possible the separation of oxygen from nitrogen.

By maintaining the temperature at about $-310°F$, the nitrogen boils off completely, leaving nearly pure liquid oxygen. The liquid oxygen is then pumped into an intermediate tank, where it changes from a liquid to a gas, and then into steel cylinders under pressure.

OXYGEN AND COMBUSTION

All living things require oxygen for oxidation, or cellular respiration, a chemical change in which elements or compounds unite with oxygen and release energy. Oxidation on a much larger scale is necessary in nearly all industry. In industry we are usually interested in oxidation that is so rapid that large amounts of heat are liberated with fire and flame. This *rapid oxidation* in which heat and light are given off is called burning, or *combustion*. Without it, iron and steel could not be made; automobiles and airplanes could not move; our civilization would be at a standstill.

For most burning operations, the diluted oxygen of the air can be used. The 21 percent oxygen of air is enough. If more oxygen is needed, it can be provided easily. Blowing or forcing a greater volume of air into a flame supplies more oxygen. Nearly all furnaces used for industrial heating, and many used for home heating, are equipped with a fan to mix more air with the burning fuel and thus obtain more heat from the fuel being burned.

Another way to increase the speed of combustion is to increase the concentration of oxygen. Although it is expensive to substitute nearly pure oxygen for the 21 percent oxygen of air, it is often worth doing. For example, acetylene burning in air produces a smoky yellow flame of rather low temperature. When acetylene is mixed with pure oxygen, as in an *oxyacetylene torch*, the crisp blue flame reaches almost $6000°F$. If you have ever seen an oxyacetylene torch cutting through steel plates like cardboard, you realize how important this high-temperature burning can be.

The flame of an oxyacetylene torch does not need air to burn, since it has its own oxygen supply. Thus, it is possible to use such a torch under water. The salvaging and emergency repair of ships are made possible because of underwater cutting.

CONTROLLING BURNING

An adequate supply of oxygen is necessary to combustion and the rate of burning can be controlled by controlling the oxygen supply. Other factors are important in combustion, too. Have you ever tried starting a fire by lighting a log? It is a nearly impossible task. But if you split the logs into kindling, they catch fire immediately.

What has the splitting done? Since combustion can take place only on the *surface* of the wood where oxygen comes in contact with the fuel, the answer is not hard to find. The surface of a log 6 inches in diameter and 20 inches long is about 434 square inches. If this log is split in two, the surface area is increased greatly. Splitting the log in two adds 240 square inches to the surface area. Splitting it into quarters adds 240 square inches more.

All fuels can be split, but the ways of splitting them are many and varied. Fuel oil is sprayed under pressure through a nozzle that breaks the stream of oil into a mist. Each droplet of oil is well surrounded by air. Coal is often powdered, which makes the use of lower-cost coal possible, and the powdered coal is blown into the furnace. Burning is practically instantaneous. An important condition controlling burning is the fineness of the fuel and the extent to which it is mixed with oxygen.

One application of this principle is in the internal-combustion engine—the engine used in most automobiles, boats, and airplanes. In an internal-combustion engine, the power comes from the very rapid burning of a mixture of fuel vapor and air. The heat produced by this rapid burning expands the gases that are produced. These, in turn, push the pistons, which are connected through the crankshaft to wheels or propellers.

HEAT AND BURNING

One condition necessary for burning is the simple matter of getting the fire going. Burning, in a limited sense, is a chain reaction. The heat produced by the combustion of each particle of fuel must be enough to start the next fuel particle burning. If not, the fire goes out.

Some substances catch fire more easily than others. It is very easy to make paper catch fire. But coal is not so easy to start burning, and setting fire to iron is quite a task. Every substance that will burn must be raised to a certain definite temperature before it will start burning and continue to burn. This temperature is called the *kindling temperature* of the substance.

When you start a campfire, you strike a match. The heat of rubbing is enough to start the combustion of the low-kindling temperature substances in the match head. The heat produced by these substances is enough to set fire to the wood of the match. The heat of the match is enough to raise the paper to its kindling temperature. The burning paper releases enough heat to start the small sticks, and the small sticks will start the heavier wood burning.

In all burning there must be something to burn. A substance used in combustion to produce heat is called a fuel. Combustion cannot exist without a fuel. Even if all conditions

233

necessary for burning are fulfilled, sand will not burn. Why? Because sand, SiO_2, is already completely oxidized.

Since oxidation is any chemical combination with oxygen, it includes many reactions that are not burning. Burning is rapid oxidation. But in many kinds of oxidation, heat is re-

Fuels are "split" in many ways.

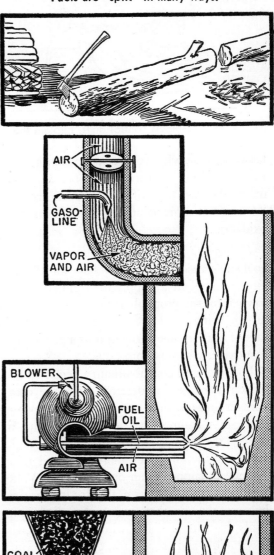

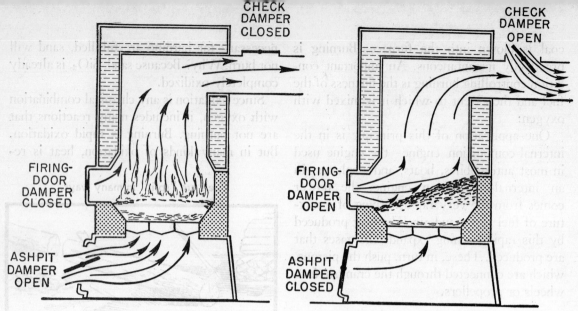

CHECK DAMPER CLOSED

FIRING-DOOR DAMPER CLOSED

ASHPIT DAMPER OPEN

CHECK DAMPER OPEN

FIRING-DOOR DAMPER OPEN

ASHPIT DAMPER CLOSED

Dampers control draft. Explain the position of the dampers in these drawings.

leased very slowly over weeks or months. The rusting of iron, the rotting of foods and other materials, formation of soil (in part), and the "drying" of some paints are examples of slow oxidation.

Firing and Banking a Coal Furnace. Every coal stove and furnace should have an adequate circulation of air to supply the right amount of oxygen for the proper burning of the coal. Improper firing and banking of a stove result in loss of heat and the formation of a gas, carbon monoxide, which is poisonous.

In firing with coal, maintain a deep fuel bed. When more heat is desired, close the check damper and open the ashpit damper. Opening the ashpit damper lets in more air and increases the burning. In banking a fire at night, shake out the ashes, add more coal, and adjust the check damper to an open position. When the check damper is open, the fire is decreased because the air that enters the smoke-pipe cools the chimney gases which, therefore, rise less quickly and prevent more air from coming up through the coal. The firing door and the ashpit damper should be kept closed.

FIRE AND ITS CONTROL

Fire is not in itself either friend or enemy. It can consume coal in a furnace or burn down an entire house. Carelessness and lack of thought are responsible for most destructive fires. Such fires are far easier to stop *before* they start.

In addition to the usual precautions about lighted matches and campfire embers, be careful about the following:

1. Never clean clothes with gasoline or naphtha indoors. The vapors mix with oxygen of the air and a spark or a light may cause this dangerous mixture to explode. If you must use a combustible or flammable liquid for cleaning, do the cleaning outside the house, where the large volume of air will dilute the gasoline vapor to such an extent that the mixture cannot explode.

2. Be sure that gas flames on stove or water heater have been put out or will not be blown out accidentally by wind or animal, before leaving the house or going to bed.

3. Fires often are started by poorly protected electric wiring. Be sure that all the electric wiring in your home is properly protected by fuses.

Firefighting. But fires do start and they must be put out. How do you put out a fire? You

234

use exactly the opposite means that you would use to promote burning: (1) remove the fuel, (2) shut off the supply of oxygen or air, (3) lower the temperature below the kindling temperature of the fuel, or (4) combinations of these three.

What to do to put out a specific fire depends on the nature of the fire. For example, if window curtains catch fire, it may be enough to pull the burning curtains down and throw them outside the house where their continued burning cannot do much damage. Or the curtains may be soaked with water from a bucket or hose. When water is poured on a fire, in becoming heated and changing to steam, it lowers the temperature of the fuel. To a certain extent, too, both water and steam keep oxygen from reaching the fire.

Water from buckets or in large streams should not be used in fighting oil or gasoline fires. The burning oil or gasoline floats on the water and continues burning. Most likely, the fire will be spread by the water. Such fires are fought by means of foamy mixtures of various kinds that blanket the burning oil or gasoline and keep out oxygen. Very fine sprays of

water—so fine that they are called *fog*—are quite effective against oil or gasoline fires.

Carbon dioxide is used in firefighting. It is heavier than air, does not burn, and keeps oxygen away from the fire. A carbon dioxide fire extinguisher consists of a steel cylinder filled with liquid carbon dioxide under pressure. By means of hose and nozzle, the substance is directed at the fire. When the liquid carbon dioxide is released, some of it changes immediately to a gas. This absorbs so much heat that part of the carbon dioxide changes to a solid—a snowy form of *dry ice*. Both gas and snow fall on the flames and put out the fire by keeping oxygen away and by cooling.

A common type of portable fire extinguisher consists of a cylinder containing a saturated solution of sodium bicarbonate. On a shelf at the top of the cylinder is a small bottle of sulfuric acid. When the fire extinguisher is used, it is turned upside down. The acid mixes with the sodium bicarbonate and produces great quantities of carbon dioxide. The pressure of the carbon dioxide forces both liquid and carbon dioxide out of the rubber hose attached to the cylinder.

WORKING WITH SCIENCE

1. Using a bunsen burner or a candle flame with blowpipe or bellows, demonstrate how increased oxygen in the draft increases combustion, and changes the color and temperature of the flame.

2. Study the school furnace or stove and find

out what means is provided for increasing the draft—or adding more oxygen to the fuel. Even a simple wood stove has such a device.

3. Visit a local garage or machine shop and see acetylene being used in cutting and welding. Find

Left: A carbon-dioxide fire extinguisher in action. Right: A special freight car for shipping dry ice.

Courtesy Walter Kidde Co.; Courtesy Air Reduction Co., Inc.

out what care is needed in using this equipment and how important it is in the work being done.

4. Attempt to light a small pile of flour. It is practically noncombustible. Light a bunsen burner and place some flour in a glass or paper tube. Blow the flour into the flame and it will burn with almost explosive violence. Why?

5. A burning splint will go out if dipped quickly into a glass filled with kerosene. Why?

6. Light a candle and set it up inside a wide-mouthed bottle. Note what happens. Now cover the bottle with a glass plate. Again note what hap-

pens during the next few minutes. Explain this.

7. Make a study of rusting—a typical process of slow oxidation. What metals rust? How can rust be removed? How can it be prevented? Make a collection of articles treated to prevent rust: tin plate, galvanized iron, painted iron, stainless steel, greased iron, and so forth.

8. Priestley prepared oxygen by heating a red powder called *mercuric oxide*. Heat a small amount of this compound in a test tube and while still heating over a bunsen burner, thrust a glowing splint into the test tube. What happens? Why?

NITROGEN FROM THE AIR

Oxidation is tied up with mining the air because air is the chief source of oxygen. But if we stopped here, we would leave more than 78 percent of the atmosphere unconsidered. Nitrogen is another resource of the air on which we constantly depend. Since nitrogen does not burn, it dilutes oxygen and slows down *all* natural oxidation. Can you imagine what the world would be like if the atmosphere were pure oxygen?

USES OF NITROGEN

Compounds of nitrogen are of great importance in industry and agriculture. Ammonia is one of them. This gas is a compound of nitrogen and hydrogen, NH_3. It dissolves easily in water. Such a solution is known as ammonium hydroxide, NH_4OH, or ammonia water, and is sold for household cleaning.

Nitric acid, HNO_3, is a powerful acid used in the manufacture of rayon, film, fertilizers, and explosives. Nitrobenzene is used in making dyes and related compounds. Sodium nitrate, or saltpeter, $NaNO_3$, is a widely used fertilizer and is a minor source of nitric acid.

NITROGEN AND AGRICULTURE

Billions of tons of nitrogen exist in the atmosphere—and yet nitrogen starvation by plants in many parts of the world has greatly reduced man's available food supply.

Nitrogen-Fixation. We add nitrogen to the soil when we turn under decaying plants or manure or when we add saltpeter or other nitrate fertilizers to the land. But the nitrogen of air cannot be used by plants. Plants need compounds of nitrogen—not the pure element—and nitrogen does not form compounds easily.

Not very many years ago, agricultural chemists and bacteriologists discovered why an old farming practice was so good for the soil. Farmers long ago knew that plowing under beans, soybeans, peas, or alfalfa enriched the soil far more than letting the fields lie idle. But it took scientists years to discover that this enrichment was the result of the action of certain bacteria in the soil. They are called *nitrogen-fixing* bacteria.

These bacteria grow in lumps, or *nodules*, on the roots of plants of the bean and pea family. Such plants are called legumes. The bacteria transform nitrogen from the air into simple nitrogen compounds in the root nodules of the legumes. These nitrogen compounds are necessary for plant life. Hence, such a crop enriches the soil considerably.

Any process by which free nitrogen of the air is changed into useful compounds is called *nitrogen-fixation*. Every scientific farmer takes advantage of nitrogen-fixing bacteria. After wheat, corn, oats, or other grain crops have been grown for several years in the same field, the nitrogen compounds in the soil are reduced and the soil becomes "poor," with low yields of crops. When this occurs, a farmer either plants a legume or adds commercial fertilizer containing nitrogen compounds.

By chemical means, man can do the work done by the nitrogen-fixing bacteria of soil. The man who made this basic discovery in 1913 was Fritz Haber [hä'bĕr], a German chemist. In the Haber process nitrogen from the air and hydrogen from water are combined:

$$N_2 + 3H_2 \rightarrow 2NH_3$$
$$\text{nitrogen} + \text{hydrogen} \rightarrow \text{ammonia}$$

Once ammonia is obtained, it can easily be converted into nitric acid, nitrates, or other nitrogen compounds that are needed in agriculture and various branches of industry.

Natural Nitrogen-Fixation. Every time there is a thunderstorm, the lightning flashes combine some of the nitrogen and oxygen in the air to form nitrogen oxides. Compounds of nitrogen are being manufactured in some parts of the atmosphere at all times, but we cannot put them where we need them most. Such nitrogen compounds are brought down in rain and amount to about 4 pounds of nitrogen per acre per year. But these nitrogen compounds fall on every acre of ocean as well as on land, so most of them are of no direct use to us. We must mine the air for our own supply.

WORKING WITH SCIENCE

1. To test for protein, place the food substance (like white of hard-boiled egg) in a test tube. Add dilute nitric acid and warm. Note the light yellow color that appears. Drain off the acid, wash and add ammonia water. Yellow changes to deep orange if proteins are present.

2. Make an exhibit of nitrogen compounds. Include the most common protein foods and such products as ammonia, nitric acid, shotgun shell (powder), rayon, camera film, and nitrate fertilizers. **Caution:** *Use care in handling nitric acid and shotgun shell.*

3. Find out how important the Haber process was during World War I. Before the Haber process was developed, the nitrate deposits of Chile were the world's main source of nitrogen.

RARE GASES OF THE ATMOSPHERE

The abundance of a material does not always determine its value. Some of the most valuable resources are rare indeed. Air is practically all oxygen and nitrogen. The presence of other gases, besides carbon dioxide, was not even suspected until about 50 years ago. Then it was found that nitrogen from air weighed just a trifle more than nitrogen made

Left: Carbon dioxide in solution helped form this cave (see page 240). Middle: Root nodules containing nitrogen-fixing bacteria. Right: Adding nitrogen-fixing bacteria to soybeans used as seed.

National Park Service; Soil Conservation Service; U. S. D. A. photo

from nitrogen compounds. Following this clue, a more searching study of air revealed five gaseous elements whose presence had escaped detection. These are rare gases, though the most common one, argon, makes up almost 1 percent of the atmosphere.

Rare Gases in Air

Gas	Percent by Volume
Argon	0.94
Neon	0.0012
Helium	0.0004
Krypton	0.00001
Xenon	0.000001

These five gases will not unite with any other element under any conditions. That is, they are chemically *inert*. This unique property makes these elements very useful. Argon is used to fill electric-light bulbs. It does not unite with the white-hot tungsten filament and prevents the filament from "evaporating." Thus argon helps lengthen the useful life of the bulb.

THE SPECTROSCOPE

To some extent, some of the rare gases are still scientific curiosities, yet we see some of their uses every day. This is because business has in part taken advantage of a scientific tool called a *spectroscope*. A spectroscope consists of a wedge, or *prism*, of glass with a viewing tube and lenses. A burning or glowing substance viewed through it reveals a pattern of lines and colors, or *spectrum*, that unmistakably identifies the substance.

With a spectroscope, a scientist can analyze substances by studying the light from them. By analyzing light from the stars, astronomers learn the composition of the stars. Any material that can be made to glow can be studied with a spectroscope.

The spectroscope is a great aid in analyzing gases. To make the gas visible in the spectroscope, a sample of the gas is placed in a narrow glass tube from which all air has been removed. This tiny bit of gas at very low pressure is sealed in the tube, which has electrical connec-

tions at each end. When electricity is passed through the tube, the gas glows. The gas can then be studied with the spectroscope and analyzed.

Neon Lights. The rare gases in glowing give off beautiful visible light. The color and brightness of the light depend on the gas and its concentration in the tube. For business use, the simple spectroscope sample tube has given way to tubes many feet in length, twisted into designs or letters. These signs glow brilliantly as electricity flows through them.

Most brilliant of all are the neon lights that glow with a bright orange-red light in the dark. This penetrating light makes neon useful in marking airports as well as in advertising signs. Tubes filled with argon give off a blue light; xenon, a lighter blue. Colors can be modified by mixing the gases.

THE SEARCH FOR HELIUM

No detective story is more amazing than the story of the discovery of helium. It was discovered in 1868 by Joseph N. Lockyer [lŏk′yẽr], an English astronomer, using the newly invented spectroscope. Lockyer saw lines in sunlight that did not belong to any element then known, and he was certain that the light he was watching came from a new element.

But Lockyer could not submit a sample of this new element to other chemists for checking. His sample was 93 million miles away. But other scientists did check Lockyer's work. There was no doubt about the new element which Lockyer named *helium*, from a Greek word meaning the *sun*.

On the earth, helium existed in name only for 21 or 22 years until a geologist studying a rare mineral obtained an inert gas from it. He put a sample in a tube, ran his current through it, and focused his spectroscope. At last! Helium was found on earth. Later, large amounts of the gas were discovered in gas wells in western Texas—so much that government engineers, who control the supply, pump it back into the earth to be stored.

Helium, like the other rare gases of the air, does not unite with any other element. It cannot burn or explode. Next to hydrogen, helium is the lightest gas known. Hydrogen-filled balloons burn and explode easily. The giant dirigible, *Hindenburg*, exploded and burned at Lakehurst, New Jersey in 1937. Nothing like that can happen to a helium-filled balloon or dirigible.

Helium has a number of interesting uses. Best known is its use in making "artificial air." Deep-sea divers and stratosphere flyers do not breathe air at normal pressures. They breathe air at much higher or lower pressures and may suffer from pressure effects.

When a flyer flies very high and when a diver returns to the surface after a deep dive, both may suffer from the "bends," a painful and often serious condition caused by nitrogen bubbles that form in the blood stream. If divers are supplied with artificial air made of helium and oxygen, this condition is prevented. Record-breaking dives have been made with the help of helium.

HYDROGEN, THE LIGHTWEIGHT CHAMPION

There is hydrogen gas in the air, too, but in very small traces only. As a part of the atmosphere, hydrogen is almost too unimportant to consider. But as the lightest and most flammable gas it is well worth knowing. Hydrogen is the lightest of the elements and one of real importance. It is most easily obtained by the electrolysis of water. Its value is not only as a pure gas, but also as a part of some of the most important chemical compounds. Hydrogen is part of the following important groups of compounds:

Acids

Nitric acid	HNO_3	All *acids* contain hydrogen combined with other elements.
Hydrochloric acid	HCl	
Sulfuric acid	H_2SO_4	
Boric acid	H_3BO_3	

Alkalies, or Bases

Sodium hydroxide	$NaOH$	*Alkalies*, or *bases*, consist of a metal united with oxygen and hydrogen.
Potassium hydroxide	KOH	
Ammonium hydroxide	NH_4OH	
Calcium hydroxide	$Ca(OH)_2$	

Carbohydrates

| Glucose | $C_6H_{12}O_6$ | *Carbohydrates* are compounds of carbon, hydrogen, and oxygen in which hydrogen and oxygen are in the same ratio as they are in water, H_2O. |
| Sucrose | $C_{12}H_{22}O_{11}$ | |

Hydrocarbons

| Methane | CH_4 | *Hydrocarbons* are compounds containing only carbon and hydrogen. |
| Gasoline is a mixture of | C_7H_{16} and C_8H_{18} | |

Those who go up in the air or down under the water do not breathe ordinary air. Left: An aviator in an oxygen mask. Middle and right: Helmeted divers with "air" lines.

Official U. S. Navy photos

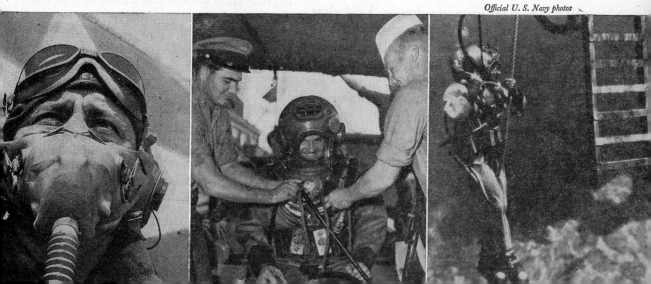

WORKING WITH SCIENCE

1. Illustrate the possibilities of spectroscopic analysis by showing the effect on flame color, by adding small amounts of salts of sodium, strontium, and copper to the flame of a bunsen burner.

2. Prepare hydrogen by the action of hydrochloric acid on zinc. Collect several bottles of the gas. Demonstrate its lightness by leaving a bottle of it open 2 minutes and then testing with a burning splint. Show the burning of hydrogen and the explosive nature of a hydrogen-air mixture. **Caution:** *Use care in handling the hydrogen-air mixture. Do not bring a flame near the apparatus while hydrogen is being formed. Be very careful.*

3. To prepare an acid by the action of a non-metallic oxide on water, prepare sulfur dioxide by burning sulfur in a bottle of air. Add water and shake. Do the same with phosphorus. Test for acid with blue litmus paper. Litmus turns red in the presence of an acid.

4. Prepare a base by the action of a metallic oxide (sodium peroxide) on water in a test tube. Test with red litmus paper and note its chemical properties. Litmus turns blue. Solution is soapy to the touch.

CARBON DIOXIDE FROM THE AIR

Two other gases of the air we seldom mine directly. However, we are greatly dependent on them and they are of very great indirect value. These two gases are the compounds carbon dioxide, CO_2, and water vapor, H_2O. Both are common enough. Some of the 2 trillion tons of carbon dioxide in the air is used directly by plants in photosynthesis.

Photosynthesis is one natural process that man has not yet been able to carry out in the laboratory. The raw materials needed are two of the lowest-cost raw materials in the world, carbon dioxide and water. All that is required is to combine these two into a single compound—a carbohydrate—such as sugar or starch.

Carbon dioxide is formed when carbon or any compound of carbon burns. It is liberated from limestone, $CaCO_3$, by the action of acids. It occurs in the gases of volcanos. A colorless, heavy gas, it neither burns nor supports combustion. Occasionally it accumulates in mines or limestone caves. Anyone who accidently enters a pocket of this odorless, tasteless gas may suffocate in it without realizing his danger.

USES OF CARBON DIOXIDE

Carbon dioxide enters into our lives in a number of other ways, too. Bread and cakes are filled with holes made by carbon dioxide given off by yeasts or baking powders. Your favorite soda-pop has its sharp, tangy flavor and its bubbly character because soda-water is a very weak acid formed by dissolving carbon dioxide in water under pressure. When the cap comes off the bottle, the pressure is released and the carbon dioxide bubbles out.

Carbon dioxide dissolves slightly in water to form the weak acid, carbonic acid, H_2CO_3. As such water runs through limestone, it dissolves the limestone, forming caves with their fantastic lime "icicles." Those that hang down are called *stalactites*. Those that build up from the floor are called *stalagmites*.

Carbon Dioxide and Ventilation. Carbon dioxide is important in breathing, too. When its percentage in air increases beyond its normal 0.04 percent, it causes more rapid breathing. In connection with health, carbon dioxide has a reputation it does not deserve. Many people believe that air in a room becomes "bad" because the amount of carbon dioxide increases. They say that this is why closed rooms with shut windows make you drowsy. Even in hospitals, flowers are often removed from rooms at night because they give off carbon dioxide then. Such beliefs are unscientific. If the amount of carbon dioxide in the air were doubled and redoubled, it would have no injurious effect on health.

Dry Ice. Dry ice is a form of carbon dioxide that is becoming more and more widely used. Much colder than ice ($-102°F$ compared with $32°F$), dry ice keeps things colder longer and with less of it than ice. In addition, dry ice changes directly into a gas without passing through a liquid state. Thus, nothing becomes wet when dry ice is used.

Dry ice is made by compressing and cooling carbon dioxide. On expansion, part of the carbon dioxide solidifies as "snow." This "snow" is then compressed, producing dry ice. It is so very cold that it is unsafe to handle without heavy gloves. Contact with the skin may cause a painful "burn."

EAT OUR CAKE AND HAVE IT TOO

As we have seen, we are dependent on the resources of the earth for our food, for the things we have, and for the kind of civilization we live in. In the past, when man's demands were small, the resources seemed boundless. However, during the last thousand years we have come nearer and nearer to using up our resources. Through new discoveries and more efficient use, we have been able to postpone the day when some of our resources are used up. But it may be only a question of time.

The answer to all this, as we all know, is conservation. Conservation means the wise use of resources so that the future as well as the present is provided for. Conservation means more than cutting down on waste. It means planning, improving utilization, searching for substitutes, developing byproducts, and everything else that makes our use of materials of the earth more efficient.

Many persons use the term conservation mostly in regard to our biological resources. However, we can use it just as well in relation to resources of the land, seas, and air. It may sound strange to talk about conserving the seas when we know that their resources are greater than those of the land. But it is not. To some extent, we are spoiling the seas when we allow industrial wastes to pollute the rivers and bays, and when we silt up the harbors because we fail to control erosion. We not only ruin the biological resources of rivers and the coast, but actually spoil areas for shipping.

We are not conserving the air as a resource when we pour factory smoke into it needlessly so that the air instead of cleaning our cities, blankets them with soot and fog.

In the long run, these points are of great importance. It is good to know that we are doing something about some of them already. If we can keep up this program, we can look forward to a future filled with more of the good things of life.

WORKING WITH SCIENCE

1. Find out more about carbohydrates, especially their value as foods. Make a temporary exhibit of carbohydrate foods that should be in every diet.

2. Find out something of the volume of sales in the soft drink industry and try to get some idea how important an industry is built on carbonated waters.

READING YOU WILL ENJOY

Faraday, Michael. *Chemical History of a Candle.* E. P. Dutton & Co., Inc., New York, 1920. Consists of six lectures given by Faraday to young boys and girls at the Royal Institution of London. The first lecture is about flames.

Freeman, Ira M. *Invitation to Experiment.* E. P. Dutton & Co., Inc., New York, 1940. Chapter 3 of this very well illustrated book deals with some simple experiments based on the weight of air.

Chapter 7 deals interestingly with "Air in Action."

Lynde, Carleton J. *Science Experiences with Home Equipment.* International Textbook Co., Scranton, Pa., 1937. Contains 29 simple and interesting experiments based on atmospheric pressure.

Slosson, Edwin E. *Creative Chemistry* (rev. ed.), pp. 14–36. D. Appleton-Century Co., New York, 1930. Discusses "Nitrogen, Preserver and Destroyer of Life."

Much of man's increasing knowledge has come from the laboratory—the symbol of modern science. There are many kinds of laboratories and many kinds of scientists. The scientists who seek new knowledge serve man in one way. The scientists who take this new knowledge and apply it to the production of new things serve in another.

In their own ways, the alchemists (1) sought the "secrets of nature." They were trying chiefly to turn lead into gold and to produce eternal life, but in their searches they did discover several elements and made surprisingly accurate studies of a number of compounds. Comparing their equipment with only a little of the equipment available to a modern research scientist (2), it is surprising that the al-

chemists made any discoveries worth considering. But they did.

As man's knowledge of the nature of matter increased, he learned how to make many substances that he had had to look for in the earth, such as coloring materials, rubies, and nitrate fertilizers. He learned to make products that had been before obtainable only from living things, such as dyes, drugs, rubber (3), cotton (5), and alcohol. And he learned to make new things that were never found in nature, such as plastics, synthetic rubber (4), nylon, rayon (6), the sulfa drugs, and DDT. No one knows where the laboratory will lead us, but what life will be like tomorrow is being determined partly in laboratories today.

20

MINING THE LABORATORY

Men first used the raw materials of nature just as they were found. But as men advanced in knowledge, they began to change these raw materials into better materials. For example, at one time men made their homes from rough logs, or mud, or both. Later on, they learned how to make bricks out of clay. Still later they learned to make better bricks by baking them in very hot ovens. Now they use steel, concrete, glass, plastics, treated woods, and various other materials to make their homes and other buildings more comfortable, more beautiful, and longer lasting.

After men had learned how to make steel from pig iron, they were not altogether satisfied with it. The steel they made rusted like iron. It was not strong enough for many uses. It was not soft enough for the inside of gears so necessary in the hundreds of machines they

had invented. It was not flexible enough for the delicate springs of their watches and other instruments.

Chemists began trying to change steel to meet modern requirements. They experimented by adding other metals in small amounts. They made a steel that does not rust by adding chromium to the steel. They added manganese and obtained a new steel so hard that it is excellent for burglar-proof safes.

When they wanted a steel that would withstand the heavy loads of locomotives and trains, they learned to add vanadium. For tools that must be used at high speed, tungsten was added. Tungsten steel, even when red hot, keeps a sharp edge. Chemists thus made new metals from old. Almost daily, new alloys come from our research laboratories to meet new needs.

IMPROVING ON NATURE

Gasoline is the fuel that keeps most of our automobiles, buses, planes, and much of our machinery going. Crude oil, or petroleum, is the source of gasoline. In the early days of the petroleum industry, only a small percentage of crude oil was converted into gasoline. As the need for more and more gasoline grew, chemists developed new methods of increasing the amount of gasoline that could be squeezed out of crude petroleum.

SCIENTISTS PRODUCE MORE AND BETTER FUELS

Petroleum is a mixture of hydrocarbons. Gasoline is made up of a few of these hydro-

carbons. By regulating the temperature and pressure during the refining of petroleum, the heavier hydrocarbons, such as kerosene, are broken down into the lighter hydrocarbons, such as gasoline. This breaking down of the heavier kerosene molecules into the lighter gasoline molecules is called *cracking*.

Polymerization. A reverse process is also used to increase our supplies of gasoline. The lighter hydrocarbons, such as various gases found mixed with the crude petroleum, are changed to the heavier gasoline hydrocarbons by joining the lighter hydrocarbons together

243

Courtesy Jones & Lamson Machine Co.; Courtesy Revere Copper and Brass Incorporated

Laboratory methods enable us to make alloys to meet almost any requirement. Left: The high-speed cutter of this machine tool is a steel that cuts steel. Right: Stainless steel cooking utensils.

until they form heavier hydrocarbons. This process of joining groups of smaller molecules into larger, heavier groups is called *polymerization*. The gasoline thus formed is called *polymer gasoline*.

Hydrogenation. Our supplies of gasoline were increased also by converting coal into gasoline. Such gasoline is called *synthetic gasoline*, and the process of converting coal into gasoline is called *hydrogenation* of coal. Coal is composed chiefly of carbon, and gasoline is made up of carbon and hydrogen. Chemists learned how to add hydrogen to coal at regulated temperatures and pressures to make large quantities of synthetic gasoline.

SCIENTISTS PRODUCE NEW TEXTILES

For centuries men used the natural fibers of plants and the wool of animals to make *textiles*, a word that refers to all the products of the loom. They used cotton from the cotton plant, linen from flax, wool from sheep, and silk from the silkworm.

Rayon. Not so long ago, men began to feel the need of a fiber that would be cheaper than silk, yet look like silk. Chemists rolled up their sleeves and went to work. After a long period of experimentation, they produced several kinds of *rayons*. They prepared these by treating woodpulp or short cotton fibers called *linters* with various chemicals, such as sodium hydroxide and carbon disulfide.

These chemicals dissolved the cellulose of the wood and formed a syrupy liquid called *viscose*. Then they squirted the viscose through tiny holes to form very thin streams, which hardened in a setting bath of liquid. Long, thin strands, or fibers, are thus formed. They are eventually woven into cloth called *rayon*.

Synthetic Wool. Other men wanted a fiber that resembles the soft, warm qualities of wool, but which is cheaper than wool. Scientists went to their laboratories and made a substitute for wool out of milk. From the *casein* of milk, the part that clumps together when milk sours, they made a fiber that looks like wool and has many of the qualities of the wool of the sheep or llama. It is called *lanital*.

Other new synthetic wools have been made from peanuts, corn, and chicken feathers. However, as yet these synthetic fibers are not as satisfactory or as low in price as sheep's wool.

Nylon. Lanital was not the last or the most spectacular of synthetic fibers. Women were looking for a fiber that could be woven into stockings that would last longer than silk and be as beautiful as natural silk hosiery. Chemists turned to their test tubes and this time, instead of starting with such natural raw

244

materials as wood, cotton, and milk, they used much simpler substances, such as coal, air, and water. From the carbon of coal, the nitrogen of the air, and the oxygen and hydrogen of water, they gradually built up *nylon.* The dream of millions of women had come true. The silkworm is no longer needed to spin its cocoon for women's hose.

With the making of nylon, rayon, and lanital, science advanced another long step. Chemists at first imitated nature by synthesizing such *natural* products as indigo. Later on they learned to create entirely new substances. Nylon, rayon, and lanital do not exist in nature. They are brand-new substances.

Cloth from Glass. Fibers have been made from glass and used to weave curtains and other fabrics. It is indeed a far cry from the raw skins and furs which covered ancient man to the richly colored fabrics prepared synthetically by our scientists. This tremendous change represents, in part, the great difference between the ancient's lack of knowledge of chemistry and other sciences and the power of modern science.

NEW DYES FROM THE LABORATORIES

Until less than a century ago, the world had to depend for its colors upon mineral colors, such as reddish iron oxide, and plant colors, such as *indigo* dye from the indigo plant. The variety of our colors was limited in both range of color and durability. In 1856, a young Englishman, William Perkin, accidentally discovered a chemical method of preparing a dye not found in nature. He made it from the tar (coal tar) left when coal is heated. This purple dye was called *mauve.*

Perkin's discovery was the beginning of a new era in dyemaking. Within the next 50 years, indigo and hundreds of new dyes were synthesized from coal tar. Synthetic indigo is purer, cheaper, and more uniform than natural indigo extracted from plants.

The manufacture of synthetic indigo killed the natural indigo industry very quickly. Thousands of men who cared for hundreds of thousands of acres of indigo plants were thrown out of work and had to find new jobs. But this was not wholly a calamity. In fact, science created thousands of other jobs by producing new chemicals and new machines.

PLASTICS: CHEMISTRY'S NEW BABY

Within the last few years, so many new plastics have been introduced that it is almost impossible to find a kitchen or any other room, an automobile, an airplane, or a radio without its variety of plastics in all kinds of colors and shapes. Actually, anything that can be molded or formed into a shape, such as clay, cement, or rubber is a plastic. However, the plastics we are now discussing are synthetic substances that can be molded and pressed into shape in dies under the influence of heat and pressure.

A good example of a synthetic plastic is "Bakelite," named after its inventor, Leo H. Baekeland [bā′kĕ-lănd], who came to the

Left: In the experimental plant of the U. S. Bureau of Mines, gasoline is made from bituminous coal. Right: Cracking and polymerization are carried on in nearly all modern petroleum refineries.

Courtesy of the Bituminous Coal Institute; Standard Oil Co. (N.J.) photo by Corsini

United States from Belgium at the age of twenty-six. Baekeland, who had already made important inventions in photography, started with two chemical compounds—both poisonous liquids. One was *formaldehyde*, a preservative with a characteristic sharp odor. The other was *carbolic acid*, a very strong germicide. When these two were heated, they formed a solid—"Bakelite"—which has all the properties of a typical plastic.

Synthetic plastics are of two classes. *Thermosetting plastics* are formed in a mold by heat and pressure and retain their hardness thereafter. They cannot be made soft again by heating. An example of this type of plastic is "Bakelite." *Thermoplastic plastics*, on the other hand, may be reformed as often as necessary. After they have cooled and hardened into one form, they may be softened again by heat and made into a new shape.

"Plexiglas" is an example of a thermoplastic plastic. It is very tough and flexible, looks like glass, and is transparent. It can be ground and machined. It is not affected by water, salt, or oils and is an excellent electrical insulator. It is used in making the nose enclosures of airplanes, table tops, glass doors, lamps, tableware, and all sorts of decorative articles. It withstands great shocks and even the sharpest blow will not shatter it.

Scores of new plastics, such as "Saran," "Styron," "Lucite," and "Polythene," are now on the market. So many plastics are still possible that it is almost literally true that a new plastic may be made to meet any requirement. Here is a world of new material never before known to man.

MAN-MADE RUBBER COMPETES WITH NATURAL RUBBER

Everyone knows that Christopher Columbus discovered America. But few know that he also took back a few rubber balls after his second visit to America. While in Santo Domingo, he noticed some boys playing with black objects made from a liquid obtained from certain trees. Some time later, Joseph Priestley, discoverer of oxygen, obtained a piece of this material which had been brought to England. He used it for erasing pencil marks and so gave it its name.

A man named Charles Macintosh took some of this rubber, dissolved it in a liquid, and spread it over some cloth from which the solvent evaporated. The fabric, now covered with a layer of rubber, was made into raincoats and sold for the first time in Scotland. Today, more important uses of rubber have been found. Rubber is the material on which the wheels of the world roll. Without it, automobiles, trucks, and airplanes would be much less comfortable. These are but a few of the thousands of uses of rubber.

What is rubber? Raw rubber is a soft,

Left: Cones and skeins of "Celanese" rayon. Middle: Determining the breaking strength of a cellulose fabric. Right: A bale of rayon fibers produced by the viscose process.

American Forest Products Industries, Inc.; U. S. D. A.; Celanese Corporation of America photo

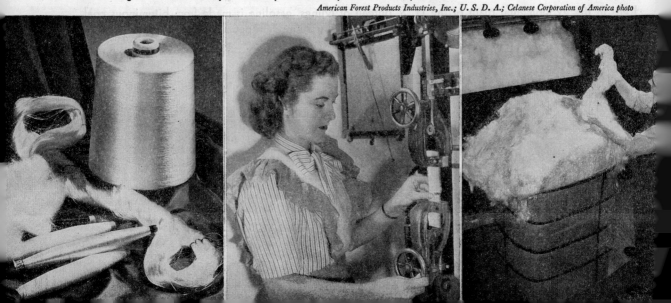

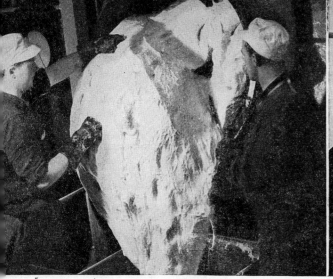

Left: One kind of synthetic rubber, "Neoprene," as it comes from the polymerization kettle. Right: Nylon has many uses beside its use as a synthetic fiber. All of these articles are made of nylon.

elastic solid obtained from a liquid, milklike sap. This sap is called *latex* and is obtained from several tropical plants. Natural rubber is soft and sticky, and wears away rapidly. How to make it harder, less sticky, and more durable was a problem which many tried to solve in the early days of its use.

Vulcanization. In 1839 an American, Charles Goodyear, was working in his kitchen in Woburn, Massachusetts. He accidentally dropped a piece of rubber mixed with sulfur on a hot stove. When this mixture of raw rubber and sulfur cooled, he found that it had new properties—just the properties he wanted. Goodyear had discovered a method of *vulcanizing* rubber with the help of sulfur. To shorten the time required for vulcanizing rubber, a substance such as zinc oxide is added. Carbon is also added, and this adds to the life of the rubber.

Synthetic Rubber. Before World War II, the United States used about 600,000 tons of rubber each year. Almost all of this rubber was imported from the Dutch East Indies and British Malaya, where 80 percent of all the world's rubber was grown.

Then came World War II and overnight our supplies of rubber were shut off. What was to be done? We had to get rubber in huge quantities. Our chemists were called in by the government. Could they make rubber synthetically just as they had synthesized new dyes, new plastics, and a thousand and one other chemicals? Their answer was, "Yes."

With government backing, American scientists went to work and before long they were completely successful. They made synthetic rubber from two raw materials, alcohol and petroleum. From alcohol or petroleum, they made *butadiene*, a gas, and from petroleum they obtained *styrene*, a clear liquid.

Both styrene and butadiene contain nothing but hydrogen and carbon. When they are chemically combined, their atoms form long chains that resemble the chemical structure of natural rubber. A new, synthetic rubber called *buna-S* came out of our factories by the tens of thousands of tons. Its cost was much higher than natural rubber had been. In 1945 we actually made a million tons of synthetic rubber—more than we had used of natural rubber in any year before the war.

Whether synthetic rubber will completely replace natural rubber, just as synthetic indigo replaced natural indigo, is a question time alone will answer. It may be that the rubber tree will remain an important source of rubber for years to come. But we now have a rival that will help make sure that the price of natural rubber does not rise too high.

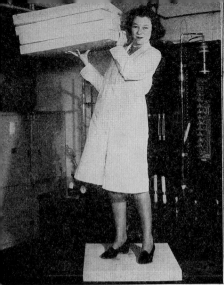

Left: A new lightweight plastic, cellular cellulose acetate, is made from the same compound as "Celanese" rayon. Middle: A nylon parachute is stronger than silk and lasts longer. Right: Testing "Teflon," a new plastic that is not affected even by acids that will dissolve gold.

CHEMURGY JOINS FARM AND FACTORY

Chemurgy is a relatively new word in our language. It was coined to apply to a movement whose purpose was to find more uses for farm products in industry. The idea behind this movement was to help the farmer get rid of surplus products and waste material from the farm. In the long run, the use of such farm materials would help not only the owners of farms and factories, but all people.

Farm products have been used by industry from time immemorial. For example, from rye, wheat, corn, potatoes, and molasses of sugar cane and sugar beet, men had learned how to make alcohol. From cotton, immense quantities of photographic films, rayon, high explosives, and quick-drying paints, such as pyroxylin, were manufactured. Alcohol made from corn has also been used, to some extent, in mixing with gasoline to make a substitute for pure gasoline.

Chemurgy wanted to find new products from farm material. Rubber was made from alcohol. Tung trees were imported and grown on the Gulf coast and several other areas of the United States. These trees supply tung oil, which is used in the manufacture of paints. The soybean was introduced from China. It supplies raw materials for several paints, plastics, cattle feeds, flours, and edible oils.

The great chemist, George Washington Carver, spent a lifetime in finding new uses for the peanut grown so widely in the South. From the peanut, he showed how to prepare oils and other substances used in the manufacture of paints, dyes, inks, glues, and many other products. The chemurgy movement was aided by the United States Government several years ago, when it set up four Regional Research Laboratories in different parts of the country. In these laboratories scientists work on new uses for farm products.

SYNTHETIC CHEMISTRY HELPS IMPROVE HEALTH

Chemistry joined medicine in attacking food-deficiency diseases. The vitamins were discovered. This great victory over death was made even more dramatic when chemists succeeded in synthesizing the vitamins from ordinary chemicals which did not come from food at all.

Chemistry also joined medicine in the study of the secretion of various ductless glands. These secretions, called hormones, are absorbed directly into the blood stream and carried to various parts of the body. Though present in very small amounts, hormones profoundly influence health, body growth, intelligence, and the whole human personality.

One of the most important of hormones is *insulin*. This is produced in a gland called the pancreas. Insulin controls the digestion of sugar and starch. If the body fails to manufacture enough insulin, the person suffers from diabetes.

Synthetic Insulin. Before the discovery and isolation of extracts of insulin by Dr. Frederick Banting, of Canada, in 1922, most diabetics died early. After the discovery of insulin, chemists went to work to prepare the pure chemical crystals of insulin. Now diabetics get their necessary insulin by injecting themselves with insulin prepared by chemists. Millions of lives have been saved.

"Magic Bullets." The German scientist, Paul Ehrlich [ār′lĭк], tried 605 different chemical compounds of the element arsenic in seeking a cure for syphilis. He finally prepared "606," *salvarsan*—a "magic bullet" which could help destroy the cause of syphilis. Salvarsan was the first chemical that could actually be placed in the blood stream to kill the germs that cause a definite disease.

Such a method of attacking the bacterial causes of certain diseases with the aid of specific chemicals is called *chemotherapy*. More recently, the "sulfa" drugs, penicillin, and streptomycin have been prepared and used successfully against dangerous streptococcus infections, pneumonia, meningitis, and other diseases.

The most recent contribution of chemistry to medicine was the synthesis of the drug quinine from coal tar. This drug is an efficient protective against malaria, a disease that attacks 800 million people each year. Two young American chemists synthesized it in 1944. Hundreds of others, over a period of a hundred years, had tried to make it and failed. Mankind can now be independent of the tropical cinchona tree from which this drug had been obtained in the past.

SCIENCE CAN MAKE A NEW WORLD

From these few examples of synthetic chemistry, we see that science has put into our hands the means of producing almost any product from raw materials that are widely and abundantly distributed. This contribution of scientists can help to prevent wars. Men fought for control of lands where natural rubber is grown because they were afraid they would be prevented from getting their needed supplies of this important substance. Today, no nation need go to war for rubber, for it can now be made in any part of the world from corn, rice, wheat, or potatoes.

New advances in science will bring about better relations among nations by making available new supplies of metals from low-grade ores. For example, the chief source of

Soybeans loom large in the chemurgy movement. Right: Pressing oil from soybeans. See if you can find out all of the uses of soybean oil.

U. S. D. A. photos

Soybean proteins are excellent nutritionally, and parts of the soybean may be made into plastics. The meat loaf contains soybean flour, while the articles at the right are all made of soybean plastics.

the metal aluminum is bauxite. Deposits of this ore are not universally distributed. Chemists, therefore, have developed a method of obtaining aluminum from a much more widely distributed ore—clay.

SCIENCE CAN PRODUCE MORE GOODS THAN EVER BEFORE

With the facts, the knowledge, and the tools that scientists have discovered and invented, the world can produce more food than ever before. It can produce enough to keep the whole world well fed. The world can manufacture all the cloth needed to keep all peoples comfortably clothed. It can manufacture all the well-equipped houses needed to keep every man, woman, and child well housed. There is really no limit to production which the world can reach if we are willing and ready to plan and work for the utilization of all the knowledge and skill of modern science.

AID FOR SCIENTIFIC RESEARCH

Most of the advances of science have come from men working in their own modest laboratories or in the laboratories of colleges, industries, private institutions, and city, state, and federal governments. More and more, large industries are employing research scientists in their well-equipped laboratories. More

and more private research groups are being organized to carry on scientific research. The government, too, is opening more laboratories and spending more money for the solution of many problems that science can tackle best.

Government research should be planned by eminent scientists as a long-range program. During World War II, government agencies, such as the National Research Council and the Office of Scientific Research and Development, mobilized the best scientific brains of the country and gave them millions of dollars for research on problems directly aimed at the successful prosecution of the war. This magnificently organized association of scientists spent $2 billion of federal funds to produce the atomic bombs that brought the Japanese to unconditional surrender in 1945. We need similar agencies at work in peacetime, for research can accomplish similar triumphs for a world fighting disease and poverty.

OPPORTUNITIES ARE STILL GREAT

Chemists have accomplished a magnificent job. But they have really only scratched the surface. There are still many rich veins to be tapped. More and more chemists will be called upon to do this work. Many local, state, and Federal agencies, private industrial organizations, colleges, and scientific foundations will be spending more money for scientific work.

You may want to be one of these research chemists. You may be interested in the chemistry of photography. The chemistry of plant culture may turn out to be your hobby. You may want to work in the chemistry of cosmetics. Chemistry in the service of criminology may attract you. Or you may want to work in some chemical laboratory as a laboratory assistant. You may even dream of joining those who today are working with test tube and beaker to enlarge our knowledge of atomic energy, to synthesize new drugs, new medicines, new dyes, new textiles, new plastics, and new alloys. Consider these fields seriously before you decide on what you intend to do as a lifework.

WORKING WITH SCIENCE

1. Prepare an exhibit of as many synthetic products as possible. Include rubber, plastics, fibers, and so forth.

2. Make a study of materials used in your kitchen. List those that are synthetic products.

3. If you live on a farm, or in a farming community, make a study to find out how many of the products grown on the farm are used as raw materials for industry.

4. Write a one-page composition on the slogan of DuPont—"Better Things for Better Living through Chemistry."

READING YOU WILL ENJOY

Borth, Christy. *Modern Chemists and Their Work*. New Home Library, New York, 1943. The story of the chemurgists who made wool from milk, silk from coal, fertilizers from peanuts, and many other new products. Chapter 9 tells the story of Baekeland, pioneer of plastics.

Haynes, Williams. *This Chemical Age*. Alfred A. Knopf, Inc., New York, 1942. A beautifully illustrated and well-written account of many of the man-made materials given to us by science, including such things as rubber, dyes, plastics, perfumes, and materials yet to be made.

Mersereau, Samuel F. *Materials of Industry*. McGraw-Hill Book Co., New York, 1947. A reference book that you may find interesting and useful in studying how materials are produced for modern industry.

Morgan, Alfred. *Things a Boy Can Do With Chemistry*. D. Appleton-Century Co., New York, 1940. More than 100 interesting experiments in chemistry.

Morgan, Alfred. *Things a Boy Can Do With Electrochemistry*. D. Appleton-Century Co., New York, 1940. A book that will give you many interesting insights into the field of electrochemistry and that will provide you with a great deal of fun in experimentation.

Pollack, Philip. *Careers in Science*. E. P. Dutton & Co., Inc., New York, 1945. A book that tries to answer the many questions raised by young people about the possibilities of choosing science as a career.

Robinson, Henry M. *Science Catches the Criminal*. Blue Ribbon Books, New York, 1935. Contains several very interesting chapters on "Crimes in Ink," "Clues in Wood," "Fingerprints," and so forth.

Rogers, Frances and Beard, Alice. *5000 Years of Glass*. J. B. Lippincott Co., Philadelphia, 1937. A comprehensive book about the types, production, and uses of ancient and modern glass.

Slosson, Edwin E. *Creative Chemistry* (rev. ed.). D. Appleton-Century Co., New York, 1930. A delightful book that tells the part science has played in industry and in our lives. Somewhat old, but still worthwhile.

1

2

Most of the things man uses must be worked on, or processed, before they become useful. Iron ore in the ground and a tree in a forest are not worth much for most of our purposes if they stay where they are as they are. But things made from the iron ore and from the tree may be very useful. Such things can be made only by processing the iron or the tree. Processing requires both work and tools—energy and machines.

Man's standard of living is tied closely to the amount of energy he controls and the efficiency of the tools and machines he uses. Earliest man had only the energy of his own muscles and no tools or machines. His standard of living was very low. Later

on, simple tools came into use (1) and still later domesticated animals supplied energy for much useful work (2) and (3). Man's standard of living improved—he had somewhat better food, clothing, and shelter.

Tools continued to be improved and finally man learned how to use the energy of wind and moving water, and coal, natural gas, and petroleum. This energy man now applies through complex machines (4) that do the work of thousands of nimble fingers and straining backs—machines that hour after hour, day after day, make more things for more people, machines that improve our standard of living.

3

4

Energy and Machines for the World of Tomorrow

21

THE MACHINES WE USE

"Do you use machines?"

"Oh no," said the housewife. "What would I do with a machine? They're too complicated for me." The music from her automatic record player almost drowned out the purr of the vacuum cleaner she was pushing and the steady hum of the washing machine in the kitchen.

"Do you use machines?"

"No, of course not," said the businessman as he sent his secretary back to her typing, took a drink at the electric water cooler, and sat down in his air-conditioned office. "Why don't you take the elevator down to the factory and talk to someone there?" He picked up the mouthpiece of his dictaphone to record some more letters.

"Do you use machines?"

"Me? Gosh no! I still go to school," said the freshman as he looked at his wrist watch. "Sorry, I'm late. I've got a date to help Henry fix his sailboat, and after that we're going to run his steam engine." Then he hopped on his bicycle and rode off.

EVERYONE USES MACHINES

You would very likely get similar answers from many people. Yet every one of us uses machines so often and in so many ways that we would be totally lost without them. Machines play a part in the production of almost everything we use. However, the devices we use are not labeled "sewing machine," or "washing machine," or some other kind of machine. And they may be as simple as a can opener or as complicated as a six-engined aircraft. In fact, we use so many thousands of different machines in every occupation that we say we are living in a *Machine Age*.

To operate these many machines, we use many kinds of energy. A housewife uses the energy of her muscles to operate a can opener. A farmer may use the energy of a horse's muscles to help him plow. Energy from burning coal, oil, or gasoline runs our trains, boats, buses, and planes. Electric energy is essential to our civilization and it gives us many comforts of living besides. Now, we have found ways to use a new energy—the energy of the atom.

But perhaps you do not care about engines, machines, and energy. Perhaps you are interested in music. Then you may be surprised to find that a piano is as much a machine as a

In building the Great Pyramid of Cheops, simple tools and simple machines were used.

tractor. If you search, you may discover very close connections between machines and music, machines and art, or machines and health, for that matter. The effects of the gasoline engine and the electric generator have been felt in every human occupation.

EARLY MACHINES OF EARLY MEN

Overnight, after a summer shower, a lawn may be covered with mushrooms, much to the surprise of the man who owns it. But a plant scientist would not be surprised. He knows that the plants that have "suddenly" appeared have been growing underground and unnoticed for some time.

The Machine Age has sprouted somewhat like mushrooms. People are surprised and astonished by what machines can now do. However, many persons are taken aback when scientists tell them that the Machine Age is not new but has been developing for a long time.

Our huge, complex, power-driven machines are new. Simple machines are not. Simple machines go back a long time. Just how long, no one knows. Recorded history begins about 5000 B.C. By that time, men were already using several very important tools—the knife, club, saw, drill, chisel, plow, scraper. All of these simple tools are machines.

The only force at the command of early men was that of their muscles. They could push and pull, hammer and tear. The first man

An early Egyptian plow.

who seized a stick and used it as a club invented the first machine. The club was a way of multiplying the force of the man's muscles and of using that force to better advantage. That is all that any *machine* can do—enable us to apply a force to a better advantage. Usually machines also multiply a force.

With a club to multiply the force of his muscles, man conquered wild beasts. He made other machines that also helped him. And because man could exert more force with machines than with his hands alone, he could accomplish more.

About 3700 B.C., the Egyptian Pharaoh Cheops [kē′ŏps] had a tomb built for himself at Gizeh. We know this tomb as the Great Pyramid of Cheops. It is 452 feet high and contains about 2 million blocks of stone. Some of the blocks weigh as much as 60 tons. These blocks were quarried with chisels, drills, and saws of bronze. They were moved on rollers and sleds by great numbers of slaves. No one knows for sure just how the job was done and how the blocks were raised into place. We do know, from pictures in Egyptian tombs, that simple tools were known at the time and were undoubtedly used.

As long as slave labor was plentiful, little effort was made to develop machines to take its place. The Greeks, comfortably supported by their slaves, toyed with many scientific ideas and worked out the science of simple machines. Foremost of the Greek scientists was Archimedes [är-kǐ-mē′dēz] (287–212 B.C.) who was also a famed student of mathematics.

Archimedes explained the principle of the *lever*, and showed just how a man could increase a force by using this simple machine. In his enthusiasm, Archimedes shouted, "Give me a place to stand, and I will move the earth." When Syracuse, his native city, was attacked, Archimedes designed giant war machines that kept the enemy off for 3 years.

254

NEW ENERGY FOR NEW MACHINES

By the time of Christ, machines had been developed to the point where new sources of energy were required. The first machines were, of course, operated by hand. They made it possible for men to apply the force of their muscles to tasks that were otherwise impossible.

It was a brilliant discovery when men found they could substitute the muscles of beasts for their own muscles. Animals were put to work. Men trained horses, oxen, camels, elephants, and even dogs to work for them. With an ox to pull his plow, an Egyptian farmer could cultivate more land than before. He could put aside his extra harvest of grain to trade for cloth or metal goods. He could save some of his surplus as a safeguard against famine.

When men substituted the muscles of beasts for the muscles of human beings, they took an important step toward the Machine Age. Men were no longer only producers of energy. They began to be controllers of energy, too.

A century or two before Christ, the Romans used the energy of running water for grinding grain. The Tiber and other Italian rivers furnished the energy to turn waterwheels that turned millstones. At first water power was used only for grinding grain and lifting water. Then it was used in sawing wood, pounding bark for tanning, and crushing ores

to make iron. For 15 centuries waterwheels were one of the most common types of machinery.

In the meantime, the Phoenicians, the Norsemen, and other seafaring peoples had found ways of using the energy of moving air to drive their boats over the mysterious oceans. This was a very important invention, for once again a plentiful, free source of energy was substituted for human muscles. Of course, sails were not the first improvement in water transportation. Both the paddle and the oar were machines that increased the force a man could apply to moving his boat.

More than a thousand years after men found ways of using the energy of wind on water, they began to use it on land. Little is known about the first windmills, but they were in use before Columbus sailed westward. The windmills of Holland are best known, but throughout Europe windmills were used wherever the wind was strong and reasonably steady.

Though the energy for a windmill costs nothing, the miller could not make the wind blow when he needed it. Often in the middle of the night he would rouse his entire family with a shout, "The wind is picking up. Everybody out of bed. There's work to be done." Soon the creaking arms would begin to turn, and grain would pour between the heavy rolling millstones.

The Machine Age really began its mush-

With ancient tools as well as modern machinery, energy of muscles is still necessary.

Soil Conservation Service photo; U. S. D. A. photo by Osborne

U. S. D. A. photos

Energy from nonhuman sources operates these products of our Machine Age. Left: A mobile rock crushing plant. Right: Huge shovels that unload ore ships.

room growth in the eighteenth century. Our progress with machines during the past 2 centuries has been far greater than anything that man has ever done before. But we must not forget that the breathtaking pace of modern times is possible only because of the long, slow, painful labors of men for perhaps a million years.

WORKING WITH SCIENCE

1. The great pyramids of Egypt are still something of a mystery. Go to the library and find out all you can about them. If you had only the simple tools of those times, how would you have tackled the job? Remember the pyramids are near the Nile River and the blocks of stone were mined many miles away. Use all the slave labor you want, and pretend you were the Pharaoh's engineer.

2. Find out about the famous war engines of Archimedes and how they worked. Cannons use gunpowder as a source of energy. What did Archimedes use? If you can find pictures of these machines, see if you recognize parts that we use in our machines today.

3. Another great scientist of the past who had very modern ideas was Leonardo da Vinci. Look up some of the inventions and discoveries that have been credited to him. It is not very often that one person brings as many new ideas to science as this one man. It has taken hundreds of years to find practical ways of making some of da Vinci's ideas work.

4. The simple machines have been considered the great inventions of ancient times. These and the discovery of fire, language, and writing made civilization possible. What do you think are the 10 most important inventions and discoveries of the past 200 years. How many of these are machines? Make a list and compare it with the lists of your classmates.

ENERGY

Behind the Machine Age is a vast and somewhat mysterious natural resource that makes it possible. Even when we name it—we call it energy—it is still rather mysterious. We know more about what it does than what it is. Energy is anything that makes objects move or changes their form. We commonly speak of energy as the ability to do work.

We usually think of energy as being associated with some kind of matter. The human body has energy. So has a stick of dynamite, a falling rock, or a running river. All these things can move themselves or other objects. But sometimes we have energy that is not matter, as we usually think of the word. For example, there is the energy of light and of electricity.

FORMS OF ENERGY

You can see the effects of energy about you all the time and it is not hard to make a list of the forms of energy. Most common is *mechanical energy*—the energy of motion. This form of energy is possessed by every moving object whether it is moving as a result of its own energy or energy applied from the outside. An automobile, airplane, dog, and sparrow carry sources of energy within them. A baseball, bullet, knife, and hammer do not. They move only when energy is applied from the outside. The wheels that turn in industrial plants are all applying mechanical energy.

Another form of energy is *heat energy*. Most of our machinery is operated by engines that use the energy of heat. *Chemical energy* is another form that energy takes. The energy in a stick of dynamite or a gallon of gasoline is chemical energy. So is the energy in a bowl of cereal or a dish of fried chicken.

Electric energy is so important in our daily living that we could hardly imagine living without it. Even *light* is a form of energy. It is hard to see how light fits our definition. Can light make things move? Can it change the form of things?

As you know, light is the energy that enables green plants to manufacture food for the living world. It changes carbon dioxide and water into a new substance—sugar. Scientists have made small motors that operate by light. And you may have seen in the windows of an optician a peculiar device that looks like an electric-light bulb with a small weather vane spinning around inside it. This device is a *radiometer*. When sunlight falls on it, the wheel spins around. In the dark it does not move at all. So you see light can change the form of things and make things move.

Sound is another form of energy with which you are all familiar.

ENERGY CAN BE TRANSFORMED

Energy can be changed from one form to another. Luckily this is possible because some kinds of energy that occur in nature are dangerous or of little value to man. Lightning is a natural form of electric energy. We have little use for it.

A waterfall is of little value until we can harness it and transform the mechanical energy of falling water into the mechanical energy of a revolving generator. By means of the generator, mechanical energy can be changed into electric energy that flows through wires to your home. There it may be transformed into heat, as in an electric stove; or light, as in an electric lamp; or back to mechanical energy, as in a vacuum cleaner.

Your body transforms the chemical energy of food into the mechanical and heat energy you need to keep you alive. Other forms of chemical energy are produced in the body from the energy of food.

A rocket transforms the chemical energy of its fuel into the mechanical energy that sends it miles high. An automobile, airplane, jet plane, and steam engine also transform chemical energy into heat energy and heat energy into energy of motion.

The transformation of energy does not necessarily require human hands. Light energy from the sun is transformed into heat when it strikes the earth. This heat energy causes the air to move and water to evaporate, resulting in wind and rain. The falling rain and the rivers it forms have mechanical energy. This energy wears down the earth and carries soil from the land into the seas. The mechanical energy of the wind causes waves that may become destructive. Some of the heat energy from sunlight winds up as the energy of lightning and thunder.

If this book had been written several years ago, we would have said that energy cannot be created nor destroyed. All that can be done

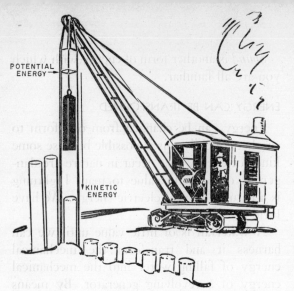

POTENTIAL ENERGY

KINETIC ENERGY

When does the potential energy become kinetic?

is to transform one kind of energy into another. However, for about a generation scientists have known and now everybody knows that, in a sense, energy can be created. Actually, matter can be converted into energy as has been done with uranium-235 and plutonium. Thus we must extend our statement and add that we can transform matter into energy and energy into matter.

KINDS OF ENERGY

In all these forms of energy the scientist recognizes only two basic kinds. The energy of motion has already been mentioned. Scientists call this *kinetic energy*. Anything in motion has kinetic energy. The heavier a substance is and the faster it moves, the more kinetic energy it possesses. Any chemical change that is going on displays kinetic energy.

The other kind of energy is the energy that an object possesses because of its position or condition. Such energy is called *potential energy*. A brick lying on the ground is just another object. But if the same brick lies on the roof of a tall building, it possesses potential energy.

Every raised object—a book on a desk, a boulder on a mountainside, an apple hanging on a tree—possesses energy because of its position. As soon as it starts to move, its potential energy is changed into kinetic

energy, or energy of motion. This energy may be put to work.

When people build a huge dam, like Hoover Dam or Grand Coulee, they store millions of gallons of water in a raised position. This water has tremendous potential energy. We let it run through pipes to waterwheels that turn electric generators. In doing this, its potential energy becomes kinetic energy, which we transform into electric energy.

We use energy of position in many ways. But if you think a bit you will see that we are really using the force of gravity. For if gravity did not constantly pull objects toward the earth, we could not use the water stored above the dams.

Objects can possess potential energy without being in a raised position. The coiled spring of an alarm clock or a mechanical toy has potential energy because it has been squeezed into a tight position. As soon as it is released, the spring uncoils and its energy runs the clock or toy.

Certain chemical compounds or mixtures have potential energy also. A mixture of sulfur, charcoal, and sodium nitrate, prepared in the proper way, is an innocent grayish powder. But because of its potential energy, this powder has changed the course of history many times. The mixture is gunpowder. Gasoline, coal, or any other fuels are examples of chemicals whose potential energy can easily be converted into heat energy.

ENERGY AND MODERN LIFE

One measure of our standard of living is the amount of energy we use. This comes to thousands of times per person as much as a human being has available through his own muscles. The steam engine, gasoline engine, electric motor—each has made man more and more of a giant. With each new invention, man was able to control and use more energy than he ever had before. Since energy is also defined as the stored up ability to do work, the more energy man can release and control, the more work he can accomplish. Machines can do the work of thousands of hands and can often do it better.

Now we are on the verge of making available amounts of energy that dwarf anything man has had at his command before. Such energy, obtained from within the atom, can make life for everyone easier and better. Unfortunately, we cannot guarantee that it will. Whether it will depends on how we use this energy.

WORKING WITH SCIENCE

1. Find out in which direction the vanes of a radiometer revolve—toward the black or toward the silvered side of the vanes? Why?

2. It has been said that all industry is nothing more than the transformation of energy from one form to another. Is this correct? How does this process work out in your father's occupation, in a baseball game, in driving a car?

3. There is reason to believe that the sun is the source of all the matter and all the energy in the solar system. If this is correct, we should be able to trace all energy back to the energy of the sun. Can you do this with (a) a peanut-butter sandwich, (b) a dog running down the street, (c) a Mississippi flood, (d) an automobile speeding along a highway, (e) a fish swimming in the ocean?

FORCE

We feel the force of the wind when it blows. We also feel the force of a current when we swim against it. It means the same thing if we say that we feel the push of the wind and the pull of the current. A *force* is a *push* or a *pull*. We can also say that a force is any kind of action that tends to produce motion or that changes the motion of an object.

You throw a ball. The muscles of your hand and arm exert a force that produces motion. You use energy obtained from food you have eaten. But try to throw a 50-pound boulder. You still exert a force, but you only tend to produce motion.

You bicycle down the street, exerting a force that sends you along. A friend whizzes by on his bike, and you exert more force to increase your motion. The traffic light changes to red. You step on the brake and apply a force that decreases your motion until you have stopped. Thus, it takes a force to produce any motion or any change in motion.

Forces surround us at all times, as energy is applied to all kinds of work. There is the force of the wind and running water. The force of expanding steam runs trains and boats. The force of exploding gasoline speeds planes and cars on their way. The force of modern explosives makes wars more deadly than ever before. The force of our pumping hearts keeps us alive. And the force of gravity tends to pull all things on earth downward.

NEWTON STUDIES FORCES

Forces were studied scientifically by Sir Isaac Newton (1642–1727). Newton experimented with bodies in motion to find out how this motion could be changed. Newton found that an object at rest will not start to move until some force acts on it. He also found that a moving object keeps on moving in a straight line without changing speed unless some force acts on it, producing a change.

It is hard to imagine any object moving onward forever without changing speed or direction. But objects in motion would do so if it were not for the forces of gravity and

What kinds of energy are shown?

259

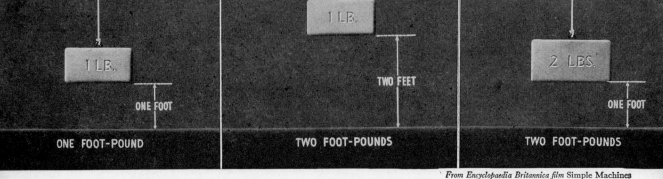

ONE FOOT-POUND   TWO FOOT-POUNDS   TWO FOOT-POUNDS

From Encyclopaedia Britannica film Simple Machines

These illustrations show the relation between force, distance, and work. How is work measured?

friction that stop them and bring them to earth sooner or later.

Newton's studies of force and motion made it easier to understand how machines work. The facts that Newton discovered are so important and are of such wide use that they are known as the *laws of motion*.

WHAT IS WORK?

The English language and all other languages, for that matter, are tools. No tool is perfect, and language is no exception. One word often has several meanings and serves several purposes. Have you ever complained that you did not feel well and did not have any "energy"? Whatever was the matter with you, you did not mean "energy" in the same sense as we have used the word in the pages you have just read.

The word *work* has even more meanings that the word *energy*. You do not mean the same thing when you say, "This is a work of art" and "It's time to go to work." For our purposes we will have to find a scientific definition of work and use that, if we want to understand work and machines. Otherwise, we may easily become confused.

It is not difficult to get anyone to admit that lifting a heavy weight is work. Lifting a 20-pound weight 5 feet in the air is a certain amount of work. Lifting a 40-pound weight the same distance is twice as much work. Lifting the 20-pound weight 10 feet requires twice the work of lifting it 5 feet. All this seems plain common sense, and it is actually the scientific way that we measure work.

Work equals a force times the distance through which that force moves an object. In the above examples we have talked of a 20-pound object moving a certain distance, but we have not mentioned a force at all. The force was, of course, exerted by your body in overcoming another force—the force of gravity. You may not have realized it, but when we said the object weighed 20 pounds, we were talking about the amount of that force of gravity.

When you stand on a scale, you measure the force that gravity exerts on your body. Because your body contains a certain amount of matter, it is pulled a certain amount by gravity. We can measure this pull in pounds and ounces or in other units of measure. If you eat a heavy meal, your body contains more matter and gravity exerts a stronger pull on it. In other words, you weigh more.

To lift a 20-pound weight, something must exert a force on the object just a bit greater than the force of gravity which makes it weigh 20 pounds. The force must be exerted in the opposite direction to the pull of gravity. The work done is equal to this force times the distance the object is moved. So to measure the work done in lifting the weights vertically, we multiply 20 pounds times 5 feet, or 40 pounds times 5 feet, or 20 pounds times 10 feet, as the case may be. The product of this multiplication gives us a number of units of work.

The units we obtain are called *foot-pounds*. A foot-pound is the amount of work done in raising a 1-pound object 1 foot vertically. Raising a 20-pound object 5 feet requires 100 foot-pounds of work. It would take the same amount of work to raise 100 pounds 1 foot or 10 pounds 10 feet.

If you carry this idea of work a bit farther, you will see that *work always involves overcoming some kind of resistance*. When you climb stairs or lift a weight, you are overcoming resistance resulting from the force of gravity. When you push a wheelbarrow or drive an automobile, you must overcome the resistance of friction that tends to keep the wheels from rolling easily. If you are going uphill, you must overcome the resistance of gravity, too. Since the force necessary to overcome these resistances can be measured, it is possible to compute the work done by the engine in driving your automobile from home to school, for example.

WHAT IS POWER?

Imagine a 10-story office building with two elevators, each weighing 5 tons. The motors of the two elevators are different, but each motor can lift the elevator from the ground floor to the roof. It is obvious that both motors can do the same amount of work, but the two motors may still be very different. One may raise its elevator to the roof in 20 seconds. The other may take 60 seconds. You would be justified in saying that the first motor is three times as powerful as the second, because it does its work three times as fast.

Time is often a very important factor when work is being done. So we need a measurement that involves both work and time, that is, the *rate* at which work is done. *Power* is the rate at which work is done. If 1000 foot-pounds of work are done by one machine in less time than another machine requires, the power of the first machine is the greater. This, of course, applies to all kinds of work, not just to the lifting of weights. More power is required to run a train at 60 miles an hour than to run the same train at 30 miles an hour.

The unit we use for measuring power is one that we have inherited from the past and it is not a very good one for modern times. It is

called the *horsepower* (abbreviated *HP*). A horsepower is 33,000 foot-pounds of work per minute, or 550 foot-pounds per second. This is the amount of work done in raising a 55-pound weight 10 feet in 1 second, or any other combination of force and distance equal to 550 foot-pounds.

SUMMARY

So far, we have only made a start in talking about machines, but the ideas in these pages are necessary to understand what machines are and how they work. Keep these ideas in mind as you read on:

Machine: a device for multiplying a force.
Energy: 1. anything that makes objects move or changes their form.
2. the stored up ability to do work.
Potential Energy: the energy an object has because of its position or condition.
Kinetic Energy: energy of motion.
Force: 1. a push or a pull.
2. anything that changes the state of

Each job requires how much work?

rest or of motion of an object, or tends to change it.

Work: 1. the result of energy being expended.

2. the result of applying a force to an object and moving or tending to move the object in the direction of the force.

3. is measured by force (in pounds) times distance (in feet) = foot-pounds.

Power: the rate of doing work; work done per unit of time.

Horsepower: a unit used in the measurement of power, equal to 550 foot-pounds per second.

WORKING WITH SCIENCE

1. The term "genius" is loosely used, but there is no doubt that occasionally some men surpass anything done by others in their fields of endeavor. Sir Isaac Newton was such a man. He solved problems that had puzzled men for years. He made discoveries in science and mathematics that seem stupendous—and he did this as a young man. Find out more about his life and his discoveries, and report on them to your class.

2. We try to suit our machines to the jobs they have to do, and so we have motors and engines

that range from a small fraction of a horsepower to several thousand horsepower. Make a list of motors and engines you can find (read the specification plate). List the horsepower of each and the purpose for which it is used.

3. Find out under what circumstances the unit of power was developed. Does a horse work at the rate of one horsepower? Can a man produce one or more horsepower? In an encyclopedia or textbook on mechanics or physics you may find more details on how power is measured.

MACHINES AND MAN

By developing machines, man became a tool-user. From a tool-user he has become a tool-controller. When a man sits behind the wheel of his car or airplane, he controls power equal to that of 50 to many thousands of horses. No king of ancient days had at his finger tips the power that any one of us can command by pushing a button or pulling a switch.

Most people are likely to think of machines as powerful devices—steam shovels, locomotives, presses, lathes, and the like. All these are machines or combinations of machines, but many machines are smaller, less

Machines transmit and apply force.

powerful, and more familiar. A housewife who uses a toaster, dust mop, egg beater, or nutcracker is using machines. Children on tricycles or roller skates are having fun with machines. A baseball bat is a machine, too.

Machines transmit force and apply this force where we want it. This may be in hammering a nail, moving a weight, or drilling a hole. A machine is not a source of energy.

An ordinary man cannot lift an automobile with his bare hands, but with the aid of a jack—a simple machine—he can raise one corner of his car and hold it up while he changes a flat tire. Human muscles can be used more effectively with the help of machines. Not many of us can lift a 100-pound barrel, but it is an easy task to raise the barrel by rolling it up a long, sloping board. The sloping board is a machine.

THE LAW OF MACHINES

A scientific law or principle is a generalized description. It tells about something we have observed so often that we believe it to be true

262

anywhere, anytime. Such a statement is called a *natural law*. We sometimes speak of the law of gravitation, the law of magnetic attraction, and so forth. These merely describe how gravitation and magnets always act.

The *law of machines* is true for all machines, large and small, weak and powerful. It sums up what we have learned by long experience— *the amount of work produced by a machine is equal to the amount of work put into it*. Or briefly, *the input of a machine equals its output*.

From a practical standpoint, the output is always something *less* than the input for some of the work is used up in overcoming friction, is lost as heat, or does not produce the effect we desire. We actually get less out of a machine than we put into it in terms of *useful* work. But if all the output is added up—useful and wasted, then input equals output. Put 100 foot-pounds of work in, and 100 foot-pounds of work come out.

Since friction and gravity are always with us, some work must be done in overcoming them. We have ways of reducing friction, but friction cannot be completely eliminated. That is why, in spite of the pipe dreams of untrained inventors, no one will ever be able to make a *perpetual motion* machine—one that will keep running of itself forever.

WHY USE MACHINES?

The law of machines raises a question even more important than perpetual motion. If the work done by a machine is only equal to the work put into it—and practically it is less— why bother using machines? You already know the answer. It is the great convenience of being able to increase or apply force in ways that would be impossible without machines. Even though some of the force is lost because of friction, we could not do without machines.

Let us put the law of machines down as a diagram. It looks like this:

$$\text{Input work} = \text{Output work}$$

But since work is the force times the distance moved,

Input force $\times$ Distance moved
$$= \text{Output force} \times \text{Distance moved}$$

As an example:

20 pounds $\times$ 50 feet $=$ 1000 pounds $\times$ 1 foot

If a man applies a force of 20 pounds through a distance of 50 feet with a machine, he can apply a force of 1000 pounds through 1 foot— or lift 1000 pounds 1 foot against the pull of gravity. That is exactly what a man does when he jacks up the wheel of a car. He multiplies his force 50 times, but he applies it through only $\frac{1}{50}$ the distance.

MACHINES OFTEN MULTIPLY FORCE

Examples of how machines multiply force are without limit. Our common hand tools are examples. Take a drill and try to turn it through a board. Put the same drill into a brace, and you can drill through the board with ease. Try pushing a spike into a plank—then use a hammer. These machines multiply your force. So does a screwdriver, a pair of scissors or pliers, a lever, a pulley, an oar, a can opener, or dozens of other simple yet very essential devices. With such machines you must exert your force through a longer distance or for a longer time but the price is well worth paying for the work the machine does.

SOME MACHINES INCREASE SPEED

For some kinds of jobs an increase in speed is more important than an increase in force. Machines will do this for us also. They will increase speed with a corresponding reduction in force. A machine may transmit only $\frac{1}{10}$ the force, but increase the speed 10 times. In sewing, not much force is needed to send the needle through the cloth. Hence speed is preferred to force. A sewing machine increases the speed, pushing the needle through the cloth several hundred times a minute. Sewing by hand, a girl can usually make considerably less than a hundred stitches a minute.

For jobs of cutting, shaping, polishing, and mixing, speed again is often more important than force. Very great speeds can be obtained

U. S. D. A. photos; Standard Oil Co. (N.J.) photo by Corsini

Which of these machines changes the force's direction or speed or both?

by means of machines. Machines can also be used to change the ratio of speed to force as required. An automobile on a level road favors speed over force. But to go up a steep hill, more force is needed. The driver uses a simple machine—the gears—to get greater force from the engine but correspondingly less speed.

MACHINES CHANGE THE DIRECTION OF FORCES

Machines not only transmit force but can also change the direction in which the force is applied. You press down on a key of a typewriter, and the type bar moves up against the paper. The force you apply has been changed in direction. In many machines it is important that the force be applied at just the right spot, at just the right time.

Can you think of any use for a few short bars of steel that move up and down for only a few inches so fast that your eye cannot follow them? Can such moving bars do any

Changing up-and-down to rotary motion.

useful work? They can. You will find them attached to the pistons in every automobile. The energy of exploding gasoline in the car pushes these rods down with the pistons. If the direction of the force could not be changed into a rotary direction, the force could not be used.

The crankshaft of the car changes the up-and-down motion into rotary motion. The rotary motion may be changed in direction, depending on whether the car goes forward or in reverse. All this makes an automobile, an airplane, or a steamship possible. Most industrial processes involve changing rotary motion to up-and-down motion, up-and-down motion to rotary motion, or other changes in the direction of motion.

ENGINES TRANSFORM ENERGY

Engines change energy from one form to another that is more suitable for doing a particular kind of work. As the energy is used, the force that is produced can be applied in different ways by machines. For most work we need mechanical energy, or energy of motion. Engines change the chemical energy of gasoline or coal to energy of motion. It may be an advantage to change chemical energy into electric energy first and from electric energy to mechanical energy. Many, many combinations and transformations are possible.

Powerful engines can either apply great

forces or produce tremendous speeds. Because these engines or motors are so compact, they can apply force in ways impossible without machines. Even if a thousand slaves turned the wheels to which the cables of the elevators in the Empire State Building are attached, their combined efforts could not begin to do as satisfactory a job as the electric motors that work silently and efficiently day in and day out.

WORKING WITH SCIENCE

1. Observe some piece of machinery in operation—a sewing machine, printing press, steam shovel, knitting machine, or something similar. See how the force is transmitted from one part to another. Often the entire secret of an important invention is a new arrangement whereby force can be transmitted so that it does some job better.

2. Demonstrate in the classroom some of the machines in common use that multiply force, change the direction force is applied, multiply speed, or perhaps do a combination of these tasks. Pick simple devices like a can opener, egg beater, or apple peeler. Explain what actually happens when the machine is used. What kind of energy is applied?

3. Make a list of the different uses of machines mentioned in this chapter, and after each put examples of well-known machines that were built primarily for this purpose.

4. Take a piece of complicated machinery like a sewing machine, automobile, or motorcycle, and show, by examples, how the different parts of it are machines, doing different jobs and illustrating the different uses of machines.

READING YOU WILL ENJOY

Bock, George E. *What Makes the Wheels Go 'Round*. The Macmillan Co., New York, 1931. The nature and operation of modern machines and power plants. This book explains the basic physics involved in modern machinery.

Harrison, George R. *Atoms in Action* (rev. ed.). William Morrow & Co., New York, 1941. A popular and accurate account of energy and how we use it.

Hartman, Gertrude. *Machines: and the Men Who Made the World of Industry*. The Macmillan Co., New York, 1939. The origins and development of modern machines that have transformed the world over the past 200 years.

Haslett, Arthur W. *Everyday Science*. Alfred A. Knopf, Inc., New York, 1937. How science affects our lives and what we might expect in the future.

Lansing, Marion F. *Great Moments in Science*. Doubleday & Co., Inc., New York, 1926. Great inventions of science, told in an interesting fashion. The book has a time table so that you can see when these great inventions were made.

Lynde, Carleton J. *Science Experiences with Home Equipment*. International Textbook Co., Scranton, Pa., 1937. A most interesting and worthwhile book to help you with science experiments using home equipment.

Lynde, Carleton J. *Science Experiences with Inexpensive Equipment*. International Textbook Co., Scranton, Pa., 1939. Another valuable book of simple experiments.

Lynde, Carleton J. *Science Experiences with Ten-Cent Store Equipment*. International Textbook Co., Scranton, Pa., 1941. Another valuable book of simple experiments with simple materials.

Reck, Franklin M. and Claire. *Power from Start to Finish*. Thomas Y. Crowell Co., New York, 1941. A detailed and well-illustrated story of power from the earliest days up to the atomic age. Explanations of all types of engines and how the power from them is used.

Yates, Raymond F. *Science With Simple Things*. D. Appleton-Century Co., New York, 1940. A good book of simple experiments.

No one knows how or when the first tools and simplest machines were discovered. It all happened a very long time ago—before any history was being written down. These first tools and simple machines were used for centuries before anyone thought very much about how they worked or how they could be combined to make better tools and machines.

We do know, though, that most of the basic tools and machines we now use were known and in use by the time the Roman Empire was flourishing. Much of our progress toward higher productivity has come about as a result of improving and combining simple machines and discovering new and better ways of applying energy to them. For example, wooden and stone drills were known to very early peoples. They were first turned by hand and later on by a bow (1).

Drills made of metal were used during the Middle Ages (2). By the nineteenth century, hard steel drills turned by belts run by waterwheels and later by steam engines were not uncommon (3). Today high-speed drills operated by electricity (4) drill two or more holes in hard steel at the same time.

22

SIMPLE MACHINES AND COMPLICATED MACHINERY

We often use machines with a good deal of skill without knowing much about how or why they operate. Often we could improve our skill in using machines if we understood the machines better. For example, anyone can row a boat, but a champion rower reaches the top, not because of strength alone, but because of skill. This skill comes partly from a very clear understanding of balance, leverage, and motion and enables him to use his oars much more effectively than most of us could.

In a way, it is unfortunate that we can operate machines and engines without knowing much about them. We lose track of the effort and ingenuity that go into the machines we are using.

SIMPLE MACHINES

Machines like wheels, levers, and inclined planes are known as *simple machines*. A better term than simple machines might be *basic machines* because most other machines and engines include these simple machines or modifications of them as important parts. Simple machines are the building blocks of the Machine Age.

OLD MACHINES IN MODERN DRESS

Here in the United States, one good sign of being up to date is to own the latest automobile. What are automobiles like today? What may we expect in the future? Look at today's models for yourself. For the future, let us see what automobile engineers have to say. In the not-too-distant future, they promise us a car so streamlined it will look like a large teardrop. The body may be built of glass fibers and plastic. You may be able to look out in any direction through a transparent top. Comfortable seats will permit you to turn in any direction.

Wheels will be smaller and safer. Tires may last much longer than they do now. Air-conditioning and radiotelephone may be standard equipment. The engine may be a small "pancake" engine beneath the floor, smaller and more powerful than engines of today. The car will use less fuel, and 50 miles to the gallon may become an everyday occurrence. Every one of these automobile improvements has already been tried out. The "car of the future" may be nearer than you think.

But let us look at this car very carefully for a minute. The engineers tell us that it has only two essential parts: the engine that provides the energy and the machines that make it possible to apply this energy to the wheels. The other devices are for safety or comfort.

Let us take this car apart—in our imagination, of course. First let us remove *all* the wheels. Not only the four wheels with their tires, but every part of the car that makes use of the idea of the wheel and axle—the steering wheel, the flywheel, the gears of the transmis-

A simple machine in operation.

sion and differential, and so forth. Now remove the levers—those that operate the brakes, the accelerator, the automatic choke, the shock absorbers, and the rest. Take out every screw and bolt also.

Why do this to our car of the future? All we have done has been to remove the simple machines that were in common use before the time of Christ. If we did this, our car would be absolutely useless. We could go farther and remove the hydraulic brakes and the parts of the engine that are pushed by the pressure of expanding gases. Both these ideas were known and used as long ago as 2 centuries B.C.

If we take all the old machines and old ideas out of the car of the future, we will have nothing left but a plastic shell and some odds and ends of metal. Of course, the screws, wheels, and levers in the car are vast improvements over the simple machines used 20 centuries ago. And although the parts are old, the very complicated combination of simple machines that adds up to an automobile is something very new. The fiftieth anniversary of the automobile was celebrated in 1946.

Probably more than 95 percent of all scientific development in the sense of inventions has taken place in the past hundred years. Some of it has been based on ideas that have remained unused for generations. Other ideas find instant application because they are needed. Sometime *you* may want to make a device to perform a task you want done. Whatever the device, the chances are that you will make use of simple machines in some way or other. And do not forget that many great inventions and discoveries have been made by young people.

THE ADVANTAGE OF SIMPLE MACHINES

We use machines to gain an advantage in work that has to be done. We usually gain this advantage by increasing the force we apply, although sometimes we wish to increase the speed. *When we apply a force, it is always to overcome some opposing force.* You apply a force in lifting a rock. You are really applying force to overcome the force of gravity. You apply force to hammer a nail. You really apply force to overcome the force that holds the particles of wood together. You apply force to push a wheelbarrow. Actually, you are overcoming the forces of friction and gravity.

We can lump together all the forces that we try to overcome with machines and call them the resisting forces, or *resistance*. We generally try to overcome a large resistance with a small effort. The gain or advantage obtained by the use of a machine is called its *mechanical advantage*. It is easily obtained by dividing the resistance by the effort. In other words, it is the ratio of the resistance to the effort used in overcoming it.

If a mason using a lever can move a 200-pound building stone with a 50-pound effort, this machine has a mechanical advantage of 4. If an electric motor operating through a series of gears makes a 100-pound effort and applies an 800-pound force to a mixing machine, the gear system has a mechanical advantage of 8.

A SIMPLE MACHINE AT WORK

Suppose we consider a very commonplace problem that will illustrate the advantage of a simple machine. Let us imagine a big church picnic where everyone has contributed something to make the occasion a success. Henry Brown, who owns the local cider mill, has brought along a few bushels of apples and a 30-gallon barrel of cider. The barrel rests on its side next to a table, and one of the ladies in charge of refreshments says in her sweetest tones, "I wish you would lift that barrel up on the table so we could start serving the cider."

You look at the barrel. Cider weighs about 8 pounds per gallon. Thirty gallons, plus the weight of the barrel, come to more than 250 pounds. You wish you were strong enough to lift it, but mere wishing does not exert the necessary force. The actual work required to get the barrel on top of the 3-foot table is 750 foot-pounds (250 pounds × 3 feet).

You get a friend to help, but the two of you together can scarcely lift the barrel. However, another friend notices a long plank on the back of Henry Brown's truck. He takes off the plank, which is about 15 feet long, places one edge against the table, and sets the other end firmly on the ground. Then he rolls the barrel around to the foot of the board and up the plank onto the table top.

By using the plank, your friend devised a simple machine. This machine enabled him to do 750 foot-pounds of work, something that you both could not accomplish by direct lifting. How did he do it? Whether the barrel was lifted or rolled up the plank, the net result was the same—250 pounds were raised 3 feet and 750 foot-pounds of work were done.

However, to raise the barrel 3 feet, your friend rolled it up a 15-foot plank. This moved the barrel 5 times the distance needed to raise it the shortest way, but because the force was expended through 5 times the distance, only one-fifth the force was needed to do the work. By applying a force of 50 pounds through a distance of 15 feet, your friend did the same work as if he had applied a force of 250 pounds through a distance of 3 feet.

The way the law of machines operated in this case can be shown by this diagram:

Input	=	Output
Applied force × Distance	=	Resistance force × Distance
50 pounds × 15 feet	=	250 pounds × 3 feet
750 foot-pounds	=	750 foot-pounds

WORKING WITH SCIENCE

1. Modern styling often misleads us about the machines we use. If you are interested in machines, study some particular machine and see what real improvements have been made in it since its invention. For example, compare a 1947 automobile with a 1937 or 1927 model. What basic changes have been made in the engine, transmission, clutch, brakes, and so forth? Compare the changes in style with real engineering changes.

2. Make a list of some of the things you do in the course of a day. These activities all involve the overcoming of resistance. In how many cases did you make use of a machine to help you? Was the machine used to gain force or to gain speed?

TYPES OF SIMPLE MACHINES

There are really only two types of simple machines. The sloping plank used to get the cider barrel on the table is an excellent example of one of them—the *inclined plane*. Any sloping surface used in performing work is an inclined plane—and there are many such surfaces. We use them all the time without recognizing them. A knife, ramp, plane, wedge, chisel, screw, and a road up a hill—all these are slopes—some are straight and some are spiral, but they work on exactly the same principle as the board against the table.

The other type of simple machine is nothing more than a bar or any solid object that rests on a point or pivot and moves up and down or back and forth. Such a machine is called a *lever*. A crowbar used by workmen to move heavy rocks or other objects is a common example. Other levers, which are not as easy to recognize, include the pulley, wheel and axle, and such simple devices as the can opener, nutcracker, baseball bat, paddle, and so forth.

Complex machines are merely combinations of these inclined planes and levers. If you learn to recognize the inclined plane and lever in all their forms, you will be surprised how often you see them in shapes and uses in which most people would not recognize them.

A loading ramp and a wedge are both inclined planes.

ROADS AS INCLINED PLANES

There are many different forms of inclined planes. The stairway in your school building, a ladder leaning against a wall, a loading ramp leading from the ground to a railway car are examples. Modern highways in hilly country are designed to use to best advantage the principle of the inclined plane.

Roads are often built so that they wind back and forth up a steep hillside, with a slope that is usually not more than 7 feet of rise for each 100 feet of road. Such a road is an inclined plane with a mechanical advantage of about 14, and most cars can go up the road in high gear. Sometimes in mountains it is necessary to have roads that rise 12 or even 15 feet per 100 feet. Then the mechanical advantage of the road is reduced, and the automobile driver may need to shift gears and go more slowly.

CUTTING AND PIERCING TOOLS

Inclined planes are not always large in size

or fixed in position. The blade of a knife or of a chisel is a movable inclined plane. When you press it against a piece of wood, the force exerted on the wood is greater than the force that you apply to the blade. If you have ever tried to cut with a dull knife, you know how important the inclined plane of a knife blade really is. A dull knife has a smaller mechanical advantage than a sharp one.

Almost every cutting tool—paring knife, cleaver, razor, ax—utilizes an inclined plane. A farmer splits a block of wood with a few strokes on a wedge which consists of two inclined planes set back to back. He might pound the same block with a blunt sledge hammer for hours without much effect. Driving the wedge exerts a terrific force that quickly splits the log.

If you mentally split a pin, needle, or nail in half lengthwise, you can easily see that piercing tools are also inclined planes. The slope of their sharp points enables them to pierce things

On what simple machine are the following based: a road up a hill? a wood plane? a chisel? How can cutting and piercing tools be considered to be inclined planes?

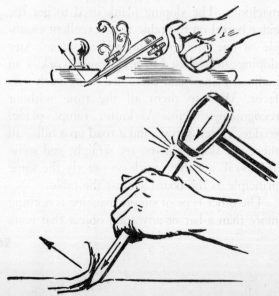

with less applied force than would be needed if the points were blunt. Piercing as well as cutting tools are force-multiplying machines.

Can you imagine several hundred chisels firmly attached one behind the other to a bar so that each cuts a bit deeper as the bar is pushed? Make the chisels very small and you have a saw. Each tooth of a saw is a chisel, and hence an inclined plane. A saw works most effectively when each tooth is set at just the right angle. Then each does its share of the job. There are hundreds of kinds of saws for many different uses, but each is a series of movable inclined planes.

SCREWS, TAPS, AND PROPELLERS

Take an inclined plane, bend it into a spiral, and you have a *screw*. You can easily see that a screw is an inclined plane. Cut a right triangle out of paper with a sloping length of 10 inches and a height of 1 inch. Now you have a low inclined plane with a mechanical advantage of 10. Color the sloping edge of the paper and wrap it, wide side first, around a pencil. The sloping edge of the inclined plane now makes a spiral up the pencil, going round and round to reach the height of 2 inches.

· Follow the thread of an ordinary wood screw and you will see the inclined plane just as clearly as in the paper model. You can also examine a machine screw, bolt, jackscrew, letter or fruit press, or meat chopper. All are screws in principle.

If you think about the propellers of a boat or airplane, you will see they are screws that twist through water or air instead of wood or metal.

Screws have spirals of different slopes. Since these spirals are inclined planes, screws may have different mechanical advantages. They are designed with a mechanical advantage suitable for the job they are to do. Wood screws generally have less threads per inch and lower mechanical advantages than machine screws.

Another device using the principle of the screw and essential to modern industry is the *micrometer*, a fine screw used in measuring. With this device it is easy to make measurements of 0.0001 inch. Skilled mechanical work is impossible without a micrometer.

Drills and augers are screws that have cutting edges. The screw extractor, tap, die, pipe threader, and pipe cutter also work on the screw principle. The screw is used to transmit power, as in the worm gear, or to move material.

Centuries ago Archimedes designed a machine to raise water into irrigation ditches. It was nothing but a screw—an oversized version of the screw that turns in a meat grinder. In northern cities, snow may be removed from roads and streets by a machine that works on this same idea. A large screw cuts into the snow, moving chunks of it back along the incline of the thread until the snow is thrown clear of the street or is loaded into trucks.

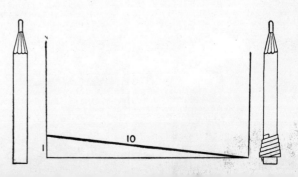

Left: A house-lifting jack is a screw with a high mechanical advantage. The slide-through handle makes the jack easy to use. Below: How to show that a screw is an inclined plane.

WORKING WITH SCIENCE

1. If there is a nearby hill so steep that the road must zigzag up it, find out the height of the hill from an official map. Also find out the length of the road from a map or by using a speedometer of a car. Compute the mechanical advantage of the road.

2. Talk with your local highway engineer or road agent. The problem of building roads of the proper slope, or grade, is very involved. See if he can explain to you some of the problems of running a road over a steep hill.

3. Measure the height and length of stairs at school, at home, and in other places. Compute the mechanical advantage of the stairs and compare them. Does mechanical advantage differ very much from place to place, or are stairs very similar? Why?

4. Make a collection or exhibit of tools that use the principle of the inclined plane—or just those that use the screw. Such an exhibit, labeled to show the principle involved, will be interesting to pupils in school who are not taking science. You can add an exhibit of screws and bolts of different sizes and shapes. With a little effort you can easily get 100 or more different specimens of tools based on inclined planes.

5. Measure the length of a large screw from the tip to the end of the thread. Measure the length of the thread by winding a string around the thread as far as it runs up the screw and measuring the string. Find the mechanical advantage of the screw by dividing the length of the thread by the length of the screw.

THE LEVER

The second of the two types of simple machines is the lever. In its most elementary form it consists of a bar that rests on a pivot, or *fulcrum*. On this point, the bar can move up and down. The resistance force is applied to one end of the bar—usually the shorter end—and the effort force is applied to the other. Such a bar is almost a natural diagram of the law of machines. Here is one example:

Resistance force × Distance
= Applied force × Distance
1000-lb rock × 1 ft
fulcrum   200 lbs × 5 ft
1000 foot-pounds = 1000 foot-pounds

This is an example of a farmer trying to dislodge a half-ton boulder from a field. He uses a 6-foot crowbar to obtain a mechanical advantage of 5. The calculation neglects the weight of the bar, the friction at the fulcrum, and the size of the stone, but it shows the principle the farmer applies.

If the farmer cannot exert a force of 200 pounds, he moves the fulcrum (actually a small stone or block) until it is, say, 6 inches from the short end of the lever. The resistance force times the distance then becomes 1000 times ½ foot, or 500 foot-pounds. The applied force, or *effort*, distance is now 5½ feet (remember that the length of the lever is 6 feet). Five hundred divided by 5½ indicates that an effort of about 91 pounds is needed to balance the 1000-pound rock.

Levers can be set up to give a mechanical advantage of almost any amount—2, 4, 6, 10, 100, 1000, or, if you desire, ½ or ¼. When the mechanical advantage is more than 1, the resistance is moved a shorter distance than the

Using a lever to move a boulder. Where is the fulcrum?

From Encyclopaedia Britannica film Simple Machines

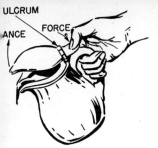

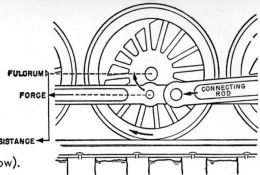

First class, second class, and third class levers (see illustration below).

effort. In the original example, the farmer can raise 1000 pounds with a 200-pound effort, but he must push down 5 feet to raise the boulder 1 foot. If the mechanical advantage is ½, the resistance moves 2 feet while the effort moves 1 foot—but the effort must be twice the resistance.

THE LEVER AS A MACHINE

The law of machines can be applied so directly to levers that you can compute the force needed to accomplish a task in an easy way. To make these computations we can fit the law of machines directly to levers and say:

Resistance × Resistance distance
= Effort × Effort distance

If we know any three of these facts, it is easy arithmetic to find the fourth. Let us try an example:

A seesaw is an excellent example of the lever. Suppose that the plank of a seesaw is 10 feet long. Two boys, each weighing 100 pounds, just balance each other when seated at the ends of the seesaw. You might express this by the equation 100 lb × 5 ft = 100 lb × 5 ft. In words, the resistance times the resistance distance equals the effort times the effort distance.

If a third boy, who also weighs 100 pounds, comes along and wants to join in the fun, he can get on one side, but both boys on that side will have to move in nearer to the fulcrum to keep the seesaw balanced. They will have to move in 2½ feet and the new situation is expressed by the equation 200 lb × 2½ ft = 100 lb × 5 ft.

Suppose a 100-pound boy wants to balance his 60-pound sister. Where should he sit?

273

KINDS OF LEVERS

Most levers do not look like a crowbar or seesaw. They are so varied in appearance and occur in such odd and unthought-of places that you can scarcely recognize them. Scissors, oars, paddles, golf sticks, doors, brakes, mousetraps, and pliers are levers. So are a wheelbarrow, a pair of tweezers, most scales, roller skates, bicycles, and your arms and legs. It is not surprising that many people have used levers for years without recognizing them or understanding how they operate.

Recognition of levers may be a bit easier if you keep in mind that the fulcrum need not always be between the resistance and the force. The resisting force may be between the fulcrum and the applied force, or the applied force may be exerted between the fulcrum and the resistance. Often it is possible to adjust the fulcrum, the resistance, and the applied force as the need demands. A farmer moving a boulder does not use a lever with a fixed fulcrum. He sets a small stone in place as the fulcrum and if his efforts do not move the

A typewriter bar is composed of many levers.

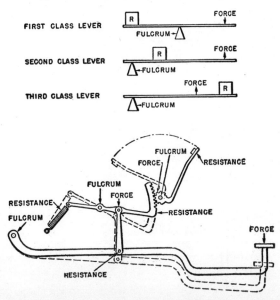

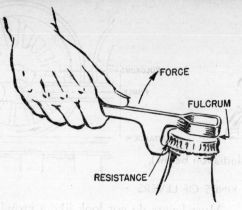

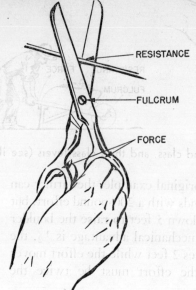

These common articles are both levers. Which class of lever is each? In considering scissors as a kind of lever, consider that one of the blades is stationary and that the other blade moves.

stone, he shoves the fulcrum in nearer the resisting boulder.

COMPLEX LEVERS

Actually, there are only three kinds of levers, as shown in the illustration on page 273. But in many machines two or three levers may be attached together to increase the applied force or to apply the force in some space where there is not room for a long lever to act. The throttle of a plane, the key of a typewriter, the arm of a steam shovel involve several levers. So do machines such as the linotype, carding machine, sewing machine,

An aneroid barometer is read through levers.

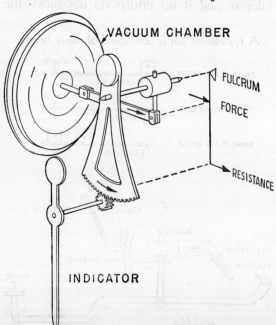

automobile, and so forth. In stepping on the brake of a car you may operate from four to eight levers, depending on the kind of brakes the car has.

BALANCE AND THE CENTER OF GRAVITY

In the seesaw kind of lever, the fulcrum is between the effort and the resistance. This lever, like all other levers, balances when the product of the effort times the effort distance equals the product of resistance times resistance distance.

This matter of balance is important in boats, airplanes, submarines, or anything that is suspended freely at the fulcrum. This may sound odd because a plane or a boat does not seem suspended, but they *act* as if they were suspended and the point at which the forces tipping the boat or plane backward or forward act is really the fulcrum of a lever. This point is known as the *center of gravity*. The entire weight of the boat or plane acts as if it were concentrated at this point.

The forces that tip a boat or a plane up or down are just like the forces that act on a lever. A small force, acting through a long distance, can balance a greater force, acting through a shorter distance, just like the boys on the seesaw. We speak of the product of a force times the distance through which it acts as the *moment* of the force. When the moments

274

that tip an object forward and those that tip it backward are equal, the object is in balance.

A simple experiment will explain the idea of balance very well. Cut an irregular piece of cardboard from the side of a cardboard box—a piece with an area of about 1 square foot but any shape you desire. Cut it with 4 sides or 5 or 6 or 11—or with curved sides if you wish. Perhaps you might like to cut it roughly in the shape of a boat.

Next make 5 or 6 small holes with a paper punch at wide intervals near the edges of the cardboard. Hang the cardboard by one hole to a nail driven in the wall. Let the cardboard swing freely until it stops. Why does it stop where it does? Simply because the moments tipping it to the left balance those tipping it to the right.

Now take a thin string with a weight on the end, a *plumb bob*, and hang it from the same nail. Draw a line along the string where it crosses your cardboard model. Remove the plumb bob and cardboard from the nail. Hang the cardboard and plumb bob from another hole, and draw the line as before. You will find that the cardboard comes to rest in a somewhat different position because the moments of force are different. The plumb bob line will be different, too, but it will cross the first line.

Repeat this procedure for four or five holes, and you will find that the lines made by the plumb bob all cross at about the same point. You should be able to balance your cardboard on the tip of a pencil at this point, which is the center of gravity.

Every object has a center of gravity, but on a ship or airplane it is not as easy to locate as on a piece of cardboard. The center of gravity is important in determining in what position a ship will float or how a car will take a turn in the road, because it is the point at which all weight seems to be concentrated.

If a plumb bob line through the center of gravity falls *inside* the base of the object or vehicle, it is stable and safe. If the line falls *outside* the base of the object or vehicle, it is unstable and will tip or turn over. Hence,

275

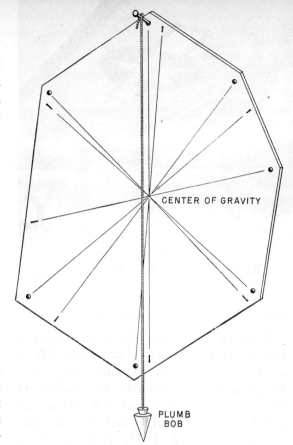

Finding the center of gravity.

modern cars are built with their heavy parts as near the ground as possible to keep the center of gravity low and make the car more stable. Boats have been known to turn over when the deck load was piled too high—a condition that raises the center of gravity so much that the push of a wave made the boat unstable.

One is very stable. Why?

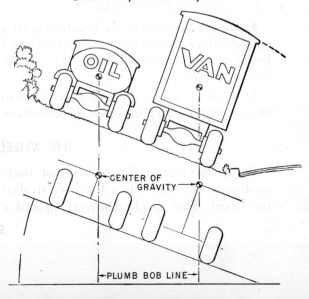

The arrow points to the right trimming tab.

SUBMARINES AND AIRPLANES

In the operation of a submarine, balance is very important. A submarine must be able to maneuver very rapidly and unless the boat is in balance, that is impossible. The moments of force acting at the bow and stern and at each side balance one another, and the submarine rides on an even keel. The boat acts like a combination of two giant seesaws in balance. Addition or subtraction of any weight upsets this balance because it alters the moments of force acting on the bow, stern, and sides.

A submarine continually acts as a lever, pivoting up and down around its own center of gravity. In every operation aboard the submarine, this fact is considered. If fuel is used from a bow tank, it must be replaced with an equal weight of water, or partly replaced with fuel from a stern tank to keep the balance of the submarine from being disturbed. Even supplies of food must be distributed so that the balance is not changed. This big job is called "keeping the ship in trim," and it is of greatest importance.

There are problems of balance in flying airplanes, too. Just before the pilot of a transport plane takes off, he receives last-minute information on his baggage and passenger load. This information enables him to judge whether there is too much weight ahead of or behind the center of balance (gravity) of his plane. For this he makes necessary allowances. A nose-heavy plane may get into difficulty in take-off and landing. Climbing, steering, and maintaining speed are also harder.

A pilot adjusts for nose heaviness or tail heaviness by the use of *trimming tabs*. These are small control surfaces attached to the trailing edge of ailerons, elevators, and rudders. On most small planes the trimming tabs must be adjusted by hand while the plane is on the ground. On larger planes the tabs are controlled from the cockpit by a series of levers.

WORKING WITH SCIENCE

1. Submarines are very ingenious inventions. Read about submarines and find out what factors in addition to those mentioned in the text are involved in the "trim" of the ship.

2. Analyze the moments of force acting on a sailboat and see if this helps you understand why a large keel is so important. What would cause the boat to tip over?

3. If you are near an airport, get permission to observe the tabs on a plane's rudder, elevators, or ailerons. How does the area of the tabs compare with that of the control surface?

4. Make a lever from a yardstick suspended by a string, and demonstrate the action of the lever by hanging weights to represent the resistance and effort at different positions. In each case, figure out the mechanical advantage of the lever.

5. Compute the mechanical advantage of some simple levers, such as a crowbar, claw hammer, or can opener.

THE WHEEL AND AXLE

Of all the ancient discoveries that made civilization possible, only a few have rivalled the wheel. This simple discovery opened a new era of transportation for early man. It is quite probable that the first wheel was also the first axle—both in the form of a smooth log.

But soon the two parts were made separately, and weight was reduced by making the axle smaller in diameter than the wheels.

A wheel is a form of lever—a rotating lever with the resistance usually between the force and the fulcrum. From your own experience you probably know that it is quite easy to turn a wheel by applying force to the rim, or *circumference*, and it is much more difficult when the force is applied directly to the axle. If the wheel has spokes, you can see that a spoke is a lever arm through which effort is applied.

The illustration at the right shows a large wheel and axle used in lifting weights. Notice where the force is applied and where the resistance acts. Which point is the fulcrum? The force is applied to the circumference, or rim, of the wheel. The *radius* (one-half the diameter) of the wheel is the distance through which the force is applied. This is the length of a spoke if the wheel has spokes.

The center of the axle is the fulcrum. Since the resisting force acts on the circumference of the axle, the radius of the axle is the distance through which the resistance acts. The mechanical advantage of this wheel is easy to compute. It is the radius of the wheel divided by the radius of the axle. If the wheel has a radius of 3 feet and the axle a radius of 3 inches, the mechanical advantage is 12.

A wheel and axle is often used to multiply a force. A winch is such a wheel and axle. It is used to lift the anchors on ships. A capstan is a winch that is operated by hand. The long

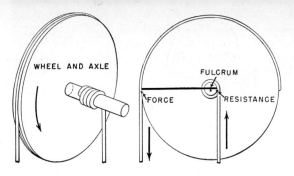

A wheel and axle is a lever.

spokes of a capstan mean that the radius is large. This gives the machine a large mechanical advantage. The spokes are removed when the capstan is not in use.

You may not have thought of it before, but a screwdriver is a wheel and axle. As long as the handle is thicker than the blade, its mechanical advantage is greater than 1. A doornob or water faucet works in the same way.

A wheel and axle can also be used to gain speed, in which case the force is applied between the fulcrum and the resistance. The pedals on the front wheel of a tricycle are an excellent example. The pedals move in a smaller circle than the circumference of the wheel. So, the radius of the applied force is smaller than the radius of the resistance. More effort is needed but the tricycle moves farther and faster because of this arrangement. In an automobile wheel, airplane propeller, electric fan, or ship propeller the force is also applied to the circumference of the shaft. As a result, the rim of the wheel, or the tip of the fan or propeller moves at a much greater speed than the shaft.

WORKING WITH SCIENCE

1. It has been said that the world moves on wheels. Make an exhibit to show the extent to which this is true. Get pictures of all of our major means of transportation, including those in which the use of wheels does not seem obvious. Underneath each picture, show by notes and diagrams just how wheels are used.

2. Take an ordinary screwdriver and by measuring the diameter and radius of the handle and stem, work out its mechanical advantage. If the

same size screwdriver bit were placed in a brace, how much would the mechanical advantage be increased?

3. The pilots of old fashioned Mississippi paddlewheel boats held their ships on course with a wheel that was more than 6 feet in diameter. To turn the ship fast, they literally had to "climb the wheel." The *Queen Mary* is steered by a much smaller wheel with much less effort. Find out how this is possible.

GEARS

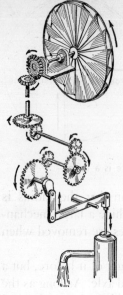

A complex train of gears.

Just as the wheel and axle is a form of lever, so are gears. They are toothed or grooved wheels so arranged that one turns another without slipping. When force is applied to a small geared wheel so that it turns a larger wheel, the small wheel makes several revolutions while the larger wheel turns only once. The resisting force on the axle circumference of the larger wheel can be overcome by a much smaller force applied to the axle circumference of the small wheel.

This situation can be reversed and the force applied to a large geared wheel that makes a smaller one spin much faster than the larger one. Force is lost, but speed is gained. A clock is a good machine in which to see the relationship of gears. If you have a broken one, take it apart and see for yourself. Count the number of teeth on the large and small gears. How many teeth are on a large gear to one on a small gear? Why?

GEAR TRAINS

Several gears acting together are known as a *gear train*. One might consist of a 10-toothed wheel that turns a 40-toothed wheel which turns a 160-toothed wheel. Sufficient force

applied to the small wheel overcomes the different resistances at each of the larger wheels and also produces several different speeds. Gear trains are found in clocks, automobiles, adding machines, printing presses, and so forth.

The mechanical advantage of a set of gears is obtained in several different ways. It can be obtained by dividing the radius of the larger gear by the radius of the smaller gear—assuming that effort is being applied to the small gear. Instead of using the radius, we can also use the diameters or circumferences of the gears. Another way to compute the mechanical advantage is by dividing the number of teeth in the larger gear by the number of teeth in the smaller one. A gear with 60 teeth being turned by a gear with 5 teeth gives a mechanical advantage of 12.

Besides a gain in force or speed, gears also offer a convenient means of changing the direction in which force is applied. A gear turning to the right rotates the adjoining gear to the left. This is the simplest arrangement, but the teeth can be built at an angle so that the applied force can be at right angles to the resisting force, or at any other convenient angle. The illustration at the left shows some of the possible arrangements of gears that apply force in different directions.

CAMS

One special device for changing the direction of a force operates on the same wheel and axle principle. However, it is hardly a gear, since it

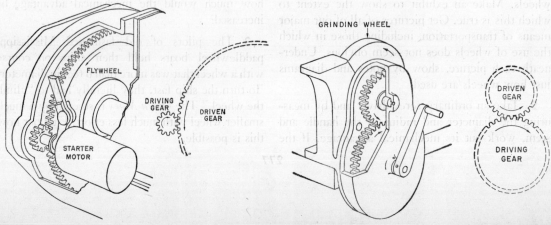

Two applications of gears. In each case which is gained, speed or force?

FLYWHEEL

STARTER MOTOR

DRIVING GEAR

DRIVEN GEAR

GRINDING WHEEL

DRIVEN GEAR

DRIVING GEAR

is usually a wheel with one or two teeth, or projections. Such projections are known as *cams*. At each turn of the wheel the cam meets and pushes a bar. The bar may be pushed upwards or to one side. Usually a spring returns it to place.

A cam transforms rotating motion into motion in a straight line. It is used to open valves or to make other movements that must be timed exactly to meet other movements of machinery. The valves of an automobile are operated by cams. If they did not open and shut at exactly the right second, the engine would not work.

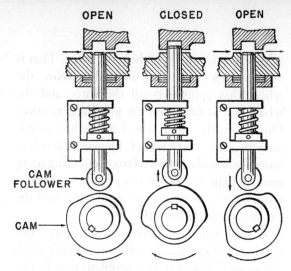

Explain how this cam operates.

GEARS IN THE AUTOMOBILE

Everyone who has driven a car or who has watched the task knows about "shifting gears." However, there are more than one set of gears in an automobile. Gears control the timing that ignites the fuel mixture at just the proper second. Gears operate the speedometer that tells you how fast you are going and how far you have gone. Gears connect the driveshaft from the engine to the rear wheels.

In older cars, in order to line the driveshaft up properly, it was necessary to run the driveshaft above the floor level of the car, producing a bulge in the rear part of the floor. To avoid this, some cars were built with a higher center of gravity, but this made them less safe on turns and at high speeds. To overcome this

difficulty, automobile engineers perfected a new type of gear that transmits the force of the engine just as well but permits the driveshaft to be lowered. This one change in gear design has made cars more comfortable and safer.

The bulge in the rear axle of a car is a complicated set of gears called the *differential*. The differential makes it possible to apply force to the rear wheels while turning. On a turn the inner wheels travel a shorter distance than the outer wheels—and hence rotate fewer times. Since no gear can operate at two speeds at once, the transmission of force to the rear wheels on a turn is a real problem.

The differential divides the applied force in proportion to the resistance. The wheel

New-type drive gears enabled engineers to lower the center of gravity of this automobile.

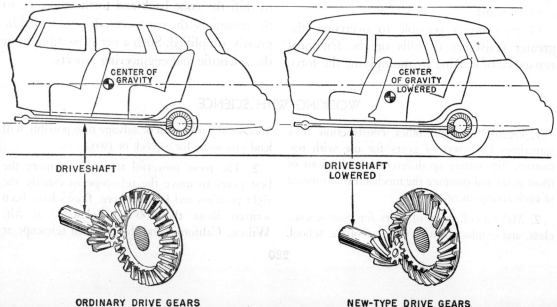

ORDINARY DRIVE GEARS   NEW-TYPE DRIVE GEARS

with *less* resistance gets the most force. That is why when a car is stuck in mud or snow, the wheel that spins gets all the force and the wheel that is firmly on the ground gets none. On a turn, the outer wheel meets less resistance than the inner wheel. Hence, it receives more force and can move faster, covering more ground than the inner wheel. On a straight road, both wheels receive equal force and the car moves ahead smoothly.

If you learn to drive an old car, your teacher will constantly tell you, "Don't clash the gears." But that is a problem that is fast disappearing. Gears are being made better and stronger. There is little danger of doing damage if you "clash" them when you attempt to shift from one set of gears to another.

Clashing is brought about when you try to mesh together two sets of gears that are spinning at very different speeds. In the latest cars this situation is automatically eliminated by a device that controls the speed of the gears while shifting is going on. The gears always slip together smoothly under this control.

Why Have Gears at All? The gears are a device to make the car practical and give it a flexibility in use that would be impossible if the force of the engine were transmitted directly to the wheels. Such a car would travel very well on a level road, but the engine would not have the force necessary to send it up a hill. There would be no way to drive the car backward.

Gears make it possible to overcome the greater resistance of hills or the frictional resistance of starting by multiplying the force of the engine. Of course, this is done at the expense of speed, but that is inevitable. Low gear gives the greatest application of force and the lowest speeds; then comes second and finally third speed, or high.

The reverse gear gives an even greater application of force than low gear. The car does not need to overcome greater resistance in going backward, but it is safer to keep the speed low when backing up.

In the future we can look forward to cars that may be quite different as far as gears go. Most cars have three forward speeds, a few have four, and trucks and buses have from 6 to 10. It would be ideal to have the right set of gears for every condition on the road. This may be accomplished by leaving out the gears entirely and putting in their place a tapering cone that would mesh with the drive-shaft at any point from the base to the tip.

The cone can be considered as a series of gears stacked one against the other, from largest to smallest. When the tip of the cone is meshed against the driveshaft, a high mechanical advantage is obtained, depending, of course, on the diameters of the cone and the driveshaft. When the large base of the cone is meshed with the driveshaft, the driveshaft turns several times for each revolution of the cone, giving the car more speed but less force.

If the cone were combined with a device, such as fluid drive, that kept the engine connected to the wheels and an automatic selector to shift the cone back and forth according to the resistance the car meets, driving would be greatly simplified. Such a car is possible from the scientific and engineering aspects.

WORKING WITH SCIENCE

1. Erector sets and other construction toys sometimes have sets of gears for use with toy motors. Try setting up different combinations of these gears and compute the mechanical advantage of each arrangement.

2. Make a collection of gears for your science class, and exhibit them to the rest of the school.

Your local garageman or salvage man possibly will lend you some for a week or two.

3. The most powerful telescopes require the best gears to move the telescope to exactly the right position and keep it there. Books have been written about the 100-inch telescope at Mt. Wilson, California and the 200-inch telescope at

Mt. Palomar, California. Read and report on the way the driving gears work on these telescopes.

4. Ask your local automobile dealer if an *overdrive* is available on the car he sells. Find out how this extra gear can save the motorist money under the right conditions. Is your locality one where an overdrive can be used to advantage?

5. The hypoid gear made it possible to lower the driveshaft of an automobile. If you are interested in cars and driving, find out how this gear works. Perhaps a garage mechanic can help you.

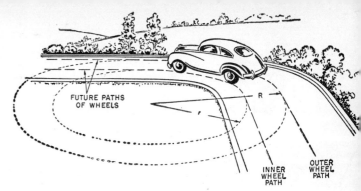

The differential in an automobile enables force to be transmitted to both inner and outer drive wheels while turning.

PULLEYS

A pulley is a grooved wheel used with ropes to obtain a mechanical advantage. The pulley may be attached to the weight to be moved or to some stable support. If more than one pulley is used, one pulley may be attached to the stable support and another pulley to the weight. One wheel and its casing is a single pulley; two wheels in a single casing are a double pulley. The pulley may be fixed or movable.

The simplest pulley setup consists of a single fixed pulley attached to a stable support and in which a force applied downward on one side of the pulley raises a weight on the other. This pulley has a mechanical advantage of 1. The force exerted is equal to the resistance, and the resisting weight is raised 1 foot for every foot that the rope is pulled downward. Since such an arrangement has a mechanical advantage of 1, no force is gained, but it is easier to pull downward than upward. The hoisting of tools or materials to a worker on a scaffold is easily done with a single fixed pulley if the load is light. Raising a flag on a flagpole is another use for a single fixed pulley.

Another pulley setup consists of a single movable pulley attached to the weight. One end of the rope is fastened to a support. The lifting force is applied upward to the other end. Pulling 2 feet on this end of the rope raises the weight 1 foot. The force is doubled, so the mechanical advantage of this pulley is 2. In spite of the advantage in force gained,

there is little use for this type of pulley since it is awkward to use.

COMBINATIONS OF PULLEYS

Pulleys, like gears, are used chiefly in combinations that give both high mechanical advantage and convenience of operation. This is usually obtained by combinations of two or more pulleys. A single fixed and a single movable pulley give a mechanical advantage of 2—the same as a single movable pulley—but there is the added convenience of a downward pull. A 10-pound weight lifted with this pulley combination requires a force of only 5 pounds, but the force must be applied through twice the distance. To raise a weight 3 feet, 6 feet of rope must be pulled.

A simple rule states that the *mechanical advantage of a series of pulleys is equal to the number of strands of rope supporting the weight.*

Pulleys may be used directly for hoisting or they may be used in combination with other simple machines. A derrick consists of a pulley system combined with a *boom,* which is a simple lever. In this combination, the

What is each combination's mechanical advantage?

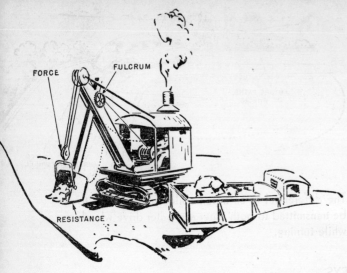

Several simple machines in combination.

pulley can be moved directly over a stockpile or some weight that is to be lifted. After the weight is raised by the pulley system, the boom can swing around and the load can be lowered at some other place.

The steam shovel is another piece of machinery in which pulleys are combined with a movable arm (usually operated by gears), giving a combination of gears, pulleys, and levers. A dragline excavator may be even larger than a steam shovel. It consists of a boom, a pulley system, and a bucket which scoops up earth. Recently one such excavator was built to remove layers of soil and sand from a bed of coal lying near the surface of the ground. It has a 9-foot bucket, big enough to hold a large car. The bucket is lowered by pulleys from the end of a 180-foot boom. At each scoop it picks up 25 cubic yards of earth—about 15 tons—doing in one day the work of 1000 miners.

WORKING WITH SCIENCE

1. The law of machines can be tested with small laboratory pulleys and a spring balance. Set up different combinations of pulleys and compute their mechanical advantage. Then lift a known weight using a spring balance as you pull. Find the actual mechanical advantage. Allowing for friction, do you expect it to be more or less than the mechanical advantage you computed?

2. Make a close study of pulleys in use, as in a sailboat, hay-loading rig, painters' scaffold, and so forth. Report on the kinds of pulleys, their mechanical advantage, and the special conveniences that the pulley serve.

3. Leonardo da Vinci, the great artist-scientist, devised pulleys of unusual size with great mechanical advantage. If you can locate a translation of his notebook in the library, look up his pulley inventions and report on them.

4. Observe and study in as much detail as you can some complex machine, such as a lawnmower, concrete mixer, cordwood saw, telegraph key, knitting machine. What simple machines and combinations of them are involved? Pay special attention to the way the complex machine has been fitted to do its special task. Note the clever ways in which the simple machines have been combined.

HYDRAULIC PRESSURE

A simple hydraulic machine.

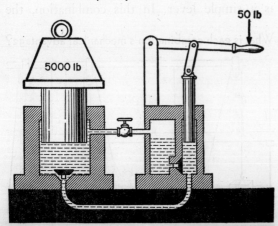

There is another and totally different type of simple machine that you have seen used many times. You enter a barber shop to get a haircut. You sit down in the barber chair. The barber pushes a simple lever two or three times, and up you go. The lever itself is of the type we have considered. But it is connected, not to the seat of the chair itself, but to a *hydraulic machine*. *Hydraulic* refers to fluids, such as water or oil.

282

When your car needs lubricating, you drive over the "lift" at a filling station and step out of the car. The attendant places blocks under the wheels. He steps back and turns the valve on a small pipe. Oil, under a few pounds pressure, flows through the pipe into a large cylinder. As the oil rises in this cylinder it pushes on the bottom of a smooth-walled piston that begins to rise. The car lift is fastened to the top of this piston and rises, carrying your car high enough for the attendant to work underneath your car.

There are many other applications of this simple hydraulic machine. The body parts of your car were stamped out in a huge hydraulic press. The car's brakes are probably hydraulic. Giant presses capable of exerting a total force of 15,000 to 20,000 tons are used in forging steel. Cotton is compressed and baled for shipment in hydraulic presses. Cottonseed oil is squeezed from the seeds by hydraulic presses. Certain types of slow-moving freight elevators, designed to lift tremendous weights, are hydraulic machines. How do these machines work?

PASCAL'S FAMOUS DEMONSTRATION

A French scientist named Blaise Pascal [păs′kăl] (1623–1662) once performed an interesting demonstration. He fastened a long pipe to the top of a strong barrel so that the entire device was watertight. He then poured water into the top of the pipe. As the water rose in the pipe, the barrel began to creak and groan in a most startling fashion. Suddenly it split apart at the seams and the water rushed out. Why? How can so little a force create so great a force?

Pascal's Law. In working with water and other fluids under pressure Pascal had found an interesting fact. He found that *pressure applied to any enclosed fluid is automatically and equally applied throughout the container.* Here is one of the experiments he performed. He constructed a huge cylinder fitted with pistons at both ends. One of these pistons had 100 times the surface area of the other one. He

DRIVING SHELL   DRIVING OIL   DRIVEN SHELL   FLUID DRIVE IN OPERATION

A fluid drive operates hydraulically.

found that one man, pushing on the small piston, was able to equal the force of 100 men, pushing on the large piston.

This experiment illustrates the fact represented by Pascal's law. Suppose the man at the small piston pushes with a force of 50 pounds. Suppose the surface area of the small piston is 1 inch. Then the man exerts a pressure of 50 pounds per square inch. Pascal's work convinced him that this pressure would be transferred equally to every part of the container.

The large piston has 100 times the area of the smaller one; that is, 100 square inches. According to Pascal there would be a pressure of 50 pounds on each of these 100 square inches. That is a total of 5000 pounds. You can see, then, why it was possible for one man to hold back the force of 100 men.

You can see, too, why the weight of the water in the slender pipe attached to Pascal's

Forming airplane parts in a hydraulic press.

A computor is a combination of simple machines.

large barrel was able to split the cask. Suppose the pipe had a cross-sectional area of 1 square inch and that it was filled with 10 feet of water. The weight of each foot of water would produce a pressure of about 4.3 pounds per square inch. The 10 feet of water would produce a pressure of about 43 pounds per square inch. Now suppose that the bottom of the barrel were 500 square inches in area. What is the total force exerted on the bottom of the barrel? You can see how easy it is to produce tons of force by exerting only a few pounds of force.

MODERN HYDRAULIC MACHINES

With a hydraulic machine do we get something for nothing? No more than with any of the other kinds of simple machines. What is gained in force is lost in distance moved, and friction cuts down the output as in any other simple machine.

Modern machines ordinarily do not require moving the small piston any great distance. Pumps are designed so that the small piston moves up and down many times instead of continuing through a long cylinder. The diagram on page 282 is of a common type of hydraulic press. Study the valves carefully. You will see that when the small piston is pushed down, it closes the valve to the oil pool and opens the valve connecting the small cylinder to the large one.

When the small piston is raised, the valve connecting the small cylinder to the large one is closed by the pressure in the connecting pipe. The valve connecting the small cylinder with the oil pool is opened so that the cylinder fills with oil and is ready for another down-stroke. If the handle of the small piston is connected to a gasoline engine or an electric motor, it can operate at high speed.

SIMPLE MACHINES IN MODERN LIFE

As we have seen, some of the most important uses of simple machines are in combinations of several simple machines. While the various levers and inclined planes are of great value by themselves, historically their most important uses were probably as simple tools that helped man to get his first slight control over his environment. A great step was taken when inventors began to understand the principles of these machines. Then they became able to combine simple machines into complex machinery with new sources of energy. In modern times these are the machines of greatest importance to us.

We sometimes do not appreciate how useful these ingenious combinations of simple machines can be. When you hear the phrase *wheel and axle*, you immediately think of transportation, and rightly so. But you can make wheels and axles practically think for you. How long would it take you to divide 3,786,945 by 0.00739? A modern calculator will accomplish that task in just a few seconds. Press the correct buttons and whirling gears will do the rest for you. When you listen to a piano, you hear an artist carefully handling a series of complex levers. The movie projector, oil burner, loom, typewriter, phonograph, washing machine, airplane, and practically every device that you can name include simple machines as essential parts of their structure.

The simple machines, applied with scientific understanding, have made our complicated machinery and our more complicated civilization possible.

WORKING WITH SCIENCE

1. Make a survey of your community to find out the different kinds of hydraulic machines that are in common use.

2. A common device for closing doors quietly is a small hydraulic machine. Probably such devices are used in your school. Ask the school engineer if he can give you a worn-out device of this kind so that you can take it apart and demonstrate its construction and operation to the class.

3. Shock-absorbers for automobiles may be of the hydraulic type. Consult a local garageman to find out how they work and report your findings to the class.

4. See if you can plan a hydraulic machine that will do some piece of heavy work. Be sure to select work that is suited to a hydraulic machine.

READING YOU WILL ENJOY

Clark, John A., Gorton, Frederick, Sears, Francis W., and Crotty, Major Francis C. *Fundamentals of Machines*. Houghton Mifflin Co., Boston, 1943. If you want further and more detailed information about simple machines, try this book.

Gail, Otto W. *Romping Through Physics*. Alfred A. Knopf, Inc., New York, 1934. A simple, lightly written book covering some very important ideas of physical science. Part of the book will help you understand better the ideas in machines.

Peet, Creighton. *How Things Work*. Henry Holt & Co., New York, 1945. A simple, well-illustrated book, dealing mostly with machines and engines, that helps make the workings of machines easy to understand.

Zim, Herbert S. *Submarines*. Harcourt, Brace & Co., New York, 1942. Chapters 8–12 deal with the principles of submarine operation and cover specific gravity, balance, "trim," and other topics related to this chapter.

In spite of our great scientific advances, we still depend on the sun for the energy to run our machines. Man has always done so. When man depended on his own muscles or the muscles of animals (1) he was one or two steps farther away from the sun than he now is. Energy from the sun, stored in foods by photosynthesis, gave energy to muscles.

One of man's greatest steps forward came when he learned to use stored-up sun energy without passing it through animals first. He learned how to burn such things as wood and coal and oil. In burning them, hot gases were produced and he learned how to harness these hot gases to do his work by means of engines, such as those run by steam (2) and gasoline (3).

An even greater discovery was the release of atomic energy (4). In a way, man now imitates the sun, for the sun's energy is probably atomic energy also. When man is able to harness the energy of the atom, he will no longer depend on the energy of stored-up sunlight. He will no longer worry about what he will do when coal and oil are gone. He will have abundant and never-ending energy to use in making more things for more people.

$$E = mc^2$$

23

ENERGY TURNS THE WHEELS

Energy makes the wheels go 'round. Modern machinery is wonderful, but only when it is in action. When the current is off or the fires have died down under the boilers, the machines are dead things. Energy is the key to the Machine Age.

THE ENERGY WE USE

In discussing simple machines and the law of machines, we said that forces were applied and resisting forces were overcome. Energy makes applied forces possible. A force *is* an application of energy. For our purposes energy is the capacity or ability to do work.

It is not feasible to attempt to run household or industrial machines with some forms of energy. For example, scientists have made a small motor that operates when a strong light is turned on a *photoelectric cell* that changes light directly into electricity. But we have no illusions about running the machinery of industry on electricity from light. The amount of energy produced is too small. Some of the other forms of energy such as x-rays, cosmic rays, and radio waves are of no value for running machinery, but they are of tremendous importance in other ways.

Heat, electricity, and mechanical energy are the three forms of energy that are used most widely in industry. In the development of the Machine Age the great milestones were discoveries and inventions that involve energy. The invention of the steam engine, the gasoline engine, the electric motor and generator, are perhaps the three greatest developments.

You will become better acquainted with electricity in Chapter 25. So here let us give our attention to the energy of motion. Heat energy is energy of motion. Heat is the result of the motion of the molecules of a material. The greater the motion of its molecules, the hotter the substance is.

Mechanical energy is energy of motion, too, but it is the motion of larger bodies—of wheels, levers, pistons—any objects larger than a molecule. Since both heat energy and mechanical energy are energies of motion, it is easy to transform one into another. In almost all industry heat energy is changed into mechanical energy.

THE ENERGY OF THE PRESENT

We use many sources of energy today. In fact, we can design and manufacture energy fuels for a specific use almost as easily as a tailor can make a suit of clothes to fit a person. For example, the gasoline we perfected over a period of some 50 years was not suitable for the high-compression engines developed for modern aircraft. So petroleum engineers made a new fuel very different from the gasoline used in automobiles and very well suited to airplane engines.

All of the fuels we use and all other sources of energy go back to two principal sources so important they outweigh all others. These are *gravitation* and the *sun*. Since there is good reason for believing that the matter of which

Left: Light shining on photoelectric cells runs this motor. Middle: A lightning flash releases solar energy. Right: Solar energy is stored behind Hoover Dam. Explain.

the earth is composed was once a part of the sun, the sun is actually our only source of energy.

SOLAR ENERGY

The sun is the source of energy that gives us life and enables us to run all our machinery. In all the past centuries we have depended on *solar energy.* We depend on it now and even if we work out better means of using the energy of the atom, we will still be dependent on the energy of the sun.

The sun's energy is released, or radiated, in all directions. We call energy of the kind that leaves the sun *radiant energy* because it is transmitted by the process of *radiation.* This energy moves as waves in all directions from the source, traveling at the enormous speed of 186,000 miles per second.

Much of the sun's energy comes to us as light. Some of the sun's energy is transformed into heat energy when it strikes the earth's surface. When it strikes the seas, it is not entirely wasted. The heat evaporates some of the ocean water, which goes into the air as water vapor and which may fall as rain thousands of miles away.

Since we must have rain for our crops, the energy from the sun that evaporates water is very useful. The rain that falls on mountains also runs some of our machinery. It finds its way into rivers, which we may convert into reservoirs by means of dams. We store water in a raised position and convert its potential energy into electric energy.

Solar heat evaporates water, makes rain possible, and warms the air and sets it into motion. Heated air may rise rapidly, carrying aloft molecules with electric charges. These electric charges may accumulate in the clouds and when the accumulation is strong enough, a huge electric arc will flash from cloud to cloud or between a cloud and the earth. This flash is *lightning,* a form of electric energy.

The brilliance and occasional destruction caused by lightning have led some people to say that man should try to harness this electricity and use it for running machines. This is not likely to be done. Careful studies of lightning show that it is an electric flash of hundreds of millions of volts. Most of our machinery operates on a few hundred volts. However, while this sounds as if lightning might be a rich source of electricity, the flash last for only about 0.000001 second, and the total amount of electricity is not great. Hence the work it could do amounts to little.

Energy from the sun also sets the winds in motion. Winds are important in determining our climate. But as a source of energy for operating machines, they are only of limited value. Wind power is of local importance, especially in regions where other sources of energy are not available. Isolated farms, weather stations, and even small communities can obtain electricity from wind power in regions where winds blow steadily.

The energy of the *tides*, which we have talked about using but have never actually used, is, in a sense, also solar energy. The tides are the result of the gravitational pull of the sun and moon upon the seas. Their combined "pull" draws water away from and lowers the shoreline. Over the ocean as a whole, water is raised only a few feet by tides. But in certain places on the earth, tides are much greater. In such places the water at high tide could be trapped behind dams and used to generate electricity as it runs out, when the tide drops.

Radiant energy from the sun is absorbed directly by the green leaves of the plants that carpet the earth. There, as you know, it provides the energy for photosynthesis. In photosynthesis only about $\frac{1}{10}$ of 1 percent of the solar energy received by the plant is transformed into the chemical energy of sugar. However, photosynthesis is the most important energy transformation we know.

Stored Sunlight. Photosynthesis is essential to all life. As you know, the food of most living things depends upon it. But more than that, nearly all our machinery is operated indirectly by photosynthesis. This may seem odd, but it is true. The coal we burn is altered plant material that accumulated in swamps and was changed by the heat and pressure of overlying rock.

It is quite likely that our petroleum deposits were formed from microscopic ocean plants or animals that were also buried. These are our principal fuels except, of course, for wood, which is plant material, too. In a sense, all these fuels are stored sunlight. When you shovel coal into the furnace or fill the tank of a car with gasoline, you are using the energy of past sunlight.

In a way, using the energy of the past is like living on savings. But coal and oil deposits cannot be replaced as can funds in a savings bank.

If solar energy could be used directly, enough reaches the earth to provide several thousand horsepower for every person—enough for all household tasks and ample for industry, too. It is enough energy to free people from much drudgery. But in the United States at present we produce—considering all sources of energy—only about 12 horsepower per person, and this country leads the world in energy production.

AMERICAN ENERGY RESERVES

We, in the United States, are very well off when it comes to energy resources. We have abundant water power, though as yet we have harnessed only about 30 percent of it. Even so, the total amount available is far from sufficient to meet our energy needs.

In 1939 the United States had about one-half the world's known reserves of coal and oil. However, we use our coal and oil faster each year and so our fuel reserves are going faster than those of other countries.

Mining coal or drilling for oil are direct ways of producing energy. But the farmer and cattle raiser are producers of energy as well. The scientist who develops a new variety of corn that will give an increased yield per acre is increasing our energy supply. So is the scientist who develops a better breed of meat or dairy cattle. Much of our industry is involved, directly or indirectly, in the production of energy.

THE TRANSFORMATION OF ENERGY

The ability to transform one kind of energy into another is the key to our use of solar energy. The changing of light energy into heat is one of the easiest changes to make. As soon as light strikes the molecules of any matter—gas, liquid, or solid—this transformation takes place. The nature of the material struck by the light makes a difference.

You can test this for yourself if you live in a region where it snows. Pick a clean spot where the snow is even and undisturbed. Place a piece of white cloth 1 foot square on top of the

Pennsylvania Railroad photo; Courtesy General Motors Corporation

Both of these locomotives run on solar energy—sunlight stored up millions of years ago. The energy of the locomotive at the left comes from wood. From what does the other locomotive get its energy?

snow. Nearby, place a piece of black cloth the same size. After the sun shines on these for a while—a day or so for best results—find out under which cloth the snow has melted most. Since sunlight fell equally on both, one cloth is better able to convert light into heat than the other.

You can provide a more dramatic demonstration of the transformation of sunlight to heat by passing sunlight through a magnifying glass. At the *focus*, the point where the rays of light come together, set some paper. At the focus, enough light is converted into heat to set the paper on fire. Fires have accidentally been started in just this way. Instead of a magnifying glass, a flaw in the window glass or the thickened glass of a chandelier has focused the light.

Attempts have been made, with some success, to convert sunlight directly into heat by means of curved mirrors turned by clockwork to follow the sun. Such solar engines are possible in places where the sun's rays are not lessened by clouds or other unfavorable atmospheric conditions. Experimental models have been used to heat water, bake bread, and do similar household tasks. We have not done more in developing solar engines because fuel is still plentiful and relatively cheap.

Keeping Energy on Tap. Our great problem is to have energy available when and where we

need it. Sunlight is available less than half the time and even if we could use it directly, we would still have to rely on something else on cloudy days and at night, unless we can find ways to store heat for future use. This is very difficult to do as you may have discovered if you have tried to keep something hot for any length of time without a fire or some other source of heat.

The best present practice is to produce the kind of energy we need on the spot, when we need it. That is why we use fuels. Their energy is released as light and heat—mostly heat. So instead of attempting to keep a reservoir of heat available for use, we keep a pile of coal or a tank of fuel oil. By burning the fuel, we convert its chemical energy into heat. Heat is changed into mechanical energy in steam, gasoline, and diesel engines.

In some cases we start with mechanical energy and merely convert it into another type of mechanical energy. Thus, the push of falling water is changed by a waterwheel or turbine into spinning, or rotating, mechanical energy. This can be used to operate machines or, as is more often the case, to produce electric energy which does not have to be used on the spot but which can be sent out over power lines.

As another example, the energy of moving air strikes the blades of a windmill and is transformed into rotating mechanical energy.

290

This is transmitted through gears and shafts to grind wheat or corn or to pump water. Some windmills have propeller-type blades that are used to turn an electric generator.

WORKING WITH SCIENCE

1. The source of the sun's energy has been understood only in the past few years. You may not be able to follow all the details, but you will discover that such common elements as carbon, hydrogen, nitrogen, and oxygen are involved. Find out more about the sun and how its energy is produced, by consulting recent books on astronomy or by visiting a planetarium or museum.

2. Sunspots are solar storms that directly affect the earth. They appear in cycles and at the time they are most numerous radio, telegraph, and sometimes telephone communications are affected. Sunspots may have other indirect effects that are interesting to know about, even though we are not so sure about them. Find out more about sunspots and report to the class.

3. Some farm products of our country may be considered as special types of fuel. Hence, the production of such crops as corn, wheat, potatoes, sugar, and sorghum gives a general picture of how efficient some plants are in converting solar energy into chemical energy. Find out the production per acre of such crops in your vicinity. Make comparisons with national and state averages. What factors enter into getting a large crop besides abundance of sunlight?

4. Every industry in your community is concerned in some way or another with the transformation of energy. Make a list of five different industries and show what energy transformation enters into the work they do or the products they make.

THE LAWS OF ENERGY

The laws of energy are similar to the law of machines and the law of conservation of matter. They deal with conditions that scientists have found true in working with energy for centuries.

THE FIRST LAW OF ENERGY

The *first law of energy* states that the total of all energy is constant. This law has been called the *law of conservation of energy*. It means much more than its few words imply. If the total energy of the earth is constant, we cannot lose energy, gain energy, destroy energy, or create energy. That leaves us only one possibility—we can transform energy from one form to another.

In transforming heat into mechanical energy or mechanical energy into electricity, we come up against difficulties similar to those we encountered with the law of machines. Some of the energy is used in overcoming friction; some escapes into the atmosphere as heat. Some electric energy is converted into heat as electricity passes through wires. In every case when we transform one kind of energy into another, we end up with *less* useful energy than

we started with. We have not destroyed or lost any energy, but some has been converted into forms that we cannot harness and use.

The loss of heat energy in an automobile is so great that we need a special cooling system to get rid of the heat that is not converted into mechanical energy. If we did not get rid of this heat, the automobile would break down.

Only about 8 percent of the total energy of a gallon of gasoline sends the car rolling forward. About 20 percent is wasted because the gasoline is incompletely burned, and another 20 percent is wasted in the hot gases that pass out the exhaust pipe. Forty percent is lost in the cooling system that is essential to keep the motor from overheating, and a final 12 percent loss results from the friction of parts within the car. This is not too bad compared with the losses of other engines, but at high speeds

How the energy of an automobile engine is used.

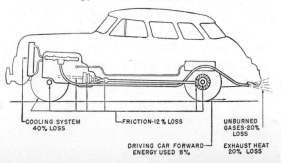

COOLING SYSTEM 40% LOSS   FRICTION-12% LOSS   UNBURNED GASES-20% LOSS

DRIVING CAR FORWARD ENERGY USED 8%   EXHAUST HEAT 20% LOSS

291

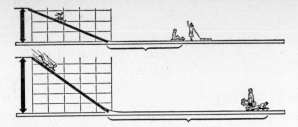

The greater the temperature drop, the greater the mechanical energy available for work.

even more of the gasoline's energy is wasted.

We can account for all the energy that enters into any energy transformation. While the input of energy is always equal to the output of energy, there is always less useful, or *available*, *energy* after the transformation. This is a state of affairs that we recognize and about which we are doing something. Laboratory workers are constantly striving to improve engines and motors so that in transforming and applying energy the loss of available energy is kept at a minimum.

THE SECOND LAW OF ENERGY

The *second law of energy* applies specifically to heat energy, but since heat is an essential form of energy, the law is important. Like the first law of energy, it is a simple statement: Heat tends to flow from objects with a higher temperature to objects with a lower temperature. The statement is so commonplace that you may wonder why it is important.

Everyone knows that to warm a pot of water you put it on the stove, not on a piece of ice. You do this because heat will flow from the place of higher temperature (about 700°F for the flame) to the place of lower temperature (perhaps 60°F of the water). As long as the water is cooler than the flame, heat passes into the water. But if you stick a white-hot bar of iron into the flame of your stove, the iron (temperature about 1200°F) gives out heat to the burning gas instead of getting heat from the flame. You would actually see the iron cool until it reached the temperature of the flame.

This second law of energy is of greatest importance. At home the furnace and heating pipes are insulated because heat energy would flow from them into the air and walls if they

were not. Your icebox is insulated, too, preventing the warmth of the kitchen from flowing to the lower temperature in the icebox.

Hot things cool off, cool things become warm. If the flow of heat were not interrupted, the earth would finally reach one uniform temperature and all activity would cease. Temperature differences make industry possible. Furthermore, the greater differences in temperature result in better engines. Consider the differences in temperature as something like the slope of a hill. A bigger temperature drop means a steeper hill. If some boys were coasting down several hills on sleds, the boy on the steepest hill would go fastest and farthest.

So it is with heat engines. The ones with the greatest temperature drop produce the greatest amounts of mechanical energy. With this second law of energy in mind, engineers have built steam engines that do not use ordinary steam at 212°F; they use superheated steam at several times this temperature. These high-temperature engines produce more energy per pound of fuel than do ordinary engines.

THE NEW LAW OF ENERGY

There is nothing really wrong with the first law of energy. In every energy reaction that we can see or measure, energy is neither created or destroyed. This is true of the law of conservation of matter which points out that matter also cannot be created or destroyed.

No scientist has discovered that these laws are in error. However, one scientist did discover that these two laws are different phases of the same law. This discovery was made by Albert Einstein in 1905 and it is regarded as one of the greatest of modern discoveries in science. The two laws are now combined into one which states that the total of energy *and* matter is constant.

Energy and Matter Are Interchangeable. This law means that energy can be transformed into matter and matter can be transformed into energy, but the total of both remains the same. This revolutionary idea indicates that energy and matter are interchangeable. The idea seems revolutionary to us because until recently the transformation had not been accomplished.

In order to understand this idea, let us consider a piece of burning wood. We take a solid chunk of oak weighing 1 pound and burn it completely. Nothing remains in our stove but some light gray ash that weighs only 0.01 pound. Haven't we destroyed the wood and changed it into heat and light as it burned? The answer is, naturally, "Yes." But while the burning has destroyed the wood, it has not destroyed the elements—chiefly carbon, oxygen, and hydrogen—of which the wood was made. These elements have formed new compounds—carbon dioxide, water vapor, and others.

If we trap all the gases that escape from the wood and weigh them and the ashes that are left behind, we will find that the weight of these products of combustion is actually more than 1 pound. In burning, the elements of the wood unite with oxygen from the air, and oxygen, too, has weight. As far as our best scales can tell us, none of the matter of the wood was destroyed in burning. However, scientists would not be surprised if a very, very small amount of matter—perhaps in the nature of a billionth of an ounce—had been converted into energy. But our scales could not detect such a small loss.

On the other hand, if the pound of wood were completely converted into energy, there would be no matter left when the process was over. No ash, no carbon dioxide, no gases of any kind. The wood no longer exists. In its place would be a flood of energy. Burning a pound of wood would scarcely provide enough energy to boil a cup of water. Converting the same wood completely into energy would give enough energy to run a 1000-watt electric heater for just about 11,300,000,000 hours. At 7 cents per kilowatt-hour, that much energy is worth about $791 million. In other units, 1 pound of matter is equal to about 15 billion horsepower hours.

Einstein's Discovery: E = mc². One pound of

any kind of matter is equal to this enormous amount of energy. One pound of rock, wood, paper, glass, beans, or anything else. That fact was the core of Einstein's discovery. Einstein worked the idea out mathematically and ended up with a simple formula that you may have seen in newspapers or books. It is a formula that is the cornerstone of the *Atomic Age*. It looks simple:

$$E = mc^2$$
energy = mass × speed of light squared

The core of this equation is the c^2. The c stands for the speed of light, a tremendously fast speed—the fastest in the universe. The c^2 means that the speed of light in centimeters per second is multiplied by the speed of light—a product that is supertremendous. Briefly, a tiny bit of matter can be converted into a tremendous amount of energy. And any kind of matter will do. It need not be uranium or other rare substances. Dirt, rock, water, wood, bones would all do equally well.

Atomic Energy. But man has not yet discovered how to transform just any kind of matter into energy. Scientists have been trying ever since Einstein said that it could be done in 1905. The first clue was the discovery of radium—the element that breaks down of its own accord into other elements, losing a small amount of its weight in the process and producing energy instead. Then came all kinds of efforts at "atom smashing" in an attempt to release some of the energy of the atom.

Removing material from an atomic pile.

As you know, scientists have found a way to release a little bit of the energy in an atom of a particular kind of uranium—uranium-235 and of atoms of the man-made element, plutonium. This atom has not been completely converted into energy, but, for example, in splitting the uranium-235 atom into an atom of barium-137 and an atom of krypton-82, some weight was lost. Actually about $\frac{1}{10}$ of 1 percent of the matter is converted into energy, but even this is the greatest release of energy that we have ever known. Even at this low rate, 1 pound of uranium-235 will produce the heat energy we now obtain from about 20,000,000 pounds of coal.

Scientists are already working on atomic engines. It is still too early to predict that someday all our industrial and home machinery will run on atomic energy, but such a thing is entirely possible in the future. The important thing is that the first steps have been taken. Atomic energy is no longer a wild dream but a reality. With patience and hard work, the next steps will come and wider use of atomic energy in industry and even in the home may come a great deal sooner than we now expect.

WORKING WITH SCIENCE

1. The events that led to the development of the atomic bomb and the use of atomic energy are as exciting as a detective story. In magazines and newspapers that appeared in the fall of 1945 and in 1946, read the story of these experiments. Prepare a report for your class.

2. Albert Einstein is a scientist who uses mathe-matics as a tool in making his discoveries. Other scientists spend most of their time performing experiments in the laboratory, but Einstein and scientists like him figure out what should happen first, and then test their ideas by experiment. Read the life of Einstein or the story of the development of some of his theories.

FRICTION AND MACHINES

Friction has entered our discussion of energy and work, like a villain in a play. Friction makes perpetual motion impossible. It keeps the output of machines from matching the work input. Is friction a villain? It has always been with us and always will be, so we had better consider friction very carefully.

Friction is a force. We can call it *frictional force*, or *resisting force*. It is the resistance of one surface rubbing against another. In machinery, surfaces rub continually against each other. Even in the simple machines there are points where friction occurs—at the fulcrum in all levers, at the point where an object is pulled or rolled up an inclined plane, as the wheels turn in a pulley.

Frictional force is the result of several factors. If we examine materials that look and even feel smooth with a microscope, we find that they are much rougher than we had supposed. Even the smooth sharp edge of a razor blade has nicks and dents in it. These roughnesses increase friction. The friction that a loaded truck creates is greater than that of an empty truck.

Weight and pressure increase friction. Weight is merely a measure of pressure due to gravity, and so the two forces are very much alike. The greater the surfaces in contact, the greater the friction between them and since the roughness of the surface is important, different materials produce different amounts of friction, other things being equal.

FRICTION AND HEAT

Probably you have observed that friction produces heat. Touch a saw after you have cut through a heavy board, or a drill after you have drilled through a 2-inch plank. Both are hot to the touch. You can produce heat by friction without tools by just rubbing the palms of your hands together vigorously. Trains are held up when a brakeman discovers a "hotbox" resulting from the friction of an axle against the wheel bearing. An auto driver can "burn out" his brakes if he uses them too much going

Courtesy Caterpillar Tractor Co.; Standard Oil Co. (N.J.) photo by Libsohn

Left: The "caterpillar" tread of this bulldozer provides tremendous friction with the ground. Right: Lubrication reduces friction between the spring leaves and eliminates squeaks.

down a steep hill. Heat produced by friction is one of the major problems in industry.

FRICTION AND EFFICIENCY

We can understand more about friction if we return, once more, to the law of machines. Work input equals work output only when friction is eliminated. In that happy state of affairs the ratio of output to input would be 1, that is, 100 percent. Such a state never exists. The ratio is always less. Often much less.

The ratio of work output to input of a machine is called the *efficiency* of the machine. If the efficiency of an automobile is 10 percent, this means that 90 percent of the energy input is lost as heat and in overcoming frictional force, and only 10 percent produces effective work in pushing the car along the road. If a lever has an efficiency of 40 percent, this means that because of friction, 100 foot-pounds of work must be done to secure 40 foot-pounds of effect.

Engineers can measure and compute the efficiency of electric motors, drills, airplane engines, presses, diesel engines, and so forth. They rarely find a machine with an efficiency as high as 50 percent. Most of the common engines and machines that you see and use have efficiencies well below 50 percent. If the efficiency of a large steam boiler can be in-creased by even 1 percent, the saving in fuel in 1 year would run into many dollars.

THE USES OF FRICTION

Perhaps by now you are saying, "Wouldn't it be wonderful to live in a world without friction?" Just stop for a moment and think what such a world would be like. No trains could run, no automobiles, no airplanes. If you slipped and·fell, as you would because you could not walk without friction, you would keep on slipping forever. If you bumped into something, you would slip in another direction. If you fell down, you could not get up. Stationary things would never move. Moving things would never stop. It is hard to imagine what such a situation would be like.

Friction has many functions. Like gravity, it sometimes makes things difficult for us, but it would be impossible to live without it. All cutting, drilling, grinding, and polishing processes depend on friction and we would have very little industry without them. When you step on the brakes of an automobile, you increase the friction on the wheels and the car's forward motion is reduced.

Often work can be done better by increasing friction, so we build tractor wheels with heavy rubber or metal lugs to increase friction with the ground. We put chains on cars when the

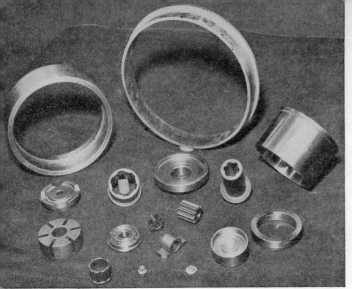

Oil-retaining metal bearings.

roads are icy, and we put wide treads on caterpillar tractors to increase the area of contact with the ground and hence, friction. Every time we take shoes to be repaired we pay tribute to the friction of our feet against the ground in walking.

REDUCING FRICTION

Since we cannot hope to eliminate friction between moving parts, we try to reduce it as much as possible. We started doing this long ago without knowing what we were doing. The man who discovered the wheel made a great discovery, even though he did not know that friction between rolling surfaces is much less than between surfaces that are sliding over one another.

Streamlining reduces friction with the air.

Rolling Surfaces Reduce Friction. Since the discovery of the wheel, we have constantly improved it so that now there is less friction between the rolling surfaces. This is done by means of ball bearings, roller bearings, or needle bearings. No matter which type is used, they all substitute rolling surfaces for sliding surfaces and thus reduce the friction. The rolling surfaces in bearings are of hard, highly polished steel, so they can support heavy weights as they move. They must be perfectly round and highly polished, so friction is necessary in making them. Polishing by friction is part of the process of making bearings that reduce friction.

Lubrication Reduces Friction. Another common way to reduce friction is by *lubrication.* Waxy and greasy compounds fill in the rough surfaces and form a protective coating, or film, on the parts so that they move not against each other but against this lubricating film. Most lubricants are petroleum compounds, by-products of the manufacture of gasoline, and just as important as fuel in running engines.

Many kinds of lubricants have been devised for different conditions. Automobiles function better when they use a light grade of oil in winter and somewhat heavier oil in summer. Lubricants that are used in high-temperature machines are made so they are not affected by the heat. They must not contain chemicals that are injurious to delicate machinery, and they must flow fast enough to keep the moving parts well oiled, yet at the same time, have enough "body" to lubricate well.

Lubrication is important in the home as well as in industry, and it is a mark of intelligence in a Machine Age to keep motors, engines, and tools well oiled so that they will run smoothly. To relieve housewives who forget to oil their vacuum cleaners or refrigerators, manufacturers now build motors with oil-retaining bearings so that the motors keep themselves oiled without attention. If the motors in your home appliances do not have bearings of this type, be sure that you oil the motors in accordance with the manufacturer's instructions.

296

FRICTION AND STREAMLINING

So far our discussion has concerned the most common type of friction—that between two solids. But we also have friction when a solid moves through a liquid, as a boat moves through water; when a liquid moves through a gas, as a raindrop falls through the air; and when a solid moves through a gas, as an airplane moves through air. The wind meets friction as it blows over the rough earth and weather scientists have known for a long time that winds blowing over the earth's surface are slower, because of friction, than those several thousand feet aloft.

We have worked out ways of eliminating much of the friction between solids and liquids, and solids and gases. In designing ships, airplanes, and automobiles, we keep this constantly in mind. We call this method of reducing friction by designing vehicles so that they create the smallest amount of resistance, *streamlining*. Streamlining by man is relatively new, but natural streamlining is not, and a falling raindrop is more streamlined than anything man has ever made.

Streamlining was not important for an ox-cart or a raft or even for the first automobiles and locomotives. Resistance of the air and water increases greatly as the speed of the object moving through it increases. So only after we began to build very fast boats, trains, cars, and planes did the problem of friction with the air become important. Now it is one of the big problems in aviation. The aeronautical engineers who plan 500- and 600-mile-per-hour transports have all kinds of friction problems.

FRICTION, STREAMLINING, AND THE AIRPLANE

All the problems of applying energy and overcoming friction seem to come to a head in the airplane. We think of this as our most modern machine, yet its principles take root in ideas worked out by the physicist, Daniel Bernoulli [bĕr-no͞o-yē′], back in 1738. Bernoulli was not concerned with planes at all but with the flow of water through pipes. He dis-

covered that if the speed of a fluid moving in a tube increased at any point, the pressure at that point decreased. This seems a long way from airplanes, but this principle is actually the key that opens up the mystery of why a plane can fly. Let us look at this principle of Bernoulli in more detail.

If a fluid flows through a pipe with a constriction that makes it narrower, the fluid moves faster through this constriction. As a result, the pressure in the constriction is less than either before or after it in the tube. The fluid may be either a liquid or a gas. The same drop in pressure results if either air or water flows through the pipe.

Look carefully at the diagram of a pipe with

Application of Bernoulli's principle produces most of an airplane's lift: 1. a pipe with a constriction, 2. two wing shapes, 3. lift.

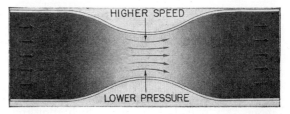

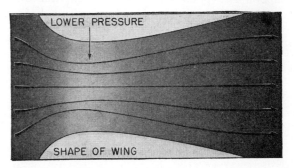

ROLL

ROLL

From Encyclopaedia Britannica film Theory of Flight

In flying, roll is controlled by the ailerons. The white arrow points at the left aileron.

a constriction, of half a constricted pipe, and the cross section of an airplane wing with its very special curve. The relationship is obvious. The airplane curve is very similar to that of the pipe. The shape of an airplane wing is such that when air moves over it, the same effect is produced as when air moves through a constricted pipe—a drop in pressure along the upper curved surface.

The blast of air from the plane's propeller actually decreases the air pressure on the top surface of the wing. The pressure on the under surface remains normal or is increased slightly. This difference is not very great. Normal air pressure is 14.7 pounds per square inch. The reduced pressure on the upper wing may be about 14.5 pounds per square inch. But this slight difference means an upward push because of the unbalanced up and down forces. It amounts to a lift of 0.2 pounds per square inch, or 28.8 pounds per square foot.

A small sport plane with a wing area of 100 square feet would have a total lift of about 3000 pounds, or a ton and a half. As long as the upward lift resulting from the difference in pressure on the wings is greater than the weight of the plane and its load, the plane will take off and fly. This is, of course, the bare essential. To act effectively, the wing must be designed to meet the air at the proper angle, and many other design problems must be solved.

The propeller which supplies the blast of air is made so that, in cross section, it has a curve similar to the cross section of the wing, and it produces the same effect as a revolving wing. In addition, the propeller acts like a giant screw which pulls the plane forward as it "bites" into the air and forces the air back over the wings.

This combination of forward pull, or *thrust*, and the lift created by lowering the air pressure on the wings makes a plane fly. Because the air has a density only about $\frac{1}{800}$ that of water, the propeller of a plane must revolve faster than that of a boat. It turns at a rate of about 2000 revolutions per minute. On large planes the angle of the propeller blades can be adjusted to make them more effective during take-off or at cruising speed.

This is enough of the background of how a plane works to let you see that friction, as a resisting force, is essential for a plane to operate. At the same time it also makes operations difficult. For part of the job of flying we need friction—for the rest we try to eliminate it. It is the density of the air that permits the propeller to work. A screw needs something to

Pitch is controlled by the elevators. The white arrows point at them.

From Encyclopaedia Britannica film Theory of Flight

PITCH

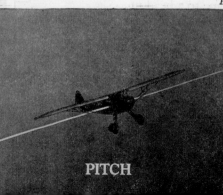

PITCH

From Encyclopaedia Britannica film Theory of Flight

Yaw is controlled by the rudder. The white arrow points at the rudder.

get a grip on. So the density of the air is essential. Propellers are less effective at high altitudes where the air is thinner and friction is less. But at the same time, the air offers less resistance to the plane moving through it.

So, as just pointed out, streamlining is essential to reduce this resistance to a minimum and thus increase the practical efficiency of a plane. The problem of the combined use and elimination of friction has no single solution. It keeps the plane designers busy to see how, in their particular model, they can design a plane that fulfills their requirements and still achieves the best compromise.

WORKING WITH SCIENCE

1. With a spring balance and a smooth table top you can do a number of experiments with friction. Using blocks of wood, metal, or stone, find out if the friction at starting is greater or less than the friction during motion. Find out how friction differs with amount of surface in contact with the table and with materials. Use rollers to see how these reduce friction. The spring balance will measure the force needed to overcome the resistance in each experiment. See if you can devise similar experiments yourself.

2. Visit a local garageman and find out how many different kinds of lubricants are used in a car. He may be able to give you practical information about lubrication and wear. Report on your discussion to the class.

3. Make a list of motors or machines in your own house that require lubrication. Find out the kind of lubrication each needs and how often it is required. Get any help you need from experts, and then post your list where you can refer to it frequently. Care of engines and machines may save your family a good deal of money.

4. Make an exhibit to show how cars, trains, planes or other vehicles have become streamlined. See if you can find out at what speed, for each vehicle, streamlining becomes important.

5. The simple atomizer operates on Bernoulli's principle, too. By blowing a jet of air across the mouth of a small tube partly immersed in water, the pressure in the tube is lowered. The air pressure on the water will force the water up the tube. Make a model atomizer, or take an atomizer apart, and study its operation.

READING YOU WILL ENJOY

Dietz, David. *Atomic Energy in the Coming Era.* Dodd, Mead & Co., New York, 1945. An interesting little book which explains atomic energy and its probable effects on our future.

Joseph, Alexander. *Fundamentals of Machines.* Charles Scribner's Sons, New York, 1943. A readable, clear explanation of machines and machinery.

Manchester, Harland. *New World of Machines.* Random House, New York, 1945. A book on recent discoveries and inventions which shows new ways that energy is transformed and applied.

Reck, Franklin M. and Claire. *Power from Start to Finish.* Thomas Y. Crowell Co., New York, 1941. A detailed and well-illustrated story of power from the earliest days up to the atomic age. Explanations of all types of engines and how the power from them is used.

Yates, Raymond F. *Atom Smashers.* Didier, New York, 1945. A very simple little book on atoms and atom smashers.

1

2

3

4

When man succeeded in making a practical heat engine, he no longer had to rely wholly on animal energy to do his work. Furthermore, heat engines enabled him to use the energy of sunlight stored up in ages past. The first heat engine of which we have good record was built by Hero of Alexandria about 200 B.C. It was a reaction engine (1) and its principle is the same as that of the latest rockets and jets. However, Hero's engine was considered a toy, and it was never used to do any work.

Little real progress was made until about the seventeenth century, when the steam engine was invented. Within the next few hundred years the steam engine was improved greatly. It drove spinning mills (2) and flour mills, railroads (3), and steamboats (4). The Industrial Revolution began, a revolution that changed the pattern of living in both Europe and America.

Gasoline and diesel engines and steam turbines, as in the power plant (5), appeared later. Soon afterward, the automobile, the airplane, and faster rail and water transportation were developed. Distances and travel time shrank. Gas turbines, jets (6), and rockets will shrink travel time still more, and in effect make the world still smaller and more interdependent.

5

6

24

HEAT ENGINES

On January 5, 1769 James Watt was granted a patent on the *steam engine* he had produced. In many ways that date is as important as October 12, 1492 or July 4, 1776. All three mark the beginnings of new eras: 1492—an era of discovery and colonization, 1776—an era of self-government, and 1769—an era of machines.

If you looked up the title of Watt's patent application, you would find it was for "A New Method of Lessening the Consumption of Steam and Fuel in Fire-Engines." Now that is a surprise! Apparently James Watt did not patent a new engine. He patented an improvement of an old one. Actually, the first steam engine was working some 100 years before Watt got his patent. But Watt's engine was such a great improvement on the earlier engine that most of us consider Watt the inventor of the steam engine.

THE STEAM ENGINE

The steam engine that Edward Somerset, Marquis of Worcester, made in 1663 could hardly be called a success. In fact, it was only half a steam engine. This engine was made to pump water. Steam forced air out of a container, or cylinder; when the steam condensed, air pressure raised water through a pipe, filling the container. This early engine and an improved model of it made by Thomas Savery in 1698 had very little in common with the steam engines we know today. But they were able to pump water and that was important.

NECESSITY: MOTHER OF INVENTION

The presence of water where it was not wanted actually caused the development of the steam engine. Water accumulating in English coal mines became such a problem that miners often could not mine coal because parts of the mines were flooded. By 1650 more horses were used in hauling water from the mines than for hauling coal.

As a result mining costs increased tremen-

dously. So, many men tried to invent a machine that would keep the mines dry at lower cost. Somerset tackled the problem. Savery followed him and Thomas Newcomen [nū-

How the Somerset engine worked.

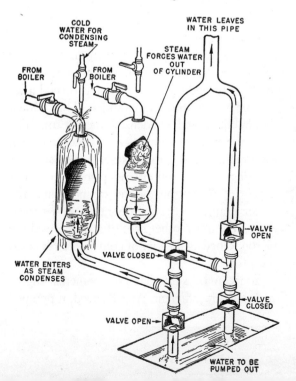

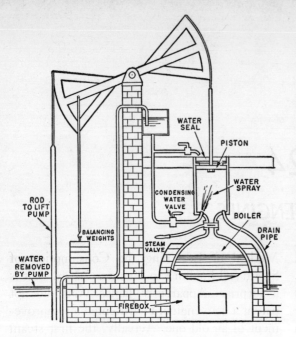

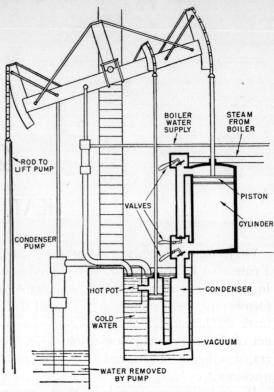

Left: Newcomen's engine. Right: Watt's engine. None of these early steam engines was very efficient. Can you explain why this was true?

kŭm'ĕn], a mechanically minded blacksmith, patented an improved engine in 1705.

Newcomen made a real improvement on the earlier engines. He included a *piston* in his engine—a movable plate of iron that was raised as the steam entered the cylinder and pushed against it. This piston was connected to a rod, the *piston rod*, which was connected by levers to the arm of a pump.

Newcomen's Engine. This is how Newcomen's engine worked. Steam from a boiler entered a cylinder from the bottom. The pressure of the steam lifted the piston. The operator then turned off the steam and turned a jet of cold water into the cylinder. This cooled the cylinder and condensed the steam. The pressure inside the cylinder was then *less* than the pressure of the air outside. As a result, air pressing on the top of the piston pushed it down to the bottom of the cylinder and the water drained out. The operator then turned the valve, and another shot of steam raised the piston. Once again a jet of cold water reversed the process.

You can be sure that Newcomen's engine was not very efficient. At full speed, it pumped

only 10 or 12 strokes a minute—but it worked. It did lift water out of the mines faster and cheaper than hauling it out in buckets and so for 30 years before James Watt was born, Newcomen's engines pumped water slowly out of the coal, tin, and copper mines.

WHAT WATT DID

For a century before Watt's invention, the steam engine was very crude and inefficient. Improvements after Newcomen's day were minor. Fuel costs were high because the cylinder was alternately heated and cooled. Thus, much of the energy of the fuel was wasted.

Watt's idea for saving fuel was very simple —do not cool the cylinder by running in cold water to condense the steam. Take the steam out of the cylinder first and then condense it. Thus, the cylinder can remain hot and fuel losses will be cut. Watt constructed a separate chamber, a *condenser*, to condense the steam in his engine. Thus, by increasing the useful energy obtained from the coal, he made a much better engine to run the mine pumps.

Steam Expansion Produces Pressure. Steam is

the lifeblood of the steam engine. Steam is a vapor formed when water is heated to 212°F. One quart of water at 212°F changes into 1700 quarts of steam, at the same temperature and pressure. But inside a boiler, steam does not have much room to·expand, so the pressure of the steam against the sides of the boiler increases as the flames burn bright beneath it. By the time the temperature has doubled (424°F), the pressure has increased 21 times. This increase in pressure would continue until the boiler exploded, except that the steam normally is removed and put to work.

To harness the force of the steam that pushes against the boiler walls for useful work, a pipe leads the steam into the cylinder of a steam engine. The steam enters the cylinder under pressure, but in the cylinder it can expand. And in expanding, it pushes the piston to the other end of the cylinder.

How Watt's Engine Worked. The steam engine made by Newcomen and the earlier engines had just one hole for steam to enter the cylinder. Watt's engine had two—one at each end of the cylinder. Watt's engine worked like this: As steam enters the first hole, it pushes the piston ahead of it and incidentally, pushes the steam on the other side of the piston out of the cylinder. When the piston almost reaches the far end of the cylinder, a valve cuts off the steam from the first hole and admits it through the second hole. At the same time, the action of this valve opens an escape route for the steam behind the piston. The steam admitted through the second hole now expands and pushes the piston back. It also forces the spent steam out the exhaust pipe.

These changes alone did not increase the efficiency of the steam engine very much. Much of the energy of the incoming steam was used to push out the steam on the other side of the cylinder. This slowed down the movement of the piston.

Watt's chief contribution was a separate, water-cooled condensing chamber near the cylinder. The exhaust steam, pushed from the cylinder, enters the condenser and immediately changes back to water. As it condenses, the steam pressure is greatly reduced. Thus, the pressure that slows down the movement of the piston is removed *without cooling the cylinder.* So, only a very small fraction of the energy of the steam is needed to clear the cylinder of exhaust steam, and more energy is made available to do useful work. Thus, Watt's improvement in the steam engine made the engine much more efficient.

Within 5 years after Watt obtained his patent, steam engines were being used to pump water from all the large mines in England. During the next 10 years, Watt made one improvement after another. He developed a method of connecting the piston rod to a wheel so that the back-and-forth motion of the piston was converted into rotary motion. By 1786 steam engines were driving the millstones of flour mills and soon the power of steam was applied to England's most important industry —the spinning and weaving of textiles.

Birth of the Industrial Revolution. Meanwhile,

1700 QT STEAM

1 QT WATER

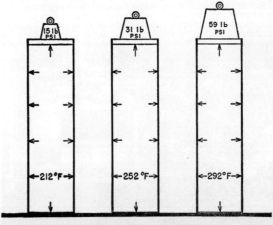

Left: A quart of water makes much steam. Right: As temperature increases, steam pressure increases.

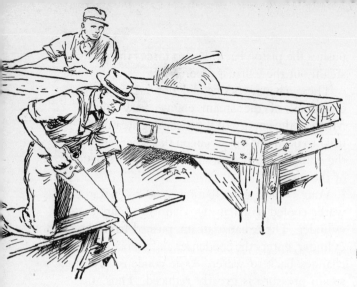

Reciprocating and rotary motion:

steam was being applied to land and water vehicles. A French army officer built a steam carriage in 1770. Experimental steamboats were tried out from 1786 to 1790, although Fulton's *Clermont* did not steam up the Hudson until 1807. Richard Trevithick [trĕv′ĭ-thĭk] made the first real locomotive in 1804, and 10

The sliding valve atop the cylinder enables steam to enter each end of the cylinder at different times.

From Encyclopaedia Britannica film Thermodynamics

years later George Stevenson began making railroads practical.

Steam was soon applied to almost every branch of industry and brought about the great changes in manufacturing and production that affected the lives of people all over Europe, Asia, and America. The great changes, resulting from the scientific development and use of the energy of steam, are known as the *Industrial Revolution*.

THE STEAM ENGINE AS A WORKING MACHINE

The steam engine first transforms the chemical energy of fuel into heat energy and then transforms the heat energy into mechanical energy. The mechanical energy produced by a steam engine is a back-and-forth, or *reciprocating*, movement. This is changed to rotating, or rotary, movement for all transportation and most industrial uses by means of a crankshaft and wheels.

The *reciprocating steam engine* was the first of modern engines. It is still one of the least efficient. Until recently most reciprocating steam engines had an over-all efficiency of about 5 percent. Only 5 percent of the energy of the fuel was transformed into mechanical energy. Even today, the efficiency of most reciprocating engines is not much higher.

The steam engine is a large, heavy engine, suited to heavy work loads. It uses a cheap, bulky, yet abundant fuel. Nowadays we are inclined to think that the reciprocating steam engine is out of date. For many uses it has been replaced by more efficient engines. However, it has been improved, and where weight is not an essential factor, it works very well.

TYPES OF STEAM ENGINES

Watt's condenser made the steam engine more efficient. As a result, the *low-pressure*, or condenser-type, *steam engine* was very widely used for many years. However, in condensing the steam much useful heat energy is lost without obtaining any useful work in exchange. This fact did not bother Watt; boilers were very poor in his day and the steam pressure and temperature were low.

304

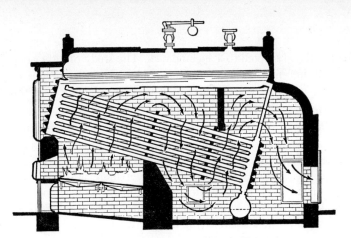

Left: A water-tube boiler. Right: A fire-tube boiler. What are the advantages of each?

Steam entering the cylinder at a pressure of 10 pounds per square inch and leaving at 5 pounds per square inch, had a working pressure of 5 pounds. The condenser dropped this final pressure to about 1 pound per square inch and gave the engine a working pressure of 9 instead of 5 pounds per square inch. That was a considerable gain. But when steam pressure and temperature are high and there is still considerable energy at the end of the piston stroke, a condenser is wasteful because that energy is lost.

Suppose that steam enters a cylinder at a pressure of 90 pounds per square inch and leaves at 20. It has a working pressure of 70 pounds per square inch. The condenser will lower the final pressure, but no one wants to waste this 20 pounds of steam pressure. Since the condenser is heavy, it is also a disadvantage on mobile steam engines, such as those on a locomotive.

High-Pressure Engines. Modern locomotives have *high-pressure steam engines* built without a condenser. They do not waste the energy of the exhaust steam but use it to heat water before it goes to the boiler and for operating low-pressure steam engines known as *pushers* or boosters.

BOILERS TO MAKE THE STEAM

Early boilers were merely tanks partly filled with water and with a fire beneath. Now two much more efficient kinds of boilers are used. The *water-tube boiler* is used chiefly for heating systems and stationary steam engines. It consists of rows of tilted pipes through which the boiler water circulates. These pipes fit beneath the boiler itself, and the flames and hot gases spread around the pipes, which provide a much greater heating surface than the bottom of the boiler. The chief advantage of a water-tube boiler is that a very large area is exposed to the radiant energy given off by the burning fuel.

In a *fire-tube boiler* the pipes or tubes conduct flames and hot gases through the water—the reverse of a water-tube boiler—and up the smokestack. The heating surface of a fire-tube boiler is greater than a boiler of the old-fashioned type. However, it does not use the radiant energy of the burning fuel as effectively as a water-tube boiler.

WORKING WITH SCIENCE

1. Look up the details of the Worcester, Savery, Newcomen, Watt, and other early types of steam engines. Make large diagrams of these engines and find out how each worked. From this information, judge the development of the steam engine from 1663 to 1763.

2. Demonstrate the principle of the Worcester engine. Fit a 500 ml Florence flask with a one-hole rubber stopper through which a 3-foot glass tube projects. Put a small amount of water in the flask. Close, and heat until steam issues from tube. Remove from flame. **Caution:** *Hot.* Invert flask and tube in a dish of water. Notice the effect as the flask cools. How could this device be used in pumping water from a mine?

3. Experiment with steam pressure. **Caution:** *Use pyrex test tubes with vaselined corks.* Put a measured amount of water in a test tube (1, 2, 3 up to 10 drops) and find out the minimum needed to pop the cork out of the test tube, when heated over an alcohol lamp or bunsen burner. The air in the test tube also expands and exerts pressure when heated. How can you be sure the effect is not caused by expansion of the air alone?

4. Make an exhibit of pictures or models showing the development of the steamship or the locomotive. In each case steam power had to be adapted to a specific task. The study of either one makes an interesting hobby. There are clubs of railroad enthusiasts who know as much as the experts about types of cars and engines.

5. Visit a factory, the boiler room of your school, or some other place where large amounts of steam are generated. Get information on the devices that are used to get more heat from the fuel, more steam pressure in the boiler, and less loss of steam in use. In a large plant what looks like a small saving may be worth several thousand dollars a year.

6. Demonstrate a toy steam engine. Study the engine carefully and see how it operates. Does it have a condenser?

THE INTERNAL-COMBUSTION ENGINE

An *internal-combustion engine* is similar to a steam engine in several ways. It is a heat engine, and it transforms heat into reciprocating, or back-and-forth, motion. The usual arrangement of piston and cylinder in a steam engine sends the piston rods back-and-forth. In *gasoline engines* the cylinders and piston rods are arranged in many ways—in line, in V-banks, in a circle, or in a "pancake." As a result, the direction of the back-and-forth movement differs in different types of engines, but in all cases it is a kind of motion that continually reverses its direction, that is, is back-and-forth.

DIFFERENCES FROM STEAM ENGINES

The principal difference between an internal-combustion engine and a steam engine is that a steam engine uses water as an intermediate step in changing heat into mechanical energy. In a steam engine, heat from the burning fuel first becomes the energy of expanding steam, and this, in turn, drives the piston. In an internal-combustion engine the fuel is burned inside the cylinder; hence the name *internal-combustion*.

The burning fuel produces hot gases, and these push directly on the pistons as they expand. This short-cut eliminates the heat loss of the boiler, a handicap that plagues all steam engines. An internal-combustion engine operates at a much higher temperature than a steam engine. For this reason, as you would expect, more heat energy is available to produce useful work.

GASOLINE ENGINES

We think of the internal-combustion engine as a relatively new invention. Your grandfather remembers the days of the first automobile. Your father remembers the first airplane. Nevertheless, a working internal-combustion engine was invented long before the early days of the automobile. In 1794

The cylinders of internal-combustion engines may be arranged in several different ways.

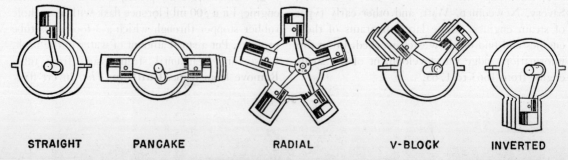

STRAIGHT   PANCAKE   RADIAL   V-BLOCK   INVERTED

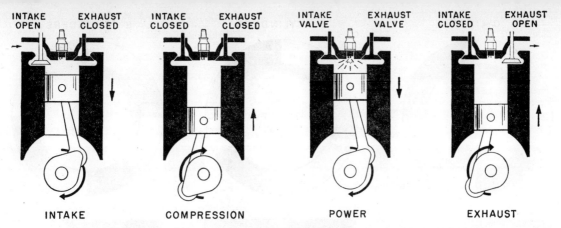

INTAKE   COMPRESSION   POWER   EXHAUST

The four strokes of a four-stroke gasoline engine.

Robert Street made an internal-combustion engine that was operated by explosions of turpentine vapor.

In the 1860's Étienne Lenoir's [lĕ-nwȧr'] coal-gas engine was used in France and about the same time Beau de Rochas [rŏ-shä'] worked out the theory of the *four-stroke engine*. Our present gasoline engine is based on this theory. In 1874 two Germans, Otto and Langen, constructed the first engine based on de Rochas' ideas, but it took another 12 years before Gottlieb Daimler [dām'lĕr] built an engine light enough to propel the first "horseless carriage."

From this time on, progress was rapid. Not only was the gasoline engine improved and made more reliable, its weight per horsepower was continually reduced. In 1883 an internal-combustion engine weighed about 1000 pounds for each horsepower it was able to produce. Today, powerful gasoline engines for airplanes produce 3500 horsepower at less than 1 pound per horsepower.

The gasoline engine, or any other internal-combustion engine, has distinct advantages over steam. Steam engines have an efficiency of about 10 percent, gasoline engines as much as 25 percent. Internal-combustion engines are easier and quicker to start. They can develop their maximum energy output after a few moments' warm-up, while it takes far longer to build up enough steam pressure to run a large steam engine. Gasoline engines usually are lighter in weight than steam engines—both in total weight and in weight per horsepower.

THE FOUR-STROKE ENGINE

Practically every gasoline engine you have seen in cars, trucks, airplanes, or motorcycles is a four-stroke engine. Most of these engines consist of from four to 24 cylinders arranged in a row, V-bank, or circle. A piston fits tightly in each highly polished cylinder. The piston can move back and forth, transmitting its energy to a crankshaft that converts the back-and-forth motion into rotating motion.

At the top of the cylinder or in a compartment at the side are two openings fitted with valves. The fuel mixture of about one part gasoline vapor to 15 parts air enters the cylinder through one of these valves. There it is exploded. The burned gases, mostly carbon dioxide, carbon monoxide, and water vapor, are forced out through the other valve. These valves are called the *intake valve* and the *exhaust valve*.

In or near the top of each cylinder is a *spark plug*—a porcelain plug from which two short wires, or *electrodes*, emerge. The electrical system of the engine sends a spark across these electrodes at the correct instant, exploding the mixture of gasoline vapor and air in the cylinder.

The force of the explosion of the compressed mixture sends the piston flying downward. Its energy is transmitted to the crankshaft and heavy flywheel which are set spinning. Each explosion in the cylinder transmits more energy to the rotating crankshaft and flywheel. The crankshaft and flywheel must have energy enough to keep moving until

4 CYLINDERS   6 CYLINDERS   8 CYLINDERS

How the addition of cylinders to an internal-combustion engine provides smoother operation.

the next explosion, or the engine will not run.

Remember that only one stroke in four produces energy. The other three strokes use some of the energy produced. A gasoline engine must produce more energy than is needed to carry through the three nonproductive strokes in order to do useful work. Automobile engines may produce from 20 to 100 horsepower or more, over and above that needed to keep the engine running.

SINGLE CYLINDERS OR SEVERAL

If you have ever listened to a single-cylinder four-stroke engine, such as those used on small pumps or washing machines, you may have noticed the repetition of sounds like "bang!— chug—chug—chug" over and over again. The "bang" is, of course, the power stroke, and the three "chugs" are the exhaust, intake, and compression strokes. The flywheel keeps the motor spinning through the nonproductive strokes.

Such an engine would not do for a modern automobile, for no one would like a car that goes "bang!—chug—chug—chug" down the street, leaping forward with each "bang." This is avoided by using engines of four, six, eight, or more cylinders. In a single cylinder the piston goes up and down twice, and the crankshaft makes two complete turns for each power stroke. In a two-cylinder engine arranged so that the power strokes alternate, a power stroke takes place for every turn of the crankshaft.

In a four-cylinder engine, energy is applied every half-turn, and in an eight-cylinder engine, every quarter-turn.

These multicylinder engines not only produce more energy per unit of time but also produce energy more steadily and smoothly. Gasoline engines have made it possible to establish a speed record for cars of almost 370 miles per hour. Airplanes, using the same type of engine, have broken the 500-mile-per-hour mark on several occasions.

THE GASOLINE ENGINE IN OUR LIVES

We are so used to associating the internal-combustion engine with the automobile and the automobile with a Sunday afternoon drive that we lose sight of the fact that the gasoline engine has had a tremendous effect on many phases of our lives. The marketing of farm crops has been revolutionized by the truck. Now a farmer in Georgia or Florida can load his truck with fresh vegetables and make a 2-day run to northern markets where he can get better prices for his products.

Nearly 10 percent of all freight moved in this country goes by truck. Buses operate on more than 2 million miles of roads and streets, carrying more than 5 billion passengers a year. In normal times we manufacture about 5 million cars and trucks annually and have about

30 million vehicles on the roads, propelled by explosions of 150 million or more cylinders.

Gasoline engines operate tractors, pumps, and a variety of small machinery. They power most of our airplanes—military, commercial, or private. They generate electric energy in isolated areas. They run washing machines and refrigerators. Passenger cars, trucks, motorcycles, tanks, buses, motorboats, and even iceboats are propelled by these light but powerful engines. In the course of some 50 years, the gasoline engine has become one of our most important sources of energy

DIESEL ENGINES

On September 28, 1913 Dr. Rudolph Diesel [dē′zĕl] packed the plans of his new and highly successful internal-combustion engine into a brief case and started for Antwerp on his way to England. This celebrated German inventor had made the submarine possible by building an engine that could handle heavier loads than the gasoline engines of that day.

The fall of 1913 was a troubled time. England and Germany were on the verge of war, and the German Navy was counting heavily on its new submarines which were propelled by the even newer *diesel engine*. And now Dr. Diesel was on his way to London to start an English diesel factory. The next evening he boarded the Channel steamer *Dresden* for the overnight trip across the Channel, and on the day following his wife received a telegram saying "Arrived safely London." The telegram turned out to be a forgery. Neither Dr. Diesel nor his important plans were aboard the *Dresden* when it docked.

You can well imagine the stories in the papers. There was reason for the excitement because Dr. Diesel was a famous inventor and the secret of his engine was very important. The mystery of Dr. Diesel's disappearance was never solved.

DIFFERENCES FROM GASOLINE ENGINE

The diesel engine is a close cousin to the gasoline engine. It differs in only two major ways. (1) It does *not* use a spark plug to ignite the fuel mixture. (2) It does *not* draw in a mixture of fuel and air during the intake stroke, but only air.

These differences are significant because they make it possible for the diesel engine to operate at higher temperatures and pressures, and hence produce more energy than the gasoline engine. The diesel is a simpler engine and is better suited to heavy work than the gasoline engine. It is also heavier per horsepower, and it uses a cheaper and less dangerous fuel than gasoline.

TWO TYPES OF DIESEL ENGINES

In construction, a four-stroke diesel engine is similar to a four-stroke gasoline engine. The engine produces one power stroke for every two full turns of the crankshaft. The differences are in the intake, compression, and power strokes. In the intake stroke, only air is drawn into the cylinder. During compression, this air is compressed about three times as much as the fuel-air mixture in a gasoline engine.

As a result of this great compression, the temperature of the air in the cylinder rises as high as 1000°F. Then fuel is injected as a fine mist and it burns instantly on contact with the heated air. The power stroke results, followed by the exhaust stroke.

The injection of the fuel oil at the end of the compression stroke is the critical time in a diesel engine. The pressure inside the cylinder is more than 500 pounds per square inch and so it takes much greater pressure than that to force in a spray of oil. This is done by a powerful pump, called a *fuel injector*, which is a very finely made piece of machinery. The parts must fit exactly. If they do not, leaks will develop at the high pressure at which the fuel injector operates.

The Two-Stroke Diesel Engine. The second type of diesel engine is a two-stroke engine. It has proved such a success that it has largely replaced the four-stroke diesels. With a two-

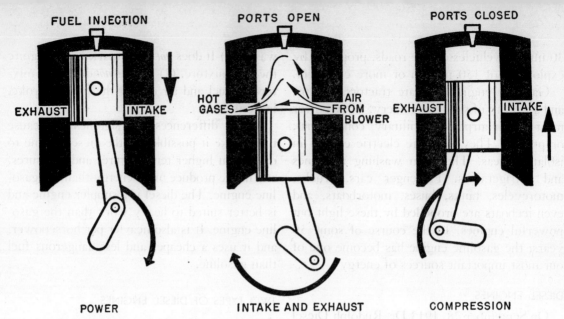

FUEL INJECTION   PORTS OPEN   PORTS CLOSED

EXHAUST   INTAKE   HOT GASES   AIR FROM BLOWER   EXHAUST   INTAKE

POWER   INTAKE AND EXHAUST   COMPRESSION

The strokes of a two-stroke diesel engine serve all of the functions of four strokes. How?

stroke engine, every second stroke is a power stroke instead of only one in four. As a result, size for size, a two-stroke diesel delivers twice as much energy per unit of time as a four-stroke diesel. There are two-stroke gasoline engines, too, but these are usually small and are used in outboard motors, motorbikes, and so forth.

The two-stroke diesel is somewhat different in appearance from the four-stroke engine. The exhaust valves may be at the top of the cylinder near the fuel injector, but the *intake* and *exhaust ports* usually are in a ring circling the cylinder just above the lowest point reached by the piston in its stroke. The secret of the two-cycle engine lies in combining the intake

Huge diesel engines in a merchant ship.

Courtesy the Pusey and Jones Corporation

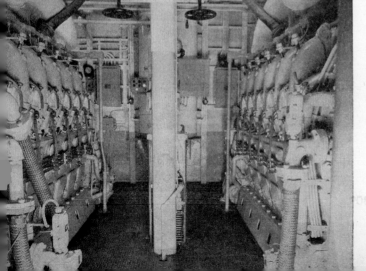

stroke with the compression stroke, and the power stroke with the exhaust stroke. This sounds a bit complicated because each stroke is so distinct in the four-stroke engine.

As the two-stroke diesel lacks a stroke in which air is pulled into the cylinder by the piston, air is supplied by a rotary blower known as a *Roots blower*. A Roots blower works like a pair of revolving doors that mesh together and push a mass of air through at each turn of the vanes. Some energy is needed to operate the blower, but the energy produced by the two-stroke diesel is sufficient to operate the blower and still do more work than a four-stroke diesel of equal size.

A few miscellaneous facts about diesel engines round out the story. Diesels are usually started by means of compressed air. A wire heated by electricity may be used to ignite the fuel if the engine is cold, but once the engine has warmed up, the heat of compression ignites the fuel and no other ignition is needed. The fuel is a carefully prepared oil and while it is heavier and less expensive than gasoline, it is a refined product and not crude oil just as it is taken from the well.

USES OF DIESEL ENGINES

Diesel engines are built in many sizes for many purposes. Airplanes have been driven by

310

experimental diesels, but as yet we do not have a practical diesel engine for airplanes. Large eight- and 16-cylinder diesel engines pull streamlined trains, which have no difficulty in reaching top speeds of more than 100 miles an hour. Fishing boats, large pleasure boats, ferries, and many modern "steamships" are diesel-powered. Many trucks and buses have diesel engines too.

The diesels in a submarine generate about 6000 horsepower. They not only operate the vessel on the surface at speeds up to 25 knots but also furnish the power for charging the submarine's storage batteries so that it can travel under water. Diesel engines operate electric plants, air compressors, refrigerating machines, tractors, tanks, bulldozers, and hundreds of other machines.

These two internal-combustion engines—gasoline and diesel—like our old standby, the steam engine, produce reciprocating motion. The pistons move at high speeds, but at the end of every stroke they must come to a dead stop and reverse their direction. This constant reversal causes loss of energy, and produces vibration and noise that must be controlled. An engine that produces direct rotary motion has distinct advantages over reciprocating engines.

WORKING WITH SCIENCE

1. Demonstrate the explosive gas mixtures that are equivalent to the mixture that enters the cylinder of a gasoline engine. Fill a quart bottle with water. Invert it in a pneumatic trough, and fill the bottle with gas from the gas petcock. Hold this bottle of gas to a flame. Watch the color of the flame as it burns and the length of time needed to burn the quart of gas. Repeat, using a bottle only half full of water. That will give a half-gas and half-air mixture. Keep reducing the mount of gas till an explosive mixture is produced. **Caution.** What proportion of gas and air produces an explosion?

2. Fit the cover of a coffee can with a two-hole rubber stopper through which you run two heavy wires arranged so that the bare ends form a ¼-inch gap. Connect by thin wires to a spark coil and batteries so that the device is actually a simple spark plug. Warm the bottom of the coffee can over a bunsen burner. Turn off the gas and drop one or two drops of gasoline on the warm bottom of the can. The gasoline will vaporize. Cover **lightly** with the top. **Caution:** *Stand back and make contact.* The spark will ignite the gasoline-vapor-air mixture. As a result, the top of the can will be blown several feet into the air.

3. Make a large cardboard model of cylinder, movable piston, crankshaft, valves, and spark plug and demonstrate action of four-cycle gasoline engine to the class.

4. Locate all the different kinds of gasoline engines you can. Besides those in autos and planes, look on power lawnmowers, pumps, air compressors, and so forth. Make a list of the size, horsepower, kind of stroke, and detailed use of each.

5. Visit a local garage when a motor is being taken down for overhauling. Get the mechanic to show you the cylinders, pistons, valves, and so forth. Note how essential it is for parts to fit exactly and to work in close timing.

6. Make a cardboard model of a two-stroke diesel engine, and explain the operation of it to the class.

7. Find out what diesel engines are used in your community. Check buses, electric plants, air compressors, large boats, and so forth. Try to learn what advantages the diesel has over a gasoline engine for the task in which it is used.

ROTARY HEAT ENGINES

The simplest *rotary heat engine* is the windmill. It may seem strange to call a windmill a heat engine. But it is a heat engine—a low-temperature, low-pressure heat engine. The heat of the sun causes the winds that push the windmill's rotating arms. It is a source of rotary mechanical energy, but a most undependable one. Waterwheels are also heat en-

An overshot waterwheel (left) is turned by *falling* water; an undershot waterwheel, by *moving* water.

gines and provide a more steady source of energy.

WATERWHEELS

Waterwheels are of two general types. Typical of American Colonial times and most often pictured in books, is the *overshot wheel*. The water flows through a trough, or *flume*, into buckets on the rim of a large wheel. The weight of the falling water rotates the wheel slowly. The overshot wheel is best adapted to situations where the water falls 8 or 10 feet or more, but the amount of water is limited. A dammed-up stream often supplies water for an overshot wheel. A good overshot wheel may have an efficiency up to 80 percent.

If there is a large flow of water and a relatively small drop, as in a rapid stream, an *undershot wheel* is used. Here the running water presses directly against the flat blades of a wide wheel and produces mechanical energy because of its push rather than because of its fall. An overshot wheel uses the potential energy of a raised body of water. An undershot wheel uses the kinetic energy of moving water. An undershot waterwheel is seldom more than 25 percent efficient.

Much larger than typical waterwheels are the *water turbines* of hydroelectric generators (see page 341). Water is led into the turbine through a large pipe, or *penstock*. It comes in on a spiral curve, strikes, and spins the turbine wheel. The water then drops out through the bottom of the turbine. These water turbines are so well designed that they convert about 90 percent of the energy of the water passing through them into electric energy.

STEAM TURBINES AND HOW THEY WORK

Steam turbines are built to utilize as much of the energy of expanding steam as possible. They are specially designed to allow steam at high temperature and pressure to expand and push until practically all its energy is converted into mechanical energy. Like other heat engines, the steam turbine is not new. One was designed in 1628, but a practical steam turbine was not built until the 1880's.

Within the following decade the steam turbine was successfully applied to boats. The *Turbinia*, first turbine steamship, broke speed records in 1894. About the same time the turbine was put to the operation of electric generators. Now about two-thirds of the electric energy used in this country comes from generators driven by steam turbines.

Modern turbines consist of two series of blades, or *vanes*. The *stator*, the stationary outside part of the turbine, is made of blades that direct the steam against the rotating blades at the proper angle. A heavy, well-balanced shaft running through the stator bears the *rotor*, which is composed of hundreds of blades attached to the shaft and which whirl the shaft around as the steam strikes them.

The tips of the large rotor blades may travel at speeds as great as the speed of a bullet. The rotor has several rings of blades, sometimes 20 or more. These rings gradually increase in diameter so that the rotor has a funnel shape.

Steam enters the turbine and strikes the smaller rotor blades first. As it gradually expands, it makes contact with larger and larger blades, each designed to act most efficiently at the steam's particular temperature and pressure at the instant of contact. By the time the steam has reached the largest blades, its pressure is down to about ordinary air pressure and its temperature is nearly down to that of boiling water.

The last remaining steam is condensed, reducing any back pressure on the turbine blades. The hot water formed by the condensed steam is pumped back into the boiler, where it is reheated, continuing the cycle. Each day only about 3 percent of the water used is lost and has to be replaced.

You must really see giant steam turbines in action to get an idea of the terrific amount of energy they produce. Steam enters the turbines under pressures of 400 to 700 pounds per square inch. In some of the latest plants this pressure has been increased to 1400 and occasionally to 2500 pounds per square inch. To achieve such pressures, the steam is heated far above the boiling point of water. Temperatures are usually in the range of 700° to 1000°F —hot enough to cause wood to burst into flame. This *superheated steam* has so much energy that it is dangerous to handle and control. A flaw in a high-pressure steam pipe is a very serious matter.

STEAM TURBINES IN USE

The energy of the steam drives turbines at speeds of 1800 to 3600 revolutions per minute. These, in turn, drive generators, producing as much as 160,000 kilowatts of electricity. A steam plant producing 100,000 kilowatts of electricity for 1 hour requires boilers that will turn 125,000 gallons of water into steam during this time. In order to cool the steam in the condenser, 7.5 million gallons of water are needed each hour. For these reasons, such plants are built along rivers, or on the ocean, where plentiful water for the condensers is available.

A steam plant of this size uses about 50 tons of coal an hour, or 1200 tons per day. The coal usually is pulverized into a dust, which is blown into the boilers or fed by an automatic feed. The boilers are so carefully planned that from 70 to 90 percent of the heat produced by the burning coal is utilized. The turbines themselves have an efficiency of about 40 percent. Hence, the total efficiency of such a steam plant is from 30 to 35 percent, depending on the relative efficiency of the boiler and turbine.

Ships often use a steam turbine to drive an electric generator and are propelled by an electric motor connected to the propeller shaft. This combination gives more flexible control than a direct turbine drive through gears. For example, the propeller can be reversed more easily, for a turbine cannot be reversed and some electric motors can.

The efficiency of a modern steam turbine depends greatly on its size, its speed, and the

Left: The rotor of a steam turbine. Right: Turbines driven by steam turn these generators.

Courtesy General Electric Company

Pennsylvania Railroad photo

A high-speed, turbine-driven locomotive, first of its kind to operate in this country.

savings that come with large-scale operation. Steam turbines are now used to operate electric generators in a new-type steam locomotive. The drive wheels are driven by electric motors.

THE GAS TURBINE

The *gas turbine* is one of the newest of the rotary heat engines. Engines of this type have been used in Switzerland for years and experimental models have been successful in Canada and in this country. Gas turbines are now being manufactured for a number of uses in which they may take the place of steam turbines. Both trains and ships have been powered by gas turbines. Engineers who know the facts are enthusiastic about this new internal-combustion engine.

Gas turbines are even simpler than steam turbines. The expanding gases that spin the gas turbine blades are produced by the combustion of gasoline, fuel oil, or powdered coal. There is no intermediate fluid, as in the steam turbine. No boilers are needed. The gases produced by combustion spin the rotor blades directly. The gas turbine is as much an advance over the steam turbine as the internal-combustion engine is over the reciprocating steam engine.

One type of gas turbine consists of an egg-shaped combustion chamber with a compressor at one end and a turbine at the other. The large compressor blows a continual blast of compressed air into the combustion chamber. Fuel jets near the entry spray oil into this air blast, and the explosive mixture is ignited. The tremendous heat expands the burned gases and the air, producing temperatures and pressures in the combustion chamber that are even higher than in the steam turbine.

At the far end of the combustion chamber is the turbine. The turbine's blades are spun by the heated gases rushing toward the exhaust. The exhaust is designed so that the gases are actually speeded up as they rush out, making the gas turbine even more efficient.

In the combustion chamber of the gas turbine, gases are produced at very high temperatures (about 1500°F) and very high pressures. As a result, the efficiency of the gas turbine is even greater than that of the steam turbine. One difficulty in perfecting gas turbines has been that the steel alloys used as blades could not withstand the very high temperatures at which such turbines operate.

The blades of gas turbines glow red-hot when in use and the steel blades tend to lose their shape, or "creep," at such temperatures. But chemists have now successfully produced new high-temperature steel alloys that make gas turbines able to run for long periods without overhaul. This is one more example of how progress in one field of science depends on progress in related fields.

The Future of the Gas Turbine. Gas turbines can be made in much smaller sizes than steam turbines. As a result, they can be used in places where limitations in size and weight exclude steam turbines. Gas turbines have already been used in operating electric plants. In addition, they have been adapted to air-

A simplified gas turbine.

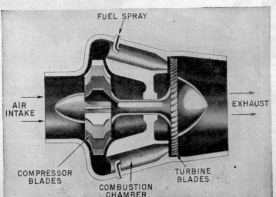

FUEL SPRAY

AIR INTAKE

EXHAUST

COMPRESSOR BLADES

COMBUSTION CHAMBER

TURBINE BLADES

314

planes and specially modified and combined with another type of engine for this use. The modified gas turbines have proved themselves in tests. Engineers predict that they are among the engines that will make 6- to 7-hour transatlantic flights at altitudes of 30,000 to 40,000 feet an everyday occurrence—and at much lower cost than at present.

WORKING WITH SCIENCE

1. Make models of overshot and undershot waterwheels from tin cans or wood. If you use wood, be sure you treat it to make it waterproof or paint it carefully. Demonstrate your models to the class.

2. Demonstrate the principle of the steam turbine by heating water in a flask with one-hole stopper through which a glass tube is drawn down to a narrow nozzle. The pressure of the steam jet can be used to turn a pinwheel.

3. More electricity is manufactured by steam turbines than by water turbines, but both are interesting to see. Find out how electricity is manufactured in your community, and arrange to visit the plant and study the process. If possible make two trips: one to study steam or water turbines and the second after you have started your study of electricity.

4. Find out more about steel alloys, especially about those that have high melting points and can be used in high-temperature gas turbines. Which elements are added to iron to produce these alloys?

5. Look up plans for planes powered by gas turbines. These have appeared in many aviation and popular science magazines. These planes will have propellers. What advantages would a gas turbine engine have over a reciprocating engine for airplanes?

REACTION ENGINES

In a sense, reciprocating engines are the heat engines of the past, rotary engines are the heat engines of the present, and *reaction engines* are the heat engines of the future.

To get an idea of a reaction engine, blow up a toy balloon. When it is full of air, release it suddenly. The balloon darts around the room before it falls empty to the floor. What sent the balloon on its wild journey? You may think that it was the air pushed from the balloon pressing against the air in the room, but that is only a minor part of the story. If you could remove all of the air in the room, the balloon would still loop-the-loop and dart around before falling.

THE REACTION PRINCIPLE

To understand what goes on inside the balloon, let us consider that it is divided into halves—a top half and a bottom half, with the neck of the balloon in the center of the bottom half. When the balloon is filled with air and sealed shut, the pressure inside the balloon is the same in all directions because such an enclosed gas presses equally in all directions. The total force against the top half of the balloon exactly balances the total force against the bottom half of the balloon. As a result, the net effect of the pressure is zero and the balloon does not move.

As soon as you open the neck of the balloon,

A balloon filled with air and then released is a good example of the reaction principle.

EQUAL PRESSURE

UNEQUAL PRESSURE

What is the reaction?

some of the air escapes through the opening. At that instant, the pressures inside the balloon become unequal. The total force against the top half of the balloon is greater than that against the bottom half. The difference in these two forces moves the balloon forward.

Newton's Third Law of Motion. Sir Isaac Newton discovered this principle in the course of his experiments. He found that *for every action there is an equal and opposite reaction.* When a bullet is fired from a gun, the gun is kicked backward with as much force as the bullet is kicked forward. This effect, called *recoil*, makes it necessary to build heavy guns with springs or hydraulic cylinders to take up this shock.

Suppose that a man loads a canoe with some large rocks and stands firmly in the back of the canoe. He then throws the rocks behind the canoe as hard as he can and finds that at each throw he pushes the canoe forward as well as throwing the rocks backward. Now increase

A rocket is a reaction engine.

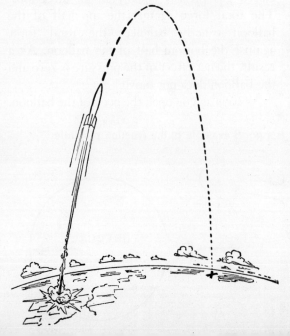

the number of rocks a millionfold and decrease their size until they become molecules, and you are back to the balloon again. The rush of the molecules of gas out the back of the balloon pushes the balloon forward. The faster the gases rush out the back of a balloon, rocket, or any other reaction engine, the greater the forward thrust.

ROCKETS

A Fourth of July skyrocket operates on the reaction principle. The powder in the rocket burns, producing large quantities of gases. Since the gases are confined, the pressure inside the rocket increases rapidly. If there were no hole at the bottom of the rocket, this pressure would cause the rocket to explode. But there is a hole and the hot gases and bits of burning powder are pushed out through it, producing enough unequal pressures inside the rocket to create the thrust that sends it zooming upward. Thrust is the reactive force that sends a reaction engine forward.

A rocket is a simple reaction engine. It operates because the unequal pressures within the combustion chamber produce the thrust that causes the rocket to rise. Whether we are dealing with a simple skyrocket, a bazooka rocket, an aerial rocket, or the giant V-2 rocket that has swished to a height over 100 miles above the surface of the earth, the principle is exactly the same. Pressure in the combustion chamber moves the rocket, and heat is the only practical way of producing gases at a continuing high pressure. Since reaction engines operate at very high temperatures, they yield much energy.

POWDER AND LIQUID-FUEL ROCKETS

The rocket is only one type of reaction engine. The rocket is a self-contained, self-propelled unit. It has a fuel supply which does not need oxygen from the outside for burning the fuel that produces the hot gases. The fuel for the rocket may be a powder similar to gunpowder, or it may be a form of high explosive similar to *cordite*. Such rockets are called *powder rockets*. In either case, the rocket does not need oxygen from the air to burn these fuels. The oxygen is already present within the fuels themselves.

Liquid-fuel rockets burn gasoline, alcohol, aniline, and similar compounds. Liquid fuels are also burned *without* air from *outside* the rocket. A tank of liquid oxygen is carried in these rockets to supply the oxygen necessary for combustion. Gasoline burned with pure oxygen releases more heat energy than the explosion of an equal weight of dynamite.

Because rockets carry their own complete fuel supply and because their energy comes from reaction within the engine, they can travel even better through a vacuum than through air. This means that rockets can travel faster at a height of 10 miles than at sea level—and still better at a height of 100 miles than at 10. They can travel through outer space where no other type of vehicle can operate.

ROCKETS IN USE

Powder rockets are of limited use. Some types, such as "JATO," have been developed to assist in the take-off of heavily loaded planes. The rockets provide a powerful thrust for only a short time—just enough to get the plane into the air. Once airborne, the engines can keep the plane going with only about half the power needed to leave the ground.

Powder rockets are also used as self-propelled weapons. They are light, cheap, and when fired have no recoil. This means that rockets, equivalent to artillery, can be fired from airplanes or from light launchers instead of from heavy expensive cannon. War rockets were used in this country by the British during the War of 1812. "The rockets' red glare" immortalized in the "Star-Spangled Banner," was caused by rockets fired during the Battle of Baltimore.

Liquid-fuel rockets are the most promising for the future. The first successful liquid-fuel rocket was sent aloft by Dr. Robert Goddard in 1926. Dr. Goddard was the pioneer rocket experimenter in this country, and while his achievements made him famous abroad, very few people here knew of him or his work.

As late as 1943 a rocket flight of a mile or so was considered very good. But the next year saw the production of a 12-ton, 50-foot rocket that rose to a height of 75 miles during a flight of 300 miles. This monster rocket, the German V-2, was an overwhelming scientific success. At maximum speed, its thrust is equal to about 600,000 horsepower. Its maximum speed has been computed to be about 3500 miles per hour.

The Future of Rockets. The V-2 clearly showed that transatlantic rockets are not only possible but they could be ready for use with only a few years of research and development. Radio-controlled rockets can be used for the rapid movement of mail. Later, passenger rockets will operate across the continent or the oceans in a few hours. Then we can really begin to plan for rockets that will leave the earth and travel far out into space—to the moon and then to nearby planets.

JET ENGINES

Related to rockets, but somewhat more limited in scope, are the jet engines. Despite their limitations for space travel, jet engines are more practical for most purposes than rockets. The distinction between rockets and jets is simple. Both are reaction engines, but jet engines do not carry a complete fuel. They use the oxygen of the air to burn the fuel oil or kerosene they use. Various kinds of jet engines use different means of getting the air supply into the combustion chamber. Some types are very similar to gas turbines and are combined with gas turbines, forming turbojet engines.

Ramjet. The simplest jet engine is the *ramjet*, which looks like a hollow cigar with a slight bulge at the center. The ramjet will function only when moving forward at speeds well over a hundred miles per hour. At such speeds, the air passing into it compresses itself. This compressed air is mixed with a fuel spray and

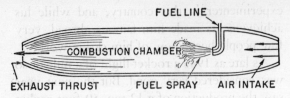

FUEL LINE

COMBUSTION CHAMBER

EXHAUST THRUST   FUEL SPRAY   AIR INTAKE

A simplified ramjet.

ignited. In burning it produces hot gases that rush out the exhaust and provide the thrust that drives the ramjet forward. A ramjet must be towed by a plane or boosted by a rocket until it reaches a speed at which the air entering it is compressed sufficiently to enable the jet to function.

Turbojet. Most jet engines use some kind of mechanical compressor that feeds compressed air into the combustion chamber. In engines like those in the P-80 *Shooting Star*, and in other jet planes that followed this first successful model, a rotary compressor is used. This is operated by a gas turbine mounted on the same shaft. The gas turbine provides energy only for compressing the air. It is not attached to a propeller. The plane is moved forward by reaction thrust. Such a combination of gas turbine and jet engine is known as a *turbojet engine*.

Turbojet engines have been built that operate both as a gas turbine that turns a propeller and as a reaction engine that provides forward thrust through an exhaust nozzle. Such an engine attempts to capitalize on the good points of both propeller and jet.

Intermittent Jet. Another type of flying jet

Rocket trips between planets may someday be made in ships like this.

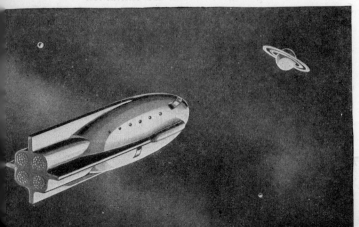

uses vanes, or flaps, on the airduct. As air enters, it mixes with the fuel and almost instantly forms an explosive mixture. This is ignited and the explosion forces the flaps shut and sends the full force of the expanding gases out the exhaust nozzle. As soon as the pressure in the combustion chamber has dropped, the air pressure forces the flaps open and more air enters the chamber, repeating the process. Repetitions occur at an enormously rapid rate, so that there may be 50 or more explosions per second. This gives the jet engine a continual forward thrust at speeds of from 200 to 1000 miles per hour. This type of *intermittent jet engine* powered the German V-1 buzz-bomb during World War II.

Jet propulsion, as applied to planes, reduces noise and vibration. Also, it provides the plane with a simpler engine that uses cheaper fuel—though more of it—than gasoline.

Both rockets and jets are best suited to high-speed, high-altitude use. A jet-propelled automobile or a rocket-driven motorboat would not be practical for many reasons. Nor should one look forward to a jet-propelled sewing machine or a rocket-propelled ice-cream freezer. However, before very long radio-controlled rockets may fly regular mail schedules to Europe, and a weekend trip to London, Moscow, or Capetown may not be an unusual thing.

THE FUTURE OF HEAT ENGINES

Each of the various types of heat engines is best adapted to certain specific conditions and to certain ranges of temperature. We cannot say that one kind of heat engine is better than another, except as we mean that it is better under certain specific conditions. We shall continue to use many types of heat engines in the future. We will still need steam and gasoline engines, but the newer types will be more widely used and will make possible a kind of transportation that has been, so far, only a dream.

Beyond the picture of future heat engines is the realm of atomic energy. Until atomic

318

energy is available—and safe—we remain completely dependent on the usual heat engines. That makes our fuel resources of prime importance. The conservation of fuel resources, through their wise and more efficient use, becomes more important every day. But someday, we may no longer need coal or oil for fuel.

WORKING WITH SCIENCE

1. Some high schools have rocket clubs whose members experiment with making and testing simple rockets. Members of the clubs study about rocket fuels and rocket designs, and conduct tests and experiments. Such a club must work under an adult director, as the chemicals and materials used in rocket experiments can be dangerous when carelessly used.

2. A chemistry textbook may contain information on the heat value of various fuels. Get the figures and see how it is possible for gasoline to produce more energy than dynamite. If this is correct, why don't automobiles explode?

3. The history of powder rockets is long and interesting, going back to about 1200 A.D. Rockets were used in battle during the wars against Napoleon and in the War of 1812. About that time nearly every country in Europe had a "rocket corps" in its army. Find out about some of these early uses of rockets.

4. Read about the possibilities of rockets to the moon. Report to the class on problems that must be solved before such flights are possible and show what is being done toward solving these problems. Some experts believe that rocket flights to the moon will be made during our own lifetimes.

5. Make charts showing the different types of rockets and jet engines. Compare each type, pointing out the advantages and limitations of each.

6. Model-airplane builders already are making models driven by jet engines. These model jet engines are of the intermittent type and are not difficult to operate. Try to locate some model enthusiast who has one of these engines, and have him demonstrate it to the class.

READING YOU WILL ENJOY

Cooke, David C. *Young America's Aviation Annual*. Robert M. McBride & Co., New York, 1946. This book, revised each year, has several chapters on aircraft engines, including data on the new turbojet engines.

General Motors. *Power Goes to Work. A Power Primer. Airplane Power*. General Motors Corp., Detroit, Mich. Well-illustrated booklets that give details on internal-combustion engines and how the power is applied in automobiles and planes.

Reck, Franklin M. and Claire. *Power from Start to Finish*. Thomas Y. Crowell Co., New York, 1941. A detailed and well-illustrated story of power from the earliest days up to the atomic age. Explanations of all types of engines and how the power from them is used.

Smith, G. Godfrey, *Gas Turbines and Jet Propulsion for Aircraft*. Aircraft Books, Inc., New York, 1946. A more technical book, for the specially interested student, about the latest types of internal-combustion engines and their special application.

Zim, Herbert S. *Rockets and Jets*. Harcourt, Brace & Co., New York, 1945. A nontechnical book on the origins, development, and application of rockets and jets.

1

2

Heat engines have limitations. For the most part, heat must be used where it is produced. Electricity, on the other hand, can be sent hundreds of miles through wires and used wherever it is needed. When man learned to transform heat into electricity, he made possible the very widespread use of energy produced efficiently and economically at central generating plants.

Like other forms of energy, electricity has been known for centuries. The Greeks produced small electric charges by rubbing amber with cloth, but they knew nothing about current electricity. Benjamin Franklin (1) was one of the early students of electricity. In 1831, Michael Faraday, (2) a British scientist, produced an electric generator. Some fifty years later, Thomas A. Edison opened the first commercial generating plant in New York City (3). At first, it was used almost wholly for lighting, but the development of the electric motor and the transformer soon placed electricity in the front rank as a source of energy for useful work. In factories, the use of electric motors (4) soon did away with the old overhead belt-and-pulley drives and increased operating efficiency by as much as 50 percent.

Because of the nature of electricity, we may someday be able to transmit it from place to place without wires. When this occurs, airplanes and automobiles will no longer have to carry heavy fuel and can carry greater payloads.

3

4

25

ELECTRICITY, THE MODERN POWER

One bright morning in 1828, Joseph Henry held something new in the palm of his hand. Many have since considered it the greatest invention of the nineteenth century—an invention that led to very great changes in our ways of living. It was not Henry's invention but an improvement on an earlier invention.

Henry thought of the idea one evening and put the device together the next morning. This was not difficult because the invention consisted of a short bar of iron around which he had wound layer after layer of thin, silk-covered copper wire. Joseph Henry had made an *electromagnet*.

Henry's was not the first electromagnet ever made. An Englishman, William Sturgeon [stûr'jŭn], had made a small one several years earlier, but Henry's electromagnet was much more powerful. When he sent an electric current through the coil of wire, the magnet would lift pieces of iron 50 times its own weight. Within a short time Henry built a much larger magnet, one that would lift more than a ton.

MAGNETISM AND ELECTRICITY

Henry, a young American, did not get the idea of the electromagnet out of thin air. Neither did he copy Sturgeon's simple magnet. He had been experimenting with electricity for several years, and was interested enough to read all the scientific books he could get, so he knew the work that had been done in England.

Henry was also familiar with the experiments of Hans Oersted [ûr'stĕd], a Danish scientist who discovered in 1822 that a wire carrying an electric current affected a *magnetic compass*. This important discovery gives us the clue that will help make much of the story of electricity clear.

OERSTED DISCOVERS ELECTROMAGNETISM

Oersted was a physics professor. One day he was lecturing to his students on the new and little understood science of electricity. Quite by accident he placed a wire through which a weak electric current was flowing over a magnetic compass that lay on his lecture table. To his surprise he noticed that the compass needle began to move. It swung around until it stopped at right angles to the wire.

Oersted lifted the wire away and the compass needle returned to its former position. Although this happened by accident, the professor's curiosity was aroused and he decided to investigate. As a result, he discovered more about this effect of an electric current on a compass needle. He reported his findings to other scientists who, like Joseph Henry, were able to use this information in their own experiments.

Electric Circuits. Just what happened on Oersted's lecture table? The professor had a battery in which chemical energy was changed to electric energy. The electric energy is produced when a wire goes from one battery connection to the second battery connection.

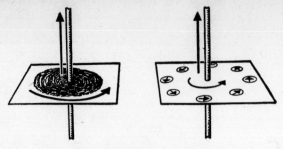

The magnetic field about a "live" wire.

When electricity can flow from its source and back again, usually through a wire, we have an *electric circuit*. In such a circuit an electric current is flowing through the wires. The wire that Oersted had on his table was such a "live" wire. It was part of a complete electric circuit, and electricity was flowing through it.

Magnetism. A compass is a magnetized needle that rests on a pivot so that it can swing freely. It points north because the earth acts as a magnet and magnets, in the right position, attract one another. As you probably know, a *magnet* is any object that has the ability to attract small particles of iron, steel, or certain other metals. Most magnets are made of metal and all possess a *north pole* and a *south pole*. The north pole of one magnet attracts the south pole and repels the north pole of another magnet.

Back in 1822 scientists believed that magnetism and electricity are not related. No wonder Oersted was surprised when he saw a wire that carried an electric current affecting a magnetic compass. But there was no mistake in that observation, and many experiments confirmed the fact that a wire carrying electricity can affect a magnet because the electric current in the wire produces magnetism. Oersted first showed that electricity and magnetism are related—a very basic relationship.

Magnetic Fields. Every wire carrying an electric current is surrounded by an area in which magnetic forces exist, that is, a *magnetic field*. Such a magnetic field disturbed Oersted's compass. You can see this yourself if you place a current-carrying wire near a compass or pass the wire through a thin cardboard on which fine iron filings are sprinkled. The filings will arrange themselves in a circular pattern following the magnetic field around the wire.

When Henry made his electromagnet, he wound hundreds of turns of fine wire in a small coil, thus bringing the magnetic field into a very small area. He wound the wire around a bar of soft iron. The soft iron served to concentrate the magnetic field still more because magnetic force flows more easily through soft iron than through air or other substances. When current passes through the coil, the concentrated magnetic field makes the soft iron a powerful electromagnet that can lift heavy iron objects or affect a magnetic compass some distance away.

MAKING AND USING AN ELECTROMAGNET

You can make an electromagnet yourself at very little cost. All you need is a large nail, bolt, or bar of iron; a length of bell wire or other fine covered (insulated) wire; and a source of electricity that flows in one direction, that is, *direct current*, such as a No. 6 dry cell. Allow about a foot of wire at the end of the coil for connections.

Wind at least 10 feet of wire neatly and tightly about your piece of iron, always winding in the same direction. Leave another foot at the end for the second connection to the dry cell. If the wire slips, tape it in place. Clean the insulation, or covering, from the two ends of the wire. Connect one end of the coil to one terminal of the dry cell and the other end of the coil to the other terminal.

Left and right: The magnetic field between a north and south pole. Middle: Between two north poles.

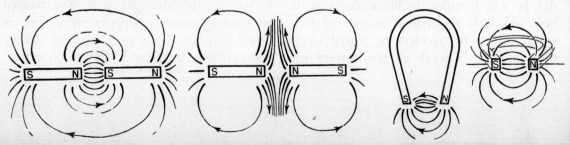

Place one end of the electromagnet near a pile of tacks. The electromagnet should pick up a good many of them.

Weigh the tacks and then weigh the magnet. What part of its weight can the magnet lift? You may notice that the wire in the magnet gets hot. This is because some of the electricity flowing through the wire is being changed into heat. If more turns of wire are used in the coil of the electromagnet, the heating effect will be less. If the magnet does overheat, disconnect it from the dry cell and use it for short periods of time only.

STRENGTH OF AN ELECTROMAGNET

Compare your electromagnet with one made by a classmate. Probably you will find that one or the other is stronger—judged on the basis of the weight it can lift. What causes this?

The strength of an electromagnet can be increased in several ways. One way is to increase the electric current flowing through it. Two dry cells, instead of one, will make your electromagnet nearly twice as strong. The dry cells must be connected so that the connecting wire goes from the *positive* (+) *terminal* of one dry cell to the *negative* (−) *terminal* of the next. Such a combination of two or more dry cells forms one kind of *battery*. The positive terminal of a dry cell is always the center terminal; the negative terminal is the outside terminal.

The wires from your electromagnet go to the negative terminal of the first dry cell and to the positive terminal of the other. Connecting the dry cells in this way is called a *series* connection. The number of dry cells connected in series may be increased as long as the current does not become so great as to overheat the coil.

You will discover that the material used to make the core of the magnet also affects its strength. Wind electromagnet coils on a bar of brass, on a piece of wood, on a fragment of cast iron, and on a bar of soft iron. What are the results? You will find that magnetic force flows most easily through the soft iron, making it the best electromagnet. The shape of the soft iron is important too. The more iron in the magnetic field, the stronger the magnet.

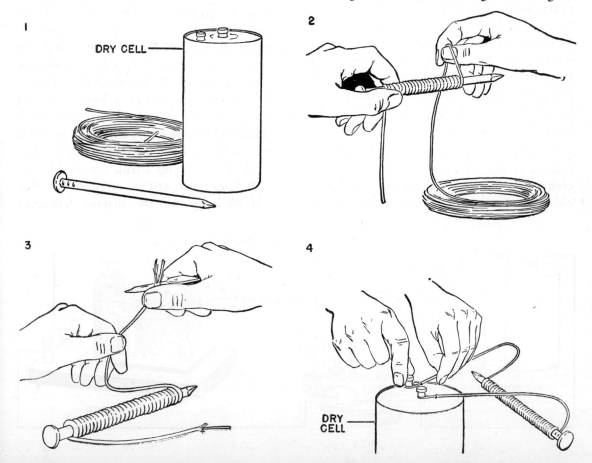

1

DRY CELL

2

3

4

DRY CELL

Increasing the number of turns of wire in the coil of the electromagnet increases the magnetic field and, hence, the strength of the electromagnet. So by controlling the amount of current, the material of the core, and the number of turns of wire, electromagnets of different sizes and strengths can be built, each adapted for a particular use.

USES OF ELECTROMAGNETS

About this time you may be saying to yourself, "What's all this about? Electromagnets are fun and they are interesting. But why should they be considered such a great invention? They don't seem very important to me."

Electromagnets are important. Without them every automobile would stop running. So would every plane and most of our locomotives. No electricity would flow from the huge generators at Hoover Dam and Grand Coulee, or from the thousands of smaller generators all over the country. All electric motors would cease to spin.

Without electromagnets trolley cars, x-ray machines, bells, radios, telegraphs, and nearly every device depending on electricity would be useless. Electric lights and heaters would still operate on batteries. But electricity which serves us in so many ways could only be used in small-scale lighting and heating and for its chemical effects. Electricity would become a novelty instead of a very necessary kind of energy.

Direct Uses of Electromagnets. The electromagnet is one of the keystones of modern civilization. However, the direct uses of the electromagnet are quite few. Large electro-magnets are used in junk yards and steel mills for loading scrap iron and for moving heavy iron objects.

Hospitals sometimes have a large electromagnet to remove bits of iron or steel that a person may accidentally get in his eye. An electromagnet attachment on a lathe or a planer permits machine work on a piece of steel without drilling and bolting it.

An even more important use of the electromagnet is in concentrating the ores of certain minerals at the mine. When ores are concentrated, they are easier to refine and, of course, cheaper to transport. Ores containing iron, cobalt, or nickel are attracted by an electromagnet. The other rocks and minerals in which the ore is found are not attracted to the magnet at all.

Indirect Uses of Electromagnets. If the electromagnet had no uses other than these few, it would still be important. But the direct uses are only a beginning.

In order to operate, an electromagnet must be in a circuit—two wires must connect it to a source of direct current. Disconnect the wires, and the electromagnet no longer works. There is nothing to limit the length of these wires. They can be an inch, a foot, or many miles in length. However, there is a loss of current that increases with the length of the wires.

By touching the end of a long wire to a battery, you could make an electromagnet pick up a nail in some neighbor's house. However, there would not be much point in doing this. Instead of picking up a nail, you could have the electromagnet attract an iron bar that would click against the magnet whenever

A simplified, one-way telegraph circuit.

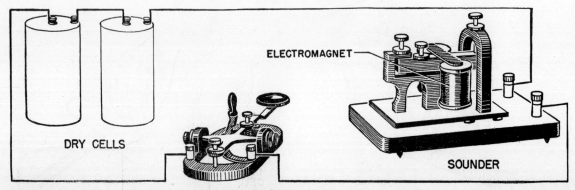

DRY CELLS

ELECTROMAGNET

SOUNDER

KEY

current was sent through the wire. You would then have a crude but effective *telegraph*.

You could improve your telegraph by using a stronger battery, and providing a *telegraph key* that opens and closes the circuit at the touch of your finger. You could mount the electromagnet on a board with a soft iron bar close to it and a spring to pull the bar away when the current is released. You would then have a telegraph set capable of sending clear signals for quite a distance.

When Samuel Morse sent his first message, "What hath God wrought?" from Washington to Baltimore in May, 1844, he used a telegraph set that was quite like the one just described. Since Morse's day, the telegraph has been improved in many ways. You can now send messages by telegraph and cable to almost any part of the world. Wire circuits that carry many messages at once have been designed.

Underwater telegraph lines, composed of heavy lead-covered *cables*, carry messages across the oceans. Even more astonishing is the *teletype machine*, a long-distance telegraphic typewriter. Messages typed on a teletype machine in one telegraph station are typed automatically on another teletype machine in another station. By means of the *telephoto machine*, it is possible to transmit pictures over telegraph wires. All of these devices use many electromagnets.

BELLS, TELEPHONES, AND CIRCUIT BREAKERS

A *telephone* is also an electromagnetic device. You can see this if you unscrew the cover of a telephone receiver, lift off the thin round steel plate, or *diaphragm*, and notice the small electromagnet immediately beneath it.

The electromagnet in a telephone has a permanent magnet for a core. This permanent magnet becomes stronger or weaker in proportion to the current flowing through the coil. If you hold the edge of the diaphragm next to the magnet, you will feel its pull. Replace the diaphragm carefully, being careful not to bend it.

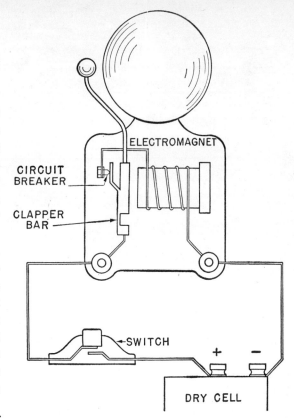

Close the switch and the bell keeps ringing. Why?

Bells. An electric bell has an electromagnet that pulls an iron clapper against a gong. As it does so, the circuit is automatically broken, the electromagnet loses its magnetism, and the clapper bar springs back. When it springs back, the circuit is established again, and the electromagnet pulls the clapper against the gong once more.

As long as you press the push button, the bell automatically makes and breaks the circuit, the electromagnet pulls and releases the clapper bar, and the bell keeps ringing. An electric buzzer operates on exactly the same

Circuit breakers protect circuits in many homes.
From Encyclopaedia Britannica film Home Electrical Appliances

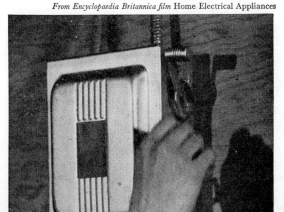

Photos courtesy Westinghouse Electric Corporation and Tennessee Valley Authority

Left: Circuit breakers in a power distributing plant. Middle: These huge generators are driven by water turbines. Right: The large motor in the foreground is part of a large motor-generator.

principle except that it has no gong. In addition, there are call bells, signal bells, alarm bells, door bells, single- and multiple-stroke bells. They all use electromagnets.

A coil of wire wound on a tube so that an iron bar can move in and out of the tube is called a *solenoid*. When a solenoid is connected in a circuit, the magnetic field produced inside the tube is so strong that an iron bar held near the mouth of the tube is pulled, or sucked, into the tube. This special form of electromagnet has many uses, as the motion or position of the iron bar can be controlled by controlling the current in the solenoid circuit.

Circuit Breakers. Often a machine or piece of electrical equipment is designed to operate on a specific electric current. If a larger surge of current should flow through this equipment, damage would result. Such equipment needs an automatic switch to cut off the current if it becomes too great. A solenoid switch does this.

The current going to the equipment passes through an ordinary switch that can be pulled open, cutting the circuit. The handle of this switch is attached to an iron rod that rests at the mouth of a solenoid. The coil of the solenoid is connected in the circuit that supplies electricity to the equipment. This coil

is so designed that normal current to the equipment creates a magnetic field just strong enough to hold the iron rod at the mouth of the solenoid.

If a stronger surge of current flows through the solenoid, the magnetic field instantly becomes stronger and the iron rod is pulled into the tube of the solenoid. Since this iron rod is attached to the handle of the switch, the switch is opened and the electricity is cut off before the equipment is damaged. Such a solenoid switch is called a *circuit breaker*.

A circuit breaker can be reset in a jiffy and the circuit is again complete. Circuit breakers are used in circuits that supply electricity to motors and heavy electrical machinery. They are frequently installed in homes to protect electric circuits and equipment.

Other Uses of Electromagnets. Probably these examples are enough to point out the usefulness of the electromagnet. We could go on and point out that not only the telephone but radio, television, and wire-photo service could not function without electromagnets. Neither could the principal instruments that are used in measuring electric current. The *galvanometer*, *voltmeter*, and *ammeter* are electric measuring instruments that depend on electromagnets.

A galvanometer is an extremely important

electric measuring instrument. Since we will be making and using electric currents, it is a good tool to have on hand. Sensitive galvanometers that measure very small amounts of electricity are delicate and expensive instruments. A home-made one is sensitive enough for our purposes.

The principle on which a galvanometer works is simple: Every electric current creates a magnetic field. If a magnet is placed in this magnetic field, the magnet will move. The resulting motion can be read from a needle that moves across a dial. Since the strength of the magnetic field and the movement of the needle vary in proportion to the amount of electricity, a galvanometer can be used to measure the current. Both voltmeter and ammeter are similar to the galvanometer.

WORKING WITH SCIENCE

1. Repeat Oersted's experiments and demonstrate that a wire carrying a current produces a magnetic field, by arranging small compasses around a "live" wire. Also sprinkle fine iron filings on a cardboard through which a "live" wire passes. Draw the pattern that results.

2. With shop equipment you can make a very powerful electromagnet at the cost of a dollar or two. You need a 4-inch pipe nipple and cap, a half-inch bolt 6 inches long, and at least a pound of magnet wire. Have a machinist drill a hole through the cap large enough for the bolt. Set the bolt in a lathe and wind a coil of wire nearly 4 inches in diameter and 4 inches long on the bolt. Set this coil inside the nipple. A magnet this size, connected to a 6-volt battery, should be strong enough to support your weight.

3. Dry cells are a source of current often used in experiments. Demonstrate connecting dry cells in parallel and series, and measure the resulting voltage and current in each case. In parallel connection of dry cells, all positive terminals are connected and all negative terminals are also connected. Demonstrate a short circuit, and show how they can be prevented.

4. The magnetic separation of ore is an essential process in our basic industries. You can demonstrate the process by using a mixture of ground magnetite (Fe_3O_4) and sand. Even a small permanent magnet will separate this iron ore from the nonmagnetic material.

5. Make and use a simple home-made telegraph set. All you need is a tin can, some nails, a board, and wire. Make home-made counterparts of the equipment shown on page 324. Bend the sounding arm and key from strips of the tin can. In about an hour, at the cost of a few cents, you can have a simple telegraph that will operate on one or two dry cells.

6. Demonstrate the principle of the electric bell and buzzer. Show how the electromagnet acts to break the circuit and ring the bell. Simple electromagnetic motors have been made to operate on the same principle. See if you can design one.

7. Demonstrate the principle of the circuit breaker, using a small home-made model. Use dry cells to supply the current for the circuit in which the circuit breaker is included.

8. Make a simple galvanometer by winding 50 turns of thin wire (No. 24 or 28) around a drinking glass. Slip the coil off and bind together with scotch tape. Mount on a block of wood, with a cork on which a compass can be placed. A current, even a weak one, flowing through the coil will cause the compass needle to move.

MAGNETIC INDUCTION

"But what is the use of this thing?" asked a polite Englishwoman of Michael Faraday in 1831. Faraday had just demonstrated his new device for producing electricity, a *dynamo*, before the Royal Society in London. "Madam," Faraday is said to have replied just as politely and certainly very effectively,

"What is the use of a newborn infant?"

If Faraday were alive today, he would be astonished at the hearty growth of the infant. Joseph Henry would be proud, too, for a full year before Faraday published the account of his experiment and invention, Henry had demonstrated the same idea himself.

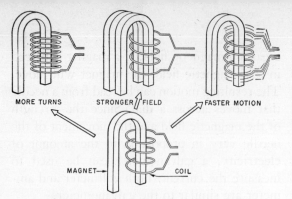

MORE TURNS · STRONGER FIELD · FASTER MOTION

MAGNET → · ← COIL

Increasing the strength of an induced current.

In making the dynamo, Faraday and Henry reversed the experiments of Oersted. The Danish professor showed how electricity might be used to produce magnetism. The British and American scientists used magnetism to produce electricity. This method of making electricity by means of magnetic force is called *magnetic induction*. It is one of the principles that have made possible the many electric marvels of the Machine Age.

GENERATING ELECTRICITY BY INDUCTION

Connect a large coil of insulated wire to a galvanometer by means of long, flexible wires. Allow the needle to become stationary. Then move the coil back and forth. Be careful not to shake the galvanometer. Moving the coil of wire will not cause the galvanometer needle to move.

Move the same coil between the poles of a horseshoe magnet and watch the galvanometer needle. As the coil of wire moves through the magnetic field, a current is produced, or *generated*, within the wire. The needle moves to one side and then drops back to zero. Move

A simplified alternating-current generator.

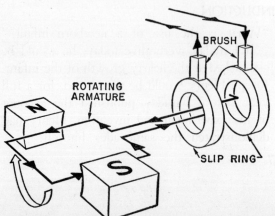

BRUSH

ROTATING ARMATURE

N

S

SLIP RING

the coil back, and the needle moves the other way and then drops back to zero.

This is the secret of the dynamo, or *generator*, the machine that produces nearly all of our electricity. *Movement*, a *magnetic field*, and a *coil of wire* are necessary.

The steps from the simple laboratory models to the powerful generators we use today were difficult. But they came very rapidly. Within 50 years after magnetic induction had been demonstrated, generators were in everyday use. To make these generators practical, it was necessary to increase the amount of electricity they produced. This was done by modifying the three basic factors that are involved in electromagnetic induction.

INCREASING THE STRENGTH OF AN INDUCED CURRENT

To produce an induced current, you need a coil of wire, a magnetic field, and movement. To induce a stronger current, the number of turns in the coil of wire can be increased, finer wire can be used, and the winding can be so arranged that more turns of the coil cut across the magnetic field at once.

Increasing the magnetic field is also a simple matter. Use three magnets, or four or eight instead of one, or use stronger magnets. The kind of magnet makes no difference; so electromagnets, many times stronger than permanent magnets, are used in most generators. Some electricity is used in the electromagnets, but the cost of this current is negligible since the generator with electromagnets is very much more efficient.

Speeding up the motion is not difficult. Swinging the coil of wire back and forth faster increases the number of times the magnetic field is cut per minute. But back-and-forth motion is inefficient. Most dynamos are so arranged that the coil of wire is rotated rapidly between the poles of the magnet. In this way, the number of wires that cut the magnetic field in a unit of time is increased. Energy from a steam or water turbine can be used to turn the coils in the generator.

328

A PRACTICAL GENERATOR

An electric current is induced as the generator coil revolves rapidly in a magnetic field. This coil and the shaft on which it rotates are known as the *armature* of the generator. If the current produced is to be used, wires from the armature must connect to electric devices, such as lights, motors, or heaters. This may seem impossible, since the connecting wires would be twisted and broken by the turning of the armature if they were connected directly to it.

Circular rings of copper, called *slip rings*, solve this problem. Each slip ring is connected to one end of the armature coil. The two insulated rings are mounted on the shaft of the generator and turn as the armature turns. The electric current flows into the slip rings.

A carbon or copper *brush* rests against each slip ring, and the electricity flows from the moving ring into the stationary brush and into the wires. Once the current is flowing in the wire, it can be used. The uses of the current depend not only on the fact that it flows in the wire, but on *how* it flows through the wire.

ALTERNATING CURRENT

When you move a coil of wire in a magnetic field, the galvanometer moves one way as you push the coil in, and in the opposite direction as you pull the coil out. The needle moves in opposite directions because the current flows in one direction on the push and in the opposite direction on the pull. The fact that the direction in which the coil is moving changes the direction in which the current flows, makes our generator a bit more complicated.

The direction of the current changes, or *alternates*, twice while the armature makes one complete revolution. This change occurs in every generator no matter what its size. Every generator makes *alternating current*—a current that changes its direction of flow as the armature revolves.

To understand why the current alternates, two facts must be kept in mind. (1) The

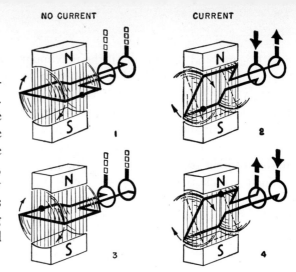

NO CURRENT   CURRENT

Why alternating current is produced.

direction of the moving coil determines the direction of the current flowing through it, and (2) the moving coil must cut across the magnetic field to generate a current within it. If the coil moves parallel to the magnetic field, no current is generated. If it moves at right angles to the magnetic field, the strongest current is generated.

The illustration above will help you see the change. In it we have put a spot on the armature (which is flattened to simplify our picture) to help you follow the movement of the armature until it returns to its original position. You can see that in a single complete turn of the armature, the current has twice increased from zero to a maximum and has changed its direction. These changes take place very rapidly and in the current you probably use in your home, you ordinarily do not notice them. But their effects are most important in designing electric machinery and in using electric energy.

CYCLES OF CURRENT

Each time an alternating current flows, first in one direction, then in the opposite direction, it completes what is known as a *cycle*. Generators are designed to produce current of a definite number of cycles per second.

Suppose that we connect a light to a generator that produces current at one cycle per second. As the armature rotates, the light gets brighter and brighter until the maximum current passes through it. Then it begins to get dim and go out. By this time, the armature has made a half-turn. In the second half-turn, the light again brightens up and again goes out. Our one-cycle generator gives us two flashes of light per second.

Such a flickering light would be of very little use to us, so we speed up our generator until the flashes of light come so fast that they blend together and our eye cannot detect them. There are always two "flashes" for each cycle, but there are ways to get more than one cycle for each revolution of the armature.

Most generators produce a *60-cycle current*, which means that current in the lights in your house changes its direction 120 times per second. Since the lamp filament does not cool down very much during that short fraction of a second while the current drops to zero and climbs up again, and since your eye cannot detect such a rapid flicker, the light seems to be burning steadily. If the generator slowed down until it was only producing a 30-cycle current, you would find the flicker noticeable and unbearable.

PRODUCING 60-CYCLE CURRENT

Perhaps you have already been doing a little mental arithmetic, thinking, "At one cycle per revolution, 60 cycles per second means 3600 revolutions per minute, and that's pretty fast for a generator to spin." It is. High-speed steam turbines, such as those described in Chapter 23 can spin generators at 3600 revolutions per minute. Water turbines cannot operate this fast. But they can produce a 60-cycle current, anyway. The method of doing this is very simple.

The current reverses itself as the armature passes the midpoint of the magnetic field between two magnetic poles. When an armature revolves between two poles, it produces one cycle for each revolution. Add another pair of magnetic poles at right angles to the first pair, so that you have *four poles*,

and the armature will produce current of two cycles per single revolution. In other words, the current will have four high spots and four low spots as the armature turns around once. With such a generator, half the speed, or 1800 revolutions per minute, will produce a 60-cycle current.

If the number of magnetic poles is again doubled, the armature will produce a current of four cycles per revolution. With this generator, 900 revolutions per minute produces a 60-cycle current. Increasing the number of coils in the armature produces the same effect as increasing the number of magnetic poles.

EFFECTIVE CURRENT

Have you been wondering about this electric current that changes from nothing at all, up to a maximum, and back again so fast? How can you measure the electric current if it is always changing? Is 110-volt alternating current actually 110 volts? Is it more or less?

An answer to these questions can be had by comparing the current produced by an alternating-current generator with the current produced by a battery. The current from the battery is a direct current that always flows in the same direction. If the direct current flows through a heating coil, the current is changed to heat. Thus we can measure the amount of heat produced by a direct current being pushed at some particular electrical pressure, or *voltage*.

If alternating current under the same pressure, or voltage, flows through the same heating coil, we do not get an equal amount of heat. We get only about 0.7 as much because the alternating current has not been at full strength all the time.

The current that we call *110-volt alternating current* is actually being pushed by a pressure of 110 volts for only a small fraction of the time. Sometimes it is less, sometimes more. Electrical engineers have found that if the alternating current varies between zero and 156 volts, it produces the same heating effect as a 110-volt direct current.

DIRECT CURRENT

For nearly all home and industrial uses, we use alternating current. Oddly enough, for many years, alternating current was a drug on the market.

Before the invention of the generator, what electricity there was came from batteries. As a result, people thought only of direct current. Besides, many uses for electricity demand direct current—electroplating of metals, electric smelting of aluminum, and certain kinds of motors. So a simple and effective way to change alternating current to direct current at the generator was devised.

Each time the current from a generator armature reaches the zero point, it reverses its direction. If some way could be found to reverse the connections to the armature at the exact instant the current reverses itself, then the current would always flow in the same direction, even though the direction of the current in the armature changed with each cycle.

That is exactly what a *commutator* does. Instead of the armature wires ending in a pair of slip rings they are connected to the two halves of a *split ring*, or commutator. The two halves of the commutator are composed of semicircular pieces, or segments, of copper mounted on the generator shaft. They come very close to each other but are carefully insulated from each other.

Two brushes rest against the commutator segments, one against each half of the split ring. The split ring reverses the connections of the brushes to the armature at the exact point at which the current in the armature reverses its direction. As a result, the current flowing into the wires from the brushes is a direct current, similar to that from a battery. The current from a direct-current generator has ups and downs as the armature revolves. However, this is remedied, as in an alternating-current generator, by increasing the number of magnets that surround the armature.

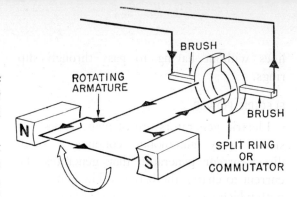

A simplified direct-current generator.

SPECIAL GENERATORS

Whether the generator produces alternating or direct current, it always has an armature that rotates in a magnetic field created between the poles of magnets. Some generators use permanent horseshoe magnets to make the magnetic field and have an armature that revolves between the poles of these magnets. This type of generator is known as a *magneto*.

A magneto is hidden inside the box of rural telephones. When you turn the hand crank on the side of the telephone box, you are actually generating an alternating current of about 20 cycles. This flows through the telephone wire and rings the bell at the operator's switchboard. Magnetos are also used to generate current for certain kinds of field radio sets. In addition, they can be modified to furnish the spark for the ignition systems of internal-combustion engines of motorcycles, motorboats, and so forth.

HIGH-VOLTAGE GENERATORS

Large alternating-current generators often are quite different in design from small generators. The current is so great that if it were to leave the armature through slip rings, continuous sparking at the brushes, overheating, and loss of current would result. To prevent this loss, large alternating-current generators are made so that the electromagnets instead of the coils revolve.

Many coils of wire connnected together are wound on the fixed part, or stator, of the generator. The current is induced in the wires of the stator, and goes directly to the power lines without having to pass through slip rings.

ELECTRIC POWER

Electric generators are of many types and sizes. Every automobile contains a small direct-current generator that generates the current to charge the battery. The generators with which we are more familiar are the larger ones that make the current used in our cities and factories.

Industrial plants often manufacture their own electric current, using steam, diesel, or hydroelectric power. Large electric power companies manufacture current and sell it, just as other companies sell other products. Eighty-five percent of the electricity produced in the United States is made and sold by private companies.

COST OF ELECTRICITY

The cost of electricity to the consumer generally runs from 3 cents to 10 cents per *kilowatt-hour*. A kilowatt-hour is enough electricity to operate twenty-five 40-watt lamps for 1 hour. Often there is a minimum charge of $1 for the first 10 kilowatt-hours or less. When the companies can sell their current in larger amounts to industrial concerns, the price drops tremendously. It may be only about 1 percent of the rate your parents pay for electricity.

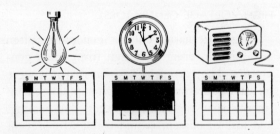

One kilowatt-hour of electricity will operate each of these 110-volt devices for the number of hours indicated.

Many cities and towns own their own electric plants. These may be operated as a byproduct of their water-supply systems. These municipal plants are often able to sell electricity at lower rates than commercial plants, partly because they are tax free. In a few cases the town power plant earns enough money for the town to pay the local taxes of its residents.

An important byproduct of the flood-control projects of the Tennessee Valley Authority is abundant, inexpensive electricity, which has benefited many rural families in the South. There are plans for building projects similar to the TVA on seven other American river systems. If these are completed, our supply of inexpensive electricity may well be greatly increased.

OUR ELECTRIC POWER RESOURCES

Our country is the world's greatest producer and user of electricity. We generate about 30 million horsepower in continuous production, day and night. In a vague way, this means that our electric-generating plants have constantly available for us the power of 30 million horses. The 18 mammoth generators at the Grand Coulee Dam on the Columbia River in Washington are designed to have an output of about 2,700,000 horsepower. Hoover Dam has an output of about 1,800,000 horsepower.

The total developed water power in our country now comes to about 19 million horsepower. This could be increased to about 40 million horsepower when we build the needed dams. At present, only about one-third of our electricity comes from hydroelectric generators. The rest comes from steam plants, except for about 1 percent produced by internal-combustion engines.

The *production* of electric energy is only part of the story. Equally important are the *transmission* of this energy and its *utilization*. There is far more to transmitting electricity than erecting tall metal towers and stringing wires across the country. The electrical engineer faces difficult problems in getting the electricity from the generators to the places where it will be used.

WORKING WITH SCIENCE

1. Demonstrate the principle of electromagnetic induction, using a permanent magnet and a coil of wire connected to a home-made galvanometer. Move the magnet near the coil and vice versa. Use a larger coil of wire, stronger magnets, and faster motion to show factors related to increasing the strength of the induced current.

2. Rural telephones contain a small alternating-current generator for calling the operator. Sometimes these may be obtained from a junk dealer. If you can get one, you can use it in many kinds of simple experiments. It operates on exactly the same principles as larger generators except that it uses permanent magnets instead of electromagnets.

3. Make a graph showing the change in strength and direction of an alternating current as the armature revolves. This curve, when carefully plotted, enables an engineer to tell much about a current.

4. On a demonstration motor, study the slip rings used on the rotor and the split ring used to convert alternating to direct current. Pay close attention to the position of the armature and the position of the brushes on the split ring.

5. Now is the time to visit your local electric plant if you have not already done so. Find out all you can about the generators—their size, operation, problems of operation, and so forth. Make a list of factors that enter into the cost of electricity to the consumer.

6. Look up your family electric bills. Find out the rate you pay for current, and see how the cost per unit decreases as the amount used increases. Make a list of all the electrical devices in your home and how much they are used. Decide whether electricity is a cheap or expensive source of energy.

7. If you know of a municipal electric system, try to find out the relative costs of private and municipal power. Why are private companies so opposed to municipal plants?

8. Get more information about the TVA and its electric power. A letter on school stationery to the TVA at its headquarters in Nashville, Tenn. will bring booklets and other information.

9. Make a list of the largest hydroelectric power projects in the world. How many of these are in the United States? What other countries use much hydroelectric power? Why?

MEASURING ELECTRICITY

Up to this point, we have talked about the "strength" and "size" of an electric current and about its "power." But there are more precise terms, such as *volt*, *ampere*, and *watt*, that we must learn to use if we are to speak scientifically.

We have already spoken of voltage as electrical pressure. Do you know the difference between a volt and a kilowatt? Can you explain what a current is? Now is the time to get these basic facts clear. You already know something about how electricity is generated and the technical terms will now have much more meaning.

FLOW OF ELECTRONS

An electric current is a flow of electrons. As you know, electrons are exceedingly small particles of matter bearing an electric charge. Electrons have been measured and weighed in spite of their infinitely small size. The weight of an electron is expressed by the

When an electric circuit is completed, electrons flow. The rate of flow is measured by an ammeter.

From Encyclopaedia Britannica film Elements of Electrical Circuits

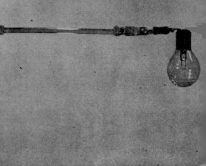

From Encyclopaedia Britannica film Elements of Electrical Circuits

When the copper wire is replaced with glass, current does not flow. Is glass a conductor?

fraction 9/10,000,000,000,000,000,000,000,-000,000 gram, and a gram is about ⅓₀ ounce. A stream of electrons may be set in motion by an electric generator or by a battery. The electrons flow from atom to atom within metals and other substances that transmit, or conduct, electricity.

AMPERES MEASURE RATE OF FLOW

A stream of electrons may be a trickle or a flood. The unit used to measure the *rate of flow* of electricity in the electron stream is the ampere. An electrician will call this unit an "amp."

An ampere is a measure of the total number of electrons passing a given point in a circuit in 1 second. You cannot count these electrons by ordinary means because in a current of 1 ampere, sufficient to light an ordinary 100-watt lamp, 6 billion electrons flow past a given point in a circuit in 1 second.

VOLTS MEASURE "PRESSURE"

All energy flows from a place of greater concentration to a place of less concentration. The rate of flow depends on the difference in concentration of energy between the two places. Electricity follows this universal pattern too. The unit used to measure the difference between two electrical forces or pressures is called the volt. The difference in concentration, or pressure, is called *electrical potential*, which determines the force of the electric current.

The number of volts indicates the current's push—the push that determines how strong the electric current will be. If the difference in potential is small, say 6 volts, the current will have a 6-volt push. This is a rather small push.

A 110-volt current has a greater push and is able to travel through circuits through which a 6-volt current could not travel. The potential of a stroke of lightning runs into millions of volts. As a result, this current is able to travel through materials that are normally considered to be electric *insulators*, or *nonconductors*.

Volts and amperes are two dimensions of an electric current. No current is composed of one and not the other. You may talk about a 110-volt current, but you are merely ignoring the amperes. Perhaps it may help you to compare a current with a waterfall. The number of volts, or voltage, represents the height of the waterfall and the number of amperes, or *amperage*, the rate at which water runs over it.

You might find a very high waterfall with little water, or a low waterfall with a torrent of water. The first would correspond to a current of high voltage and low amperage; the second, to a current of low voltage and high amperage.

The currents we know may involve various combinations of volts and amperes. For example, a small flashlight bulb uses a low-voltage current and requires only a low amperage. The starting motor of an automobile uses a 6-volt current, but it may require 30 or more amperes to crank the engine. Here we have a combination of low voltage and high amperage.

The current used in your doctor's x-ray or in the neon signs on Main Street is pushed by a very high voltage, 10,000 volts or more, but it is usually a small fraction of an ampere. In the electric furnace or in making artificial lightning, we may use a current of both high voltage and high amperage.

WATTS MEASURE POWER

When you talk about electric power, you are talking about *both* volts and amperes. The unit of electric power is the watt, named after James Watt. It simply combines or multiplies electrical pressure and current flow. It is equal to the electrical pressure multiplied by the number of amperes.

If you remember the formula *Watts = Volts × Amperes*, or $W = V \times A$, you can solve many simple problems dealing with electricity. You can immedia ely compute the fact that a 110-volt 550-watt motor requires a current of 5 amperes. If you know that an electric iron consumes 7 amperes on 110-volt current, it uses electricity at the rate of 770 watts. Since 746 watts equal 1 horsepower, we can compare electric power with mechanical power. Furthermore, if watts are multiplied by units of time, a unit of work is obtained.

WATT-HOURS MEASURE WORK

A watt used for an hour is a *watt-hour*. This is a unit of *work*. But since it is a small unit, we generally use 1000 watt-hours, or a kilowatt-hour, as a practical unit. When you buy electricity, you pay so much per kilowatt-hour. It makes no difference to the electric company whether you run a 1000-watt electric iron for 1 hour, a 100-watt lamp for 10 hours, or a 2-watt electric clock for 500 hours. One kilowatt-hour of work is done, and you are charged for it.

OHMS MEASURE RESISTANCE, THE FRICTION OF ELECTRICITY

In an electric circuit, the electricity must flow through something. No matter what the substance is, it is not a perfect conductor of electricity. Every object offers more or less resistance to an electric current, and so a unit

335

of resistance is necessary. The unit is the *ohm*, named after George Ohm [ōm], an early experimenter who discovered the relation between voltage, amperage, and resistance. This relation is now known as *Ohm's law*.

The resistance offered to an electric current by a piece of No. 30 copper wire 10 feet long is about 1 ohm. No. 18 copper wire (the lower the number, the thicker the wire) offers less resistance. One hundred sixty feet of No. 18 wire has a resistance of 1 ohm. A table giving the resistance of wires of various sizes appears on page 336.

If you had some No. 30 nichrome wire, the kind that is used in electric heaters, you would find that only about 2 inches of this wire has 1 ohm of resistance. Thus, you see that the thickness of the conductor affects the resistance and so does the material of which the conductor is made. The length of the conductor also affects the resistance: 100 miles of wire naturally offers more resistance than 10 miles.

These drawings illustrate Ohm's law. Explain.

From Encyclopaedia Britannica film Elements of Electrical Circuits

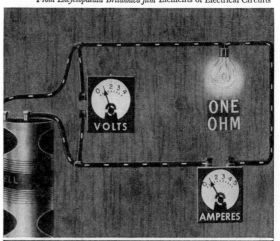

Resistance of 1000 Feet of Copper Wire

Wire Number	Diameter in Inches	Resistance in Ohms
0	0.32	0.1
5	0.16	0.4
12	0.08	1.6
18	0.04	6.4
24	0.02	25.6

Silver is an excellent conductor of electricity; copper is next; gold, aluminum, and iron follow. Substances like wood, paper, oil, or glass that do not conduct currents except under tremendously high voltages, are called insulators. Most electric wires are insulated with rubber, cotton, or enamel to prevent short circuits.

The number of amperes of current flowing through an electric circuit or device equals the voltage divided by the resistance. This is Ohm's law. It can be written as:

$$Amperes = \frac{Volts}{Resistance}$$

or

$$Resistance = \frac{Volts}{Amperes}$$

or

$$Volts = Resistance \times Amperes$$

Knowing any two of the three quantities—volts, amperes, or ohms—it is easy to compute the third. By measuring the electric pressure with a voltmeter and the current with an ammeter, you can easily figure out the resistance. A 40-watt lamp has a resistance of about 300 ohms; an electric bell, only 2 or 3 ohms. Many questions on the use of electricity involve Ohm's law, and it is used frequently both by the scientist and the practical electrician.

RESISTANCE AND HEAT

When an electric current meets a resistance, heat is produced. This heat may or may not be desirable. We build electric stoves, heaters, and irons with wires of high resistance so that much of the current is converted into heat. But in the transmission of electricity, the heating effect causes a loss of current that we try hard to prevent. If wires are too small for the current, overheating can become so great that the wires become red-hot. They may set fire to anything flammable they touch.

Electric wiring in houses and other buildings must be protected in such a way that this danger is reduced. Putting a *fuse*, or a circuit breaker, in a circuit provides protection against overheating of wires. A fuse contains a bit of metal with a low melting point. This piece of metal is of such size that a current of a certain number of amperes will pass through it without causing the metal to overheat.

If a short circuit or an overload permits more current to flow through the line, the fuse overheats and melts, breaking the circuit before the wires get a chance to overheat. As the fuse wire is safely enclosed in an insulating can, there is no danger of causing a fire.

This matter of resistance and heating causes difficult problems in our use of electricity. You may appreciate it more if you understand that the heat produced by electricity increases very rapidly as the current increases. Doubling the amperage through a circuit increases the heat produced by four times. If a short circuit permits 10 times the current to flow, 100 times as much heat is produced. You can see that this can mean either a great loss of current or a dangerous source of fire.

A frayed cord may produce a short circuit, causing a fuse to melt. Why does the fuse melt?

From Encyclopaedia Britannica film Elements of Electrical Circuits

The resistance of a wire increases with its temperature. When wires are cooled to about −450°F, their resistance decreases to nearly zero, and they become almost perfect conductors. But as their temperatures go up, their resistance increases. On a hot summer day, transmission lines actually carry less current than in winter because the temperature of transmission lines in the hot summer sun is very much higher.

WORKING WITH SCIENCE

1. Experiment with measuring the conductivity of different substances. Connect a lamp in a circuit so that the circuit remains incomplete unless a gap is bridged by a conductor. Test the conductivity of some of the following in a 110-volt circuit:

Solids	Liquids	Gases
iron	water	air
copper	weak acid	
lead	weak base	
graphite	salt solution	
wood	gasoline	
porcelain		
silver		

2. Connect different lamps and a heating coil in simple circuits. Measure the voltage and amperage across the device, using a voltmeter and ammeter. **Caution**: *Always connect a voltmeter in parallel with the lamps or heating coil; connect an ammeter in series.* Does the electric potential change in the circuit?

Does the amount of current used vary with each device?

3. Examine lamps and various electric appliances. On each you will usually find some indication of current requirements as "110 volts, 500 watts." From the data compute the current (amperes) used by each device. Which household devices use the most current?

4. From the data you have obtained by looking at appliances, make a list of different devices and the length of time you can use them for 1 kilowatt-hour of electricity. For example, a 100-watt lamp can operate 10 hours; a 1000-watt heater, for 1 hour; and so forth.

5. Using a voltmeter and ammeter, make current measurements on devices in simple circuits as in Exercise 2 above. From the information you gather, compute the resistance of the device, using Ohm's law. Make a list of common devices in order of their increasing resistance.

TRANSMITTING ELECTRIC CURRENT

From long experience, engineers have found that a current of 110 or 115 volts is most satisfactory for home or small industrial use. The potential, or push, is not great enough to be dangerous if proper care is taken, but it is sufficient to operate small motors, heaters, lights, and other devices quite effectively. As a result, 110-volt current is widely used, and most common electric appliances are made for it.

TRANSMISSION PROBLEMS

It might seem proper to have 110-volt generators at our big power plants and send the current they produce through transmission lines to homes and factories. However, the large generators produce currents of several thousand amperes. The resistance that such a current would meet in even the heaviest wires would be so great that the wires would melt.

The only way a current of 110-volts and several thousand amperes could be distributed would be through heavy bars of copper or silver. The cost would be prohibitive and the current dangerous. The alternative would be to have many small generators for every home or group of homes.

The first electric generators were small, and they could only supply current to houses within a few blocks of the generating plant. Imagine what a city such as New York would be like if it were necessary to have a power plant in every other block.

A very high voltage and low amperage are preferred for sending current over great distances with the lowest loss resulting from

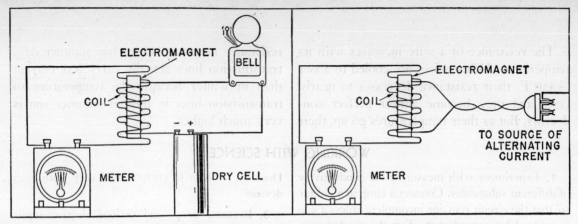

Two ways of changing the voltage of a current. What kind of current is produced?

resistance. But generators cannot be made to produce extremely high voltages since such currents are hard to insulate and the generators would short circuit. Besides, high-voltage currents are dangerous and have only a limited use. Thus, we see that a current that can be generated most efficiently cannot be transmitted well. In addition, a current that can be transmitted most efficiently cannot be generated easily.

Solving the Problem. This seems to be an impossible situation. But it is not. The solution of the problem lies in another device that operates by electromagnetic induction. It is a simple device, too, and probably you already realize its importance.

A magnet moving in a coil of wire induces a current in the coil. If the motion stops, so does the current. If we could dispense with the movement and still induce a current, we could effect a real saving. A method of doing this has been found.

If an electromagnet is placed within a coil of wire, a galvanometer shows that a current is induced in the coil as soon as the electromagnet is connected to the battery. The galvanometer needle moves when the connection is made. But the needle quickly returns to zero, showing that even though the electromagnet is operating, no more current is induced. But disconnect the electromagnet and as you take the wire from the battery, you will notice that another current is momentarily induced. If you keep making and breaking the

circuit, you will induce a current in the coil each time you do so.

Why is the current induced? Before the electromagnet is connected to the battery, it is not a magnet at all. It is just another coil inside a larger coil. As soon as the battery contact is made, current flows through the electromagnet, and the magnetic field begins to form. It takes only the tiniest fraction of a second for this to happen, but during this time the magnetic field *spreads out* from the poles of the electromagnet. As it spreads, it cuts across the wires of the larger coil.

When you break the circuit, the magnetic field *contracts* and disappears. The field shrinks across the wires of the coil, cutting them again. Every making and breaking of the circuit is the equivalent of moving the electromagnet, because the magnetic field cuts across the wires of the coil. But if you leave the electromagnet connected, the magnetic field forms and then does not change. Since there is no more cutting of the coil by the magnetic field, current is not generated.

CURRENT INTERRUPTERS

It is not necessary to make and break the circuit by hand. This can be done mechanically. Connect an electric bell or buzzer in series with the electromagnet so that the current from the battery must go through *both* to complete the circuit. This device will automatically make and break the circuit many times per second. The bell does this as its vibrator moves back and forth.

Engineers go this device one better. Instead of using direct current from a battery and a bell to interrupt it, they use alternating current, which cuts itself off and turns itself on twice in every cycle. This is 120 times per second for 60-cycle current. Sending an alternating current through the electromagnet is the equivalent of turning the current on and off rapidly. Thus, the current in the coil is generated, in effect, continually.

We now know how to induce a current without moving magnets as in a generator. This is an important step. One more step and we will have the solution to our electric power problem.

TRANSFORMERS AND HOW THEY WORK

The voltage of an induced electric current depends on the number of wires cutting the magnetic field. An armature with many turns of wire will produce a higher voltage than one with fewer turns. If we put an electromagnet into a coil that has only a few turns of wire, we will induce a current of relatively low voltage. If the coil has many turns of wire, the voltage will be greatly increased. This fact is of great significance, since it gives us a way to control the voltage of an induced current by inducing the current in either a larger or a smaller coil of wire.

We can now combine the electromagnet and the coil in an instrument to change voltage and current. Take a bar of iron or a large nail bent into a U-shape. Around one arm of the U, wind 20 turns of bell wire. Connect this coil to a source of low-voltage alternating current, such as a model train transformer, or to a low-voltage direct current with an interrupter. Using thinner wire, wind 200 turns on the other arm of the U. Connect this to an alternating current voltmeter or to a lamp.

The instrument you have made is a *transformer*. It transforms current. If we send a 6-volt alternating current into the electromagnet's 20-turn side, we will get an alternating current of about 60 volts out of the 200-turn

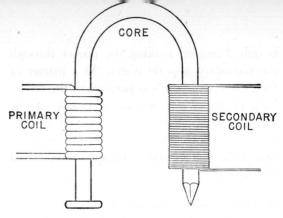

A simple transformer is easy to make.

side. The wire on the second side of the transformer has 10 times as many turns as the first. Since 10 times as many wires cut the magnetic field, the voltage is stepped up 10 times, that is, from 6 to 60. If we reverse the connections and send the 6-volt current through the 200-turn coil, the current induced in the 20-turn coil is about 0.6 volts or $\frac{1}{10}$ the original.

The winding of the transformer through which the original current flows is called the *primary* of the transformer. The winding from which the induced current is taken is called the *secondary*. In our transformer we sent 6 volts into the primary and took about 60 out of the secondary. However, do not think that we increased the amount of the electric current and got something for nothing. Not even a transformer can do that.

If our 6-volt current was of *10 amperes*, the power through the primary was 60 watts. The 60-volt current taken from the secondary

From generator to home involves step-downs.

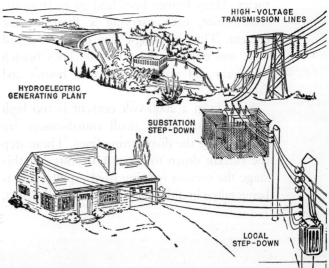

HIGH-VOLTAGE TRANSMISSION LINES

HYDROELECTRIC GENERATING PLANT

SUBSTATION STEP-DOWN

LOCAL STEP-DOWN

is only *1 ampere*, making the power through the secondary also 60 watts. As a matter of fact, there will be a loss because of the resistance of the wires and arrangement of the magnetic fields. You never get out of a transformer as much energy as you put in, even though the voltage and amperage can be raised or lowered.

MODERN POWER TRANSMISSION

Now we are ready to see how electrical engineers solve the problem of power transmission. Consider a waterfall in the mountains where a hydroelectric plant with a large generator has been built. The generator produces a current of about 8000 volts at 200 amperes. This amounts to 1,600,000 watts of power. The 200-ampere current would be too much for the transmission line, so we pass this current through a 1:20 transformer.

The transformer increases the voltage 20 times to 160,000 volts and reduces the strength of the current to 10 amperes. This current is sent out over the transmission lines. By using large porcelain insulators and spacing the wires far apart, this high-voltage current is kept from jumping from the wire to the poles and hence to the ground.

As the transmission line nears a city, where such a high-voltage current might be dangerous, it passes through a step-down transformer of 80:1 ratio. This brings the current down to 2000 volts and increases the amperage to 800. At this substation, the current is divided and sent in various directions to nearby factories. Many branch lines lead away from the transformer, each carrying a share of the current. Thus, no single line carries the full load, and every little while the lines branch off again and send current into homes and factories.

Since even a 2000-volt current is too high for most use, many small transformers are strung along the distributing lines. These step the current down to about 110 volts. At this stage the current is being used rapidly, and is being taken in different amounts by industries, public buildings, homes, stores, and so forth.

The use of step-up and step-down transformers enables us to send current a distance of 100 miles or more with little loss. The city, miles from the waterfall, could not have used this hydroelectric power if it had not been for the transformer and the transmission system. The power from Hoover Dam is stepped up to 287,000 volts, and this superhigh voltage is carried more than 200 miles before it is used.

The power lines you see threading their way across the country carry 2300 volts or more. The larger transmission lines with their tall steel towers may carry current in the neighborhood of 100,000 to 200,000 volts.

Electric energy can be transmitted more cheaply and faster than any other kind of energy. If we want to transmit heat energy, we must heat some liquid or gas, which we can send through a pipe. For a longer distance we must ship the fuel and convert it into heat energy on the spot. Electric energy is far more flexible. We can send it wherever we can string a wire. We can send it through wires hanging in the air or buried under the ground.

HIGH-VOLTAGE PROBLEMS

The imposing transmission lines that loop their way from the giant generators to the big cities are troublesome affairs. When electricity has a push of 100,000 or 200,000 volts, it is capable of much mischief. This is because currents under such pressure will flow through substances that are ordinarily insulators. The power lines cannot be insulated by coating the wire with rubber or cotton. Nothing that you can wrap around the wire would insulate such voltages. You may have noticed the long porcelain insulators that are needed to keep the current in the wires where it belongs.

The wires of the power lines are $\frac{1}{2}$ to $\frac{3}{4}$ inch in diameter and to reduce their weight are often made of aluminum instead of copper. The largest power lines consist of flexible pipes—hollow tubes conduct the current just as well as solid wires.

WORKING WITH SCIENCE

1. Using the electromagnet that you made earlier, see whether you can induce a current in a coil. The coil can be made from a piece of mailing tube about 8 inches long around which 100 or more turns of wire have been wrapped. Connect the coil to a galvanometer and see if you can induce a current in the coil.

2. Connect your electromagnet to an electric bell. See if the current induced in the coil is more continuous than in Exercise 1.

3. Look up an account of some of the early generating plants, as described in the life of Edison. What were some of the difficulties in running the first direct-current generators?

4. Make a transformer by winding 20 turns of bell wire around a large spike for the primary. Tape this coil in place and wind 200 turns of finer wire over it for the secondary. Test this transformer with batteries and an interrupter.

5. You will find transformers in many unexpected places. Notice a transformer is connected to every neon sign to step up the voltage to a high level. Your radio includes several transformers. Your home may have a bell-ringing transformer or you may have one for an electric train. Make a list of all the transformers you can locate, and from the data plates on each, record the ratio of primary to secondary windings.

6. If a "high line" passes nearby, find out where it starts and where it ends. How high a voltage does it carry? What are some of the problems encountered in transmitting such current?

7. You may be able to find accounts of making artificial lightning for use in high-voltage experiments. Your class will be interested in the accounts of how this high-voltage current is made and what results have come from the many experiments that have been carried out with it.

USING ELECTRICITY FOR BETTER LIVING

We have very little direct use for electric energy. Electricity becomes useful to us chiefly as we convert it to other kinds of energy—light, sound, heat, or motion. Most of all, we convert electricity into rotary motion to operate machinery.

Scarcely a home today does not have at least one electric motor. Many homes have a dozen or more. Count them—refrigerator, vacuum cleaner, washing machine, electric clock, electric shaver, perhaps a pump, a fan or two, and a mixer in the kitchen. If you have a modern oil-burner or a coal furnace with forced draft, an electric motor is part of it, too. You may have an electric drill or other power tools if you have a workshop. The starter in the family car is a motor, too.

HOW A MOTOR WORKS

An electric motor is not difficult to understand. It is very much like a generator. In a generator, a coil of wire moves in a magnetic field, producing electricity. In a motor, electricity is sent through a coil of wire in a magnetic field, producing motion. Some of the

earlier motors were often reversed and used as generators. Now we make them more efficient by designing each for its own purpose.

A highly oversimplified motor consists of a magnetic compass and a magnet. If you put the south pole of your magnet near the north-seeking end of the compass, the compass needle is repelled and pushed away. If you follow the needle with your magnet, you can

The water turbines of hydro-electric generating plants produce electric current at about 8000 volts. Before this current reaches the home it is stepped up at least once and then stepped down several times. Why are these voltage changes necessary?

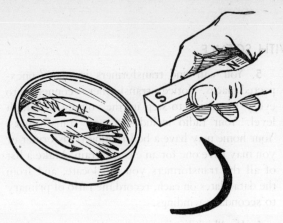

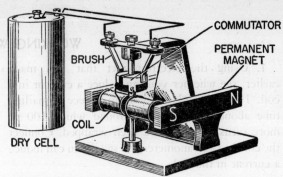

BRUSH
COMMUTATOR
PERMANENT MAGNET
COIL
N
S
DRY CELL

Left: A highly oversimplified electric motor. Right: A laboratory motor. Why is the commutator necessary?

keep it spinning around and around. In a sense, this is a simple motor. The needle is constantly repelled by a rotating magnetic field.

A series of electromagnets so connected that the magnetic field rotates is more practical than our moving magnet. An armature consisting of such electromagnets will rotate continuously in a magnetic field. The magnetic fields can, of course, be formed by electromagnets instead of permanent ones.

Does this sound familiar? It is very much like the problem of the direct-current generator. We can build a motor that consists of several electromagnets arranged in a circular field with an armature rotating within them. We can put a commutator on this armature and connect it to a battery. At each turn of the armature, the current will be reversed and the polarity of that part of the armature will change also. The armature will be constantly repelled and attracted by the electromagnets (*field magnets*) and will keep spinning as long as current is supplied.

When we use alternating current, it is

How many kilowatt-hours does this meter read?
From Encyclopaedia Britannica film Elements of Electrical Circuits

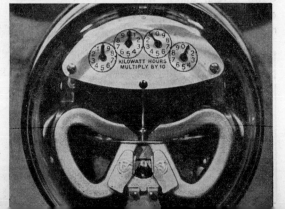

possible to get along without the commutator in some forms of motors. If the alternating current is connected to the field magnets, the automatic reversal of the alternating current will induce a current in the armature. The reversal of the current in the field coils produces the effect of rotating the magnetic field. Hence, the armature also rotates, following the rotating magnetic field but never moving quite as fast as the field does. As a result, the changing magnetic field is continually cutting the wires of the armature and inducing a current in it. Such a motor is called, as you would expect, an *induction motor*.

KINDS OF MOTORS

There are many kinds of motors. We can mention only a few. A *synchronous motor* is very similar to an alternating-current generator. It operates at fixed speed, regardless of its mechanical output. Besides being used for production of electricity, a synchronous motor can be used in relaying information. As such it is used in submarines and airplanes to transmit directions from a master compass to auxiliary instruments. Synchronous motors are also used in electric clocks.

Electric Meters. An electric meter with its revolving disk is a small induction motor. The motor turns dials that show the amount of electricity being used. The speed of this motor is proportional to the current used, but the motor itself uses very little current.

A kilowatt-hour meter is easy to read. As you look at the meter the dial on the left indicates the number of thousands of kilowatt-hours. The next dial to the right indicates the number of hundreds of kilowatt-hours. The second dial from the right indicates the number of tens of kilowatt-hours. The dial at the extreme right indicates the number of units of kilowatt-hours. These four digits are combined to obtain a number, as for example 1352 kilowatt-hours.

Such a meter must be read on two occasions to find out how much electricity has been used. In most cases the meters are read each month. To find out how much electricity has been used the reading at the beginning of the period of use is subtracted from the reading at the end of the period. The difference is the number of kilowatt-hours of electricity used.

Motor-Generators. Motors and generators are sometimes built together in one housing and used to transform one kind of electric current into another. For example, a 110-volt alternating-current motor is mounted on the same shaft as a 6-volt direct-current generator, or a 12-volt direct-current motor may operate a 220-volt alternating-current generator. As the motor turns, it operates the generator. Such an arrangement of motor and generator is called a *motor-generator*. Special currents to meet a great variety of needs can be generated on the spot by the use of motor-generators.

Electric motors are made in literally thousands of different sizes. Some use only a small fraction of an ampere of current—for example, motors in electric meters. Others operate heavy machinery and use more current than an entire small town. Special motors are built for airplanes so that a very small light motor can operate rudders, flaps, and other controls.

The use of electricity is not at all confined to motors, even though motors are the principal consumers of electric current. As our standard of living increases and more and more people share the benefits of science, more and more small electric motors will be used in the home: to keep us cool in summer and warm in winter, wash the dishes, help iron our clothes, dispose of the garbage, and keep us entertained.

ELECTRICITY AND HEAT

Electricity is easily converted into heat. To do so the current is sent through material which is a poor conductor of electricity. Certain alloys meet this specification exactly. As the current passes through them, it is effectively converted into heat. The heating unit may be in an electric iron, stove, electric blanket, hot-water heater, soldering iron, hot pad, or embedded in walls or floors for use in radiant heating.

ELECTRICITY AND LIGHT

For more than 60 years now we have obtained light by heating a piece of high-resistance tungsten wire, or *filament*, in an evacuated bulb. Electricity heats it so hot that it glows with white heat and gives us light. Such lamps are called *incandescent lamps*. The electric light is probably *the* greatest electric convenience, and one that is enjoyed by the most people. Even so, in 1947 hundreds of thousands of families living in the United States could not afford to use electricity even for lighting or lived in areas without electricity.

Electric lights have been continually improved so that they use less current and give more light. They are indispensable to us. But we realize that the ordinary electric light has many shortcomings. It is very inefficient— far more heat than light is produced. The color is too yellow, and glare is a problem. Filament lamps are not the final answer to our lighting problems.

The new *fluorescent lamps* are a great improvement in many ways. They not only give better light but operate at lower cost for the amount of light produced. These lights produce invisible ultraviolet light as the electric current passes through an evacuated tube containing a small amount of mercury vapor. The ultraviolet light causes the fluorescent

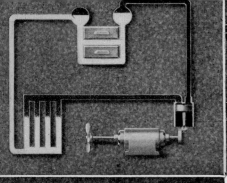

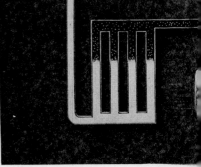

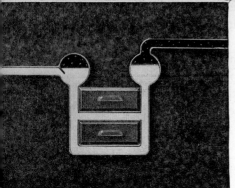

From Encyclopaedia Britannica film Home Electrical Appliances

An electric motor changes electric energy into mechanical energy. In an electric refrigerator, the mechanical energy is used to pump heat out of the refrigerator. A simplified but complete refrigerator system is shown above at the left. The electric motor turns a compressor and a fan. In compressing the refrigerating gas, as shown in the middle drawing, heat is produced. This heat is removed and the refrigerating gas is condensed in the condenser, as shown above at the right. In the evaporator at the left, the refrigerating liquid expands and changes back into a gas. This absorbs heat and cools the interior of the refrigerator. The heat pumped from inside is released to the air in the room.

material with which the inside of the lamp tube is coated to glow. A soft illumination is the result. Very little heat is produced and, for general lighting, these lamps are a real improvement over filament lamps.

X-RAYS AND CYCLOTRONS

Even newer uses of electricity lie in creating kinds of "light" that are invisible to the human eye, but which are, nevertheless, exceedingly important. By the use of transformers that create currents up to 4 million volts, it is possible to operate *x-ray tubes* of extraordinary strength. This high voltage sends a stream of electrons against a metal target. The electrons strike the target with such energy that they produce the invisible radiations known as *x-rays*.

Everyone knows that x-rays will pass through human flesh and, hence, are used in medicine. Many do not know that x-rays can be used to "see" inside heavy steel castings and other metal articles to discover flaws or weaknesses that might otherwise pass unnoticed. The industrial use of x-rays is a new and important use and one that is increasing every day.

Another use for high-voltage current is in the remarkable instrument, the *cyclotron*. The cyclotron is used to bombard atoms and study their structure. Voltages of 50,000 or more are applied to the machine. These start atomic particles moving at ever-increasing speeds, and by the time the particles have gone through the machine, each particle may have a push of 5 million volts or more.

Electricity is widely used in the science of *electronics*. Radio, radar, television, and many other kinds of electronic devices are operated by electric currents. Nearly all of these instruments include transformers, which step the alternating current up or down to the different voltages required for the operation of the electronic device.

ELECTRICITY FOR TOMORROW

Electricity is our most flexible kind of energy. It is easily produced, easily transmitted, and can be used in a greater variety of ways than any other form of energy. In many ways it is ideal, and we cannot see anything in the future that will take its place. One great use of atomic energy can be in the production of low-cost electricity. New inventions and discoveries will make more electricity available and show us new uses for it.

WORKING WITH SCIENCE

1. Make a list of all the electric motors in your home and the use of each. If you can locate the plate on the motor, find its power rating. What is the largest motor you use at home? the smallest?

2. Illustrate the laws of magnetic attraction and repulsion by use of compass and two bar magnets. This is the principle on which motors operate.

3. Make a toy motor out of nails, cork, and wire. Operate the motor on one or two dry-cells. What type of motor is the one you made? Directions can be found in a number of books on electricity that you can find in the library.

4. Report to class on the number and kinds of motors used in a large aircraft, such as a DC-4 or Constellation. Such information may be obtained from books and magazine articles.

5. Make a list of, and observe if possible, many different kinds of electric heating appliances from hot pads and electric blankets to welding outfits. Find out how much current each uses.

6. Get samples of pictures of different types of filament lamps, and find the use for which each type is intended. Such an exhibit will be an interest-

Courtesy General Electric Company

An industrial x-ray unit.

ing one for your classroom. You should be able to exhibit at least 50 kinds.

7. Measure the resistance of 40-, 60-, and 100-watt lamps, using the voltmeter-ammeter method described on page 336.

8. Demonstrate the action of fluorescent lights, using a spark coil operated by dry batteries as a source of current.

READING YOU WILL ENJOY

Harrison, George R. *How Things Work: Science for Young Americans*. William Morrow & Co., New York, 1941. An authentic source book that takes up many questions, including machines, engines, and power.

Manchester, Harland. *New World of Machines*. Random House, New York, 1945. A book on recent discoveries which shows new ways that energy is transformed and applied.

Neill, Humphrey B. *Forty-Eight Million Horses*. J. B. Lippincott Co., Philadelphia, 1940. The story of electricity pictured through the development of one of our largest manufacturers of electrical equipment. Emphasis on power and the uses of electric energy.

Potter, Robert D. *The Atomic Revolution*. Robert M. McBride & Co., New York, 1946. Includes much clearly presented, well-organized information on atomic energy and the ways it may be obtained and used.

Reck, Franklin M. and Claire. *Power from Start to Finish*. Thomas Y. Crowell Co., New York, 1941. A detailed and well-illustrated story of power from the earliest days up to the atomic age. Explanations of all types of engines and how the power from them is used.

Samuels, Maurice M. *Power Unleashed*. Dorset House, Inc., New York, 1944. An experienced engineer describes how electricity is made and used. A book for adults, but a student interested in electrical engineering will find it very worthwhile.

Yates, Raymond F. *A Boy and a Motor*. Harper & Bros., New York, 1944. A good source of experiments and games to show the relation between electricity and magnetism.

Yates, Raymond F. *The Boys' Book of Magnetism*. Harper & Bros., New York, 1941. A brief history of the development of electric motors and directions for building simple motors.

1

2

When early man made something, his measurements, if any, were not very accurate. Since he usually made only one article at a time, each article was different from every other article like it. In this respect production did not change much until almost the beginning of the nineteenth century. Most things were made one at a time by hand. As a result, the parts of one musket, for example, would not fit any other musket (1). For repair, a new part had to be made.

Eli Whitney, an American inventor, helped change our methods of making things. Whitney decided that a lot of problems could be solved by making things exactly alike so that the parts of one would fit another. His particular problem was the making of 10,000 muskets for the United States Army. Whitney was successful (2). Exact measurements made his success possible. Parts produced in this way are called standardized parts. They are so exactly alike that when one part breaks, the broken part can be replaced with another just like it.

Nearly everything we buy today is made of standardized parts. Consequently, continual checking of measurements is necessary as parts are made. This checking has brought into being many kinds of gages used by workmen and inspectors (3). Measurements made with gages such as these make it possible for you to buy a new part for your car at the local garage (4), rather than having a new part made.

3

4

Time, Measurement, and Mass Production

26

PRECISION MEASUREMENT FOR MODERN SCIENCE

A great bombing plane lifts itself from the earth and roars away. Over the target, the bombardier rather than the pilot flies the plane. The bombsight, through which the bombardier sights the target, moves the control surfaces on the wings, tail, and rudder of the plane as the bombardier tilts and turns the bombsight.

Suppose you are the bombardier in that plane. You are flying 300 miles an hour and getting near the target. Three hundred miles an hour is 440 feet—more than two city blocks—per second.

If the plane is flying 30,000 feet above the ground, the time required for the bombs to fall (disregarding wind resistance) is a bit more than 43 seconds. But, as your plane and the bombs are traveling forward at the rate of 440 feet per second, the bombs continue to travel forward, while dropping, for about 3.6 miles from the time you release them until they hit the target. You must release the bombs in a split second, at some precise point 3.6 miles before you reach the target. The bombsight does the figuring if you set such factors as your speed and height, and direction and speed of the wind into the mechanism.

PRECISION DEMANDS IN MODERN PRODUCTION

The accuracy required of the bombardier is far less than that required in the manufacture of the bombsight he uses. If your plane were traveling at 300 miles per hour at 20,000 feet, you would miss your target by several hundred yards if any of the tiny balls in the *bearings* that support the bombsight and enable it to tilt and turn were "out of round" or had scratches more than 0.000010 (ten millionths) inch deep.

There are six of these balls in a bearing. They must be round to within 0.00001 inch greater or less than $\frac{3}{32}$ inch in diameter. And each of these tiny bearing balls must be able to stand a pressure of 300,000 pounds per square inch! That is another kind of accuracy —far more important to all of us than accuracy in bombing.

PRODUCTION AND CHECKING OF TOLERANCE

In the example of the bearing balls, variations of more than 0.00001 inch greater or less than the exact size are not allowable. Allowable variations are called *tolerances*. In this case the tolerance is 0.00002 inch, the total from the *upper limit* of 0.00001 inch greater than desired to the *lower limit* of 0.00001 inch less than desired. How is such

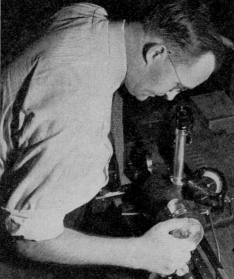

Courtesy SKF Industries, Inc.

Left: An electrolimit gage used in checking tolerances of precision-made bearing balls. Middle: A special gage used in checking tolerances of bearing races. Right: Very accurate gage blocks are used in checking the gages that check the tolerances of bearing parts.

accuracy produced and how are the bearing balls checked? The story is fascinating, and the production and checking of these bearing balls are typical examples of precision production.

Before 1940 tolerances of 0.0001 inch were common in precision machinery. But many new devices demanded much greater precision. All modern machinery moves on roller or ball bearings. These tiny rollers or balls rest snugly between axles and the wheels that rotate on them and, in general, lie between all moving parts. Thus, mechanical parts do not rub or slide over one another. The tiny balls or

This device sorts bearing rollers into six size groups differing by only 0.00002 inch.

Courtesy SKF Industries, Inc.

rollers allow them to *roll* over one another with a minimum of wear.

Even your bicycle requires bearings. Its axles would wear out in a few weeks if it were not for the smooth balls in the bearings which roll along between the wheel and axle.

But the tolerances of 0.0001 inch—which were sufficient for most machinery—were not good enough for modern aircraft engines and certainly not for bombsights. The designers of the bombsight wanted it so accurately balanced that it would turn and tilt if breathed on from a distance of 2.5 feet! They got it, too! How was the job done and checked?

CONTROL OF THE ALLOY

The first requirement was an alloy steel of the highest and most uniform quality. The tiniest flakes, pits, or differences in composition of the metal would make the bombsight worthless! A satisfactory alloy steel was developed after long years of effort.

Every batch of steel that arrives at a ball-bearing plant is carefully sampled and checked to be sure that it meets the rigid specifications set. The steel is checked under powerful microscopes and x-rays that show up the slightest flaws.

348

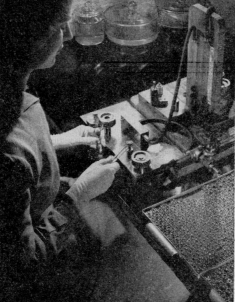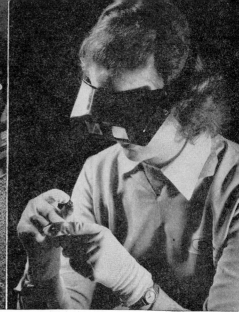

Courtesy SKF Industries, Inc.

Left: Bombsight ball bearings are so small that they are lubricated with a hypodermic needle by a worker wearing lint-free gloves. Middle: Testing how easily an assembled bearing turns by means of an air stream. Right: Inspecting a bearing for surface defects with magnifiying goggles.

SHAPING THE BALL

Then a wire of approved steel of proper size is fed into a forming machine that automatically cuts off pieces and feeds them between cup-like dies to give them a ball shape. When a sufficient number of these are formed, they are run through "filing" machines that remove excess metal, including the "flash" band caused by the pressing operation. Next, the "filed" balls are transferred to machines that grind them between grooved wheels, one of which is stationary, until they are uniform in size and comparatively round. As the one wheel turns, the balls rotate thousands upon thousands of times, removing excess material and surface defects.

Then the balls are placed in large tumbling barrels, immersed in a mixture of cutting powders and water, and tumbled, depending upon size and quantity, from 30 to 40 hours. This makes the balls smoother and reduces them to the size required for heat treating.

The balls are then heated to approximately 1500°F and immediately cooled in oil to give them the hardness and strength they must have. They then go to another precision grinder using finer wheels. Tests show that the balls at this stage are only about 0.00004 inch from desired size.

Finally, the balls are rolled for about 20 hours between two grooved wheels with polishing powder and oil. This operation, known as *lapping*, polishes the balls and brings them to within the 0.00002-inch tolerance allowable.

CHECKING ALONG THE WAY

But how do we know that these balls will be so accurate in shape and smoothness? At every stage in their manufacture, samples are taken and measured with precision gages.

Each inspector has a chart with lines on it to indicate the tolerances allowed. In this instance, there would be a line indicating a 0.00001-inch bump as the upper limit and another indicating a 0.00001-inch scratch as the lower limit. Such a chart is called a *quality control chart*. As the inspector takes samples at random, he measures them with precision instruments and records the roundness of each sample ball on the chart by a dot.

From the chart the inspector knows that the chances are good that all of the balls from which he had taken his samples are within the tolerance limits set. However, suppose he finds one sample ball that exceeds the upper tolerance limit. He would immediately throw out the entire batch of balls from which the sample was taken.

Sometimes an inspector finds that each sample ball he examines seems to be a little closer to the tolerance limits than the one before it. Under such circumstances, the inspector would undoubtedly have all the machinery used in producing the balls checked, for it would appear that some part or parts of the machinery were becoming worn and would soon allow the balls being produced to exceed the tolerance limits. By repairing the machinery *before* the samples are beyond the tolerance limits, a tremendous amount of time and material is saved.

FINAL INSPECTION

Sample inspection, as described, is ordinarily sufficient for most kinds of equipment and materials. It is used extensively in modern manufacturing. But every bearing ball for a bombsight must have its own final inspection.

After the balls have had a final sampling inspection, and all manufacturing operations have been completed, they are taken into a room for a final inspection of every ball for roundness, diameter and surface defects. The temperature in this room is kept constant and the humidity controlled since any change in temperature would cause a change in the size of the balls and high humidity would cause rust. Precision gages and microscopes are used in checking the balls in this department. The balls are now ready to be fitted into their ring-like *races* to form a completed ball bearing.

THE MACHINES THAT MAKE THE MACHINES

A bombsight is a marvelously adjusted combination of simple levers and inclined planes combined with optical systems and electric devices. Essentially, each part of the bombsight is simple. But the way these simple parts fit and work together is far from simple.

The manufacture of only one tiny part of the total bombsight has been discussed here. The machines that grind and polish these ball bearings are marvels of ingenuity and precision. The machines behind the bombsight form a more complex pattern of precision-made parts than their product.

But that is not the end of the matter. Someone had to make the machines that make the bearing balls for the bombsight. The *tool-making machines* that did this job were, in themselves, precise and complicated. Finally, behind the tool-making machines are the simple machines, such as levers in the form of wrenches, screwdrivers, and hammers, and inclined planes in the form of bits, knives, saws, gages, screws, and so forth. In other words, behind all of the machinery of modern science and production are the simple machines of which all machines are composed and with which man will continue to make more and more complex machines.

WORKING WITH SCIENCE

1. Observe the wide use of bearings in modern machinery. Check bicycles, washing machines, roller skates, electric motors, automobiles, and similar common devices. Where direct inspection is not possible, use diagrams.

2. Arrange for a trip to a machine shop and observe the use of precision gages in the machin-

ist's work. Report to the class on the gages used.

3. Study the ball-bearing action of a bicycle wheel or a skate wheel as the wheel rotates. Remove the ball bearings and study their action in more detail. Note how the balls change a sliding motion to a rolling motion. Can you explain how this lowers friction?

INTERCHANGEABLE PARTS

The tolerances of the bombsight ball bearings are about as small as can be produced in machine production at present. But even the tolerances of the parts of your automobile are extremely small. For example, diameters of piston pins, pistons, cylinders, valves, steering-knuckle pivots, crankshafts, and camshafts are generally made to a tolerance of 0.001 inch.

Very small tolerances are required for the long-lasting, fast-operating machinery of modern life. But the chief reason for such precise measurement in modern production lies in the very nature of modern production. This is illustrated by the story of Eli Whitney, inventor of the cotton gin and—of far greater importance—one of the first men to make parts that could be interchanged.

ELI WHITNEY AND HIS GUNS

Eli Whitney had a streak of hard luck. Probably you know that he invented a cotton gin that removed the seeds from cotton with a great saving of time and labor. But he received little money from his invention because others infringed on his patents.

In 1795 when Whitney was deeply in debt, some of his friends secured a contract for him to manufacture 10,000 muskets for the United States Army. Up to that time, firearms had been manufactured largely by hand. Each trigger, firing pin, breech, and barrel had to be produced and fitted, with much filing and shaping, to each other piece of the gun. For example, a trigger was made to fit a gun by a slow process of filing, fitting, filing, and fitting. When finished, it worked well enough in that particular gun but would not fit in other guns of the same general pattern, for no two triggers were ever exactly the same size and shape.

Whitney had a deadline to meet. The government wanted all 10,000 guns by a certain date. But Whitney had produced only a few hundred guns, and the deadline loomed dangerously near. His friends became worried. What had he been doing with his time? How was he to finish all of the guns in the short time remaining?

Whitney had not been loafing. He had been doing some important thinking and experimenting. It had occurred to him that if he could produce 10,000 triggers exactly alike, and 10,000 breeches exactly alike, and 10,000 exact copies of all other parts of the gun, a tremendous saving in time would result. For such *standardized parts* would be *interchangeable*. The long hours of filing and fitting parts together would be saved. Workers could then take any trigger from a large stock-pile and fit it into the rest of a gun made of other standardized and interchangeable parts.

Perhaps it would be possible to build machines to make each standardized part so that handwork would be necessary only in assembling the parts. Almost as important—ran Whitney's thinking—if a soldier should break the trigger or any other part of a gun made of standardized parts, it would not be necessary to spend long hours shaping and filing a replacement. *Spare parts*—a totally new idea then—could be kept near at hand and replacement made quickly.

Not only had Whitney thought this problem through (he borrowed some ideas from the British), but he had been spending most of his time inventing the machines and setting up a factory to produce such standardized parts.

Whitney asked for a meeting with the Washington representatives of the War Department to explain his work and its advantages to them. It must have been a dramatic meeting! Whitney talked with the men for a few minutes and then produced an almost-finished gun. He threw down a handful of triggers. "Pick out one," he said, "and I'll finish putting the gun together."

"Pick out one?" they echoed. "What are you talking about—only one of these triggers is the one made for that gun, surely!" But one was selected, and swiftly and easily Whitney fitted it into the gun. Then he replaced it with one after another of the triggers in the pile. He had demonstrated conclusively the value of standardized and interchangeable parts in manufacture.

ADVANTAGES OF STANDARDIZED PARTS

To us it seems most natural to take our automobiles, vacuum cleaners, fans, or what-

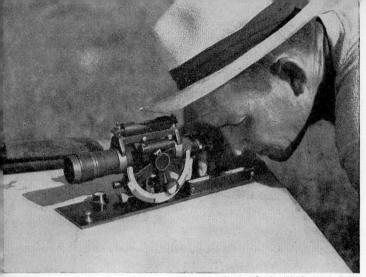

Mapping is made possible by accurate instruments for measuring angles and plotting distances.

careful work of hundreds of highly-skilled craftsmen, working for months. A car that now costs about $1800 would possibly cost 20 to 100 times that amount.

Few of us could afford such an automobile. Even if we all could afford one, it would not be possible to produce them, for enough men could not be taken from other work to make all the cars we need. But with standardized parts, a relatively small number of men—each with his particular job to do—can assemble a modern car in a matter of hours rather than months.

And we can expect speedy, efficient repair because of standardization. Your local garageman will have in stock a part identical to the part which must be replaced. It can be inserted with very little trouble. Think of the time wasted and the cost if he had to make that part by hand and fit it into your automobile.

Standardized Parts Demand Precise Measurements. These advantages would not be ours without the precision of measurement that modern science has made possible. To produce hundreds of thousands of automobile parts that do not vary more than 0.001 inch in diameter or automobile-engine parts that do not vary more than 0.0001 inch in diameter is quite a feat!

not to the repair station to have broken or worn parts replaced. But we have Eli Whitney to thank for introducing the idea to America and for providing the basis on which our modern factories turn out thousands of different products cheaply and dependably.

Imagine for a moment what it would cost to purchase a modern automobile if it were made largely by hand and by the slow and laborious process of fitting each part to the other parts. It would still be possible to have a fairly smooth-running car. But to produce the equivalent of a modern car would require the

WORKING WITH SCIENCE

1. Arrange a trip to an automobile garage. Observe the work of the mechanics and the stored spare parts ready for replacement in automobiles. If possible, watch valve-grinding operations or the

reboring of cylinder walls. Determine, from the mechanics doing the work, the tolerances to which they fit the parts they are working on. How do these tolerances affect the lubrication of a car?

HOW MEASUREMENT MAKES SCIENCE POSSIBLE

Modern production is not the only field where precise measurement is required. Measurement is the basis of almost all scientific work. It is not enough for a doctor to know that a small amount of a chemical injected into the human body will kill disease germs but not seriously harm the body, while a larger amount will kill the person into whom it is injected. A doctor must know *precisely* how much chemical he can inject with safety.

It is not enough to know that a "lot of voltage" is required to push electricity through a wire "of a pretty fair size" to produce the current required in a house—with no danger of fire to the house and its occupants. Voltage, current, and resistance must be determined exactly and surely. And so it goes. Science in action demands precision in measurement. And scientists have devised machines and instruments that make such precision possible.

SCIENTIFIC EXPERIMENTS DEMAND PRECISE MEASUREMENT

Suppose you plan to be a mechanical engineer. Someday you may have to design a great bridge to span a swift-flowing river. You have determined the strength of the materials and the design of the bridge. But you realize that the steel of the bridge will expand as it gets hot under the summer sun and will contract as it cools at night and during the winter. How much must you allow for expansion?

In an engineering handbook you turn to a table headed "Coefficient of Linear Expansion." Under this heading you find "Steel— 0.000013 per degree centigrade." This means that 1 foot of steel will expand 0.000013 of a foot for each degree centigrade increase in temperature. Now to determine how much the bridge will expand for each degree of temperature rise, multiply the total number of horizontal feet of steel by 0.000013. You can find the maximum change in temperature at that particular place from local records and add a few degrees for a margin of safety. Multiply the expansion per degree rise in temperature by this figure and you will know how much you must allow for expansion.

Very precise experiments were necessary to prepare the table you used. Bars of steel of various lengths and widths were placed in an apparatus such as the one shown below.

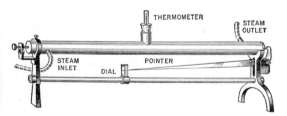

A coefficient-of-expansion apparatus.

Coefficient-of-Expansion Apparatus. This apparatus is so arranged that a bar of metal can be placed in the hollow tube. A gage at one end is turned until the metal touches the tip of the base at the gage end and the end of the lever at the other end. Water is heated in the flask and steam rushes through the rubber tubing and into the tube surrounding the bar of metal.

A thermometer in the tube enables the experimenter to read the temperature of the steam. The experimenter checks the temperature and the position of the pointer on the dial. Then he runs steam through the tube long enough to be sure that the bar of metal is evenly heated to the temperature of the steam. As the temperature rises, the bar expands. The slight expansion causes the bar to push on the end of the lever. Since the pivot, or fulcrum, is much nearer this end of the lever than the end that forms the pointer, a slight expansion of the bar causes a larger motion of the pointer, which can be read on the dial.

Let us say that the bar is steel exactly 1 foot long, and that the temperature change is 80°C. Suppose that the lever moves far enough to indicate 0.00104 foot expansion. By dividing this number by the number of degrees (80 in this example) the *coefficient of expansion* of this steel is, as you see, 0.000013 per degree centigrade.

Many such experiments—using far more exact apparatus—have shown that, regardless of the shape, length, or width of this kind of steel, a temperature change of 1°C will produce 0.000013 of a foot expansion or contraction for each foot of the steel. An engineer can work successfully by knowing such precise figures on the strength, expansion, and so forth of construction materials.

Chemistry Balance. You may decide to take a course in chemistry someday soon. In chemistry you will find another example of the necessity of precise measurement in scientific work. For example, you may want to know how much oxygen combines with a certain amount of magnesium in forming magnesium oxide. To do this you will need to weigh accurately the dish in which the magnesium is burned, the magnesium you will use, and the magnesium oxide that forms when magnesium burns. You will weigh the dish, then the dish and the magnesium. You will then heat the dish strongly until all of the magnesium has burned. From this you will be able to determine the original weight of the magnesium, the weight of the magnesium oxide, and from this the weight of the oxygen which combined with the magnesium.

WORKING WITH SCIENCE

1. Find out if there is a scientific laboratory in your community. Many factories and industries maintain scientific laboratories in connection with their work. If one is located near you, arrange a trip to see the precision work that goes on in the laboratory.

SYSTEMS OF MEASUREMENT

In order to make measurements there must first be a unit to compare with and a tool with which to make the comparison. If you want to tell someone exactly how long a table is, you do not say, "Well, it is longer than I am, but not quite as long as a horse." Even if you were so inexact, you would be using units, or *standards*, of measurement. Your height and the length of a horse would be the standards.

Some of the old standards of measurement are about as inexact as the example just given. Horses used to be measured, and still are in many cases, by how many "hands" high they were. The unit of measurement was the width of a human hand. Obviously, this standard varies and is not accurate enough for general usage.

THE ENGLISH SYSTEM

You are already familiar with the *English system* of measurement. Distance is measured in inches, feet, yards, and miles. Weight is measured in ounces, pounds, and tons. Volume is measured in fluid ounces, pints, quarts, and gallons; also in cubic inches, cubic feet, and so forth.

The English system is used extensively only in the United States and England at the present time. The reason for not using it elsewhere is good. Did you ever try to change inches into yards, or determine the number of cubic inches in a gallon? Figuring with the English system requires much arithmetic.

THE METRIC SYSTEM

The *metric system* is used in most countries except England and the United States and it is used for scientific work everywhere. This system was developed in France during the time of the French Revolution. It is a decimal system—based on multiples of 10—and is very easy to use. You know how easy it is, for we use a system based on 10's in our money "measurement."

If you are asked how many cents or how many dimes there are in a dollar, you immediately know the answers. You know these answers because our money system is based upon the decimal system and the decimal point is simply moved in changing to a different unit of the system. A dollar is written $1.00. A dime is $0.10. A cent is $0.01. A mill, commonly used in figuring taxes, is $0.001. Note that a mill is one-thousandth of a dollar, a cent is one-hundreth of a dollar, and a dime is one-tenth of a dollar. Now try to figure what part of a mile a yard, a foot, and an inch are. Finding the answers requires a lot of figuring. The same is true for weights in the English system.

The metric system carries out the ease and logic of the decimal system to length, volume,

How some units of measurement in the English system compare with similar units in the metric system.

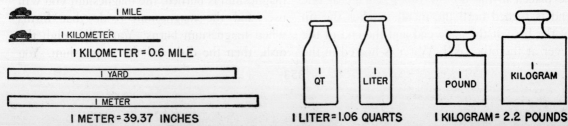

I MILE

I KILOMETER

I KILOMETER = 0.6 MILE

I YARD

I METER

I METER = 39.37 INCHES

I QT   I LITER

I LITER = 1.06 QUARTS

I POUND   I KILOGRAM

I KILOGRAM = 2.2 POUNDS

and weight. At the International Bureau of Weights and Measures, near Paris, France there is a metal bar made of an alloy of platinum and iridium. On this bar are two parallel scratches. The distance between these scratches is the *standard meter*. A meter is 3.28 feet, or 39.37 inches—just a bit more than a yard in length.

Just as a dime is one-tenth of a dollar, a *decimeter* is one-tenth of a meter. Just as a cent is one-hundreth of a dollar, a *centimeter* is one-hundreth of a meter. A mill is one-thousandth of a dollar, and a *millimeter* is one-thousandth of a meter. Therefore, 10 millimeters (*mm*) make 1 centimeter; 10 centimeters (*cm*) make 1 decimeter; 10 decimeters (*dm*) make 1 meter (*m*).

You can see how convenient this system is and why it is the official measuring standard of science. One hundred thirty-two centimeters are 1.32 meters; 20.35 meters are 2035 centimeters. You can figure quickly and accurately with the metric system. One thousand meters make a *kilometer*. In France or in Germany or in Italy or in Mexico, you will not find signposts saying so many miles to such and such a place. Instead, you will find signs saying so many kilometers to this or that place.

The metric system is equally convenient for weighing things. The unit of weight is the *gram*. A *kilogram* is 1000 grams. It is equivalent to about 2.2 pounds in the English system. A new five-cent piece weighs almost exactly 5 grams. The same prefixes are used here:

deci-, centi-, milli-. What part of a gram is a *milligram*?

The metric unit used in measuring capacity is the *liter*. A liter is equal to 1000 *milliliters* (1000 *ml*) and is a little larger than a liquid quart in the English system (940 ml).

We can hope that people in the United States will more and more use the metric system in measurements. It is easy to learn, easy to remember, and easy to use accurately. If you take science courses in high school and in college, most of your work will be done with the metric system.

CHANGING STANDARDS OF MEASUREMENT

How far is it from Chicago to New York? If you look it up, you will probably find that it is about 831 miles by automobile. What does that mean? So many inches, feet, and miles in which to plant crops, build factories, or use for some good reason.

But that is not why you ordinarily ask distances, is it? Usually you want to estimate how long it will take to go from one place to another. This fact has made it increasingly common to speak of the distance between two points in terms of hours of travel time. After all, which makes better sense: to say it is 831 miles from New York to Chicago, or that it is 5 hours by plane or 18 hours by train? The time it takes to travel the distance is the important point, and that time is steadily being whittled down. As you can see, we sometimes change our units of measurement—in this instance replacing distance units with time units that have more meaning.

WORKING WITH SCIENCE

1. Measure the length, width, and thickness of various objects, such as tables and books, using both English and metric measuring sticks. Which is easier to work with? Determine the number of cubic inches in a block of wood and then, using metric measuring sticks, determine the number of cubic centimeters in the same block of wood. Which is easier?

2. If scales and balances are available, weigh

small objects in ounces and pounds and then in grams and kilograms. Using the block of wood you measured in Exercise 1, determine the weight in ounces per cubic inch and then the weight in grams per cubic centimeter. Which is easier?

3. If cylinders and beakers marked with metric scales are available, measure out a certain number of milliliters of water and weigh it on a metric scale. What is the weight of a milliliter of water?

Measure out a certain number of fluid ounces of water and weigh this amount in ounces. What is the weight of a fluid ounce of water? Which figuring is easier?

4. Study the construction of a vernier caliper and measure the inside and outside diameters of a small water glass. Repeat your measurements with a measuring stick. Which measures more finely? (Your teacher will show you how to read the vernier scale of the caliper.)

5. If a micrometer caliper is available, study its action and measure small objects with it. How fine a measurement can you make with the micrometer caliper?

TIME IN THE MODERN WORLD

A savage in the jungle is said to have once remarked that civilized man must not be very smart since he has to look at his watch to tell when it is time to eat. Of course, your watch does not tell you when you are hungry. But you have adjusted your eating habits to the clock, and you know how hungry you can get if you do not eat at the usual time.

How important is time in our modern world? A savage does not bother about time. He sleeps until he wants to get up and eats when he is hungry. Not a bad idea, you say. But how far would you get if you tried to live so informally?

SCHOOLS WITHOUT CLOCKS?

Suppose that you and all the other students in your school decided to live without watches and clocks for a week. What time would you get up? Wait a minute—there is no way for you to know. Your mother or father could not wake you at your usual hour. There is not a watch or clock in the house. Eventually, however, some member of the family gets all the sleep he wants, wakes up, and gets you out of bed.

After dressing, you go into the kitchen, expecting breakfast. But mother, not having any clock, is not in the kitchen. So you decide

These time zones and the clocks show how time differs in various parts of the world. Why are the time zones 15 degrees wide? Why are some of the boundary lines not straight?

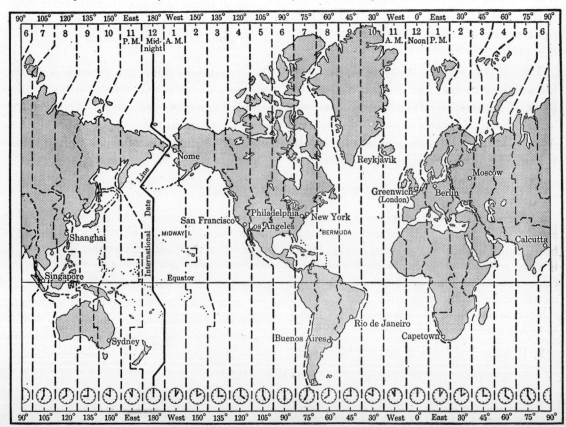

to cook your own eggs this morning. You like them soft-boiled—3-minute eggs. But what do you get? You did not judge the time very well, and the eggs are not to your liking.

You finally wander off to school. Your father's boss has just called and wants to know why he is not at work—the factories still have clocks, you see. You think that you may be a bit late for school. When you get there, you find it in an uproar. The principal's office is filled with students who want to know, "Is it time to go to Miss Jackson's class, or do we eat lunch now?" "Lunch!" you think. "I've just had breakfast."

Finally you find out what period it is and go to class. The room is only half filled. In about 3 minutes, in comes another student. Then another and another. By this time, Miss Jackson has decided to give up teaching and open a hamburger stand. There, it will not matter when people come in. She can cook another hamburger at any time.

This story could be continued, but we think you see the point already. Think how impossible it would be for a factory to operate if time could not be measured accurately enough so that work could be geared together and assembly schedules maintained. And what if nobody came to work on time?

What would happen if modern industry did not have calendars as well as clocks? Think of the exact timing that keeps trains rolling and planes flying on schedule and that helps get food, clothing, and other goods produced and distributed to where we want them *when we want them.*

TRANSPORTATION DEMANDS PRECISION TIME

Before railroads began threading across the country, time was a local matter. In ancient times sticks thrust upright in the ground, or *sundials*, gave reasonably good indication of when "high noon" had arrived by the shadow they formed. Later on, instruments for sighting the sun and measuring its angle overhead were used. But each local community had its own time. This practice created little difficulty

Courtesy American Airlines

The pilot checks his watch before taking off.

before the days of modern, fast transportation.

When trains began travelling across the country, local time became an impossible situation. Standard time belts were established so that all communities within one time belt had the same time. A person who travels across the country in a bus, train, or airplane, has only to look at the elaborate time schedules to understand how precisely the buses, airplanes, and trains run. If you could spend a few weeks in the office of the traffic manager of a major railroad, trucking service, or airline, your respect for the importance of precise timing would increase.

A giant airliner depends for the very safety of its flight upon exact timing. Weather reports from all over the United States are wired into central headquarters every 6 hours. These reports must be placed on the wires within 3 minutes of the exact time they are supposed to be filed.

In this way comprehensive weather reports and forecasts can be available at exact times. These reports and forecasts are important items considered by the flight dispatcher in determining time of departure, flight route, and time of arrival of airliners.

COMMUNICATION AND TIMING

You have undoubtedly noticed how precisely radio programs begin and end. Even programs that include audience participation or unrehearsed conversation stop precisely at the end of the time allowed them.

Radio time is expensive time. A few seconds may mean several thousand dollars to some of the national chain broadcasts. Every one of those precious seconds must be used. But not a single extra second can be allowed.

INDUSTRY RUNS ON TIME

In Chapter 27 you will read of the beautifully interlocked program of modern mass production. Timing is a chief factor in such production. A modern automobile rolls off the end of the assembly line, finished and gleaming. Some of the metals of which it was made were toughened by heat treatment that required accurate timing. Some of them were "pickled" to prevent rusting under processes requiring exact timing of chemical action. The lacquers that provide lasting beauty and protection to the metal surfaces were prepared and applied by means of many processes, some

This balance determines weights to 0.000001 gram.
Courtesy E. I. du Pont de Nemours & Co.

of which required exact timing. The tires on which the automobile rolls were formed of crude rubber mixed with other materials and "cooked" for a precise amount of time to make them tough and lasting.

The car, which was assembled on one particular assembly line, actually depended upon the closely timed production of parts at many other factories in other places. If one supplier of parts—the factory producing certain of the bolts, for example—does not produce and deliver the number of bolts needed at exactly the time they are needed, the entire automobile assembly line must stop. Timing is thus a keyword in modern mass production.

THE DOCTOR AND TIME

A doctor without a watch would seem as odd as a doctor without pills or a stethoscope. He needs a watch because one important symptom of illness is a marked change in the body's timing of certain functions. In an examination, one of the first things a doctor does is to take the patient's pulse. The rate of heart beat rises in many illnesses and goes down in a few illnesses. The rate of breathing is another index of the state of a person's health.

Modern medicine depends in many ways on precise time measurement. If x-ray exposures were not timed correctly, conditions in the body would not show up on the x-ray plates. When radium or x-rays are used to combat cancerous tissue, an overdose might actually cause cancer or destroy tissues directly. Thus, x-rays must be timed precisely.

Dental surgery and other types of operations often depend upon local anesthetics to relieve pain. The amounts of these pain killers have been determined according to known times in which the average person's sensory nerves are deadened by any particular amount of anesthetic. These are but a few examples of the place that exact time determination plays in medical science.

SCIENCE DEMANDS PRECISION TIMING

Scientific research depends heavily upon exact timing. It is one thing to know that any object falls toward the earth with ever-increasing speed. But such knowledge would be rather useless because it is not precise enough. When we say that any object falls toward the earth with a speed that increases 32 feet per second every second that it continues to fall, we have a precise knowledge of the increase in speed for each unit of time. That knowledge can be —and has been—put to a wide variety of important uses.

Research in mechanics, light, sound, electricity, and many branches of chemistry and biology often seeks to find more precise determinations of change of some sort per unit of time. Moreover, modern research into each of these fields depends very heavily upon knowledge we have already gained on the time required for certain things to take place or changes to occur.

Time is often as important to the scientist as matter and energy. The precision of his knowledge about all three is a clue to the state of our usable knowledge about the world.

NEW FRONTIERS OF MEASUREMENT

Scientists have measured, with accuracy sufficient to make their measurements useful, distances so vast that they baffle the imagination. In addition, they have measured objects so small that they defy the great magnifying powers of even the new electron microscope.

Besides such distance and size measurements, scientists have "weighed" the sun and the earth, and molecules, atoms, and electrons. Electrons are so very small that many billions could be packed together on the head of a pin with room for billions more.

No one has taken a tape measure to measure the distance to a star. No one has placed the sun or the earth or an electron on scales to determine its weight. But there are indirect ways to measure these things. The distance to the moon may be measured in the same general way as the height of a tree—by comparing similar triangles.

The sun can be weighed by knowing accurately its composition through the use of spectroscopes (see page 238) and weighing those identical substances here on the earth. The earth can be weighed by a gravimeter (see page 203), which determines the gravitational attraction of objects on each other. The size of a molecule of gas can be determined with fair accuracy by reasoning from a common law of physics.

The story of these frontier fields of measurement is long and complicated. But the probing fingers of science have reached to the farthest corners of the universe and to the remotest particle of matter. Through precise measurements, the new world of science is constantly developing. Some of you may contribute to its advance.

WORKING WITH SCIENCE

1. Recall the number of times that precise timing is necessary in your daily life. Consider such things as the making of candy, cooking of eggs, taking of photographs, and developing and printing of them in case you have a home photographic laboratory. How many of these things could be done successfully without a watch or clock?

2. Take your pulse and that of a classmate. Determine your breathing rate or that of a classmate. Now exercise violently for a few minutes. Again take your pulse. Explain the purpose of the mechanisms of the body that speed up or slow down its functions according to individual need.

3. Secure a time schedule from the local depot, bus station, or airport. Note how exactly these transportation schedules are timed. Consider the many types of problems that would arise if all trainmen, bus drivers, and transport pilots were to leave their watches at home for just 1 day.

4. Investigate some local industry to determine to what degree precise timing is involved in its operation. Discuss the effects of 1 day's operation of that industry without the use of watches or clocks.

Even after standardized parts were developed, mass production did not spring up overnight. In fact, it was quite a long time in coming, for mass production involves much more than just standardized parts.

Of course, among other things, mass production does require a product that can be assembled from standardized parts. New products are designed that way; old products usually must be redesigned (1). Then the parts must be made. This may be done by the assembly-line operator or he may buy the parts from parts manufacturers. Then the assembly line must be planned (2) so that it moves at the right speed and the right parts reach the assembly line just where and when they are needed. Of course,

the right kind of labor—skilled or unskilled as necessary—must be on hand to put in the parts as the assembly line rolls forward (3). Since the assembly line uses up parts at a rapid rate—and must shut down if it does not have them—great care must be taken to make sure that an adequate supply of parts is on hand at all times.

Mass production, as its name implies, produces goods in large quantities. Therefore, mass production depends on mass distribution. One cannot exist without the other, for there would be no point in mass producing something that cannot be sold in great quantities nor in selling great quantities of something that cannot be mass produced.

3

27

PRODUCTION FOR ALL

Manufacturing begins with raw materials. It changes their form and condition and ends up with products that are useful in ways that the raw materials were not. For example, through manufacturing, aluminum, magnesium, copper, limestone, coal, oil, soybeans, rubber, cotton, and many other raw materials end up as a "Superfortress" that can fly at 30,000 feet. Through manufacturing, or processing, raw materials are so changed that they either become more useful to us or become useful to us in other ways.

AN EXAMPLE OF MASS PRODUCTION

As an example of mass production, we are considering the production of the "Superfortress" because it is an interesting story of the largest and most complex mass-production job ever undertaken anywhere at any time.

In a large plane the number of parts reaches a staggering total. A "Superfortress" has 55,000 different parts, 10 miles of electric wiring, 152 different electric motors, 600,000 rivets, and a multitude of nuts and bolts. Each of its four engines has 18 cylinders, and the push of 72 moving pistons gives the plane a total of 8800 horsepower.

ASSEMBLY-LINE PRODUCTION

Many of the smaller parts of a "Superfortress" were made by different manufacturers. The parts produced by these subcontractors were shipped to assembly plants where the huge planes were assembled. The process of assembling products in a quick, low-cost, efficient way is a symbol of modern times. It was first applied to the production of automobiles by Henry Ford in making the "Model-T" for which he became famous.

In ordinary production, a man or group of men work on a product from beginning to end. For example, a shoemaker took leather and from it fashioned a finished shoe. With the possible exception of the nails he used, the shoe was entirely handmade. Such production was slow and costly.

Henry Ford adopted Eli Whitney's idea of interchangeable parts and carried the idea even farther. He set up an assembly line in which each worker had only a small, specialized job to do in assembling the finished product. Perhaps this job consisted of tightening a single screw or connecting a few wires. The unfinished automobile moved along the assembly line from worker to worker until the last man completed the assembly and the "Model-T" was ready for the paint shop.

In this way, production was speeded up very greatly. No longer was it necessary for each worker to be a skilled mechanic. All a worker needed to know was how to do his own small job rapidly and skillfully. So production costs and the time necessary to produce finished products were both reduced. As a result, assembly-line production was adopted by many industries. Production on an assembly line from interchangeable parts is called mass production.

Courtesy Boeing Aircraft Company, Wichita Div.

A plane in the air and a car on the road are the results of years of careful planning. Left: A "Superfortress." Right: Making machine tools to be used in making aircraft parts.

BUILDING A "SUPERFORTRESS"

"Superfortresses" were not built on the kind of assembly line that Henry Ford made popular. The huge planes, 100 feet long and with a wingspread of 140 feet, took up too much space. Production in a single line would have spread the unfinished planes over miles of factory and would have created difficulties in supplying materials and power. Much of the work was done on subassembly lines, where small parts were combined into major units of the plane. Only in the last hours of construction were the main subassemblies brought together and joined into the finished plane.

BEHIND THE ASSEMBLY LINES

Behind the final assembly and even the subassemblies is a long story. This story emphasizes two things that make such production possible. One is *cooperation* and the other is *planning*. The planning becomes clear when you know that paper work that led to the "Superfortress" began in 1936, eight years before the big plane was officially announced in June, 1944.

In 1936 Boeing aircraft engineers began plans for larger, long-range planes with pressurized cabins. In early 1939 Air Corps generals told airplane manufacturers the kind of war planes they wanted. They said what they wanted in terms of speed, range, size, power, maneuverability, and other factors. Boeing submitted its model No. 341. But as fast as sketches and plans were submitted, the requirements were stepped up because of military needs. Model No. 345 was larger, and Boeing Aircraft was finally commissioned to go ahead with the new plane of this design, a design very different from the plane the Air Force generals had wanted in 1939. It was different—and much better.

In September, 1942 the XB-29, an experimental model, was taken up for its first flight, and within a year the new plane was rolling off the production line. But the new plane that was produced in 1943 was not the same as the experimental model. Nine hundred distinct improvements were made as the experimental model was developed and 240 more before the plane was put into production. Later on, hundreds more improvements were made.

That required real planning. It was not easy to design a monster plane like the "Superfortress" and bring together all the materials, tools, and spare parts to assemble it. Every time the design was changed, new supplies and tools were needed, and the assembly line

Courtesy Boeing Aircraft Company

Left: This machine does the work of many men in making a part for the "Superfortress." Right: Sub-assemblies and prewired cables simplify wiring problems and speed up production.

had to be reorganized while the planes were moving along. Such planning is possible only when the entire production system is organized so that it runs like a well-oiled machine.

COOPERATION IN PRODUCTION

Though Boeing Aircraft made the plans and the experimental models, so many "Superfortresses" were wanted that other companies were brought in to help. Four large manufacturers undertook the big jobs of subassembly and final assembly. Plants were put in operation at Wichita, Kansas; Omaha, Nebraska; Marietta, Georgia; Chicago, Illinois; Seattle, Washington; and Cleveland, Ohio. These were only the plants where finished engines and planes were produced. Smaller parts and raw materials were obtained from plants in many states and from several foreign countries as well.

To help coordinate the production, a committee was set up, with the major companies and the Army represented. This committee did the planning—it obtained materials, worked on changes in design, passed on new ideas, and saw that bottlenecks did not develop. All this was behind the production lines that turned out "Superfortresses" in a stream during 1943, 1944, and 1945. A total of 2744 of these giant planes was produced.

PRODUCTION AND ASSEMBLY

A "Superfortress" is constructed of seven major assemblies. The *fuselage*, or main body of the plane, is built in four sections; the wings, in five. That totals nine, but the two wingtips made by a subcontractor are not counted. These are the major assemblies.

Smaller subassemblies were used in providing the parts for the major assemblies. Wooden patterns, or *templates*, were made to speed the work of electrical wiring. The electric wiring was laid out over painted guide lines and around wooden pegs. Wires were spliced, connections made, and the individual wires bound together into cables. An electrical subassembly was made to fit into each section of the fuselage. The wires were connected to terminal boxes, where wires from instruments and motors were also connected as they were installed. This saved much time compared with wiring each light, instrument, and motor separately.

When the major assemblies were ready, they moved toward the final assembly lines. Instead of one line, as for automobiles, four parallel assembly lines were used to conserve space. Movable cradles and frames, or *jigs*, held the assemblies until they were ready for final connection. An overhead crane lifted the fuselage assemblies, or sections, into line.

Courtesy Boeing Aircraft Company

Left: Storage of completed assemblies and subassemblies requires much space and planning. Right: One step in assembling a "Superfortress" from major assemblies.

They were brought together and accurately fitted. Electric cables and other connections were made from section to section. The wheels were lowered and the fuselage moved forward. The bases of the wings were built into the fuselage. The wing sections and tips were added during final assembly when the engines were already in place and the fuselage was complete.

Plant Design. All this moved along like clockwork, because everything in this production scheme had been planned and coordinated. The planning involved *space* and *time* as well as *materials.* All three were important. Materials must be on hand—this involved storage. Such storage must be near the place where materials are used, and production must be so timed that everything moves into the final assembly lines at just the right moment. To do this, the working space must be planned as carefully as a scientific experiment.

For a "Superfortress," the amount of space allotted to production was: storage of raw materials and supplies received from producers, 10 percent; fabrication of parts from these raw materials by stamping, riveting, welding, cutting, and so forth, 30 percent; subassembly lines for small assemblies and closely related parts, 28 percent; storage of

assembly parts waiting major assembly, 6 percent; major assembly of wings and fuselage in jigs and cradles, 8 percent; installation of instruments, armament, and special parts in sections, 11 percent; final assembly of main sections into the finished plane, 7 percent.

Tools for Production. To produce on such a scale required special tools and equipment. In the production of "Superfortresses" more than 100,000 special tools were designed and built, and an equal number of standard tools were purchased. By finding the best tool and method for each job, work was speeded and errors reduced. For example, wings were assembled in large three-story jigs that permitted the mechanics to work freely on any part of the wing surface. The jigs were accurately adjusted so that the wings received full support while they were being made. There were special tools for drilling, cutting, punching, riveting, and welding. One machine punched 19 different holes in one operation on the ribs that support the fuselage. It punched these holes 45 times as fast as the job had been done before this special punch was developed.

New methods of casting, molding, and assembling saved time and materials. For example, at one time in making the door to the

One of the rooms in which "Superfortresses" were assembled. Final assembly lines at the extreme right and left; lines for major assemblies in the center.

tail-gunner's compartment, 30 parts were assembled by welding and riveting. Engineers studied this process and worked out a way to stamp out the door from a sheet of metal. Twenty-six of the 30 parts were eliminated, and the finished door was even better than before. In addition, both time and materials were saved by the new process.

When changes were made, new tools, new dies, and new assemblies were required. And all changes had to be set up without interrupting normal production of the planes.

Continual inspection and checking were required—of raw materials as they came in, of subassemblies, of instruments, and of the finished planes as they rolled off the final assembly line.

The building of this big plane is only one dramatic example of a method of production that helps make the materials and discoveries of science available for all to use. This kind of production has given us telephones, radios, washing machines, refrigerators, automobiles, fountain pens, and hundreds of other products. The problems differ with each product, but the basic methods are the same.

Industry has called in thousands of men with scientific training to help make production more efficient and, hence, less expensive.

Science is involved not only in discovery and invention but also in the equally important task of making the fruits of invention and discovery available to all of us.

DISADVANTAGES OF MASS PRODUCTION

It is hard to see any disadvantages in mass production, isn't it? Factories all over the country turn out thousands of products to make our lives more safe, easier, and more fun, and do it so inexpensively that almost all of us can afford a few of the gadgets as well as the necessities. Mass production has helped to make the *gadgets* and *luxuries* of yesterday the *necessities* of today. Radio is an example of this.

What are the problems of mass production, if any? In the first place, there is the danger that as machines take over, men will be forced out of work. But most experts agree that the machine need not throw men out of work. For it takes men to invent, manufacture, run, and service the machines. Machines create more jobs than they destroy. Furthermore, the Machine Age has meant that most people are working shorter hours so that all profit from the time saving and the labor saving of modern machines.

Another important problem of mass production is that expensive machinery is required to make such a product as a modern car or a modern airplane. And it takes a long time between the designing of a modern product and the time the product starts rolling off the assembly lines.

Suppose that a new type of plane is wanted. Expert engineers and draftsmen must design machinery to produce the thousands of parts on a standardized mass-production basis. That takes many months of work. Then the machinery to make the parts must be manufactured and installed in a great factory. This takes many more months. Then men must be trained to organize the flow of materials along the assembly lines, and others must be trained to do each small job in assembling the plane. All of this costs much money.

Finally the asembly lines are working at top speed. Every hour a plane rolls off the final assembly line, is tested, and takes to the air in its maiden flight. By then the designers have plans for new models that will fly faster, farther, higher, or otherwise better than the plane that is rolling off the assembly lines.

Do you see the problem? Can we afford to junk all the machinery, or modify that which can be changed? Can we afford to hold up production long enough to get the new machinery designed, installed, and workmen trained to handle it? Can we afford the extra millions of dollars to keep changing our machinery for new and better designs so that we can continue mass production but with ever better and better planes, automobiles, or washing machines?

It should be clear that in mass production, industry cannot alter designs too frequently. It cannot be expected to produce automobiles, airplanes, rat traps, or can openers that are the latest and best that have been designed. If they tried to do this, such products as cars would cost a small fortune and few of us could afford them.

WORKING WITH SCIENCE

1. There is nothing quite as exciting in industry as to see an assembly line in operation. Products take form before your very eyes. Arrange to visit some factory where this method of production is used. Talk with the foreman or some other company official to find out about the problems that come up in keeping "the line" moving.

2. In almost every factory, machine shop, or garage you will see specialized tools designed to do a specific job better. Instead of ordinary hammers, wrenches, and screwdrivers, there may be tools designed to make a particular job a bit easier. Ask your garageman or some other tool worker to show and explain to you the special tools he uses and how these tools make his work easier.

3. The proof of the value of mass production lies in the worth of the products. Search through attics or cellars and try to find some typical products that are at least 25 years old—a camera, electric fan, electric iron, sewing machine, electric-light socket, and so forth. Compare these with products made recently. Pay special attention to small differences: number of screws and bolts, how parts are fitted together, weight of appliance, and so forth. Summarize your findings. Do you think it is true that the older things were "made better"?

SCIENCE HAS NOT CREATED THE WORLD WE WANT

The aviation industry is only one example of what scientific, planned production can do. Many new industries show how science can increase employment, wealth, and happiness. But merely because science *can* help increase employment, wealth, and happiness, we cannot conclude that it has always done so. Science has been a great force for good, but there is another side of the story. Great scientific effort has gone into the development of guns, bombs, poison gases, and other tools of warfare. The cost of World War II for a single day would be sufficient to provide the funds needed for research that would almost certainly lead to at least partial solution of many of our most pressing problems.

Let us consider some of these problems. In 1940 there were about 35 million dwelling units in the United States. Nearly half of these lacked a bathroom. Almost a fourth of them lacked gas and electricity; 12 percent did not have central heating; and nearly 20 percent needed major repairs.

In spite of the millions of jobs that science has created and the billions of dollars worth of products that have come from scientific inventions, many people have not benefited greatly. For example, in 1940 about 25 percent of the families in the United States had an income of $1000 a year or less. About 8 percent had an income of $500 or less. An average family in our country consists of 3.8 persons. What do you think of their chances of sharing the benefits of science on such incomes? What are their chances of having good food and shelter, adequate medical care and education?

SCIENCE AND BASIC CHANGE

While we are mentioning such basic problems of living as food, clothing, and shelter, we should note that science has not always been applied directly to these problems. Our clothing is still very much the same as it was 1000 years ago. Of course, styles have changed, and we sew by machines rather than by hand. But for the most part, we still gather fibers from plants and animals, weave them into cloth, and cut and fit them into garments much as our forefathers did. One scientist has pointed out that it is already possible to make molded plastic garments that need no sewing, at such a low price that they could be worn for a short time and then discarded. No more washdays; no more laundries!

Our houses, too, are very similar in design to those of 1000 years ago. We have made modifications and improvements, but our experts have done little to tackle the real problem of designing the most useful kind of shelters for man and designing them for mass production so that good homes can be within reach of all.

We still gather plants and slaughter animals for our food. We feed our chickens and cows and pigs more scientifically than we feed ourselves. And when we do make scientific discoveries about our diet, such as the discovery of the vitamins, we permit this discovery to be misused.

LIMITATIONS ON SCIENCE

How can we account for this state of affairs? Science has done so much, and yet the world is far from perfect. There is no answer. Our world is so complex that there are many causes for our troubled state. Some of them will give you an idea of why the good effects of science have not been more widespread.

A scientific invention or discovery does not arise in a vacuum. An inventor does not retire to an attic and come out with a brand-new idea. If he goes to an attic at all, he takes with him knowledge of problems and needs—things that do not work or things that should work better. He has a problem because he sees a need for change. Most inventions come in response to the knowledge of such needs.

Occasionally a discovery that is unrelated to the needs of the time is made. But such discoveries and inventions may wait many years before being put to practical use. The ancient Greeks knew something about electricity, steam, and water power, but since they had enough slave labor, there was no need for them to try to develop other sources of energy.

PUTTING SCIENCE TO WORK

Getting an invention or a discovery used is often a difficult task. Many inventors have spent years trying to prove the worth of their ideas or inventions. Their greatest efforts were not in making the discovery but in convincing a banker, merchant, or manufacturer that the invention would be profitable. Few inventors or scientists have seen the fruits of their labor made available to the public until

Mobile Communications Division, Farnsworth Television & Radio Corporation

Two-way radio enables a trainman to communicate with other crewmen, control centers, and radio-equipped trains. Such equipment has been installed by many railroads.

someone was convinced that a profit could be made from the idea. There are today many ideas which would go far to improve man's lot and increase his happiness if they could be put into action.

Of course, a scientist or inventor can always go into business for himself. But many scientists prefer to continue with research. Besides, our industrial world is so organized that it is hard for a newcomer to get a start and to compete with the giant industries already underway. In certain fields, large corporations have such complete control that for all practical purposes it is impossible for a newcomer to enter. Improvements or changes must fit in with the plans of such organizations if they are to have a chance.

RESISTANCE TO CHANGE

In addition to these difficulties, both people and industry often resist new ideas and inventions. At times, major industries seem to have discouraged inventions that later turned out to be of great benefit to them. For example, at first the railroads would have nothing to do with the Westinghouse airbrake. The inven-

tors of the automatic-signaling device and the car-coupling device had a hard time getting their inventions adopted. The two-way system of radio communication now used on trains was technically possible many years before it was adopted.

MONOPOLIES MAY LIMIT SCIENCE

Our system of industry is based on ideas of competition and free enterprise. But these basic ideas have often been pushed aside by companies that have banded together and resisted the advance of science when it has served their own purposes to do so.

Similar agreements have been brought to light in several industries. Agreements of this kind have discouraged the wider application of science for the benefit of most people. Charges have been made that large companies have deliberately bought up and suppressed patents that would interfere with their particular product. Probably you have read about combines, cartels, and trade associations whose actions have sometimes interfered with free competition and the application of scientific inventions.

OPPOSITION TO LABOR-SAVING METHODS

In some cases labor organizations have opposed scientific inventions and improvements. There are unions that do not permit their members to use mechanical devices which improve their work and cut costs heavily. Some insist that work be done by hand when with the help of machines a man can do a better job at lower cost. There are many instances of rules that protect an immediate job but are short-sighted in regard to scientific improvements that would create even more employment. If we are to use the achievements of science to the fullest, we must carefully consider such practices.

SCIENTISTS AND THE USE OF SCIENCE

Until recently many scientists have not given much thought to problems such as those just mentioned. But they are finding that they cannot ignore the world around them. They see that their ideas and discoveries must fit into the world as it now exists. So they are more and more concerned with the place of science in the world and the way in which science is used. They are equally concerned about the world of tomorrow, because they know that science can do great and wonderful things, and they are afraid that the opportunity may be lost or that their efforts may be hampered or misused.

WORKING WITH SCIENCE

1. World War II cost this country about $500 billion besides the loss of lives and negative effects on the home, family, and industry. Find out (from *The World Almanac* or similar sources) how much we spend each year on education, hospitals, scientific research, old-age insurance. How much progress do you think we could make on our basic problems with even $1 billion.

2. You have had a chance to check your own diet (Unit 3). Now find out what you can about the scientific feeding of cattle, dogs, or poultry. Where is our knowledge of nutrition applied more effectively, with animals or with man? Can you think of reasons for this? List some of them.

3. Everybody, everywhere seems to resist change. We like the old shoes and old clothes that we are used to wearing. We do not care to try new foods or change our daily paper. Sometimes we say, "It was good enough for Grandfather, and it's good enough for me." Find out some of the opportunities for your community to change—in transportation, water supply, industry, and so forth, and find out what kind of resistance has been offered. Examine the "reasons" given. Are they satisfactory or do they only cover up a desire to keep things the way they have been?

SCIENCE FOR TOMORROW

Science can go, and has gone, far to improve the physical conditions of man and make his life easier. What of the future? How will science be applied to building the world of tomorrow? You already know that there is no single answer. Science *already has* the means to produce marvelous changes in our way of life IF—and, of course, the IF is very big. So let us look at some of the factors bound up in this IF to see quickly the complex world in which science must operate.

SCIENCE NEEDS CAPITAL

In our kind of civilization, money or capital is required, often a great deal of it, to start an industry and keep it going. This capital usually comes from private sources, but in recent years government has provided considerable capital directly or indirectly.

Interest must be paid for the use of capital, and because investments are large, the owners of capital desire a guaranteed return for a long period of time. Recognizing that this is the case, if science is to help produce the new world of tomorrow, it must have the cooperation of those who control our nation's wealth.

SCIENCE NEEDS LABOR

Labor is just as essential as capital. Here the responsibilities of science are more complicated. It is comparatively easy to control an invention so that it will yield a good profit. It is much harder to keep the invention or discovery from throwing thousands of people out of work while industry becomes reorganized around the new idea. We could easily develop the mechanical cotton picker so that within 5 years the need for southern farm help could be drastically reduced. Would that solve or create problems?

Science needs the cooperation of labor. Ways must be found to maintain wages while labor-saving devices are introduced. Workers cannot be discarded like outmoded machines, although sometimes that has been the practice. Workers are entitled to the security of steady employment and the opportunity to increase their skill and earning power. The world of tomorrow will remain a dream unless a satisfactory solution is found to some of these problems.

SCIENCE NEEDS MANAGEMENT

Management is essential to industry and science. It is concerned with organizing, planning, and distributing. It can be a strong force in promoting efficiency and developing new methods and products. Management can help solve the problems of both science and labor, and it will improve the financial structure of the industry in doing so. We have not given enough thought to education for effective management. But good management is essential in the teamwork that will make scientific progress a reality.

SCIENCE IS FOR THE CONSUMER

Then there is that often ignored but highly important person, the consumer. *He* is labor, management, capital, housewives, old folks, government employees, and even scientists and students.

The consumers' income is the purchasing power of the nation. Industry must know consumers' demands and interests and their ability to pay. Consumers must educate themselves so that they can wisely choose— or just as wisely reject—the many products offered for sale. They must learn how to distinguish truths from half-truths in advertising and how to evaluate goods in terms of their quality and price.

Consumers, who should be the most powerful of all groups in our country, are not a powerful group at all. This is because they are not a group. They are, in general, unorganized. They require protection against adulterated food, injurious or ineffective medicines, and fraudulent claims of all sorts. But more and more, consumers are banding together to help get their share of things fairly produced and at a fair cost.

THE GOVERNMENT MUST USE ALL OUR RESOURCES

Interwoven into all of this is government, which affects industry, labor, management, consumers, and many aspects of our personal lives. By the use of public projects and by the development and conservation of our natural resources, our government has gone very far in helping to see that each citizen gets some share of the things that science has produced. Government research programs have improved our crops and livestock; they have shown how to prevent erosion; and they have helped us toward sound health. There is still much to be done, of course, but much has been done already.

Government enforcement of laws that already exist helps to prevent monopoly and the control of industry for the benefit of the few at the expense of the many. The government, which represents you, has the difficult job of blending and guiding many of the forces that are involved in our very complex society.

THE NEW WORLD OF TOMORROW IS YOUR RESPONSIBILITY

How will all these interests fit together in making our new world? No one knows. Many have suggested solutions. Industry has its own, so has labor. The different political parties each feel they have the answer. Advocates of all kinds of social reform believe their particular point of view is the key to the situation.

But one thing is clear. By itself, science cannot produce a better world. This is certain, though science has already devised, or can devise, means of improving almost every aspect of our lives. No one wants to do this more than the scientists, who know that science is dedicated to the good of all men.

Just how this can be achieved is a problem for America to work out in a democratic way. If this is to be done, *you* must help in solving the complex problems involved. As a citizen, you can do no less. And as an individual who faces the possibility of a life far better than people have ever enjoyed before, you have nothing to lose and much to gain.

WORKING WITH SCIENCE

1. Cheap and rapid transportation of materials and energy is essential in mass production. List all the ways materials and energy are moved in some of the typical industries of your community. Do not forget the things we take for granted, like water through pipes.

2. Every community depends on storage to fill the gap between supply and the use of materials. Investigate the kinds of storage used in your school and in your community. Besides food of various kinds, look at storage of fuels, metals, raw materials of industry. Go to the lumber yard, coal yard, gasoline station, hardware store, and so forth.

3. We often lose sight of the very basic industries of this country because we are more attracted to the gadgets and materials which we, as consumers, use. Make a list of what you consider to be the 10 or 12 more basic industries in the United States. Be prepared to defend your choices because others will have different opinions.

4. If a factory or industrial plant in your community has a laboratory for research or testing, arrange to visit and find out the kind of work done there and why it is important.

As long as man has existed, he has wondered, worried, and complained about the weather. Bad weather often meant the difference between enough food and little or no food, between fairly comfortable living conditions and very miserable living conditions. As a result, early man studied the weather and attempted to foretell and control it. He was not very successful.

Not until man had learned considerable about the composition and characteristics of the atmosphere was much progress toward an understanding of weather possible. And little of this progress was made before the seventeenth century. Torricelli invented the barometer and showed that air exerts pressure in 1643. In 1648, Pascal had one of Torricelli's barometers carried to the top of a moun-

tain (1) and showed that air pressure decreases with altitude. In 1660, Otto von Guericke (2) successfully predicted an approaching storm as a result of a sudden drop in atmospheric pressure.

Joseph Priestley, (3) who discovered oxygen in 1774, was an early student of the composition of the air. As early as 1784, balloon flights to explore the atmosphere began. One famous flight of this nature was made from Paris by Tissandier (4) and two companions in 1875.

From this knowledge, we have gradually learned much about how the atmosphere produces our changing weather. Today atmospheric data are collected in many local weather stations (5) and transmitted to central stations (6) where short-range predictions of remarkable accuracy are made.

UNIT EIGHT

The Weather and What We Can Do About It

28

THE ATMOSPHERE

The weather is a common topic of conversation. When we do not know what else to talk about, we talk about the weather. We unconsciously realize that the weather interests everybody. So a comment such as, "Nice day, today," or, "It looks like rain," is one very widely used way to start a conversation.

WEATHER IN OUR LIVES

There are good reasons for our concern with weather. Weather is extremely important. It affects all of us. Consider a rain—an ordinary rain—as an example. Perhaps you have missed a ball game or a picnic because of a steady all-day rain. Next day when the sky is clear the newspaper may state, "Elmsville High School postponed its scheduled baseball game with Aldwin yesterday on account of rain. The game will be played next Saturday at 3 p.m. The rain also interrupted plans for the picnic supper of the Women's Auxiliary of the Reid Avenue Church. The Weather Bureau reported 1 inch of rainfall at Elmsville during the past 24 hours."

AN INCH OF RAINFALL

What does a 1-inch rainfall mean? Briefly, it means that a standard-sized can, or *rain gage*, set in the yard of the local weather observer was filled with 1 inch of rain between Saturday and Sunday mornings. This much rain may fall in one severe thunderstorm. Sometimes a half-dozen wet, drizzly days do not yield 1 inch of rain. There are places in the world where the rainfall averages more than 1 inch daily, and others where less than 1 inch of rain falls in an entire year.

If rain stayed where it fell, like glue, at the end of this rain in Elmsville there would have been a layer 1 inch deep over everything—houses, plants, roads, and lake. How much water does 1 inch of rain amount to? Consider only 1 square mile of land—a good-sized farm but very small compared with the more than 51 million square miles of the earth's total surface.

One inch of rainfall on 1 square mile of land amounts to about $2\frac{1}{3}$ million cubic feet of water—enough to make a 133-foot cube of water. Since each cubic foot of water weighs 62.5 pounds, the weight of this amount of water is 72,600 tons. At 7.5 gallons per cubic foot, the 1-inch rainfall amounts to about 18 million gallons of water. This is enough to meet one day's needs for drinking, washing,

A little rain is a lot of water.

bathing, and so forth (50 gallons per person) of a city the size of Seattle, Washington or Rochester, New York. It is enough water to fill a 6-foot pipe 15½ miles long.

EFFECTS OF WEATHER

Weather is big business. For example, an unpredicted change in weather can endanger the Florida or California orange crop, valued at several hundred million dollars. The New England hurricane of 1938 caused damage amounting to about $300 million. The hurricane of 1944 followed a similar path, killed 46 persons, and did $100 million damage. To be sure of the best time to spray crops or harvest grains, fruits, and vegetables, a farmer must know what to expect in the way of weather.

Sudden rain can change a carnival, fair, or outdoor meeting into a dismal failure. So promoters of fairs and owners of resorts often carry weather insurance to protect themselves against losses from bad weather. When a thundershower spreads over a large city, light after light is turned on. The overcast sky may double the demand for electricity. Unless the power plant is forewarned, it may not have time to start additional generators to take care of the extra load.

Before a snowstorm starts, the streetcar company, the street-cleaning department, and big stores want to know all about it. Will the snow be "wet" or "dry"? How long will it last? Will it freeze or turn into slush? Why are such questions important?

WEATHER AND FLIGHT

In 1934 about 14,000 persons had pilot's licenses. Today it is estimated that approximately half a million persons know how to fly, and many more are learning or want to learn. No one can fly safely without understanding the weather. Weather knowledge is as important to a flier as his knowledge of maps, mechanics, and flight instruments. Even today weather controls the airways. But some of our best scientists and engineers are working on the problem of making flying "weatherproof."

VALUE OF WEATHER INFORMATION

Savings and profits of more than $3 billion a year result from scientific weather predictions. But even this sum does not represent the total value of weather forecasts if they could be fully utilized in all branches of farming, industry, and commerce.

A few examples of how people use weather forecasts show the dollars-and-cents value of weather information. One of the largest baking companies in New York City follows weather predictions carefully and saves a million dollars a year by reducing returns of stale baked goods. How does weather information enable them to make this saving?

The answer is simple. About half the sales of bread and baked goods are made in New York City and about half in the surrounding suburbs. In the suburbs, housewives take care of the shopping while their husbands are in town. If the weather is stormy, the women are not likely to go shopping. Instead, they telephone their husbands to pick up a loaf of bread or an apple pie in the city and bring it out on the train. So, in stormy weather city sales of baked goods boom and suburban sales drop sharply. By knowing the weather 24 hours or more in advance, the baking company can send most of its goods to the proper stores and, hence, prevent unnecessary loss.

Dairymen, too, watch the weather. When a warm spell is predicted they can expect the sales of milk to rise. When a cold spell is ahead, milk sales drop, and more milk can be sent to cheese or ice-cream plants. Candy companies hold back shipments when unusually hot weather is predicted.

Dealers in antifreeze, insect sprays, coal and fuel oil, bathing suits, and rubbers all keep an eye on weather reports. Restaurant owners do, too, for what people eat changes as the temperature goes up and down. Builders of roads, bridges, airports, and railroads need weather data. A safe bridge cannot be built unless the engineer knows the average and maximum rainfall expected in the region, its past history of floods, and something about the force of local winds.

In World War II it was very important to have accurate knowledge of weather in planning troop movements, long-range bomber attacks, invasions, and transportation of supplies. As a result, one of the first training programs set up by the Army was for weather experts, or *meteorologists*.

WEATHER AND ATTITUDES

All aspects of life are affected by weather and *climate*, which is the average weather of a region over a long period of time. Obviously air, water, and rail transportation are delayed by fog, rain, snow, and floods. We know what weather means to farmers. But people do not realize fully how weather concerns them personally, affecting their emotions and their health.

Doctors who have studied the matter believe that weather has much more to do with the way we feel and act than we generally believe. Temperature, air circulation, relative humidity, and amount of light affect us all. Dr. Raymond H. Wheeler, of the University of Kansas, placed colonies of rats in rooms at different temperatures and tested how fast they could learn to find their way through a maze. He found that rats raised in a cool room at 55°F learned from three to six times as fast as rats raised in a warm room at 90°. Other studies have shown how weather affects blood pressure and blood chemistry. Certain mental illnesses seem to become worse with weather changes.

WHAT WE DO ABOUT WEATHER

Since weather affects us every minute of

our lives, it is worth understanding. Weather is said to be one thing that man can do nothing about, but this is not strictly true. People have been doing something about the weather for thousands and thousands of years. The first man who built a fire or wore the skin of an animal for warmth was doing something about the weather. The first house, stove, sailboat, and windmill were efforts either to use or to resist the effects of weather.

Some scientists believe that the changeable weather of the temperate zones has stimulated their inhabitants to greater activity than people in other parts of the world. The distribution of the world's cities and the places where great inventions or discoveries were made bears this out. However, most of man's reactions to the weather have been defensive. In general, he has sought to protect himself from bad weather and to prepare himself by forecasting the weather.

The newer methods of weather forecasting are a tremendous step forward. They will enable us to know more about coming weather than has hitherto been possible. Those who understand the weather can use it and, consequently, have an advantage over those whose lack of knowledge leaves them at the mercy of sudden rains, storms, winds, floods, and drouths. Acquiring weather information and using it are an important step in learning to know and to use *all* phases of the environment.

A farmer, sailor, mountaineer, or any person of long outdoor experience can often make weather forecasts merely by looking at the sky. But these forecasts are suited only to the

Early man sought protection from the weather.

immediate vicinity. No local observer, even the best, can foretell weather changes over large areas or long in advance. So the Federal government has taken over the job of forecasting weather and distributing the information on a nation-wide basis. The cooperation of foreign countries and ships at sea makes more data available than could be gathered within the boundaries of this country and results in more accurate predictions.

WORKING WITH SCIENCE

1. The next time a good rain occurs, find out the amount of rainfall and the area of your town. Figure out how many tons or gallons of water fell.

2. Obtain the following information about your local rainfall: How much does it average yearly? Does it come seasonally? What crops do best with this amount and distribution of rain? Do weather records show that the climate of your town is becoming wetter or drier?

3. Make a rain gage from a No. 10 tin can and a funnel. Set up the gage so that rain can fall into it directly. Measure rainfall with a ruler and compare with an official Weather Bureau gage.

4. Consult the local newspaper files about damage by storm, flood, drouth, hail, or any other weather conditions during the past year. Can you estimate the cost of bad weather in your vicinity?

5. Find out what local businesses or industries are dependent on the weather and how. See if you can get figures on how business was affected by favorable or unfavorable weather.

6. Ask a local insurance agent about policies that provide insurance against damage by hail, storm, or flood. Try to find out how the premiums are fixed.

7. Obtain information about the role of weather in the invasion of Europe and in other military operations of World War II.

UNITED STATES WEATHER BUREAU

The weather map and weather prediction that appear daily in the newspaper are something we take for granted. We take them so much for granted that we complain violently when the weather does not turn out exactly as the meteorologist figured it should. But because the weather forecast is correct from 89 percent to 95 percent of the time, we plan and do things with reasonable certainty of having the weather with us. This ability to predict the weather with such accuracy is no accident. More than half a century of experience and scientific research lie behind it.

The United States Weather Bureau was established in 1890. Before that time, the War Department and local groups gathered weather data independently. As established, the Weather Bureau was a part of the Department of Agriculture. But in 1940 it was transferred to the Department of Commerce—an indication of the increasing importance of weather information to commercial and business interests, including aviation.

WEATHER FORECASTING

At Weather Bureau stations weather data are plotted on maps. From these maps a trained observer can determine weather conditions anywhere in the United States almost at a glance. He can use this information in making his own local predictions.

The importance of weather maps can be realized if you consider weather to be the sum of many factors that fit together something like a huge jigsaw puzzle. The observations of one weather observer make only one piece of the puzzle—a piece so small that it does not give many clues as to the complete picture. But as data from more and more observers become available, the picture becomes more and more complete. With an up-to-the-minute weather map, a meteorologist in, say, Portland, Oregon, can predict the weather at Miami, Florida, at Portland, Maine, or at any other place in the country.

Weather data are collected at least four times daily at more than 300 major weather stations of the United States Weather Bureau and at many Army and Navy posts and airfields. In addition, more than 5000 volunteer observers submit data on local weather. To help the professional observers at large stations, the latest equipment is used. Instruments automatically record changes in temperature, air pressure, humidity, surface wind speed and direction. Gas-filled balloons are sent aloft from many of the larger stations to determine the direction and speed of winds at high altitudes.

Radiosonde. Many of the larger stations obtain high-altitude weather data. These data are obtained by means of an ingenious miniature weather station carried aloft by a hydrogen-filled balloon. This device is called a *radiosonde.* It contains lightweight weather instruments and a midget radio set that automatically broadcasts their readings. When the balloon bursts because of decreased pressure 10 or more miles above the earth, the radiosonde falls. Its speed is checked by a light parachute. If you should ever find a radiosonde, bring it to school. Your class and your science teacher will find it interesting.

The Weather Bureau has developed special services, in addition to its forecasts. It issues flood warnings, forest-fire warnings, and frost warnings. It provides special reports to farmers who grow cotton, tobacco, citrus fruits, and other crops that are quickly affected by weather changes. Its observers watch for hurricanes and storms that imperil navigation and it broadcasts details of a storm's power, path, and speed.

Conditions for Accurate Forecasts. Perhaps you may be tempted to ask, "Why did we wait until 1890 to start a Weather Bureau? Why wasn't one started 100 years earlier?" The answer lies in the way in which scientific progress is made. New applications of science usually come in response to human needs. Until travel, commerce, agriculture, and other endeavors were far enough advanced, accurate weather information was not really necessary. Invention of the airplane and introduction of semitropical crops, such as oranges and grapefruit, created a need for weather predictions of far greater accuracy than had been available. As the need for accurate weather information increased, more research became necessary and was undertaken.

But real progress in the study of weather was impossible until people learned the nature of air and its physical properties, a task that took several hundred years. The development of accurate weather instruments was another long task. But oddly enough, progress in electricity and communication made modern weather forecasting possible. Invention of the telegraph in 1844 was the first step. Without

Left: At the far left is an aneroid barometer. The girl is examining an **anemometer,** an instrument for measuring the speed of the wind. Right: Pilots receiving the latest weather data.

Lil and Al Bloom; Courtesy American Airlines

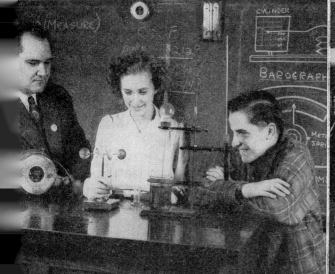
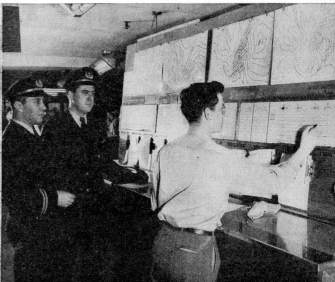

the telegraph and its more modern counterparts, telephone, teletype, and radio, rapid collection of weather data from hundreds of stations would be impossible. Without these data, even the best meteorologist could not make a reliable prediction.

Weather data were first collected by telegraph in the 1850's. As the system was perfected, the data were assembled into weather maps. Nowadays, a surface map of atmospheric conditions over the United States can be made within 2 hours after observers go out to read their instruments. More than anything else, rapidly assembled weather data make modern and accurate weather science possible.

WORKING WITH SCIENCE

1. Report to the class on the organization and work of the United States Weather Bureau. A booklet giving the history of the Bureau and details about what it does can be obtained by writing to the United States Weather Bureau, Washington 25, D.C.

2. Visit your local Weather Bureau station or observer. Find out how long records have been kept and how they are kept. If the station sends in daily reports, ask about the code that it uses to transmit weather information quickly.

3. Ask at your local telegraph office how long it takes for the actual sending of a message for distances of 1000, 2000, or 3000 miles. See if the answer helps explain the importance of the telegraph in collecting weather data.

THE AIR AROUND US

It is much easier to talk about the atmosphere than to get a real picture of what it is like. The atmosphere is so close to us, so much a part of our everyday life, that we seldom think much about it. If every molecule of air were miraculously colored red, then we would see that air not only surrounds us but penetrates into our bodies and clothing, into substances that we commonly regard as solid, and into many liquids as well.

THE LAYER WITHOUT A TOP ·

Some persons describe the air around us as an "ocean" and point out that we live at or near the bottom of this ocean of air. Others consider the atmosphere as a blanket, or layer. But, as you know, these terms are only partly true. The atmosphere extends completely around our earth. Its lower surface fits against the earth's physical features. The atmosphere does not have a distinct upper surface.

As you learn more and more about the air, it will become evident why words such as *ocean, blanket,* or *layer* cannot fully describe the atmosphere. Properties of the atmosphere are those things about it that can be observed and measured. The *weight* of the air is one property. The total weight of the atmosphere has been estimated at $5\frac{1}{2}$ million billion tons. Of course, small amounts of air weigh very little—a quart weighs only 0.04 ounce.

As you know, air is *elastic.* That is, it can be compressed and will expand to its original volume when the pressure is released. It is composed of molecules of various gases. These molecules are in constant motion, and there are vast spaces between them. The motion of the elastic molecules, and the spaces between them account for the elasticity of air.

At the outermost limits of the atmosphere there is very little weight above the molecules. Consequently, their constant motion spreads them far apart. There is, in other words, more space by far than molecules. Near the earth, as a result of the tremendous weight of the air above, air molecules are pushed much closer together. That is, the air is compressed, owing to its own weight. That a good deal of space still exists between the molecules is demonstrated by the fact that air can be squeezed into a much smaller space and the compressed air will expand when the pressure is released.

If air were not compressible, it would be of no use in automobile tires.

OUR COMPRESSED ATMOSPHERE

These two properties, weight and elasticity, acting together produce the condition of our atmosphere. The weight of the upper air presses on the lower levels of the atmosphere. The lower layers are compressed until the pressure at sea level is about 15 pounds on every square inch. This means that there is more air in the lower atmosphere than higher up. A quart of sea-level air weighs three times as much as a quart of air at the top of Mount Everest.

Because air is compressed, half the atmosphere lies within $3\frac{1}{2}$ miles of sea level, and 90 percent of the air lies within 10 miles of the earth's surface. The amount of air decreases above the 10-mile mark, but there are definite traces of atmospheric gases at great heights. Exactly how high is an unanswered question.

UPPER LIMITS OF THE AIR

Twilight, which brightens the sky after sunset, is a scattering of sunlight by the upper layers of the atmosphere. Measurements have shown that this light is scattered at heights up to 44 miles. Hence, there are traces of air at least that high.

Meteors, or "falling stars," are masses of rocky material that tear through space. When a meteor enters our atmosphere, friction with the air heats it *white-hot* and makes it visible as it speeds across the sky. By careful observation of a meteor from at least two places on the earth, it is possible to compute its height. Results show that there is enough air at a height of 190 miles to produce the friction needed to make a meteor white-hot.

One other bit of evidence indicates that air exists at even higher levels. Scientists have found that the *aurora borealis*, or northern lights, that occasionally glows in the arctic skies, is an electric discharge. It can be duplicated in a laboratory when electricity is passed through a tube from which all air, except the barest trace, has been removed. Hence, the upper height of this beautiful display indicates the level at which only the barest traces of air remain. This height is more than 600 miles from the earth.

WORKING WITH SCIENCE

1. If air does penetrate into many solids and liquids, we should be able to prove it is there. Can you devise a way to prove that there is air in a brick? Or, to go farther, can you measure how much air is in a brick? Can you do the same with a quart of water?

2. Fill a balloon with air. Now release the air carefully into quart bottles filled with water and inverted over a pneumatic trough. Be careful not to let any air escape. In this way, you can measure how many quarts of air were in the balloon. Put a funnel in the mouth of the balloon, and try to fill the balloon with that many quarts of water.

What happens? Can you explain the result?

3. Compressed air can be used as a source of power. It can be carried from the compressor to portable tools through pipes. Find out about compressed-air drills and other tools. What particular advantage do they have?

4. Man has constantly tried to get higher and higher into the atmosphere. Look up some of his records for climbing, for balloons, for open-cockpit planes, for pressure-cabin planes, for sealed gondolas, for rockets. Make a graph showing these records.

PROPERTIES OF AIR

Man is adapted to live in air at a pressure of about 15 pounds per square inch. But this was not realized for many years. Men, accustomed to the lowlands, who climbed the high peaks of the Alps got "mountain sickness," but they did not know what caused it. In 1783 the Montgolfier [mŏnt-gŏl'fĭ-ēr] brothers in France, made the first practical balloon. Soon

From Encyclopaedia Britannica film The Atmosphere and Its Circulation

Left: How a mercury barometer works. Middle: This aneroid barometer measures altitude (see page 382). Right: As altitude increases, air pressure decreases.

men were rising to unheard-of heights in flimsy baskets swinging from these hot-air bags. These man also experienced "mountain sickness." Sometimes they even lost consciousness.

In 1875 the French meteorologist Gaston Tissandier [tē-säɴ-dyā'] and two companions cast off on a balloon flight. They suspected that lack of oxygen, resulting from low air pressure, was dangerous at high altitudes, so they took along a flask of oxygen. But by the time the balloon reached 20,000 feet, the men were too weak to open the oxygen flask. The balloon rose to 28,000 feet. When it descended, Tissandier was unconscious and his two companions were dead. There was not enough pressure at that height to force life-giving oxygen from the air into their blood.

HIGH-ALTITUDE FLYING

Army and Navy fliers use oxygen masks at altitudes of more than 10,000 feet. A "Superfortress" can cruise at 35,000 feet, but the crew cannot live in the "thin" air at that altitude. As a result, this and other high-altitude planes have pressurized cabins. Air is pumped into these airtight cabins and compressed until the pressure is about that at sea level. Thus, the crew is protected from the deadly effects of low oxygen pressure. If a leak in the pressure system develops, the crew must put on oxygen masks immediately.

WEIGHT AND PRESSURE

The enormous weight of the atmosphere is the total weight of untold billions of exceedingly small molecules of gases, such as nitrogen, oxygen, carbon dioxide, and water vapor, that make up the air. A chemist is interested in these gases because they are essential to both plant and animal life. A meteorologist is interested in the gases not so much as chemicals, but in the ways they mix, move, and conduct heat and electricity.

The direct effect of the weight of air is its pressure. This is the same pressure you feel when a book or any object rests on the palm of your hand. It is the direct effect of the most universal force on earth—gravity. The pull of gravity on the air gives it weight. Because of its weight, air presses on all things submerged in it.

Air Pressure. Pressure may be caused by forces other than weight. The pressure of a screw or a wedge may be thousands of times its own weight because of the mechanical advantage of these simple machines. Pressure may result from the potential energy of a coiled spring or a compressed gas. It may also come from the kinetic energy of objects in motion, such as a baseball hitting a window or the wind blowing against an umbrella. Since this is true, the pressure of air is not always the pressure resulting from weight alone. The pressure of air may be increased or decreased if the air is moving, especially if it is moving up or down.

Quiet air at sea level exerts a pressure of 14.7 pounds per square inch. Usually air pressure and the weight of an air column are the same. But if the air is moving downward, as it often does, it is actually piling up and *compressing* the column of air, so there is more air in the 1-square-inch column. When this happens, the pressure is slightly *greater* than 14.7 pounds per square inch. The reverse can happen, too. Air often moves upward on hot days. Then there is *less* air in the column and consequently less pressure. This relationship between the movement of air and the resulting pressure is most important in weather forecasting and in flying.

Barometer. Anyone can easily demonstrate that a basketball filled with air weighs slightly more than one that is deflated. As early as 1643, Evangelista Torricelli [tŏr-rĕ-chĕl′lĕ], an Italian scientist, discovered a practical way of "weighing" the air by balancing it against a column of *mercury*, a silvery, liquid metal 13 times as heavy as water. His device, known as the *barometer*, is even more important today than it was when it was made.

To construct a barometer, seal a narrow glass tube not quite a yard long at one end. Fill the tube with mercury. Place a finger over the open end of the tube, and invert the tube in an open dish filled with mercury. When the finger is removed, the mercury in the tube falls to a level of about 30 inches and remains there, supported by the pressure of the air on the surface of the mercury in the dish. If the air pressure decreases, so does the level of the mercury in the tube. An increase in the air pressure causes the mercury to rise.

The modern mercury barometer used in scientific laboratories and weather stations consists of a reservoir and tube of mercury mounted on a wooden support or in a metal case. A ruled scale enables air pressure to be read to hundredths of an inch. Other adjustments make the mercury barometer a highly accurate and dependable instrument.

Another kind of barometer, the *aneroid barometer*, consists of a chamber about the size of a silver dollar made of springy metal, from which the air has been partly removed. The normal pressure of the atmosphere forces the sides of the chamber together. When the air pressure decreases, the springy sides bulge out. With increased pressure, the sides are forced farther in. This movement of the metal walls is very slight, but levers magnify the change and move a needle across a dial which is marked so that pressure can be read.

Left: Laboratory mercury barometers. Middle: An accurate hair hygrometer (see page 385) indicates relative humidity. Right: Movements of radiosonde balloons are followed by radar to get information on the winds aloft.

U. S. Weather Bureau photos

Uses of Barometers. Barometers have two principal uses. Since air pressure decreases with height, a barometer at Denver, Colorado (elevation 1 mile) will indicate lower pressure than one at Miami, Florida (elevation 10 feet). Thus, a barometer can be used to measure altitude. When used for this purpose, the scale of the barometer (usually an aneroid barometer) is marked directly in feet, and the instrument is known as an *altimeter*. If carried up a mountain or installed in a plane, an altimeter will indicate the altitude to within 10 or 20 feet.

How Pressure Changes with Elevation

Inches of Mercury	Elevation in Feet
30	0
29	950
28	1,900
27	2,900
26	3,900
25	5,000
20	11,000
15	18,000
10	25,000

The figures given in the table above are average figures. Actually, the drop in pressure varies slightly from summer to winter. Because air is more compressed at low altitudes, a drop of 1 inch on the barometer indicates less change in altitude than a drop of 1 inch at higher levels where the air is thinner.

Another use of the barometer is in weather-forecasting. A recording barometer, called a *barograph*, records the changes in air pressure as different bodies of air move past a weather station. These changes in pressure are related to storms, cold waves, and other air movements. Hence, air pressure is one of the important factors in predicting weather.

The pressure of the air may be written in several ways. It may be given in pounds per square inch or in inches of mercury—29.92 inches is the *normal pressure* at sea level. Air pressure is often recorded in metric units. Thus, the normal sea-level pressure is 760 millimeters of mercury, since 25.4 millimeters equal 1 inch.

When pressure is used to indicate height, as in an altimeter, the scale is read directly in feet or in inches of mercury. But for meteorology none of these measures is satisfactory. On weather maps, which are used to make all weather predictions, pressure is indicated in *millibars*, a unit of force. About 34 millibars equal the pressure of 1 inch of mercury. Hence, normal sea-level pressure (29.92 inches) is 1013 millibars. This new unit is being used more and more, and familiarity with it is necessary for a flier or anyone else who uses weather maps.

WORKING WITH SCIENCE

1. Prepare a mercury barometer according to the instructions on page 381. Mark the height of the mercury column and check for up or down movement over a period of several days. Compare the readings with official Weather Bureau figures.

2. Construct an aneroid barometer by stretching a piece of balloon rubber across the top of a quart milk bottle and tying it tight. Glue a long, straw pointer to the center of the rubber. What limits the accuracy of this instrument?

3. If any buildings in your town are five stories high, you may be able to measure their height with a mercury or aneroid barometer. Make several careful readings of the instrument at the

The "greenhouse" effect.

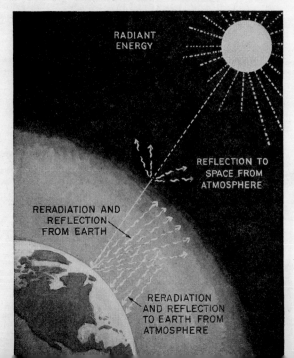

RADIANT ENERGY

REFLECTION TO SPACE FROM ATMOSPHERE

RERADIATION AND REFLECTION FROM EARTH

RERADIATION AND REFLECTION TO EARTH FROM ATMOSPHERE

street level and then again at the top floor. Determine the drop in pressure as a fraction of an inch, and compute the building's height, knowing that a height of 950 feet produces a drop of 1 inch on the barometer.

HEAT AND WEATHER

Heat (see Unit 10) is actually the result of the motion and consequent collision of molecules. If the rate of molecular collisions of an object is doubled, its heat is doubled.

The atmosphere is warmed by the heat of the sun, but not directly. Energy pours out from the sun in amounts almost beyond understanding. The earth receives only 1 two-billionth of the sun's energy but much of this is "wasted."

HEAT FROM THE SUN

The sun's energy reaches us in the form of visible and invisible light, but clouds reflect about 40 percent of the light the earth receives. Some light rays are scattered through the air, making the sky, which is actually colorless, seem to be blue. About 40 percent of the energy reaches the surface of the earth and is absorbed.

On striking the earth, some of the radiant energy is transformed into *heat waves* that heat the earth's surface. These waves strike molecules of the earth's surface and increase the speed of their motion. This increased molecular motion of the earth bombards the molecules of air, increasing their speed and thus heating the air in contact with the earth. As these molecules hit other molecules above them, the heat gradually moves out into space. Thus, the atmosphere acts as a gigantic greenhouse for the earth, blanketing it with a warm, protective layer of air but slowly losing heat into outer space.

The earth is unevenly heated by the sun. This is because various substances, such as water, soil, and rock, require different amounts of radiant energy to be heated equally. Consequently, the air over a large land mass, like Asia, heats and cools faster

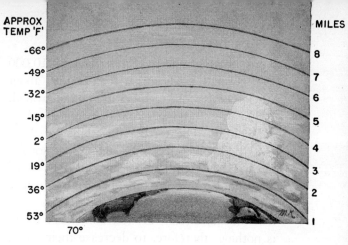

APPROX TEMP 'F'		MILES
-66°		8
-49°		7
-32°		6
-15°		5
2°		4
19°		3
36°		2
53°		1
70°		

Up to about 8 miles, temperature drops steadily.

and is generally hotter or colder than air over the nearby Pacific Ocean.

The daily and seasonal movements of the earth affect the spread of the energy received from the sun. This energy is called solar energy. Generally, the regions near the equator receive the greatest heat, but not all of the time. In our summer, the region 30 to 35 degrees north of the equator receives the most heat. In our winter, a similar region south of the equator is warmest.

If any one condition is the basis of the weather, it is the *unequal heating of the earth's surface*. This unequal heating causes unequal heating of the air which results in winds, rain, lightning, snow, tornadoes, and other storms. The importance of heat and heat distribution cannot be overestimated in considering weather.

TEMPERATURE AND ALTITUDE

Heat is, of course, a form of energy. Really it is a form of motion—the motion of molecules. When a molecule strikes another molecule, it increases the speed of the molecule but loses some of its own speed. As the second molecule hits a third molecule, and it, in turn, a fourth, and so on, the original energy is spread among many molecules. In other words, each molecule in succession is hit somewhat less hard than the one preceding it. For this reason, temperature decreases rapidly with height. The average temperature drop in quiet air is about 3°F per 1000 feet, or 17°F per mile.

Thus, the thermometer in a plane at 10,000 feet normally indicates a temperature about 30° lower than the temperature on the ground.

The drop in temperature does not continue indefinitely. The temperature falls to about −67°F at 50,000 feet and usually does not fall much farther with increasing altitude. This may be because the number of molecules relative to the spaces between them is so small that they have relatively few collisions. There is nothing, therefore, to decrease their speed or heat energy.

This constant temperature layer exists all over the world—in the tropics as well as in the arctic. The region where temperature no longer drops with altitude is the *stratosphere*. It generally begins at a height of about 30,000 feet but may begin as high as 50,000 feet. The exact height varies from day to day, with the season and with the distance north or south of the equator.

The lower region of the atmosphere, where the temperature drops with the altitude, is the *troposphere*. It extends from sea level to the base of the stratosphere. It is the region of storms, clouds, wind, and rain. It is the part of the atmosphere we live in and in which most flying is done.

HEATING AND COOLING BY PRESSURE

The drop in temperature of 3°F per 1000 feet takes place only in quiet air. When air is moving upward or downward, as it often does, a new condition holds. As air descends, as when it flows down from a mountain, it is pressed by the air pushing down upon it and is compressed. The molecules are forced closer together. As they collide more frequently, their heat is increased. You may have noticed that a bicycle-pump hose gets hot when you pump (compress) air into a tire. The rapidly colliding air molecules heat the pump hose.

The reverse is also true. As air rises, it expands and cools, and its temperature is lowered. Your electric refrigerator works on the same principle. A fluid is expanded so rapidly that the molecules collide relatively very few times in a minute, thus cooling the refrigerator. This heating and cooling of air as a result of compression and expansion have a marked effect on climate, because they are important in the formation of clouds, rain, wind, and storms.

Death Valley. The prevailing west wind that blows across southern California provides a good example of the cooling effect of expansion and the heating effect of compression. This wind is forced up the west slopes of the high Sierra Nevada Mountains. As it rises, it expands, cools, and loses much of its moisture. (Cold air cannot hold as much water vapor as can warm air.) By the time it has reached the crests of the Sierras, at a height of about 15,000 feet, it is very dry and cold.

Then the air pours over the crest and down the steep eastern slope into Death Valley. The air descends a full 15,000 feet. It is compressed and warmed about *5°F for each 1000 feet it falls.* The falling air is heated 75°F, more or less. The resulting hot, dry air is one reason why the region to the east of the Sierras is a burning, parched desert. Death Valley is one of the lowest regions of land in the United States. The air which pours into Death Valley has just passed over one of the highest regions of the United States. The tremendous drop and compression of the air passing into Death Valley makes it the hot, dry region it is.

WORKING WITH SCIENCE

1. The "greenhouse" effect results from the fact that light rays penetrate the air more easily than the longer heat rays. The atmosphere becomes a sort of one-way screen. The same principle is used in heating houses, greenhouses, and cold frames. How does it operate in each of these cases?

2. It is easy to demonstrate that compression produces heat. Pump up an automobile tire, and notice the temperature of the pump barrel before and after you do the job. Also visit the nearest

garage and look at the air compressor. You will notice that it is built with a special design to dispel the heat generated when it is in action.

3. From weather reports in the daily paper or from weather maps, compare the temperature at several cities of the same latitude. Do this on several different days, as there may be daily variations resulting from different air conditions. How does the temperature at Philadelphia usually compare with the temperature at Columbus, Ohio, or that at Boston with Sioux City?

4. The principle of heating and cooling by compression and expansion is widely used in industry.

Why Death Valley is extremely dry.

Your electric refrigerator is an example. Find out how your refrigerator works, and report to the class. Exactly what does the motor do?

WATER IN THE AIR

Changes in air temperature produce marked effects since they affect the amount of moisture in the air. This moisture is the source of our rain, snow, hail, and frost. The moisture in the air is another clue to the secret of the weather. Visible moisture, suspended as clouds or falling as rain or snow, is a part of weather that everyone has seen and the importance of which everyone knows.

Water vapor is always present in air. This water vapor is invisible—just as invisible as oxygen and nitrogen that make up most of the atmosphere. It differs from the *water droplets* that are visible and make up clouds and fog.

Water vapor is always present in air but not in any fixed amount. It may be almost completely absent, or it may make up as much as 5 percent of the total weight of the air. This is not a large percentage, but the total weight of water in the air averages something like 225 thousand billion tons.

RELATIVE HUMIDITY

The total amount of water in the air is not as important as the amount of water actually in the air compared with the amount the air at that temperature can hold. This relationship is known as *relative humidity*. When air contains as much water as it can possibly hold, the relative humidity is 100 percent. If air contains only half the water it can possibly hold, the relative humidity is 50 percent.

Hygrometer. Relative humidity is measured by an instrument known as a *hygrometer*. A hygrometer contains a fine, blonde, human hair or a plastic fiber that stretches as the moisture in the air increases. The stretching of the hair moves a lever and sends a needle across a dial, thereby giving a direct reading of the relative humidity of the air.

Another type of hygrometer consists of two thermometers. Around the bulb of one is a moist cloth. The "wet" thermometer usually gives a lower reading than the "dry" thermometer. The difference in temperature measured by the two thermometers enables one to compute the relative humidity.

Capacity of air to hold water increases with its temperature. Warm air will take up more moisture than cold air if water is available. If the temperature of a mass of air rises and more water is not available, the relative humidity of the mass of air drops and its ability to take up water is increased. This is what happens to the air that tumbles over the steep eastern slope of the Sierras. When air is warmed by compression, it becomes relatively drier. It takes up moisture from the land, helping to create desert conditions.

Dewpoint. If the temperature of a mass of air decreases, its relative humidity *increases*. It may continue to increase until its relative humidity is 100 percent. At this point, the air is said to be saturated. It cannot hold more moisture. The temperature to which air must be cooled to raise the relative humidity to 100 percent is the *dewpoint*. The dewpoint is the temperature at which the invisible water vapor condenses into visible water droplets, forming dew, clouds or fog, and finally rain or snow.

A Pound of Water. Imagine a small room, 8¼ feet long, 8¼ feet wide, and 8¼ feet high—more a cell than a room. On a summer day when the temperature is 84°F and the air is saturated, the air in this space—560 cubic feet—holds a pound of water vapor. If the temperature drops 20°F, as it might at night, the temperature becomes lower than the dewpoint. And part of the water vapor in the air condenses on the walls, ceiling, and floor.

Air usually cools during the night and the relative humidity increases. When air is sufficiently cooled, its relative humidity reaches 100 percent, and the air contains all the moisture it can hold at that temperature. If the air cools more, the excess water vapor present condenses, forming water droplets if the temperature is above the freezing point of water, or ice crystals if it is below. The next morning you will probably find dew on the grass or, if the temperature has dropped below the dewpoint and below freezing, frost will cover the ground.

Saturation, which produces dew or frost at the dewpoint, also produces clouds. Clouds form at the level where the air is saturated and where condensation takes place. The weatherman, who knows the humidity of a mass of air and the way it is moving, can predict what kind of clouds will form, at what height, and when.

PRODUCTS OF CONDENSATION

Products of condensation are formed when part of a mass of air is cooled to its dewpoint. Cooling and condensation are not uniform throughout the atmosphere because of differences within the atmosphere. You have proof of this when you see it raining in one spot and not raining a few blocks away.

Another factor is involved. Scientists have found that condensation will take place only when the air contains many small particles upon which the water vapor can condense. These may be dust or smoke particles, or even the microscopic bits of salt picked up as winds blow over an ocean. Fortunately, such particles are generally present.

Clouds. Clouds are the most familiar condensation product. There are many types of clouds, each with a special meaning in the weather. Clouds are *not* water vapor, but are usually made up of tiny droplets of water averaging about 0.001 inch in diameter. About 200 million of these droplets are equal to one teaspoonful of water.

While most clouds are composed of water droplets, they are far from being all water. A cubic foot of water weighs 62.5 pounds. The water droplets in a cubic foot of average cloud weigh less than 0.001 pound. When the dewpoint of a mass of air is below 32°F, as it usually is at heights above 20,000 feet, clouds are made up of tiny crystals of ice instead of droplets of water.

Cloud Types. Clouds are classified according to their height and form. High clouds are 20,000 to 40,000 feet above the ground. Middle clouds are generally found from 6500 feet to 20,000 feet, and low clouds lie from the ground surface up to 6500 feet.

There are three principal types of clouds, and these exist in several combinations. *Cirrus* (curly) clouds are light, fleecy, or stringy. They are too fine to cast shadows. *Cumulus* (heaped) clouds are lumpy and billowy, like white woolpacks. They may be gray underneath and cast shadows as they move along. *Stratus* (layered) clouds are sheetlike, flat layers of clouds that may cover the horizon or the entire sky. *Nimbus* (rainstorm) clouds are those from which rain and snow fall. As they are a combining form with stratus or cumulus clouds, they may be sheetlike or merge into towering, dense, mountainous clouds that form a typical "thunderhead."

CIRRUS
30,000 FT

CIRRO-STRATUS
35,000 FT

CIRRO-CUMULUS
20,000 FT

CUMULO-NIMBUS
2,500 TO 20,000 FT

ALTO-STRATUS
15,000 FT

ALTO-CUMULUS, 12,000 FT

CUMULUS
2,500 TO 20,000 FT

STRATO-CUMULUS
5,000 FT

CUMULO-NIMBUS
2,500 TO 20,000 FT

NIMBO-STRATUS, 2,500 FT

STRATUS 2,000 FT

Cloud types and the altitude at which they are normally found.

Besides these basic cloud types, there are cloud combinations, such as cirro-stratus (cirrus clouds in layers) and cumulo-nimbus (cumulus clouds that develop into a summer thunderstorm). Other combinations are equally simple. The general cloud classification is given in the illustration above. The heights given are average heights to the base of the cloud, except in the case of cumulus and cumulo-nimbus clouds. These grow vertically and may be found anywhere between the heights given.

An air-mass fog along a coast.

Clouds generally are higher in summer than in winter. Several types may be in the sky at one time. The actual height of clouds depends on many local conditions. Average heights as given on page 387 are only a general indication of the cloud level.

Both the types of the clouds and their order as they pass across the sky give a clue to the kind of mass of air present. Learn to know the principal cloud types. They are quickly identified, and they will tell you how the weather is changing when you do not have a weather forecast handy.

As you might expect from their extreme height, cirrus-type clouds are composed of tiny ice crystals, so small that they scarcely interfere with the passage of sunlight. The clouds of middle height may contain ice crystals, water droplets, or a mixture of both, depending upon the season and upon local conditions. The lowest clouds are nearly always composed of water droplets and are, with the middle clouds, the source of much of our rain and snow. Low clouds are often low enough to cut visibility and hamper the use of airways.

The cloud classification is not perfect because clouds, like all other natural objects, vary in form. They are constantly changing from one type to another as the weather changes.

Fog. A good question for a quiz program might be, "When is a cloud not a cloud?"

The answer is, "When it is on the ground." A cloud on the ground is *fog*. Fog may form in a number of different ways, but it is of two general types.

Air-mass fog forms *within* a large body of air, usually by local cooling as the air comes near, or in contact with, cold land or water. Land cools quickly at evening, and warm, moist air that blows against this land is cooled on its lower surface. As condensation takes place, it may be in the form of fog. Air-mass fog is the common fog often seen in the evening or early morning. It is the type of fog most common over the Newfoundland fishing banks and off the coast of California. The other, more limited, type of fog, is the *frontal* fog, which may form when a warm mass of air meets a cold mass of air.

Weather forecasters are still studying the conditions under which fog forms. Under certain special conditions, fog forms even before the air is saturated. As meteorologists learn more about the conditions causing fog, they will be better able to predict its appearance. In an age of flying, fog is a serious hazard.

Drizzle. Water droplets in fog are somewhat smaller than those in clouds. They are less than 0.001 inch in diameter. About 7 billion fog droplets would form a teaspoonful of water. These droplets are too small to settle. Droplets that are somewhat larger, up to 0.002 inch in diameter fall gradually, though the slightest air movement will carry them aloft. Such droplets, falling from low stratus clouds, are called *drizzle*.

Rain. Though meteorologists are still uncertain as to the exact way rain forms, they classify drops larger than fog as *rain*. Usually they are so large that they fall at a speed of at least 10 feet per second and there are fewer than in drizzle. If the rain is of short duration and the drops are especially large, the result is a *shower*. Showers usually come from isolated clouds that develop rapidly during warm summer days.

Hail. Summer cumulus clouds often mark an area where air, warmed by the heated land, is rising rapidly. Often it is rising so rapidly that when rain begins, the drops are carried *upward* instead of falling down. The drops are carried up so high that they may freeze, since the upper levels of a thunderhead may be higher than 20,000 feet and the temperature well below freezing. The frozen drops, or *hailstones*, may gather moisture and grow in size as they fall.

Hailstones may be carried aloft several times before falling to the ground. Examine a hailstone, and you will see that it is composed of layers of ice, somewhat like an onion. Each layer of ice marks a movement into the freezing level of the cloud. Hailstones may become as large as several inches in diameter. Such size alone indicates the strength of the updraft in the thunderhead.

Snow. Rain, drizzle, fog, and hail generally form when the dewpoint of the air is *above* freezing, though it is possible, for example, to have a fog composed of ice crystals. Usually when condensation occurs *below* freezing, condensation forms as *snow* or ice. Snowflakes grow in size as water vapor condenses, and several snowflakes may cling together.

Snowflakes form a characteristic six-sided or six-pointed crystal of rare beauty and complexity of design. Snowflakes can be studied easily by catching them on a dark cloth and observing them through a small magnifying glass or microscope. Individual snowflakes will gradually evaporate even at below freezing temperatures. Above freezing, they will quickly melt.

Sleet, Glaze, and Ice. Sleet forms when raindrops freeze while passing through cold air near the ground. The term is also loosely used to describe a mixture of snow and rain. *Glaze,* or *ice,* forms as drizzle or rain freezes on contact with objects below freezing temperatures. If glaze forms on the control surfaces of wings, propeller, or in the carburetor of a plane, the effects may be serious enough to cause a crash. Ice storms have caused enormous damage to telephone and telegraph lines, trees, and crops.

HEAT TRANSFER

All forms of condensation depend upon *heat transfer* within the atmosphere. To fully understand them, it is necessary to know the ways in which the atmosphere is heated and cooled.

Radiation. The sun's energy reaches the earth by radiation. Energy radiated from the sun, called radiant energy, is transformed into heat when it is absorbed by some substance. The surface of the earth absorbs it and transforms it into heat. Much of this heat passes into the air as *all* warm solid bodies radiate heat. This direct transmission of heat makes us comfortable in front of a fireplace or near a stove on a cold day.

Under what conditions do snow (left) and dew (right) form?

Convection. Fluids, that is, liquids and gases, transfer heat by *convection*. This is heat transfer by means of currents set up by *unequal heating*. A heated fluid expands and, because it becomes lighter than the surrounding fluid, rises and is replaced by colder fluid. This action produces a current that moves vertically or horizontally. Convection currents may be easily watched by setting a pot of water over a small flame and dropping bits of colored paper into the water. As the water is heated, the movements of the paper mark the path of the convection currents.

Since air is a fluid and since it is constantly being heated by the warm land and water, convection currents are set up in the atmosphere. These currents are the means by which the unequally distributed solar heat is spread out over the surface of the earth.

Conduction. Conduction is the third method of heat transfer. This is the method of direct contact. In conduction heat energy passes from molecule to molecule through a substance, like a bucket brigade passing water at a fire. Conduction is best illustrated by solids. Some, such as copper, silver, and iron, are excellent conductors of heat. The part of the atmosphere that is in actual contact with the earth may be heated or cooled by conduction. But in general, radiation and convection are of far greater importance in the heating of the atmosphere.

THE INGREDIENTS OF WEATHER

The air—its weight, pressure, humidity, temperature, and movement—is the basis of our weather. However, the effects of these factors are modified by the movements of the earth, the relationship of land and water bodies, mountain ranges, and other physical features of the land. Weather is complicated because all these things are involved. A meteorologist must know not only the basic facts about the atmosphere, but also the local conditions as they affect weather at his post. Such familiarity leads to a more complete understanding of weather and to the ability to make weather predictions for longer periods.

So far, we really have been looking at the raw materials of the weather—the essential ingredients. Our picture is still very incomplete. To help round it out, we must consider what happens to these ingredients. How is weather made from humidity, temperature, and pressure? What makes the machinery of the weather tick? From the ingredients we must turn our attention to the practical elements of the weather—the masses of air that, by their movement and mixing, make our days hot or cold, wet or dry, windy or calm. The story of these masses of air is a new one. It has a new point of view that considers a three-dimensional atmosphere—one in which the height of the atmosphere is as important as its width and length.

WORKING WITH SCIENCE

1. Make an artificial cloud under conditions that approximate those in nature. All you need is a bicycle pump and a milk bottle with a cork. Drill the cork so that the tube from the pump will fit tightly through it. Wash out the inside of the bottle to moisten it—then hold down the cork and pump until the air in the bottle is compressed. Remove the cork suddenly or let it blow out because of the pressure. As the air decompresses, condensation will take place and a "cloud" or fog will fill the bottle.

2. If some blonde girl in the class will contribute a few long strands of hair, you can make a simple hygrometer. Glue one end of the hair to a nail in a board, and fasten a small weight, such as a split BB shot, with a paper pointer to the other. As the hair stretches and contracts with changes in the humidity, the small differences can be noted as the pointer moves up and down.

3. Another type of hygrometer can be made from two cheap thermometers. Remove one thermometer from its scale and cut the scale off at the 20° mark. This permits the bulb to extend beyond the scale when you remount the thermometer. Wrap some absorbent cotton around this bulb and moisten the cotton. Fan both thermometers and compare the readings. Tables are available to convert the difference in temperature into relative humidity.

4. Those who are interested in flying can follow up the important problems of icing on planes. All large planes are now equipped with various kinds of de-icing equipment, yet the basic problem is still unsolved. Report to the class on the conditions under which icing occurs and how serious this icing may be to aircraft.

5. Snowflakes are perhaps the most unusual of all weather products. Their infinite variations in design, all based on the same pattern have long attracted attention. A camera enthusiast can have fun attempting to photograph snow crystals. The task requires careful organization so that it can be done rapidly. You can make quick sketches of snowflakes even if you do not photograph them. These make an interesting exhibit.

6. Cut a column of snow from a recent snowfall. The snow column may be cut with a large sized fruit-juice can, opened top and bottom. Measure its height, and then melt the snow. Pour the water into a container of the same diameter and find out how many inches of snow equal 1 inch of water. Try several samples and get an average answer.

7. Convection currents can be demonstrated by heating a large beaker or pot of water over a low bunsen burner or alcohol lamp. Tiny bits of paper or a crystal or two of potassium permanganate dropped in the water show the direction of the currents.

READING YOU WILL ENJOY

Baer, Marian E. *Rain or Shine*. Rinehart & Co., Inc., New York, 1940. An interesting and well-written book about the weather and the men who study it.

Brooks, Charles F. *Why the Weather?* Harcourt, Brace & Co., New York, 1935. If you think that clouds float or the groundhog determines the weather, read this interesting book. It will give you accurate and understandable information about weather at various times of the year.

Gaer, Joseph. *Fair and Warmer*. Harcourt, Brace & Co., New York, 1939. The work of the United States Weather Bureau and the scientific study of the weather. Includes interesting discussion of popular superstitions and suppositions about the weather.

Pickwell, Gayle B. *Weather*. McGraw-Hill Book Co., New York, 1938. Beautiful, large photographs of clouds and weather conditions make this book particularly useful.

Attempts at forecasting the weather began long before the day of recorded history. Early man was always on the lookout for weather signs such as winds, clouds, flights of birds, and various activities of animals.

The weather lore of the ancients was not very reliable because the things actually responsible for weather were not then known. In fact, only now are we beginning to understand much about them. By 1899, de Bort (1), a French weather scientist, had completed studies that set off the stratosphere from the warmer air beneath and placed all of our weather in this lower layer of air from 5 to 8 miles thick. During World War I, Vilhelm Bjerknes and his son (2), Norwegian meteorologists, studied the movements of tremendous air masses and the effects produced when air masses meet. From their work, the idea of air mass analysis—the basis of modern weather forcasting—was born.

Air-mass analysis requires observations taken at various levels of the air in many parts of the world. One of the instruments used in obtaining such data is the radiosonde (3) a small balloon that sends data automatically to the weather station by radio. From weather stations in air-mass source areas, such as the far north (4), weather data are transmitted by radio.

29

THE AIR MASSES

Weather is chiefly the result of the unequal distribution of heat throughout the atmosphere. The movements of air caused by this unbalanced heating are the basis of atmospheric circulation. These air movements are both horizontal and vertical. The horizontal movements of the air produce what we commonly call *wind*. Winds are the currents in the ocean of air. Winds might be compared to the Gulf Stream, Japan Current, or other streams of warm or cold water that move within the seas.

GENERAL AIR MOVEMENTS

To understand air movements, let us first assume that the earth does *not* rotate. In the equatorial regions of such a nonrotating earth, air is warmed by contact with the warm land and water. The warmed air expands and, becoming lighter, rises. Cooler air flows in from both sides to replace the warmed air, which rises less rapidly as it cools and finally ceases to rise at all once its temperature equals that of the surrounding air. The pressure of the rising warm air pushes the cooled air off to each side of the warm air belt, and this air flows north and south at high altitudes. As this air flows northward or southward, it is so thoroughly cooled that it begins to sink and return to the surface of our nonrotating earth.

In the arctic and antarctic regions of this nonrotating earth, the reverse condition is true. Air over the poles is constantly cooled. It becomes relatively heavy and sinks, flowing out over the land surface. Other air from warmer latitudes flows in at high levels, replacing the air that has descended and setting up a system of circulation.

Between the tropical and polar regions lie the middle latitude regions where warm and cold air continually meet. It is here on our nonrotating world, that most storms originate and here that weather is most variable.

Left: Air movements on a nonrotating earth. Right: Circulation cells on a rotating earth.

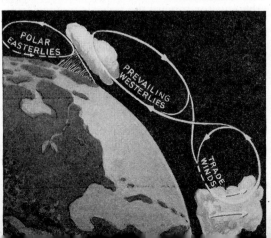

Winds aloft (white arrows); surface (black).

WINDS ON A ROTATING EARTH

The path of the air that rises and falls and moves horizontally across the earth is changed by the fact that the earth is constantly spinning on its axis. In addition, the speed of rotation varies with the distance from the equator.

The earth rotates once in 24 hours. At the equator, the distance around the earth is about 25,000 miles. To cover this distance in 24 hours, the earth rotates at a speed of more than 1000 miles per hour. About 4 miles from the poles, the distance around the earth is only 24 miles. This distance also is covered in 24 hours, but at a speed of only 1 mile per hour. The speed of rotation of the earth varies from more than 1000 miles per hour to zero, as one moves from the equator toward the poles. At 60 degrees north or south latitude, the earth's speed is half that at the equator.

The variation in speed of rotation has a marked effect on the winds. Air moving from the equator toward the poles is moving from a region of greater speed to a region of less speed. As it starts toward the north, it has an easterly speed of about 1000 miles an hour. As it moves north, it pushes forward over an earth whose rotation, or easterly movement, is steadily decreasing.

At 60 degrees north latitude the speed of the earth rotating toward the east is about 500 miles per hour. This causes air currents from the equator to swing to the *east* in the Northern Hemisphere and to the *west* in the Southern Hemisphere. Thus, the air moving northward forms a *west* wind (winds are named for the direction *from* which they blow) and the air moving southward forms an *east* wind.

The shifting in wind direction caused by the rotation of the earth is known as *deflection*. It determines the direction of the *general*, or *prevailing*, *winds*. These prevailing winds have had a great effect on our history. In the days of sailing ships they handicapped trips from Europe to America. Today they speed planes across the Atlantic from America to Europe. Planes making the westward trip take slightly different routes to avoid headwinds. These same prevailing winds control much of our rainfall, thereby determining whether lands are moist or dry, fruitful or barren.

The deflection owing to rotation affects not only the major wind movements but the smaller and less important ones too. All air movements in the Northern Hemisphere are deflected to the right and in the Southern Hemisphere to the left.

Pressure Gradients. The movements of winds are easier to understand if you realize that, like water, winds always flow "downhill." The downhill in this case does not refer to any visible hill or valley but to the pressure slope, or *gradient*, of the atmosphere.

A hill, or *high*, in the atmosphere is an area where the air pressure is higher than in the surrounding air. A high may be the result of air being cooled or moving downward. Winds blow down and *outward* from such a high-pressure area. There are also low-pressure, or *low*, areas in the atmosphere that are comparable to valleys or basins. Here the air may be moving upward, thereby reducing pressure. Winds blow into these valleys and down their invisible slopes. But in this case, winds blow *toward* the center where the pressure is less.

Winds should, therefore, blow in toward

low-pressure areas and out from high-pressure areas. They do, but their direction is modified by the rotation of the earth, which always deflects them to the right in the Northern Hemisphere. This deflection makes the wind shift *clockwise* from a high-pressure area and *counterclockwise* toward a low-pressure area.

Locating a Storm Center. Here in the Northern Hemisphere there is a good rule to determine the low-pressure area involved in a storm. When a person stands with his back to the wind, the low-pressure area is to his *left* and *slightly ahead*. If you are out in the open during a storm, try this several times during the storm and you will see that the center of the storm (the low-pressure area) moves onward, generally to the east.

The illustration on page 394 shows the general pattern of winds. Each belt of wind has its own kind of weather, depending on the nature of the land or water over which the wind blows. Moving masses of air are modified somewhat by contact with the land and water over which they pass. This is especially true when the areas of land or water over which the masses of air pass are large.

Air that passes over the warm waters of the Caribbean Sea and the Gulf of Mexico gradually becomes warm and moist. Air moving over the cold lands of northern Canada and Alaska becomes cold and dry. Air farther to the west, over the Aleutian Islands and the North Pacific, is typically cold and moist. Regions *large enough* to modify the air that moves over them are called *source regions*, and a widespread body of air that takes on its characteristics from such a region is called an *air mass*.

WORKING WITH SCIENCE

1. The basic wind movements resulting from unequal heating can be demonstrated over an ordinary kitchen stove, bunsen burner, or radiator. Each one of these creates a strong updraft. Very small bits of absorbent cotton or milkweed floss tossed into this updraft will be carried upward, and if conditions are right, they will move out along the ceiling, descend, and may even move back toward the source of the heat.

2. Set a small block of "dry ice" over the north pole of a globe. **Caution:** *Do not touch the "dry ice" with your hands.* Notice how the vapor spreads southward in all directions. This is similar to the movement of air from the polar high-pressure area.

3. In understanding weather, relationships are most important. These can be discovered by getting a good physical map of the world. Prepare a piece of cellophane big enough to fit over the map by coating it with a gelatin solution. After coating, you can paint on the cellophane with water colors or draw with India ink. Draw the principal wind belts. Set the overlay on top of the physical map, and see what relationships are evident between winds and deserts, mountain ranges, ocean currents, or other physical features.

AIR MASSES OF NORTH AMERICA

The power of an air mass should not be underestimated. People travel from New York to Florida in winter to escape the harsh effects of one air mass, while they enjoy the soothing effects of another.

An air mass covers a large area of the earth's surface—large enough to be measured in thousands of square miles. Its temperature, pressure, and humidity are generally uniform, not throughout but at specific levels only. Hence, comparisons of air masses can be made only by referring to a specific level. You might compare two air masses and say, for example,

Air movements around a high and a low.

that at the 10,000-foot level, the air mass over northern Canada is colder and drier than the air mass over the Gulf of Mexico. But you might easily find a level in the air mass over the Gulf of Mexico (perhaps at 20,000 or 30,000 feet) that would be colder and drier than the 10,000-foot level of the air mass over northern Canada.

The important thing about an air mass is that its characteristics are generally constant at specific levels and that when they change, they do so very slowly. When cold polar air moves southward across warm land, it is not altered immediately by the heat of the surface over which it moves. The lower layers of the polar air mass are warmed and altered, but the mass as a whole is affected only gradually.

SOURCES OF AIR MASSES

There are two general source areas of air masses: *polar* and *tropical*. These correspond roughly to the high-pressure areas of the earth, characterized by the *subtropical highs*, or *horse latitudes*, and the *polar highs*. Air piles up and constantly moves out from these regions. Then there are two types of surfaces over which an air mass forms: land, or *continental*, and water, or *maritime*. These facts are used in naming and classifying the world's air masses.

CONTINENTAL POLAR AIR MASS

Continental polar air forms over the great expanse of North America that extends northward from the region of Hudson Bay to the far islands of the Arctic Ocean. This air is cold and dry. It is stable and generally free of clouds. As this continental polar air (abbreviated *cP* on weather maps, charts, and tables) moves southward, its lower layers become warmed. Consequently, their ability to hold moisture increases, and additional moisture is picked up over the Great Lakes region. Clouds or fog may develop. The increased moisture may result in snow flurries during winter as the air rises and cools in passing over the Allegheny Mountains. Pilots flying air routes over these mountains know how dangerous flying conditions there can be.

Residents of central or eastern United States and Canada recognize continental polar air as a *cold wave*. The cold air actually pushes beneath and lifts the warmer air off the surface.

Areas in which air masses originate and the general directions in which they move.

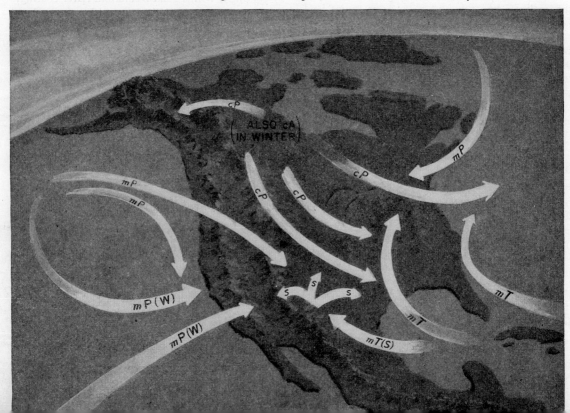

There is little mixing when this contact is made. Because of its greater density, continental polar air pushes between the ground and warm air like a wedge. This line of contact between the two distinct air masses is called a *front*. It is here that storms originate.

Continental polar air is generally confined east of the Rocky Mountains and the Cascade Range because it is a shallow air mass. It may move directly south with great rapidity, carrying freezing weather across the plains into Texas, or into the rich orange groves of Florida. It occasionally breaks across the mountains and gives Californians a taste of cold. Then the orange growers, forewarned by the Weather Bureau, light hundreds of fires in their orchards in an effort to save their delicate and valuable trees by surrounding them with a protective blanket of warm air.

CONTINENTAL ARCTIC AIR MASS

During the winter, air from the polar regions becomes even colder at its source area. This is *continental arctic* air (*cA*)—even colder and drier than continental polar air. As continental arctic air moves southward, it is warmed and it picks up moisture. It becomes similar to continental polar air.

MARITIME POLAR AIR MASS

Maritime polar air (*mP*) develops over the cold waters of the North Atlantic and North Pacific. Since water heats and cools more slowly than land, the temperature of this air mass is more moderate than that of continental air. A maritime polar mass is more moist than a continental air mass because it forms and moves over water and because its higher temperature enables it to absorb and hold more moisture. The properties of this air mass differ from summer to winter as in all air masses, but in our brief survey we will have to ignore these important seasonal changes.

The cool, moist maritime polar air swings in from the North Pacific so laden with moisture that condensation occurs as it passes over the cold ocean current that parallels the

A "northeaster" involves maritime polar air.

California and Oregon coast. The fog thus formed frequently blankets the Golden Gate during summer, often cutting visibility to zero all along the Pacific coast and handicapping both plane and sea transportation. This moist fog aids certain types of farming. Near Salinas, California it aids the rapid growth of hundreds of acres of lettuce that often ends up in winter or early spring salads.

Farther north, the moist maritime polar air is lifted over the steep Cascade Range. Condensation occurs rapidly, giving this area a rainfall of more than 100 inches annually in some places. This, more than any other single factor, accounts for the dense forest growth of the Pacific Northwest, where the largest stands of redwood, fir, spruce, and pine are found today.

As the maritime polar air descends the eastern slope of the Cascade Range, it is warmed, partly by compression. Once again it takes up moisture. This time from ground that is already too dry for good farming. In this region dams like the Grand Coulee are needed to provide water for irrigation so that the miles of rich volcanic soil may produce wheat, fruit, and other crops. If it were not for the Cascade Range, the moist maritime

Continental arctic air "dripping with cold."

Cool air passing over warmer land.

polar air would give this area sufficient rainfall.

Moving still farther east, the maritime polar air rises to the crown of the Rocky Mountains, cooling again and dropping still more of its moisture on the western slopes of the Rockies in Montana and Idaho. The west slope of the Rockies is a region of moderate rainfall with good forests and rich natural pastures. As the maritime polar air descends the east slope of the Rocky Mountains, it heats up once more. Maritime polar air rarely gets farther east than this because it encounters the colder continental polar air moving down from the north. The warmer, lighter maritime polar air is pushed up *over* the colder, continental polar air, forming clouds but generally with little or no condensation. From here on, the air from these two distinct source regions is very similar in its properties. Maritime polar air occurs over the Atlantic also.

MARITIME TROPICAL AIR MASS

Farther south, the maritime air is warm as well as moist. This *maritime tropical* air (*mT*), as it is called, develops over the Pacific Ocean west of Mexico, over the Atlantic Ocean east of the Carolinas and Florida, and over the Gulf of Mexico. Moving from the Pacific high-pressure area toward the coast, the water vapor in the moist maritime tropical air condenses as it passes over cold ocean currents. Low coastal fogs form. When the land is cool in winter, condensation may produce stratus clouds, mist, and rain.

A similar condition exists on the Atlantic coast. Warm tropical air pushing up from the Gulf or the Atlantic may produce heavy fogs or bring slow drizzling rains.

These are the major air masses that control the weather of North America. The facts you have learned about them are so brief that they cannot be of use in predicting the weather. It takes years of study to master the details that a professional meteorologist must know. But these facts are enough to make us realize that our weather does not just "happen." It is mainly the result of air-mass movements.

WARM AND COLD AIR

On weather maps, air masses are not referred to as simply *mP* or *cA*. A letter *k* or a *w* is always included as *mPw* or *cAk*. The *w* stands for *warm*, and the *k* is the abbreviation for the German world *kalt* meaning, of course, *cold*. These terms apply to the temperature of the lower levels of the air mass. If the air in the lower levels is warmer than the ground over which it is moving, the air mass is considered to be *warm*. When the

This illustration and the one on the next page show some of this country and some winds that blow.

lower levels of an air mass are colder than the ground beneath, the air mass is considered to be cold.

Cold Air. As you would expect, a cold air mass is warmed by the land below, and a warm air mass is cooled by the land beneath it. Cold air is generally clear. But the lower air, if warmed enough, will rise, producing clouds and, perhaps, rain or snow flurries. If the weatherman knows that the path of a cold air mass will take it over warmer land, he may predict increased cloudiness with probable showers or snow.

Warm Air. A warm air mass is cooled as it

Warm air passing over cooler land.

passes over cold land, but since cooled air is denser than warm air, it remains at low levels. Clouds, or fog, that form stay near the ground. If there is rain, it will be a long drizzle instead of a quick shower. While conditions on the ground may be bad and visibility poor, the upper warm air is usually smooth and stable.

WORKING WITH SCIENCE

1. Compare a weather map of 5 years ago with the kind used today. How many differences can you notice? These differences illustrate important changes in gathering and reporting weather data. Find out more about them.

A weather map is something like a diagram of the plays in a football game. Unless you know each symbol and its meaning, the whole diagram does not mean very much. If you take the trouble to learn the rain, wind, temperature, cloud, and other symbols used on official maps, you can use the maps in getting weather data.

2. Locate the principal summer and winter air masses on an outline map of North America. Which of these have the most effect on weather in your vicinity?

3. The United States Department of Agriculture Yearbook for 1941 is a survey of the climate and its effects. Using it as a reference, find out how climate and weather are important in such agricultural fields as cotton, vegetables, livestock, sugar beets, forests, tobacco, corn, and small grains.

4. On a large physical map locate the major deserts of the world. These are the result of adverse climatic conditions. How many seem to be influenced by air warmed by compression as it descends over mountains?

5. Some local winds are interesting in the way they originate and because of peculiar effects they sometimes produce. Find out about *mistral*, *chinook*, *froehn*, and other famous local winds.

Account for the precipitation indicated in terms of what you have learned about weather factors.

Air masses are important for two reasons. First, because of the weather they bring as a direct result of their physical properties and second, because of the storms that are born at the contact between two different masses of air. This contact occurs as constantly moving polar and tropical air masses meet.

When polar and tropical air masses meet, they do not mix easily. The two masses may remain as separate as layers of oil and water in a bottle. The cold, heavy polar air retains its properties and so does the lighter, tropical air. The place where one air mass meets another is called a front. The front is the line on the ground that separates the warm air from the cold air. Since the cold air is usually beneath, a front may also be considered as the *forward surface of the cold air mass*. Along a front, air is continually being disturbed. Warm air is continually pushed over cold air.

THE POLAR FRONT

The best known front is at the contact of the winds moving from the polar highs and the westerlies, moving from the subtropical highs. This is the famed polar front which, in several main segments, surrounds the arctic regions.

The cold air mass or the warm air mass advances in a surge that disturbs the entire front and sets up a wavelike motion within it. These surges, or waves, of air are large, extending from 600 to 3000 miles in width.

For a general idea of what happens, consider the air movement between two high-pressure areas. Air moves out from each high and from each is deflected by the earth's rotation so that the winds along the front *blow in parallel but opposite directions*. A zone of friction forms, and into this already disturbed area, cold air surges forward. The smooth, stationary front is disturbed by a series of waves not very different from those produced by pushing your hand through the water in a bathtub. As soon as the first ripples appear, the front is no longer stationary. It breaks up into a cold front, where the cold air is advanc-

ing, and a warm front, where the warm air is advancing.

ORIGINS OF STORMS

The ripple, if we should follow one as it progresses, grows into a wave. The wave brings a shift in the wind direction and produces a *local area of low pressure around which the winds move with a counterclockwise movement*. This area is a storm or, technically, a *cyclonic storm*. A cyclonic storm, once started, moves across country along rather well-defined paths from west to east. Storms have other origins, too, especially in the tropics.

The counterclockwise movement that is set up in a storm is the result of the deflection of our rotating earth and other forces. Perhaps you can see this better if you imagine a middle-latitude storm as a target mounted on a pivot that is moving eastward with the earth at about 500 miles per hour. A person near the North Pole, where his speed is very much less, will not hit the bull's eye if he aims at the target and shoots, because the target is moving faster than he is. He will hit to the *west* of the target.

A person shooting from the equator, where his speed is about 1000 miles per hour, is moving faster than the target and his bullets will hit to the *east* of the target instead of in the bull's eye. As the target is on a pivot, free to swing around, the bullets coming from opposite directions and hitting the edges of the target because of differences in rotational speed, send the target spinning in a counterclockwise direction. Actually, storms move much slower because of the friction of the air.

While the cyclonic storm is moving, there is movement within the cyclone as well because the cold front advances more rapidly than the warm front. The cold air gradually overtakes the warm air and lifts it off the ground, thereby producing an *occluded front*. By the time this has happened, the storm has lost much of its vigor. Soon the remnants of the wave dissolve into the general air circulation; air aloft moves parallel to the front and, hence, does no lifting.

From its beginning the cyclonic storm may have lasted a week or perhaps two. In this time it may have moved several thousand miles across the United States and out over the Atlantic Ocean. Meanwhile, new waves have formed along the polar front. Thus, we have a continual procession of storms, causing the changeable weather with which most of us are familiar.

WARM FRONT

At all fronts, warm air is forced above cold air. The front is a *warm front* only where warm air is actually replacing cooler air. The wedge of cold air under a warm front is almost like a chisel, with the warm air being pushed slowly over it. The slope of the cold-air wedge is so slight that warm air moves many miles behind the warm front before it is lifted 1 mile. This rise is slow and steady and hours pass before the air is lifted enough to produce cloud formations.

If warm air is stable, a definite series of clouds forms as the air is lifted. This series is so characteristic that even an inexperienced observer can recognize an approaching warm front and predict the weather from the clouds. You can do it yourself after you have studied the next few pages.

Warm-Front Clouds and Weather. The first clouds that an observer, standing in a cold air mass, sees are high cirrus clouds—at about 25,000 to 30,000 feet in altitude. From the general slope of the warm front, these high cirrus clouds indicate that the front itself is from 500 to 1000 miles away. The cirrus

Looking down on the origin of a cyclonic storm. Cold air is indicated by white arrows; warm air by black. Left: The two currents merge. Right: Cold air surges forward.

Above left: The ripple grows into a wave. Right: The wave produces a low-pressure area. Below: Counterclockwise winds develop and the storm moves eastward.

COLD AIR MASS   WARM AIR MASS

These cloud formations indicate the approach of a warm front.

clouds gradually change to cirro-stratus clouds and by the next day to alto-stratus clouds.

Each of these cloud layers is a bit lower than the preceding one, indicating that the region of contact between the cold and warm air is getting lower and lower. This means that the front is coming nearer and nearer. Soon the alto-stratus clouds thicken and descend even lower, forming nimbo-stratus clouds. With these come drizzle and rain.

Up to this point in our observations, all the clouds will be in the warm air, but as rain begins to fall, it passes through the cold air which is relatively dry. In the cold air the rain partly evaporates and condenses again in tiny droplets, forming stratus clouds within the cold air mass. So, as the warm front reaches the observer, there are heavy stratus clouds with rain or snow.

Knowing this series of clouds and their meaning, an observer can estimate that rain may be coming in 1 to 3 days after the high cirrus clouds first appear. A warm-front rain is slow in starting and slow in stopping. Rain may last from less than a day to nearly a week.

Aviators look askance at all warm fronts for, while they may bring farmers the long, slow rain that plants need, they bring only trouble to fliers. A warm front produces widespread stratus clouds and poor visibility. The warm, moist air cools at night and causes fog. If temperature is low enough, dangerous icing may occur.

COLD FRONT

In a *cold front* the cold air does the active pushing. It forces its way into a mass of warmer air, producing marked changes in the weather. Again the nature of the warm air and its stability are important. In structure a cold front differs in several ways from a warm front. The slope is generally steeper—about two to five times as steep as a warm front.

The cross section of a cold front is different because the cold air near the ground drags as a result of friction. The air higher up moves along more freely and faster than warm-front air. This speed causes the cold front to bulge forward. Cold fronts generally move faster than warm fronts. A fast-moving cold front travels from 15 to 20 miles per hour, or up to about 500 miles a day.

Cold-Front Clouds and Weather. The weather of a cold front, like that of a warm front, is determined largely by the nature of the overlying warm air. As a cold air mass pushes down from Canada during the winter, it plows into the warm air lying to the south. If this warm air is stable, a heavy stratus-layer of clouds forms against the steep, forward surface of the cold front. These thick stratus clouds may extend sideways for hundreds of miles just ahead of the cold front, but they are found only 50 miles or so in front of the cold front because of the steepness of the front. Such a line of clouds is known as a *squall line*.

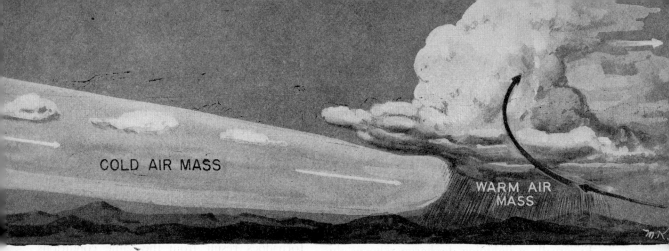

These cloud formations indicate the approach of a cold front.

A squall line brings showers or snow without giving the 24- to 72-hour cloud warning that accompanies a warm front. A cold front brings a sudden shower or snow flurry as it passes, followed by prolonged cold as the cold air mass spreads over the country.

If a cold front moves into unstable air, the effects are exaggerated, and the formations of cumulus thunderheads pile higher. This condition is common in summer, when a cold front may be marked by a line of thunderstorms that are dangerous to fliers. A pilot may alter his course to fly directly across a cold front, since the disturbance is not wide and there is a chance of crossing the narrow, cold front between two thunderstorms.

WORKING WITH SCIENCE

1. See if you can follow the cloud changes as a warm front approaches. Your weather map may show the front some distance to the west. At the same time, you may notice the high cirrus clouds which move farthest ahead of the front. During the next 24 hours you should notice definite changes in the types of clouds that appear over your region.

2. Using the weather maps that appear in the daily paper, follow a cold front from the time the cold air starts pushing forward till it has moved completely around and occluded a warm front. You will need to follow the maps for several days.

MORE AND MORE STORMS

So far we have centered our attention on the basic features of our weather—types of air movements that produce the major effects. But what about lightning and thunder, typhoons, hurricanes, blizzards, and the many other kinds of winds, storms, and precipitation?

THUNDERSTORM

Thunderstorms offer some of the greatest flying hazards. One Army pilot reported his experience in a thunderstorm, "While flying blind in the vicinity of Sunbury, Pennsylvania at 10,000 feet, we hit a downdraft and fell 4000 feet absolutely out of control. We regained control for about 15 seconds and then hit another draft almost as violent as the first.

We regained control from this one at about 3000 feet, and the hills here are about 2000 feet high." Another pilot got caught in the thunderstorms along a squall line in Texas. "I ran into the storm at 6000 feet," he reported, "and came out the top, tail first, at 14,000 feet. Had absolutely no control of the ship."

Thunder and Lightning. At least three general sets of conditions of the atmosphere produce thunderstorms, but they all result in the same thing—a strong upward movement of air into a column of cumulo-nimbus clouds. This strong updraft of air is the heart of the thunderstorm.

Experiments have shown that under normal conditions raindrops do not fall through air that is moving *upward* faster than 25 feet per second (17 miles per hour). The raindrops are blown to pieces by the upsurging air and are carried aloft as spray. This breaking-up process produces both positive and negative charges of electricity. Gradually a thunderhead, which may extend upward as high as 30,000 feet, becomes positively charged at the top and negatively charged at the bottom. Eventually a lightning discharge relieves this difference in electric charge. The flash may be within the cloud, between clouds, or from cloud to earth. The action of lightning has been studied carefully. Scientists have learned how to keep the current from damaging power lines, homes, and factories.

Thunder is the result of lightning. It is caused by the sudden and almost explosive violence of the flash. The molecules of air surrounding the flash are pushed apart so violently that a sound wave of great strength is produced.

Flying in a Thunderstorm. The updraft in a thunderstorm is caused by heated air rushing skyward. It may attain speeds as great as 200

A cross section through a thunderstorm.

miles per hour—faster than most horizontal winds. Planes caught in this updraft are practically impossible to control. Pilots report being carried *upward* in the updraft while diving their planes *down* into a thunderstorm.

TORNADO

All through the central United States, from Minnesota to the Gulf of Mexico, farmers watch the sky during the tornado season, which is late spring and early summer. Tornadoes result from the same conditions that produce thunderstorms and are usually associated with them. Conditions are right when a steep cold front moves into warm, moist, unstable air. A tornado develops in the upper air and is fed by a convection updraft until a compact, whirling mass of air is formed.

The elongated cone of the tornado moves along with the prevailing wind, which is usually from the southwest. It may touch the ground in one place and skip to another. The speed of wind in the storm center has been estimated at more than 500 miles per hour. The whirling motion lowers the pressure in the funnel, or *vortex*, so greatly that the walls of buildings hit by the tornado are pushed *outward* because of the relatively greater pressure from within.

Hurricane, Waterspout, and Typhoon. A tornado that occurs over the ocean is called a *waterspout*. The whirling, moist air condenses and looks like a column of water. Such a storm can be just as dangerous to a ship in its path as a tornado is on land.

In the Far East tropical cyclones are called *typhoons*. In the West Indies they are called *hurricanes*, and occasionally they sweep over the Gulf of Mexico and up the Texas or Florida coasts, spreading a path of destruction as they go.

The weather that is so typical for most of the United States—that changing weather of alternating calm and storm—is not found in many other parts of the world. It does occur in Europe, but in Asia the weather is modified by the heating and cooling effects of the massive Asiatic continent. In equatorial regions there is little frontal weather. The heat is relieved only by torrential rains of the thunderstorm type, resulting from updrafts and convection currents. The middle latitudes of the Southern Hemisphere do not have as much variation in weather as we do. There the vast amount of water in the Pacific, Atlantic, and Antarctic Oceans is a modifier because it changes the winds and makes the frontal zone weaker.

Many local conditions affect weather and, in some areas, overbalance the factors in the general weather picture.

U. S. D. A. photo

A tornado approaching.

WORKING WITH SCIENCE

1. If you have the opportunity to see a thunderstorm as it approaches, keep a careful record of changes in temperature, pressure, and wind directions until the storm passes. Note also the amount of rain, its pattern, and the size of the raindrops.

2. Watch water run down a drain or pour it through a funnel. Notice the kind of circular motion that is set up. Which way does the water rotate? Can you do anything to make it rotate in the opposite direction? Compare this rotary motion with the movement of air in a tornado.

3. Find out from your local Weather Bureau observer or from books or magazines what is being done with long-range weather forecasting. How far in advance are forecasts made? What is the accuracy of a 24-hour forecast as compared with a 3-, 6-, 48-, or 72-hour prediction?

4. A good deal of interesting data can be obtained if you set up your own weather bureau. As a class or club project there is much that can be done. A number of instruments can be made cheaply in a shop or at home. Keep careful records and make graphs of your data. Compare your figures with the official ones and see what factors cause your figures to differ from the offical figures, if differences exist.

READING YOU WILL ENJOY

Bureau of Aeronautics of United States Navy. *Aerology for Pilots.* McGraw-Hill Book Co., New York, 1943. As one of a series for the training of pilots, this clear, well-illustrated book makes weather knowledge simple and fun to read. There is a touch of humor, excellent diagrams, and clear presentation of weather facts.

Kimble, George and Bush, Raymond. *The*

Weather. Penguin Books, Inc., New York, 1946. A clear and reasonably nontechnical description of the weather and its causes.

Vetter, Ernest G. *Visibility Unlimited.* William Morrow & Co., New York, 1942. More than a weather book, for it also tells of the art of flying. But the first 18 chapters deal with the weather from an airman's viewpoint.

1

2

In science, observation and experiment pave the way to understanding. And understanding is necessary before any kind of prediction or control is possible. Because of our increased knowledge, we are even beginning to think that someday we may be able to control at least some phases of the weather.

Without an understanding of basic facts, efforts at control seem foolish. We smile at the efforts of primitive peoples who tried to control the weather without really getting at the causes of it. When rain was needed, sometimes they shot arrows at clouds (1) or sprinkled water on the ground to set a good example to the clouds. Sometimes they made offerings to frogs or fish in the hope that these animals could somehow attract rain. Fairly recently, professional "rainmakers" set off explosives and fired cannons (2) on the mistaken notion that the loud sounds produced, similar to thunder, might cause rain.

Our efforts at weather control are beginning to be more successful. Smudge pots protect citrus groves from early frosts (3). This is control on a very limited scale. But of far greater importance has been the successful production of snow crystals that melt into rain by means of dumping a small amount of dry ice by airplane in certain kinds of clouds (4). No one knows yet just where such efforts may lead. But two things are certain. Such methods are scientific and they produce results.

3

4

30

CAN WE CONTROL THE WEATHER?

Many persons say that everybody talks about the weather, but no one does anything about it. It is true that we cannot control the weather, but we have been actively doing something about it ever since the first cave man discovered fire.

ADAPTATIONS TO WEATHER

Much of what we do about the weather consists of adapting ourselves to its changes. The part of the world where we live sometimes gets too hot or too cold for our comfort. So we do things to protect ourselves from extremes of temperature.

HOUSING

We can create artificial weather within our homes. No longer do we merely heat houses in winter. Complete control of temperature, humidity, and circulation of air is possible. With such control, the atmosphere within a house or factory can be kept healthful and invigorating all through the year. Windows are no longer necessary for ventilation or lighting and many of the most recent buildings have been built without them. Modern lighting and air-conditioning may so alter the design of buildings that they will be unlike those you see today. An excellent example of what such buildings may be like is shown on page 412.

Solar Heating. Experts on housing tell us that houses can be built so that they *use* the weather. Much of the heat during the winter can be supplied by the sun. But the heat of summer can be just as effectively excluded. New methods of design may enable us to save considerable fuel by using solar heat to help heat our homes in winter.

FOOD AND CLOTHING

Adaptations to weather also include the foods we eat. Long ago people learned to suit their food habits to their need for heat and energy. The Eskimos' diet of fat meats from walruses, seals, and whales supplies more heat than our less fatty diet.

Our clothing, too, is adapted to the weather. Properly designed clothing helps to conserve or get rid of body heat. Loosely woven fabrics permit freer circulation of air than those that are tightly woven. With this circulation of air much heat is removed. Dark colors absorb more heat from radiant sources than do light colors.

INSULATION

The methods of controlling heat in buildings and by clothing are based on the three ways that heat is spread—conduction, convection, and radiation. If we wish to *insulate*, or keep heat from spreading, we must cut down conduction, convection, or radiation. The use of small dead-air spaces, that confine air and keep it from circulating, cuts down convection. Many materials have been designed to enclose millions of small air spaces. Such materials are used to insulate walls and roofs of houses.

To cut down conduction, materials that are poor conductors are used. These include wood,

DEAD-AIR SPACE

Polar bears and hollow tiles have what in common?

of heat is, in a way, a control of weather. But it is a very limited control—limited to areas we can insulate and heat artificially.

PLANTS AND ANIMALS

It is possible to alter plants and animals so that they can resist cold, heat, or drouth and live and grow in regions where they are not native. New varieties of cotton that are more resistant to cold have been developed. Thus, the cotton belt has been enlarged. Drouth-resistant varieties of wheat and corn make the more arid sections of the West productive.

Wheat can now be grown in regions of central Canada and Alaska where no one formerly would have believed farms possible. The government of the U.S.S.R. has announced that an apple has been developed that will grow so far north that the ground is perpetually frozen to depths of about 6 feet. In these and hundreds of other ways, we attempt to push aside the limitations of weather and climate—to produce, in effect, the same results as if all parts of the earth had a mild climate.

brick, slate, asbestos, rock wool, glass brick, and so forth. To cut down radiation, the under surfaces of roofs have been painted with smooth aluminum or white paints. Dull, black surfaces are the best absorbers and radiators of heat. Smooth, bright surfaces are the poorest absorbers and radiators of heat.

The use of our knowledge of heat transmission makes it possible for us to produce the artificial weather we need in refrigerators, greenhouses, homes, and schools. This control

WORKING WITH SCIENCE

1. Manufacturers of air-conditioning systems advertised in magazines may send you information about their products for home and factory use. Find out about the importance of air-conditioning in industry. How are the principles of air-conditioning related to the weather principles about which you have studied? Report to your class.

2. Some architects have gone so far as to say that windows for ventilation are no longer needed for homes. They favor large, sealed windows whose only purpose is to give a view from the inside. Arrange a debate on "Are Windows Necessary?" Gather information for arguments on both sides of the case.

3. You can test the ability of various materials to conduct heat by placing equal-sized rods of

copper, iron, glass, and wood in a glass of nearly boiling water. Which rod feels hottest after 1 minute in the hot water?

4. Make a collection of different insulating materials used in home construction. Find out of what natural materials they are made and on what principle they operate. How effective is each kind of insulating material in reducing heat loss?

5. Get information from your county agricultural agent or from the United States Department of Agriculture about cold-resistant or drouth-resistant plants which are or could be grown in your vicinity. If one particular plant is important in local agriculture, find out what varieties have been developed to meet a wider range of climate and soil conditions.

ATTEMPTS AT WEATHER CONTROL

When primitive peoples wanted rain, they tried to imitate or suggest rain or things that

go with rain. Sometimes they beat on drums to imitate thunder or painted designs showing lightning and clouds. Sometimes they sprinkled water on the ground or cut themselves and let blood drip. Some caught frogs, ducks, or other water-loving animals in the hope that these would attract water from the sky.

Such methods are bound to fail because they are not related to the cause of the lack of rainfall. Any method of controlling weather or climate must affect the causes if it is to produce results. This is far more difficult than it sounds. Even with our scientific knowledge of weather, we have been unable to control it, except on a limited scale.

MODERN WEATHER-MAKERS

Experimentally, however, scientists have produced snow. In 1946 Dr. Schaefer, a scientist working for the General Electric Company, climbed into an airplane carrying a small box filled with tiny pellets of dry ice. Dry ice, as you know, is solid carbon dioxide and is very cold. Dr. Schaefer had his pilot fly into a cloud floating high above the earth. Ordinarily this cloud would have drifted by without losing its moisture in the form of rain or snow. But this cloud was one of the many "super-cooled" clouds whose temperatures are actually below the freezing point of water. Such clouds do not lose their moisture, probably because they are so stable that crystals of snow do not start forming. In other words they need a "shock treatment" or some crystals to start a sort of chain reaction.

Once in the cloud, Dr. Schaefer simply threw his pellets of dry ice overboard. Almost immediately the plane was engulfed in a blinding snowstorm. The crystals of dry ice had caused the molecules of water vapor to begin forming crystals. The change was dramatically sudden.

Later it was found that dry ice was not needed. Early in 1947 it was discovered that compressed air, suddenly expanded, would do the trick. Dr. Bernard Vonnegut, another General Electric scientist working on the problem simply walked out of his house into a super-cooled fog. In his hands he held a toy popgun. He fired it into the fog. For some 30 feet the fog changed immediately to snowflakes.

Dry ice can be used easily. Before very long it was being widely tried whenever drouth became a local problem. The spring and summer of 1947 were dry, and in many parts of the country, men went up in small private planes to sprinkle clouds with dry ice pellets. When conditions in the clouds were right, their efforts were successful. Rain began to fall before the plane had time to land. With this encouragement, more and more people are trying to produce rain locally.

Silver Iodide and Snow. The only trouble with the popgun or dry ice treatment of clouds is that it is time consuming and costly to attack each super-cooled cloud independently and as it arrives overhead. So the weather-makers began working on the possibility of developing or discovering some substance that could be sprayed into the air in any region and that would hang there "waiting" for a super-cooled cloud to come along.

They developed a laboratory with a cold room in which super-cooled clouds could be produced at will. Then they tossed all kinds of things into the air of the room. They finally discovered that crystals of silver iodide would work very well. Snowflakes are six-sided (hexagonal) crystals. So are the crystals of silver iodide. Snowflakes or raindrops will not form unless there are tiny grains or particles for them to form on. It was found that they would form much more easily if tiny crystals were available. The silver iodide worked so well that an extremely small amount was able to produce a good-sized laboratory snow storm.

What the future of this cloud treatment will be cannot be predicted accurately. Scientists have figured, however, that about 200 pounds of silver iodide would be sufficient to fill the entire atmosphere of the United States with snow-activating crystals. Furthermore these crystals are so tiny (a billion billion will fit into an eggshell) that they will hang suspended almost indefinitely. Scientists estimate that if 1 pound of silver iodide per hour were shot into the atmosphere, the atmosphere could be kept filled sufficiently with silver iodide crystals to produce snow from all super-cooled clouds as they form.

STOPPING DESTRUCTIVE HAILSTORMS

For the present, however, the uses of this snow-maker are more modestly considered. One of these more limited uses is to prevent hailstorms which produce millions of dollars of damage to crops every year in the United States.

You will recall that hail is formed as falling raindrops are pushed upward at great speeds in rising currents of air. Quickly they reach altitudes of low temperature and freeze. Down they drop only to be covered with a film of water and then, again, to be forced upward and this film of water frozen. Giant hailstorms are formed by many such trips. Suppose that clouds of such turbulent character were shot full of silver-iodide crystals. As the raindrops were forced upward, they would freeze in the form of harmless snowflakes before they had a chance to form destructive hailstones.

This is one immediately proposed use of this man-made weather-maker. Future uses will be even more dramatic. It may be found possible to knock snow and rain out of air masses over desert areas and drouth-ridden croplands. Thus, we may have achieved the ability to "irrigate" directly from the sky rather than to wait helplessly while clouds carry rainwater to mountainous areas, and then pipe it back for hundreds of miles into an expensive ground-irrigation system.

CONTROLLING EFFECTS OF WEATHER

Scientists point out that man's advancement has been a series of conquests of conditions that people had long been used to considering "natural." For many years it was considered natural that nearly half the children born died in their first year, and that adults rarely lived beyond the age of fifty. It was natural to have to work 12 and 14 hours a day to obtain the bare necessities of life. But these things have changed. We still look on floods, storms, and drouths as "acts of God" and do not do much about them. But we do know the ways to control floods, and we have reduced their number. By persistent efforts, we can prevent or quickly control fires in our homes or forests.

In the control of floods, we have made a definite, although limited, attack on a specific problem. Floods have a history filled with death, destruction, and waste, but for years our efforts were confined largely to issuing flood warnings to save life and property. Even now these warnings are important because progress in flood control has been limited.

Left: The propellers keep the air moving in this citrus grove and help to prevent frost damage. Middle: A rainstorm produced by "seeding" with dry ice. Right: A regional water control system.

U. S. D. A. photo; Hugh Ackroyd; Tennessee Valley Authority photo

In flood control, two alternatives are offered. The first is control of precipitation—rain or snow—and that, at the present, is still in the experimental stage. The second, is control of the disposal of this water. We have controlled this to some extent and can do much more if we will but do it.

Scientific studies have been made to find out what happens to rain and snow when it falls: how much evaporates, how much sinks into the soil, how much runs off over the surface, how much is held back by plants. These and hundreds of other small facts show that floods can be prevented and the runoff of water controlled so that it will be of use to man for crops and pastures, in river navigation, in generating electricity, in maintaining wildlife, and in preserving and building up the soil.

As a result of these studies, definite action has been taken to prevent floods. Soil-conservation experts advise farmers on the kinds of crops that will best hold soil and on ways to prevent erosion and gullying on their farms. Such action catches the flood at its very source. As a next step, small dams are built in gullies and washes to slow the flow of water after a rain and give it opportunity to soak into the ground. Slowing the speed of running water reduces its power to wear away the land and carry off the soil.

Larger dams on larger streams hold back the water of spring rains and melting snows. When the season becomes drier, this water can be gradually released to maintain the water level in a river or to provide for irrigation. As water is released to run downstream, it turns giant turbines, generating low-cost electricity for the surrounding area.

On great streams, such as the Mississippi, *dikes* and *levees* keep the river moving in the desired course. When the pressure of flood waters threatens the levees, *spillways* make it possible to release water where it will do least harm. The river is so controlled that its deep channels are kept clear by the current and do not fill with silt and mud that hamper shipping and help produce floods.

CONTROL OF WEATHER OR CLIMATE

When people have considered weather control, they have usually considered one specific phase of the weather. For example, the problem was to make rain or to stop rain, to prevent cold, or to calm a wind. However, many factors act together to produce weather. Hence, the many factors must be considered together in attempting to control weather.

Two approaches to the problem of what to do about the weather are possible. One is an attempt at weather control, that is, control of the atmosphere so that at a given time and place there would be rain, snow, or sunshine. The other possiblity is control of climate—a control that would affect the *total weather* over an area but not immediate weather details.

Scientists who are looking far ahead have turned their attention to the problem of controlling climate. The reasons for this are clear, considering the value of climate control. Adequate rainfall, a growing season of reasonable length, and freedom from undue extremes of temperature are of tremendous value to a region.

NEED FOR CLIMATE CONTROL

In our own country alone, the fertility of thousands of square miles of land would be greatly increased by more rainfall. In Siberia an average increase in temperature of only a few degrees would open thousands of square miles of land to agriculture and more intensive settlement. If the need for such land becomes great enough, efforts of scientists to solve the problem may be intensified. What are some of the possible ways in which this can be done?

One must immediately go back to the factors involved in weather and see which of them can be altered. Obviously, alteration of the air masses themselves would be an impossible task, perhaps forever beyond the skill of man and the energy he can command. Greater possibilities may lie in other factors that modify climate—altitude, nearness to sea or large body of water, prevailing winds, vegetation, evaporation.

CLIMATE HAS CHANGED

Climate *has changed* in the past, but the changes have been very slow. Fossil remains of plants and animals buried in ancient rocks tell us this. For example, coral thrives in warm, shallow, salt water. If coral fossils are found in the rocks that make up the Catskill Mountains in New York State, there are only two possible explanations. Either that part of New York was once under warm, shallow, salt water, or the living habits of coral have greatly changed. Other evidence makes it clear that it was the land surface and climate and not the coral that changed.

Gradual climatic changes only 30,000 or 40,000 years ago led to the formation of huge ice sheets, which spread over Europe and North America. At the time of their greatest extent, some 25,000 years ago, 12 million square miles of earth were icebound. We know that widespread glaciers have formed not once, but at least three times on the Northern Hemisphere.

It might seem that greatly lower temperatures than are now normal are required to produce the giant glaciers. All evidence points out that this is not true. Probably the decrease in the earth's total temperature during any period of glaciation was between 5°F and 8°F, possibly less. Great glaciers exist even today. One expert has calculated that if the earth's total temperature were increased 2°F, the polar ice caps would disappear. If the polar ice caps melted, experts state that the level of the oceans would rise about 100 feet.

In general, evidence points out that throughout most of the earth's existence the climate of the earth was warmer and more moderate than it is now. Fossils of semitropical plants and animals have been found in Alaska, Greenland, and Antarctica. At various times New York State has had a climate similar to that of Florida, Arizona, and Alaska. Such changes have been world-wide. At times, glaciers were present in Africa and tropical plants and animals in the Arctic and Antarctic.

CAUSES OF CLIMATIC CHANGES

The causes of changes in the earth's climate are not well understood because not enough clues on which scientists can work have been discovered. A few things are clear, borne out by study of both past and present climates.

Most outstanding is the fact that climatic changes seem to occur with changes in the earth's geography—the appearance of new mountain ranges, the flooding of lowlands, the drying up of shallow seas, and so forth. This is not surprising, since the location and size of bodies of land and water profoundly influence climate today. Changes in ocean currents with changes in the earth's geography

Plants can be bred and buildings erected to control the effects of climate. Left: One plant variety is resistant to cold. Right: Climate outside has little effect on "climate" inside this building.

U. S. D. A. photo by Killian; Courtesy The Austin Company

probably produced climatic changes. Today, ocean currents influence climate along the eastern shores of the Pacific and along the northern coast of Europe. Any change in these currents would change the climates, too.

Maps of the floor of the Atlantic Ocean show a prominent mountain ridge sweeping from northern Scotland to Iceland. This ridge is far enough below water that the warm waters of the Gulf Stream flow right over it on the way to the coasts of Norway and Sweden. The warm water of the Gulf Stream (called *North Atlantic Drift* as it approaches Europe) modifies the climate of these northern countries and keeps some of their ports ice-free all year. For example, around North Cape, in northern Norway, the average January temperature is about 25°F.

However, 6000 miles to the east, at the same latitude in Siberia, the January average is from 50° to 60°F colder, roughly −30°F. If this oceanic mountain ridge were above water, as it is believed to have been in the past, then the warm current would be deflected southward. This would give England a much warmer climate but would deprive the Scandinavian countries of much warmth. Under such conditions, Norway and Sweden would probably get colder in winter, but as long as the climate there is influenced by the ocean, it would remain more moderate than Siberia.

WORKING WITH SCIENCE

1. Talk with your parents, friends, and classmates. Find out some of their weather beliefs. How many of them are superstitions? How many common beliefs have a basis in facts? Can you check them against weather records? Make a list of weather beliefs that have, and those that do not have, a basis in facts.

2. Flood-control projects are not undertaken until a region has been scientifically investigated to determine all the local factors that enter into the flood problem. If you have a flood-control project in your region, find out why it is there, what is being done, and the results that have been obtained or are expected.

3. Books on historical geology tell about the changes that have taken place on earth during past ages. They include some information on climates of the past. Refer to one of these books and report to the class on how the climate in different parts of the world has changed and how we know that this has happened.

4. Your teacher may be able to help you work out some of the climatic changes that have taken place in your own region during past ages. This involves a knowledge of local rocks and when they were formed, plus a knowledge of past climates, which you can find in reference books on geology.

5. If you live in a region that was once covered with glacial ice (generally north of the Ohio River), study the evidence that a glacier was present. Collect samples of the rock, gravel and other materials brought or formed by the glacier.

THE FUTURE OF WEATHER CONTROL

These examples illustrate the relationship of land masses and oceans to climate. They bring us to an important question: Can man produce artificial bodies of water or alter ocean currents so that modifications in climate may be produced?

No one knows for sure. Projects that were considered quite impossible even 25 years ago have been carried out successfully. And we do not know what we shall be able to do in the future.

ARTIFICIAL LAKES

Hoover Dam and others making huge artificial lakes may affect climate. Hoover Dam holds back 10½ trillion gallons of water, forming Lake Meade—120 miles long and the largest artificial lake in the world. The water in this huge lake may be expected to have some effect on the local climate, but records have not been kept long enough to be sure. In Montana, Fort Peck Dam holds back more than 6 trillion gallons of water and makes the upper Missouri River a lake 189 miles long. After their effects on climate have been observed and studied, these two dams may indicate that we can alter the land to produce climatic changes.

Irrigation projects do not produce changes in climate, but give the effect of greater rainfall. Already our irrigation projects have put millions of acres of wasteland into use. For example, Grand Coulee Dam will provide good water sufficient to convert 1,200,000 acres of sagebrush into farm land and provide livelihood for an estimated 350,000 people. New projects in the planning stage include one to provide irrigation for 5,300,000 acres in the Missouri River Valley and for large areas of the Arkansas River basin.

CHANGING OF OCEAN CURRENTS

Another suggestion that has received serious consideration is the building of barriers at places where ocean currents might be deflected. At places where seas are shallow and currents are near the shore, this is considered possible. Russian scientists have proposed one such project to extend southward from the Kamchatka Peninsula and deflect the cold ocean currents from the eastern coast of Siberia.

SHELTER BELTS AND FORESTS

The planting of forests and cover crops may produce climatic changes. For example, the Prairie States Forest Project of the United States Forest Service planted 220 million shelter-belt trees, forming more than 7000 miles of shelter belts throughout the midwestern states, where erosion and dust storms were becoming serious problems. While this planting was not made for its effect on climate, it may result in minor climatic changes.

Windbreaks and shelter belts are designed to protect nearby farm land from the effects of strong winds. Eight to 10 acres of windbreak will protect an average 160-acre midwestern farm. Shelter belts slow down the speed of winds and thus reduce the evaporation of soil moisture. Slowing down air movement permits the temperature to rise a bit higher than it otherwise would. In winter this is important, since cattle require more food when the weather is cold. Crops are protected from wind damage, snow is kept from drifting, and soil erosion is decreased.

CITY PLANNING

Cities have many problems. In general, these congested areas have grown without plan or with only the simplest kind of planning. As a result, cities have many health, transportation, housing, and efficiency problems that might be reduced or eliminated by city planning. Even the climate of cities has been made worse by the cities' planless growth.

Large cities are generally a few degrees warmer than the nearby country. Smoke and dust often blanket the area and intensify the heat. The gridwork of streets either breaks the wind entirely or sends it rushing down narrow canyons between buildings with even greater force than it would have in the open.

Experts have suggested that the climate of a city might be partly controlled by the use of materials to reflect heat, by devices to eliminate smoke, and by planning that would permit free and easy circulation of air. This is not visionary. Electronic devices to control smoke are already in use. Newer factories and offices are built with tile and glass which

A plan for a city of the future.

admit light but keep out much of the summer heat. City planners think about spreading buildings farther apart with more parks, parkways, and open spaces. In such cities, the streets will no longer be at the bottom of hot steep canyons in which the wind is constantly stirring up dirt and dust.

COOPERATIVE EFFORTS

Most possible climate controls are community, national, or international, rather than individual, affairs. If it were possible for our country to alter the course of the Gulf Stream at Newfoundland, we could not act without realizing the serious effects such action might have on the climates of Iceland, England, Norway, and Sweden. Control of climate on a large scale means that large groups of persons must cooperate to produce results that will benefit the greatest number of people and harm the fewest.

An individual can do very little except to control his own personal weather. By designing his home to use the sun for heating, by the use of air-conditioning, comfortable clothing, and the like, each person can surround himself with a pocket of weather that he can control to some extent. A farmer who irrigates his land or who grows his tobacco crop under cloth is extending this idea farther. But an individual can do only so much. Action by large groups is necessary if the results are to be successful.

The larger aspects of climate and weather control are still far in the future. But man in some distant future may be able to alter the physical features of the earth and the covering of the soil sufficiently to modify climatic conditions.

Scientists who want science to be used to make everyone's life better and happier do not scoff at such ideas. They patiently examine the problems and see what methods, information, skill, and knowledge are needed to solve them. Gradually the facts will be pieced together, and sooner or later the problems may be solved.

WORKING WITH SCIENCE

1. Find out about soil-reclamation projects and the work that has been done to reclaim waste swamps and arid lands in this country.

2. If you have shelter belts in your region, find out when they were planted, how fast they have grown, and what is expected as they mature.

3. Find references to modern city planning. Compare ideas of future cities with cities that you know.

4. Make a list of the kinds of science that are involved in city planning. How many of these are related to weather and its effects?

READING YOU WILL ENJOY

Blair, Thomas A. *Weather Elements*. Prentice-Hall, Inc., New York, 1942. A sound, well-organized textbook in meteorology that covers in detail a number of topics on which this Unit touches lightly. It may be rather difficult to read, but the student interested in the weather will find this a good reference.

Humphreys, William J. *Ways of the Weather*. The Ronald Press Co., New York, 1942.

Written by a leading American weather expert, this book brings together an amazing amount of weather knowledge: wind, precipitation, temperature, pressure, and so forth.

Stewart, George R. *Storm*. Random House, New York, 1941. The dramatic and exciting biography of a cyclonic storm and how it affects the country and the lives of people. This is a book that you will find well worth reading.

By the time of the Greeks, many things about the sun, moon and stars had been observed. Ptolemy of Alexandria, in the second century A.D., collected much of this information in a book. He described the earth as a sphere around which the sun, stars (and planets) revolve. He believed that these heavenly bodies revolved at great distances from the earth (1). Aristotle and other students held the same opinion.

Our present idea of the sun at the center of the solar system is chiefly the result of the work of four men: Copernicus, Brahe, Kepler, and Newton. After a lifetime of observation and study, Nicolaus Copernicus, a Polish priest-physician of the six-teenth century, became convinced that the sun is actually at the center of the solar system and that the planets revolve about it (2). However, his ideas were not widely accepted until the next century, after the observations made by Tycho Brahe (3) and his one-time assistant, Johann Kepler (4). A little later, Sir Isaac Newton's Law of Gravitation and his mathematics provided a thorough-going explanation of Kepler's conclusions.

Thus our own earth has gradually shrunk in importance. Once it was thought to be the center of the universe. Now we know it is only a tiny part of the solar system, all of which was once part of a star.

UNIT NINE

Astronomy

31

THE SOLAR SYSTEM IN WHICH WE LIVE

A Connecticut Yankee in King Arthur's Court, by Mark Twain, tells how a Yankee foreman in a pistol factory was transplanted from nineteenth-century America to King Arthur's court in sixth-century England. In the course of his experiences, the Yankee got into trouble. He was thrown into prison, and there awaited execution. To save his life, he thought of a scheme.

"Go back and tell the king," he shouted from his prison cell, "that I will smother the whole world in the dead blackness of midnight; I will blot out the sun . . . and the peoples of the earth shall famish and die, to the last man!"

Soon the sky actually began to grow dark. The king and his people were frightened. King Arthur begged the Yankee to stop this terrible catastrophe and to name his terms. "You shall appoint me your perpetual minister and executive," came back the answer.

This was indeed a very great demand. The king hesitated. The sky grew darker. It became pitch black, and the stars came out. Then the king agreed to the terms. The Yankee lifted his hand and "the silver rim of the sun pushed itself out." The darkness disappeared.

You may know why the Yankee's scheme worked. The Yankee had remembered the date of a total solar eclipse (see page 427), which, fortunately, was due to take place at that moment. No one else at the king's court knew about it. So the Yankee was thought to have supernatural powers.

BEGINNINGS OF ASTRONOMY

The story of the Yankee, of course, is only a story. But there are real values in a knowledge of astronomy. In fact, the science of astronomy had its beginnings in real, everyday needs. Thousands of years ago, men learned that seeds must be sowed at certain seasons or they do not produce good crops. They found that they had to plan ahead for planting and for other seasonal activities. Such activities included plowing, harvesting, starting on long voyages, and the many religious festivals that accompanied these activities.

So it became necessary for people to keep track of the seasons. Some wise men discovered that the position of the stars and the shadows cast by the sun gave clues to changing seasons. As soon as this was learned, they could plan for seasonal activities. So they built pillars, pyramids, and temples with openings so arranged that when the light from some star just reached them or threw a certain shadow, it was time for certain festivals.

Early astronomers were given the job of preparing calendars. As early as 4241 B.C. the Egyptians, by just such observations, concluded that a year consisted of 365 days. The Aztecs' stone calendar, independently invented in the fifteenth century in the Western Hemisphere, was also based on a year with 365 days.

Astronomy came into being, too, because knowledge of the changing positions of the stars gave men directions for locating and traveling to many faraway places of the earth. Astronomy was a very practical sort of business.

MODERN ASTRONOMY IS BORN

The ancients collected many facts dealing with astronomy. Their measurements were fairly good, and their theories and explanations worked fairly well. But more exact information and greater advances in astronomy were not possible because of their crude instruments and mistaken notions. For example, up to the sixteenth century, most people believed the earth to be the center of the universe. According to this belief, the other planets and the sun moved around the earth.

People liked to believe that the earth was the most important body in the universe. This theory is known as the *geocentric theory*, from the Greek *geo*, meaning *earth*. It gave men a feeling of great importance. Very few people

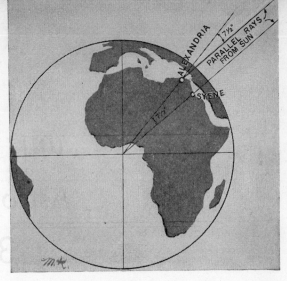

With some additional information from an atlas, you can figure out the circumference of the earth as the early astronomers did.

questioned the accuracy of this idea for another—and very good—reason. This theory seemed to explain the most commonly observable facts.

Nicolaus Copernicus [ko-pûr′nĭ-kŭs] was a Polish astronomer and mathematician. He was one of the few men of his day who would not accept the geocentric theory. The facts he had collected did not agree with the geocentric theory. His measurements and observations of the changing positions of the heavenly bodies led him to conclude that the sun, and not the earth, is the center of the solar system.

By this time, Copernicus was an old man. However, he felt that the truth had to be

Early peoples built things to help them keep track of the seasons. The structure at the left is early English; that at the right, Egyptian. See if you can find out how these structures were used.

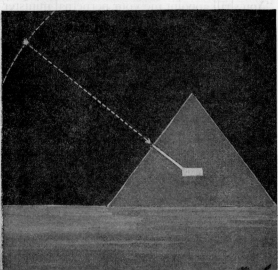

announced. He wrote a book advancing this idea, and on the morning of May 24, 1543 the printed book was brought to him as he lay on his deathbed. In this book, published less than half a century before the first English colonists landed on Roanoke Island, Copernicus presented the evidence for his conclusion that the sun was the center of the solar system.

Copernicus was not the first to insist that the earth moved around the sun. Long before Copernicus, some of the Greeks had believed the same thing. Pythagoras [pĭ-thăg′ô-răs] (582–500 B.C.) and Aristarchus [ăr-ĭs-tär′-kŭs] had both come to this conclusion. But they did not have enough facts to convince other astronomers of their day.

Announcement of the *heliocentric theory*, from the Greek term *helio*, which means *sun*, had a tremendous effect. A few people accepted it at once on the basis of the evidence. Most people, however, refused and continued to follow the teachings of the old authorities. An Italian teacher, Giordano Bruno (1548–1600), actually was burned at the stake, in part because he dared to teach the new theory in contradiction of the old authorities. Many generations passed before the heliocentric theory was finally accepted by all.

WHAT IS THE SOLAR SYSTEM?

The earth is a sphere that moves around the sun, making a complete trip once a year. The earth is not the only body that moves around the sun. Eight other similar bodies do also. These bodies are called planets.

Around six of the planets, including the earth, move smaller bodies. These smaller bodies are called *moons*, or *satellites*. The earth has one moon; Jupiter has 11.

The planets and their satellites are not the entire solar system. About 1500 smaller planets, or *planetoids*, as well as many comets and thousands of meteors, also belong to the solar system. So you see, it is quite a large family.

How large is the solar system? The distance between the sun and the outermost known planet is 3680 million miles. This distance is the same as the radius of the solar system. The diameter of the solar system is about twice this distance. In other words, the solar system is roughly a circular area 7360 million miles across.

To get some idea of the distance of the sun from the planets, imagine an airplane that can travel indefinitely at a speed of more than 600 miles an hour, or 10 miles a minute. This speed

The solar system. Distances are not in the correct scale. Do you know why?

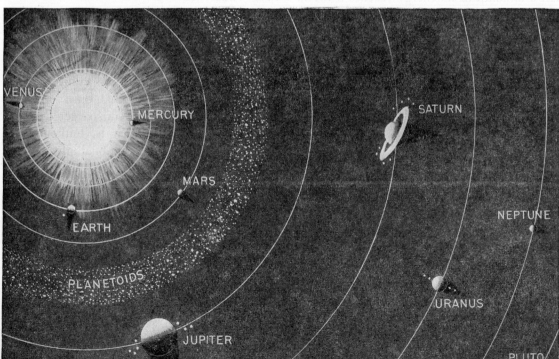

has already been surpassed by some planes. Such a plane would actually take about 18 years to fly from the earth to the sun. It would require somewhat more than 700 years to fly from the earth to the outermost planet, Pluto. And such a plane would have to keep flying for 1500 years to fly across the solar system.

THE SUN

The sun is a medium-sized star or sphere of glowing and gaseous material 866 thousand miles in diameter. Actually, it is so immense that almost a million earths could fit into its interior. The temperature of its surface is at least as high as 10,000°F, much hotter even than molten iron. However, its surface is cool, compared with the temperature of its interior, which has been estimated to be about 60 million degrees Fahrenheit. Just below the surface, in areas called *sunspots*, tremendous electric and magnetic storms rage. Sunspots are more than spots. They are really areas ranging from about 500 miles to 150,000 miles in diameter.

At various places on the sun's surface great tongues of glowing gases extend outward, in some cases more than half a million miles. These *solar prominences*, as they are called, are composed of glowing hydrogen.

The sun is the chief source of light and heat received by the earth, although only about one-half a billionth of its energy reaches us. This energy at any instant is equivalent to about 60 thousand horsepower for each of the earth's inhabitants.

Like the earth, the sun is made up of many chemical elements. On the surface of the sun the elements exist in the form of vapor. These include iron, calcium, silicon, copper, zinc, nickel, gold, and many others.

The sun spins, or *rotates*, about a fixed but imaginary line, or *axis*. Any point on its equator takes 24⅔ days to complete one *rotation*, that is to return to its original position.

HOW WE HAVE LEARNED ABOUT THE SUN

August Comte [kôNT], a great French scientist and philosopher, once wrote, "There are some things of which the human race must forever remain in ignorance; for example, the chemical composition of the sun and the other heavenly bodies." But he was wrong.

Comte knew that it would be impossible to approach the sun without being burned to a cinder. Consequently, he believed that scientists would never get this information. But Comte neglected to take into account the instruments that men of science could invent. Improved telescopes, cameras, and photographic films help scientists to get information that years ago was considered "impossible!"

Such scientific instruments open up new worlds. With them, scientists get needed information indirectly, that is, without actually going to the sun. Additional information is obtained by reasoning based on the facts revealed by scientific instruments. For example, scientists learned about the elements present in the sun by means of the spectroscope, which was invented in 1859, 2 years after Comte died.

The spectroscope really brings the sun right down to earth. How? An American

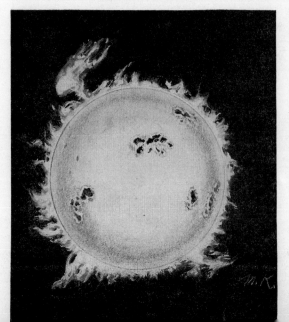

"Ol Sol," our sun.

physician, David Alter, had noticed that when chemical elements burn or glow they give off a definite color. For example, when copper is heated, it gives off a green light. Sodium produces a yellow flame, and potassium a violet flame. Dr. Alter suggested that these different flame colors could be used to identify the burning elements in the sun. Later the spectroscope was used to make a more careful study of these flame colors.

The colors produced by the elements are the same regardless of where the elements come from. When scientists pointed the spectroscope at the sun, they found the same elements in the sun that exist on our earth.

The Spectroheliograph. George Ellery Hale, an American scientist, made an improved spectroscope called the *spectroheliograph.* With the spectroheliograph, additional information about the sun was obtained.

Hale was the son of a wealthy manufacturer. He could have followed his father into business. But, he wrote, "The nature of the sun held me spellbound. I gave up the huge, humming factories of my father and entered the laboratories of science." He built a large solar observatory on the top of Mount Wilson, in California, and with his spectroheliograph investigated the nature of sunspots.

SUNSPOTS

Hale discovered that sunspots are regions of tremendous electric and magnetic disturbances. The largest of them appear near the equator of the sun. They grow in size and in number approximately every 11 years, and then decrease greatly during the next 11 years. This appearance and reappearance of sunspots in a definite period of time is known as the *sunspot cycle.* No one has as yet given a satisfactory explanation for this cycle.

Sunspots affect the earth by throwing out tremendous bursts of electric particles, or

White light broken up into light of other colors.

electrons. When sunspots are large and numerous, electric disturbances, or storms, disrupt telegraph and power lines and other electric equipment, and radio transmission is confused by static. They have a slight effect on the weather conditions on earth.

The aurora borealis, or northern lights, is believed to be caused by such disturbances.

WHAT PRODUCES THE TREMENDOUS HEAT OF THE SUN?

Many different theories have been offered to explain the great heat of the sun and why the sun does not burn up. The most generally accepted theory, proposed in 1938, is that of Professor Hans Bethe [bā′tĕ] of Cornell University. According to this scientist, hydrogen in the interior of the sun is converted into helium. During this transformation some hydrogen is converted into energy in the form of heat, in accordance with the Einstein mass-energy conversion equation. A small amount of carbon in the sun helps in this change. We can understand then why such a huge body as the sun can continue to radiate energy for millions of years without any noticeable cooling off in, let us say, 500 years.

Actually, the sun is cooling very, very slowly. It has been estimated that many millions, perhaps trillions, of years will pass before the sun completely cools. Long before that happens, the earth, too, will have become so cold that life will have disappeared.

WORKING WITH SCIENCE

1. Obtain the spectrum of sunlight by placing a glass prism in the path of a narrow beam of light.

2. Dip a clean nichrome wire (or platinum wire) in some table salt and then place in the tip of a clean bunsen-burner flame. Note the color of the flame. Repeat using other chemicals, such as copper sulfate, potassium chlorate, and lithium chloride.

THE EARTH

Before we go zooming out into space to take a look at some of the other celestial bodies, let us get a good look at the earth. To see the earth as a globe, we would have to rise nearly 20,000 miles. It would look like a perfect sphere. However, it is flattened somewhat at its poles and bulges a little at its equator. Because of flattening and bulging, its diameter is not the same at all places. For example, the diameter from pole to pole is 7899 miles, while the diameter at the equator is 27 miles longer, or 7926 miles.

The average density of the earth is 5.6. The density of water at 4°C (39.2°F) is 1. Thus the earth material weighs 5.6 times as much as the same volume of water at 4°C (39.2°F). The core of the earth is even denser. It is about 10 times as dense as water. The density of the earth's crust averages about 2.7. The density of the planet Jupiter is a little more than 1, and that of Saturn is actually somewhat less than 1.

ROTATION OF THE EARTH

The earth spins, or rotates, about a fixed but imaginary line, or axis, the ends of which are its poles. This spinning motion is not noticeable because we are held firmly to the surface of the earth by the *gravitational pull* of the earth (see page 426). The speed of the earth's rotation is very high. At places near the equator, it amounts to about 1000 miles per hour—faster than the fastest plane. As we approach the poles of the earth, the speed of rotation becomes less and less, since an object has less distance to cover in the same time. At New York City (latitude 41 degrees north) the speed of rotation is about 750 miles per hour. At the geographic poles a person would merely be turned completely around every 24 hours.

Day and Night. As a result of rotation, part of the earth's surface faces the sun, while the part away from the sun gets no sunlight at all. Thus, one half of the earth is illuminated by the sun while the other half is in darkness.

The uniform rotation of the earth gives us a basis for telling time. The length of a day is determined by noting the interval that elapses between two passages of the sun over any given point.

You may have noticed something that the ancients, too, observed. The shadow that the sun's light casts behind a vertical pole varies in both length and position with the time of the day. The shortest shadow occurs when the sun is at its highest position overhead. This is

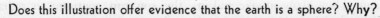

Does this illustration offer evidence that the earth is a sphere? Why?

noon, or 12 o'clock *solar*, or *local*, time. You can test this on any sunny day. Before clocks were introduced, men determined the time of day by sundials. A sundial gives the time by means of a shadow cast by a rod, or *gnomon*.

When men could not depend on sundials, because of cloudy weather or the very short days of winter, other methods of measuring time were used. Eventually, clocks were invented.

HOW WE LOCATE A PLACE ON EARTH

Early astronomers realized that the position of the heavenly bodies was the key to a yearly calendar. They also saw that a knowledge of the sky could be used to locate places and make possible the drawing of maps. For example, they observed that the *time* when the sun cast its shortest shadow changed as the observer moved *east* or *west* of his position. They also found that the position of the sun in the sky changed as the observer moved *north* or *south* of his position.

We can locate a corner drugstore by saying that it stands at the intersection of Ninth Street and Avenue C, which run at right angles to each other. In the same way we can locate a place on earth, only in this case the lines we use are imaginary circles drawn around the earth at right angles to each other.

Map-makers drew circles parallel to the equator. These circles are called *parallels of latitude*. The latitude of the equator is 0 degrees, and that of the North Pole is 90 degrees north latitude. Through the poles, they drew circles called *meridians of longitude*. Since there was no such natural starting point for longitude as the equator is for latitude, it was agreed to start at the Royal Observatory then at Greenwich, England (near London), and call the meridian passing through this place the *prime*, or *zero*, *meridian*. Since there are 360 degrees in any circle, 1 degree of latitude is $\frac{1}{360}$ of 25,000 miles (the circumference of the earth), or about 70 miles. Near the equator, 1 degree of longitude is also about 70 miles.

STANDARD TIME BELTS

Probably you know that when it is 5 P.M. in New York, in Chicago it is 4 P.M., in Denver it is 3 P.M., and in San Francisco it is 2 P.M. You may have wondered why this is the case. Since the earth rotates from west to east, the sun appears to rise in the east and set in the west. Therefore, the sun rises a little later any place to the west of an observer.

In 4 minutes the sun appears to travel through 1 degree of longitude. Hence in two towns, one of which is 1 degree west of the other, there is an actual difference of 4 minutes in solar, or local, time. A full hour elapses between the rising of the sun at places separated by 15 degrees of longitude. With every step westward or eastward, local, or sun, time changes.

Since travel is so extensive today, and buses, autos, and airliners cross and recross the continent so frequently, it would be a nuisance to keep changing watches to agree with the local, or sun, time. A timetable in Chicago reading 3 P.M. would not mean the same to a person in Omaha, Nebraska or Albany, New York. This would be very confusing. People would be constantly missing their trains, planes, and buses. To prevent this, the earth was divided into zones, or standard time belts. These belts are 15 degrees apart, and the difference in standard time between two adjacent time belts is always exactly one hour. Hence, we change our watches only when we pass from one time zone into the next standard time belt.

Locating a place on earth.

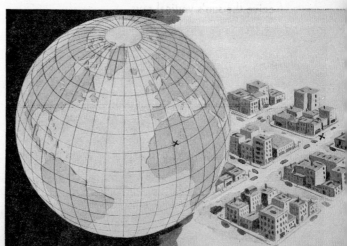

Vertical rays concentrate light and heat in a smaller area than do slanting rays.

REVOLUTION OF THE EARTH

At the same time that the earth is rotating on its axis, it is also moving around the sun. This movement is called *revolution*. The earth takes approximately 365¼ days, or 1 year, to make one complete revolution around the sun. You may recall that both the Egyptians and the Aztecs discovered this 365-day period many centuries ago.

In making a revolution, the earth travels about 580 million miles. Its speed is about 1100 miles a minute—much faster even than its speed of rotation. Its path around the sun is called an *orbit*. Its orbit is not a circle but an *ellipse*, a sort of flattened circle. The sun is not at the center of the orbit but rather to one side.

Cause of Seasons. Three facts account for the changing seasons. One is that the earth revolves around the sun. Another is the *inclina-*

As the earth moves in its orbit, different parts receive the sun's vertical rays.

tion of the earth's axis. A third is that the inclination of the earth's axis does not change while it is revolving around the sun and rotating on its axis. In other words, the earth does not wobble around.

Let us see how these facts combine to produce a change of seasons. First, how does the earth's inclination affect the seasons? If you draw a curved line to show the orbit of the earth and extend the earth's axis to meet this path, you will see that the axis does not meet the path at right angles but at a different angle. We say that the earth's axis is inclined 23½° to a perpendicular drawn to the plane of the earth's orbit. This 23½° is called the earth's *angle of inclination*.

If the earth's axis were not inclined, the same half of the earth would receive the same amount of sunlight every day of the year. As a result, there would be no change of seasons, since a change of seasons results from the fact that the same part of the earth receives *different* amounts of sunlight and, hence, heat at *different times of the year*.

Not all parts of the half of the earth facing the sun receive the same amount of heat. This unequal distribution is caused by the fact that one part of the earth, near the equator, receives the *vertical* rays of the sun, while another part, near the poles, receives only *slanting*, or *tangent*, rays. Vertical rays heat an area faster than slanting rays because vertical rays are concentrated in a smaller area than slanting rays (see illustration at the left above). Since the same amount of solar radiation heats a smaller area, the area becomes warmer than an area that receives only slanting rays. We are assuming, of course, that both areas receive solar radiation for the same length of time.

The length of the seasons depends upon the time required for the earth to make a revolution about the sun. If it took the earth ½ year instead of a full year to make one revolution around the sun, the length of the seasons would be one-half what it is.

424

WORKING WITH SCIENCE

1. Make a sundial on the basis of actual observations of the shadow cast by the sun at different hours of the day. The sloping edge of the gnomon should be at an angle equal to your latitude (in New York City it would be 41°). At noon the shadow cast would be the shortest. With a watch in front of you, mark off the hours as shown by the moving shadow on a semicircle.

2. To illustrate the unequal distribution of heat, throw a light from a flashlight against the blackboard from a foot away. With a piece of chalk, mark the outline of this bright spot. Now turn the flashlight so that its light strikes the blackboard with slanting rays. Mark the outline of this lighted area with a piece of chalk. How do the two spots compare in area? In relative brightness?

3. With the help of a large globe of the earth, find the latitude and longitude of New York, Moscow, Paris, Chungking.

4. Throw a beam from a large lamp or strong flashlight against a large globe of the earth in a semidarkened room. Now rotate the globe and

How the earth and its moon might look from outer space. Distances are not in the correct scale.

notice how much of the earth is always in darkness and how different parts of the earth are illuminated.

5. Make a sextant, that is, an instrument to measure the position or "altitude" of the sun or any star. Obtain a protractor and paste a soda straw securely to its straight edge. Hang a small weight from a thread attached to the midpoint of the protractor. Sight through the straw (use smoked glass to protect your eyes), and note the angle between the straw and the thread.

THE MOON, COMETS, AND METEORS

The earth has an interesting neighbor. At an average distance of about 240 thousand miles from the earth, is a smaller body called the *moon*. The moon revolves around the earth in the same counterclockwise direction as the earth revolves around the sun. The moon is our nearest celestial neighbor. Why does the moon move in the same direction as the earth? Probably because at one time the moon was part of the earth and was formed by a bit of the earth breaking away from the main body.

The moon is a sphere about 2163 miles in diameter. With the aid of a large telescope, its surface can be seen clearly and photographed. It is not a smooth surface. It has mountains and valleys; it is pitted and pock-marked. Galileo, who was the first to see mountains on the moon, wrote, "It is a most beautiful and delightful sight to behold the body of the moon."

Many of the moon's peaks are higher than

Mount Everest. Some *craters,* which are depressions shaped like cups, on the moon are 150 miles across. They may have been formed by some ancient volcanic action or by the explosion of meteorites that fell into the moon.

The moon does not shine by its own light as the sun does. That is, it is not a luminous body. Like the earth, the moon shines by light reflected from the sun. That part of the moon's surface facing the sun is actually hotter than boiling water, while the half turned away from the sun has a temperature as low as −250°F. There is no water on the moon. Hence, there are no clouds, no rain, no snow. The moon does not have an atmosphere, since it is not heavy enough to hold any atmosphere.

The moon, like the earth, revolves and rotates. It revolves around the earth once in every $27\frac{1}{3}$ days. It rotates on its axis in exactly the same period of time. Because its period of rotation and its period of revolution

Gravitation keeps the earth in its orbit.

are exactly the same, only one half of the moon—always the same half—is turned toward the earth.

WHY DO WE NOT SEE A FULL MOON ALL THE TIME?

Half of the moon is illuminated by the sun. But we on earth do not see all of this illuminated half of the moon. The movement of the moon around the earth produces an effect that we call the *phases* of the moon. When the moon is between the earth and the sun, an observer on earth cannot see the part of the moon that receives light from the sun. The moon is said to be in the phase called *new moon*. As it slowly moves out of this position, we begin to see the moon as a *crescent*, then as a *half-moon*, then as a *full moon*. Then the moon begins to wane in brightness and soon disappears. The time between new moon and full moon is about 14 days.

WHAT KEEPS THE MOON AND EARTH IN PLACE?

You may have wondered why the moon keeps moving around the earth. Why does it not fly out into space and disappear? The answer is that the gravitational pull of the earth holds it. But why does it not then fall into the earth? Similar questions may have occurred to you with regard to the sun and

The moon and the tides.

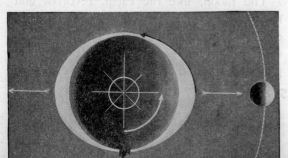

the earth. The answers to these questions may be found in recalling Newton's laws of motion which we studied in Chapter 21. Newton's laws of motion state that *a body remains at rest or continues in its motion in a straight line at a constant speed unless some outside force compels it to change its state of rest or motion.*

Newton's Law of Gravitation. Newton also formulated the law of gravitation to explain *how one body attracts another body.* The amount of this attraction depends on (1) the distance between the bodies—if the distance is doubled, the attraction becomes only one-fourth as great—and (2) their masses (weights)—a heavier body has a greater attraction than a lighter body. An apple falls to the ground because the earth has a very much stronger attraction for the apple than the apple has for the earth.

Since the sun is a much heavier body than the earth, it would seem that the earth should fall into the sun. This would happen if it were not for another force. This is the force that tends to throw a rapidly rotating body away from its center of revolution. This force is called *centrifugal force.* Because of centrifugal force, mud flies off an automobile tire that is in rapid motion. If you tie a heavy weight to the end of a string and whirl it, you feel a tug on your fingers. This tug is caused by the attempt of the ball to fly away from the center of rotation (your fingers holding the string).

The earth does not fall into the sun but continues to revolve around the sun for two reasons. First, because an object continues to move forward unless disturbed by an outside force such as friction (Newton's laws of motion). Second, it continues to move in a curved path around the sun, because the force of gravitation pulling it toward the sun just equals the centrifugal force pulling it away from the center of revolution—the sun. In radiating energy the sun is slowly losing weight. As a result, the earth actually is moving farther away from the sun at the rate of about 1 inch every 3 years!

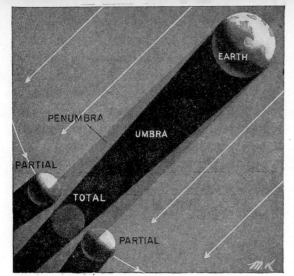
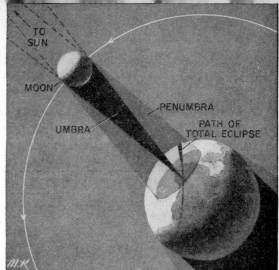

Left: A lunar eclipse in several stages. Right: A solar eclipse.

EFFECT OF THE MOON ON OUR LIVES

Romance and the moon have been coupled for thousands of years. Even so, the moon does not control our individual actions directly. However, the moon affects us indirectly in many ways. For example, the light of the moon helps to illuminate the earth to some extent during the night. The moon also produces the daily tides which are so important to us because they affect shipping and fishing.

Tides. The gravitational force that pulls the earth toward the sun also pulls the earth toward the moon. The attractive force of the moon pulls the water in the earth's seas toward the moon, causing *tides*. When the moon is in a position almost directly overhead or directly opposite from overhead, it exerts the greatest attractive force on the water of the earth. This produces *high tide*. Approximately intermediate positions of the moon produce *low tide*. The place and time of greatest pull change from day to day, because the moon revolves around the earth. The position also changes because the earth itself is rotating on its axis. There are two high tides and two low tides every 24 hours and 52 minutes.

The time of low and high tide and the positions of the tides are accurately predicted by astronomers and mathematicians years in advance and are printed in almanacs and newspapers for the use of fishermen, ships'

captains, and other people concerned. This sort of prediction is sound and accurate, for it is based on exact laws and arrived at by careful mathematical calculations.

ECLIPSES

For centuries, those moments when the sun was temporarily blotted out in broad daylight were very dreadful for millions of people. Superstition surrounded such events. Great calamities were feared. Some people even believed that the temporary blotting out of the sun was a sign that the end of the earth was at hand.

About 200 years ago, astronomers showed that such an occurrence, called an eclipse, was the result of natural, explainable causes.

Why the moon does not always look the same.

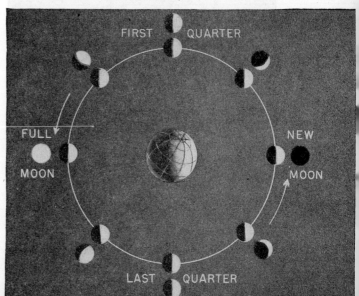

Furthermore, they were able to determine in advance not only the time of the next eclipse but the place from which it could be seen best. When predictions of astronomers proved true time after time, people began to lose their fear of eclipses.

Light cannot pass through the moon. Hence, when the moon passes between the earth and the sun, an eclipse of the sun, or *solar eclipse*, takes place.

When the moon comes within the earth's shadow, as shown in the illustration on page 427, an eclipse of the moon, or *lunar eclipse*, occurs. If all of the moon falls within the darkest part, or *umbra*, of the earth's shadow, the eclipse is called a *total lunar eclipse*. If part of the moon is inside the less dark area, or *penumbra*, of the earth's shadow, a *partial lunar eclipse* occurs. Because the orbits of the moon and the earth are not perfect circles and because they do not lie in the same plane, the number of solar and lunar eclipses varies from year to year. But there are never more than three lunar and five solar eclipses each year.

Men travel thousands of miles to witness eclipses. During the time that the sun is temporarily blotted out due to an eclipse (seldom longer than 7 minutes), the region around the sun can be observed more clearly than normally. Better photographs can be obtained from which to study the region of very thin gas around the sun, that is, the *corona*.

So important are these short moments of total eclipse that scientists have braved jungles, mountains, and the dangers of war to be on the right spot to see the eclipse best.

We no longer depend altogether on eclipses to study the corona. A new instrument was invented in 1930 called the *coronagraph*, which makes possible almost daily study of the corona.

COMETS

In 1759 a strange object appeared in the night sky over New England. An eerie light flashed in the dark heavens. It was not a star or any other heavenly body that the Colonists had ever seen. Most observers felt that it was something new—something ominous. People whispered that some strange being from outside the solar system—some dragon of the sky—was approaching the earth to strike and destroy it in one terrific crash.

Many of the Colonists believed that the end of the world was at last at hand. But some level-headed men of science among them, John Winthrop in particular, did not believe this. Winthrop preached a sermon in the chapel of Harvard College at Cambridge on this visitor from outer space. He told his listeners that this visitor from space was a natural occurrence—a harmless *comet*. This quieted the Colonists, and the people went about their business as usual.

All through the early centuries men feared comets. One of the ancient sages, Seneca, wrote, "Comets bring with them and leave behind them the seeds of blood and slaughter."

When astronomers began to study comets, they found them to be very light bodies, even though they are tremendously large in size. The head of a comet is composed of tiny fragments of matter.

Behind the head of a comet is a huge tail of extremely "thin" gas. This tail, often millions of miles long, always points away from the sun. It is visible because it reflects light from

A comet in its orbit around the sun.

ORBIT OF COMET

SUN

428

the sun. The pressure of the sun's light forces the tail away from the head of the comet.

The comet that had frightened the people in Winthrop's day was *Halley's comet*, whose return had been predicted. The distance, speed, and orbit of comets can be accurately determined by astronomers. If they know how long it will take a body to make a complete trip around its orbit, astronomers can predict when it will return.

METEORS, OR "FALLING STARS"

You have probably seen so-called "shooting" or "falling stars." They are not stars at all. They are pieces of material that, like the planets, were once parts of the sun or other stars or comets and passed into the earth's atmosphere. As these pieces of material, called meteors, enter the upper atmosphere they become heated by friction between them and molecules of air. At an altitude of about 190 miles, friction produces enough heat to make them glow. On any night you might see one or two an hour. During August as many as 50 to 100 may be seen every hour because of the return of the Perseid shower of meteors.

Most meteors are burned up and disappear as gases into the atmosphere before they reach the earth's surface. However, some of them occasionally reach the earth. Fragments of meteors which reach the earth are called meteorites. They vary in size from several feet across to just a fraction of an inch.

In times past, meteorites several hundred feet in diameter have hit the earth. A large hole in Arizona, *Meteor Crater*, is believed to have been formed by the crash of such a huge meteorite. It is $\frac{3}{4}$ mile wide and 600 feet deep. Admiral Peary many years ago brought from Greenland a 10-foot meteorite, which weighs about 36 tons. It is at the American Museum of Natural History in New York City. Several fairly large ones fell in the Philippines in 1938.

Meteorites are interesting because they tell us something about the nature of material that may have come from outside the solar system. Scientists have found that certain kinds of meteorites contain almost pure iron and some nickel. Other meteorites, called *stone meteorites*, are made up of the materials similar to those in the rocks of the earth. Some meteorites are mixtures of iron and stone.

WORKING WITH SCIENCE

1. Show the changing position of the sun from day to day as follows: Cut a hole about the size of a dime in a cardboard. Place this against a window facing south. Mark the spot where the sun's light, passing through the small hole, falls on a table top or floor. Repeat this for several days in succession at the same hour, and report on your findings.

2. Demonstrate the appearance of the moon to an observer on earth at the different phases, as follows: Shine a bright light against a large globe in a darkened room. Move slowly around the globe at a distance of 10 feet, and notice the changing appearance of the lighted portion of the globe visible to you.

3. Demonstrate a lunar eclipse with the aid of a strong flashlight, a globe, and a baseball.

4. If you live near the sea-shore, observe the time of high and low tides over a period of a week. Report on your observations to the class.

5. If you live near a large museum, visit its exhibit of meteorites and report on what you have learned.

6. Make a graph showing the time of sunrise and sunset, and the length of daylight and darkness for 30 consecutive days. What conclusion can you draw from these observations?

OTHER PLANETS AND PLANETOIDS

The ancients knew six planets. They had observed and studied *the earth, Mars, Venus,* *Jupiter, Saturn,* and *Mercury*. On the night of March 13, 1781, a seventh planet was discovered. William Herschel [hûr′shĕl], using a 6½-inch reflecting telescope, was the lucky astronomer. Herschel had been an oboe player with a Hanover regiment, but after his first battle he fled to England to escape the tumult of war. He taught music to keep himself alive, and on the side busied himself with astronomy. The discovery of the new planet which he named *Uranus*, god of the sky, brought him great fame and a wealthy wife. Thus, he became able to devote all his time to study of the heavens.

THE DISCOVERY OF NEPTUNE

Almost 60 years later, in 1840, the position of an eighth planet was discovered. Two astronomers, working independently, found that Uranus was not behaving as it should in its motion around the sun. On the basis of Newton's laws of motion and universal gravitation, Uranus should have moved around the sun in a definite orbit, but it did not. Some outside force, perhaps resulting from the attractive force of an unknown body, seemed to be interfering with its expected motion.

Using mathematics as a tool, these two scientists concluded that a planet behind Uranus was the culprit. These men, John C. Adams, who was an Englishman, and a Frenchman named Urbain Leverrier [lĕ-vĕ-ryā′], figured out by mathematics exactly where this new planet would be found. Several astronomers began hunting for it, and finally, 6 years later, it was actually seen by an astronomer named Johann Galle [gäl′ĕ]. This was a remarkable achievement, both for astronomy and mathematics, two sciences that are very closely related. The new planet was named *Neptune*.

PLUTO

The ninth and last of the planets to be discovered so far is called *Pluto*, god of darkness. Its presence had been suspected by several astronomers and many had searched for it for years. On January 21, 1930 a young amateur astronomer working at the Lowell Observa-

tory in Arizona found a bright spot on a photograph of the heavens. This spot had never been identified as anything new until this boy, Clyde Tombaugh, announced it as the image of a new planet. Here was a great discovery made by a young man who had taken up astronomy as a hobby. He had picked out this bright spot from millions of stars shown on the same photographic plate. Tombaugh was awarded a medal in 1931 by the Royal Astronomical Society of England, and later became a professor of astronomy at the University of California.

There may be other planets in our solar system even farther out in space than Pluto. Maybe some day one of you may have the thrill of discovering a new planet. The study of any branch of science is a great adventure.

PLANETOIDS

After studying the motions of the nearer planets, astronomers, again using mathematics, calculated that there should be a planet between Mars and Jupiter at about 28 million miles from the sun. Many people watched the skies but could not find this theoretical planet. Actually, the mathematical law on which the belief that such a plant existed was based was later found to be questionable. However, on the first night of the year 1801, 25 years after the prediction was made, a Sicilian astronomer named Giuseppe Piazzi [pyät′sĕ] found a body between Mars and Jupiter.

It was no wonder others had failed to see this object. It is very tiny, as heavenly bodies go, only about 485 miles in diameter (smaller than Texas). It was named *Ceres*. A few months later, an even smaller body was found nearby. Since then, more than 1500 similar small bodies have been found. Most of them revolve around the sun between the orbits of Mars and Jupiter. They are called planetoids, meaning *planet-like*.

MARS

Many people have wondered whether planets other than our own are inhabited by beings similar to ourselves. A few have insisted that Mars not only has vegetation growing on its surface but also that beings with intelligence may be living on it.

The red appearance of this planet is caused, they say, by large arid regions similar to the painted desert in Arizona, which has a brilliant red coloration. We are also told that large masses of ice or dry ice (frozen carbon dioxide) appear to collect around its poles and then diminish as the warm season approaches.

These astronomers point out that the period of rotation of this planet is 24 hours, 37 minutes, and 22 seconds. This makes the Martian day slightly longer than our own. Its period of revolution around the sun is 686.9 days, something less than twice our own year. The axis of Mars is tilted like that of the earth.

Mars has an atmosphere that contains very little oxygen—as little as that at the top of Mount Everest, more than 7 miles above sea level. The surface temperature of Mars is below freezing during the night, but it rises above the freezing point during the day, making possible the growth of vegetation.

Dr. Percival Lowell, of Boston, built a splendid observatory at Flagstaff, Arizona, after being convinced of life on Mars. He could see straight lines on the surface of this planet, which he thought might be deep channels built by some intelligent beings to carry away into reservoirs the huge quantities of water formed when the polar ice caps melt. It is still an open question whether Lowell was right or not. But most astronomers today do not believe that intelligent beings exist on Mars.

SATURN

Is it possible that living things—one- or many-celled—may exist on other planets? Apparently not on Saturn. For one reason, it is probably altogether too cold, because Saturn is so very far away from the sun. Furthermore, its atmosphere contains not oxygen but two poisonous substances—marsh gas and formaldehyde.

Saturn would be an interesting planet to live on, for it is the only heavenly body that has rings around it. Galileo, the famous Italian scientist, was the first to observe these rings, and he and the millions who have looked upon Saturn since his time have thrilled at the beautiful sight. Its three rings are separated by wide gaps. Each ring is about 10 miles thick and from 11,000 to 18,000 miles wide. The rings are not solid but are composed of dust and rocks, swarms of tiny bodies swinging around Saturn. Saturn also has nine moons, the last of which was discovered by an American astronomer, W. H. Pickering, in 1904.

JUPITER

This planet, larger than all the others combined, is surrounded by a thick, cloudy atmosphere (containing no oxygen) that makes it impossible for us to see its surface. It, too, is a very cold body whose surface temperature is about −220°F. It is very improbable that any living things exist on Jupiter.

Its four largest moons were first observed by Galileo. They are so large that they can be seen with ordinary field glasses. An American astronomer, Edward E. Barnard, discovered the fifth moon in 1892. In 1914 Jupiter's ninth satellite was reported by Seth B. Nicholson, of the Mount Wilson Observatory in California. Its tenth and eleventh moons were also discovered by Nicholson in 1938.

MERCURY AND VENUS

Life on Mercury is also highly improbable. The same half of this planet is always turned toward the sun, while the other half is always turned away from the sun. The part that faces the sun is extremely hot; the part turned away is always frightfully cold.

Venus has no free oxygen in its atmosphere. However, there is plenty of water and carbon dioxide, and the variation of temperature on this planet is not so great as to make impossible some form of life.

Since these two planets follow orbits between the sun and earth, they sometimes pass between us and the sun. When this occurs, observers on earth see them as tiny black dots moving across the face of the sun. The movements of Mercury and Venus across the face of the sun are called *transits* and are followed with great interest by astronomers. In fact, the first observatory set up in the United States at public expense was erected in Philadelphia in 1769 for the purpose of observing and studying such transits.

OTHER WORLDS

Some scientists believe that "our solar system is a freak" in the sense that there is no other such solar system in the universe. They point out that the stars are so far apart that the possibility of other solar systems having been formed by collision is very remote.

Other astronomers feel that it is altogether possible that other solar systems exist around other stars out in space.

If we accept the theory that planets were formed by the approach of stars, then why could not other stars have approached each other and torn out other planets among the millions of stars way out in almost limitless space during the millions of years of time? At the present stage of our knowledge of the heavens, we cannot be certain whether other solar systems exist, although in 1943 an extra-solar planet was reported. An American astronomer reported the presence of a planet accompanying the double star Cygni 61. This report is still being checked. Perhaps with better instruments and more information we will learn whether worlds other than our own exist.

WORKING WITH SCIENCE

1. With the help of an almanac or some book on astronomy, locate a planet near the western horizon at sunset. Such a planet is called an "evening star." On a piece of graph paper make a heavy dot for the planet and two small crosses for two stars near the planet. Locate the planet several nights in succession. What is your conclusion?

2. Make a large chart showing the relative sizes of the moon, planets, and the sun. Try to make your chart to the correct scale.

3. Consult the latest book published on astronomy or your local observatory or planetarium scientists for the latest information on other solar systems. Write a report on your findings.

READING YOU WILL ENJOY

Fabre, Jean H. *This Earth of Ours*. D. Appleton-Century Co., Inc., New York, 1923. One of the classics of popular science. It was first written many years ago, but its material on mountains, rivers, volcanos, earthquakes, and geysers is still wonderful reading.

Gamow, George. *Birth and Death of the Sun*. Penguin Books, Inc., New York, 1945. Rather difficult reading, but contains much information about the sun not found in the other books. It explains the heat of the sun from the point of view of the energy inside the atom.

Newcomb, Simon. *Astronomy for Everybody* (rev. by Robert H. Baker). New Home Library, New York, 1942. A simple, up-to-date survey of astronomy. Includes a very interesting chapter on Mars.

Nininger, Harvey H. *Our Stone-Pelted Planet*. Houghton Mifflin Co., Boston, 1933. A very unusual book that tells of the work of a man who spends his time searching, collecting, and studying meteorites by the hundreds.

Stetson, Harlan T. *Sunspots and Their Effects*, pp. 12–26. McGraw-Hill Book Co., New York, 1937. A discussion of some interesting effects of sunspots on human behavior.

THE PLANETS
In Order of Nearness to the Sun

	Mercury	Venus	Earth	Mars	Jupiter	Saturn	Uranus	Neptune	Pluto
Distance from sun (millions of miles)	36	67	93	141	483	886	1783	2793	3670
Diameter in miles	3000	7600	7900	4200	89,000	75,000	31,000	34,000	6000
Number of moons	0	0	1	2 discov'd by Asab Hall in 1877	11	9 moons, 3 rings	4	1, discovered in 1846	?
Period of rotation	88 days	?	24 hours	24½ hours	10 hours	10¼ hours	10.7 hours	15.7 hours	?
Period of revolution	88 days	225 days	365¼ days	687 days	12 years	29 years	84 years	165 years	700 years
Temperature	Facing sun: 660°F. Not facing sun: −250°F	?		?	?	?	Very cold	?	−380°F
Atmosphere	Practically none	Almost as dense as earth's—heavy clouds		?	Marsh gas and formaldehyde	Marsh gas and formaldehyde	Marsh gas and formaldehyde	Marsh gas and formaldehyde	?
Tipping of axis	Almost zero	?	23½°	25°	3°	27°	98°	?	?
Special charac.	Nearest the sun	Twin sister to earth		Appears red	Largest planet	Famous for its rings			Last to be discovered
Relative weights of objects 100 lbs on earth	25 lbs	85 lbs	100 lbs	36 lbs	264 lbs	117 lbs	92 lbs	112 lbs	?

1

2

The sun and billions of other stars shine every day, year in and year out. And they have been shining for many, many years—probably for 2 or 3 billion. Simple as these facts are, their explanation puzzled man for centuries.

Ancient Greek mathematicians figured out the distance to the sun. Eratosthenes (1), who lived in the second century B.C., was one of the first to come close to the modern figure, 93 million miles. In the seventeenth century, Sir Isaac Newton (2) formulated the Law of Gravitation. Knowing this law and the distance to the sun, astronomers were able to figure out the mass (weight) of the sun. Knowing this, they showed that if the sun's energy came from

combustion, the sun would have become a burned-out cinder after a few thousand years.

A clue to the energy of the sun came in 1896, when Becquerel (3) discovered the radioactivity of uranium. Later studies showed that tremendous sources of energy lie within the atoms of which all things are composed. However, almost half a century passed before Dr. Hans Bethe (4), an American nuclear scientist, worked out the now generally accepted theory that the energy of the sun and similar stars comes from the "carbon cycle," a series of nuclear changes in which an atom of carbon "helps" four atoms of hydrogen to become one atom of helium. In these reactions, mass is converted directly into energy.

3

4

32

BILLIONS OF STARS AND OTHER UNIVERSES

Excluding the sun, which is also a star, *Proxima Centauri* is the star nearest to us. If a colossal flashlight were set up on this star and pointed toward the earth, light from the flashlight would take more than 4 years to reach us. At this speed it takes light from the sun only 8 minutes to reach us and only about 5 hours to reach the outermost planet, Pluto.

The sun is about 93 million miles away from the earth. Proxima Centauri is about 25 trillion miles away. Even this distance is very small compared with the distance to other stars. Their distances are so great that in miles they mean nothing to us. Astronomers who deal with such distances use another unit of length. This unit is based on the distance that light can travel in one year. It is called a *light-year*.

Light travels at a speed of 186,000 miles per second. In one minute it covers 60 times 186,000 miles and 60 times this in 1 hour. Calculations show that light travels about 6 trillion miles in 1 year. This distance is a light-year. Therefore, Proxima Centauri, which is a little more than 25 trillion miles away, is about 4.3 light-years away from us.

STARS AND OTHER HEAVENLY BODIES

Stars are much farther away from us than are the planets. In addition, stars appear to be motionless in the sky; their changing positions throughout the year are caused chiefly by the earth's revolution. On the other hand, planets, from a word meaning *to wander*, are not fixed in space. They are revolving around the sun and changing their positions in the sky from day to day. Since planets are so much nearer to us, a telescope shows them as circular disks, or plates. But even the most powerful telescope cannot increase the size of a star to anything larger than a bright dot.

A few thousand stars can be seen on any clear night with the naked eye. Some are brighter than others. The brightest stars seen, such as Sirius and Arcturus, are said to be of the *first magnitude*, and astronomers talk of the faintest star as being of the *twenty-first magnitude*. Without the aid of a telescope, an average person can see stars no dimmer than the sixth magnitude. A star is one magnitude lower than another if it is 25 times as bright as the other.

Planets are either very cold, or at most, as hot as 700°F. Visible stars, on the other hand, are extremely hot bodies. Blue stars are the hottest of all; their surface temperatures are in the neighborhood of 50,000°F. The red stars are comparatively cool stars, with surface temperatures of about 3000°F. Yellow stars, such as the sun, are hotter than red stars.

Stars differ not only in color and temperature but also in size. We can measure the diameters of the planets fairly easily. However, measuring the diameters of stars is one of the most difficult jobs for an astronomer. This is because of their enormous distances from us.

CONSTELLATIONS

Some of the brighter stars are so located that lines drawn between them might, with some stretch of the imagination, be made to represent some object, person, or animal. The ancient watchers of the skies gave names to several of these groups of stars, which we call constellations. For example, the constellation *Cassiopeia* was named after a character from mythology. Another group of stars was called *Pegasus*, after a mythological horse with wings. *Ursa Major*, the Great Bear; *Ursa Minor*, the Little Bear; *Cancer*, the Crab; and *Draco*, the Dragon, are other widely known constellations.

Constellations have more than romantic value. It is often easier to locate individual stars by referring to their position in one of these constellations. For example, the North Star (*Polaris*) can be located by looking for the end of the handle of the *Little Dipper*. When you face Polaris, you face north. Sailors from Phoenicia steered their ships by Polaris. Caravans crossed the deserts by this same star. Pilots of planes roaring through the night and captains of ships sailing the seas still use this star as a guide.

During World War II the United States Government charted 27 other stars which were used by army and navy men as sighting points. They helped determine latitude, longitude, and time, in every corner of the globe.

Among these stars were *Andromeda*, *Betelgeuse*, *Sirius*, *Antares*, and *Vega*.

THE TELESCOPE

To get entirely new information and more exact data, scientists have invented instruments such as the clock, the camera, the spectroscope, and the telescope. Without such tools, most of the newer knowledge of astronomy would still be unknown.

In 1609 Galileo built a telescope which was an improvement of an original design of Jan Lippershey and two other Dutch scientists. These three men had each invented the telescope independently in 1608. The telescope consisted of a tube containing two lenses, one to produce an image of the distant object and to collect and concentrate the feeble light. The other lens, the eyepiece, served to enlarge this image. The first telescope was about 18 inches long and magnified three or four diameters. Lenses were very crude affairs at first, and only a few new stars could be picked out with their help.

Stars too faint to be seen with the unaided eye began to be seen by astronomers using telescopes. The telescope with which Galileo discovered the mountains of the moon, the rings of Saturn, and four of the moons of Jupiter, had a $2\frac{1}{4}$-inch lens. As the years went by, larger and better telescopes were constructed, and thousands of new stars were studied. The largest telescope ever constructed has a mirror, or "eye," 200 inches in diameter.

PRINCIPLE OF THE TELESCOPE

There are two main types of telescopes in common use: the *refracting* (lens) *telescope* and the *reflecting* (mirror) *telescope*. As shown in the illustrations on page 437, light from a distant star is concentrated by a lens in such a way that a very faint star appears as a brighter point of light.

No matter how powerful the telescope is, a star, because of its tremendous distance, appears as only a point of light. Planets appear as large circles, or disks, because they are relatively very near the earth, and the eyepiece

Two well-known constellations.

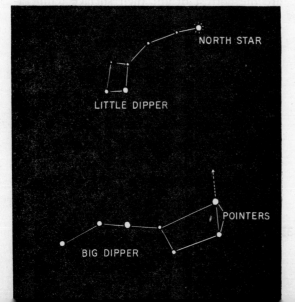

NORTH STAR

LITTLE DIPPER

POINTERS

BIG DIPPER

can enlarge the image formed by the other lens of the instrument.

THE GREAT EYE OF PALOMAR

On Mt. Palomar is a 200-inch reflecting telescope—the largest telescope in the world. It enables astronomers to look at the moon as if it were only 25 miles away and reaches out into space to stars never before seen by men. It gathers 640,000 times as much light as the human eye and will enable scientists to do many things they have long wished to do; for example, take color photographs of solar prominences.

It took many years to plan and construct this instrument, and it cost many millions of dollars. American philanthropists and American scientists made the completion of this 500-ton instrument possible. It was not built for profit or immediate industrial use. It was built to enable men to learn more about the size and shape and construction of the *universe*, the total of heavenly bodies and space.

THE MILKY WAY

If you look at the sky on a clear night, you will notice a band of light which stands out against the blackness of the heavens. Galileo thought that this band of light was made up of many stars close together which his crude telescope could not separate into individual stars. This was only a guess, however, until William Herschel built larger mirrors for his telescopes. He ground the glass himself, never

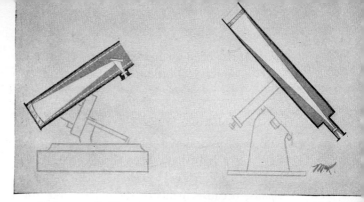

Reflecting (left) and refracting telescopes.

taking his fingers off as he polished them for hours at a stretch.

With a 19-inch telescope of his own construction, Herschel carefully examined this belt of light and, in 1784, announced that this belt of light, called the *Milky Way*, was really "a most extensive stratum [layer] of stars of which our Sun and the solar system is but a part." Herschel's telescope enabled him to pick out thousands of individual stars in the Milky Way. Galileo was right.

A person on earth sees the Milky Way as a thing apart from the earth, but in reality *the earth and the whole solar system are actually a part of the Milky Way.* (The Milky Way goes all the way around the sky. We see only half of it at a time—part of it in summer and another part in winter.) Herschel calculated that the sun was somewhat away from the center of the Milky Way, which could be pictured as a huge, flattened, double-convex watch-shaped system of stars. We see only the edge of it. The Milky Way is also called a *Galactic System*, after a Greek word meaning

Left: The home of the "Great Eye" of Palomar. Right: Looking up at the telescope.

Press Association, Inc.

milk. It has been estimated that this system of stars contains 200 billion stars and is 300,000 light-years in diameter.

OTHER GALACTIC SYSTEMS

Beyond our own galactic system, other patches of light have been discovered. These patches are called *nebulas*, which means *clouds*, because many of them look like thin, wispy, shapeless clouds. Some are spiral in shape; some look like flat dishes. Astronomers wondered whether these nebulas were other systems of stars even farther out in space than the Milky Way.

While some astronomers were making a deeper study of the Milky Way, others devised new methods of examination and built better telescopes and larger instruments with which to examine strange patches of light beyond the Milky Way. They found that some nebulas are clouds of luminous gases, but most of them are tremendous groups of stars. Thus, some of these nebulas are galactic systems far out in space. Harlow Shapley, of Harvard University, found many globular star clusters. And there are thousands of these star systems, or "island universes," as far away as our telescopes can reach.

HOW LARGE IS THE UNIVERSE?

It is almost impossible to get a clear picture of the immensity of the universe. One famous astronomer has tried to give us some idea of its size by stating that if a map the size of a nor-

mal city block were made of the known universe, the earth would be too small even to appear on such a map. If an ordinary period were printed on such a map, that period would be more than 50,000 times too large to represent even the outermost limit of the solar system.

In terms of light-years, our telescopes have shown the presence of stars so far away that the light from these stars takes more than 220 million years to reach us. Such distances dwarf our earth into less than a pin point. We have found that this "huge" earth, on which we live, is only a speck of dust in the universe.

THE EXPANDING UNIVERSE

Two American astronomers, Edwin P. Hubble and Milton Humason, have studied hundreds of star systems by means of the 100-inch telescope at Mount Wilson Observatory. With the aid of a spectroscope and special cameras attached to their telescope, they discovered that these nebulas seem to be rushing away from the earth at tremendous speeds. The universe, in other words, seems to be expanding. Astronomers hope that with the new 200-inch telescope on Mount Palomar in southern California a further study of these nebulas will supply us with some explanation of this phenomenon.

INTERPLANETARY TRAVEL—IS IT POSSIBLE?

On January 10, 1946 men made contact with

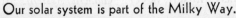
Our solar system is part of the Milky Way.

the moon for the first time in history. Army scientists at Belmar, New Jersey shot a beam of high-frequency radio waves (radar) at the moon. The radar waves struck the moon and bounced back to the earth. A series of jagged lines on an instrument called an *oscilloscope* showed that the round trip of about 477,000 miles had taken 2.4 seconds, exactly as calculated. Predictions soon followed the startling news. Men would map the moon, contact other planets, and prepare again for interplanetary communication.

Many men have long dreamed of traveling to the moon or to other planets in rockets. Some have actually tried to invent rockets that could be used for such a purpose. Rocket societies in 17 countries, among which are the British Interplanetary Society and the American Rocket Society (founded in 1930 as the American Interplanetary Society), are interested in the problem.

In 1944 an eminent scientific writer concluded that ideas of space travel had reached a rather high state of perfection. Rockets capable of attaining a speed of 1 mile a second had already been made. The fuel used was alcohol and pure liquid oxygen. This was before the world knew that the energy of the atom's nucleus had been unlocked and could be used to propel rockets with much greater speeds. There is no doubt any more about the requirements and the principles for the fulfillment of space travel. No problems connected with the project appear unsolvable.

To consider a flight to the moon or to another planet impossible of eventual achievement is contrary to the spirit of science. A great scientist, Liebig, once wrote, "The secret of all who make discoveries is to look upon nothing as impossible." Modern engineers are saying, "Whatever the mind of man can conceive, he will some day do!"

WORKING WITH SCIENCE

1. On the next clear night pick out the constellation called the *Big Dipper*. Make a diagram of the most visible stars in this constellation.

2. Repeat the above observation every night for a period of several weeks. Report on the apparent change of position of this constellation.

3. Start constructing a small telescope, using the directions in one of the books on astronomy mentioned in the reading list. Report on your progress from time to time, explaining just what you have done.

4. Make a visit to your nearest observatory or planetarium, and report on the type or types of telescope used there.

5. There is a star-map printed in each issue of the magazine, *Science News Letter*. Examine five or six of such consecutive star-maps, and report on what these maps tell you about the position and motion of stars and constellations. If possible, bring the magazines to class to illustrate your conclusions.

6. Make a sky chart showing a few important constellations observable in the northern hemisphere. Use a blue or black background for the cardboard chart.

READING YOU WILL ENJOY

Gable, J. H. and Swezey, G. D. *Boys' Book of Astronomy*. E. P. Dutton & Co., Inc., New York, 1936. One of the best written and most clearly illustrated books in this field of science. Chapter 3 deals with "The Astronomer's Workshop."

Lockwood, Marian and Draper, Arthur L. *The Earth among the Stars*. Basic Books, Inc. New York, 1935. A small book, but it contains a wealth of information on stars and nebulas, excellently written and skillfully illustrated.

Woodbury, David O. *The Glass Giant of Palomar*. Dodd, Mead & Co., New York, 1939. The opening chapter of this book has the title, "Jules Verne Becomes a Piker."

Zim, Herbert S. *Rockets and Jets*. Harcourt, Brace & Co., New York, 1945. Three excellent chapters, 15–17, are devoted to the problem of interplanetary travel. The latest available information is used to answer many questions on this fascinating topic.

1

2

Some great inventions consist of combining several earlier ones. Combining the use of fire for heat, and shelter for protection, was a big step forward. An open fire in a cave or a rude shelter provided some warmth, but smoke made the place almost unbearable. Holes in the roofs were not much help in getting rid of the smoke (1). Perhaps the greatest single advance was the invention of the chimney. This long tube over the fire carried out the smoke and provided a draft that made the fire burn better. Chimneys were built against walls for support and a special structure was developed beneath them for the fire. This resulted in the fireplace (2).

When Benjamin Franklin invented a metal stove to take the place of the fireplace, he developed a much more effective heating system. The sides and back of the stove (3) radiated heat and less was lost up the chimney. From Franklin's day, we have made great progress in home heating. The stove, now a furnace, was moved from the living room to the basement (4). We burn improved fuels and have devices to start and stop the furnace automatically. Modern heating methods warm all the rooms of the house from a central heating plant. However, the goal of a healthful steady indoor temperature, with proper humidification, free of drafts, yet providing enough fresh air to make us feel our best—all at low cost—has not yet been reached.

3

4

UNIT TEN

Science for Our Homes

33

HEATING OUR HOMES

Home means much to all of us. We like a change, but we like even more to come back home again. Many things make home what it is, but first of all home is some kind of building to provide shelter. When homes are considered scientifically, questions about dozens of things that most of us take for granted must be asked. Why does your house have a cellar or an attic? Why do people want a fireplace in the living room? Does a house need windows? Why does an electric light often hang from the middle of the ceiling? Questions like these start people to thinking about their homes and why they were built as they are.

OLD IDEAS HANG ON

Consider the attic, for example. It is a room and still not quite a room. Roasting hot in summer and freezing in winter, it is a dumping ground for old trunks, broken chairs, and things we cannot quite decide to throw out. Why do houses have attics? They are used mostly for storage, but surely it would be hard to design a worse kind of storeroom.

Attics exist because the roofs of most houses slant upward at an awkward angle. But not all building have sloping roofs. Why do the roofs of most houses slant upward? We must look into the early history of housing to find a

reason. This reason ties in with the climate of north and central Europe, whence many of our ideas on how to live have come.

Primitive, traditional, and "modern" homes.

441

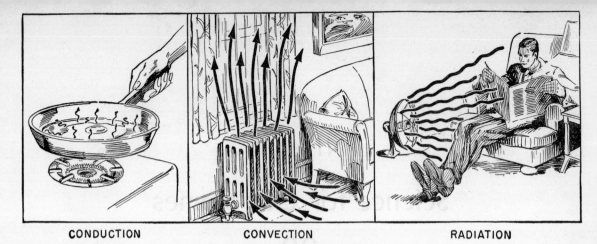

CONDUCTION   CONVECTION   RADIATION

Heat travels in three ways.

Nowadays, with modern materials, a house with a flat roof can be built more easily and less expensively than one with a peaked roof. Instead of an attic, a storage room suited to its purpose can be included.

By following the development of a few ideas—heat, light, electronics, and sound—you will see how these things are used today and how they may be used tomorrow in our homes. As you might expect, these stories cannot be completely separated because modern inventions are the result of ideas that have been taken from many of the various branches of science.

HEAT AND LIFE

Life is possible on the earth chiefly because the temperature averages from about 40°F to 110°F. Some such moderate amount of heat is necessary for all plant and animal life. By burning fuel foods we keep our bodies warm enough to function most effectively. By burning fuels such as coal, oil, and wood, we control the temperature of our homes and buildings so that we can live and work.

WHAT IS HEAT?

Let us review what is known about heat before considering heat transfer. Heat, as you know, is a form of energy. In other words, heat can be used to do work, that is, produce motion. In fact, *heat is motion*—the motion of molecules. When we say that water taken from a teakettle is hotter than tap water, we mean that the billions of molecules in the water from the teakettle are moving faster than those in the tap water. If the hot water is mixed with the tap water, the speed of the moving hot-water molecules will slow down and the speed of the tap-water molecules will increase. To make the water molecules keep completely still, we would have to cool them to a temperature of −459°F. At this temperature, known as *absolute zero*, the motion of molecules stops.

TRANSFER BY CONDUCTION

The nature of heat means that all heat transfer is a matter of speeding up or slowing down molecules. But doing this quickly, inexpensively, and effectively is not always easy. The fire in the fireplace of the pioneer's cabin causes the molecules of the bottom of the iron kettle to move faster. The rapid motion of the molecules on the bottom surface is transferred to those alongside, and on and on until the whole kettle has been heated.

This method of heat transfer in which the heat is transferred from molecule to molecule without any motion of the object (in this case, the kettle) is called conduction. Metals are the best conductors of heat. Iron conducts heat about 2500 times as well as air, and silver conducts heat even better than iron. If you could afford to make soup in a silver kettle, it would warm faster than in an iron one.

TRANSFER BY CONVECTION

As the kettle warms, it warms the water in it. The molecules of water move faster. Since water is a liquid, these molecules have room to move and, being heated, they push more and take up more room. The heated water *expands* and becomes lighter than an equal volume of cold water. The lighter, expanded water rises to the top of the kettle and is replaced by heavier, colder water flowing from the top of the kettle down along the sides. In this way a current called a *convection current* is set up. Thus, heat is transferred through the water of the kettle.

The transfer of heat through liquids and gases by means of currents is called convection. A room is warmed by convection, as heated air over a stove rises and is replaced by cooler air flowing in across the floor. Stoves, oil heaters, and radiators warm chiefly by convection.

TRANSFER BY RADIATION

The rapidly vibrating molecules in a flame give off energy in the form of waves. Light is one form of wave energy. However, much of the energy given off by the flame is invisible and is composed of waves that are longer than light waves. These energy waves travel at great speeds through empty space as well as through air. When the energy waves strike objects, much of the energy is converted into heat. This method of transferring heat is called radiation. The energy given off is known as radiant energy. Radiant energy from the sun warms the earth in the same way that radiation from the fire in the fireplace warms a room.

WORKING WITH SCIENCE

1. Find out about scientific attempts to reach absolute zero in laboratories for the study of low temperatures.

2. Test the speed with which different metals conduct heat by holding in a flame several wires of the same diameter but made of different metals. Before placing the wires in the flame, put small balls of wax or paraffin at one end. Hold with pliers and stick the bare ends of the wires in the flame. Note the approximate time required for the wax to melt.

3. Make a list of places in the home where good and poor heat conductivity are desirable.

4. By means of bits of sawdust or crystals of potassium permanganate, trace the convection currents in a large beaker of water being heated over a bunsen burner.

5. Trace the convection currents in a room by means of smoke or tiny bits of absorbent cotton dropped over a hot radiator.

6. Obtain samples of materials commonly used in insulating furnaces and pipes. Explain how these improve a heating system.

7. Make a survey of heating in homes of your classmates. How many have central heating? How many use stoves? What fuels are used?

HOW WE HEAT OUR HOMES

When we moved the source of heat to the basement, we had to work out ways to transfer heat from the basement to upstairs rooms. This has been done by three different systems, each of which has its own advantages. All are a great improvement over having a fireplace or stove in nearly every room of the house. Each of these systems may use coal, oil, or gas as fuel with slight modification in the firebox.

HOT-AIR SYSTEM

One heating system uses air as a conductor of heat. The firebox of the furnace is surrounded by a metal jacket which is insulated from the outside air. Cold air flows in at the

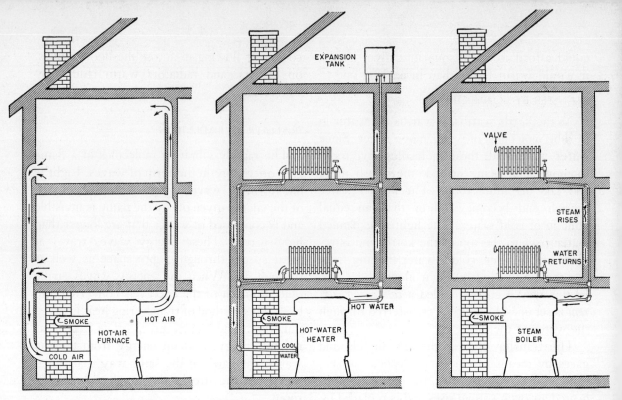

Three types of heating systems: hot-air, hot-water, and steam.

bottom of this jacket, is warmed, rises, and passes upward through pipes, or *ducts*, that lead to the various rooms. Such a system is called a *hot-air system*.

In some hot-air systems, an electric fan gives the air a boost and sends it faster and more surely to its destination. A hot-air system heats quickly, but unless a fan is used, some of the rooms may not receive enough heat. Bulky ducts are needed and, unless care is taken, the heated air will be drier than is considered healthful.

HOT-WATER SYSTEM

In a *hot-water system*, water instead of air is the conductor of heat. This system is a bit more complicated than a hot-air system. The water must be confined at all times, forming a *closed system*. A boiler, or *water-jacket*, surrounds the source of heat.

The heated water rises from the boiler through pipes to radiators, which provide a large heated surface in contact with the air of the room. The air at the radiator is warmed rapidly, and soon the room is heated by con-

vection currents from the warm radiator. As the water in the radiator loses heat, it becomes cool and flows back to the boiler through return pipes, is reheated, and starts its journey again.

A hot-water heating system must be filled with water at all times. If a radiator is half-filled with air, the hot water cannot enter. Why? Furthermore, water expands when heated, and an expansion tank must be connected to the hot-water pipes to allow for the expansion of the water.

Some modern hot-water systems have an electric pump to circulate the hot water. Such a system is very satisfactory. It does not heat a room as fast as a hot-air system, but it gives a steadier heat and is easier to control.

STEAM-HEATING SYSTEM

In a *steam-heating system*, the fire heats water in a boiler, which often consists of a series of tubes, so arranged that a large surface is presented to the flames. The boiler tubes are not completely filled with water, and once a temperature of 212°F is reached, steam forms.

444

The pipes fill with steam, and if the heat is sufficient, steam pressure of 2 to perhaps 5 pounds per square inch is produced. This pressure drives the steam up through pipes to radiators. In the radiators the steam condenses back to water, giving out much heat in the process. The warmed radiator warms the room, largely by convection.

The water formed by the condensing steam may be returned to the boiler through the pipe in which the steam comes to the radiator. However, in some steam systems, a separate return pipe is provided. Steam moves through the system faster if no other gas, such as air, interferes. In large buildings an air pump is connected to the steam-heating system to pump the air out of the pipes and make circula-

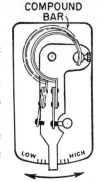

A thermostat and a metallic thermometer.

tion of the steam easier. A steam system operates at a higher temperature than either hot-water or hot-air systems. Steam will heat a room more quickly than hot water, but the control of temperature is not quite as satisfactory.

WORKING WITH SCIENCE

1. Visit a house with a hot-air heating system. Locate the cold-air intake and the ducts. Find out how the owner likes it. Make a sketch of how it works.

2. Study a hot-water heating system as you did the hot-air system. Locate the risers, return pipes, water boiler, water gage, and expansion tank, and make a diagram of the system.

3. Construct a model steam-heating system of glass tubing and flasks. Demonstrate its operation to the class.

4. Study steam heating as you have the other two systems. If your school is a large one, it probably has a steam system. If so, study it in detail. Find out the yearly cost of heating your school. Sketch a section of the heating system.

CONTROL OF HEATING

A modern furnace is a vast improvement over earlier furnaces. Some modern furnaces are no longer dependent for air supply on a draft created by a tall chimney. An electric fan or blower provides a more easily controlled supply of air. This forced draft makes it possible to control combustion and to produce or cut off heat at will.

Better control is provided by a *thermostat*, one of the simplest and most convenient heat-

ing aids that man has invented. A thermostat enables us to keep a room at about any temperature we may desire.

A thermostat works because not all substances expand the same amount when heated. For example, brass expands more than iron for each degree rise in temperature. This merely means that if a bar of brass and a bar of iron are exactly the same length at 60°F, at 80°F the bar of brass has expanded more and

How a thermostat controls the temperature of an electric iron. Explain.

From Encyclopaedia Britannica film Home Electrical Appliances

become slightly longer than the bar of iron.

Suppose we take two bars, one of brass and one of iron, and make a *compound bar* by riveting them together. Now heat them. What do you think happens? On heating, a compound bar bends. Since the iron expands less than the brass, the iron will be on the *inside* of the bent compound bar.

If you attach a needle, or pointer, to a compound bar in such a way that the pointer moves across a dial as the bar bends, you have a *metallic thermometer*, a kind widely used. If you connect the compound bar in an electric circuit, so that it will complete the circuit when it bends enough to touch a contact point, you have a thermostat. You can construct the thermostat in such a way that the distance between the compound bar and the contact point can be regulated. As a result, the bar will have to move a greater or smaller distance before it makes contact. In this way, the temperature at which the thermostat completes a circuit can be varied.

USES OF THERMOSTATS

A thermostat can be set to control an electric motor that opens the draft or turns on a blower when the temperature drops. When the temperature increases sufficiently, the thermostat will cause the motor to close the draft or turn off the blower. A thermostat provides automatic temperature control when connected with the heating system.

WORKING WITH SCIENCE

1. Make an air thermometer as follows: Insert 3 feet of glass tubing through a one-hole stopper. Insert stopper and tube in a Florence flask. Warm the flask slightly and invert. Place the end of the tube in a beaker of colored water. As the flask cools, the colored water will rise in the tube. This air thermometer will respond to temperature changes that heat or cool the flask.

2. The same materials can be used to make a large water thermometer. Fill the flask completely with colored water. Insert the stopper. Heating the water-filled flask will cause water to expand and rise higher in the tube.

3. The different rates of expansion of metals have important uses. See if you can devise an experiment which will show that metals expand at different rates when heated. Remember that the amount of expansion will be very small. So some method of measuring it is essential.

4. Take apart a cheap metallic thermometer to see the structure of the compound bar and how it is connected to the pointer.

New-type furnaces give us more heat for less fuel. From left to right: A new furnace for bituminous coal, a new furnace for anthracite, and a new oil burner.

Photos courtesy of the Bituminous Coal Institute; Anthracite Institute; General Electric Company

SUMMER RAYS

WINTER RAYS

A solar house. Explain how heat from the sun is used in winter but kept out in the summer.

5. You can make a simple compound bar by riveting together a thin sheet of brass and a thin sheet of iron. Use sheets of metal about ½ inch wide and 8 inches long.

6. Using your home-made thermostat made from a compound bar, see if you can connect up a circuit in which the thermostat controls the ringing of an electric bell such as a door bell.

7. You will probably find in your own town that there are industries in which temperature control is important—for example, the bakery or some manufacturing plant. Find out exactly how this temperature control is achieved and why it is important.

NEW HEATING SYSTEMS

In the past few years, more and more has been heard of another method of heating, which differs somewhat from those discussed so far. This method is not new. It has been used successfully in Europe for some time but has been introduced into America only recently. In the common heating systems, a room is heated largely by convection currents and mechanical mixing of warm and cold air. A steam or hot-water radiator radiates heat only to a limited extent. Its effectiveness is chiefly the result of the convection currents that are set up over the warm radiator.

RADIANT HEATING

The new method of heating, known as *radiant heating*, warms a room through large radiating surfaces, usually the entire floor, the walls, or floor and walls. This method of heating results in more uniform heat than other

systems. It warms persons or objects in a room without raising the air temperature as high as is necessary in other systems to obtain the same degree of comfort.

A radiant-heating system does not have radiators. During construction of the house, the floors may be filled with crushed rock or cinders. On the layer of rock a flattened pat-

A radiant heating system.

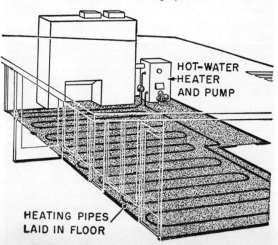

HOT-WATER HEATER AND PUMP

HEATING PIPES LAID IN FLOOR

447

tern of pipes is laid. The pipes cover the entire floor. The pipes from the different rooms are connected to a hot-water heating system. Concrete is poured over the pipes, and after it has set, a wood or linoleum floor is laid on top. Hot water at about 130°F is circulated through the pipes, usually by means of a circulating pump. The floor and walls are warmed and radiate heat. As a result, there are no hot or cold spots, and the temperature can be maintained easily at a comfortable level. Because the room can be kept cooler and still be comfortable, there is a saving of fuel.

SOLAR HEATING

If a house were built with many windows or with large glass surfaces facing south, much of the sun's heat could be trapped during the day to keep the house warm. But there are two difficulties. Such a house would be unbearably hot in summer and would cool off at night almost as fast as it heated up during the day.

How do these illustrations relate to the "Zone of Comfort"?

From Encyclopaedia Britannica film Control of Body Temperature

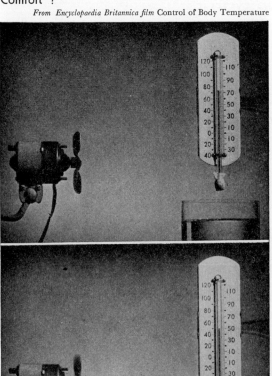

These difficulties can be overcome. The possibility of trapping too much heat can be eliminated by the design of the house itself. You have probably observed that the path of the sun as it crosses the sky is a low arc in winter and that it moves on a longer, higher path in summer. If a house is built facing south with large windows and overhanging eaves, much sunlight enters during the winter because of the low angle of the sun. In summer the sun is higher and, instead of entering the house, the rays are cut off by the overhanging eaves. Such a house would benefit from solar heat in winter but would not be overheated in summer.

Rapid cooling at night is prevented by the use of double-glass windows built with a sealed dead-air space. Dead-air space serves as an effective insulator. The dead-air space between the double glass permits sunlight to pass through but prevents the heat from escaping. A window with double glass is a kind of permanent storm window. If it is covered by drapes at night, it is further insulated to prevent loss of heat.

Solar heat alone is not enough to completely warm a house in the northern parts of our country. It must be used in conjunction with some other heating system.

ZONE OF COMFORT

We have looked at only half the picture of heat in our homes. We have been concerned with adding heat. Often it is just as important to be able to take away heat. The goal of household heating is an even, comfortable temperature. The important thing is how people *feel*, not what the thermometer says the temperature is.

Heating engineers and doctors have conducted many experiments and have found certain limits of temperature and humidity within which people are most comfortable. The temperature limit varies a bit from season to season, but it is generally from 63° to 75°F. Often mentioned as the best indoor temperature is 68°F.

448

Humidity is also important. Excessive humidity prevents evaporation of the perspiration that is constantly given off through the skin. A person feels hot and sticky and actually irritated by excess moisture. Indoors a relative humidity of 40 to 60 percent is desirable. Certainly it should not be more than 10 percent above or below those figures. But this goal is hard to achieve. The air in most houses is too dry in winter and too moist in summer for comfort and health.

AIR-CONDITIONING

How is this comfortable zone of temperature and humidity to be obtained? In summer, cooling may be as necessary as heating is in winter. The entire process of maintaining air in a comfortable and healthful state is known as *air-conditioning*. This term is often loosely used, but it means more than cooling or circulating air with a fan.

A complete air-conditioning system passes air over heating coils to warm it during winter and over cooling coils to cool it in summer. During the summer, water is removed from the air by chemical or mechanical means until the relative humidity is brought within the comfortable range. In winter when the air is heated, water is added until the humidity is up to the required level. In addition, air may be washed or filtered to remove dust, pollen, and bacteria. Dust, pollen, and smoke may also be removed by an electronic device known as a "Precipitron."

WORKING WITH SCIENCE

1. If a local dealer handles furnaces and heating systems, visit his store and examine the kinds he handles. Ask him questions about the advantages, costs, and efficiency of each system. He will be glad to explain these things to you.

2. New developments in heating and heat control are being made all the time. Obtain information from advertisements and circulars about new-type furnaces for oil, coal, and light oils.

3. Make a brief study of the heating systems used in airplanes or in automobiles. Would such a system have advantages in a home?

4. Compare the size, weight, cost, and efficiency of copper and iron radiators. Any local building contractor will give you the facts. Decide for yourself which type you would prefer in your home.

5. More modern houses are being designed with radiant heating. You may find a book on modern housing in your library which will give more of the practical story of radiant heating. Read this and report to the class. If any new factories have been built in your town the last few years, find out whether radiant heating is used.

6. You may have noticed that a thermometer in direct sunlight reads much higher than a shaded thermometer nearby. Sometimes when the shaded thermometer is below freezing, the one exposed to direct sunlight may read 70° or 80°F. Explain this difference.

7. Make a chart, showing how hot beds, cold frames, and greenhouses operate. All three make use of the principle of solar heating.

8. The "Precipitron" has two distinct uses. In industrial plants it keeps smoke and dust from going out into the air; in homes it removes smoke and dust from the air that enters the air-conditioning system. Find out more about this interesting device from advertisements or from a local dealer.

9. There are many different types of air-conditioning. Try to obtain booklets from manufacturers of different air-conditioning devices. Compare what they have to say. What do all air-conditioning devices have in common? How do they differ?

READING YOU WILL ENJOY

Nelson, George and Wright, Henry. *Tomorrow's House.* Simon and Schuster, Inc., New York, 1945. Written for people planning new homes, this book touches on solar and radiant heating, illumination, and other scientific developments that are real contributions to the home.

For centuries most work and leisure activities came to a halt with darkness. Unsteady light from an open fire made work almost impossible. The improvement of lighting has made evenings more enjoyable and has made occupations such as mining possible.

A great, but now hardly appreciated invention, was the oil lamp (1). Its secret is a wick that soaks up a liquid fuel so that it may be easily vaporized. The candle was another step forward. It uses a solid fuel and hence is more convenient to carry about and to store. The knights of old may have lived in grand style, but a cold drafty castle lighted only by torches (2) and candles is no place to be on a winter's night.

The search for better light sent men to remote parts of the world. In the Atlantic, Pacific, and Antarctic men hunted whales for oil to burn in lamps. About 1800, gas, manufactured from coal, was first used for lighting. It soon was widely adopted for lighting both streets (3) and homes. Gas lighting was later improved by an invention of Carl von Welsbach who made a mantle (4) that glowed a brilliant white in the gas flame and increased the light tremendously. In the meanwhile, people discovered how to prepare kerosene, or "coal oil," (5) from thick, black petroleum. When the first oil well was successfully dug in 1859, a steady supply of fuel for lamps was assured.

Several kinds of electric lights had been tried before Edison's invention (6) in 1878. Early models used a great deal of current and were not very dependable. Continued improvements in the manufacture of electric lights have produced better illumination at lower costs. The modern lights are the fluorescent lamps in which a glowing gas produces excellent light with very little heat. Now, at the flick of a switch, light, almost equivalent to daylight, is ours to use. Light makes our homes more livable and much safer.

34

LIGHTING OUR HOMES

Fire is a source of both light and heat. The cave man's fire warmed his crude shelter and gave him light that, in effect, increased the length of his day. In addition to the fact that light and heat may both be produced by combustion, they are produced at the same time in many other ways. In fact, a chief problem in modern lighting is to produce light *without* heat. Reducing the amount of heat produced has resulted in many new types of lamps.

DEVELOPMENT OF ARTIFICIAL LIGHT

The exact nature of light has puzzled scientists for hundreds of years. It still puzzles them in certain respects. However, all scientists agree that light is a form of energy. Usually it acts as if it consists of very short waves that travel 186,000 miles a second. Light waves are so short that the thickness of this sheet of paper is about equal to the combined length of several hundred of them.

LENGTH OF LIGHT WAVES

Let us be more specific about the length of light waves. They have been measured with great care. Like most other scientific measurements, the length of light waves is recorded in the metric system. The unit used is 0.000001 meter. It is called the *micron* and is equal to about 0.00004 inch. The micron is a convenient unit for measuring light waves, just as the mile is a convenient unit for measuring large distances.

How long is a light wave? Not even 1 micron. Light waves range from 0.4 to 0.8 micron in length. Within that narrow range are all the kinds of light that the eye can see— all colors, shades, and tints.

Heat waves are just a bit longer than light waves. Heat waves average from 1 to 100 microns in length. The longest heat waves gradually merge with the ultrashort radio waves and, as you have probably guessed, the longest light waves merge with the shortest heat waves. The longer the waves, the less energy they possess. When sunlight strikes the earth, the light waves hit the molecules that make up the ground, the sea, and other matter. Some of their energy is directly changed into heat in this process.

ELECTRIC LIGHT

When Edison invented the electric light in 1879, it was a very dim affair, judged by present standards. The light produced was a dull yellow, and there was less of it than from gas. The bulbs were expensive, burned out quickly, and the cost of electricity itself was very high.

Improvements in electric-light bulbs during the past 50 years have been remarkable. Their light output compared to current used has increased more than 500 percent, and the cost of bulbs and electricity has decreased greatly.

Nearly everybody in the United States has seen and operated an electric light. But many persons do not know how electricity makes

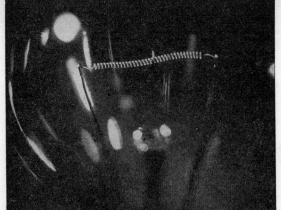
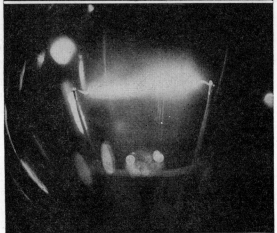

From Encyclopaedia Britannica film Home Electrical Appliances

Cold and hot filaments.

the light work. Let us begin our study of modern lighting by getting a clear idea of what goes on inside the frosted-glass bulb when the switch is turned on.

As you know, metals are generally good conductors of heat and electricity and non-metals are poor conductors. Silver, the best conductor of heat, is also the best conductor of electricity. Silver conducts electricity twice as well as aluminum, 70 times as well as nichrome.

When an electric current meets a resistance, work must be done to overcome the resistance. This work reveals itself as heat. Part of the current is transformed into heat. If you send a current through a nichrome wire, the wire becomes hot. Increase the current, and the wire becomes red-hot. Increase the current still more, and the wire glows with white heat for a short time, then melts and burns in two.

No matter what kind of wire you use, you will not find anything that will produce a good

452

source of light in the open air for more than a few seconds. Your choice of wire is limited to a few substances with very high melting points. Using these at a temperature high enough to make the wire glow white-hot, oxygen of the air unites with the hot metal and completely oxidizes it, causing the wire to "burn out." But how about removing the oxygen?

EDISON'S LAMP

Edison got the filament away from oxygen by mounting his thin wire, or filament, in a glass bulb and pumping out as much air as he could. When the oxygen is removed, an electric current big enough to make a filament glow white-hot can be sent through it safely. This was the secret of Edison's electric light— a high-resistance filament sealed in a bulb from which nearly all air has been removed. Edison used a filament of charred bamboo in his first electric lamp.

TUNGSTEN-FILAMENT LAMPS

The modern filament lamp is a modification of the original. Instead of a charred bamboo filament, a specially coiled tungsten wire is used. Tungsten has a very high resistance, a very high melting point, and converts far more electricity into light than the earlier carbon filament. Air is still removed from inside most bulbs and is replaced by argon or nitrogen gas,

The structure of a filament lamp.

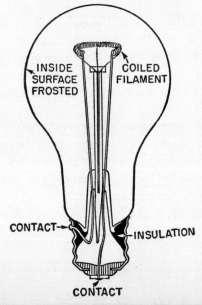

INSIDE SURFACE FROSTED

COILED FILAMENT

CONTACT

INSULATION

CONTACT

neither of which gases supports combustion.

Tungsten-filament bulbs gradually blacken because heat causes the tungsten molecules to "boil off" from the filament and deposit on the glass. Filling the bulb with an inactive gas causes some of the tungsten molecules to bounce back to the filament as they are shot off, and the bulb can be used longer without blackening. Examine a used bulb and notice the dark coating on the inside of the frosted glass.

Some electric-light bulbs are not gas-filled. As much air as possible is pumped out of them. Oxygen that remains behind is removed by means of compounds called *getters* that unite with the oxygen. Getters also convert much of the evaporated tungsten inside the bulb into a white compound. This prolongs the life of the bulb.

WORKING WITH SCIENCE

1. Your class can make an interesting exhibit on illumination, showing as many different kinds of lamps as you can borrow. A search through attics and cellars is worth making. Make models of early clay lamps for yourself.

2. Welsbach gas mantles can be obtained from mail-order houses. Demonstrate how they operate, using a bunsen-burner flame.

3. A replacement heating coil for an electric toaster or heater can usually be obtained from a hardware store at low cost. This is made of nichrome wire. Connect such a heating coil in a 110-volt circuit and notice the effect. **Caution:** *Hang the heating coil in air or lay on an asbestos board.*

4. Connect three dry-cells in series. Run the current from them through a fine copper wire. Notice the effect. If a rheostat is available, connect this in the circuit, and build the current up gradually.

5. If you work carefully, you can file a hole in the glass at the base of an electric-light bulb or you may be able to break the glass away without injuring the filament. Connect such a bulb in a circuit. Explain what happens.

LIGHT IN THE HOME

How can you tell what size bulb to use for a specific purpose? There is always the trial-and-error method of finding the bulb you think gives enough light. This method is generally unsatisfactory because few people have enough knowledge of illumination and of eyesight to know their own requirements. Accurate scientific studies of the light needed for home and industrial use have been made, and it is easy to check the light requirements in your own home.

CANDLEPOWER

In order to talk about light requirements, you need to know a few more facts about light. First, brightness, or *intensity*, of light is meas-

Enough light is as important in a modern kitchen as in a factory.

Courtesy Sylvania Electric Products, Inc.; The Austin Company

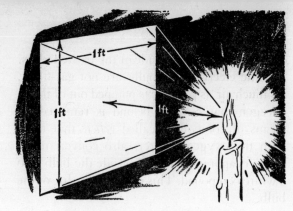

One foot-candle of illumination.

ured in terms of *candlepower*. That is, a lamp is compared in brightness to a standard-sized candle that burns at a definite rate. A 10-candlepower lamp has the intensity of 10 standard-sized candles. Some of the flares used for aerial photography have an intensity of 8-million candlepower.

FOOT-CANDLES

The amount of light from any source that reaches you depends on how far away you are from the light source. The farther away you are, the dimmer the light appears. The amount of light received on an area or surface, that is, *illumination*, is measured by a unit called a *foot-candle*. A piece of cardboard held 1 foot from a standard candle receives 1 foot-candle of illumination. The farther away you move the cardboard, the less light falls on it.

The amount of illumination *decreases* as the *square* of the distance from the source. That is, if you move the cardboard 2 feet from a standard candle, it will not receive ½ as much light as before but only ¼ as much. Three feet away, it will receive ⅑ as much. Four feet away, ¹⁄₁₆ as much. This means that if you move your chair twice as far away from your reading lamp, you get only ¼ as many foot-candles on the pages of your book.

RECOMMENDED ILLUMINATION

If this matter of illumination is clear, you can understand all anyone needs to know about correct lighting in the home. Careful studies show just how many foot-candles are needed. For simple rough work or other work that does not require seeing fine details, 10 foot-candles or less may be sufficient. Reading fine type, continual reading, or doing fine work requires about 20 foot-candles. Still closer work requires from 20 to 50 foot-candles.

School classrooms should have from 12 to 20 foot-candles on desks and blackboards. At home, less light is needed for general illumination, but concentrated spots of light should be available where they are necessary. Sometimes the use of three-way bulbs helps. These large bulbs contain three filaments, for example, 40, 60, and 100 watts, or 100, 200, and 300 watts. At the turn of the switch, you can make the lamp lighter or dimmer to suit your needs.

MEASURING ILLUMINATION

Knowing about foot-candles does not tell you whether you should use a 40-watt or a 100-watt bulb in a specific place. However, you can make actual measurements of foot-candles if you can borrow a *light-meter* from a friend who is a camera enthusiast. A light-meter often is marked in foot-candles and is similar to a scientific instrument known as the *foot-candle meter*. It is a photoelectric cell connected to an electric meter which gives readings directly in foot-candles.

When held facing the surface to be tested, a needle on the dial of the light-meter points to the number of foot-candles of light being received by the surface. With a light-meter you can quickly tell whether your desk lamp is giving you enough light to do your homework without eyestrain. If the papers on your desk are not receiving at least 10 foot-candles, you can either move your lamp a little closer or replace the bulb with one of larger size.

DIRECT LIGHTING

The glare or dazzle of an intense light is very tiring to the eyes. Thus, while *direct lighting*, using a bulb with or without a reflector, is the most efficient and least expensive kind of lighting, glare from the filament is often very great. Glare may be so great that this method is unsatisfactory unless the light is so placed that direct rays do not reach the eye.

Most bulbs for household use are frosted on the inside by chemical treatment. This frosting spreads, or *diffuses*, the light, so that the filament cannot be seen. Glare is partly reduced and illumination is made more uniform. Even so, direct lighting using frosted bulbs may be very harsh and irritating.

INDIRECT LIGHTING

Some lighting fixtures are so constructed that you cannot see the light bulb at all. Light is reflected upward against the ceiling or against a reflector that is part of the fixture. If the upper walls and ceiling are painted a light color, about half the light is reflected to lower parts of the room, giving a softer and more even light than direct lighting. Larger bulbs are used in *indirect lighting* because more light is diffused throughout the room than in direct lighting. Thus, indirect lighting is more expensive. However, the absence of glare makes it very satisfactory.

SEMI-INDIRECT LIGHTING

Semi-indirect lighting, which you probably use in your own home, is a compromise between direct and indirect lighting. Some of the light from the bulb shines directly through a diffusing glass globe that cuts down the glare. The remaining light is reflected up to and down from the ceiling and walls. This system combines features of both direct and indirect lighting. It requires larger bulbs than are used in direct lighting but not as large as those used in indirect.

It is difficult to say which lighting system is "best." Many factors enter the picture. On the whole, indirect lighting is preferred, with spots of glare-free direct light for specific uses. The semi-indirect system is a good compromise.

Surveys have shown that most American homes do not have enough light, and what they do have is not used effectively. Part of this difficulty results from cost. While electricity is not expensive, people still use it as if it were.

It is surprising that in this country today many families still cannot afford electricity and use kerosene lamps, even though their dwellings are wired. Thousands of rural families are still without electricity. Our government has made special efforts to bring electricity to farm communities.

WORKING WITH SCIENCE

1. Your class can collect an exhibit of different types of electric bulbs. It will not take much effort to find 25 different kinds. Some classes have brought in more than 100. Label each bulb to show

Direct, semi-indirect, and indirect lighting. What are the characteristics of each?

the current it uses and the purpose for which it is used.

2. Make a list of the number and size of the light bulbs in each room of your house. How many light bulbs do you have in your home? Get the total number for the class and the average.

3. With a foot-candle meter or light meter take readings at equal distances from a small light source. Do your readings bear out "the inverse-square law"?

4. Take readings around your school with a foot-candle meter or light meter. Report on the illumination in the gymnasium, shop, library, and classrooms. See how the illumination varies during the day. If your readings indicate there is not sufficient illumination, have your teachers check further.

5. Make a survey of lighting used in some of the neighborhood stores, shops, movies, factories, and so forth. How often is direct lighting used? Indirect? Semi-indirect?

OTHER KINDS OF LIGHTS

Light, as most of us use it in our homes today, comes from an electric-light bulb. The light is produced by a white-hot filament, and the light source must be shaded and the light diffused before we can use it comfortably. In spite of these difficulties, home illumination is far better today than it was in our grandparents' time.

PERFECT LIGHT

In spite of all the improvements in artificial lighting, there is no light like sunlight. Normal sunlight includes all the rays to which the eye is sensitive in a proportion and at an intensity that give very satisfactory illumination. Sunlight, excluding direct glare from the sun, is the perfect light. Scientific measurements are backed by the opinions of artists, color workers, photographers, and so forth. This gives us a standard to go by. We can measure the success of artificial lighting by its ability to duplicate sunlight.

MERCURY-VAPOR LAMPS

Vapor lamps and fluorescent lamps probably will eventually replace filament lamps in most home illumination. Some types of vapor lamps have been in use for years, while other types are relatively new.

The *mercury-vapor* lamp is one of the oldest of these lamps. You may have seen them at photographers' studios, in printing plants, or in factories. The bluish-green color of the light is very easy to recognize.

A mercury-vapor lamp is a narrow glass tube, sometimes as much as 4 feet long. This

Left: Fluorescent lamps provide soft illumination. Middle: This new sunlamp operates in any 110-volt a-c socket. Right: This lamp glows by electricity transmitted without wires.

Courtesy Sylvania Electric Products, Inc.; Courtesy Westinghouse Electric Corporation

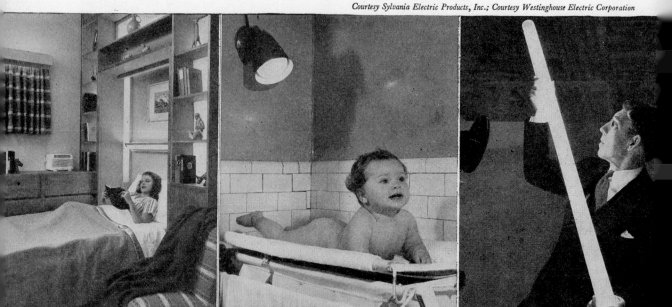

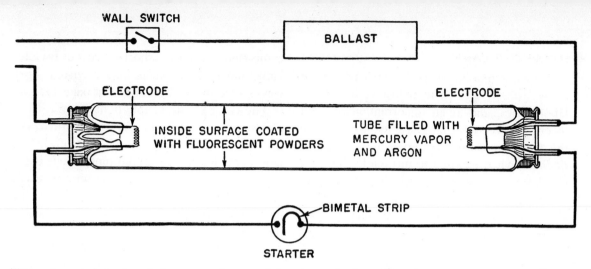

WALL SWITCH

BALLAST

ELECTRODE

ELECTRODE

INSIDE SURFACE COATED
WITH FLUORESCENT POWDERS

TUBE FILLED WITH
MERCURY VAPOR
AND ARGON

BIMETAL STRIP

STARTER

When the switch is closed, the starter closes and the electrodes heat. Then the starter opens, current flows from one electrode to the other through mercury vapor inside the tube, and the tube glows.

tube contains connections to the electric current (electrodes) and a small amount of mercury. All air has been removed from the tube. When the tube is tilted, the drop of mercury makes contact between two terminals, or electrodes, and is vaporized by the current passing through it. The mercury vapor fills the tube and serves as a path for the electric current. It glows with a characteristic bluish-green light.

The ultraviolet light produced by a mercury-vapor lamp cannot be seen, but it produces many physical and chemical effects. Ultraviolet wavelengths are roughly from 0.02 to 0.4 micron, just shorter than visible violet light. No one gets sunburned by the ultraviolet light produced in an ordinary mercury-vapor lamp. The short waves are all absorbed by the lamp's glass tube, and only the visible colored radiations escape.

Some mercury-vapor lamps are made with quartz tubing instead of glass. Ultraviolet light penetrates quartz easily. It passes through the lamp's tube, and ultraviolet rays can be detected easily under a quartz mercury-vapor lamp. Such a lamp is commonly known as a *sunlamp* because its light and sunlight both contain ultraviolet light.

Ultraviolet rays are used medically. Under their influence, the cells of the skin produce a substance similar to vitamin D. If a doctor thinks that a child is not getting enough of this vitamin or cannot absorb it from cod-liver or other oils, he may prescribe short sunlamp treatments. Such treatments are often given to children who have rickets and to miners who work underground. Long exposure to ultraviolet rays produces severe sunburn and may seriously injure the eyes, so a sunlamp must be used exactly according to directions.

Vitamin D *irradiated milk* is produced by flowing the milk through an area of intense ultraviolet radiations. Such milk is often used in the feeding of infants. Direct exposure to ultraviolet rays kills many kinds of germs and molds. Special kinds of ultraviolet lamps thus provide a very satisfactory way of sterilizing the air in a room. Food products are often sterilized before packaging by ultraviolet irradiation.

See if you can find out how an arc lamp works and where such lamps are used today.

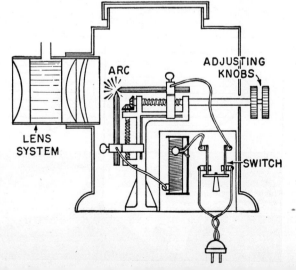

ARC

ADJUSTING
KNOBS

LENS
SYSTEM

SWITCH

457

FLUORESCENT LAMPS

A quartz mercury-vapor lamp has a great many uses. It is used in industry, in science laboratories, and as an important instrument in crime detection. This last use depends on the fact that certain materials will glow, or *fluoresce*, when exposed to ultraviolet light. A check written with fluorescent ink or on paper containing a fluorescent dye will immediately show erasure or any alteration under ultraviolet light. Forgeries, raised checks, changes in documents, passport frauds, and many other crimes have been solved by the use of ultraviolet light.

Ultraviolet light makes fluorescent lamps possible. Fluorescent lamps are relatively new. They are widely used in stores, offices, restaurants, factories, and homes. They produce a near equivalent to daylight at a cost considerably lower than filament lamps.

Every fluorescent lamp contains a small amount of mercury. When the current is turned on, the glowing mercury vapor produces ultraviolet and visible bluish-green light. But this is not the color that we see in a fluorescent tube. The inside of a fluorescent tube is coated with compounds that fluoresce, or glow, when struck by ultraviolet light. These compounds absorb short-wave ultraviolet light, and reradiate it as longer, visible light waves (see illustration at top of page 457).

The color of the visible light given off depends on the fluorescent materials with which the inside of the tube is coated. To produce a blue-white light, magnesium tungstate is used. For a pink light, cadmium borate is used. Coatings of mixed compounds are used to produce a light that is very much like daylight, the perfect light for our eyes.

Fluorescent lamps can be used for direct lighting, since they produce almost no glare. Because the light source is long instead of concentrated, as in a filament lamp, fluorescent lamps produce far less shadow. But one of the chief advantages of fluorescent lamps is their efficiency. Per watt of energy used, they produce from two to three times as much light as filament lamps. This means more light for your money.

Many modern homes now have built-in fluorescent fixtures. You can have a bar of light above the kitchen sink or alongside the mirrors in the dressing room. Fluorescent desk lamps give a soft even light that makes reading easier. Schools, shops, homes, stores, and factories also use fluorescent lighting.

WORKING WITH SCIENCE

1. Demonstrate a simple arc light, using two carbon electrodes and a resistor. Do not look at the arc without shielding your eyes.

2. If mercury-vapor lamps are used in a factory near your school, get permission to see them and find out how they work and why they are used.

3. Find out about the medical value of ultraviolet lamps for growing children and for adults. Should these lamps be used in the home?

4. If a quartz mercury-vapor lamp, or sunlamp, is available, demonstrate fluorescence of minerals, inks, salts, teeth, and so forth. **Caution:** *Use the*

Different kinds of curved mirrors have different uses.

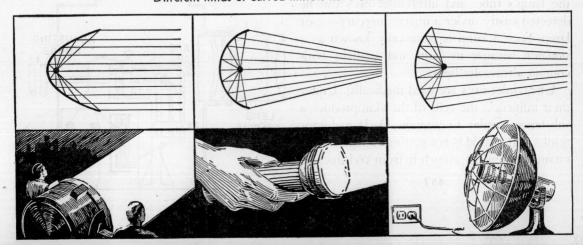

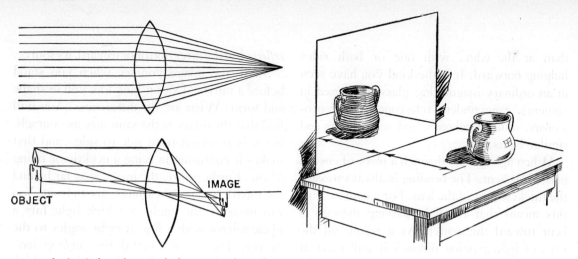

Left: A lens focuses light rays and produces images. Right: Reflection in a plane mirror.

ultraviolet lamps with care to prevent sunburn or eye injury.

5. Use a battery and a Ford spark coil to demonstrate fluorescent lighting with fluorescent lamps.

6. Survey the use of fluorescent lamps in your community. If storekeepers have installed them to replace filament lights, find out why and whether the fluorescent lamps have been as good as expected.

LIGHTS THAT FOCUS

Suppose you want a stronger light on a picture or over the armchair where you like to read. You can put a floor or table lamp nearby to give this illumination. If you feel that the lamp will spoil the appearance of the room, you can use a spotlight, which will gather most of the light from a filament lamp and send it in a strong beam just where you want it. Such a spotlight can be built into the wall or the ceiling and can be adjusted to send its beam in any direction.

MIRRORS

The spotlight itself consists of a filament lamp behind which is placed a polished curved mirror. Light from a filament normally spreads in all directions, but the part that hits the curved mirror is reflected, and all the light rays are sent in the same direction. Every automobile headlight has such a curved mirror to throw the light ahead of the car. Searchlights, flashlights, spotlights, and floodlights use the same principle.

The curve of the mirror is important in determining the way that light will be reflected from it. If the mirror has a spherical curve—

that is, if it is part of a sphere—light rays striking it will be reflected back to a point known as the focus. Here the rays meet and cross. If the curve of the mirror is shallow, the focus is some distance from the mirror. If the curve is deep, the focus is close to the mirror.

For most purposes a mirror with a long focus, and hence a very shallow curve, is best. If a beam of parallel light rays is desired, a *parabolic* mirror is used, and the source of light is placed at the focus of the mirror. Light is reflected in parallel rays from a parabolic surface. Parallel light rays are concentrated by a parabolic mirror at its focus. Such mirrors are used in automobile headlights and as the mirrors of giant telescopes.

A curved mirror behind a filament lamp bends a beam of light in one direction. But the beam can be made even more intense by putting a lens in front of the bulb as well as a mirror behind it.

LENSES

There are many kinds of lenses. The kind used in a spotlight is known as a *convex* lens. This is the kind that is thicker at the center than at the edge, with one or both sides bulging outward. It is the kind you have seen in an ordinary magnifying glass. It is used in cameras, rangefinders, telescopes, movie projectors, some eyeglasses, and searchlights and similar lights.

When light passes through a piece of curved glass, it is bent. The bending is always toward the thickest part of the lens. For a convex lens, this means that the light passing through is bent toward the center. As a result, all the rays of light passing through it will meet at some point beyond the lens. This point is the focus.

The distance of the focus from the lens depends on the curve of the glass. The greater the curve, the shorter the focus. Lenses used in spotlights usually have a fairly long *focal length*, that is the light passing through the lens forms a long narrow beam before it reaches the focus. At a short distance on each side of the focus, the light is still concentrated in an intense beam; farther on, it spreads out again.

The intensity of the spot of light at the focus depends on the amount of light produced by the filament and the ability of the lens to concentrate the light. A spotlight, consisting of a lamp, a curved mirror, and lens, can be used to supplement the general illumination obtained from vapor lamps, and combinations of both types of illumination are finding places in homes.

MIRRORS AND LENSES IN THE HOME

Look around your own house and you are sure to find some mirrors and lenses. There is a lens in the camera, possibly someone wears eyeglasses, and you may also have a magnifying glass or pair of binoculars. Curved mirrors include those in flashlights and automobile headlights, and some men use a mirror with a shallow curve for shaving. Why?

Every house has ordinary mirrors, or *plane mirrors*. You will find several, perhaps a dozen, in your own home. A plane mirror is a flat piece of glass, silvered on the back so that nearly all light that strikes it is sent back, or *reflected*, in the direction of, or toward, its source.

Study the image you see when you stand before a mirror. Does it look like you in shape and form? What are the differences? You will find that the image is the same size as yourself, but it is reversed from side to side—and that makes it confusing in tying a necktie or fixing a bow. Furthermore, the image is as far behind the mirror as you, the object, are in front. You can measure the angle at which light hits a plane mirror with a line at right angles to the mirror. This angle—called the *angle of incidence*—is always equal to the angle at which the light leaves the mirror. This angle is called the *angle of reflection*.

Plane mirrors are widely used because in them we can see ourselves very much as others see us. They also have a use in illumination. Since light striking a plane mirror is reflected, mirrors properly placed, will lighten a dark corner of a room. They will also make a small room seem as if it were much larger.

LIGHTS FOR TOMORROW

Much more can be done to improve our lighting. Hints of things that may come are truly amazing. For example, scientists have already demonstrated a light that glows without being connected to wires. This light operates by electricity that may be transmitted through the air. It may be possible someday to have a source of such electricity in one part of your house that will operate lights wherever you wish.

Even more intriguing is the idea of "cold light." You will recall that about 94 percent of the electricity used in a filament lamp produces heat. In a fluorescent lamp, much less heat is produced. But none of these lamps is as efficient as the common firefly, or lightning bug, which converts 96 percent of its chemical energy into light. Chemists have long attempted to solve the secret of the firefly's highly efficient light. They have made some progress, but as yet there is no way to put their findings to practical use. Perhaps someday an entirely new method of chemical lighting will be available. It may not involve electricity at all and may be much cheaper than lighting is today.

Another possibility is the production of light from a central source much as we produce heat today. The light can be "piped" wherever it is needed by means of rods of certain plastics, such as "Lucite" or "Plexiglas."

At the beginning of this unit, we asked the question, "Does a house need windows?" Right now windows are needed, but if you look ahead to the time when houses are com-pletely air-conditioned and when we can produce the exact equivalent of sunlight at very low cost, what need will we have for windows then? If we want to see what is happening outside, we can always turn on the television receiver. The fact that many modern homes are built with great expanses of insulated windows illustrates, however, that windows have an important value to most of us. We simply enjoy the view and the feeling of spaciousness. Television can hardly give us a similar feeling, nor should we expect it to.

WORKING WITH SCIENCE

1. Hold a curved mirror behind a small light source, and study the effects of the mirror on the light. Find the focus by moving a piece of cardboard back and forth in front of it.

2. Find the focal length of a simple convex lens by holding it toward a window or other light source. Move a sheet of paper back and forth behind the lens. The point at which the image is most distinct is the focus. The distance from there to the lens is the focal length.

3. Demonstrate the projection system of the school movie projector. Show the class the curved mirror behind the projector bulb and the system of lenses in front of it.

4. Make a simple spotlight from a tin can and a cheap convex lens. Such a light is useful for photo-graphic work and may also be useful in the production of school plays.

5. Draw a line across a piece of paper. Set a small plane mirror upright on this line. Stick a pin in the paper a few inches in front of the mirror. Lay a ruler on the paper, sight along the edge with your eye level with the paper toward the image of the pin in the mirror. Draw a line along the ruler to the mirror's edge. Do the same from one or two other points. These lines will converge toward the mirror. Lift the mirror off the paper and, with a ruler, extend the lines beyond the one where the mirror stood. Measure the distance from the point where these sighting lines crossed to the mirror line and from the pin to the mirror line. What do the measurements indicate about the position of the pin's image in the mirror?

READING YOU WILL ENJOY

Luckiesh, Matthew. *Torch of Civilization*. G. P. Putnam's Sons, New York, 1940. The dramatic story of man's conquest of darkness, written by a man who has done a great deal of research in light.

Neblette, Carroll B., Brehm, Frederick W., and Priest, Everett L. *Elementary Photography for Club and Home Use* (rev. ed.). The Macmillan Co., New York, 1944. A valuable book if you are in-terested in photography as a hobby. It gives practical and clear instructions on many kinds of photographic work.

Teale, Edwin, W. *Boys' Book of Photography*. E. P. Dutton & Co., Inc., New York, 1939. An excellent book for the beginner in photography. Information is given on how to make a pin-hole camera and how to set up and use a darkroom.

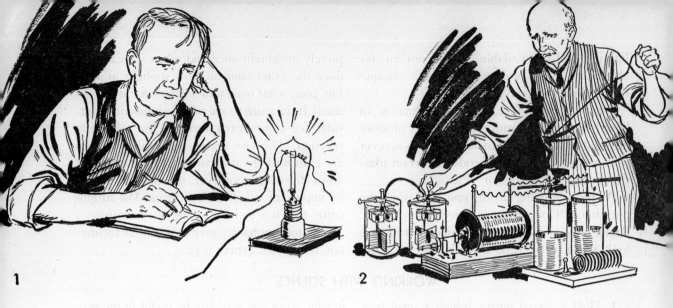

Perhaps the beginning of electronics was a peculiar effect that Thomas A. Edison (1) noticed during his experiments with electric lights in 1883. After noting this effect in his record book, Edison did not explore it further. The beginnings of radio stimulated research that finally led to the making of the first electronic radio tube—the Fleming valve, or diode. In 1904, Professor John Ambrose Fleming (2) discovered that the rapidly alternating current sent out by radio transmitting stations could be changed into a weak direct current by passing from the filament to the plate of a vacuum tube. This change was an improvement over the early crystal receiving sets.

In 1906, Dr. Lee De Forest (3) improved the Fleming valve by adding a third element to the tube. This element—the grid—made it possible for the weak radio current placed on the grid to control a much stronger current moving from filament to plate through the three-element tube, or triode. The new tube strengthened, or amplified, the current greatly, and De Forest's invention, more than any other, made modern radio possible. Modern transmitting (4) and receiving tubes can all be traced back to De Forest's triode.

Electronics has brought new wonders to industry and the home. We can now enjoy radio, television, record players, and sound recorders. Electronic devices eliminate dust, open doors, and charge the battery of the family car. The future will bring rapid electronic cooking and heating, plus improved means of communication that will put a person, no matter where he is traveling on land, sea, or in the air, in quick contact with his home.

35

ELECTRONICS IN THE HOME

Most of you are now familiar with the term *electronics*. Broadly speaking, it is the science of the use of electrons. Ten years ago not many persons had ever heard of electronics. The science existed, of course. But most persons even today believe the term to be merely another name for radio.

Electronic devices or their products are in every home today, in ways that few people recognize. They help make the food we eat, the clothes we wear, and the automobiles we drive. They are involved in the operation of railroads, telephones, airplanes, television, aluminum refining, and in literally hundreds of industries that contribute directly and indirectly to making your home more livable and your standard of living higher. The science of electronics includes many of the greatest discoveries and inventions of the first half of the twentieth century.

WHAT IS ELECTRONICS?

MINIATURE SOLAR SYSTEMS

As you know, all matter is made up of elements, that in turn, are made up of atoms. Each atom is composed of smaller particles. At or near the center of the atom is the *nucleus*, the "heavy" part of the atom. Around the nucleus, still smaller particles move in orbits somewhat like the planets around the sun. These sub-microscopic planets are electrons. Each electron is exceedingly small, exceedingly light, and each bears a negative electric charge. Some thirty thousand trillion electrons weigh an ounce.

Some electrons are bound strongly in the atoms. Others are bound less strongly and can easily be released. Certain electrons in atoms of metals belong to this second group. Some (not all) can be loosened from the atom of which they are normally a part.

It may be a bit confusing to think of an electron as both matter and electricity at the same time, but it is. All matter is made up of tiny, subatomic particles. Some of the particles have a positive, or plus, charge and are called protons. Some have a negative, or minus, charge, and are called electrons. Some are electrically neutral and are called neutrons.

In a normal atom, the plus and minus charges balance one another and the entire atom is neutral. However, if electrons are knocked out of an atom, the atom loses negative charges, and more positive than negative charges remain. Such an atom is *positively charged*. If the electrons lost are regained, the atom again becomes neutral. A substance with more electrons than protons is *negatively charged*. If a wire connects two objects, one charged negatively and one charged positively, the excess electrons from the object with the negative charge will flow through the wire to the object that is positively charged. This flow of electrons is, of course, an electric current.

There are several ways to drive electrons out of metals. Most common are ways involving light, electricity, and heat. Heat a

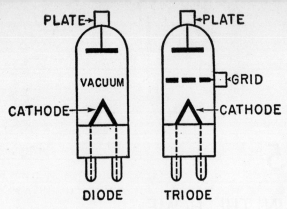

Modern versions of the Fleming valve, or diode, and the DeForest "Audion," or triode.

piece of metal red-hot and electrons leap from it. Every time you turn on a filament lamp, electrons flow out of the white-hot tungsten wire. Soon the space in the bulb becomes crowded with electrons. Since these negative charges repel one another, as many are bounced back into the filament as come out of it.

Light will drive electrons from only a few metals. Such metals are used in converting light into electricity, as in a photoelectric cell.

THE EDISON EFFECT

While experimenting with the electric light, Edison made a discovery that paved the way for the science of electronics. Edison noticed an unusual glow near the carbon filament of one of his early lamps. Experimenting to find out the cause of this glow, he inserted a metal plate near the filament inside

When the cathode of a diode is heated, electrons flow from the cathode to the plate.

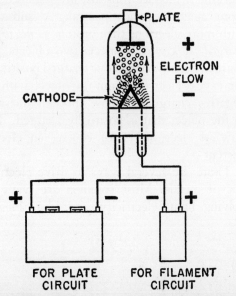

the bulb, connected a wire to it, and sealed it in place. When the negative pole of a battery was connected to one end of the filament and the positive pole to the other end, the lamp lit, but the metal plate was not affected. Edison connected this metal plate to the positive pole of another battery. He connected the negative pole of this battery to the negative side of the filament. He also connected an instrument that detects an electric current, a *galvanometer*, in the circuit between the plate and the battery.

Then Edison again turned on the filament current. As soon as the filament began to glow, the galvanometer indicated that a current was flowing in the circuit from filament to plate. This puzzled Edison since there was no connection between the filament and the metal plate. It puzzled him so much that he wrote a description of what had happened. The occurrence was later termed the *Edison effect*. However, since this effect did not seem to be related to the problem of perfecting the electric light, Edison did not continue his experiments. From 1883 to 1903 the Edison effect was merely a scientific curiosity.

During that 20-year period, other things were happening. When the Edison effect came to the attention of an English physicist, Ambrose Fleming, he saw possibilities in this curious action. The next year, Fleming produced the *tube*, or *valve*, that bears his name. This simple Fleming valve became the first practical radio tube. Within 2 years, an American, Dr. Lee DeForest made a very significant improvement on the Fleming valve. DeForest's tube made possible the rapid development of modern radio.

WORKING WITH SCIENCE

1. Small as it is, the electron is of tremendous importance. Find a book on modern physics and read the story of the discovery. Prepare a report for class.

2. Electrons have been weighed and their electrical charge has been measured. Find out how these two measurements were made and report to the class. Both are complicated tasks and you will need a good understanding of science to grasp the details.

3. The production of positive and negative charges can be demonstrated by rubbing a rod of hard rubber with fur and a rod of glass with silk. Charged rods can be used to attract pieces of paper or their charge can be transferred to other non-conductors.

4. Tear two strips of newspaper about 1 inch wide and 18 inches long. Hold the ends in one hand. Rub the strips briskly between your two fingers. Explain what happens in terms of electrical charges.

5. A radio enthusiast can set up a demonstration of the Edison effect, using a simple triode tube and an A and B battery. Demonstrate this effect to the class.

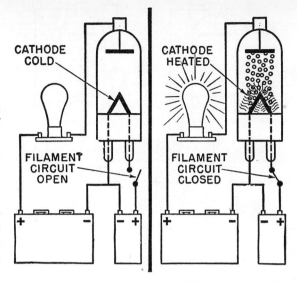

A diode operating as a switch. When the cathode circuit is closed, the cathode is heated and current flows in the plate circuit.

DIODES AND PHOTOELECTRIC CELLS

Let us consider in detail the kinds of tubes that are most like the Fleming valve. These tubes have two essential parts, or *elements*, and are known as *diodes*. The two elements are the filament, or cathode, and the metallic *plate*. Other electron tubes have three, four, five, or more elements.

A diode is simply a modern version of the tube made by Edison and improved by Fleming. The metal plate is no longer perched awkwardly on one side of the tube. Usually it consists of a cylinder that fits closely around the filament. The filament is very different from the filament of Edison's lamp, since the filament of an electron tube is not made to produce light.

HOW A DIODE WORKS

Let us connect up a diode and see how it operates. We will use direct current, since that makes it easier to trace the tube's operation. Direct current moves only in one direction. Experiments show that the electrons flow from the minus pole of a battery to the plus pole, from the place where there is an excess of electrons to the place where there is a lack of them.

Connect the plus pole of the battery to a small lamp and connect a wire from the lamp to the plate of the diode. Connect the negative side of the battery to the filament of the diode. Look at the illustration above. As you see, the circuit is incomplete. The filament of the diode does not touch the plate, and the current cannot flow over this gap. You can be sure of this because the lamp does not light.

Now connect another battery so that its negative pole is connected to the same end of the filament as the negative pole of the first battery. Connect the positive pole of the second battery to the other end of the filament. The filament begins to glow. As soon as the filament warms up, the lamp begins to light. When the filament current is turned off, off goes the lamp, just as if we had put a switch in the place of the diode tube.

As you know, electrons can be driven out of metals by heating them. As soon as the filament is hot, electrons pour from it. The electrons repel one another because of their negative charges. These negative charges are opposite to the charge on the plate, which is connected to the positive pole of one battery.

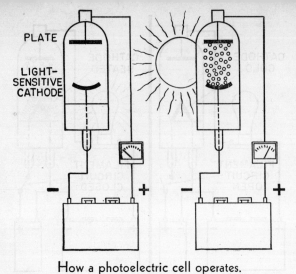

PLATE

LIGHT-
SENSITIVE
CATHODE

How a photoelectric cell operates.

Since there are less electrons on the plate, the electrons from the filament flow in a steady stream to the positively charged plate. This flow of electrons is an electric current, completing the circuit and hence lighting the lamp. As soon as the filament is turned off, the electron flow from filament to plate ceases, and there is a gap that breaks the lamp circuit. The filament current of a diode carries the heavier plate current and controls it like a switch. Cut off the filament current and the plate current instantly ceases.

THE PHOTOELECTRIC CELL

Let us look at a diode that is a bit different in construction to see what an amazing switch a diode can be. In this diode, the negative element, or cathode, is made of selenium, caesium, or a similar metal. Such a cathode gives off electrons when light shines on it.

When a beam of light hits a selenium cathode, electrons are released. If there is a positively charged element, or anode, to attract them, a stream of electrons will flow from cathode to anode. This electron stream can be used to operate an electromagnetic relay that acts as a switch in a circuit with stronger current. When no light falls on the cathode, no electrons are released and no current flows. This diode, known as a photoelectric cell, acts as a switch controlled by light.

USES OF PHOTOELECTRIC CELLS

No doubt you have seen persons in restaurants, offices, and railroad stations step into a beam of light whereupon a door opens. The beam of light is focused on a photoelectric cell. As soon as the light is cut off, current in the tube stops, a relay held open by current from the tube closes, and a motor or solenoid swings the door open. A man dips his head toward a drinking fountain. As his head cuts the light beam, the water is turned on. As he lifts his head when finished, the photoelectric cell turns off the water.

Until recently the operation of punch presses, multiple drills, metal shears, and

A diode can be used to change alternating current to a pulsating direct current. Using these drawings, see if you can figure out how this change is accomplished.

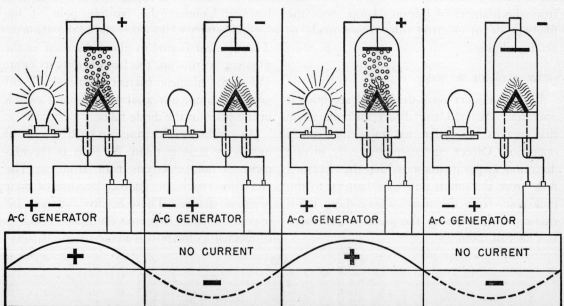

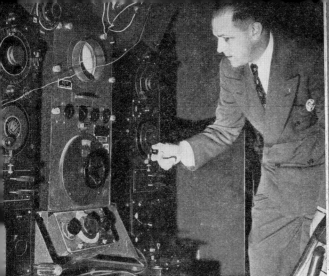
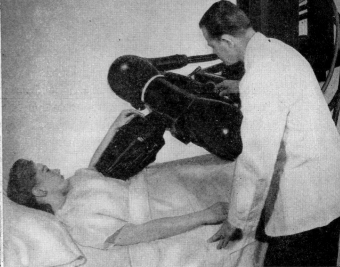

Press Association, Inc.; American Cancer Society photo

Left: Adjusting a search-type radar set. With this set, Army scientists sent radar waves to the moon and back. Right: Using x-rays in treating cancer.

similar machines was regarded as hazardous work. The employee who was the least bit careless took the risk of losing a finger or hand. Now such machines are hemmed in by a beam of light focused on a photoelectric cell. If the operator's hand is in a dangerous position, it cuts the beam of light, and the machine will not operate. Only after the hand is withdrawn to safety will the machine operate normally.

X-RAYS

When a stream of electrons flows from the cathode of an electron tube to the plate, the electrons bombard the plate like so many bullets. Certain experimental tubes, called *cathode-ray tubes*, show this by using the electron stream to spin a small, bladed wheel inside the tube. When the speed of the electrons is increased, as at high voltages, they hit the plate with such speed that their effects are very marked.

In 1895 William Roentgen [rûnt'gĕn] noticed that fluorescent material glowed when placed near an experimental electron tube, even though the stream of electrons was entirely inside the tube. Roentgen covered the tube completely with black paper so that no light could be seen, and still the fluorescent material glowed when brought near the tube. "This glow must be produced by some

mysterious ray," thought Roentgen and so he named the mysterious and unknown rays x-rays.

PRODUCING X-RAYS

X-rays are produced when high-speed electrons hit the plate of a diode. The higher the speed of the electrons, the more penetrating are the x-rays produced. Dr. William C. Coolidge perfected the x-ray tube in use today. It is a very specialized diode from which practically all the air is removed. Electrons are set free from a small, heated cathode and are speeded on their way to the plate by the push of several thousand to a million or more volts. The plate itself is a heavy piece of tungsten set so that the x-rays produced come out one side of the tube. X-rays are very penetrating and pass through many substances through which light will not pass. Among these substances are flesh, many metals, wood, paper, and others.

How x-rays are produced.

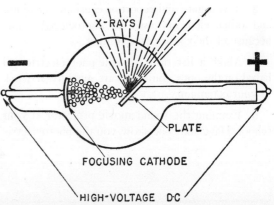

USE OF X-RAYS

As soon as x-rays are mentioned, people think of doctors. And they are right in doing so. X-rays are very useful in medicine and dentistry. X-rays remove all guesswork from the treatment of fractures and many internal injuries. Conditions that had long been mysterious to the physician and that he could not identify until the symptoms became serious, can now be detected early and examined thoroughly by means of x-rays.

A doctor may examine a patient directly by placing the patient between a source of x-rays and a fluorescent screen. Such an instrument is called a *fluoroscope*. The x-rays pass readily through the flesh and cause the fluorescent screen to glow. Bones and more solid parts of the body are not penetrated as easily by the x-rays and produce shadows on a screen. Since the silver compounds of a film are as sensitive to x-rays as they are to light, x-ray photographs may be taken easily.

X-rays do more than help the doctor to diagnose illness by exposing conditions which he could not otherwise notice. They are also used in the treatment of disease. Fungi and molds that cause a number of skin diseases are quickly killed by short applications of x-rays. Certain other infections and inflammations are benefited also. But of far greater importance is the use of x-rays in the treatment of certain kinds of cancer. These rays are more injurious to cancer cells than they are to normal tissue, so, if carefully used, they can sometimes destroy the cancer without seriously affecting the surrounding normal cells.

X-RAYS IN INDUSTRY

Metals, as well as people, can be diseased. A turbine casting may have a hidden flaw that cannot be detected by ordinary inspection. A propeller shaft, a high-pressure steam pipe, a welded seam, or some vital machine part may break down at a critical time as a result of some inner weakness. By the use of x-rays in industrial inspection, flaws are discovered before they can cause trouble.

DIODES DO ALL THIS

These devices, the electronic switch, photoelectric cell, x-ray tube, and the others, exist in many varieties. All of them are diode tubes or modifications of diodes. Expensive and complicated auxiliary equipment often is needed to make these devices work. But the same principle operates in all cases.

WORKING WITH SCIENCE

1. Connect a diode so that it will control a 110-volt 40-watt lamp. Vary the filament current by using a rheostat. What effect does varying the filament current have on the brightness of the lamp?

2. Connect up a demonstration photoelectric cell so that it will control a lamp. Show how the cell, acting through a relay, can function as a light switch.

3. Investigate and report on caesium, selenium, and other elements used in photoelectric cells because of their sensitivity to light.

4. Make a list of uses of the photoelectric cell based on the ones you know are actually at work in your community.

5. Examine the sound movie projector in your school. Have someone show you the photoelectric cell and demonstrate it in action with a sound film.

6. Prepare a report on the use of photoelectric controls in some specific industry, such as steel manufacture, coal mining, printing, textile weaving, or whatever industries occur in your community.

7. Make your own photoelectric invention. Describe or draw the plan for some use you think could be made of a photoelectric control in home, school, or industry.

8. If a mercury-vapor battery charger can be obtained, examine it and then study the charger in operation. Measure the current input and output. How efficient is the charger?

9. Investigate how electricity is used in our basic metal industries—aluminum, steel, magnesium, and copper. Which involve direct current?

TRIODES

In 1906 Dr. Lee DeForest added something new to the diode. He added a thin screen, or *grid*, of metal between the cathode and plate. Such a tube has three elements and is called a *triode*. Like cathode and plate, the grid has a connection leading outside the tube so that an electric charge can be placed on it. Neither grid, cathode, nor plate touch each other, but they are all bound together into a remarkable team.

HOW A TRIODE WORKS

When a diode is connected in a circuit, the cathode sends a stream of electrons to the positively charged plate. When a grid is inserted between the cathode and plate, it can act as a controlling switch, or valve.

The grid, when uncharged, does not affect the flow of electrons from cathode to plate. However, when an electric charge is placed on the grid, the grid affects the electron stream. Consider a grid with a negative charge. As the electrons approach the grid, they are *repelled* because both they and the grid are charged negatively. The electrons cannot pass the negatively charged grid to reach the plate. The thin metal screen has become as impenetrable as a stone wall. No current can pass to the plate as long as the grid, with its negative charge, bars the way.

Change the charge on the grid to positive, and the grid attracts electrons, making it even easier for the electrons to reach the plate. A positive charge on the grid thus increases the current to the plate.

The charge on the grid—positive or negative—does not have to be large to control the current from cathode to plate. On the contrary, it may be very small, yet it can completely control the cathode-to-plate circuit. Even the slightest change in the grid's charge produces a change in the cathode-to-plate current, even though this current is usually thousands of times that in the grid circuit. If the charge on the grid changes the least bit

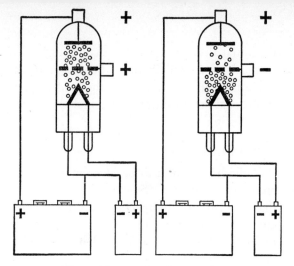

The grid controls electron flow.

either positively or negatively, there is a corresponding, but far greater, change in the plate current. The changes in the charge on the grid are reproduced exactly but on a much larger scale, in the plate current.

GRIDS AND RADIO

The use of the grid as a control over the plate current makes the triode capable of tasks that a diode cannot perform. Since the plate current reproduces on a larger scale any changes in the grid current, the triode is used chiefly in *amplification*, or "making larger." This function makes the triode tube the key to radio reception.

Radio waves set up an alternating current of varying strength in an antenna. From the antenna, this alternating current passes through coils and condenser to a detector tube. This detector tube often is a diode that changes the alternating current to direct current. This direct current then passes to the grid circuit of the first triode. This exceedingly weak direct current of varying strength continually changes the amount of negative charge on the grid, and this in turn is reproduced on a larger scale in the plate current.

The plate current, which is many times stronger than the incoming grid current, passes to the grid of the next radio tube, and again it affects the still larger plate current in this tube. This may take place several times, depending on your set. The strength of the initial alternating current may be amplified as much as 25 billion times before you hear voice and music coming from the loudspeaker. Additional details on radio are included in the next chapter.

RADIO IN USE

Radio has many uses besides entertainment and communication. Suppose, for example, that a plane is approaching an unattended emergency airfield. The pilot sends out a radio signal and instantly the landing area is ablaze with light. An amplified radio signal from the plane operated the lighting switch. When the pilot has landed safely, the lights go off again.

Airline pilots depend on radio as they fly the big transports along the airways. They fly on invisible paths called *radio beams*, or "ranges." They can determine their position by means of a *radio-compass*, an instrument that shows very accurately the direction of the source of incoming radio signals. If a pilot must land in fog, a radio *runway localizer* and *glide path* will set him down safely on the runway that he cannot see.

These uses of radio do not receive much attention. We seldom listen to police radio reports, but radio is essential in crime prevention and detection. Radio-equipped police cars are a common sight. Most of us never use the accurate time signals that are broadcast from the Naval Observatory in Washington, but these are quite necessary to the accurate navigation of ships at sea and are used on land by many industries and transportation companies.

RADAR

Many new uses of radio were developed during World War II. Outstanding are the locating devices using very-short-wave radio beams. The term *radar* is applied to such instruments. A radar sending set transmits very short radio waves that behave somewhat like a beam from a searchlight, except that they penetrate fog, clouds, and darkness with equal ease.

When a radar beam strikes an obstacle, it is reflected, and the reflected radio waves are picked up by the radar receiver, which is located near the transmitter. Since radio waves travel with a speed of 186,000 miles per second—that is, with the speed of light—the distance to the reflecting object can be determined. It is equal to the time required for the beam to travel to the object and back to the receiver multiplied by 186,000 and divided by 2. These computations are made automatically by the radar set and the distance to the

In landing in "ceiling zero" weather, pilots may be "talked down" by means of GCA or may land "on instruments" by means of ILS.

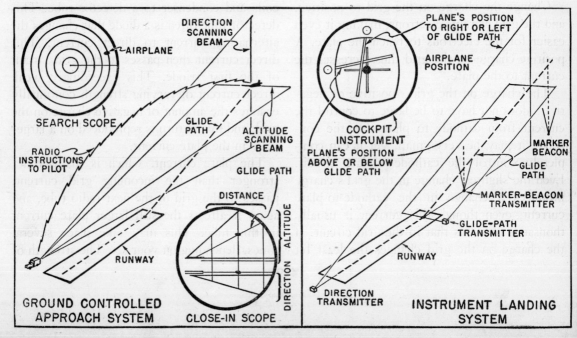

GROUND CONTROLLED APPROACH SYSTEM

INSTRUMENT LANDING SYSTEM

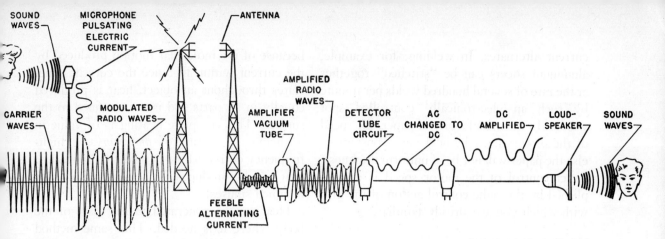

Radio transmission and reception, from the sound transmitted to the sound heard by the listener. Both transmission and reception depend on electron tubes.

reflecting object is read by the observer on dials on the instrument.

In 0.001 second a radio wave travels 186 miles. If that amount of time elapses between the outgoing signal and the returned reflection, the reflecting surface must be half of 186, or 93 miles away.

Radar works with such precision that the beam can follow a moving plane. It informs the radar operator which way the plane is going and how fast. Planes and ships 50 to 100 miles away can be detected and their movements followed by radar. From a plane, a radar beam can locate tall buildings or mountains, measure the height of the plane above the ground, and locate other planes in the air.

Peacetime uses of radar are as striking as military uses. Collisions between ships and other ships, ships and icebergs, or ships and rocks will not occur when all ships are equipped with radar. And both ships and aircraft will be able to reach their destinations safely regardless of fog or other conditions of low visibility.

TRIODES IN INDUSTRIAL CONTROL

Amplification has many industrial uses also. Devices have been perfected that amplify vibrations produced by machine parts. A crankshaft that is not exactly balanced produces vibrations that will rapidly cause it to wear out. The same is true of motor armatures and airplane propellers. By using ampli-

fiers, such defects can be detected and remedied before the part is installed. Amplifiers are also used with the photoelectric cell in circuits that accomplish all kinds of inspection, counting, and checking of materials.

The grid controls the plate circuit so completely in a triode that many forms of industrial control are based on this simple fact. Anything that can be converted into an electric current and can be used to change the charge on the grid, can automatically control machinery or processes. For example, high temperatures can be measured by a sensitive instrument known as a *pyrometer* which produces a weak electric current that is measured on a galvanometer marked in degrees.

If an electric furnace must be held at exactly 2300°F, a pyrometer can be connected to the grid of an amplifier tube in such a way that current operating the electric furnace is controlled. If the temperature rises higher than 2300°F, the slight increase in the charge on the grid (making it more negative) will cut down the current entering the furnace. If the temperature drops a bit, the grid becomes more positive and the current is increased.

Speed, time, temperature, pressure, weight, to mention only a few things, can all produce changes that will turn on, turn off, or modify the working current in some way. If an alternating current is put on the grid, the working current is turned on and off as fast as the grid

471

current alternates. In welding, for example, aluminum sheets can be "stitched" together at the rate of several hundred welds per minute by such an electronically controlled spot welder. In the manufacture of paper, the speed of the motors must be held very constant or else the paper will not be of uniform thickness. Exact control of the motor speed is accomplished by the same control action of the grid with which you are already familiar.

ELECTRONIC HEATING

A triode can generate high-frequency alternating currents, just as the diode can produce direct currents. This is done by sending part of the plate current of a triode back into its *own* grid. When a certain voltage is reached, the tube *oscillates*, or produces alternating current. Alternating current for household use is produced at 60 cycles per second. With the proper triode tubes, alternating currents of millions of cycles per second can be produced.

These high-frequency currents are widely used—for example, in radio broadcasting and for their heating effects. An object within one of these high-frequency fields is heated because of the molecular motion produced by the current within it. Since the current penetrates throughout an object, heat is produced equally in all parts and is not confined to the surface. This complete heating is of value in medicine. By means of *diathermy*, as high-frequency currents used in medicine are called, heat can be produced inside sore muscles or inflamed sinuses.

Heat can be generated in any part of the body where it is needed. This same method may be used to produce *artificial fever*, which is of value in treating certain kinds of diseases. High-frequency currents are used in a new machine that cooks steaks, roasts, cakes, cookies, and all kinds of foods in just a few seconds instead of minutes and hours.

By controlling the frequency, heat of almost any degree can be produced—mild enough to warm an injured knee or hot enough to melt steel and platinum. The heat can be applied so that it penetrates the entire object or so that it will affect only the surface and not the interior. Thus, steel can be hardened by heat treatment at the surface to reduce wear, while the interior of the axle or gear still remains soft and tough.

WORKING WITH SCIENCE

1. If there is a public-address system in your school or a motion-picture projector, see if the person in charge of it can show you how it operates. Someone who knows radio can point out the

Left: Electronic heating equipment used in heat-treating a gear. Middle: An iconoscope, heart of the television camera. Right: Modern high-power transmitting tubes.

Photos courtesy General Electric Company; National Broadcasting Company; Westinghouse Electric Corporation

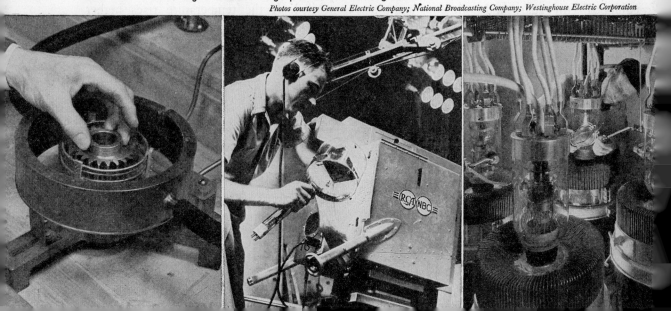

amplifying tubes and can tell you how they work.

2. If your town has an airport, you may be able to see a radio beacon in operation, or someone may be able to explain to you the radio guide used in blind flying.

3. The perfection of radar was a thrilling wartime activity. Read the story of this invention which was "top secret" for several years. Report its wartime uses and how it can be used in peace.

Why are its peacetime uses slow in coming?

4. Ask your doctor about diathermy and how it is used. For what diseases or conditions is it most beneficial. Find out the difference between diathermy and "a heat lamp."

5. Plywood is becoming more and more important in building homes, making furniture and boats, and for use in industry. Find out how electronic heating or bonding is used in making plywood.

TELEVISION AND ELECTRONIC BEAMS

The oscillating current produced by a triode may be controlled to produce the waves used in radio broadcasting. Every radio transmitter is built around these oscillating tubes, some of which are so powerful that they must be continually cooled by circulating water to keep them from overheating. These powerful tubes, rated at up to 50,000 watts, send such a current to the transmitting antenna that the signals can be detected thousands of miles away.

TELEVISION

Home *television* is a well known application of electronics. We want to see as well as hear events occurring at a distance. Many types of television transmitters, tubes, and receivers have been developed. Research is still continuing. Such terms as *iconoscope, orthicon, image dissector*, and *kinescope* refer to the different kinds of tubes used. The discussion that follows refers chiefly to just one type of transmitting tube and just one type of receiving tube.

What does television involve anyway? More than a little oversimplified, television transmission involves changing light into an electric current and changing the electric current into radio waves. In television reception, the reverse process goes on; radio waves are changed to an electric current, and the electric current is changed to light.

If the light were steady, this would be no problem, but when we attempt to send out the light reflected from a group of people acting in a play, the problem becomes very difficult.

The amount of light is constantly changing and each section of the scene varies from second to second. To translate such a changing pattern of light into radio waves is indeed a task.

ICONOSCOPES

The commonly used television sending tube, or iconoscope, meaning *image observer*, and the receiving tube, or kinescope, are far more complex in their operations than the usual electron tubes. They can best be described by recalling some of the characteristics of electrons. These tiny negative particles of electricity can be produced in a flood or a trickle. They flow from the cathode to the plate, but if the grid is positively charged, its extra attraction speeds up the electrons.

In television tubes a series of "accelerating anodes" with positive charges speeds up the electrons and helps form them into a close "beam" that might be compared to a thin beam of light. This beam of electrons can be sent the length of the iconoscope or kinescope tube. What is more, it can be directed with great precision to any particular spot on the flat end of the tube.

Control of the electron beam is accomplished by two pairs of electrically charged plates set at right angles to each other in the neck of the television tube. The beam of electrons passes between them. Let us suppose that the top plate has a slight positive charge. The beam of electrons bends up toward it. Put the positive charge on the bottom plate and the electron beam bends down. If you want the electron beam in the upper right-

An electron microscope. On the wall are photographs taken with this powerful instrument.

hand corner, the charge goes on the right plate and the upper plate.

By varying the charge, the beam of electrons can be moved across the end of the tube in line after line, just as your eyes follow the lines of type on this page. This motion of the electron beam is known as *scanning*. The idea is ingenious—and when you learn that an electron beam will scan an entire television screen back and forth in 525 distinct lines all in $\frac{1}{30}$ second, you can appreciate how rapid this scanning really is.

In the iconoscope tube is a thin screen of mica, an excellent electric insulator. On this screen are thousands of small droplets of silver, and on each droplet is a coating of caesium, a metal that emits electrons when struck by light. These droplets do not touch one another and are insulated by the mica. Each is a miniature photoelectric cell. The back of the mica sheet is covered with a coating of metal which is connected to a wire leading outside the tube.

In action, the image of the television performers is focused by a lens, like that of an ordinary camera, on this sensitized electronic screen. As soon as the light strikes these many miniature photoelectric cells, each cell gives off electrons, and becomes positively charged. The more intense the light hitting a particular spot on the screen, the more electrons it will give off and the more positively charged it will become.

By suitable means of scanning, the varying charge on different parts of the iconoscope screen affects the charge on the grid of an amplifying tube. Thus, the movement of the actors is translated into an electric current which acts on the grid of an amplifying tube and produces the high-frequency radio waves that carry the television signals.

KINESCOPES

The television reciving tube, or kinescope, must change the incoming high-frequency radio waves back to light. The television signals are amplified by triodes to increase their strength. They are then fed into the kinescope. In the kinescope is a beam-producing cathode and auxiliary equipment for speeding up the electrons. However, the flat end of the tube is coated with fluorescent materials instead of with miniature photoelectric cells. The fluorescent materials glow when struck by the electron beam. The beam also passes through a grid to which the incoming television current is fed.

The kinescope electron beam scans at exactly the same speed as the iconoscope and in the same pattern. As the beam passes the grid, the charge on the grid will either attract or repel some of the electrons in the beam, making it easier or more difficult for them to reach the screen. If the electrons are attracted by the grid, they will make a brighter splash of light when they hit the fluorescent screen. If they are repelled, the light will be relatively dim. Thus, the grid controls the intensity of the light, and it is these differences in intensity that produce the image on the television screen, which is in one end of a kinescope tube.

How can a spot of light moving across 525 lines on a screen in $\frac{1}{30}$ second give the appearance of people moving and things happening? The kinescope can only produce this rapidly moving spot of light. The rest is up to your eyes and luckily your eyes are much slower than the scanning beam. The effect is an optical illusion. It is a case of the electron beam being faster than the eye. Your eye cannot detect the changes that occur in $\frac{1}{30}$ second. They blend together and give the appearance of motion. In fact, all the motion pictures you have ever seen consist of 24 still pictures per second, flashed in succession on a movie screen. Action in both movies and television is an optical illusion.

THE ELECTRON MICROSCOPE

Another use of the electron beam is in the electron microscope. Beams of light can be focused through glass lenses and used to magnify small objects. A good microscope will magnify an object 2000 times, but even the best microscopes cannot be used to see objects that are shorter than a single wavelength of light. However, the waves produced by electrons are very much shorter than light waves. They are used in the electron microscope to magnify objects that would otherwise be invisible. The electron beam is focused by charged plates similar to those used in the television tubes.

Many new discoveries in medicine have been made with the electron microscope. The agent that causes influenza has been seen for the first time. New information about bacteria and viruses is constantly appearing. Studies of metals and liquids have already led to new industrial processes based on a better knowledge of the surfaces of materials. Since the electron microscope is 50 to 100 times as powerful as the best light microscope, we can continue to expect new discoveries from it.

ELECTRONICS IN THE HOME

When you read about heat, light, and sound in the home, the applications are very clear. However, many of the electronic devices mentioned in this chapter never have, and never will, appear in the home. But many products, which would be more costly or even non-existent without electronics, play an important part in home life. The role of electronics in refining metals has been mentioned, so check off every piece of aluminum, magnesium, copper, and some of the steel in your house as the result of electronics. Then there are the plastics, bonded plywoods, and welded materials. Electronic controls in spinning and weaving make low-cost cloth and clothing available. Electronic devices are essential, too, in food production and in protecting your health. You depend on electronics far more than you realize, even though the only electronic instrument you use may be your radio.

WORKING WITH SCIENCE

1. Obtain commercial booklets on television and find out what may be expected of this new electronic instrument. How have new television receivers been improved over the models that were produced several years ago?

2. High-frequency radio waves can travel only as far as the horizon. Find out why this is true and how it affects television transmission and reception.

3. Experiments with color television have gone so far that this new kind of television has already been demonstrated. Find out what you can about it.

4. Find out more about the electron microscope and its use. If an ordinary microscope is available, look at some small object through it—and imagine a microscope at least a hundred times more powerful.

READING YOU WILL ENJOY

Caverly, Donald P. *A Primer of Electronics.* McGraw-Hill Book Co., New York, 1943. A general introduction to a systematic study of electronics.

Hudson, Ralph G. *An Introduction to Electronics.* The Macmillan Co., New York, 1945. A very short, elementary book that stresses the principles of electronics.

Stokley, James. *Electrons in Action.* McGraw-Hill Book Co., New York, 1945. An excellent and understandable book on all phases of the interesting subject of electronics.

We are so accustomed to continual sounds that complete silence would seem very strange to us. Sound is an important part of the home, the school, and the world at work. It is the means through which we make contact with other people for business or for pleasure. The telephone and radio are ways of making our voices carry over great distances. Music, drama, sound movies, and even family conversation are all based on sound.

Sound in communication has brought people and their problems closer together. The "talking drums" of Africa (1) and the latest automobile telephone (2) both involve getting a message across through sounds that can be heard.

Sound in the form of music makes a lasting impression on us. Music is created by building sounds together to produce a pleasing effect. Different people have different ideas of what is pleasing, but all agree that music is something to be enjoyed. Music can create moods and arouse emotions even better than words. Probably you have seen a crowd stirred by music as a band goes marching by (3) or have seen how a symphony orchestra enraptures the listeners (4).

The opposite of music is noise—a mixture of unpleasant, jarring sounds often a byproduct of our Machine Age. Noise produces fatigue and lowers morale and industrial production (5). So the elimination of noise in factories (6), restaurants, and even in homes has become important. This control is possible through devices based on a knowledge of the way sounds are produced and transmitted. The use and control of sound are other ways in which science has affected our lives.

36

SOUND IN THE HOME

Our world seems familiar to us partly because we are familiar with its sounds. Without thinking much about them, we listen for familiar sounds—footsteps, rustling leaves, rain, and distant automobiles. Such sounds are very much a part of our lives. If we suddenly entered a soundproof room where there was no noise, the room would seem strange and we would be likely to feel somewhat, or even very, uneasy.

THE NATURE OF SOUND

Let us make some sounds and see, or rather hear, what they are like. You can talk, bang on the table, blow into a bottle, snap a rubber band, whistle, or make sounds in dozens of ways. But no matter how you make the sounds, how low or how high or how loud or how soft the sounds, to make a sound you always set something in back-and-forth motion. Such motion is called *vibration*.

SOUND WAVES

As an object that emits a sound vibrates, it produces sound waves in the air around it. You are already familiar with radio, light, and heat waves and water waves, but sound waves are not very much like them.

Light, heat, radio, and water waves all vibrate at *right angles* to the direction in which they travel. For example, if someone turns a flashlight on you, the beam of light comes toward you, but the light waves in the beam vibrate up and down, and from side to side never toward you and away from you. On the other hand, if someone shouts at you through a megaphone, the sound is directed toward you, and the sound waves vibrate back and forth in the same path as the sound beam.

The first type of wave, like heat, light,

sound, and water waves, is known as a *transverse wave*, a wave that vibrates at right angles to, or *across*, its own path. The second type of wave is known as a *longitudinal wave*, a wave that vibrates in its own path. This kind of wave is sometimes called a *compression wave*, and in a moment, you will see why this name is a good one.

Stretch a rubber band 8 inches or more, and pluck it. A sound is produced. You can hear it, and if you touch the rubber band, you can feel it vibrating. When you pluck the rubber band, it starts to vibrate. As it comes forward, the rubber band squeezes, or compresses, the molecules of air in front of it, packing them into a smaller space. As the rubber band moves

Two types of wave motion.

TRANSVERSE WAVE

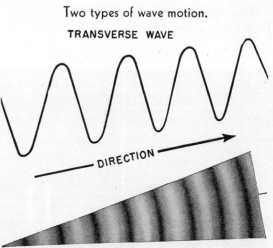

LONGITUDINAL WAVE

477

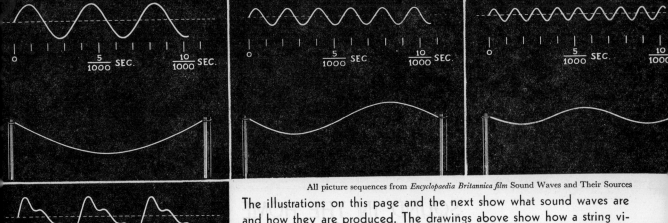

All picture sequences from *Encyclopaedia Britannica film* Sound Waves and Their Sources

The illustrations on this page and the next show what sound waves are and how they are produced. The drawings above show how a string vibrates as a whole, in halves, in thirds, and as all three at once. The appearance of the waves is shown at the top of each drawing. The drawings below show how sound waves are produced by a tuning fork. The white dots represent air molecules. The drawings at the bottom of the next page show how these air molecules hit a diaphragm and make a "picture" of a sound wave. The drawings at the top of the next page show a sound wave of a certain frequency and amplitude, then two sound waves of the same amplitude but different frequency, and finally two sound waves of the same frequency but different amplitude.

back, the pressure is relaxed and the molecules remaining occupy more space. Again it comes forward, sending a wave of compressed air out before it, and so on. The waves spread out in all directions, like ripples from a stone dropped in a pond.

SYMPATHETIC VIBRATION

Let us stretch a small sheet of rubber a short distance from the vibrating rubber band. The compression waves, traveling from the vibrating rubber band, soon hit the rubber sheet. As the first compression wave strikes, the rubber sheet bulges forward. As the wave passes, the sheet springs back. The second compression wave hits, and again the rubber sheet, or diaphragm, moves forward. As the second wave passes, the rubber sheet comes back once again. The sheet of rubber begins to vibrate at the same rate as the rubber band.

Such vibration is known as *sympathetic vibration*, or *resonance*. As the rubber band loses its energy and its vibrations become weaker, the rubber sheet receives weaker vibrations and vibrates less. Finally both come to a halt. Many substances vibrate sympathetically, reinforcing the original sounds. For example, pieces of furniture in a room may vibrate sympathetically with music or conversation, producing a pleasant effect. Lack of resonance produces an unpleasant "deadness."

The rubber band you snapped probably vibrated between 100 and 500 times per second, depending on how tightly it was pulled. You could not see the vibrations, but you could feel them, and they could have been recorded and measured with the proper apparatus. Such records have been made of thousands of kinds of sounds.

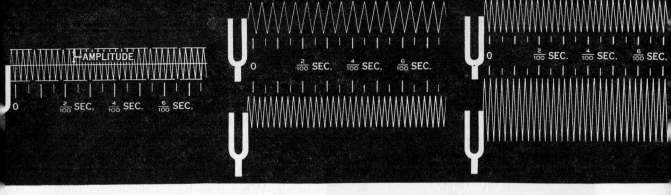

TUNING FORK VIBRATIONS

In studying sound, scientists use a special piece of U-shaped metal with a short handle, known as a *tuning fork*. A tuning fork is made to vibrate at a definite rate, for example, 256, 384, or 512 times per second. These vibrations produce a simple humming sound, quite pleasant, and easy to study. You can use a tuning fork to study how sound travels and how it is heard.

INTENSITY OF SOUND

A tuning fork will vibrate steadily when it is struck against the side of a table or when the ends are "plucked." Strike a fork labeled "C-256," and you will hear a sound close to middle C on a musical instrument, produced as the fork vibrates 256 times per second. Strike the fork lightly and the sound is weak. Strike it harder and the sound is louder. The fork vibrates 256 times per second in both cases, but after the fork is struck hard each vibration is larger and pushes the air with more energy. This simple demonstration shows one characteristic of sound—its *intensity*. The intensity of sound depends on the energy of the sound wave.

Intensity is not exactly the same as *loudness*. Loudness is the way in which the intensity of a sound wave is interpreted by the ear. The intensity of a sound depends on the distance sound travels and decreases with the square of the distance from the source of the sound.

If a shipload of high explosives blew up in the middle of the Atlantic, sound waves of very high intensity would be produced. To a survivor, the noise would have been ear-splitting. By the time the sound reached a ship, say, 10 miles away, it might still have been loud enough to blot out momentarily all other sounds. The crew on a ship 50 miles away might have heard the sound as a soft rumble, or not at all.

PITCH

Suppose that you strike a C-256 tuning fork, then an E-320, a G-384, and any others that are available. You hear *different* sounds, for each tuning fork vibrates at a different rate, or *frequency*. The ear interprets the frequency of sound as *pitch*. You can easily see for yourself that the greater the number of vibrations per second, the higher the pitch. Conversely, the lower the frequency, the lower the pitch.

This relationship between frequency and pitch is true no matter what vibrates. The lowest tones of an organ are produced by columns of air vibrating about 20 times per second. People normally can hear shrill sounds of 20,000 vibrations per second. Some people can hear sounds with somewhat greater frequencies.

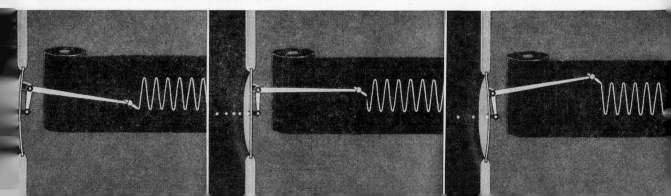

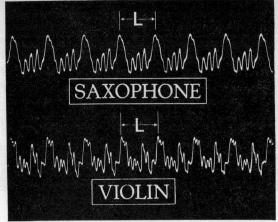

From Encyclopaedia Britannica film Sound Waves and Their Sources

The same note, but different overtones.

What determines the frequency of a sound wave? Look into a piano, and you will quickly see the difference between the strings that produce low-frequency tones and those that produce tones of high frequency. The low-frequency strings are heavy and long; the high-frequency strings are thin and short. Compare the pipes of an organ, the strings of a guitar, or the blocks of a xylophone, and you will see that a similar condition holds true. In strings of the same length and tension, it is always the heavier ones that produce the lower-frequency tones.

Increasing the stretching force on a vibrating string increases its frequency of vibration and, hence, its pitch. Have a friend pluck a rubber band as you pull it tighter and tighter. What happens to the frequency? The frequency of a drum can be regulated by tightening the drumhead. When a piano tuner adjusts the strings of a piano, he does not make them thicker or thinner to regulate the pitch; he merely loosens or tightens them a bit.

The length of a vibrating string or column of air determines the frequency with which it vibrates. Look at the piano again, and see which strings are longer. A violin or guitar player can increase the frequency of one of his strings by pressing his finger against the string and thereby shortening it. Watch a trumpet, saxophone, flute, recorder, or clarinet being played. By opening and closing holes, the player lengthens or shortens a vibrating column of air. When does he get the higher pitch?

TONE QUALITY

Besides intensity and pitch, most sounds have another important characteristic. This is *quality*, a complex characteristic very important to a musician. You can buy a violin for $15, but a violin made by Stradivarius is worth $15,000 or more. Why? Both have the same number of strings and the same shape. The answer lies in the quality of the tones they produce.

If the same note, say C-256, is produced on a violin, piano, flute, and trumpet with the same intensity, anyone can tell the difference between the flute and the piano, the violin and the trumpet, and so forth. That difference is in the quality of the tones produced. On the other hand, two tuning forks, each sounding C-256, sound exactly alike. The tuning forks produce sound composed of vibrations of one frequency only and, hence, sound alike.

But this is not true of musical instruments. The tone of each musical instrument is a blending of many vibrations which mix harmoniously with a tone when it is played. These other tones, called *overtones*, that mix and blend with each simple tone produce the differences in quality of sound from different sources. People's voices have very different

Sounds are produced as air sets the vocal cords in the glottis, or voicebox, to vibrating.

From Encyclopaedia Britannica film Sound Waves and Their Sources

GLOTTIS

qualities. They vary so much that you can learn to recognize a person by the quality of his voice when you hear it over the telephone.

HOW SOUND WAVES TRAVEL

Sound waves travel through many substances even more readily than through air. However, some kind of matter through which compression waves can pass is necessary. Light will travel through absolutely empty space, and so will heat and radio waves. But sound waves will travel only through matter—through either a solid, a liquid, or a gas.

We know that sound travels through air very well. However, at an altitude of 30,000 feet, where there is much less air than at sea level, sound does not travel very well, and you would have to speak very loudly to be heard. If you could go into a tunnel where sand-hogs work under compressed air, you would find that the compressed air carries sound waves even better than air at normal pressure, and even whispers are clearly audible at a considerable distance.

The ability of air to conduct sound depends on both its density and temperature, but under any circumstances air is not one of the best conductors of sound. The speed of sound is 1089 feet per second in air at 0°C, but the speed increases with the temperature.

The speed of sound through air is so much less than the speed of light that the difference is easily noticed. Perhaps you have seen a man hammering some distance away. If you watched closely, you noted movements that were out of step with the sounds you heard. The flash of light or the puff of smoke from the firing of a gun or cannon at a distance can be seen some time before the sound of the explosion is heard.

The same effect occurs during a thunderstorm when the thunder rolls in some seconds after you see the lightning flash that produced it. With a little practice, you can learn to judge the distance of a lightning stroke. As soon as you see the flash, begin counting—one thousand and one, one thousand and two, one

thousand and three, and so forth. The extra "and" slows you down so that each phrase is about equal to 1 second. Stop when you hear the thunder. Since sound travels about a mile in 5 seconds, divide the time in seconds by 5 and you will have a rough estimate of the distance of the lightning flash in miles.

The next time you go swimming, have a friend bang two stones together under the water. You will not hear them, until you duck under. Then you will hear them clearly, because sound is conducted about four times as well through water as through air. Sound travels at approximately 4500 feet per second through water.

Sound travels better through metals and most other solids than through air. If you put your ear to a railroad track when a train is coming, you will be able to hear it through the rails before you can hear it through air. The reason is that steel conducts sound 15 times as well as air. Through steel sound travels at about 15,400 feet per second. Why do you think Indian scouts occasionally stopped, got off their horses, and put their ears to the ground?

Solid objects that are very elastic are the best conductors of sound. Glass is much more elastic than most of us think. Sound travels through it at almost 20,000 feet per second.

How are its different tones produced?

Courtesy National Broadcasting Company

481

A decibel meter measuring the intensity of sound.

Sound travels less than 1500 feet per second through wax, cork, or tallow—about as fast as in air.

WHAT IS NOISE?

Noise is sound we do not like or that seems unpleasant to us. If your brother is practicing on his saxophone while you are doing your homework, you are more likely to shout, "Stop that noise," than to say, "Stop that music." What is music to your brother, is noise to you. On the other hand, this is stretching our definition a little too far. There are many unpleasant, irregular, jarring sounds that nobody seems to like. These are noise. In most homes there is always some noise. In schools, restaurants, and public buildings, there is likely to be more.

ELIMINATION OF NOISE

When noise interferes with our usual occupations, we must do something to get rid of it. That can easily be done. We can surround the source of noise by padding that absorbs the sound waves. We mount motors and machinery on blocks of rubber so that they do not make floors and walls vibrate. Modern machinery is designed so that vibration and noise are kept at a minimum. For example, compare an old typewriter with a new "noiseless" model.

Noise is even more bothersome when it is

loud. Loudness of sounds has been carefully studied. The loudness of sound depends on the intensity of the vibration or the amount of energy put into producing it. The unit used to measure the loudness of sound is the *bel*, named after Alexander Graham Bell, who experimented with sound, in addition to inventing the telephone. In actual use, sound engineers use the *decibel*, or 0.1 bel, a more convenient unit. An increase of 1 decibel in the intensity of a sound is the smallest increase in loudness that the ear can recognize.

The softest sound that can be heard is the faintest rustling of leaves, which is about 2 decibels. A whisper runs from 10 to 15 decibels, and the average noise in a house where clocks are ticking and people are walking is about 25 decibels. Schools and offices are noisier—from 30 to 35 decibels. The sound of a conversation scores 50, and a modern automobile makes just about the same noise. The noise in a busy street is about 60 decibels, a train comes to about 80, and an airplane engine comes close to 110. A nearby clap of thunder may be 125 or more decibels.

Once the intensity of sound has been measured, it is possible to predict how effective noise elimination will be. Soundproofing in offices may reduce the noise level as much as 40 to 60 decibels. Though an airplane engine produces a very loud noise, good sound insulation keeps the noise level inside a modern plane at only about 50 or 60 decibels.

SOUND ENGINEERING

If noise cannot be eliminated at the source, it can be restricted and absorbed. The compression waves will bounce, or reflect, from smooth or hard surfaces, and travel back and forth across a room many times before their energy is lost. In moderation, this reflection is good; sounds are stronger and deeper because of it. Excessive reflection produces disturbing echoes that can be eliminated only by cutting down the reflection. Soft draperies can be hung over plaster walls. The ceiling can be covered with sound-absorbing material containing a special pattern of holes which breaks up and absorbs sound waves.

Theaters, radio studios, and auditoriums are carefully designed so that sound is reflected only in desirable ways. The curved shell behind the orchestra in a concert hall directs the sound so that the audience receives most of it. Without sound engineering, there would be echoes and confusing noises that would interfere with the music or speakers.

Fortunately, even with younger brothers and sisters, most homes are not noisy enough to require special sound treatment. But people in apartment houses are often bothered by sounds from their neighbors or the radio in the next apartment. After an apartment building has been built, it is difficult and expensive to reduce such sounds. However, modern apartment and office buildings usually are so constructed that sounds do not pass readily from room to room. Dead-air spaces and cinder or concrete blocks in walls and floors are effective sound insulators. Such substances are used in constructing modern buildings.

WORKING WITH SCIENCE

1. With two identical tuning forks, sympathetic vibrations can be demonstrated by setting the two forks on sounding boxes a foot or so part. When one tuning fork is struck, the second will begin to vibrate. Stop the first tuning fork by touching it and the sound of the second will be heard distinctly.

2. Make sounds of different intensities by blowing, banging, or plucking, or watch how a drummer secures different effects by varying intensity only. What are the limits to increasing intensity of sound?

3. If a "silent" dog whistle is available, demonstrate it to the class. Such a whistle produces a high-pitched sound, too high for most people to hear. However, dogs can hear these higher vibrations and can be taught to respond when the "silent" whistle is blown.

4. Compare the strings of stringed instruments, such as violin, cello, mandolin, and guitar to see if you can account for differences in quality of tone. Also compare bells of different pitch and see how the size and weight of the bell affects its pitch.

5. Stretch a steel wire in a vice or by using the frame of a small jig saw. Test the pitch as you tighten the wire. If you have means of measuring the pull on a wire, notice the change in pitch as you double the tension and then redouble it.

6. If your school has an orchestra, watch at rehearsal and have players demonstrate how they vary the pitch of their instruments. Have students who play instruments bring them to class and explain the principles underlying their use.

7. Put an electric bell under a bell jar and connect it to a vacuum pump. Turn on the bell, and start pumping out the air. The sound of the bell diminishes as the air is removed. Why?

8. Find out how submarines were detected by listening devices during World War II.

9. Does your town have antinoise ordinances? Find out whether noise is a community problem and what is done about it. Many towns have zoning regulations to aid in controlling noise.

10. Some schools test students' hearing by having them listen to a phonograph record in which numbers are repeated more and more faintly. Find out about hearing tests and how hearing is measured.

11. Find out about "soundproofing" or "acoustical treatment." Do the contractors in your town sell soundproofing materials? Try to find buildings where they have been used.

An acoustical shell spreads sounds properly.

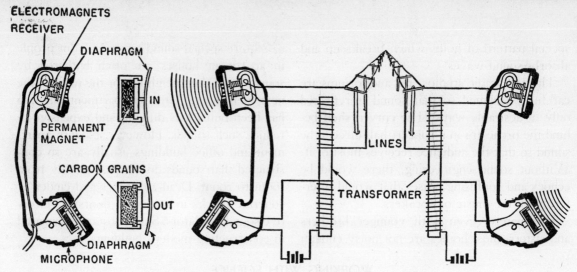

A modern telephone handset and telephone lines.

12. Find out about whispering galleries, orchestra shells, echoes, and other situations involving sound reflection.

13. By means of reflected sound waves, ships can measure the depth of water beneath them. Find out how this is done.

SOUND EQUIPMENT

As far as the home is concerned, sound is used primarily in communication. Of course, you can open the window and call across the street to a neighbor, but it is much more convenient to use a telephone. If your neighbor is a considerable distance away, as neighbors are in many parts of the United States, a telephone is a necessity.

PARTS OF THE TELEPHONE

The telephone begins and ends with sound, but sound does not go through the wires. Electric currents carry the message. Besides the wires and the batteries that supply the current, a telephone has two other essential parts—the *receiver* and the *microphone*. The part of the telephone into which you talk is a microphone, even though it does not look like the kind used by radio announcers.

THE CARBON MICROPHONE

A microphone is a device for changing sound waves into a changing electric current. A microphone is a conductor of electricity, but its ability to conduct changes in keeping with the sound waves that hit it. The wire carrying the telephone current, a low-voltage direct current, leads into the back of a small metal box containing tiny grains of carbon. Another wire leads from the front of the box. Electricity flows through these grains of carbon without much difficulty as long as they touch one another. The more grains that touch, the better the conductor.

In front of the metal box of carbon grains is a thin sheet of flexible metal. This sheet, or diaphragm, exerts a slight pressure on the carbon grains, just enough to maintain the current. When you speak into a telephone, thousands of compression waves strike the diaphragm. Each wave pushes the diaphragm against the carbon grains, and for that slight fraction of a second, the grains of carbon are pushed closer together and more electricity flows through the circuit. The flexible diaphragm moves back, releasing the pressure, and then another wave hits it, and another, and another. The diaphragm vibrates with every sound you speak and changes the sounds into a fluctuating electric current. If you speak loudly, the diaphragm vibrates harder and a greater change in the current is produced. If you raise the pitch of your voice the diaphragm vibrates more rapidly, and more fluctuations of current per second travel through the circuit.

THE TELEPHONE RECEIVER

At the other end of the telephone is the receiver. Inside this part of the instrument is an electromagnet, against which rests another thin metal diaphragm. You are already familiar with the electromagnet and how it works. You know that the strength of the electromagnet depends on the strength of the current in it. If the electric current is variable, the pull of the magnet changes as the current changes.

That is exactly what happens in a telephone receiver. The variable current changes the strength of the electromagnet, and the pull on the diaphragm is increased or decreased. When the current becomes stronger, the diaphragm is pulled toward the magnet. As it becomes weaker, the diaphragm bends away. Thus, the diaphragm reproduces exactly every vibration of the microphone diaphragm. The diaphragm of the receiver pushes the air as it vibrates, and produces compressional waves. These compressional waves are sound waves, and so you are able to hear what is being said into the telephone microphone.

Such a simple telephone can operate only over relatively short distances. For long distances, transformers and triode amplifiers are used to make the variable electric current strong enough to reproduce sounds without loss.

Years of scientific study have gone into making the telephone what it is today. But the principles involved in modern telephones are the same that Alexander Graham Bell developed in 1876. Bell had connected a little telephone from one room to another in his laboratory. It was almost ready for testing when Bell accidentally spilled some acid from his battery near the microphone. He called out to his assistant, "Come here, Watson, I need you." Mr. Watson working in the other room had his ear near the receiver. He distinctly heard the first message to be sent by telephone and ran to Bell's assistance.

OTHER TELEPHONIC DEVICES

The telephone is first cousin to dozens of other devices, all of which operate on the same principle. Hearing aids for the hard of hearing, public-address systems, interoffice communication systems, phonograph pickups, and radio loudspeakers all use, in part at least, the basic principle of the telephone.

The hearing aid for persons who are hard of hearing usually consists of a small sensitive microphone, a pocket-size amplifier, and a receiver. Public-address systems used in schools, churches, and auditoriums have sensitive microphones somewhat different in design from that of the telephone, but doing the same work. The public-address system includes an amplifier to increase the strength of the microphone current and loudspeakers which are more powerful but quite similar to telephone receivers.

RADIO AND SOUND

In radio there are no wires for the current to travel through from transmitter to receiver so an additional step is involved. At the transmitter, sound is converted into a variable electric current by means of a microphone. This electric current is transformed into radio waves, which vary from 1 foot to about 5 miles in length. These radio waves are picked up by the radio receiver, and amplified, and changed back into an electric current again. The electric current operates the loudspeaker, reproducing sounds picked up by the microphone

A tube for a hearing aid.

Courtesy Sonotone Corporation

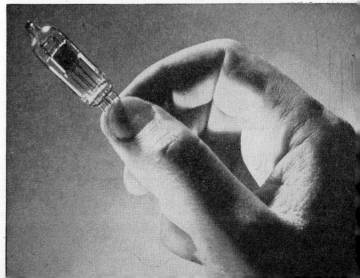

at the studio and transmitted by radio.

Microphones for broadcasting use are a far cry from the carbon telephone microphone. Broadcast microphones are much more sensitive. Some are specially designed for speakers or singers; others are made to catch the entire tonal range of an orchestra.

Once the sound has been picked up by the microphone and transformed into a variable direct current, the microphone current is sent into a grid circuit of a triode. It is greatly amplified and is impressed on the oscillating current produced by the transmitting tubes. Each change in tone or pitch is transformed into a change in the amplitude of the constant-frequency carrier radio waves. The frequency of these changes in amplitude corresponds to the frequencies of the sound source.

In a receiving set the radio waves pass through tuning coils or condensers, which pick out carrier waves of a certain frequency coming from a certain station, into the detector tube. In the detector tube the alternating current of the radio waves is changed into a variable direct current in the plate circuit. This variable direct current must be amplified by several tubes before it can operate the loudspeaker.

This description of radio is greatly oversimplified, but it does describe the basic principles of present broadcasting (called *amplitude modulation*, or *AM*). Tubes used in modern radios are usually more complicated than the simple diodes and triodes we have discussed. Some of them are designed to do two or three jobs at once. Often one tube is the equivalent of two simple diodes or triodes put under the same glass or metal cover.

The design of radio sets is a rather complicated business, and radios are now so specialized that each radio cabinet may house two or three kinds of radios—a short wave, a long wave, and a *frequency modulation*, or *FM* set, all using the same amplifier but differing in many other respects. The FM sets are especially interesting because FM radio waves involve changes in frequency of the carrier waves rather than in amplitude modulation of carrier waves of a constant frequency. FM sets have distinct advantages in reception of clear signals, free from interference, or "static."

THE PHONOGRAPH

Have you ever seen a picture of an early phonograph with a cylindrical record and a large tin horn? Such early phonographs are funny to look at and even funnier to hear. However, the principle on which they operate is still widely used for home entertainment and in making radio transcriptions.

In making a record the music or voice causes a diaphragm in the recording apparatus to vibrate. These vibrations (often amplified) are transferred to a needle which moves over a revolving wax disk. The vibrating needle draws a wavy line in the wax, each wave in the line representing a change in the sound waves. From this wax record, a metal master record is prepared, and from the master record, thousands of copies may be produced, each of which will duplicate the original sounds.

On some early phonographs, records were played by placing them on a revolving turntable and placing the needle of a reproducer in the groove. As the turntable revolved, the vibrations of the needle were transmitted directly to a mica or metal diaphragm at one end of a horn. The sounds produced by the vibrating diaphragm were not as lifelike as those

AM (left) and FM waves. Top: Sound wave. Middle: Carrier. Bottom: Transmitted waves with sound.

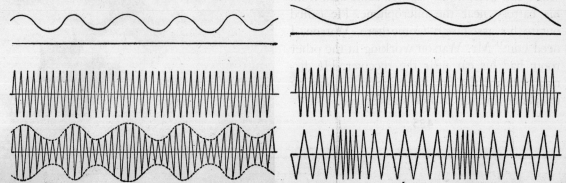

produced by modern phonographs, in which the sound is reproduced electronically.

In a modern phonograph the needle transmits the vibrations from the record groove to a crystal or magnetic pickup. In a crystal pickup, changes in pressure corresponding to the original sounds are converted into a fluctuating electric current. This current is amplified and used to drive a loudspeaker.

A modern phonograph or radio sounds better than earlier models chiefly because it is able to reproduce more of the original sounds. For example, an orchestra produces sounds with frequencies that vary from about 20 to 20,000 cycles per second. Early phonographs and radios could not duplicate this range of vibrations. They reproduced sounds from only about 250 to 5000 cycles per second. The music from the record or the radio did not have the low tones and the high tones of the orchestra that was playing. Only part of the music was reproduced. Improvements in mass-produced phonographs and radios have increased the range of sounds reproduced from as low as 50 cycles per second to as high as about 7000. As a result, reproduction of music and voice is much improved. High-fidelity phonographs and radios have much greater tonal ranges, from as low as 20 cycles per second to as high as 18,000 to 20,000 cycles per second.

Entirely new methods of recording are now being perfected. These use either a steel wire or a strip of metallic paper tape instead of records. These methods may someday entirely replace records. Such a machine will play for several hours from a roll of wire or tape.

WORKING WITH SCIENCE

1. Using a flashlight bulb, two dry cells in series, and two pieces of pencil lead with connecting wires, demonstrate the principle of the carbon microphone.

2. If someone in the class is a radio enthusiast, have him investigate and report on types of microphones other than the carbon microphone.

3. Open a telephone receiver or radio headset and demonstrate the electromagnet in them to the class.

4. Make a string telephone by stretching a string through paper diaphragms fastened over the ends of opened tin cans. Such telephones can be made to carry a voice clearly for 15 or 20 feet. How do such telephones operate, and how are they different from our usual telephone?

5. Look up the diagrams of actual telephone circuits. How many wires are used for each phone? How strong is the current used?

6. Visit your local telephone exchange. Find out how it operates and what some of the problems of the telephone company are.

7. Investigate hearing aids. Manufacturers will be willing to supply the class with literature which will give much interesting information about sound and hearing and aid to the hard of hearing.

8. Visit the nearest radio station, and have an engineer explain the station's organization, operation, and principles.

9. Find out how common sound effects are produced and try to make some and demonstrate them to the class. Demonstrate behind a screen and see if the sounds can be recognized.

READING YOU WILL ENJOY

Bragg, Sir William. *The World of Sound*. G. Bell & Sons, London, 1925. Though old, this book by a world-famous scientist is still worth reading.

Reck, Franklin M. *Radio from Start to Finish*. Thomas Y. Crowell Co., New York, 1942. A fine book on the story of radio. Does not cover *how* a radio works but does an excellent job on how our modern radio system came to be as important as it is as a method of mass communication.

Tyler, Kingdon S. *Modern Radio*. Harcourt, Brace & Co., New York, 1944. Covers every phase of radio and television.

Tyler, Kingdon S. *Telecasting and Color*. Harcourt, Brace & Co., New York, 1946. Discusses the most recent development in television—color television.

1

2

Like all living things, man has two inheritances. From his parents man receives the genetic inheritance that provides the promise and to an extent sets the limits of what he will become. The other inheritance consists of the environment and the conditions in which he will live. If the environment is favorable, he may fulfill or even surpass the possibilities of his genetic inheritance. If the environment is unfavorable, he may not live up to them.

Suppose some fine seed corn is separated into two equal parts. The genetic inheritances of each part are equal. One part (1) is planted in poor, unfertilized soil. It gets little rain and little cultivation. The other part (2) is planted in rich, fertilized soil.

It gets the right amount of rain and proper cultivation. Will the yields be the same?

The same thing is true of people. Identical twins develop from the same fertilized egg cell and have the same genetic inheritance. Suppose that the twins are separated at birth. One twin (3) is raised by ignorant foster parents in a poor home. He receives poor food, no education, and no contact with people and books. The other twin (4) grows up in a good foster home. He has good nourishing food and excellent physical care. He goes to good schools and has pleasant social and cultural opportunities. In spite of identical genetic inheritances, these twins will be very different physically and in personality and intelligence.

3

4

37

SCIENCE AND PEOPLE

Making a modern airplane requires the services of men and women all over the world. In addition, the fact that modern airplanes with world-shrinking speeds exist and can be used to spread death and destruction demands that we make a fundamental choice. We must either learn to cooperate fully with the peoples of the world, or we must expect endless strife and wars of great violence. We choose the path of cooperation, of course. But we cannot cooperate with peoples whom we do not understand. Real cooperation cannot be built on suspicion, fear, or feelings of superiority or inferiority.

The German Nazis and their leader, Hitler, brought death and destruction to millions at least in part because of their idea that the Germans were superior to all other peoples. Years of propaganda convinced many Germans that they belonged to a superior "Nordic race." One way to prevent such ideas is for all peoples to learn the scientific facts regarding various races, peoples, and nationalities, and what makes them alike and different.

THE RACES OF MAN

You know that the term *nationality* refers to the nation of which a person is a citizen. If you are a citizen of the United States, your nationality is American. You may be white, black, or yellow, but you are an American. Your parents may be of German, Scotch, English, or Mexican descent, but you are an American. But what do we mean when we speak of the *races* of man?

A race is a group of people having a common descent and, therefore, bearing common physical characteristics. Race is another name for *variety*, as geneticists use the term. Mendel crossed two races, or varieties, of peas when he crossed a tall variety (which was purebred and always produced tall offspring when mated with a similar purebred variety) with a dwarf race, or variety.

If a variety of pea plant, generation after generation, produces white flowers, we might properly say that it is a race, or variety, of pea plant distinct from another race that always produces red flowers. But if pea plants produce offspring that are both red and white, pink, or other colors, we can be sure that we have a hybrid rather than a pure variety, or race.

What do we find when we apply the term *race* to mankind? Are there groups that have

Two Caucasian types, a Caucasian from India, Negroid types from South Africa and from North Africa.
Courtesy E. I. du Pont de Nemours & Co.; British Information Services; Union of South Africa Goverment Information Office

distinct color differences from other men, or that have other physical characteristics that cause them to form a distinct group? Using the term in this sense, we have four races, but *many, many hybrids exist in each race.*

Caucasian. One race of man is the *Caucasian,* or white, race. The skin color varies from white to dark brown, for East Indians are Caucasians, and their skin is darker than that of many American Negroes. The nose of the Caucasian is typically high-bridged and generally narrow. The hair varies in color and texture. The shape of the skull varies from long to round. Other physical features are also involved in the classification of a human being as a Caucasian.

Negroid. The Negro belongs to another race. *Negroid* is the scientific name of this race. The racial characteristics of the Negroid are clear. The hair is black and kinky. The skin is black or dark brown. The skull is long and the nose broad. Purebred Negroes exist in some parts of the world, but most American Negroes show clearly that they are hybrids with modified distinguishing characteristics.

Mongoloid. Another race is the *Mongoloid,* to which belong the Chinese, Japanese, Eskimos, and American Indians. The skin is yellowish or yellow-brown. The hair is straight and dark. The skull is usually broad, and the nose is wide and low-bridged.

Australoid. The fourth race is the *Australoid* which is made up of a people commonly called *Australian bushmen.* They are brown or coppery in color and have long, narrow skulls and low brows. In terms of physical characteristics and evidence of common descent, this small group of people, who have lived in isolation for many generations in Australia, might be said to be the purest race of man.

DO RACES AND NATIONALITIES DIFFER PSYCHOLOGICALLY?

Race is a scientific term that refers to common descent and the inheritance of similar physical characteristics. It does not refer to psychological characteristics, such as personality and intelligence. Yet it is a proper question to ask whether or not racial and national groups do differ in such traits. But it is very important that we check the scientific facts to get our answer. The German Nazis did not bother to check scientific facts. They merely *assumed* that the German people were superior. What is known about the psychological differences of peoples?

Attempts have been made to compare racial and national groups as to psychological traits. Most such studies have employed *intelligence tests.* Such tests vary greatly but generally they consist at least in part of questions of many kinds. Scores are given on the basis of the number of questions correctly answered.

Racial and national groups have shown differing abilities, as a group, to score highly on these tests. However, scientists generally agree that such scores do not indicate the native, or inborn, *intelligence* of these groups of people. The cultural or environmental differences are too great for this to be possible. East Indians, for example, have rather different cultures and types of education than Americans. Thus, when tested on intelligence tests made by Americans for Americans, they are

An Australoid type, a pure Australoid, two Mongoloids from China and one from North America.
Courtesy Australian News and Information Bureau; American Museum of Natural History, New York; U. S. D. A. photo by Knell

almost certain to score lower, as a group, than Americans. In addition, each race contributes at least some individuals who make very high scores and others who make very low scores on intelligence tests.

If exactly the same environment could be provided to groups of people, it might be possible to test them and to assume that any differences were the result of inborn differences in ability. But this is totally impossible. All we can say is that peoples do vary in their scores on intelligence tests and that those with the most similar backgrounds have the most similar average scores.

Intelligence, in the broader sense, cannot be tested in a few hours with a paper and pencil test. Definitions of intelligence vary, but the most commonly accepted definition refers to the adaptability or successful adjustment that an individual can make to a situation in which he finds himself. It refers, too, to an individual's ability to control his environment and adapt it to his needs. An Eskimo who has lived all of his life in the Arctic region would score very low on an American intelligence test. But the Eskimo has shown remarkable ability to adapt himself to the difficult living conditions of an ice-bound environment.

How many Americans could adapt themselves swiftly and successfully to the Eskimo's way of life? If the Eskimo should construct an intelligence test, how high a score would an American be likely to make on it? Who is more intelligent, the Eskimo or the American? We can only say that both seem to be capable of adjusting very successfully to their environments.

DO RACES AND NATIONALITIES DIFFER IN PERSONALITY TRAITS?

Peoples of different racial, national, and religious groups do differ somewhat in personality traits, but their likenesses are far greater than their differences. It is easy to say that the Scotch are "tight," the Chinese "clever," the French "artistic," and the Negro "musical." But if you have known many persons of these national and racial stocks, you have probably found that they did not fit the "pattern" at all. Yet, there are undoubted slight differences in peoples. Easterners, southerners, and westerners differ slightly in certain personality traits. The big question is what makes them differ as groups?

Lower animals, such as insects, are born with tendencies to act in certain ways. Such patterns of behavior are called *instincts*. A particular type of solitary wasp, for example, is hatched, grows as larva, pupates, and emerges as an adult which immediately starts getting food, making nests in which it places paralyzed spiders on which it lays its eggs. It does all this and much more without any other wasp giving it the slightest instruction. And its procedures are always just the same as those of other wasps of the same type. These wasps do not have to learn to do these things.

Man, on the other hand, has very few instincts to act. Almost everything he does is a result of training and education. As a newborn baby, he obtains food by sucking. This action is the result of a sucking instinct, and he does not have to be taught how. Only a very few such elementary things are instinctive to man.

Man must learn. He can learn to be warlike or peaceful, to be kind or vicious, to be generally happy or generally sulky. His individual inheritance is involved in this, it is true, as are such matters as his diet and health.

When large groups of people are considered, the traits of individuals range from one extreme to another. But group behavior may be quite a different matter. When we find nations or cultural groups that are mostly warlike, peaceful, mechanically minded, or agricultural, such traits are the result of traditions, history, goals, materials at hand, and general training.

Man is extremely adaptable. As a group, men and women are neither good nor bad, wise nor stupid, musical nor mechanical. They may be any of these things. They are, in large part, what their culture and specific training make them. Individuals vary tremendously as a result of genetic inheritance, but the group pattern is set by the culture.

INHERITANCE IN ANIMALS AND MAN

What an animal or plant becomes depends not only upon its biologic, or genetic, inheritance, but on the environment in which it lives. The biologic inheritance sets the limits on what an organism can become and what it can do. But the environment and the cultural inheritance determine the extent to which the biologic inheritance can be fulfilled. The best wheat seeds in the world will not produce wheat plants with ripe grain if water is withheld or if they are planted on bare rock.

The best native abilities in the world will produce little if proper environment for their development is lacking. The best native intelligence imaginable would not result in an intelligent human being without proper food, attention to physical needs, and education. Peoples of the world vary tremendously in their environments. Millions of human beings have been denied any education as we know it. Millions of others live in perpetual half-starvation. Millions have died of malnutrition and starvation. Such peoples have had little chance to develop great scientists, artists, businessmen, writers, and scholars.

WE CAN LEARN FROM OTHER PEOPLES

The airplane and other modern inventions have made the people of this world closer together than they have ever been. We can never hope to have lasting peace unless we recognize that all the peoples of the world are natively much like ourselves. All peoples have contributed to the greatness of the modern world in one way or another.

Our future depends now, more than ever before, on cooperating with all the peoples of the world. Such cooperation will give us increased understanding of the worth of other peoples. The flow of commerce, study, and travel, which modern science and such cooperation will make possible, should enable us to enrich our own lives by contact with representatives of other cultures.

WORKING WITH SCIENCE

1. Undoubtedly there are young people in your school of various nationalities and races. Perhaps you can arrange to have the parents of some of these boys and girls discuss with you some of the interesting things they knew about their countries and their peoples. If some of these parents grew up in foreign lands, they should be able to provide valuable and interesting accounts of how they lived, went to school, worked, and so forth, in their native lands.

2. Check in encyclopedias or other references to determine the nationalities and racial origins of some outstanding men and women. You may be particularly interested to study the backgrounds of some of the great men of science. References at the end of this chapter will help you.

READING YOU WILL ENJOY

Benedict, Ruth and Weltfish, Gene. *The Races of Mankind*, Public Affairs Pamphlet No. 85. Public Affairs Committee, Inc., New York, 1943. An interesting and important booklet on races and the facts and superstitions about them, written by two foremost scientists in the field.

Kendall, James. *Young Chemists and Great Discoveries*. D. Appleton-Century Co., New York, 1940. Interesting and brief biographies of the work of well-known chemists when they were young men.

Lewis, Elizabeth F. *Young Fu of the Upper Yangtze*. John C. Winston Co., Philadelphia, 1932.

If you would like to know something of what it would be like to grow up as a Chinese youngster in China, read this interesting book about Young Fu.

Nash, James V. *Races of Men*. Thomas S. Rockwell Co., Chicago, 1931. A readable, reliable book about the races of men. Gives information about the migrations of men and their probable origins.

Pope, Clifford H. *China's Animal Frontier*. The Viking Press, New York, 1940. An interesting book about collecting animals in Asia for the American Museum of Natural History. Gives information about the animals and about the Asiatic people encountered.

INDEX

As you use this index, you will see that entries are in three kinds of type: **boldface**, *italic,* and roman. The boldface entries indicate pages on which definitions of terms are given. By turning to these pages, you can read both the definitions and the materials from which the definitions were developed. Definitions looked up in this way will mean a great deal more to you than if you merely looked them up in a glossary.

Some words have several boldface entries. The reason for this is that many scientific terms expand in meaning as you learn more about them. The first boldface entry refers to the simplest definition of the term; other entries refer to more advanced definitions—definitions that have grown as your understanding of the terms has grown. Italic entries indicate illustrations or their captions, and roman entries are ordinary references.

Pronunciations are given for all words with which you might have difficulty. The respellings for pronunciation are based on material in Webster's *New International Dictionary,* Second Edition, Copyright 1934 and 1939 by G. & C. Merriam Company, and are used by permission.

Abdomen, *49;* of grasshopper, **126**
Absorption, 41–42, 91
Accidents, 73, 115, 116, 206; alcohol and, 115; deaths from, 73; first aid and, 116–119; in mines, 206
Accommodation, of eye, **69**
Acetate, cellular cellulose (sĕl′ū lẽr sĕl′ū lōs ăs′ḗ tāt), *248*
Acetylene (ă sĕt′ĭ lēn), 232
Acids, 235, **239,** 240
Acne (ăk′nḗ), **105,** 106
Action: involuntary, **63;** vasomotor, **53;** voluntary, **64–65**
Adam's apple, 40, **102**
ADAMS, JOHN C., 430
Adaptation: **33,** **137–142,** 379; and reproduction, 139; for food getting, 138–139; for protection, 139; of man, 141, 379, 491; of plants, 139; to weather, 407
Adolescence, **105;** problems of, 101–107
Adrenals, (ăd rē′nălz), *103*
Advantage, mechanical, **268, 270,** 272, 273, 277
Aeration (ā′ẽr ā′shŭn), **226**
Afterimage, **67**
Agriculture, 4, 216, 236, 237, 411
Air: 58, 71, 117, 122, 137, 154, 179, 191, 196, 207, 209, 213, 215, 224, 226, 229–241, 288, 290, 297, 298, 299, 301, 302, 307, 309, 310, 314, 317, 350, 375, 377, 379, 382, 383, 384, 385, 386, 388, 397, 398, 400, 401, 402, 403, 429, 443, 445, 452, 453, 457, 467, 480, 481; "artificial," 239; cold, **398,** 399, 400, 402; compressed, 409, 481; continental arctic (*cA*), **397;** continental polar (*cP*), **396,** 397, 398; energy of, 255, 290; maritime polar (*mP*), **397,** 400; maritime tropical (*mT*), **398,** 400; masses, 393–405; movements of, 380, 382, 393; pres-

sure of, 58, 72, 229, 239, 298, 301, 302, 303, 330, 377, 379, **380, 381, 382,** 389, 390, 394; warm, **398,** 399, 400, 401; weight of, 58, 378, 379, 380, 381, 385
Air-conditioning, 267, 449
Airplanes: 11, 13, 73, 145–146, *163,* 210, 222, 232, 243, 246, 287, 297–299, 317, 342, 343, 347, 348, 357, 361–366, 377, 389, 409, 436; ailerons of (ā′lẽr ŏnz), *298;* balance and, 276; Bernoulli's principle, and, 297; energy and, 297; engines of, 307, 310, 314–315; friction and, 297, 299; jet-propelled, 169; mass production and, 361–366; pitch and, *298;* roll and, *298;* thrust of, **298;** trimming tabs of, **276;** weather and, 374, 377, 378–383, 389, 394; World War II and, 361–363; XB-29, *362;* yaw and, *299*
Airport, 238, 377
Air sac, *57, 58, 127*
Alcohol, 114, 146, 247, 248, 317, 439
Algae (ăl′jē), **132, 133,** 154
Alkalies, **239**
Alloy, **208,** 209, 210, 222, 243, 244, 314, 343, 348
ALTER, DAVID (ôl′tẽr), 421
Altimeter (ăl tĭm′ḗ tẽr), **382**
Altitude, 377, 380, **382,** 383, 384, 401
Alumina (à lū′mĭ nà), **210**
Aluminum (à lū′mĭ nŭm): 154, 180, 184, 210, *211,* 212, 222, 250, 336, 340, 408, 452, 472, 475; oxide, **210**
Ameba (à mē′bà), **36,** 130, 139
American colonies and colonists, 5, 8–9, 10, 13, 14, 428
Amino acids (ă mē′nō), **94**
Ammeter (ăm′mē′tẽr), **326,** *333*
Ammonia, **220, 236, 237**
Ammonium: chloride, **220;** hydroxide (hī drŏk′sīd), **236, 239**

Amperage (ăm pẽr′ĭj), **334,** 336
Ampere (ăm′pẽr), 333, **334,** 335, 336, 337, 339, 340, 343
Amphibians (ăm fĭb′ĭ ănz), **124**
Amplification, **469,** 471–472
Amplitude modulation, **486**
Andromeda (ăn drŏm′ḗ dà), 436
Anemometer (ăn′ḗ mŏm′ḗ tẽr), *377*
Aneroid barometer (ăn′ẽr oid), *274, 380, 381,* 382
Angle: of incidence, **460;** of reflection, **460**
Aniline (ăn′ĭ lĭn), 317
Animals, 4, 36, 61, 79, 80, 81, 83, 84, 121, 138, 139, 141, 150–153, 154, 163, 169–170, 200, 211, 212, 255, 380, 491; carnivorous, **138,** 139; cold-blooded, **123;** conservation of, 150–153; crossbreeding of, **172;** herbivorous, **138,** 139, 151; inbreeding of, **172;** jellyfish and corals, **129–130;** jointed-legged, **125;** mutation and, **172;** one-celled, **36,** 61, 79, 130; predatory, **151;** sea urchins, sand dollars, starfish, 129; warm-blooded, **123**
Anode (ăn′ōd), **222,** 466, 473
Antares (ăn târ′ēz), 436
Antennae (ăn tĕn′ē), **126, 127,** 469
Anthracite, **190,** 196
Anthrax (ăn′thrăks), **80,** 81, *82*
Antibiotics (ăn′tĭ bī ŏt′ĭks), *115*
Antibodies, **86,** *87*
Antitoxin (ăn′tĭ tŏk′sĭn), **86,** 109
Ants, 164, 165
Anvil, of ear, **71**
Aorta (ā ôr′tà), **51**
Appendix, **42**
Arachnids (à răk′nĭds), **126–127**
ARCHIMEDES (är′kĭ mē′dēz), 254, 271
Arcturus (ärk tū′rŭs), 435
Argon, 231, 238, 452
ARISTARCHUS (ăr′ĭs tär′kŭs), 419
Armature (är′mà tụ̄r), **329,** 330, 331, 339, 342
Arsenic, 95, **163,** 249
Arteries, *49,* **50,** 51, **52,** 53, 118

Artificial respiration, 117–118
Asbestos, 210, 220, 408
Ascorbic acid (á skôr′bĭk), 92
Asphalt (ăs′fôlt), 212
Asphyxia (ăs fĭk′sĭ á), 117
Assembly line, 361, 362, 363–365
Assimilation, 91
Astigmatism (á stĭg′má tĭz′m), 70
Astronomers and astronomy, 192, 238, 417–439
Atabrine (ăt′á brĭn), 109
Atlantic Ocean, 5, 10, 215, 394, 397, 398, 405, 413
Atmosphere, the: 191–192, 229, 236, 378, 379, 383, 389, 390, 409–410, 425, 429, 431; pressure of, 379; weight of, 378, 380
Atom, 3, 4, 18, 27, 180–181, 182, 211, 220, 247, 293, 294, 334, 344, 439, 463; charges of, 463; discovered, 18; energy of, 3, 4, 27, 181, 211, 294, 344, 439; nucleus of, 463; "smashing," 293
Atomic: Age, 393; bomb, 1–4, 18, 28, 169, 180, 205; engines, 294; energy, 3, 27, 181, 203, 211, 223, 253, 259, 293–294, 318, 344; fission, 181; pile, 3, 293
Auricles (ô′rĭ k′lz), 50, 51
Aurora borealis (ô rō′rá bō′rĕ ā′lĭs), 379, 421
Australoid (ôs′trá loid), 490
Automobiles: 11, 28, 73, 209, 232, 243, 246, 267, 279, 283, 287, 291, 308, 311, 332, 352, 365; care of, 280; cooling system of, 291; engines, 308, 311; heat energy and, 291; mass production and, 361, 365, 366; tolerances and, 350
Aviation: 376; Age of, 11
Axis: earth's, 394, 424, 427; sun and, 420; of Mars, 431
Axle, 267, 269, 276–277, 284, 348. See also Wheel.
Aztecs (ăz′tĕks), 418, 423

Bacilli, bacillus (bá sĭl′ĭ), 81
Bacteria: 42, 79, 80, 115, 121, 132, 154, 200, 224, 229, 236, 475; nitrogen-fixing, 236, 237
BAEKELAND, LEO H. (bā′kĕ länd), 245–246; "Bakelite," 245–246
Balance, 274–275, 276
Balloon, 229, 239, 377, 379, 380
BANTING, DR. FREDERICK, 249
Bar, compound, 446
Barium (bâr′ĭ ŭm), 95
Barium–137, 294
BARNARD, EDWARD E., 431
Barograph, 382
Barometer, 380, 381–382
Bases, 239
Basining, 157

Battery: 330, 331, 332, 334, 338, 339, 342, 465; dry cell, 322, 323, 325, 338
Bauxite (bôks′ĭt), 210, 250
Bearings: 296; ball, 296, 347–350; needle, 296; roller, 296, 348
Beavers, 196
Bees, 131, 132, 166
Beetles, 162, 164, 165
Bel, 482
BELL, ALEXANDER G., 482, 485
Bells, 325–326, 338
Benzine (bĕn zēn′), 212
Beriberi (bĕr′ĭ bĕr′ĭ), 92, 93
BERNARD, CLAUDE (bĕr′när′), 49
BERNOULLI, DANIEL (bĕr′nōō′yē′), 297
BESSEMER, HENRY (bĕs′ĕmĕr), 208
Bessemer process, 208, 209
Betelgeuse (bē′t′l jōōz), 436
BETHE, HANS (bā′tĕ), 421
Bile, 41
Birds, 47, 122, 152, 165
Bivalves (bī′vălvz), 127
Blast furnace, 207
Bleeding: 118; arterial, 118
Blood: 37, 39, 41, 45–47, 48, 49, 50, 51, 52, 53, 54, 58, 103, 114, 118, 119, 124, 163, 224, 380; cells, 36, 37, 46, 85–86, 87; clots, 46; platelets, 46; pressure, 115, 375; stream, 239, 248, 249; vessels, 92; weather and, 375
Blubber, 141
Boats and ships, 10, 11, 13, 304, 311, 312, 313, 314
Body (machine): 31–73, 83, 112–115, 257; alcohol and, 114–115; and energy, 257; and fatigue, 112; and personal hygiene, 112–113; tea and coffee and, 114; tobacco and, 113
BOHR, NIELS (bōr), 18
Boilers, 305
Boiling and boiling point: 182, 183, 232; of liquid air, 232; of liquid nitrogen, 232; of liquid oxygen, 232; of water, 182
Bombsight, 347, 348, 350
Bones, 94, 95
Boom, of a derrick, 281, 282
BOONE, DANIEL, 10
Borax, 185, 210
Boric acid, 239
Boron (bō′rŏn), 95, 154
BOYLSTON, DR. ZABDIEL (boil′stŭn), 17
Brain, 63, 64–65, 103, 114, 141
Brass, 209
Breeding, of plants and animals, 170–176
Broadcasting, radio, 485–486
Bromides (brō′mīdz): 106; magnesium, 221, 222

Bromine (brō′mĭn), 210, 217, 221, 222, 226
Bronchi, bronchus (brŏng′kī), 58
Bronze, 209, 254
BRUNO, GIORDANO, 419
Brush, 329, 331
Bubonic plague (bŭ bŏn′ĭk), 79, 84, 89, 163
Bulb, electric light, 28, 238, 343, 451, 452, 454, 455, 456
Buna-S, 247
Butadiene (bū′tá dī′ēn), 247
Burning, 232, 233–234, 305
Butterflies, 162
Byproducts, 211, 241, 332

Cable: 325; electric, 364
Cadmium (kăd′mĭ ŭm): 184; borate, 458
Caffeine (kăf′ēn), 114
Calcium (kăl′sĭ ŭm): 94, 154, 184, 216, 217, 420; hydroxide, 239; symbol for, 183
Calendar, 418, 423
Calories, 91
Cams, 279
Canals, semicircular, of ears, 71
Cancer: constellation, 436; disease, 468
Candlepower, 454
Capillaries (kăp′ĭ lĕr′ĭz), 42, 48, 49, 57, 58, 118
Capillary action, 147
Carbohydrates (kär′bō hī′drāts), 91, 92, 136, 239, 240
Carbolic acid, 246
Carbon: 91, 154, 179, 180, 183, 184, 207, 208, 210, 211, 212, 244, 247, 293, 329, 484; dioxide (dī ŏk′sīd), 45, 51, 58, 91, 124, 136, 154, 187, 191, 207, 216, 220, 230, 231, 235, 237, 240–241, 257, 293, 307, 380, 409, 431; disulfide (dī sŭl′fīd), 244; monoxide (mŏn ŏx′īd), 207, 209, 234, 307
Carbonates (kär′bŏn āts), 217
Carbonic acid (kär bŏn′ĭk), 240
CARVER, GEORGE WASHINGTON, 248
Casein (kā′sē ĭn), 244
Cassiopeia (kăs′ĭ ō pē′yá), 436
Cathode (kăth′ōd); 222, 464, 465, 466, 469, 473; -ray tubes, 467
Caucasians (kô kā′shănz), 141, 490
Cellophane (sĕl′ō fān), 145
Cells: 34, 35, 37, 38, 50, 51, 59, 121, 457; and food, 94; connective, 36; epithelial, 36, 37; fat, 36; many-celled organisms, 36; membrane, 35; muscle, 36, 37, 50; nerve, 36, 61, 126; nucleus of, 35–36; of a plant, 132; one-celled organisms, 36; photo-

electric, 287, *288*, 464, 466, 471, 474; sex, 171, 173; specialized, 36; structure of, 35; tissues and, 36; Vorce, 220

Cellulose (sĕl′ū lōs), 136, 145, 244

Cement: 245; natural, 187

Centrifugal force (sĕn-trĭf′ū găl), 426

Ceramics (sĕ răm′ĭks), 210

Cerebellum (sĕr′ĕ bĕl′ŭm), 65

Cerebrum (sĕr′ĕ brŭm), 64, *65*, 66, 114, 115

Ceres (sē′rēz), planetoid, 430

Cesium (sē′zĭ ŭm), 95, 179, 466, 474

CHADWICK, SIR JAMES, 18

CHAMBERLIN, THOMAS C., 193

Changes: chemical, 181–182; in directions of force, 264; in forms of energy, 264–265; in temperature, *195*; nuclear, 181; of composition, 181; of earth, 193–197; of form, 181; physical, 181

Characteristics, physical, 173–175

Charcoal, 146, 179, 258

Chart, quality control, 349–350

Chemical: change, 181; compounds, 180, 183, 185, 186, 188, 190, 192, 207, 210, 211, 215, 217, 218, 220, 224, 225, 229, 236, 237, 239, 240, 246, 249, 258; equation, 187, 207, 220, 222, 231, 237; weathering, 194

Chemists and chemistry: 222, 243, 244, 245, 247, 248, 249, 250, 251, 353–354, 383, 460

Chemotherapy (kĕm′ō thĕr′ȧ pĭ), 249

Chemurgy (kĕm′ŭr jĭ), 248

CHEOPS, PHARAOH (kē′ŏps), 254

Cherrapunji (châr′ȧ pŭn′jĭ), 224

Chest, 58

Chlorination, of water, 226

Chlorine: 154, 179, 180, 183, 210, 217, 218, 220, 221, 222, 226; gas, 220

Chlorophyll (klō′rō fĭl), 135, 136, 137

Chloroplasts (klō′rō plăsts), *137*

Cholera (kŏl′ēr ȧ): 84; chicken, 80

Chromium (krō′mĭ ŭm), 208, 212, 243

Chromosomes (krō′mŏ sōms), 173

Cilia (sĭl′ĭ ȧ), 47, 139

Cinchona (sĭn kō′nȧ), 23, 249

Circuit: electric, 321–322, 324, 325, 326, 334, 335, 336, 338, 465, 486; breakers, *325*, 326, 336; short, 336

Circulation: 38, 47–54; and arterial bleeding, 118; atmospheric, 393; cells, *393*; of air, 407; systems, 38, 47–49, *56*

Circumference, 277

Civilization: machines and, 255, 284; resources and, 241; science and, 5–18, 26–28, 249–251, 369–371, 414, 438, 489–492

Clams, 127, *128*

Clay, 187, 210, 225, 245, 250

Climate: 204, 216, 219, 288, 375, 384, 408, 409, 411, 412, 413–415; and adaptation, 140; and mining, 204; changes in, 412; cities and, 414–415; control of, 409, 411, 413; roofs, and, 441

Clocks, 423

Clothing, 367, 407

Clouds: 224, 383, 384, 385, 386–388, 396, 398, 399, 401, 402, 403, 409, 470

Coagulation (kō ăg′ū lā′shŭn), 225

Coal: 190, 196, 205, 207, 211–212, 213, 232, *233*, 244, 245, 258, 264, 289, 294, 301, 313, 314, 318, 361, *442*, 443; gas, 211; tar, 211, 245, 249

Coastal plain, 195

Cobalt (kō′bôlt), 95, 324

Cochlea (kŏk′lē ȧ), 71, 72

Cocoon, 162

Coefficient-of-expansion apparatus, 353

Coil, 321, 322, 323, 324, 326, 328, 329, 331, 338, 339, 341, 342

Coke, 207, *208*, 209, 211

Cold wave, 396

Color, 421, 435

COLUMBUS, CHRISTOPHER, 212, 246

Combustion: 232, 233, 293; chamber, 314, 316

Comets, 419, 428–429

Communication: 12–13, 28, 377; interplanetary, 439

Commutator, 331, 342

Compass, magnetic, 321, 322

Composition, 181

Compounds. *See* Chemical compounds.

Compression: 229, *307*, 309, 310; of air, 229, 317, 318, 378, 379, 380, 384, 385, 397, 409, 477, 478; stroke, 309

Compressor, *344*

Computor, *284*

COMTE, AUGUSTE (kônt), 420

Concentration: electrical energy and, 334; of oxygen, 232

Concrete, 243

Condensation and condensing, 182, *223*, 386, 389, 397

Condenser, 302, 303, 304, 305, 313, *344*, 486

Conduction, 390, 407, 442

Conductor, *334*, 335, 336, 337, 343, 390, 407, 452, 481, 485

Cones, 68, *188*

Conjunctiva (kŏn′jŭngk tī′vȧ), 68

Consciousness, 62

Conservation: of energy, law of, 291; of forests, 149; of matter, law of, 292; of resources, 241; of soil, 155–157, 411; of wild life, 150–153

Constellations, 436

Constipation, 42

Consumer, science and, 27, 370

Convection, 390, 404, 407, *442*, 443, 444, 445

Conversion, 156

COOLIDGE, DR. WILLIAM C., 467

Cooperation: 18, 27–28, 226, 249–250, 363, 489, 492; and control of climate, 415; of peoples of world, 489, 492

Coordination, of nervous system, 61

COPERNICUS, NICOLAUS, (kŏ pûr′nĭ kŭs), 418

Copper: 95, 154, 179, 180, 184, 189, 209, 210, *211*, 212, 220, 221, 222, 329, 331, 336, 337, 340, 361, 390, 420, 421, 475; carbonates of, 209; oxide, 209; sulfate, 209; uses of, 209

Corals, 129, 187, 196, 200, 201, 216, 412

Cordite, 316

Corn, *171*, 408

Cornea, of eye (kôr′nĕ ȧ), 68

Corona, of sun (kŏ rō′nȧ), 428

Coronagraph (kŏ rō′nȧ grȧf), 428

Corpuscles, 46, 48, *58*, 86, *87*

Cosmic rays, 287

Cotton, *171*, 244, 248, 283, 336, 340, 351, 361, 377, 408; gin, 351

Cowpox, 17

"Cracking," 243, *245*

Crankshaft, 233, 307, 309

Craters, of moon, 425

Cricket, Mormon, *165*

Crops: 149, 153, 154, 155, 156, 157, 160, 161, 370, 377, 397, 410, 411, 414

Cryolite (krī′ō līt), 210

Culture: of bacteria, 80; pure, 80

CURIE, PIERRE and MARIE (kü-rē′), 180

Current: air, 229, 394; alternating, *328*, 329, 330, 331, 339, 342, 343, 344, 469, 472; convection, 390, 443, 444, 446; direct, 322, 330, 331, 339, 343, 465, 484; electric, 321, 322, 323, 324, 326, 327, 328, 329, 330, 331, 332, 334, 342, 343, 344, 452, 457, 463, 464, 466, 469, 471, 474, 484, 485; grid, 469; induced, 328, 339; ocean, 216, 229, 412, 413, 414; plate, 469; 60-cycle, 330; winds and, 393

Cutworms, 164
Cycle: of current, **329**, 330, 339, 472, 487; of sunspots, 421
Cyclonic storm, **400**, 401
Cyclotron (sī′klŏ trŏn), **344**
Cygni 61 (sĭg′nī), 432
Cylinder, **301**, 302, 303, 305, 306, 307, *308*, 309, 310

Daimler, Gottlieb (dām′lĕr), 307
Dampers, of a furnace, **234**
Day, **422**
DDT, **165**
Decibel (dĕs′ĭ bĕl), **482**
Deeps, of the ocean, **215**
Deflection, **394**, 395, 400
De Forest, Lee, 28, 464, 469
Density: of air, 298, 299, 397; of planets, **422**; of water, **422**
Dermis, **86**
Derrick, **281–282**
Desert, 3, 216, 384, 385, 410
Diabetes (dī′à bē′tēz), **249**
Diameter, 277, 278
Diamond: 185, 204, *205*; drills, **204**
Diaphragm (dī′à frăm): *57*, 58, *59*; of telephone, **325**; 484, 485, 486; sound waves and, *478*
Diathermy (dī′à thûr′mĭ), **472**
Diesel engines, **309–310**, 332
Diesel, Rudolf (dē′zĕl), 309
Diet, 91, 93, 94, 96–98, 106
Differential, of automobile, **279**
Diffusion, **41**
Digestion, **39**, 40–42, 54, 101
Dike, **219**, 411
Diode (dī′ōd), *464*, **465**, 466, 467, 468, 486
Diphtheria (dĭf′thẹr′ĭ à), 86, 87
Diseases: 7, 17, 21, 22, 56, 72, **75**, 76, 77, 79–89, 109, 112, 113, 248, 249, 468, 472; and forests, 148; communicable, **75**, 79–89; deaths from, 87, 88; deficiency, **91**; germs, 86, 225; noncommunicable, **75**; rules to prevent, 88–89; x-rays and, 468
Distance: 260, 263, 269, 272, 273, 274, 284, *419*, 425, 435; and work, **260**; around the earth, 394; measurement of, **354–355**; of stars, 435, 438
Distillation, *223*, **224**; destructive, '**211**
Dominance, in hybridization, **173**
Draco (drā′kō), constellation, 436
Drake, Colonel Edwin, 212
Drizzle, **388**, 389, 402
Dry ice, **235**, **241**, 409, 431
Ducts, **56**
Dwarfism, **102**
Dyes, 146, 207, 211, 220, 236, 245, 248

Dynamite, 27, 202
Dynamo (dī′nà mō), **327–328**. *See also* Generator.
Dysentery (dĭs′ĕn tĕr′ĭ), 84, 225

Ear, 71–73; of grasshopper, 126
Eardrum, **71**, 72
Earth: 135, 179, 184, 186, 191–197, 199–213, 359, 378, 379, 383, 390, 393–395, 412, 418, **419**, 420, 421, 422–425, 426, 427, 429, 431, 437, 438, 451
Earthquake, **195**, 203
Eclipse, 417, **427–428**
Edison, Thomas, A.: 28, 451, 452, 464, 465; effect, **464**
Education, science and, 5
Efficiency, **295**, 304, 307, 313, 458
Effort, 268, **272**, 273, 274, 276. *See also* Force, applied.
Eggs: of animals, **173**, 174; of insects, *161*, 162, 163; of plants, **132**, 173, 174, 175
Ehrlich, Paul (ār′lĭk), 249
Einstein, Albert (īn′stīn), 18, 292, 293, 421
Elasticity: of air, **378**, 379; of lungs, 58; of rubber, 247
Electric: bell, **325–326**; buzzer, 324–325, 338; current, 321, 322, 323, 324, 325, 326, 327, **329**, **463**, 485; disturbances, **421**; energy, 253, **257**, 290, 332, 334, 340, 341, *344*; generator, 254, 257, 328, 329, 331; industries, 209, 332; light, **451–453**, 456; light bulbs, 238, **451–452**; meters, 342–343; motor, 287, 341–343; plants, 313, 314, 332; power, 329, 334; wiring, 209, 210, 234, 321, 322, 328, 329
Electrical potential, **334**
Electricity: 6, 17, 28, 184, 203, 209, 210, 218, 220, 222, 231, 238, 287, 288, 289, 310, 313, 321–345, 367, 374, 377, 379, 380, 404, 411, 451, 455, 460, 473, 484; and metals, 203, 334; cost of, 332; discovery of, 18; energy of, **257**; meter for, 342; TVA and, 332; uses of, 344
Electrode (ê lĕk′trōd), **222**, 307
Electromagnet: **321**, 322–327, 331, 338, 342, 466, 485; iron as, 323
Electronic, and electronics (ê lĕk′trŏn′ĭk): **344**, 463–475; devices, 414, 449, 463, 475; copper and, 209; screen, 474
Electrons (ê lĕk′trŏnz): **180**, 203, 333, 334, 344, 359, 463, 464, 465, 466, 467, 469, 473; "beam" of, 473, 474, 475; of sunspots, 421; weight of, 333–**334**, 463

Elements: **91**, 95, 154, 179, 180, 181, 183, 184, 186, 188, 190, 192, 199, 203, 209, 215, 216, 217, 220, 222, 229, 231, 238, **239**, 293, 420, 421, 463, 465, 466; chemical, **91**, 420, 421; combinations of, 180; inert, **238**
Elevators: 283; of airplane, **298**
Ellipse, **424**
Enamel, 96, **336**
Energy: **3**, 4, 50, 136, 137, 180, 181, 211, 223, 232, 253, **256**–259, 267, 284, **287–299**, 302, 303, 307, 308, 311, 312, 451; atomic, 3, 4, 27, **181**, 203, 211, 223, 253, 259, **294**, 318, 344, 439; chemical, **257**, 264, 289, 290, 304, 321, 460; controllers of, **255**; electric, 253, **257**, 264, 288, 290, 309, 312, 321, 332, 334, 340, 341, *344*; kinetic, **258**, 261, 380; laws of, 291–294; matter and, 292; mechanical, **257**, 264, 287, 290, 304, 306, 311, *344*; of heat, **257**, 287, 304, 306, 341, 383, 384, 442; of human body, 91, 92, 94, 135; of light, **257**, 341, 451, 460; of muscles, 253, 254, 255; of sun (*solar*), 137, **287–289**, *290*, 383, 420, 421; potential, **258**, 261, 380; producers of, **255**; production in U. S., 289; radiant, **288**, 305, 383, 389, **443**; sound, **257**, 341, 479; transformation of, **257**, 264, **289**, 291, 292, 293
Engines: 267, 289, 291–292, 301–319; and energy, 264–265; and force, 265; and speed, 265, 308, 311, 313, 317, 318; coal-gas, 307; diesel, **309–311**; gasoline, 254, 287, *291*–292; high-pressure, **305**; internal-combustion, 233, **306–311**, 331, 332; jet, **317–318**; low-pressure, **305**; multicylinder, 308; reaction, **315–318**; reciprocating, **304**–311; rotary heat, **311–315**; solar, 290; steam, 287, 292, **301–305**, 306
Environment, 491, 492
Enzymes (ĕn′zīmz), **39**, 138, 139
Epidermis (ĕp′ĭ dûr′mĭs), **85**, *137*
Epiglottis (ĕp′ĭ glŏt′ĭs), **40**
Epsom salts, 222
Equator: 383, 384, 394, 400, 423; of sun, 421
Erosion, soil: 146, 147, 156, **194**, 195, 196, 200, 215, 226, 241, 370; prevention of, 156, 411, 414
Esophagus (ê sŏf′à gŭs), *39*, 40, 58
Ethylene dibromide (ĕth′ĭ lēn dī brō′mīd), 221

Eustachian tube (ŭ stā'kĭ ăn), 57, 58, 71, 72
Evaporation, **182,** *183,* 186, 200, 201, 219, 224
Exercise, value of, 53, 112
Expansion of: air, 384; steel, 353
Experimentation, nature of, 17, 21–25, 26–28, 79–82, 135, 170–176, 243–251, 259, 297–299, 301–310, 316–318, 321–323, 350, 352–354, 361–366, 373–378
Experiments: **22;** control, **23,** 25
Explosives, 27, 207, 236, 248, 259
Extrusive rock (ĕks trōō'sĭv), **189**
Eyes, 68–70, 125, **126,** 127, 324, 330, 474, 475

Faraday, Michael (făr'*à* dā), 28, 327, 328
Farmers and farming, 248, 289, 374, 375, 397, 404, 411
Fats, 37, 41, 92, 136, 141
Fault, of rock, 195, *196*
Fermentation, **79**
FERMI, ENRICO (fär'mĕ), 18
Ferns, 132
Fertilization: animals and, 173, 174; of plant cell, **132,** 174, 175
Fertilizer, **156,** 236, 237
Fever, 84, *88, 89,* 163, 225, 472
Filaments, 145, 343, 452, 456, 464, 465; tungsten, 453
Filtering, water, 225–226
Fire: 4, 148, 149, 179, 233, 234, 377, 410; control, 149, 234–235
Firefly, 460
First aid, **116–119**
Fish, 47, **124**
Fleas, 163
FLEMING, JOHN AMBROSE, 28, 464, 465; tube, or valve, **464,** 465
Flies, 163, 165, 174
Flint, 185, 212
Floods: 146, 375 410–411
Flow, rate of, **334**
Fluid: 229, 283, **297,** 298, 390; Bernoulli's principle and, 297; drive, of automobile, 280; in body, 38; Pascal's law, and, **283**
Flume, **312**
Fluorescence (flōō'ŏ rĕs'ĕns), **203,** 467
Fluorescent: lamps, 343, *456,* 458; materials, 474; uses of, 458
Fluorine (flōō'ŏ rĭn), 95, 154
Fluoroscope (flōō'ŏ rŏ skōp), **468**
Flying, 374, 381, 384, 388, 403, 404
Flywheel, 307, 308
Focus, 69, **290,** 459
Fog, 216, 235, 241, 375, 385, 386, 388, 389, 396, 397, 398, 399, 409, 470
Folds, of rock, 195, *196*

Foods: 5, 38–44, 45, 49, 51, 54, 79, 80, 90, 109, 135, 141, 162, 196, 226, 241, 250, 257, 289, 367, 407, 475; fuel, 442; pasteurization of, 80; protective, **96;** rotting of, 234; science and, 5, 367
Foot-candle, **454;** meter, **454**
Foot-pounds, **260,** 269, 272, 295
Force: **259–261,** 262, 263, 264, 265, 268, 269, 273, 277, *282,* 283, 284, 294, 299, 382; and direction, 264, 278; and law of machines, 269; and work, 260; applied, 268, 269, **272,** 273, 277, 279, 280, 281; centrifugal, **426;** energy and, 287; frictional, **294–**299; gears and, 278; inclined plane and, 270, 271; lever and, 272, 273; moment of, **274,** 276; of electric current, 334; of wheel and axle, 277; resistance, 269, 272, 278, **294,** 229; unit of, **382**
FORD, HENRY, 361, 362
Forests, 145–150, 155, 156, 397, 398, 414
Form: changes in, **181;** of air masses, **396;** of clouds, 386, 388
Formaldehyde (fôr măl'dĕ hīd), **246,** 431
Formula: chemical, **183,** 207, 209, 216, 220, 222, 236, 239, 240; Einstein's, **293;** of electricity, **335**
Fort Peck Dam, 413
Fossils, **169,** *187,* **188,** 412
Four-stroke engine, **306,** 307, 309
FRANKLIN, BENJAMIN, 5, 13, 17, 27
Freezing: 183, 389; point, **183,** 386
Frequency: of a current, 472, 486; of sound, 479, 480, 487
Friction: 260, 263, 268, 284, 291, 294–299, 379, 429; and air front, 400; and bearings, 296; and lubrication, *295,* 296; uses of, 295
Fronds, of fern, **132**
Front, air, **397, 400–**403, 404
Frost, 377, **386,** *410*
Fruits: 42, 93, 96, 209, 397; citrus, **92,** 377
Fuel: 135, **211,** 212, 232, **233,** 235, 243, 257, 258, 267, 287, 289, 290, 302, 305, 306, 309, 316, 317, 318, 439, 448; as source of energy, 135, 287, 290; injector, 309; mineral, 212; oil, 232, 314, 317; splitting of, **232**
Fulcrum, **272,** 273, 274, 353
FULTON, ROBERT, 303
Fungi (fŭn'jī), **133,** 154, 468
Furnace, **207,** 234, 334, 443, 444, 445, 471
Furrows, **157**

Fuse, 336
Fuselage (fū'zĕ läzh'), **363,** 364
Gage: precision, 349; rain, 373
Galactic System (gà lăk'tĭk), **437**
GALILEO (găl'ĭ lē'ō), 425, 431, 436, 437
GALLE, JOHANN (gäl'ĕ), 430
Gallium (găl'ĭ ŭm), 179
Galvanometer (găl'và nŏm'ĕ tēr), **326,** 328, 329, 338, 464, 471
Gamma rays, 203
Ganglia, ganglion (găng'glĭ à), **62**
Gases: 179, 182, 184, 189, 191, 199, 207, 209, 216, 221, 224, 229, 230, 231, 233, 234, 237–241, 247, 291, 297, 306, 316, 318, *344,* 378, 379, 380, 390, 420, 428, 438, 443, 481; compression of, 229; friction and, 297; from petroleum, 212; inert, **238;** marsh, 431; natural gas, 196, **212,** *213;* of comet, 428; of sun, 420, 428
Gasoline, 212, 213, 221, *233,* 234, **239,** 243, **244,** *245,* 248, 254, 259, 264, 287, 291, 292, 306–311, 314, 317
Gastric juice, **41**
Gears: 267, 268, 271, **278–280,** 291
Geiger counter (gī'gēr), *3,* **204**
Gelatin, 80, 94
Generator: 254, 257, 287, 291, 312, *313,* 314, *326,* 328, 329, 330, 331, 332, 342, 343, 374; alternating current, *328;* direct current, *331;* electric, 332, 334; high-voltage, 331; hydroelectric, 332; motor, *326,* 343
Genes, 173–174, 175
Genetics and geneticists (jĕ nĕt'ĭks), **172,** 177, 489
Geocentric theory (jē'ŏ sĕn'trĭk), **418**
Geologist (jē ŏl'ŏ jĭst), 190, 192, 195, 202, 203, 204, 212, 238
Geology (jē ŏl'ŏ jĭ), **204**
Germanium (jûr mā'nĭ ŭm), 179
Germs: 21, 79–82, 83, 84, 85–86, 87, 113, *115,* 225, 226, 249, 457
Getters, 453
Giantism, 103
Gills and gill slits, **124,** 127, *128*
Glacier, *181,* *195,* 412
Glands, 36, **37,** 39, 45, 56, 102–**103,** 105, 122, 126, 248
Glass, 243, 244, 246, *334,* 336, 456, 457, 459, 481
Glaze, 389
Glottis (glŏt'ĭs), *480*
Glucose (glōō'kōs), **39,** 239
Glycogen (glī'kŏ jĕn), 49, 50
Gneiss (nīs), **190**

Gnomon (nō'mŏn), 423
GODDARD, DR. ROBERT, 317
Goiter, 95
Gold: 179, 180, **184**, 185, 189, 192, 200, 201, 205, 209, 212, 236, 420; panning for, **200**, 205
GOLDBERGER, JOSEPH, 93
GOODYEAR, CHARLES, 247
Gophers, pocket, 160
Gradient, of atmosphere (grā'dĭ ĕnt), **394**
Gram, **334**, **355**
Grand Coulee Dam, 332, 397, 414
Granite, *184*, **189**, 190, 194 *195*
Grasshoppers, 164
GRASSI, BATTISTA (gräs'sē), 22
Gravel, 205, 225
Gravimeter (gră vĭm'ē tēr), **203**, 359
Gravity and gravitational pull: 203, 258, 259, 260, 263, 268, 287, 289, 294, 380, 422, **426**, 427; center of, **274**, 275, 276, 279; law of, 263, **426**, 430
Great Salt Lake, 200, 218
"Greenhouse effect," *382*, **383**
Greenwich (grĭn'ĭj), England, 423
Grid, **28**, **469**, 471, 472, 474, 486
Gulf Stream, **215**, 393, 413, 415
Gunpowder, **258**
Gypsum (jĭp'sŭm), **185**, 210

Haber, Fritz (hä'bēr), 237
Hail, **389**, 410
Hair cells, of ear, **72**
HALE, GEORGE ELLERY, 421
Halite (hăl'īt), 185
HALL, CHARLES MARTIN, 210
Halley's comet (hăl'ĭz), 429
Hammer, of ear, **71**
Hands, 141, *142*, 351, 352
Health: 5, 38, **75–78**, 83, 91–100, 101, **109–117**, 240, 3'70, 475; national, **109–111**; science and, 5; weather and, 375
Hearing, **71**
Heart: *39*, 47–49, 50–51, 53, 56, 59, 115, 358; force of, 259
Heat and heating: 91, 182, 184, 211, 212, 215, 216, 219, 222, 224, 232, 233–234, 246, 257, 263, 287, 288, 289, 290, 291, 306, 311, 323, 330, 336, 343, 349, 379, 380, **383–384**, 389, 390, 393, 407, 408, 420, 429, 441–449, 451–461, 463, 472; conduction of, **390**, 442; convection of, **390**, **443**; copper, and, 184, 209; electricity and, 343; friction and, **294**; law of energy of, **292**; of rocks, 188, 190; radiant, **447**; radiation of, **389**, 443; resistance and, 336; solar, **407**, 421, 448; solar en-

ergy and, **238**, 289, 290; transfer, 389, 390, 442
Height: of air, 379, 383; of clouds, 386, *387*, 388
Heliocentric theory (hē'lĭ ō sĕn'trĭk), **419**
Helium (hē'lĭ ŭm), 180, 203, **238–239**, 421
HELMONT, JAN BAPTISTA VAN (vän hĕl'mŏnt), 135
Hematite (hĕm'ȧ tīt), 206, 207
Hemisphere, 394, 395, 405, 418
Hemoglobin (hē'mō glō'bĭn), **46**, 95
HENRY, JOSEPH, 321, 327, 328
HERSCHEL, WILLIAM (hûr'shĕl), 430, 437
HERTZ, HEINRICH (hĕrts), 28
Home, science and, 5–7, 441–487
Honeydew, **164**
HOOKE, ROBERT, 34
Hoover Dam, *288*, 332, 340, 413
Hormones, **103**, 248
Horses: 169, 175; horse latitudes, **396**; horsepower, **261**, 262, 307, 309, 332
Houses and housing: 5, 6, 7, 8, 407, 441–442, *447*; science and, 5, 6, 367, 441–487
HUBBLE, EDWIN P., 438
HUMASON, MILTON (hŭ'mȧ sŭn), 438
Humidity: 350, 375, 377, 395, 407, 448, 449; relative, **385**, 386, 449
Humid regions, **194**
Humus, **154**, 157
Hurricane, 374, 377, **404**
Hybrids and hybridization (hī'brĭdz), **171**, 172–175, **490**
Hydraulic (hī drô'lĭk): mining, 205, *206*; machine, **282**, 284; pressure, 282–284
Hydrocarbons, (hī'drō kär'bŏnz), **239**, 243
Hydrochloric acid (hī'drō klō'rĭk), 239
Hydroelectric power and power plants (hī'drō ē lĕk'trĭk), 332, *339*, 340
Hydrogen (hī'drō jĕn), 154, 180, *181*, 184, 207, 211, 212, 220, 236, 237, 238, **239**, 244, 247, 293, 420, 421
Hydrogenation of coal (hī'drō jĕn ā'shŭn), 244
Hydrosphere (hī'drō sfēr), **192**, 229
Hygrometer (hī grŏm'ē tēr), **385**

Ice: 182, 194, **389**, 412, 431; crystals, 386, 388
Inconoscopes (ī kŏn'ō skōps), **473**

Igneous rocks (ĭg'nē ŭs), 188–189, 191, 196
Illumination, **454**
Immunity, specific, **86**, 87
Impulse, nerve, **62**, 71
Inclination of earth's axis, **424**
Inclined plane, 269–272, 350
Incubation period, 87
Indians, 212, 490
Indigo, 244, 247
Induction, **328**, 338
Industrial Revolution, 73, 303–304
Industry, 216, 220, 231, 232, 236, 237, 248, 287, 289, 292, 295, 303, 304, 366, 368, 370, 468
Infections, 113, 118, 249, 474
Inheritance, 492
Inoculation and inoculating (ĭn ŏk'ŭ lā'shŭn), **17**, *86*, 87, 89
Insecticides (ĭn sĕk'tĭ sīdz), **163**
Insects: **22**, 47, 87, 88, 89, 123, **125–126**, *127*, 131, 132, 148, 161–166, 491
Inspection, sample, 349–350
Instincts, 491
Insulation, 292, 322, **407–408**
Insulators, 210, 246, 334, **336**, 340, 474
Insulin (ĭn'sŭ lĭn), **249**
Intake ports, *307*, 310
Intelligence: 141, 490, *491*; tests, **490**, 491
Intensity: of light, 453–454, 460, 474; of sound waves, 203, **479**, 482
Intercellular spaces (ĭn'tēr sĕl'ŭ lēr), **54**, 56
Internal-combustion engine, **233**, 306–311, 331
Intestine, *39*, 40, 41, 42, 48, *128*
Intrusive rock, **188**, *200*
Inventions and discoveries, 16, 18, 73, 79–82, 136, 173–175, 193, 230, 237, 238, 244–249, 254, 255, 259, 283, 297, 301–304, 307, 309, 321, 351, 361, 362–365, 375, 381, 409, 418, 419, 420, 421, 426, 428, 429, 430, 431, 436, 437, 438, 451, 464, 46'
Invertebrate animals (ĭn vûr'tē brȧt), **125–131**
Iodine (ī'ō dīn), 95, 118, 154, 22
Ions (ī'ŏnz), **220**
Iris (ī'rĭs), of eye, **68**
Iron: 91, 94, 95, 154, 179, 180 **184**, 185, 187, 192, 200, 201 205, 206–209, 212, 217, 234 245, 322, 323, 324, 336, 390 420, 429, 442
Irrigation, **156**, 271, 397, 410, 411 414

Jefferson, Thomas, 27
JENNER, EDWARD (jĕn'ēr), 87

Jet engines, 169, **317–318**
Jig, **363**, 364
Joint, of rock, **195**
JOLIOT, IRÈNE and FRÉDERÍC, (zhô′lyō′), 18
Jupiter, 419, 422, 429, 431, 436

Kapitza, Peter (ká′pyĭ tsŭ), 18
KELLY, WILLIAM, 208
Kelp plants, 221
Kerosene, 243
Kidney, *39, 128*
Kilowatt and kilowatt-hour (kĭl′ô wŏt): 313, **332;** meter, **343**
Kinescope (kĭn′ĕ skōp), **473**, 474
Kinetic energy, **258**
KOCH, ROBERT (kŏk), 80–81
Krypton (krĭp′tŏn), 238, 294; krypton–82, 294

Labor, science and, 365, 369
Lamp, **343**, **452**, 453, 456, 457, 458
LANGEN, EUGENE (läng′ĕn), 307
Lanital (lăn′ĭ tăl), **244**
Larvas, larva (lär′vảz), 161, 162, 163, 164
Latex (lā′tĕks), **247**
Latitude, 393, 394, 396, 423
Lava, 186, **189**, 195
Law: 25; natural, **263;** of energy, 291–294; of gravitation, 263, **426**, 430; of machines, **263, 269,** 273; of motion, **260, 316, 426,** 430; Ohm's, **335,** 336; Pascal's, **283**
LAWRENCE, ERNEST O., 18
Laxatives (lăk′sả tĭvz), **42,** 76, 77, **102**
Lead, 179, 180, 184, 189, 200, 212, 220
LEEUWENHOEK, ANTON VAN (vän lā′ vĕn hōōk), 79
Legumes (lĕg′ūmz), **156,** 236, 237
LENOIR, ÉTIENNE (lĕ nwár′), 307
Lens: convex, **459,** 460; focal length of, **460;** of human eye, 69; of insect's eye, *126;* of spectroscope, 238; of telescope, 436; of television set, 474
Levels, of air masses, 395–396
LEVERRIER, URBAIN (lĕ vĕ′ryā′), 430
Levers, 254, 268, **269,** 272–276, 278, 281, 284, 302, 350, 353, 381, 385
Lice, 163
LIEBIG, JUSTUS VON (lē′bĭk), 439
Life-expectancy, science and, 7
Life-functions, **33,** 91, 135
Light: **66, 67,** 68–70, 136, 222, 238, **257,** 287, 289, 290, 375, 383, 420, 437, 443, 463, 464, 466, 474; absorbed, **67;** "cold,"

460; electricity and, 343–344; glare of, 454, 455; mirrors and, 459; reflected, **66;** solar energy and, 288; speed of, **293, 435;** television and, 473–475; white, 67
Lighting, 451–461
Lightning, 17, 257, **288,** 334, 335, 383, 403, 404, 481
Light-year, **435,** 438
Lignin (lĭg′nĭn), **145**
Lignite, or brown coal, **211**
LILLIE, DR. RALPH (lĭl′ĭ), 62
Lime, *155,* 187
Limestone, **187,** 188, 193, 194, 207, 216, 240, 361
Linters, **244**
LIPPERSHEY, JAN (lĭp′ĕrs hī), 436
Liquid air, **232**
Liquids, 179, **182,** 199, 221, 231, 247, 297, 378, 390, 443, 475, 481
Liter (lē′tĕr), **355**
Lithosphere (lĭth′ô sfḗr), **191,** 192
Liver, *39,* 41, 49–50, *128*
Living: standard of, 258; things, 4, *33,* 121–178
Lockjaw, **87**
LOCKYER, JOSEPH N. (lŏk′yĕr), 238
Locomotive, 304, 305, 314
LONGFELLOW, HENRY W., 12
Longitude (lŏn′jĭ tūd), **423,** 436
Loudspeakers, 485
LOWELL, DR. PERCIVAL, 431
Lubrication, *295,* **296–297**
Lucite (lū′sīt), 246, 461
Lungs, **39,** 45, 51, *57,* 58, 122, 124, 206
Lye, 220
Lymph (lĭmf), *42,* **51,** 56, 85
Lymphatics (lĭm făt′ĭks), **56**

Machine Age, **253,** 254, 255, 267, 287, 296, 328, 365
Machinery, 253, 288, 309, 343, 347–359, 366, 482
Machines: 4, 9, 15, 212, 243, 245, 253–299; and energy, 264; and force, 262, 263, 264; and speed, 263; complex, **269,** 284; efficiency of, **295;** law of, **262, 269,** 273, 295; perpetual motion and, 263; progress and, 256; simple, **267, 268, 269–285,** 350, 380; tool-making, 350
MACINTOSH, CHARLES, 246
Magic, 16
Magma (măg′mả), **188,** 196, 199
Magnesium (măg nē′ zhĭ ŭm): 154, 179, 180, 184, 210, 217, *221,* 222, 223, 226, 353, 361, 475; bromide, 222; chloride, 222; oxide, 353, 354; tungstate, 458

Magnet: 321, **322,** 328, 331; field, **342;** horseshoe, 328, **331**
Magnetic compass, 321, 322
Magnetic field, **322,** 323, 324, 326, 327, 328, 329, 330, 338, 341, 342
Magnetic induction, **328**
Magnetism, **322,** 328
Magneto (măg nē′tō), **331**
Magnitude, of stars, **435**
Malaria, **21–24,** 85, 249
Malnutrition, **91,** 92, 96
Mammals, **47, 122,** 153
Man, 121, 262, 141, 407, 489–491
Manganese (măng′gả nēs), *95,* 154, 208, 212, 243
Manufacturing, 361
Maps: 423; weather, 376, 378, 398
Marble, 190
MARCONI, GUGLIELMO (mär kō′nē), 28
Mars, 429, 430–431
Mass-energy conversion equation, 293, 421
Mass production: 9, 15, 358, **361– 366;** disadvantages of, 365–366
MATHER, COTTON (măth′ĕr), 17
Matter: 291, 292, 293, 463, 481; conservation of, 291, **292**
MAXWELL, JAMES CLERK, 28
Meade, Lake, 413
Measurement: of air, **381,** 382; of rainfall, **373;** precise, 347–359; systems of, **354–355**
Mechanical advantage: **268,** 270, 272, 273, 277, 278, 281, 287, 380
Mechanical energy. *See* Energy.
Medicine and medical care: 5, 16, 38, 83, 109, 110, 111, 115, 211, 231, 248, 475; Blue Cross Hospitalization Plan, 111; electron microscope and, 475; Group Health Association of Washington, D. C., 111; group health plans, 110–111; Hospital Service of California, 110; National Health Insurance Plan, of England, 110; problems of, 111; science and, 5; timing and, 358; x-rays and, 468
Medulla oblongata, (mĕ dŭl′ả ŏb′ lŏng gä′tả), 65
Melting: **182;** point, **182,** 183, 188, 199, 336, 452
Membrane: 58; mucous, **39,** 41, *42,* 93, 114; of a cell, **35;** of the ear, 72
MENDEL, GREGOR (mĕn′dĕl), 173– 175, 489
Mercury: metal, 179, **381,** 382, 457, 458; planet of, 429, 431, 432; vapor, 343, 456, 457, 458
Meridian: 423; prime, 423

Metabolism (mě tăb'ŏ lĭz'm), 33, 37, 91, 135

Metals: 184, 199, 200, 203, 207, 212, 218, 222, 226, 334, 353, 442, 463, 464, 468, 475, 484

Metamorphic rocks (mět'à môr'fĭk), 190, 191, 207

Metamorphosis (mět'à môr'fŏ sĭs), 161–162

Meteor Crater, Arizona, 429

Meteorites (mě'tĕ ĕr īts), 192, 425, 429

Meteorologist (mě'tĕ ĕr ŏl'ŏ jĭst), 375, 376, 378, 390

Meteors, 230, 379, 419, 429

Meter, 342, 343, 355, 454

Methane (mĕth'ān), 212, 239

Mica (mī'kà), 185, 190, 207, 486

Mice, 160, 161, 474

Micrometer (mī krŏm'ĕ tẽr), 271

Micron (mī'krŏn), 451

Microorganisms, 75, 79, 80, 81, 84

Microphone, 484, 485, 486

Microscope: 79, 80, 348, 350, 359; electron, 359, 474, 475

Milk, 84, 89, 93, 94, 95, 96, 109, 122, 244, 438, 457

Milky Way, 437, 438

Millibars, 382

Mind, 101

Minerals, 38, 94, 136, 154, 155, 156, 157, 185, 186, 190, 192, 194, 196, 199, 200, 203, 212, 213, 215, 217, 226

Mining and mineral deposits, 199–213, 301, 302, 303

Mirrors, and light, 459–460

Mist, 398

Mixture, 181

Modulation, frequency, 486

Moisture, 224, 384, 385, 386, 396, 397, 398

Molars, of a deer, 138

Molds, 114, 133, 457, 468

Molecule (mŏl'ĕ kūl), 180, 181, 182, 183, 224, 229, 244, 287, 378, 383, 442, 443

Mollusks (mŏl'ŭsks), 127

Molybdenum (mŏ lĭb'dĕ nŭm), 154, 184, 208

Mongoloid (mŏng'gŏl oid), 490

Monopolies, 368, 370

Montgolfier, Joseph and Jacques (mŏnt gŏl'fĭ ēr), 379

Moon, 359, 419, 425–428, 431, 439

Mosquitoes: 22–25, 85; anopheles, (à nŏf'ĕ lēz), 22, 23, 24, 26, 130; culex (kū'lĕks), 22, 23

Moth, clothes, 162–163

Motion: 18, 50, 182, 257, 258, 259, 260, 264, 304, 328, 341, 378, 383, 477; changes in direction of, 264, 279; energy of (kinetic), 257, 258, 341; force

and, 259; heat and, 442; laws of, 260, 314, 426, 430; molecular, 383, 472; of electron beam, 474; of winds, 394; sound wave and, 477

Motor: 341–343; -generator, 343

Moulton, Forest R. (mōl'tŭn), 193

Mouth: 39; of animals, 138; of insects, 163; of a squid, 127

Muscles, 36–37, 40, 42, 53, 58, 62, 65, 68, 102, 127, 128, 129, 253, 254, 255

Mutations, 172, 176

Naphtha, (năf'thà), 234

Nasal cavity, 40, 58

National Health Survey, 110

Nationality, 489

National Park Service, 153

Nebulas (nĕb'ŭ làz), 438

Negative: charges, 463, 469; pole, 465; terminal, 323

Negroes, 141, 490

Negroid, 489, 490

Nematode, golden (nĕm'à tōd), 164

Neon lights (nē'ŏn), 238, 334

Neoprene (nē'ŏ prĕn), 247

Neptune, planet, 430

Nerves, 37, 53, 61–65, 114

Nervous system: 38, 61–65, 73, 114; alcohol and, 114–115; central, 62; involuntary, 63; 64; voluntary, 64–65

Neutral charges, 463

Neutrons (nū'trŏnz), 180, 181, 463

Newcomen, Thomas (nū kŭm'ĕn), 301

Newton, Sir Isaac, 18, 259, 260, 316, 425, 430

Nicholson, Seth B., 431

Nichrome (nī'krōm), 452

Nickel, 95, 192, 208, 210, 212, 324, 420, 429

Nicotine (nĭk'ŏ tēn), 113–114, 164

Night, 422

Nitrates (nī'trāts), 154, 237

Nitric acid (nī'trĭk), 236, 237, 239

Nitrobenzene (nī'trŏ bĕn'zēn), 236

Nitrogen (nī'trŏ jĕn): 154, 155, 156, 179, 180, 191, 230, 231, 232, 236–237, 238, 239, 380, 452; fixations, 236, 237; liquid, 232; oxides, 237

Nobel, Alfred (nŏ bĕl'), 27

Nodes, lymph, 56

Nodules (nŏd'ūlz), 236, 237

Noise, 482

Nonconductors, 334

Nonmetals, 184, 212

North Atlantic Drift, 413

North Star, 436

Nuclear change (nū'klĕ ẽr), 181

Nucleus: of atom, 180, 181, 463; of cell, 35, 36

Nutrition, 91

Nylon, 244–245, 247, 248

Observatory, 421, 430, 431, 432, 438

Oculist, 70

Oersted, Hans (ûr'stĕd), 321, 322, 328

Ohm, 335, 336

Ohm, George (ōm), 335, 336

Oil: 196, 202, 212, 213, 232, 235, 282, 283, 284, 289, 310, 336, 349, 361, 442, 443; crude, 243; edible, 248; fuel, 232 233, 314, 317, 318; lubricating, 212. See also Petroleum.

Open-hearth process, 208, 209

Open-pit mining, 205, 307

Ophthalmologist (ŏf'thăl mŏl'ŏ jĭst), 70

Oranges, 374, 377, 397

Orbit: of comets, 428, 429; of earth, 424; of particles, 463

Ore, 189, 199, 200, 201–204, 205, 212, 223, 324

Organic material, 194

Organs: 38; abdominal, 49, 54, 58; internal, 39; reproductive, of plants, 131; sense, 62; vital, 63

Oscilloscope (ŏ sĭl'ŏ skōp), 439

Osmosis (ŏs mō'sĭs), 41, 42, 224

Otto, Nikolaus August, 307

Overtones, 480

Oxidation (ŏk'sĭ dā'shŭn), 46, 50, 232, 233, 236

Oxyacetylene torch (ŏk'sĭ à sĕt'ĭ-lēn), 231, 232

Oxygen (ŏk'sĭ jĕn): 45, 46, 48, 51, 58, 91, 124, 154, 179, 180, 181, 184, 191, 193, 201, 206, 207, 208, 209, 210, 216, 220, 226, 229, 230, 231, 232, 233, 234, 235, 236, 239, 246, 293, 317, 353, 380, 452, 453; liquid, 232, 317, 439; masks, 239, 380

Oysters, 127, 221

Pacific Ocean, 129, 221, 222, 383, 395, 397, 398, 405, 413

Paint, 408

Palate, 40; soft, 40, 58

Pancreas and pancreatic juice: 39, 41, 103, 249; pancreas islets, 103

Panning, gold, 200

Paper, 145, 336, 472

Parachute, 377

Paraffin (păr'à fĭn), 212

Parallels, of latitude, 423

Paramecia (păr'à mē'shĭ à), 61, 130

Parasites, 79

Parathyroid (păr′à thī′roid), *103*

Particle, 180, 220, 233, 344, 463

Parts, **351**–**352**, 361, 363

PASCAL, BLAISE (păs′kăl′), 283; law of, **283**

Pasteur, Louis (päs tûr′), 79, 87

Pasteurization (păs′tēr ĭ zā′shŭn), **80**

PAULI, WOLFGANG (pow′lĕ), 18

Peanut, 248

PEARY, ADMIRAL ROBERT E., 429

Pébrine (pā′brēn′), 80

Pegasus (pĕg′à sŭs), 436

Pellagra (pĕ lā′grà), **93**

Penicillin (pĕn′ĭ sĭl′ĭn), 28, 109, *114, 115,* 249

Penstock, **312**

Penumbra (pĕ nŭm′brà), *427,* **428**

Peristalsis (pĕr′ĭ stăl′sĭs), **40**, *41*

PERKIN, WILLIAM, 245

Perseid shower (pûr′sĕ ĭd), 429

Personality: 91,**101**, 105–106, 249, 490; and race, 491–492

Pests, 159–167

Petroleum, 211, 212, *213,* 243, 247, 289, 296

Pharynx (făr′ĭngks), *57,* **58**

Phases, of moon, **426**

Phonograph, 485, 486–487

Phosphates, 212

Phosphorus, 91, 94, 154, 155, 156, 184, 207

Photoelectric cell, **287**, *288,* 464, 466–467, 471, 474

Photography: 246, 420, 437, 454; films for, 236, 248; photoflash bulbs for, 222

Photosynthesis (fō′tō sĭn′thĕ sĭs), **137**, 230, 240, 289

PIAZZI, GIUSEPPE (pyät′sĕ), 430

PICKERING, W. H., 431

Pistil, **131**, 132

Pistons, 233, 264, 283, 284, **302**, 303, 306, 307, 310, 311

Pitch, sound and, **479**, 480

Pituitary gland (pĭ tū′ĭ tĕr′ĭ), 103

Plane, inclined, **269**–**272**, 284

Planet, 192, 317, 418, **419**, 429–*433,* 435

Planetoids, **419**, **430**

Plants: 4, 83, 84, **131**–**133**, 135–137, 154, 169, 193, 194, 200, 209, 211, 212, 221, 230, 236, 289, 380; adaptation of, 139

Plasma (plăz′mà), 45, 46, 54, 220

Plastic and plastics, 145, **188**, 213, 243, **246**, 248, *250,* 475

Plate, metallic, *464,* **465**, 469, 473

Plexiglas" (plĕks′ĭ glăs), **246**, 461

Plumb bob, **275**

Pluto, planet, 430, 435

Plutonium (plōō tō′nĭ ŭm), 181, 184, 258, 294

Plywood, 146, 475

Poisons, 119, 160, **163**, **164**

Polar regions, 393, **396**

Polaris (pō lā′rĭs), 436

Pole: **322**, 330, 331, 338, 393, 394; North, 423

Pollen, and pollination, **131**, 132

Polymerization (pŏl′ĭ mĕr ĭ zā′shŭn), 243–**244**, *245,* 247

Polythene (pŏl′ĭ thēn′), 246

Pore-bearers, **130**

Positive: charge, 469; pole, 465; terminal, 323

Potash (pŏt′ăsh), 212

Potassium (pō tăs′ĭ ŭm): 154, 155, 156, 184, 210, 217, 421; hydroxide, 239

Power: 261, 262, 271, 307, 332; resources of, 332; stroke, 307

Precipitation (prē sĭp′ĭ tā′shŭn), *399,* **411**

Precipitron (prē sĭp′ĭ trŏn), 449

Precision measurement, 347–359

Pressure, *182,* 232, 235, 238, 239, 240, 268, 282, 283, 284, 297, 305, 309, 314, 316, 395, 478; and friction, 294; Bernoulli's principle, and, 297; electrical, 330, 332; high-pressure areas, **394**, 396, 400; low-pressure areas, **394**, 395, 400; Pascal's law, and, 283; on rocks, 188, 190, 193, 195; points, *118*

PRIESTLEY, JOSEPH, 230, 246

Principle, **25**

Prism, **238**

Production: biological, 177; mass, 9, 15, 358, **361**–**366**

Propellers, 233, 271, 277, 298, 299, 313, 318

Proteins (prō′tē ĭnz), **40**, 91, 94, *95,* 96, 136

Protons (prō′tŏnz), **180**, 181, 463

Protoplasm (prō′tō plăz′m), **34**

Protozoa (prō′tō zō′à), 79, 121, 130

Proxima Centauri (prŏk′sĭ mà sĕn tô′rī),435

Ptyalin (tī′à lĭn), **39**

Pulleys, **281**–**282**

Pulse, **52**

Pupa (pū′pà), *161*

Pus, **86**, 93

Pushers, 305

Pyrometer (pī rŏm′ĕ tēr), **471**

Pyroxylin (pī rŏk′sĭ lĭn), 248

PYTHAGORAS (pĭ thăg′ō răs), 419

Quality, of tones, **480**

Quarantine, 79

Quarries, 205

Quartz (kwôrts), **184**, 185, 194, 199, 457

Quartzite (kwôrts′ĭt), **190**

Quinine (kwī′nīn), *23,* **109**, 249

Races: of ball bearing, **350**; of man, 489–490, 491

Radar (rā′där), 169, 344, *381,* 439, *467,* **470**

Radiant: energy, **288**, 305, 383, 389, **443**; heating, 447–448

Radiation, **288**, 38℃, 390, 407, 408; 424, *442,* **443**

Radio (rā′dĭ ō): 13, 28, 209, 210, 326, 344, 365, 368, 377, 378, 469–470, **485**–**486**; beams, 470; compass, 470; FM, 486; long wave, 486; runway localizer and guide path, **470**; short wave, 486; sunspots and, 421; time and, 357; tube, 464

Radioactivity, **181**

Radiometer (rā′dĭ ŏm′ĕ tēr), **257**

Radiosonde (rā′dĭ ō sŏnd′), **377**

Radiotelephone, 13, 267

Radium (rā′dĭ ŭm), 180, 203, 204, 294

Radius, **277**, 278

Railroads, 11, 13, 304

Rain and rainfall: 147, 154, 156, 157, 192, 193, 194, 201, 217, 224, 237, 257, 288, 373, 375, 383, 384, 386, 388, 389, 397, 398, 399, 402, 404, 408, 409, 410, 411, 414

Ramjet engine, **317**

Rate: of flow, **334**; of molecular collisions, 383; of work, **261**

Rats, 160

Rayon: 145, 220, 236, 244, *246,* 248; Celanese (sĕl′à nēs), *246*

Receiver, of telephone, **484**, 485

Reciprocating motion, 303, **304**, 306, 311, 328

Reducing: agent, **207**; medicines, 102

Reflex arc, **62**, *63*

Regeneration, of starfish, **129**

Regions: antarctic, 393; arctic, 393, 400; polar, 393; source, 395; tropical, 395, 396

Reproduction **33**, **131**, **132**, 139

Reptiles, **123**–**124**

Reservoirs, 225, 288

Resistance, general: 85, **261**, **268**, 272, 273, 274, 277, 279, 280, 281, 297, 299, 335, 336, 337, 338, 340; distance, **273**; of friction, 261, 299; of gravity, 261; to electric current, 335, 336, 337, 452; work and, 261

Resonance (rĕz′ō nǎns), **478**

Resources, natural: 146, **179**–**197**, 229, 370; and other nations, 212; biological, 241; energy as, **256**–**259**, 289; forests as, 146; mineral, **199**–**213**; of atmosphere, **229**–**241**; of electric power, 332; of fuel, 318; of water, 215–227

Respiration, system of: 57–59, 65; artificial, 117–118; cellular, 232

Retina, of eye, 68

REVERE, PAUL, 12

Revolution: of earth, 424, 435; of moon, 425, 426; of planets, 431, 435

Riboflavin (rī′bŏ flā′vĭn), 93

Rickets, 92

Rings: slip, 329, 331, 332; split, 331

ROCHAS, BEAU DE (rŏ shä′), 307

Rockets, 230, 257, 316–317, 439

Rocks, 4, 154, 155, 185, 186–191, 193, 194, 195, 199, 200, 201, 202, 203, 207, 212, 215, 219, 222, 225, 383, 408, 429

Rodents, 153, 159–161

Rods, of eye, 68

ROENTGEN, WILLIAM (rûnt′gĕn), 467

Roots, of plants, 135, 136, 147

Roots blower, 310

Rosin (rŏz′ĭn), 146

ROSS, RONALD, 21

Rotary blower, 310

Rotary motion, 264, 279, 303, 304, 307, 311, 328

Rotation: of crops, 156; of earth, 393, 394, 395, 422, 424; of Mars, 431; of moon, 425; of sun, 420

Rotor (rō′tēr), 312, 313

Rubber: 210, 212, 245, 246–248, 249, 336, 340, 361; and raincoats, 246; synthetic, 212, 247

Rubies, 185

Sachs, Julius von (fŏn zäks′), 136

Safety rules, in mining, 206

Saliva (sȧ lī′vȧ), 39, 41, 139

Salt, 180, 183, 185, 200 210, 216, 218–220, 223–224

Saltpeter, 236

Salvarsan (săl′vēr săn), 249

Sand, 154, 180, 184, 186, 205, 207, 225, 223

Sandstone, 187, 188, 190

Saran (sȧ răn′), 246

Satellites, 419, 431

Saturation, of air, 386

Saturn, 422, 429, 431, 436

SAVERY, THOMAS (sā′vēr ĭ), 301

Scale insects, 165

Scanning, of electron beam, 474

SCHAEFER, DR., 409

SCHLEIDEN, MATTHIAS (shlī′dĕn), 34, 35

SCHWANN, THEODOR (shvän), 34

Science and scientists: 1–19, 26, 184, 190, 213, 221, 222, 238, 244, 247, 249–251, 268, 289, 361–371, 409, 410, 411, 412, 415, 436, 437, 438, 463, 489–

492; and civilization, 5–18, 249–250, 369–371, 415; and democracy, 27–28; and labor, 245, 365, 367, 369, 370; abuse of, 27; biological, 4; capital and, 369; growth of, 16–19, 245, 268, 314; management and, 370; mass production and, 361–366; modern problems and, 367–369; physical, 4; research and, 3, 250, 254–256, 259, 283, 293, 301–304, 307, 309, 316, 317, 321, 351, 362, 365, 376, 377, 409, 413–415, 418, 421, 430–432, 438, 464, 470; tomorrow and, 369–371

Scientific methods: 21, 24–25, 202; of making steel, 208

Screw, 271, 298

Scurvy, 92

Seas, 192–193, 212, 213, 215–227, 229, 241, 257, 288

Seasons, 417, 418, 424

Sedimentary rocks, 186–188, 189, 190, 191, 195, 222

Seed, 131, 132, 135, 139, 140

Seismic methods of mining (sīz′-mĭk), 202–203

Seismograph (sīz′mŏ gráf), 203

Selenium (sĕ lē′nĭ ŭm), 466

SENECA (sĕn′ē kȧ), 428

Sense, organs, 62, 64, 66, 73

Series connection, of a battery, 323

Shadows, 417, 422–423, 428

Shaft mining, 201, 205–206

Shale, or mudstone, 187, 190

SHAPLEY, HARLOW (shăp′lĭ), 438

Shock, physical, 54, 116–117

Shower, 388, 403

Silica (sĭl′ĭ kȧ), 187, 206, 207

Silicon (sĭl′ĭ kŏn): 95, 154, 184, 207, 210, 420; dioxide, 184

Silicosis (sĭl′ĭ kō′sĭs), 206

Silk, 80, 244

Silver: 95, 179, 189, 220, 221, 224, 336, 337, 390, 442, 452, 474; bromide, 221; iodide, 409, 410

Siphon, of clam (sī′fŏn), 127, 128

Sirius (sĭr′ĭ ŭs), 435, 436

Sky, 383, 409, 423, 437

Slag, 207–208

Slate, 190, 408

Sleet, 389

Smallpox, 17, 88

Smelting: copper, 209; iron, 207

Snakes, poisonous, 124, 153, 160

Snow: 374, 375, 383, 386, 388, 389, 403, 409, 410, 411; snowflakes, 389, 409

Soaps, 220

Socket, of eye, 68

Soda, 180, 220

Sodium: 180, 184, 216, 217, 218, 220, 421; bicarbonate, 220, 235;

carbonate, 220; chloride, 185, 220; hydroxide, 220, 239, 244; nitrate, 236, 258

Soil: 146–147, 153–157, 191, 194, 195, 234, 236, 237, 257, 397, 411; conservation of, 155–157

Soil Conservation Service, 156

Solar heating, 448

Solar prominences, 420, 437

Solar system, 193, 192, 417–439

Solar-system arrangement of the atom, 181

Solenoid (sō′lĕ noid), 326, 466

Solids, 179, 182, 199, 215, 216, 217, 247, 297, 378, 390, 481

Solution, 183, 219, 220, 230

Solvay process, 220

Solvents, 207

SOMERSET, EDWARD, 301

Sound: 72, 257, 477–487; waves, 71, 202, 403, 477, 478, 481, 485

Soybean, 237, 248, 249, 361

Space, 317, 364, 378

Spark plug, 307, 309

Spectroheliograph (spĕk′trŏ hē′lĭ ŏ gráf), 421

Spectroscope (spĕk′trŏ skōp), 238, 359, 420, 436, 438

Spectrum, 238

Speech, man and, 141

Speed: 263, 265, 277, 279, 280, 284, 291, 297, 311, 312, 313, 344, 383, 394, 402, 404, 422, 424, 443, 467; Bernoulli's principle and, 297; of light, 293 435, 481; of a liquid, 297; o molecules, 383; of radio waves 470; of sounds, 481; of wheel 277

Spermatophytes (spûr′mȧ tŏ fīts′) 131

Sperms, 132, 173, 174, 175

Spillways, 411

Spinal cord, 62, 63, 64, 65, 121

Spinnerets, of spider, 126

Spleen, 39

Sponges, 130

Spore: of fern, 132; of germ, 87

Spotlight, 459, 460

Squall line, 402, 403

Stalactites (stȧ lăk′tīts), 240

Stalagmites (stȧ lăg′mīts), 240

Stamens (stā′mĕnz), 131

Starch, 39, 41, 49, 50, 96, 136, 13' 139, 240, 249

Stars, 4, 238, 379, 417, 420, 42 435–439

Static, of radio, 421, 486

Stator (stā′tēr), 312, 331

Steam: 199, 224, 235, 259, 30 302, 303, 312–314, 332, 35 367, 444, 445; boats, 304, 31 heating system, 444; pressur 304, 305, 312; turbines, 312

Steel: 207, 208, 232, 243, *244*, 283, 322, 324, 353, 481; alloys, 314, 348

Sterile dressing, 118

Stethoscope (stĕth'ŏ skōp), 50, *52*

STEVENSON, GEORGE, 304

Stimuli (stĭm'ū lī), 61

Stirrup, of ear, 71

Stoma (stō'mà), *137*

Stomach: *39*, 40–41, 45, 58, 101, 115, 140, 224; of clam, *128*; of starfish, 129; poisons, 163

Stones: 429; meteorites, 429

Storms: 377, 382, 383, 384, 389, 393, 397, **400**, 403–405, 409, 410, 414; cyclonic, **400**–401; dust, 414; hail, 410; snow, 409; sunspots and, 421; thunder, 403

Stratosphere, *230*, **384**

Streamlining, *296*, **297**–299

STREET, ROBERT, 307

Streptomycin (strĕp'tŏmī'sĭn), 249

Strip: cropping, *156*, 157; mining, **205**, *206*

Structure, 34

STURGEON, WILLIAM (stûr'jŭn), 321

Styrene (stī'rēn), 247

Styron (stī'rŏn), 246

Subassembly, 362, 363

Submarine: 276, 309, 311, 342

Subsoil, 153

Sucrose (sū'krōs), 239

Suffocation, **117**–118

Sugar: **39**, 49, 50, 91, 136, 137, 154, 180, 183, 240, 249, 257, 289; in vein, 49; simple, 39, 50

Sulfa drugs, or sulfonamides (sŭl'fŏn ăm'īdz), 28, 109, 249

Sulfates, 217

Sulfur (sŭl'fēr): 154, 179, 184, 185, 206, 207, 209, 210, 247, 258; dioxide (dī ŏk'sīd), 209

Sulfuric acid (sŭl fū'rĭk), 235, 239

Sun and sunlight: 135–137, 192, 216, 219, 224, 226, 238, 257, 288–289, 311, 359, 379, 383, 419, 420, 422, 424, 425, 426, 428, 429, 431, 437, 451, 456; sundial, 357, 423; sunlamp, 457; sunspots, 420, 421

"Superfortress," 361–365

Superstition, **16**–17

SUTTER, JOHN A. (sŏŏ'tēr), 200

Switch: electric, *325*, 326, 469; automatic, 326; solenoid, 326

Symbols, 183

Synthetics (sĭn thĕt'ĭks), 109, **145**, 212, 244–245

Syphilis (sĭf'ĭ līs), 82, 249

System: **37**; central nervous, 62; circulation, **38**, *49*, *56*; digestive, **38**, 138; English, 354; heating, 443–449; hot-air, 444; hot-

water, 444, 448; lymph, **56**; metric, **354**, 451; nervous, *38*, **61**–65; of measurement, 354; respiration, *38*, **57**–59; solar, *192*, **193**, 417–439; steam-heating, 444; water-supply, 332

Takaki (tä kä kĕ), 92

Talent, **101**

Tea and coffee, 114

Tear glands, of eye, **68**

Teeth: of animals, **138**; of a gear, 278, 279; of man, 75, 76, 78, *94*

"Teflon," *248*

Telegraph, 13, 209, *324*, **325**, 377

Telephone, 13, 209, **325**, 326, 331, 365, 378, 482, 484

Telescopes, 420, **436**–437, 460

Teletype machine, **325**, 378

Telephoto machine, **325**

Television, 13, 209, 326, 344, 461, **473**–475

Temperature: 216, 232, **233**, 235, 292, 303, 306, 309, 313, 314, 316, 337, 350, 353, 375, 376, 383, 385, 386, 389, 393, 395, 397, 398, 407, 411, 412, 413, 420, 425, 431, 435, 442, 444, 448, 471, 481; control of, 446; kindling, **233**; mechanical energy and, 292; second law of energy and, 292

Templates, **363**

Tennessee Valley Authority (TVA), 322, *410*

Tentacles of squid, **127**

Terminal, of battery, **323**, 363

Terracing, 157

Tetanus (tĕt'à nŭs), **87**

Tetraethyl lead (tĕt'rà ĕth'ĭl), 221

Textiles, 244, 303

Theobromine (thē'ŏ brō'mēn), 114

Theories, working, **22**, 25

Thermometer, 385, **446**

Thermostat, 445, 446

Thiamin (thī'à mĭn), **94**

Thorium (thō'rĭ ŭm), 184

Thunder, 257, **404**; storm, 403, 481

Thyroid gland (thī'roid), **95**, 102

Tides, **289**, 427

Time: 356–359, 422, 423, 427, 436, 470; belts, *356*, **423**; mass production and, 361, 364, 366; of low and high tides, 427; science and, 359; signals, 470

Tin, 179, 180, 184, 200, 209, 212

TISSANDIER, GASTON (tē'sän'dyā'), 380

Tissues, 36, *37*

Titanium (tī tā'nĭ ŭm), 184

Tobacco, 113, 377

Tolerance, 347–348, 349, 350

TOMBAUGH, CLYDE (tŏm'bô), 430

Tone, quality of, **480**

Tonsils, 56

Tools: 5, 8, 14–15, 254, 263, 362, 364–365; science and, 15

Topsoil, 153, 156

Tornadoes, 383, **404**, *405*

TORRICELLI, EVANGELISTA (tôr rĕ chĕl'lĕ), 381

Tourmaline (tŏŏr'mà lĭn), *185*

Tourniquet (tŏŏr'nĭ kĕt), **118**

Toxins (tŏk'sĭnz), 42, 83, 86, 87, 112, 113

Toxoid, **87**, 109

Trachea (trā'kĕ à), 40, *57*, 58

Transformer, **339**, 340, 344, 485

Transfusion, blood, 54

Transits, of planets, **432**

Transmission, of electricity, 332, 337, 340

Transmitter, of radio, 485

Transportation: 5, 10, 276, 357; science and, 5, 10; wheel and, 276

Trees, 131, 146, 148, 152, 160, 165, 249

TREVITHICK, RICHARD (trĕv'ĭ thĭk), 304

Triode (trī'ōd), **469**, 471, 474 485, 486

Troposphere (trŏp'ŏ sfēr), *230*

Tung, 248

Tubercle bacillus (tū'bēr k'l bà sĭl'- ŭs), 81

Tuberculosis, 81, 84, 113

Tungsten (tŭng'stĕn), 184, 208, 238, 243, 343, 452, 467

Tuning fork, **479**

Turbines (tûr'bĭnz), **312**, 313, 314, 317, 318, *326*, 328, 330

Turbojet engine (tûr'bô jĕt), 317, **318**

Turpentine, 146, 307

TWAIN, MARK, 417

Twilight, **379**

Typhoid fever, 84, 225

Typhoon, **404**

Typhus fever, 84, *88*, *89*, 163

Ulcers, 93

Ultraviolet light, 203, 457, 458

Umbra, **428**

United States: Department of Agriculture, *24*, 93, 96, 97, 148, 153, 159, 160, 161, *166*, 376; Department of Commerce, 376; Fish and Wildlife Service, 153; Forest Service, 148, *149*, 153, 414; Geological Survey, 190; Government, 247, 248, 250, 370, 376, 397; Public Health Service, 93, 110, *166*; Weather Bureau, 376–378, 397

Units, **34**

Universe, **437**, 438

Uranium–235, 181, 184, 203, 258, 294
Uranium ore, 203–204, 294
Uranus, planet (ū′rȧ nŭs), 430
Ursa Major, Ursa Minor (ûr′sȧ mā′jŏr, mĭ′nŏr), 436
U.S.S.R., 408
Uvula (ū′vŭ lȧ), 40

Vaccination, 88. See Inoculation.
Vacuum, 58
Valves: 303, 469; exhaust, 307, 310, 314, 318; Fleming, 464; intake, 307, 310; of automobile, 279; of heart, 50, 52, 56; of hydraulic press, 280
Vanadium (vȧ nā′dĭ ŭm), 184, 243
Vanes, 312, 318
Vapor, 182, 191, 224, 230, 233, 240, 293, 303, 307, 343, 380, 385, 386, 389, 409, 456, 457, 458
Variations: 169, 170–175
Vaseline, 212
Vasomotor action (vȧs′ō mō′tēr), 53
Vega (vē′gȧ), 436
Vegetables, 42, 92, 93, 94, 95, 96, 141, 209
Veins: of body, 48, 49, 52, 53, 56, 118; of rock, 199, 200
Ventricles (vĕn′trĭ k′lz), 50, 51
Venus, planet, 429, 431, 432
Vertebrate animals (vûr′tē brât), 121–124
Vibrations: 202–203, 477, 479, 482, 485, 486; sympathetic, 478
Villi (vĭl′ī), 41, 42, 49
Viruses (vī′rŭs ĕs), 35, 83, 475
Viscose (vĭs′kōs), 244, 246
Vitamins (vī′tȧ mĭnz), 92–94, 98, 248, 367, 457
Volcano, 186, 188, 189, 190, 195, 240, 425
Volt, 333, 334, 335, 336, 337, 340, 344, 467
Voltage, 330, 336, 337, 338, 339, 340, 341, 344
Voltmeter, 326, 336
Volume, measurement of, 354, 355
Vonnegut, Bernard, Dr., 409
Vortex, of tornado (vôr′tĕks), 404

Vulcanization, of rubber (vŭl′kȧn-ĭ zā′shŭn), 247

War of 1812, rockets and, 317
Washington, George, 10, 27
Wasps, 162, 165
Watches and clocks, 356, 357, 358
Water: 41, 45, 152, 154, 155, 156, 157, 179, 180, 181, 182, 186, 192, 193, 194, 196, 200, 203, 205, 209, 215, 216, 217, 220, 221, 223–227, 229, 231, 235, 237, 239, 255, 257, 282, 283, 288, 289, 297, 301, 302, 306, 313, 349, 353, 381, 383, 385, 386, 397, 409, 410, 411, 426, 428, 431, 442, 443, 444, 448, 481; and disease, 84; and the earth, 193; and evaporation, 182; and forests, 147; and mining, 200; and rocks, 186, 193; and solar energy, 288; boiling point of, 182; cycle, 223; distilled, 224; droplets, 385, 386, 388; force of running, 259; freezing point of, 183; in plants, 136; jacket, 444; power, 210, 220, 225, 289, 290, 332, 367; sea, 215–227; supplies of, 224–226, 332; transportation, 255; turbines, 312, 341; vapor, 182, 191, 224, 230, 240, 293, 303, 307, 380, 384, 386, 389, 409
Waterspout, 404
Waterwheels, 255, 311–312
Watt, electric, 332, 335, 473
Watt, James, 301, 302, 304, 335
Waves: carrier, 486; cold, 396; compression, 477, 478, 482, 484; energy, 443; heat, 383, 451; light, 443, 451, 457; longitudinal, 477; of air, 400; of ocean, 257; radio, 287, 469–470, 471, 474, 486; transverse, 477
Weather: 357, 373–415; air masses and, 393–405; and heat, 383; artificial, 408; cold front and, 402; control of, 408–415; flying and, 374; forecasting, 374, 375, 376, 381, 388; map, 376, 396, 398; U.S. government and, 376–378; warm front and, 401

Weeds, 159, 165, 166–167
Weight: 58, 104, 283–284, 294, 359, 379; electromagnet and, 321, 323; friction and, 294; measurement of, 354, 355; of engines, 307; Pascal's experiments and, 283; of persons, 104
Westinghouse airbrake, 368
Wheat, 170, 175, 397, 408
Wheel: 16, 233, 246, 267, 276–277, 278–280, 281, 284, 296, 303, 312, 348, 349, 364. See also Axle.
Wheeler, Dr. Robert H., 375
Whitney, Eli, 351, 352, 361
Wildlife, 150–153, 176, 411
Wind: 194, 216, 230, 255, 257, 259, 288, 297, 347, 377, 383, 384, 393, 394, 400, 404, 405, 414; energy of, 255; force of, 259; power, 288; prevailing, 394, 404; resistance of, 347
Winding, of a transformer, 339
Windmills, 255, 290, 311
Wings, of airplane, 364
Winthrop, John, 428
Wire and wiring: 321, 322, 328, 329, 331, 332, 335, 336, 337, 338, 339, 340, 343, 363, 452, 464, 484, 487; -photo service, 326; resistance of, 337
Wood: 145–147, 179, 243, 244, 290, 293, 336, 407, 442
Wool: 244; synthetic, 244
Work: 260, 261, 262, 263, 287, 295, 306, 335
World War II: radio and, 470; science and, 18, 27, 84, 165, 169, 247, 250, 318, 366, 436, 470; weather and, 375
Worms, 127–129, 154, 162
Wright, Orville and Wilbur, 27

Xenon, (zē′nŏn), 179, 238
X-rays: 111, 203, 287, 334, 344, 348, 358, 467, 468; tubes, 344

Year, 424
Yeast, 93

Zero, absolute, 442
Zinc: 154, 189, 209, 212, 420; oxide, 247

48